A Grammar of Southern Unami Delaware
(Lenape)

Ives Goddard

Mundart Press

2021

Copyright © 2021 by Joshua Jacob Snider
Mundart Press, 807 Howard Street, Petoskey MI 49770

All rights reserved. No part of this book may be reproduced or
transmitted in any form or by any means, electronic or mechanical,
including photocopying, recording, or by any information storage
and retrieval system, without permission in writing from the publisher.

The publisher hereby grants such permission to the Delaware Tribe of
Indians and the Delaware Nation of Western Oklahoma for any tribal
educational or cultural purpose.

A publication of the Recovering Voices Program of the Smithsonian
Institution, supported in part by a gift from the Shoniya Fund.

Publisher's Cataloguing-in-Publication Data

Names: Goddard, Ives, 1941- author.
Title: A grammar of Southern Unami Delaware (Lenape) / Ives Goddard.
Description: Petoskey MI : Mundart Press, [2021] | Includes bibliography.
Identifiers: ISBN: 978-0-9903344-3-9 | LCCN: 2021902974
Subjects: LCSH: Delaware language--Grammar. | Algonquian languages--Grammar. | Delaware Tribe of
          Indians--Language--Grammar. | Delaware Nation, Oklahoma--Language--Grammar.
Classification: LCC: PM1032 .G63 2020 | DDC: 497/.31--dc23

Table of Contents
(**sections** and examples)

Preface.   xvii

Abbreviations and Conventions.   xviii-xxii

1. Introduction.   1-2
    §1.1.
    §1.2. Name.
    §1.3. Dialects.
    §1.4. Sources.

2. Sound System.   3-38
    §2.1. Phonemes.   3-4
        (2.1) The segmental phonemes of Southern Unami   3
    §2.1a. Spelling.   3
    §2.1b. Consonant clusters.   3-4
    §2.1c. Nasal clusters.   4
    §2.1d. Long fricatives.   4
    §2.1e. Constraints; /ɔ/ and /ɔ·/.   4
    §2.2. Blanchard's orthography.   4-5
        (2.2) The Delaware alphabet used by Blanchard   5
    §2.3. Weak and Strong Syllables.   5-6
    §2.4. Weakening and Loss of Vowels.   6-7
        (2.3) Syncope (loss) and weakening of short vowels in weak syllables   6
    §2.4a. Loss of underlying strong short vowels.   6-7
        (2.4) Syncope of short vowels before clusters containing a voiceless fricative   6-7
    §2.5. Underlying |h|.   7-8
        (2.5) Some treatments and effects of underlying |h| 7-8
    §2.6. Other Consonant Changes.   8
        (2.6) Initial-syllable reduction and loss   8
    §2.7. Effects of weakened |a|.   8
        (2.7) Secondary effects of the weakening of |a| 8
    §2.8. Long Consonants in Metathesized Syllables.   8-9
        (2.8) Secondary lengthening after metathesized sequences   9
    §2.9. Word-final changes.   9-11
    §2.9a. Word-final |-l|.   9
        (2.9) Loss of final |l|.   9

§2.9b. Word-final |-w|.   **9-10**
    (2.10) Loss of final |w|.   9-10
§2.9c. Word-final |-h|.   **10**
    (2.11) Loss of final |h|.   10
§2.9d. Word-final post-vocalic /-i/.   **10**
    (2.12) Word-final negative suffix   10
    (2.13) Assimilation and non-assimilation of /-i/ outside the negative   11
§2.10. Vowel Replacement and Vowel Coloring.   11-17
§2.10a. Vowel-shortening before clusters.   **11**
    (2.14) Vowel-shortening before voiced consonants in clusters   11
§2.10b. Contraction of |w| and |a| or |ā|.   **11-12**
    (2.15) Contraction of |wa| and |wā| to /ɔ/, /ɔ·/, and /ɔh/   11-12
    (2.16) Contraction of |wa| to /o·/ and /ɔ/ with |-ak| anim. pl.   12
    (2.17) Contraction of |wa| with |-a(l)| inan. pl. to /u/ (older /o·/) in verbs, and to /ɔ/ in nouns   12
    (2.18) Contraction of |wa| with |-a(l)| obv. to /-o·/, /-u/, and /-ɔ/   12
§2.10c. Contraction of |əwə|.   **13**
    (2.19) Contraction of |ə-wə| and |əw-ə| to |o·| 13
    (2.20) Non-contraction of |əwə| in prefixes before nasal clusters   13
§2.10d. Contraction of |əyə|.   **13-14**
    (2.21) Contraction and non-contraction of |əy-ə| 13-14
§2.10e. Contraction of |awə| in verbs and nouns.   **14**
    (2.22) Contraction of stems in |aw| with |ə| 14
§2.10f. Contraction of |ayə|.   **14**
§2.10g. Contraction of |Cw| in TA verbs.   **14**
    (2.23) Contraction with TA stems in |Cw| 14
§2.10h. Vowel changes before |w| and |y|.   **14-15**
    (2.24) Vowel changes in third person forms   15
    (2.25) Replacement of |ī| by /ə/ before |y| 15
    (2.26) /ə/ and /u/ for |ə| before |w| 15
§2.10i. Treatment of |ə| before |kw| and |hw|.   **16**
    (2.27) /u/ for |ə| before |kw| and |hw|, and before |k| and |h| in rounding environments   16
§2.10j. Treatment of |ə| before |nk|.   **16**
    (2.28) /u/ and /i/ from |ə| before |nk| 16
§2.10k. Weakening of |a| between /h/ and /m/ or /n/.   **16-17**
    (2.29) /ə/ replacing weak-syllable |a| and |wa| before |m| and |n| 16-17
§2.11. Loss of intervocalic |w| and |y|.   17-21
§2.11a. Intervocalic |w|.   **17**
    (2.30) Loss of intervocalic |w| 17
§2.11b. Loss of intervocalic |y|.   **17-18**
    (2.31) Loss and retention of |y| 17-18
§2.11c. Intervocalic /y/ replacing |w|.   **18**
    (2.32) Replacement of |w| by /y/ before /u/ or /o·/   18
    (2.33) Replacement of |w| by /y/ before |-əm| POSS.TH   18

Table of Contents

§2.11d. Intervocalic /y/ for |w| by analogy.	**19**
(2.34) Analogical secondary /y/ before /ə/	19
(2.35) Analogical secondary /y/ before /k/	19
§2.11e. Treatments of |wəy|.	**20-21**
(2.36) Retention and loss of |w| in TA and AI stems	20
(2.37) Variation in |kawī-| AI 'sleep'	21
§2.12. Other miscellaneous phonological changes.	**21-26**
§2.12a. Treatment of |w| potentially followed by |h|.	**21-22**
(2.38) Potential |w| followed by |h|	21
§2.12b. Treatment of |x| following |w|.	**22**
(2.39) Potential |w| followed by |x|	22
§2.12c. Replacement of |y| by |h|.	**22**
(2.40) |y| followed by |h| or |s|	22
§2.12d. Underlying |ōx| and |ōxw|.	**22-23**
(2.41) Examples of |xw| (with and without |ō|) and |ōx| (without |w|)	23
§2.12e. Secondary /hi/.	**23**
(2.42) Secondary, anomalous /hi/	23
§2.12f. Treatment of |-hmənā| 1p,12.	**23-24**
(2.43) The realizations of |-(ə)hmənā| 1p,12	23
§2.12g. Assimilation of |m| before |k| and |t|.	**24**
(2.44) /nk/ from |m-k|	24
(2.45) /nt/ from |m-t|	24
§2.12h. Metathesis of |w| and |k| 3s.	**24**
(2.46) Metathesis of |w| and |k| to |kw|	24
§2.12i. Replacement of |t| by |č|, |h|, and |s|.	**24-25**
(2.47) Replacement of |t| by |č| in inflectional endings	24-25
(2.48) Replacement of |t| by |h| before |k|, and loss of the |k|	25
(2.49) Replacement of |t| by |s| before certain finals	25
§2.12j. Other restricted processes of cluster reduction.	**25-26**
(2.50) Replacement of nasal consonant by |h| before |l|	25-26
(2.51) Word-final |-hl| from |m| + |l| replaced by |-h|	26
(2.52) Replacement of |l| by |h| before |k|	26
§2.12k. Irregular preterite singular ending.	**25-26**
(2.53) First and second singular preterite	26
§2.13. The realization of the pronominal prefixes (and homophonous syllables).	**26-33**
(2.54) Combinations of pronominal prefixes and initial syllables	26-27
(2.55) Metathesis of the |w| of |wə-| 3	27-28
(2.56) Retained /wt-/, /ws-/, and /wən-/ before /a/ and /a·/ in Blanchard	28
(2.57) |wə-| 3 retained as /w-/ or /wə-/	28
(2.58) |w| of |wə-| 3 assimilated to /p/, /k/, and /m/	29
(2.59) |w| of |wə-| 3 contracted with |ə| to /u/	30
(2.60) Loss of |wə-| 3 before /təl-/, /tən-/, and intercalated |t|	30
(2.61) Retention of |wə-| 3 before /təl-/, /tən-/, and intercalated |t|	30-31
(2.62) Prefix |nə-| 1 before voiceless consonants, |n|, and |l|	31
(2.63) Prefix |kə-| 2 before voiceless consonants other than |k|	31
(2.64) Prefix |kə-| 2 before |k|	31-32

(2.65) Contraction of prefixes with stem-initial |wə-|	32
(2.66) Non-contraction of prefixes with stem-initial |wə-|	32
(2.67) The treatment of stems beginning with |wə-|, |nə-|, and |na-|	33

§2.14. Variation in stem shape with and without prefixes.   33-35

(2.68) Stems with an added syllable after prefixes	34
(2.69) Retention and leveling of weak and strong syllables	34
(2.70) Partial unprefixed stem shape after a prefix	35
(2.71) Weak vowel after syncopated short vowel	35

§2.15. Static words, syllables, and segments.   35-38

(2.72) Static demonstratives and noun substitutes	36
(2.73) Static free particles	36
(2.74) Static preverbs	36
(2.75) Static numeral pre-particles	37
(2.76) Particles with a static diminutive suffix	37
(2.77) Nouns with static non-productive diminutive suffixes	37
(2.78) Static vocatives	37
(2.79) Static loanwords	37
(2.80) Static nicknames and the like	38

3. Grammatical Categories.   39-50

§3.1.   39
§3.1a. Parts of Speech.   39
§3.1b. Stem Components.   39
§3.1c. Grammatical Categories.   39

§3.2. Gender.   39-41

(3.1) Animate nouns (predictable categories)	39-40
(3.2) Animate nouns (objects)	40
(3.3) Animate nouns (natural phenomena)	40
(3.4) Animate nouns (body parts and the like)	40-41
(3.5) Inanimate nouns	41

§3.3. Number.   41-42

(3.6) Singular and plural distinguished	41-42
(3.7) Singular and plural not distinguished	42

§3.4. Obviative.   42

(3.8) Obviative marking	42

§3.5. Absentative.   43

(3.9) Uses of the absentative	43

§3.6. Pronominal Persons.   43-44

(3.10) Emphatic pronouns and pronominal categories	43
(3.11) Coreferential indefinites	44

§3.7. Verbs: Formal and Syntactic Types.   44-50
§3.7a. Arguments.   44

(3.12) Primary and secondary objects	44

§3.7b. Obliques.   44-46

(3.13) Relative roots and obliques	45-46

§3.7c. Instrumental Obliques.   **46**
    (3.14) Instrumental obliques   46
§3.7d. Instrumental Obliques and Adjuncts.   **46-47**
    (3.15) Adjuncts with no morphological link to a verb   47
    (3.16) Adjuncts indexed by n-endings   47
    (3.17) Adjuncts as heads of participles   48
§3.7e. Intransitive and Transitive Verbs.   **48-49**
    (3.18) Intransitive stem pairs   48
    (3.19) II stems derived from AI stems   48
    (3.20) Transitive stem pairs   49
§3.7f. Secondary Object.   **49-50**
    (3.21) Verbs with secondary object   49
§3.7g. Inanimate Subject with Non-Sentient Object.   **50**
    (3.22) Animate inflection for inanimate transitive subject   50

4. Inflection.   **51-113**
§4.1.
§4.2. Inflection of Nouns.   **51-58**
    (4.1) Peripheral (outer) suffixes   51
    (4.2) Noun paradigms   52-53
§4.2a. Possessed Nouns.
    (4.3) Inflection for possessor   53
    (4.4) Possessed inanimate noun (ahpóˑn 'bread; loaf of bread'; ahpánši 'pole'; xkán 'bone'; mhúkw 'blood'; múxˑoˑl 'boat'; lačˑeˑsˑəwáˑkˑan 'possessions, clothes')   53-54
    (4.5) Possessed animate noun (|-nīčān| 'child', later esp. 'daughter'; |ələnəw| '(man); brother of female'; |-kahēs| 'mother'; |-tēh| 'heart')   54
    (4.6) Possessed forms of nouns with stems in |-y| or |-əw| 54-55
§4.2b. Dependent Nouns.   **55**
    (4.7) Dependent nouns   55
§4.2c. Absentative Possessed Nouns.   **55-56**
    (4.8) Absentative possessed nouns   55-56
§4.2d. Locative.   **56-57**
    (4.9) Additional locative forms with /-ink/   56
    (4.10) Locative plural forms   56
§4.2f. Vocative.   **57**
    (4.11) Vocative forms   57
§4.2g. Obviative Plural.   **57-58**
    (4.12) Obviative plural   57-58
§4.3. Inflection of Pronouns.   **58-60**
    (4.13) Emphatic pronouns ('too' set)   58
    (4.14) Reflexive pronouns (forms)   58
    (4.15) Reflexive pronouns (examples)   59
    (4.16) Demonstrative pronouns   59
    (4.17) Interrogative demonstrative   60

(4.18) Indefinite-interrogative pronouns	60
§4.4. Inflection of Verbs (Basic Categories).	**60-61**
§4.4a. Orders and Modes.	**60**
§4.4b. Preterite and Present.	**60**
§4.4c. Negative and Prohibitive.	**61**
§4.4d. Theme Signs.	**61**
§4.4e. Absolute and Objective.	**61**
§4.5. Independent Order Paradigms and Examples.	**61-78**
(4.19) Independent order central endings	62
§4.5a. Independent Indicative.	**62-74**
(4.20) Independent indicative: AI and II paradigms	62-63
(4.21) Independent indicative AI and II (examples)	63
(4.22) Independent indicative, TA direct (inflections)	64
(4.23) Independent indicative, TA direct (forms of |nōtəm-| TA 'guard')	64
(4.24) Independent indicative, TA direct (examples)	65
(4.25) Independent indicative, TA inverse (inflections)	65
(4.26) Independent indicative, TA inverse (forms of |nōtəm-| TA 'guard'; |pōl-| TA 'escape from')	65-66
(4.27) Independent indicative, TA inverse (examples)	66-67
(4.28) Independent indicative, TA first and second person passive (inflections; forms of |nakal-| TA 'leave behind')	67
(4.29) Independent indicative, TA first and second person passive (examples)	67
(4.30) Independent indicative, TA theme 3 and theme 4 (inflections)	67
(4.31) Independent indicative, TA theme 3 (forms of |wīčəm-| TA 'help')	67
(4.32) Independent indicative, TA theme 4 (forms of |wīčəm-| TA 'help'; |maxkaw-| TA 'find'; |nēw-| TA 'see')	67-68
(4.33) Independent indicative, TA theme 3 and theme 4 (examples)	68
(4.34) Independent indicative TI absolute (inflections)	68
(4.35) Independent indicative TI absolute (forms of |pən-| TI(1a) 'look at'; |məšən-| TI(1b) 'get'; |pēt-| TI(2) 'bring'; |mīčī-| TI(3) 'eat'; |nēm-| TI(3) 'see')	68-69
(4.36) Independent indicative TI objective with singular object (inflections)	69
(4.37) Independent indicative TI objective (forms of |pən-| TI(1a) 'look at'; |məšən-| TI(1b) 'get'; |pēt-| TI(2) 'bring'; |mīčī-| TI(3) 'eat'; |nēm-| TI(3) 'see')	69
(4.38) Independent indicative TI absolute (examples)	69-70
(4.39) Independent indicative TI objective (examples)	70
(4.40) AI+O with definite secondary object (examples)	71-72
(4.41) TA+O with definite secondary object (examples)	72
(4.42) AI and II with definite oblique (examples)	72-73
(4.43) TA with definite oblique (examples)	73
(4.44) TI with definite oblique (examples)	73
(4.45) Inflection for definite adjunct (examples)	73-74

§4.5b. Subordinative.   74-78
    (4.46) Subordinative: AI and II (inflections;
         forms of |pā-| AI 'come'; |pənīhlā-| II 'fall')   74-75
    (4.47) Subordinative TA (inflections)   75
    (4.48) Subordinative TA (forms of |nōtəm-| TA 'guard')   75
    (4.49) Subordinative without |əlī| PV '{so}' (examples)   75-76
    (4.50) Subordinative with |əlī| PV '{so}' (examples)   76-77
    (4.51) Subordinative with ná PRES and |əlī| PV '{so}' (examples)   77-78
    (4.52) Subordinative as main verb (examples)   78

§4.6. Conjunct Order Paradigms and Examples.   78-89
    (4.53) Conjunct modes: formation and uses   79
    (4.54) Conjunct order central suffixes   79

§4.6a. Plain Conjunct and Subjunctive Paradigms.   80-82
    (4.55) Plain conjunct and subjunctive of AI and II
         (|pā-| AI 'come'; |ləmatapī-| AI 'sit'; |pənīhlā-| II 'fall')   80
    (4.56) Plain conjunct TA
         (forms of |nōtəm-| TA 'guard'; |mīl-| TA 'give to')   80-81
    (4.57) Subjunctive TA
         (forms of |nōtəm-| TA 'guard'; |mīl-| TA 'give to')   81
    (4.58) Plain conjunct TI
         (forms of |pən-| TI(1a) 'look at'; |məšən-| TI(1b) 'get';
         |pēt-| TI(2) 'bring'; |mīčī-| TI(3) 'eat'; |nēm-| TI(3) 'see')   81
    (4.59) Subjunctive TI
         (forms of |pən-| TI(1a) 'look at'; |məšən-| TI(1b) 'get';
         |pēt-| TI(2) 'bring'; |mīčī-| TI(3) 'eat'; |nēm-| TI(3) 'see')   82

§4.6b. Conjunct Examples.   82-89
    (4.60) Plain conjunct (examples)   82
    (4.61) Changed conjunct (examples)   83
    (4.62) Changed Subjunctive (examples)   83-84
    (4.63) Subjunctive (examples)   84-85
    (4.64) Participle (proximate examples)   85-86
    (4.65) Participle (obviative examples)   86-87
    (4.66) Participle (second person and inanimate examples)   87
    (4.67) Participle with oblique head (examples)   87-89

§4.7. Independent and Conjunct Preterite.   89-97
    (4.68) Independent indicative preterite AI and II (examples)   89-90
    (4.69) Independent indicative preterite TA (examples)   90-91
    (4.70) Independent indicative preterite TI (examples)   91
    (4.71) Independent indicative preterite AI+O and TA+O (examples)   92
    (4.72) Independent subordinative preterite   92
    (4.73) Changed conjunct preterite   92=93
    (4.74) Subjunctive preterite   93
    (4.75) Preterite participle (AI, II)   93-94
    (4.76) Preterite participle (TA direct and inverse)   94-95
    (4.77) Preterite participle (TA themes 3 and 4)   95-96
    (4.78) Preterite participle (TI)   96-97

§4.8. Present.	**97**
(4.79) Present (examples)	97
§4.9. Negative Suffix and Particles.	**97**
§4.10. Independent Negative.	**97-102**
(4.80) Independent indicative negative, AI and II inflections and paradigms	97-98
(4.81) Independent indicative negative, AI and II (examples)	98
(4.82) Independent indicative negative, TA direct (inflections)	98
(4.83) Independent indicative negative, TA direct (examples)	99
(4.84) Independent indicative negative, TA inverse (inflections)	99
(4.85) Independent indicative negative, TA inverse (examples)	99-100
(4.86) Independent indicative negative, TA first and second person passive (inflections, forms)	100
(4.87) Independent indicative negative, TA first and second person passive examples)	100
(4.88) Independent indicative negative, TA theme 3 and theme 4 (inflections)	100
(4.89) Independent indicative negative, TA theme 3 and theme 4 (examples)	100-101
(4.90) Independent indicative negative, TI absolute (inflections)	101
(4.91) Independent indicative negative, TI absolute (examples)	101
(4.92) Independent indicative negative, TI objective with singular object (inflections)	101-102
(4.93) Independent indicative negative, TI objective with singular object (examples)	102
§4.10a. Subordinative Negative.	**102**
§4.11. Conjunct Negative.	**102-105**
(4.94) Conjunct order negative, AI and II (endings)	103
(4.95) Conjunct order negative, all modes, AI and II (examples)	103
(4.96) Conjunct order negative, TA (endings)	103-104
(4.97) Conjunct order negative, all modes, TA (examples)	104
(4.98) Conjunct order negative, TI (endings)	105
(4.99) Conjunct order negative, all modes, TI (examples)	105
§4.12. Imperative Order Paradigms and Examples.	**105-113**
§4.12a. Imperative Mode.	**105-109**
(4.100) Imperative mode, AI and TI(3) (endings)	106
(4.101) Imperative mode, TA (endings)	106
(4.102) Imperative mode, TI(1a), TI(1b), and TI(2) (endings)	106
(4.103) Imperative mode, AI (examples)	107
(4.104) Imperative mode, TA theme 1 (examples)	107-108
(4.105) Imperative mode, TA theme 3 (examples)	108
(4.106) Imperative mode, TI (examples)	108-109
§4.12b. Prohibitive Mode.	**109-111**
(4.107) Prohibitive mode, AI and TI(3) (endings)	109
(4.108) Prohibitive mode, TA (endings)	109-110

(4.109) Prohibitive mode, TI(1a), TI(1b), and TI(2) (endings)	110
(4.110) Prohibitive mode, AI (examples)	110
(4.111) Prohibitive mode, TA (examples)	110
(4.112) Prohibitive mode, TI (examples)	111
§4.12c. Injunctive Mode.	**111-112**
(4.113) Injunctive mode (endings)	111
(4.114) Injunctive mode (examples)	112
§4.12d. Future Imperative Mode.	**112-113**
(4.115) Future imperative mode (endings)	112
(4.116) Future imperative mode (examples)	113
5. Derivation.	**114-187**
§5.1. Stem Composition.	**114**
§5.1a. Primary Stems.	**114-116**
(5.1) Primary stems (examples)	114
(5.2) AI stems consisting of an initial with no segmentable final	115
(5.3) AI stems without a recurring initial	115
(5.4) TA and TI stems without a recurring initial	115-116
§5.2. Formation of Components.	**116-132**
§5.2a. Underived Initials.	**116-117**
§5.2b. Initials Formed from Stems.	**117-118**
(5.5) Initials formed from noun stems	117
(5.6) Initials formed from verb stems	117-118
§5.2c. Initials Formed from Initials.	**118**
(5.7) Initials formed from initials by extensions	118
(5.8) Initials formed by initial change	118
§5.2d. Finals and Medials Not Derived from Stems.	**119-125**
(5.9) Underived noun finals	119
(5.10) Abstract AI and II verb finals and final pairs	120-121
(5.11) Significant AI and II verb finals and final pairs	121-122
(5.12) Underived transitive verb finals	122-124
(5.13) Underived medials	125
§5.2e. Finals and Medials Formed from Stems and Components.	**125-132**
(5.14) Noun finals from non-dependent noun stems	126-127
(5.15) Noun final from prefinal + final:	127
(5.16) Noun final from medial (with added |w|)	127
(5.17) Verb finals from verb stems	127-128
(5.18) Verb finals from verb finals	128-129
(5.19) Medials from noun finals	129-130
(5.20) Medials from non-dependent nouns	130
(5.21) Medials from dependent nouns	130-131
(5.22) Medials from medials	131-132
§5.3. Particles.	**132-187**
§5.3a. Underived Particles.	**132-134**
(5.23) Unanalyzable free particles and preverbs	132

(5.24) Enclitics (complete set)	132-134
§5.3b. Particle Finals.	**134-136**
(5.25) Particles with |-ī| PF (not also used as preverbs)	134
(5.26) Particles incorporating |-ənk| LOC	134
(5.27) Preverbs with |-ī| PF	134
(5.28) Particles with |-ī| PF used also as preverbs	134-135
(5.29) Particles and prewords with |-īwī| PF	135
(5.30) Particle with variation in the particle final	135
(5.31) Particle finals derived from medials	135-136
(5.32) Particle finals derived from nouns	136
(5.33) Particle finals without an abstract final	136
§5.4. Reduplication.	**136-144**
§5.4a. Plural Reduplication.	**137-139**
(5.34) Plural reduplication	138
(5.35) |amank-| 'big (pl.)' with prefixes and initial change	139
§5.4b. Repetitive Reduplication.	**139-141**
(5.36) Repetitive reduplication (consonant-initial stems with a short vowel in the initial syllable)	139
(5.37) Repetitive reduplication (stems beginning with |ə-| and some with |a-|)	140
(5.38) Repetitive reduplication (stems with a long vowel in the first syllable, and some with |a-|)	140-141
(5.39) Stems with fossilized plural or repetitive reduplication	141
§5.4c. Continuative Reduplication.	**141**
(5.40) Continuative reduplication	141
§5.4d. Habitual Reduplication.	**141-143**
(5.41) Habitual reduplication (without initial change)	142
(5.42) Habitual reduplication with initial change	142-143
§5.4e. Extended Reduplication.	**143-144**
(5.43) Extended reduplication (for removed past)	143
(5.44) Extended reduplication (with a negative)	143-144
§5.4f. Rare Patterns of Reduplication.	**144**
(5.45) Rare reduplication types	144
§5.5. Secondary Derivation.	**144-175**
§5.5a. Nouns Formed from Nouns.	**144**
§5.5b. Diminutives.	**144-146**
(5.46) Diminutive nouns with |-ətə̀t|	145
(5.47) Possessed diminutive nouns	145
(5.48) Nouns with a non-productive diminutive suffix |-(ə)s|	145
§5.5c. Pejoratives.	**146**
(5.49) Nouns with a pejorative suffix	146
§5.5d. Objurgatives.	**146**
(5.50) Objurgative nouns	146
§5.6. Secondary Derivation: Nouns Formed from Verbs.	**146-151**
§5.6a. Nouns with |-ən| NF.	**146-147**
(5.51) Nouns with |-ən| NF added to an AI stem	146-147

§5.6b. Nouns with |-ənay| NF. **147**
(5.52) Nouns with |-ənay| NF added to an AI or TI(3) stem   147
§5.6c. Nouns with |-wən| NF. **147**
(5.53) Nouns with |-wən| NF   147
§5.6d. Nouns with |-wan| NF. **147**
(5.54) Nouns with |-wan| NF   147
§5.6e. Nouns with |-kan| NF. **147-148**
(5.55) Nouns made with |-kan| NF   148
§5.6f. Nouns with |-īkan| NF. **148**
(5.56) Nouns made with |-īkan| NF   148
§5.6g. Nouns with |-ākan| NF. **148**
(5.57) Nouns made with |-ākan| NF   148
§5.6h. Nouns with |-wākan| NF from Primary Stems. **148-149**
(5.58) Abstract nouns made with |-wākan| NF from primary stems   149
§5.6i. Nouns with |-wākan| NF from Derived AI Verbs. **149-150**
(5.59) Abstract nouns made with |-wākan| NF from secondary AI stems in |-ē| and invariant |-ā| 149-150
(5.60) Abstract nouns made with |-wākan| NF from secondary stems with |-(ə)tī| AI   150
§5.6j. Nouns with |-w| NF from AI and TA Verbs. **150-151**
(5.61) Agent nouns with |-w| NF   150
(5.62) Agent nouns with |-əs| NF   150
(5.63) Nouns of undergoer with |-āw| NF   150
(5.64) Noun of undergoer with |-əkw| NF   151
§5.6k. Lexicalized Participles. **151**
(5.65) Lexicalized participles   151
§5.6l. Agent Nouns in |-s|. **151**
(5.66) Agent nouns in |-s| 151
§5.7. Secondary Derivation: Verbs Formed from Nouns. **151-155**
§5.7a. Verbs of Being or Becoming. **152**
(5.67) Verbs of being or becoming   152
§5.7b. Verbs of Having as an Attribute. **152-153**
(5.68) Verbs of having as an attribute   152-153
§5.7c. Verbs of Speaking a Language. **153**
(5.69) Verbs of speaking a language   153
§5.7d. Verbs of Making. **153**
(5.70) Verbs of making or acquiring   153
§5.7e. Verbs of Possession (AI). **153-154**
(5.71) Verbs of possession (AI)   153-154
§5.7f. Verbs of Possession (TA). **155**
(5.72) Verbs of possession (TA)   155
§5.8. Secondary Derivation: Verbs Formed from Verbs. **155-175**
§5.8a. Diminutive Verbs. **155-157**
(5.73) Diminutive verbs   156-157
§5.8b. Pejorative Verbs. **157**
(5.74) Pejorative verbs   157

§5.8c. Collective Verbs. **157-158**
 (5.75) Collective verbs   158
§5.8d. II Verbs Derived from AI Stems. **158-159**
 (5.76) II verbs derived from AI stems   159
§5.8e. Causatives. **160-163**
 (5.77) Causatives derived from AI stems with |-h| TA, |-ht|, TI(2)   160
 (5.78) Causatives derived from AI stems with |-l TA|, |-t| TI(2)   160
 (5.79) Causatives derived from AI stems with |-wəhē| AI+O   161
 (5.81) Causative derived from an AI stem with |-ənahē| AI+O   161
 (5.82) Causatives derived from AI stems with |-wəhāl| TA (/-hɔ·l/)
  and |-hāl| TA (/-ha·l/)   161
 (5.83) Causatives derived from AI stems with |-hāl| TA   162
 (5.84) Causatives derived from AI stems with |-(ə)mahāl| TA   162
 (5.85) AI+O causatives derived from AI stems   162
 (5.86) TI causative derived from a TA taken as a passive   162
 (5.87) Causatives derived from transitive stems   162-163
§5.8f. Applicatives. **163-164**
 (5.88) Applicatives derived from AI stems with |-l| TA, |-t| TI(1a)   163-164
 (5.89) Applicatives derived from AI stems with |-m| TA   164
 (5.90) Applicatives derived from AI stems with |-aw| TA   164
 (5.91) Applicatives derived from AI stems with |-htaw| TA, |-ht| TI(1a)   164
 (5.92) Applicatives derived from AI stems with |-htam| TA   164
 (5.93) Applicative derived from an AI+O stem with |-māl| TA (irregular)   164
§5.8g. Double-Object Verbs. **165-166**
 (5.94) Double-object verbs derived from TI(1a) and TI(1b) themes   165
 (5.95) Double-object verbs derived from TI(2) stems   165-166
 (5.96) Double-object verb derived from a TI(3) stem   166
 (5.97) Ostensible double-object verbs not derivable from TI stems   166
§5.8h. Benefactives. **166**
 (5.98) Benefactives   166
§5.8i. Joint-Action Verbs. **166-167**
 (5.99) Verbs of joint action or inclusion.   166-167
§5.8j. Detransitives. **167-169**
 (5.100) General detransitives in |-īkē| AI   167-168
 (5.101) Indefinite intransitives in |-əwē| AI (verbs and derived nouns)   168
 (5.102) Indefinite intransitives in |-kē| AI   169
 (5.103) Indefinite intransitives in |-āsī| AI (replacing |-aw| TA)   169
§5.8k. Middle-Reflexives. **169-170**
 (5.104) Middle-reflexives (types and examples)   170
§5.8l. Derived Passives. **170-172**
 (5.105) AI and II passive stems derived from TI(1) stems   171
 (5.106) II passive stems derived from TI(2) stems   171
 (5.107) AI and II passive stems derived from TA stems with
  |-əkwəsī| AI, |-əkwat| II   171-172
 (5.108) Stems with |-īnākwəsī| AI, |-īnākwat| II 'seem, appear'   172

(5.109) Stems with |-əhtākwəsī| AI, |-əhtākwat-| II 'have a sound, use or be a voice'	172
§5.8m. Reciprocals.	**172-174**
(5.110) Reciprocals on different stem shapes	172-173
(5.111) Reciprocal with singular inflection	173
(5.112) Reciprocal form not literally reciprocal	173
(5.113) Reciprocal stems with indefinite subject (reciprocal and passive meanings)	173
(5.114) Nouns derived from reciprocal stems (ostensibly active)	173-174
(5.115) Nouns derived from reciprocal stems (with passive meaning)	174
(5.116) Nouns derived from reciprocal stems (possessed forms)	174
§5.8n. Verbs of Environmental Effect.	**174**
(5.117) Verbs of environmental effect and the like with |-(n)amī| AI	174
§5.8o. Objurgative Verbs.	**175**
(5.118) Objurgative verbs	175
(5.119) Objurgative verbs euphemistically altered	175
§5.9. Compounds.	**175-187**
§5.9a. Compound Nouns.	**175-179**
(5.120) Prenouns with underived initials and -i PF	176-177
(5.121) Prenouns with underived initials and -í·i PF	177
(5.122) Prenouns from noun stems and -í·i PF	177
(5.123) Prenouns from lexicalized participles and -í·i PF	177-178
(5.124) Prenoun from locative noun or particle	178
(5.125) Prenouns from verb stems with |-w| NF	178
(5.126) Derived particles matching prenouns with -í·i PF	178
(5.127) Prenoun in -í·i PF with a derived noun,	179
§5.9b. Compound Verbs.	**179-186**
(5.128) Preverbs with grammatical functions	179-182
(5.129) Other underived preverbs	183-186
(5.130) Preverb from prenoun	186
(5.131) Preverb from free particle	186
(5.132) Preverbs from verb stems	186
§5.9c. Particle Compounds.	**186-187**
(5.133) Particle compounds	186-187

6. Sentence Structure. 188-198
§6.1. Kinds of Sentences. 188
§6.2. Sentence Components. 188-191
§6.2a. Noun Phrases. 188-189

(6.1) Noun phrase without a noun or participle	188-189
(6.2) Noun phrase with a noun or participle	189
(6.3) Quantifier and adjunct	189
(6.4) Possessor and possessed	189
§6.2b. Verbal Phrases.	**189-190**
(6.5) Verb with adverbial particle	189

(6.6) Verb with negative or prohibitive particle	190
(6.7) Verb with complement of relative root	190
(6.8) Conjoined verbs	190
§6.2c. Particle Phrases.	**190-191**
(6.9) Particle phrases	190-191
§6.3. Verbless sentences.	**191-192**
§6.3a. Substantive Sentences.	**191-192**
(6.10) Substantive sentences	191-192
§6.3b. Equational Sentences.	**192**
(6.11) Equational sentences (Given + New)	192
(6.12) Equational sentences (New + Given)	192
(6.13) Equational sentences with New term emphasized	192
§6.4. Subordinate Clauses.	**192-193**
§6.4a. Conditional Clauses.	**192**
§6.4b. Complement Clauses.	**193**
(6.14) Direct discourse complement	193
(6.15) Indirect discourse complement	193
§6.5. Sentence-Initial Focus and Emphasis.	**193-195**
§6.5a. Focus-Fronting.	**193-194**
(6.16) Focus-fronted subject or object followed by enclitic host	193-194
§6.5b. Focus Peg.	**194**
(6.17) ná P PRES not in sentence-initial focus position	194
§6.5c. Presentational Pronoun.	**194-195**
(6.18) Forms of nánal (nál) 'he, she, it is the one that'	194
(6.19) Examples of nánal (nál) 'he, she, it is the one that'	194-195
§6.5d. Presentational Particle as Emphatic.	**195**
(6.20) šé· P EMPH	195
§6.6. Discontinuous Constituents.	**195-197**
(6.21) Discontinuous particle compound	195
(6.22) Discontinuous compound verb	195-196
(6.23) Discontinuous noun phrase (demonstrative and participle)	196
(6.24) Discontinuous noun phrase (noun or pronoun and participle)	196
(6.25) Discontinuous noun phrase (particle and noun or participle)	196
(6.26) Discontinuous noun phrase (possessor and possessed noun)	196
(6.27) Discontinuous noun phrase (locative)	197
(6.28) Discontinuous noun phrase (oblique complement of the included relative root)	197
(6.29) Discontinuous subordinate clause	197
(6.30) Two discontinuous clauses intertwined	197
§6.7. Gapping.	**197-198**
(6.31) Conjoined verbs with gapping	198
(6.32) Conjoined verbs: second head verb gapped after preverb with prefix	198

Bibliography.   **199-200**

Preface

This grammar of the Eastern Algonquian language Southern Unami (Delaware; Lenape; ISO **unm**) has been completed to accompany the edition of Ira D. Blanchard's Harmony of the Gospels printed in Indian Territory (now Kansas) in the years 1837-1839 (Blanchard and Conner 2021). It is based principally on Blanchard's Harmony (and his three primers) and materials collected from Oklahoma Delawares in the twentieth century by C.F. Voegelin and myself.

The principal aim has been to make it possible for those interested in this language to recognize and understand the considerable complexities of its inflected forms. Full paradigms are given, along with many examples. The basic processes of stem formation and derivation are also presented. Special attention is also paid to topics that may be considered unusual or challenging, such as discontinuous constituents, focus constructions, equational sentences, and gapping. A formal account of syntax is not included, however.

This work would not have been possible without the patient assistance of the Delaware speakers I worked with from 1966 to 1970, especially Ollie Beaver Anderson and Martha Snake Ellis. Other speakers I worked with and those heard in the Lenape Talking Dictionary (see p. 2) are named on pp. 1-2. I have also benefited from the collegial assistance of Jim Rementer, Todd Thompson, and Raymond Whritenour, who provided useful and sometimes critical materials on more than one occasion. The text of Blanchard's Harmony was entered by Oana David and Stephanie Hasselbacher. Miles Beckwith compiled the *Glossary* to Blanchard's publications and aided with the preparation of the final text of the edition and the grammar. I am indebted to David J. Costa for comments on an earlier draft of this book.

Southern Unami is the heritage language of the Delaware Tribe of Indians (Bartlesville, Okla.) and the Delaware Nation of Western Oklahoma (Anadarko). The last two speakers died in 2000 and 2002.

Washington, February 2021

Abbreviations and Conventions
(unified list, including some from related works)

Abbreviations (grammatical terms and references)

A.	Albert Anthony
Acts	Acts of the Apostles
AGTV	agentive (**§5.6.l**)
AI	animate intransitive (**§3.7e**)
AI+O	AI stem taking a secondary object (transitivized AI; **§3.7f**)
AN, AN, anim.	animate (**§3.2**)
/b	Blanchard text as printed
B, B.	Blanchard (esp. Blanchard 1837[-1839])
B&A	Brinton and Anthony (1889)
BPL	Bartlesville Public Library
CC	changed conjunct (**§4.6**)
cf.	compare
CNJ	the conjunct indicative or PLAIN conjunct (**§4.6**)
COLL, coll.	collective (**§5.8c**)
CONT	continuative (continuative-attenuative) (**§5.4**)
Cor	Corinthians
/cp	Anglican *Book of Common Prayer* (1662)
CS	changed subjunctive (**§4.6**)
DIM, dim.	diminutive (**§5.5b**, **§5.8a**)
dict.	O'Meara (1996), a Munsee dictionary
/e	emended text
EAb	Eastern Abenaki (esp. Penobscot dialect)
em.	emended, emendation, to be emended
EMPH	emphatic (**§3.6**; **§6.5d**)
exc.	exclusive (**§3.6**)
EXT	extended (**§5.4**)
FI	future imperative (**§4.12d**)
FOC	focus (5.24o)
FUT	future (5.24b)
Gr.	Grammar
HAB	habitual (**§5.4**)
Heb	Hebrews
HRSY	(evidential for hearsay account) (5.24g)
IC	initial change (**§4.6**)
II	inanimate intransitive (**§3.7e**)
Ill	Illinois

IMP, imp.	(ordinary) imperative (**§4.12a**)
IN, IN, inan.	inanimate (**§3.2**)
inc.	inclusive (**§3.6**)
IND, ind.	independent indicative (**§4.4a**)
indef.	indefinite (**§3.6**)
INJ	injunctive (**§4.12c**)
IPA	International Phonetic Alphabet
ital.	italics
Jn	John
JR	Jim Rementer
/k	King James text (Authorized Version)
KHS	Kansas Historical Society (online scan of B)
KJV, K	King James Bible
/kl	King James and Lieberkühn texts combined
L.	Lieberkühn
L.1	Lieberkühn (1771)
L.2	Lieberkühn (1823)
/l	Lieberkühn text (1823)
Lk	Luke
LOC	locative (**§4.2d**)
Mah	Mahican
Mass	Massachusett
MEP	*Morning and Evening Prayers* (Wampum and Hogg 1847)
Mes	Meskwaki
MH	*A Collection of Hymns in Muncey and English* (Halfmoon 1874)
Mk	Mark
Mt	Matthew
ms.	manuscript
Mun	Munsee
Narr	Narragansett
NEG	negative (**§4.4c**)
NF	noun final (**§5.1**)
O1	primary object (**§3.7a**)
O2	secondary object (**§3.7a**)
OBL	oblique (**§3.7b**)
obv., OBV	obviative (**§3.4**)
OBV.POSS	obviative possessor (**§4.2a**)
Oj	Ojibwe
om.	omitted
p	plural
P	particle (**§3.1a**)
/p	phonemic interpretation
PA	Proto-Algonquian
PC	plain conjunct (**§4.6**)
PEA	Proto–Eastern Algonquian
PERF	perfective

PL	plural reduplication (§5.4)
pl	plural
PN	prenoun (§5.9)
PF	particle final (§5.1)
poM	postmedial (§5.2)
poR	postradical (= postinitial) (§5.2)
POSS.TH	possessed theme (§4.2)
PP	preparticle (§5.9)
PPL, ppl.	participle (§4.6)
PRES	presentational (§6.5b; 6.10h-q)
PRET, pret.	preterite (§4.4b)
prF	prefinal (§5.2)
prM	premedial (§5.2)
PROH, proh.	prohibitive (negative imperative) (§4.12b)
prox.	proximate (§3.4)
PRST	present (§4.8)
PST	past (5.24m)
PV	preverb (§5.9)
Q	question (5.24eh)
R	(abstract marker of reduplication formula; §5.4)
/r	Revised Standard Version
redup.	reduplication (§5.4)
REP	repetitive (repetitive-intensive) (§5.4)
RSV	Revised Standard Version
s	singular
SB1	Spelling-Book, first edition (Zeisberger 1776)
SB2	Spelling Book, second edition (Zeisberger 1806)
s.b.	should be
SBD, sbd.	subordinative (§4.4a)
SBJ	subjunctive (§4.6)
sg	singular
Sh	Shawnee
smthg	something (place-holder for the complement of a relative root)
smwh	somewhere (place-holder for the complement of a relative root)
s.o.	someone (third person animate; 'him', 'her', or animate 'it')
/t	translation of line "/p"
TA	transitive animate (§3.7e)
TA+O	TA taking a secondary object (double-object stem; ditransitive stem; §3.7f)
TH	theme (§4.2a, §4.4d)
TI	transitive inanimate (§3.7e)
TI-O	TI stem not taking an object (syntactically objectless TI; §3.7f)
VOC, voc.	vocative (§4.2f)
Z.	Zeisberger (1887)
Z. 2014	Zeisberger (2014)

Abbreviations (speakers and other sources)

AD	Anna Davis
AP	Anna Parks
APh	Anderson Pheasant (Munsee)
B	Ira D. Blanchard
BF	Blanche French
BS	Bessie Snake (in LTD)
CH	Charles Halfmoon (Munsee)
CW	James C. (Charlie) Webber
EJ	Enoch Jacobs (Munsee)
EJo	Emily Johnson (Munsee)
ER	Elijah Reynolds
FE	Frank Exendine
FF	Fred Fallleaf (in LTD)
FW	Freddie Washington
JA	John Armstrong (Munsee)
JM	Josephine Martinez (in LTD)
LB	Lucy Blalock (in LTD)
LHW	Lillie Hoag Whitehorn (in LTD)
LTD	Lenape Talking Dictionary (http://www.talk-lenape.org)
ME	Martha Ellis
MR	Mary Riley (Munsee)
ND	Nora Dean (fieldnotes; "LTD ND" if in the LTD)
NP	Nicodemus Peters (Munsee)
OA	Ollie Anderson
SP	Stella Parton
V	C.F. Voegelin (V* = inflection attested on another stem)
VJ	Vester Jacobs (Munsee)
WL	Willie Longbone
WP	Winnie Poolaw
WS	Willie Snake (in LTD)
WT	Willard Thomas (LTD)

Symbols

*	(before a stem or word) Reconstructed for a protolanguage but not attested; conjectured correct spelling of a misprinted word.
*	(after a stem or word) Unattested shape or form (supported by other forms).
†	Phonemic shape conjectured.
/	In line /b, separates the printed lines; in lines /p and /t, separates segments of text that do not cohere idiomatically.

|..|	enclose the underlying form (§2.1)
/../	enclose a phonemic transcription (§2.1)
[..]	enclose a (more detailed or specific) phonetic transcription (§2.1 end); in lines /k, /kl, or /l these enclose untranslated words
⟨..⟩	enclose the exact spelling of the source
{..}	enclose the conventional gloss of an oblique complement (§3.7b)
(..)	enclose the pronominal gloss of the indefinite object (or inverse subject) of an absolute form

>	becomes (becoming), develops to, changes to, making the derivative
<	coming from
←	the realization of, the recategorized use of
-	separates the parts of a compound stem, or flags parts that are not contiguous
=	marks the following word as an enclitic (§5.3a)

Bullets

- ▪ (square bullet)   marks the section for a stem type or the like
- • (round bullet)   indicates a change of stem shape
- ♦ (diamond bullet)   indicates a comment on usage or related words
- ▶ (arrow bullet)   directs readers to a cross reference or other note

Person-marking

Persons: 1 first person; 1s first singular; 1p first plural exclusive; 12 first plural inclusive; 2 second person; 2s second singular; 2p second plural; 3 third person animate; 3s third person animate singular; 3p third person animate plural; 3´ third person animate obviative; 0 third person inanimate; 0s third person inanimate singular; 0p third person inanimate plural; X indefinite person.

Inflection for arguments: 3s third singular subject or possessor; 1s–2s first singular subject acting on second singular primary object; 3s–(0) third singular animate subject acting on inanimate object (absolute); 3s–0s third singular animate subject acting on third singular inanimate (objective); 3p–3´+0 third plural animate subject acting on third obviative primary object plus inanimate secondary object (objective).

1. Introduction

§1.1. This grammar describes some aspects of the Southern Unami dialect of the Delaware language, in varying degrees of detail. Unami is the name applied to the Eastern Algonquian language spoken at the time of European contact over most of the area of the present state of New Jersey and in adjacent areas in the Delaware River Valley and west of Delaware Bay. Its sister language Munsee was spoken to the north and east, and the more distantly related Nanticoke language was spoken to the south.

§1.2. Name. There is no universally accepted name for the Unami language. "Unami," the term used by German-speaking Moravian missionaries in the eighteenth century, is from the Munsee name *wə̆náˑmiˑw*, literally 'person from downriver'. The name Delaware, sometimes used for both Unami and Munsee, is from the name of the Delaware River, a designation originating in English. Speakers of Unami called themselves Lenape (Unami *lənáˑpˑe*), and this term is also commonly used in English for the language, but its earlier meaning, still used by Blanchard, was 'person, human being'. Unami *alləníˑxsu* is used for 'he or she speaks Delaware (Unami)', and Blanchard has the related expression *énta-ləníˑxsink*, literally 'in the ordinary language', on his Delaware title page. A more recent label is *lənapˑeˑíˑi-liˑxsəwáˑkˑan*, literally 'language of the Lenape (Indian)'. The term Unami is used here because it can be applied unambiguously to all varieties in all time periods.

§1.3. Dialects. There is evidence for three major dialects of Unami. In the eighteenth century the missionary David Zeisberger included in his dictionary three variants of the word for 'wolf' (⟨Tumme⟩, ⟨Tímmeu⟩, and ⟨Mĕtümmeu⟩; Zeisberger 1887:234), which can be transcribed phonemically as *tə́me*, *tə́meˑw*, and *mətə́meˑw*. The first of these is the word used by Blanchard and later in Oklahoma. The third of these was used on the "upper part" of the Delaware River, presumably in the area of the falls where Trenton now is (found as ⟨Metumnu⟩, evidently misread at the end; Jameson 1909:58-59). Zeisberger was giving the variants from south to north, and the dialects of Unami they represent can be identified as Southern Unami (with *tə́me*), the dialect described here, and two varieties of Northern Unami, both of which are reflected in the writings of the Moravian missionaries. The northernmost of the three dialects must be the one the Moravians called Unalachtigo (Munsee *wə̆naláhtkoˑw* 'person of the upper (tidal) river'); its location is shown by documents and connections unearthed by Hunter (1974:151).

There was minor variation among the last speakers in Oklahoma, much of it apparently due to relatively recent divergent innovation. Speakers occasionally pointed to lexical differences between "Dewey" and "Anadarko" speech. They seem never to have volunteered differences in pronunciation or grammar, but archaic usages of other speakers were sometimes rejected.

§1.4. Sources. Ira D. Blanchard's translation of the revised English version of Samuel Lieberkühn's (1823) harmony of the Gospels has been used extensively (Blanchard 1837 [1839]; "B"), as have, to a lesser extent, his three primers (Blanchard 1834a, 1834b, 1842). The various publications and writings of C.F. Voegelin ("V"), almost entirely derived from Willie Longbone (WL), were also important sources. Some forms were taken from the fieldnotes of Truman Michelson (1912). Materials obtained during my fieldwork (1966-1970) are referred to by the speakers' initials where it seemed appropriate to indicate who used a particular form or sentence: Ollie Anderson (OA), Martha Ellis (ME), Anna Davis (AD), Anna (pronounced "Annie") Parks (AP), Freddie Washington (FW), Elijah Reynolds (ER), Bessie Snake (BS), Willie Snake (WS),

Stella Parton (SP), Winnie Poolaw (WP), Blanche French (BF), and Frank Exendine (FE). Words documented by sound clips from native speakers in the Lenape Talking Dictionary (LTD; http://www.talk-lenape.org) are marked with their initials, mostly Lucy Blalock (LB) and Nora Dean (ND), but also Fred Fallleaf (FF), OA, BS, and WS. Some forms cited were recorded by Frank G. Speck from James C. (Charlie) Webber (CW).

2. Sound System

§2.1. Phonemes. The inventory of the phonemes of Southern Unami is in (2.1). The phonemes are the distinctive sounds of a language, those which contrast in at least some environments to distinguish different words. Slashes are used to specify a phonemic transcription (/a/, /p/).

(2.1) The segmental phonemes of Southern Unami
  Consonants:
    voiceless stops and affricate   p   t   č   k
    voiceless long stops and affricate   p·   t·   č·   k·
    voiceless fricatives   s   š   x   h
    voiceless long fricatives   s·   š·   x·
    voiced nasals   m   n
    voiced approximants   w   l   y
  Vowels:
    short vowels   i   e   a   ɔ   u   ə
    long vowels   i·   e·   a·   ɔ·   o·   (ə·)

It can also be useful to cite UNDERLYING forms, abstract representations that factor out the grammatical variation in the phonemic shapes of related forms; these are enclosed in bars (|a|, |p|). Underlying long and short vowels do not correspond directly to phonemic long and short vowels; underlying long vowels are marked by macron (|ā|, |ī|). Underlying |i| and |u| are written where phonemic /i/ and /u/ are not accounted for by the phonological processes described in §2.5. Other underlying segments treated irregularly are underlined. Formulaically |C| refers to any consonant.

Phonetic detail can be indicated by phonetic transcriptions, given in square brackets ([ʌ], [d]).

§2.1a. Spelling. The letters that represent the phonemes have the pronunciations that are standard in technical linguistic usage, except that /n/ is pronounced [ŋ] (like English "ng") before /k/. /č/ is like English "ch" in *church* (or more precisely like the unaspirated "ch" in Spanish), and /š/ is like "sh" in *ship*. /x/ is a velar fricative (IPA [x]), like the "j" of Spanish or the "ch" in German *Bach*; Unami /x/ is articulated further forward than Munsee /x/, which is consistently a back velar (IPA [χ]). A raised dot marks a long consonant or vowel; these are generally less than twice the length of the corresponding short phonemes, and in fact good speakers in the 1960's disfavored overly long pronunciations of consonants. A long consonant after a vowel is perceived as "ambisyllabic" (Voegelin 1946:131): both at the end of the preceding syllable and at the beginning of the following syllable. In contrast, when a short voiceless consonant follows a long vowel and is followed by a vowel, the preceding vowel is heard as having a slight to prominent falling pitch and decreasing amplitude (loudness), and the consonant begins the following syllable. The /ɔ/, called "open oh," is technically described as an open-mid back rounded vowel; this is the vowel in English *law* in the speech of those that distinguish this from *la*. The /ə/ (schwa) is a mid central vowel, like the unstressed vowel in the first syllable of *connect* and *polite* or the last syllable of *bottom* and *rhythm*.

§2.1b. Consonant clusters. The primary clusters of true consonants are: *sk, sp; šk; xp, xk; mp, nt, nč, nk, ns, nš; hp, ht, hč, hk, hs, hš*. In addition *p, k, x, h*, and *m* as single consonants or the second members of cluster may be followed by *w* (though not all combinations are attested). The secondary clusters (those that arise from the loss of an intervening short vowel) include the geminates *pp, tt, čč, kk, šš, hh, mm, nn, ww, ll*. These are doubly articulated or extra-long. (Potential geminate *ss* [from |s|+|s| and |š|+|s|] always seems to be restructured as long *s·*.) The geminates other than *tt, čč, šš,* and *hh* may occur word-initially, where /pp-/ is [p:] and /kk-/ is [k:] (i.e., longer than /p·/ and /k·/). Word-initial /pp-/ always includes an assimilated third person prefix (underlying |wə-|), /kk-/ always includes a second person |kə-| or (only before /w/ or /o·/) a third person |wə-|, and /nn-/ and /ll-/ always include a first person |nə-|, but not all speakers assimilate /nl-/ (underlying |nə-l-|) to /ll-/. In transcribing Blanchard's spellings, initial geminates have been written following the conservative pronunciation of Martha Ellis, heard in the 1960's. Some of the initial geminates were also sometimes heard from other speakers.

§2.1c. Nasal clusters. The voiceless consonants have variant but contrasting pronunciations after homorganic nasals (those pronounced at the same point of articulation). In this environment, the plain (non-long) stops and affricate are partially to fully voiced (before a vowel /mp/ is pronounced [mb], /nt/ is [nd], /nč/ is [ř̝], and /nk/ is [ŋg]), and the phonemic long consonants are short and voiceless (e.g., /nt·/ is [nt], [nᵗt], [n̥t]). The clusters with plain second members are word-initial clusters (necessarily secondary), and word-medial and word-final primary clusters; the clusters with long second members are secondary clusters. In the pronunciation that predominated in the twentieth century /ᴠns/ and /ᴠnš/ (using /ᴠ/ for any vowel) were [ṽ·s] and [ṽ·š] (with nasalized vowels conventionally written as phonemically long, including /ə·/, found only in such words). There were still some speakers, however, (e.g. SP) who had an older pronunciation like that of the other nasal clusters, with short, oral vowels and voiced consonants (/ᴠns/ [ṽnz]; /ᴠnš/ [ṽnž]). This is what Blanchard's spellings point to: e.g. ⟨Kxuns⟩ 'your older brother' (Jn 11.23), evidently for /kxáns/ rather than the later /kxá·ns/. Other speakers had a range of pronunciations for these clusters (e.g. BS).

In secondary clusters with a non-homorganic nasal or an /l/ as first member the first consonant is pronounced as in secondary clusters that have homorganic nasals, with some degree of devoicing in the nasal or /l/, but the second member is, by convention, written as short, since there is no contrast between short and long consonants in such clusters: e.g., *šəwánpi* 'salt water' (for *šəwánp·i*, with partly devoiced [n] and short voiceless [p]); *čəmámsak* 'rabbits' (for *čəmáms·ak*); *wi·k·əwámtət* 'little house' (OA; with /mt/ for /mt·/); *ntakwímkwən* 'he blamed me for it' (V; with /mk/ for /mk·/); *nhiltúwak* 'they killed each other' (OA; with /lt/ for /lt·/).

§2.1d. Long fricatives. Length was not considered to be phonemic for the fricatives by Voegelin (1946), though he sometimes noted long fricatives in his early transcriptions, but it eventually became evident (during my fieldwork in 1969 and 1970) that these contrasts existed and had to be written (Goddard 1979: Foreword viii; p. 22). The contrast between /s/ and /s·/, for example, is clearly heard in *sa·sap·ís·ak* 'fireflies' (with /s/ and /s·/), *hilo·sós·ak* 'old men' (with /sós·/), and *xawši·sósak* 'old women' (with /sós/) as pronounced by Lucy Blalock (in LTD). A clear example of a short /š/ between long vowels is in *ši·ší·p·e·* 'it is stretchy' as pronounced by the same speaker, which contrasts with the prominent long /š·/ in *ní·š·aš* 'seven' (ND).

§2.1e. Constraints; /ɔ/ and /ɔ·/. The phonemes do not combine freely in making words, and many sequences do not occur. For example, the long consonants only occur between vowels, or between a homorganic nasal and a vowel. Some tendencies do not involve absolute constraints. For example, the occurrence of long vowels in word-final position is restricted, and a process of shortening word-final vowels can be observed, but word-final long vowels do occur under some circumstances. The vowels /ɔ/ and /ɔ·/ are the realizations of underlying |wa| and |wa·| (**§2.10b**) and are subject to the same processes of weakening, lengthening, and shortening in related forms as /a/ and /a·/.

§2.2. Blanchard's orthography. The alphabet used by Blanchard (2.2) was devised by the printer Jotham Meeker, who had learned some Potawatomi and even more Ottawa, and who developed a series of alphabets for Indian languages that assigned arbitrary values to unneeded letters (McCoy 1835:26; Pilling 1891:351–356; McMurtrie and Allen 1930; Walker 1996:168–169). In (2.2) the "English values" are those implied by the English words given (Blanchard 1842:[3]).

(2.2) The Delaware alphabet used by Blanchard

	English values	Unami phonemes (recurring values)
a	[a]	/a·/; also /a/
b	[yu(w)]	/yu/, /yo·/, /yə/ (before /m/, /w/), /yəw/
c	[ɛ]	/e/, /ə/; /e·/ before /x·/
e	[i(y)]	/i·/, /i/; also /y/
f	[ŋg]	/nk/; /n/ before /k/
h	[č]	/č/, /č·/; also ⟨th⟩ for /č/ and especially /č·/
i	[ɪ]	/i/, /ə/, /-e/
j	[š]	/š/, /š·/
k	[k]	/k/, /k·/, /kk-/
l	[l]	/l/, /ll/
m	[m]	/m/, /mm/
n	[n]	/n/, /nn/
o	[o]	/ɔ/, /ɔ·/, /o·/
p	[p]	/p/, /p·/, /pp-/
q	[kw]	/kw/, /k·w/, /kkw-/; /kəw-/, /k·əw/
r	[e(y)]	/e·/, /e·y/, /e/
s	[s]	/s/, /s·/
t	[t]	/t/, /t·/
u	[ʌ]	/a/, /ə/, /ɔ/
v	[h]	/h/; rarely /x/; also indicates devoicing (e.g. ⟨lvk⟩ for /lk/)
w	[u(w)]	/o·/, /o·w/, /ɔ/, /u/, /əw/; /ə/ before /m/ or /p/; /ə/ after /w/; also /w/, /ww/
y	[ay]	/ay/, /ai/; /a/ before /y/ or /i/
x	*	/x/, /x·/

*"This character denotes an aspirate guttural sound." (Blanchard 1834b:2); "This letter denotes a guttural sound peculiar to the Delaware, and is quite indescribable." (Blanchard 1842:[3]).

The short, long, and geminate consonants are written the same, except that /č·/ is often written ⟨th⟩. When ⟨kk⟩ is written it always spells /kwk/ (the last time on p. 50); later this was written ⟨qk⟩ (first on p. 39). Ostensible ⟨tt⟩ is once written for /t·/, but this is at a line break: ⟨wrt-|tunan⟩ for /-wé·t·əna·n/ (p. 111). The only writing of a double consonant for a geminate is in ⟨tuntu skuppalao⟩ for /tə́nta-skappalá·ɔ/ 'he wet it (anim.) in (something)' (p. 207). The phoneme /x/ was generally kept distinct from /h/, and Blanchard became quite reliable at writing /h/ (⟨v⟩) before a consonant and often writes the generally non-distinctive word-final aspiration. Distinguishing the vowels was a problem (2.2), but over time Blanchard became more consistent and reliable, and he eventually came to write sequences of multiple vowels quite accurately.

§2.3. Weak and Strong Syllables. A pervasive feature that governs many alternations of vowels and consonants is the contrast between weak and strong syllables in what is referred to as the metrical structure of words. Basically, a syllable is strong if its vowel is long, or if it ends in a consonant cluster or is word-final. Other syllables are weak if they follow a strong syllable, and strong if they follow a weak syllable (including some originally weak syllables that now lack a vowel). Still others are strong because of special circumstances: they may have a short vowel that alternates with a long vowel in related forms (and can therefore be identified as an underlying long vowel), or they may simply be unpredictably strong, as often when patterns of alternation in related forms are leveled out (2.69, 70), or when they follow certain anomalous weak vowels (2.71). Some words or parts of words have short vowels and consonants where long phonemes would otherwise be expected; these are called STATIC words, syllables, and segments (§2.15). One syllable in each word bears a pitch accent (marked with an acute: ´), which has contrastively greater stress and loudness. The accent usually falls on the last non-final strong syllable, or the only strong syllable, but many words have the accent on the next preceding syllable, and it is not rare for either of two syllables to bear the accent.

§2.4. Weakening and Loss of Vowels. One widespread metrical effect is the weakening or loss of short vowels before voiceless consonants. This may have consequences for the adjacent consonants as well. Underlying |ə| is lost in a weak syllable before all voiceless consonants (2.3ac), except that it is retained in a word-initial sequence /mə-/ or /lə-/: məkó·s 'awl'; ləpákw 'he weeps'. It is also lost in the sequences |ləl| (2.5n), |lən| (with assimilation to /nn/; 2.3b), and |yəl| (with assimilation to /ll/; 2.14a); word-initially in the sequences |nən| (if |nə-| is the first person prefix; 5i) and |nəl| (giving /nl-/ and /ll-/ for different speakers; 2.3c); and in |wəw| in all positions (2.3d), with some exceptions (**§2.11d**). (|lən| remains as /lən/ if the |l| is in the TA theme sign |-əl| marking a second person object [2.19f].) Underlying |a| in a weak syllable is usually retained as /a/ before a voiced consonant, but it is replaced by /ə/ after /h/ (unless restored by analogy); it is usually retained as /ah/ before a voiceless consonant (2.3eg), but it is lost before |h| (2.3f) and |x|. Phonemic /ɔ/ (underlying |wa|) is affected the same way as |a|, its weak equivalent being /ɔh/ (2.3g). (In the underlying forms given in these examples, the vowels that are lost are crossed out with a slash (|ə̸|, |a̸|), and the ones that are weakened (adding /h/ or, before a voiced consonant, becoming /ə/ [**§10j**]) are marked with a breve accent (|ă|).)
(2.3) Syncope (loss) and weakening of short vowels in weak syllables
    (a) kwtə́k·i·w (|kwə̸təkī-w|) 'he went back'; nkwə́tki (|nə̸-kwətə̸kī|) 'I went back'
    (b) nkənnə́mən (|nə̸-kələ̸n-əmən|) 'I carried it';
        kələnínke (|kələn-ənkē|) 'if he carries it'
    (c) nlúnkɔhsəs and llúnkɔhsəs (|nə̸lənkwăsəs|) 'my nephew'
    (d) kó·li-wwa·háwwa (|kōlī wə̸wāh-āwə̸wā|) 'you (pl.) know him well'
    (e) kahtúnkɔ·m (|kătənkwām-w|) 'he is sleepy';
        nkat·únkɔ·m (|nə̸-katənkwām|) 'I'm sleepy'
    (f) nkəphámən (|nə̸-kəpa̸hamən|) 'I shut it'; kpahánke (|kə̸pahankē|) 'when he shuts it';
        kpahəmáne (|kə̸paha̸manē|) 'when you (sg.) shut it'
    (g) tahkɔ́č·u (|tăkwačī-w|) 'he is cold'; ntákɔhči (|nə̸-takwăčī|) 'I'm cold'
A short |a| or |ə| that is not subject to weakening or loss is indicated in underlying forms with a grave accent (`): təpčéhəla·s (|tə̀pə̸čēhlās|) 'wagon' (with |tə̀p-| 'around, circling'); see also (2.4a). A vowel may be weak in some forms and strong in others: |aləm-| (2.10c), but áləmi PV 'begin'.

§2.4a. Loss of underlying strong short vowels. Short vowels are also sometimes lost in underlying strong syllables that are not preceded by a weak syllable (that is, they are either preceded by a strong syllable or they are word-initial). This vowel loss takes place before clusters that begin with a fricative (/sk/, /sp/, /šk/, /xp/, /xk/).

(2.4) Syncope of short vowels before clusters containing a voiceless fricative
- (a) təp·i·nxké·p·i (|təpīnə̸xkēpəy|) 'bracelet'; cf. nnáxk 'my hand'
- (b) ɔ́·pskɔ (|wāpə̸skw-a|) 'corn husks'; cf. ɔ́·p·askw (|wāpaskw|) 'corn husk'
- (c) nkát·a-kwtə́kskaɔ (|nə̸-kata|, |kwə̸tə̸kə̸skaw-ā|) 'I tried to drive him back';
   cf. nkwətkə́skaɔ (|nə̸-kwətə̸kəskaw-ā|) 'I drove him back'

The alternations produced by the process in (2.4) are very commonly leveled out by the restoration (or non-deletion) of the vowel. These retained vowels may also be marked in underlying forms with a grave accent (|ə̀|, |à|), though this has not been done uniformly: askáskwe· (|àskàskwē-w|) 'it is green'; ma·laxkwsí·t·a (|mālàxkwəsīt-a|) 'beans'; kaxpí·s·u (|kàxpīsī-w|) 'he is tied up'. A retained vowel may be deleted in a related form: káski PV (|kàskī|) 'be able to', but máta kí·kski (|kī+kaskī|) 'be not ever able to'; |ə̀| in 5.9c but |ə| in 2.10a.

§2.5. Underlying |h|. Metrical structure and other factors affect underlying |h|, which is not always realized as a phonemic /h/. A long vowel and a following underlying cluster of |h| and voiceless consonant are realized as a long vowel followed by a short consonant, the |h| being lost (2.5a). If a short vowel precedes the |h|, the treatment is the same (with the vowel being lengthened) as long as the preceding syllable is weak (2.5bc). But if the preceding syllable is strong (or there is no preceding syllable), the |h| metathesizes (changes places) with the vowel, which stays short, and the consonant is also short (2.5bc). If the consonant after the underlying |h| is voiced and followed by a phonemic vowel, a phoneme /ə/ is inserted to break up the underlying cluster (2.5defg), but if the voiced consonant in the underlying cluster comes to stand before a consonant (because an intervening |ə| was deleted) or is word-final, the |h| is lost (2.5eijk). Metathesis occurs under the same conditions as with a voiceless consonant (2.5di). When a long vowel precedes an |h| that has a /ə/ inserted after it, the underlying long vowel is shortened (2.5fg), but its status as an underlying long vowel blocks it from metathesizing (2.5f). The same shortening takes place if the /ə/ after the /h/ is an underlying |ə| followed by |l| or |w| (2.5h). If the short vowel originally before an underlying |h| is |ə|, it is replaced by /i/ (or lengthened to /i·/) in most environments (2.5il), but it is replaced by /u/ (or lengthened to /o·/) if the cluster is |hp|, |hkw|, |hm|, or |hw| (2.5mn).

(2.5) Some treatments and effects of underlying |h|
- (a) pá·pu (|pāhpī-w|) 'he (she) is playing', mpá·pi (|nə̸-pāhpī|) 'I'm playing'
- (b) mahtá·ke·w (|mātahkē-w|) 'he fights'; nəmatháke (|nə̸-matahkē|) 'I fight'
- (c) hatá·p·i 'bow' (|ahtāpəy|); nta·tá·p·i (|nə̸t-ahtāpəy|) 'my bow'
- (d) hál (|ahl|) 'put him, them (you sg.)!'; ntáhəla (|nə̸t-ahl-āw|) 'I put him'
- (e) wəlahəlánkwe (|wəlahl-ankwē|) 'if we (inc.) marry (*lit.*, keep) him';
   wəlaltiénke (|wəlahlətī-yēnkē|) 'if we (exc.) get married (to each other)'
- (f) pəníhəle·w (|pənīhlā-w|) 'he fell'; kpəníhəla (|kə̸-pənīhlā|) 'you fell'
- (g) ktəlawéhəmɔ (|kə̸t-ələwē-hmwā|) 'you (pl.) say {so}';
   ntələwéhəna (|nə̸t-ələwē-h(mə)nā|) 'we (exc.) say {so}';
      cf. lúwe·w and lúwe· (|ələwē-w|) 'he says {so}'
- (h) kpehəlúhəmɔ (|kə̸-pēh-ələhmwā|) 'I waited for you (pl.)';
   péhəwe·w (|pēhəwē-w|) 'he (she) is waiting' (V); cf. kpé·həl 'I waited for you (sg.)';
- (i) nníhəla (|nə̸-nəhl-āw|) 'I killed him'; nhíl (|nəhl|) 'kill him, them (you sg.)!';
   nnílko·k (|nə̸-nəhl-ə̸kōk|) 'they killed me'
- (j) wíl (|wīhl|) 'name him, them (you sg.)!';
   cf. kwíši-wihəlawwá·a 'they had named them' (OA)
- (k) wí·k·əwam (|wīkəwahm|) 'house'; cf. wi·k·əwáhəma (|wīkəwahm-a|) 'houses'

(l) mhitó·x·we·w (|məhtōxwē-w|) 'he's going on foot';
    nəmi·tó·x·we (|nə-məhtōxwē|) 'I'm going on foot'
(m) íka ló·kwe· (|ə̷ləhkwē-w|) 'he looked there' (íka 'there' [not deictic]);
    ná íka təlhúkwe·n (|wət-ələhkwē-n|) 'then he looked there' (ná 'then')
(n) ktəllúhəmə (|kə̷tələ̷ləhmwā|) 'I tell you (pl.)';
    kpənuntələlhúmə (|kə̷-pənōntələləhmwā|) 'I showed you (pl.)'

Although underlying |hC| is eliminated, clusters of /h/ and a voiceless consonant (not from weakened |a| [**§2.4**]) are not rare. These clusters are always preceded by a short vowel, an underlying long vowel being shortened. (A unique exception is the diminutive stem of 'heart': 5.46q.) They occur where |ə| is lost from an underlying |həC|, in certain kinds of reduplication, and in imitative and expressive words: ma·č·ihtí·t·e (|māčīhətītē|) 'when they went home'; kihkəmó·tke·p 'he had been a thief'; tíhtəs 'small woodpecker'.

§2.6. Other Consonant Changes. Some of the changes that affect the adjacent consonants when a vowel is deleted have been illustrated (2.3bc). Another such effect is the replacement of a long consonant in a secondary cluster by its short counterpart (2.4b), except after a homorganic nasal (**§2.1c**). Potential word-initial clusters may be reduced (2.6a), and in some cases a word-initial syllable is deleted even though syllables of the same or similar shape are retained in other words (2.6bc). If a word-initial /mh-/ or /nh-/ would potentially result from the metathesis of |ah| or |əh|, the nasal is lost in some cases (2.6def) but retained in others (2.5il, 2.8d).

(2.6) Initial-syllable reduction and loss
    (a) kší·k·an (|pə̷xkə̷šīkan|) 'knife'; mpaxkší·k·an (|nə̷-paxkə̷šīkan|) 'my knife' (V)
    (b) tá·x·an (|mə̷tāxan|) '(piece of) wood'; nəmət·á·x·an 'my (piece of) wood' (V, OA, ME)
    (c) kəhó·k·an (|tə̷kwahākan|) 'corn mortar'; ntakhó·k·an 'my corn mortar' (OA);
         also regularized nkəhó·k·an 'my corn mortar'
    (d) hitamí·x·ən (|nəhtamīxən|) 'it is first';
         cf. ne·tamí·x·ink (|nēhtamīxənk| < |IC+nəhtamīxən-k|) 'one (inan.) that is first'
    (e) hít·ukw (|məhtəkw|) 'stick'; cf. nəmí·tkəm (|nə-məhtə̷kw-əm|) 'my stick' (ME)
    (f) hákhakw 'bottle'; cf. nəmá·khakw 'my bottle' (V)

Extreme variation in shape has generally been leveled out (2.6c), and the cases that survive may best be considered as simply irregular patterns. There are more examples in **§2.14** of stem variation resulting from the presence or absence of the pronominal prefixes.

§2.7. Effects of weakened |a|. The weakening of |a| to /ah/ or /ɔh/ has other secondary effects. A preceding long or potentially long consonant (an underlying plain consonant subject to lengthening) is shortened, and before this consonant a long vowel is also shortened (2.7abc). A consonant without a long counterpart (2.7de) or a consonant that is underlying |hC| (2.7f) does not have this effect. Also, if a weak /ah/ is preceded by an underlying |hl|, the |h| is lost (2.7g).

(2.7) Secondary effects of the weakening of |a|
    (a) čípahkə (|(ma)čīpăkw-a|) 'shoes'; čí·p·akw (|(ma)čīpakw|) 'shoe'
    (b) pásahpɔ·n (|pāsăpwān|) 'light bread'; pá·ste· (|pāsə̷tē-w|) 'it puffs up in cooking'
    (c) či·mákɔhtu (|čīmākwătō|) 'they (inan.) stink'; či·má·k·ɔt (|čīmākwat-w|) 'it stinks'
    (d) ɔ́·lahkat (|wālăkat-w|) 'it is a hole'
    (e) ká·hahpɔ·n (|kāhăpwān|) 'corn bread'; ká·han 'it (a river or pond) is dry, shallow'
    (f) ktá·pahpi·n (|kə̷t-ahpăpī-n|) 'you (sg.) sit on it';
         hápahpi (|ahpăpī-(l)|) 'sit on it (you sg.)!'
    (g) wi·kwílahta·w (|wīhkwīhlătā-w|) 'he has his horse tire under him' (V);
         wi·kwíhəle·w (|wīhkīhlā-w|) 'he is tired' (V)

§2.8. Long Consonants in Metathesized Syllables. In a two-syllable word with metathesis in the first syllable a following voiceless consonant becomes long. This lengthened consonant may be extended to longer words based on the two-syllable word (2.8b, 5.13b).
(2.8) Secondary lengthening after metathesized sequences
    (a) hák·i (|ahkəy|) 'land, earth', loc. hák·ink; ntá·ki (|nət-ahkəy|) 'my land';
          cf. hakiá·lakw (|ahkəyālakw|) 'cellar', "dugout" (*lit.*, 'earth hole')
    (b) hát·e· (|ahtē-w|) 'it exists, is (somewhere)'; hat·é·k·e (|ahtē-kē|) 'if it exists'
    (c) khík·ay (|kəhkay|) 'old person'; cf. khíkayak (|kəhkay-ak|) 'old people'
    (d) mhúk·u (|məhkwī-w|) 'he, it bleeds'; cf. mhukwí·tam 'he has a nosebleed'

The irregular pronominal form nhák·ay 'myself' (khák·ay 'yourself'), which does not have metathesis (underlying |n-ə́hakay|), is treated in the third singular form as if it did: hɔ́kaya 'himself, herself' (but hɔk·ayúwa 'themselves'). This treatment seems at odds with Voegelin's (1946:131) claim that the secondary /t·/ in (2.8b) was ambisyllabic but "neither long nor fortis."

§2.9. Word-final changes. An underlying word-final long vowel is shortened (2.3abfg, 4c, 5abefhj, 8b). But a long vowel may or may not be shortened if it comes to be word-final because of the loss of a final consonant (|l|, |w|, |h|). The conditions under which these consonants are lost are complex and differ depending on their grammatical function.

§2.9a. Word-final |-l|. The imperative singular suffix |-l| is optionally lost, and when this happens the preceding long vowel is treated like an underlying final vowel and shortened (2.9a). The imperative form with retained /-l/ is not a free variant, however; it predominates in Blanchard and was later apparently established as an alternative, more emphatic form. Ordinarily, word-final /-l/ is retained (2.5c, 5j, 19e), but the homophonous suffixes |-a| INAN.PL and |-a| OBV each also have an archaic variant |-al| that is attested by Blanchard, especially in his earlier work, but extremely rare later (2.17c). When these suffixes are contracted with |w| to |-ōl|, the younger variant without the |l| undergoes the same word-final vowel shortening as in the case of the imperative (2.17ab, 18b), but the forms with /-l/ appear to be rare, archaic free variants, with no distinct function.
(2.9) Loss of final |l|.
    (a) kawí (|kawī|) 'sleep (you sg.)!', beside (more emphatic) kawí·l (|kawī-l|)
    (b) ahsə́na 'stones' (B 10x, V, OA, ME, ND); older ahsə́nal (B 4x)
    (c) kkwí·s·a 'his or her son or sons' (B 36x, OA, ME); older kkwí·s·al (B 31x)

§2.9b. Word-final |-w|. A stem-final |w| in nouns is always dropped word-finally after an unstressed long vowel, and the vowel is shortened (2.10a). The formative element |-w| of the TA w-endings (marking definite animate objects in the independent indicative; **§4.5**) is also dropped word-finally with vowel-shortening, but this happens even if the vowel is stressed (2.10b). The independent indicative third singular suffix |-w| (4.20) had begun to disappear in Blanchard's day, but it continued to be occasionally heard in the twentieth century; a preceding vowel always remains long (2.10c). After the negative suffix |-(ō)w(ī)| the third singular |-w| was lost word-finally with vowel shortening, like the formative |-w| (2.12). The |-w| in the TA passive is treated like the third singular |-w|; it is always dropped, but there is no shortening (2.10d). The nouns with stress on the final syllable are also treated the same way; there are few attestations of the final |w|, but the vowel is always kept long (2.10e). In contrast to all these other cases of word-final |w|, a stem-final (or analogical) |w| that is word-final in a TA singular imperative is always retained (2.10f, 11c). Imperatives of this category are also unique in retaining word-final |-əw| (as /-əw/ or /-úw/); this is otherwise always replaced by /-u/ (2.10g). An underlying |w| preceded

by a consonant is lost word-finally (2.3e, 17a) unless it is preceded by k; word-final |-k(-)w| is retained as /-kw/ (2.16cdf).
(2.10) Loss of final |w|.
    (a) skí·xkwe (|wəskīxkwēw|) 'young woman'; pl. ski·xkwé·ɔk (|wəskīxkwēw-ak|) (B, V)
    (b) nníhəla (|nə-nəhl-āw|) 'I killed him', nnihəlá·ɔk (|nə-nəhl-āwak|) 'I killed them' (V);
          íka ntəli-lá (|nət-əlī əl-āw|) 'I sent him word' (íka 'there' [not deictic];
            |əlī| PV 'to'; |əl-| 'say {so} to') (OA)
    (c) pé·w and pé· (|pēw| < |pā-w|) 'he came' (B); pé· (later)
          aləmske·w (|aləməskā-w|) 'he left' (B, V); aləmske· (B and later)
    (d) thwə́na· (|tạhwən-āw|) 'she was arrested' (B)
    (e) pəlé·w (|pəlēw|) 'Turkey Clan member' (V, AP); pəlé· (others)
          xkwé· (|axkwēw|) 'woman' (all sources); xkwé·w (AP after prompting)
          məté· (|mətēw|) 'man of great spiritual power' (more commonly məte·ínnu) (OA)
    (f) wí·č·e·w (|wīčēw|) 'go with him (you sg.)!' (OA, ME, LB);
          né·w (|nēw|) 'see him (you sg)!' (V; not used by others)
    (g) pé·š·əw (|pēšəw|) 'bring him, them (you sg.)!' (ME, LB);
          cf. ahpú (|apəw| < |apī-w|) 'he is there, exists'; lə́nu (|ələnəw|) 'man' (pl. lə́nəwak)

§2.9c. Word-final |-h|. Word-final /h/ is found only in a few uninflected words with final stress. An underlying word-final |h| is otherwise deleted, with a preceding long vowel remaining long (2.11a). When this happened in a TA singular imperative, the resulting shortened form was originally used (2.11b), but it was later analogically reshaped with an added /-w/ (always retained) or /-haw/ (2.11c).
(2.11) Loss of final |h|.
    (a) nté· (|nətēh|) 'my heart' (V, OA; cf. wté·ha 'his heart')
    (b) ké·nahki· (|kēnakīh|) 'take care of him (you sg.)!' (B; cf. nke·nahkí·ha 'I — him')
    (c) pó·ni·w (|pōnī(h)- + -w|) 'leave him alone (you sg.)!' (OA, ND); cf. po·ní·haw (OA)

§2.9d. Word-final post-vocalic /-i/. In negative verbs of the independent indicative the suffix |-(ō)w(ī)| NEG is almost always /-i/ word-finally in Blanchard and Voegelin (and note Goddard 1979:26). In the 1960's this /-i/ had assimilated to the preceding vowel (-ó·wi becoming -ó·u) for most speakers, with only a few occasionally retaining /-i/, and in fact Voegelin's recordings of WL also sometimes have this assimilation.
(2.12) Word-final negative suffix
    (a) takó· no·wa·há·i (|nə-wəwāh-āwīw|) 'I don't know him' (B, WP, BF [with ɔkó·])
          kó· no·wa·há·a (|nə-wəwāh-āwīw|) 'I don't know him' (others in 1960's)
    (b) pé·i 'comes (neg.)' (|pēwī| < |pā-wīw|); later pé·e:
          tá=á· šá·e pé·i 'he won't come right away' (B);
          tako· káski- íka -pé·i. 'he (she) could not come there' (V);
          tá=á· awé·n kí·xki íka pé·e 'no one would come near there' (ME)
    (c) takó· wəntamaɔ́·i (|wəntamaw-āwīw|) 'he was not taught' (B);
          kó· awé·n nne·ɔ́·i. (|nə̄-nēw-āwīw|) 'I didn't see anyone' (⟨nne·yó·i⟩ V 2x);
          kó·=húnt káhta-ne·ɔ́·i 'don't let anyone see him' (ME)
          xú máta kpalhɔ́·ɔ (|kə̄-palahw-āwīw|) 'you won't miss him' (ME)
    (d) tá=á· .. wələt·ó·wi (|wələt-ōwīw|) 'it would not be good' (B);
          takó· kəwi·nəwaməló·wi (|kə-wīnəwam-əlōwī|) 'I do not ask you (sg.)' (B);
          akó· háši kéku awé·n ntəlkó·wi (|nət-əl-əkōwīw|) 'nobody told me anything' (AP)

takó· wəli·x·ənó·wi 'it is not lawful' (verb 6x); also takó· wəli·x·ənó·u (3x) (B);
takó· káski- tə́ntay -milló·u. 'I can't give you (sg.) fire.' (WL recording)
akó· wəlǝt·ó·u (|wǝlǝt-ōwīw|) 'it is not good' (OA);
akó· kǝwinkalló·u (|kǝ-wīnkāl-ǝlōwī|) 'I don't like you' (OA)

Particles may also assimilate a final /-i/ to a long vowel (2.13ab), but in some /-i/ seems always to be retained (2.13cd). If a word-final /-i/ is part of a verb stem it is never assimilated (2.13e).

(2.13) Assimilation and non-assimilation of /-i/ outside the negative
  (a) kahtəné·i P 'year(s)' (B 10x); kahtəné·e (OA, ME)
  (b) məsəč·é·i P 'whole' (B); məsəč·é·e (B 1x; OA)
  (c) mayá·i P 'really, very', PN 'true' (B, OA, AD)
  (d) nahkó·i P 'any' (B, V, OA, ME)
  (e) nta·té·i (|nǝt-ahtēwī|) 'I stooped over' (OA);
      cf. haté·yu (|ahtēwəw| < |ahtēwī-w|) 'he stooped over' (OA)

§2.10. Vowel Replacement and vowel coloring. In some cases vowels are changed or replaced because of an adjacent underlying consonant or sequence, and often depending on the grammatical categories involved.

§2.10a. Vowel-shortening before clusters. A long vowel is shortened (|ō| becoming /u/) before a primary cluster of a nasal and a stop or affricate (2.14c, 2.19fg, 2.20a), and before a secondary cluster of two voiced consonants: /ll/ (2.12d, 2.14a), /nn/ (2.14b), /ww/ (2.3d, 2.5j, 2.14d), and /mm/ (2.14e, 5.35f). (Long vowels occur freely before the primary cluster /mw/. For shortening before |h| see **§2.5**.)

(2.14) Vowel-shortening before voiced consonants in clusters
  (a) ktalo·kallúhəmɔ 'I send you (pl.)' (B; |alōhkāl-| TA 'send', |kət–ǝlǝhmwā| 1s–2p/IND);
      cf. ntalo·ká·la 'I send him'
  (b) énnink=á· (|ēlə́nənk| < |IC+ǝlǝn-ǝnk|; =á· POT) 'what he could do' (B)
  (c) é·ank (|ēyānk| < |IC+ā-nk|) 'the way', *lit.* 'where one goes'; cf. é·a·t 'where he goes'
  (d) a·s·úwwak (|āsōwə́w-ak|) 'they sing' (WS); a·s·uwwá·k·an (|āsōwə́wākan|) 'song' (LB);
      cf. a·s·ó·u (|āsōwǝw|) 'he sings'
  (e) úmma· 'grandmother (voc.)'; cf. nó·həm 'my grandmother'

§2.10b. Contraction of |w| and |a| or |ā|. A |w| may contract with a following vowel or with vowels on either side to produce a vowel of a different quality.

Very generally |wa| is realized as /ɔ/ and |wā| is realized as /ɔ·/, vowels that undergo the same processes of weakening, shortening, and lengthening as underlying |a| and |ā| (2.3cg, 4b, 5ghn, 6c, 7abcde, 9bc, 12c, 15abc). The /ɔ/ quality spreads to a following |a|-quality vowel across an intervening |h| (2.6c), and in some cases across a |x| (2.15d). This contraction does not take place if the |w| is preceded by |ǝ| or |ō| (2.3d, 12ad), or in a few exceptional cases (2.15e). If contraction would have resulted in an alternation between /wa/ and /ɔ/ at the beginning of a stem, the variants are apparently always leveled, generalizing /ɔ/ (2.15f) or /wa/ (2.15g), but some speakers have doublets (LB in 2.15fg). Underlying stem-initial |wā| apparently always generalizes /ɔ·/ (2.15h), and similarly stem-initial |wah-| (/hɔ-/) is realized as /ɔ·/ after prefixes (2.15i).

(2.15) Contraction of |wa| and |wā| to /ɔ/, /ɔ·/, and /ɔh/
  (a) ktəskaɔ́k·e (|kə́tǝskaw-àkē|) 'if I cast them out'; cf. lák·e (|ə́l-àkē|) 'if I say to him'
  (b) ne·ɔ́·t·e (|nēw-ātē|) 'when he saw him, them; if he sees him, them' (B ⟨nrotc⟩ 26x; ND);
      cf. lá·t·e (|ə́l-ātē|) 'if he says to him'
  (c) pəntá·k·ɔt (|pəntākwat|) 'it is heard'; pəntákɔhto·p (|pǝntākwat-ōp|) 'it was heard';
      cf. wəláskahto·p (|wǝlaskat-ōp|) 'there was nice grass' (B)

(d) ná kóx·ɔ·n (|wə-kwax-ān|) 'then he feared him' (ME); kóx·a·n (same) (OA);
     cf. kɔx·á·a (|wə-kwax-āwa|) 'he feared him' (OA, ME); nkóx·a 'I fear him' (OA, ME)
(e) né·wa 'four' (presumably influenced by ní·š·a 'two' and naxá 'three'; cf. 2.30d);
     wá, wáni 'this (anim.)', wáka 'this (abs. anim.)' (cf. Penobscot owa [əwa?] 'this (an.)')
(f) nóni·n 'I forgot it' (OA, LB); stem /ɔni·-/ as in wóni·n 'he (she) forgot it' (OA),
     énta-ɔní·t 'when he (she) forgot it' (V)
(g) wáni· 'he forgot' (ME); stem /wani·-/ as in nəwáni·n 'I forgot it' (ME, ND, LB)
(h) ɔ́·psu (|wāpəsī-w|) 'he is white'; analogical: nó·psi 'I am white'
(i) hópanak (|wahpan-ak|) 'lungs'; nó·panak 'my lungs' (OA), wɔ·panə́ma 'his lung(s)' (V)

The |a| in the animate plural suffix |-ak| contracts with |w| to |ō| (appearing as /o·/) when the sequence |-wak| follows a consonant in the inflection of nouns (2.16abc) and verbs (2.16de), except that the plural of some nouns with stems in |kw| has /-ɔk/ (2.16f). Other suffixes beginning with |a| do not have contraction to /o·/ (2.16gh).

(2.16) Contraction of |wa| to /o·/ and /ɔ/ with |-ak| anim. pl.
(a) a·yhámo·k (|āyəhamōk|) 'eagles'; cf. sg. á·yham (|āyəhamw|) (OA, ME),
     a·yhamwí·i PN 'of eagle' (FW)
(b) ní·ləmo·k 'my sisters-in-law (of a man), my brothers-in-law (of a woman)' (OA);
     wí·ləmɔ 'his sister(s)-in-law, her brother(s)-in-law' (OA); cf. ni·ləmwə́t·ət (voc.) (ME)
(c) hítko·k (|məhtəkōk| < |məhtəkw-ak|) 'trees'; sg. hít·ukw (|məhtəkw|), obv. hítkɔ
     (B ⟨vetko⟩ 3x)
(d) nnílko·k (|nə-nəhl-əkōk|) 'they killed me' (V, ME);
     cf. kəníhəlukw (kə-nəhl-əkw|) 'he kills you (sg.)' (B)
(e) kanše·lə́ntamo·k (|kanšēlənt-amōk|) 'they were astonished';
     cf. kanše·lə́ntam (|kanšēlənt-amw|) 'he was astonished'
(f) alánkɔk (|alankw-ak|) 'stars'; cf. alánkw 'star' (V)
(g) lúk·ɔne (|əl-əkwanē|) 'if he tells you (sg.)'
(h) mhók·e (|məhw-àkē|) 'if I eat it (anim.)' (ME);
     méhɔk (|mēhwak| < |IC+məhw-ak|) '(anim.) which I ate' (ME)

Similarly, in the inflection of verbs the |a| in the inanimate plural suffix |-a(l)| contracts with post-consonantal |w| to |ō|, giving archaic /-o·l/ and more commonly /-u/ (already the only variant in Blanchard); this sequence was probably found only with verbs in |-n| and |-t| (2.17abc). In nouns the |a| in this suffix contracts with post-consonantal |w| to /ɔ/, giving /-ɔl/ (2.17e) and /ɔ/ (2.17d).

(2.17) Contraction of |wa| with |-a(l)| inan. pl. to /u/ (older /o·/) in verbs, and to /ɔ/ in nouns
(a) aləmí·k·ənu 'they (inan.) continue growing' (B)
(b) to·xkí·x·ənu 'they (inan.) got torn'; sg. to·xkí·x·ən (AD)
(c) ɔwə́lto·l 'they (inan.) are good' (OA; V ⟨ɔwəltú·l⟩; reduplicated stem |wawələt-|)
(d) čípahkɔ 'shoes' (B ⟨hepavko⟩ 3x, V, 1960's), mɔč·ípahkɔ 'his shoes' (B ⟨muthepavko⟩)
(e) mɔč·ípahkɔl 'his shoes' (B ⟨mothepavkul⟩)

The obviative suffix |-a(l)| after post-consonantal |w| has contraction to /-ɔ/ in noun inflection (2.16bc), but after the TA inverse ending (with the inverse theme sign |-əkw|) it retained the older contraction to |-ō(l)|, giving /-o·l/ archaically (2.18a) and commonly /-u/ (2.18b), though at least one speaker in the 1960's had /-ɔ/ (2.18c).

(2.18) Contraction of |wa| with |-a(l)| obv. to /-o·/, /-u/, and /-ɔ/
(a) tə́lko·l (|wət-əl-əkō(l)|) 'he (obv.) said to him' (B ⟨tclkwl⟩ 1x)
(b) tə́lku (same) (B ⟨tclkw⟩ 28x, ⟨tulkw⟩ 20x; V, ME)
(c) tə́lkɔ (same) (OA)

§2.10c. Contraction of |əwə|. Underlying |əwə| often contracts to |ō|, realized as /o·/ (2.12a, 2.19abcde) or /u/ (2.19fghi). The sequences affected arise when the prefixes |nə-| 1, |kə-| 2, and |wə-| 3 precede stems beginning in |wə| (see also 2.65), when endings beginning with |ə| follow a verb or noun stem in |-əw|, and in |-əkōnā(n-)| 3–1p/12 (4.25, 26). The third person prefix |wə-| contracts with |wə-| to |ō|, with loss of the initial |w| (2.19ac). (No word begins with /wo·-/.)
(2.19) Contraction of |ə-wə| and |əw-ə| to |o·|
  (a) no·wá·to·n (|nōwāhtōn| < |nə-wəwāht-ōn|) 'I know it' (B, V, OA, FW, ME);
     o·wá·to·n |wə-wəwāht-ōn| 'he (she) knows it' (B, OA, ME);
     cf. kə́t·a-wwá·to·n |wə-kata wəwāht-ōn| 'he wanted to know it' (B);
     ó·li-wwá·to·n (|ōlī wəwāhtōn| < |wə-wəlī wə́wāht-ōn|) 'she well knew' (B)
  (b) ko·lá·məwe (|kōlāməwē| < |kə-wəlāməwē|) 'you tell the truth';
     cf. wəlá·məwe·(w) 'he tells the truth'
  (c) no·txúk·o·k (|nə-wətax-əkōk|) 'they come to me' (B);
     o·txá·ɔ (|ōtạ́xāwa| < wə-wətạx-āwa|) 'he came to them' (B, V);
     cf. tɔx·í·t·e (|wə́tax-ītē|) 'if he comes to me' (B)
  (d) íka pe·š·ó·k·one (|pēšōkwanē| < |pēšəw-əkwanē|) 'if he takes you (sg.) there'
     cf. mpé·š·əwa (|nə́-pēšəw-ā|) 'I bring him'
  (e) kpé·š·o·l (|kə́-pēšəw-əl|) 'I brought you' (OA); cf. 17d
  (f) kuntamo·ləné·ɔ (|kōntamōlənēwā| < |kə-wəntamaw-ələnēwā|) 'I tell you (pl.) it';
     cf. wəntamaí·ne·n (|wəntamaw-īnēn|) 'tell us!'
  (g) pe·š·únte (|pēšōntē| < |pēšəw-əntē|) 'when (anim.) is brought' (V); cf. 17d
  (h) sí·p·unk (|sīpōnk| < |sīpəw-ənk|) 'river, creek (loc.)'; cf. sí·p·u 'river, creek', pl. sí·p·əwa.
  (i) lənúnka (OA), lənúnkahke (ME) (|ə́lənəw-ənka(ke)|) 'men (abs.)'

The sequence |əwə| is kept within stems (2.20ab) and when an |ō| resulting from the contraction of |wə-| 3 and stem-initial |wə-| would be reduced to /u-/ because of a following |nt| or |nč| (**§2.10a**). In the latter case, in Blanchard and all later sources |wə-| 3 is added as before any other stem-initial |w| (2.20cd, 57e); Blanchard is transcribed as having /wwə-/, although this was usually heard as /wə-/. In the 1960's the non-contraction had generally spread to all prefixes (2.20ef) in forms where a contracted |ō| would surface as /u/, but some forms with the old contraction of |nə-| 1 and |kə-| 2 were used (2.65jkl). The non-contraction was also heard in cases where the sequence |əwə| was followed by a consonant cluster (2.20gh).
(2.20) Non-contraction of |əwə|
  (a) nkəš·əwə́na (|nə-kəšəwən-āw|) 'I scratch him'
     (|kəšəwən-| TA 'scratch' < |kəšəw-| 'itch, scratch' + |-ən| TA 'by hand')
  (b) šəwə́l 'it (anim.) is sour' (< |šəw-| 'sour' + |-əl| AI abstract [for taste, etc.])
  (c) wwə́nči-pá·ne·p (|wə-wə́nči pā-nēp|) 'he came because of it' (B ⟨Wunhi panrp⟩);
     cf. núnči-pá·n (|nōnči pān| < |nə-wənči pā-n|) 'I came because of it' (B ⟨Nwnhi pan ⟩)
  (d) wwəntamáɔ·n (|wə́-wəntamaw-ān|) 'he told him' (B ⟨wuntamaon⟩); cf. 2.19f
  (e) nəwə́nči-=č -wəlamalsí·ne·n 'so that we'll keep well' (OA)
  (f) kəwə́nči- ní -lə́s·i·n 'the reason you're like that' (ME)
  (g) nəwəškinkwí·ne 'I have sore eyes' (OA)
  (h) nəwə·nsá·ɔk (|nə-wəns-āwak|) 'I boiled them (anim.)' (OA)

§2.10d. Contraction of |əyə|. The only opportunity for a sequence |əyə| to arise would be when a noun stem ending in |-əy| is followed by a suffix the begins with |ə|, notably |-ənk| LOC (2.8a, 21abc): |əyə| contracts to |ī|, and this is shortened to /i/ (**§2.10a**). Some nouns in |-əy| are also attested without this contraction (2.21c).

(2.21) Contraction and non-contraction of |əy-ə| (with |-ənk| LOC)
- (a) mpínk (|nəpīnk| < |nəpəy-ənk|) 'in the water'; cf. mpí (|nəpəy|) 'water'
- (b) ktə́k·ink (|kə̸təkəy-ənk|) 'on your shoulder'; cf. 2.31f
- (c) hwíkwink (|wihkwəy-ənk|; for |i| see **§2.12e**) 'on his chin' (OA); (2.42b);
  cf. nhwíkwiyink (as if |n-wihkwəy-ənk|) 'on my chin' (ME)

Before other suffixes that begin with |ə|, nouns replace stem final |-əy| with |-īw| in the attested cases (2.33d, 34g).

§2.10e. Contraction of |awə| in verbs and nouns. TA verbs with stems ending in |aw| have contraction of |aw-ə| to |ā| or |ō| depending on the ending. With the inverse theme sign |-əkw| and the passive theme sign |-əkē| the contraction is to |ā| (2.22abc). With the theme sign for second person object |-əl| and the third person passive suffix |-ənt| the contraction is to |ō| (2.19f, 22de). Contraction of |awə| to |ō| is also found with |-ənk| LOC (2.22f).

(2.22) Contraction of stems in |aw| with |ə|
- (a) no·t·é·ka·kw (|nōtēhkākw| < |nə-wətēhkaw-əkw|) 'he comes after me';
  cf. tə́ləmi-wte·kaɔ́·ɔ (|wət-alə́mī wətēhkaw-āwa|) 'he began to follow behind him'
- (b) nnəná·k·o·k (|nə̸-nənaw-əkōk|) 'they recognize me';
  cf. nnənaɔ́·ɔk (|nə-nənaw-āwak|) 'I recognize them'
- (c) palí·i ktəlska·k·éhəmɔ (|kə̸t-ələ̸skaw-əkēhmwā|) 'you (pl.) are driven away';
  cf. palí·i təlskaɔwwá·ɔ (|wə̸t-ələ̸skaw-āwə̸wāwa|) 'they drove him away'
- (d) kənat·o·xto·lhúmɔ (|kə-natōxə̸taw-ələhmwā|) 'I ask you (pl.)';
  cf. nɔt·o·xtaɔ́·ɔ (|wə̸-natōxə̸taw-āwa|) 'he asked them'
- (e) énta-máxkunt (|ēnta maxkōnt| < |maxkaw-ənt|) 'when he (she) was found' (V);
  cf. nəmáxkaɔ (|nə-maxkaw-āw|) 'I found s.o.'
- (f) lé·k·unk 'in the sand' (OA); cf. lé·k·aw 'sand' (OA, ND)

Stem-internally |awə| is kept: šawə́s·u 'he is weak'; pi·tawə́nte· 'it has many rooms'.

§2.10f. Contraction of |ayə|. An |ay| that is not stem-initial contracts with |ə| to |ē|. The only examples of this sequence have a noun stem in |-ay| with |-ənk| LOC, and |ē| is shortened to /e/ (**§2.10a**): nəmó·t·ay 'stomach'; nəmó·t·enk (|nə-mōtay-ənk|) 'in, on my stomach' (V; 4.6b).

§2.10g. Contraction of |Cw| in TA verbs. The TA verbs with stems ending in a post-consonantal |w| (|pw|, |mw|, |sw|, |šw|, |hw|) and suffixes beginning with |ə| have contraction of |wə| to |ō|. The |w| in the underlying |sw| and |šw| drops when followed by |a| or |ā|.

(2.23) Contraction with TA stems in |Cw|
- (a) mpə́mo·kw (|nə̸-pəmw-əkw|) 'he shot me with an arrow' (V, ME);
  kə́nč pəmó·lane (|pəmw-əlanē|) 'I must shoot you' (ME);
  cf. kpə́mwi (|kə̸-pəmw-ī|) 'you shot me' (V);
  mpə́mɔ (|nə̸-pəmw-āw|) 'I shot him' (V, OA, ME)
- (b) wəlo·s·o·k·u (|wə-lōsw-əkō(l)|) 'he (obv.) burned him' (ME); nlɔ́·s·a 'I burned him'
- (c) kwi·skšó·k·wən (|wə̸-kīskə̸šw-əkwən|) 'it cut him' (OA); cf. nkí·skša 'I cut him' (OA)
- (d) nsihó·k·e (|nə̸-sihw-əkē|) 'I was beaten, I lost' (ME);
  cf. nsíhɔ (|nə̸-sihw-āw|) 'I beat him' (ME)
- (e) énta-psakhwitéhunt (|ēnta pə̸sakwəhtehw-ənt|) 'where he was crucified' (B)

§2.10h. Vowel changes before |w| and |y|. A vowel may be changed before |w| or |y|, sometimes automatically and sometimes because of the grammatical status of the adjacent phonemes. Intervocalic |w| and |y| are often lost (**§2.11**), but they may leave behind an effect on a preceding vowel.

A stem-final |ā| or |ī| is replaced in some verbs before the suffix |-w| 3,0 (marking third person animate and inanimate in the independent modes). The intransitive stems (AI and II) that do not keep these vowels unchanged replace |ā| with |ē| (2.24abc) and replace |ī| with |ə| (2.24de). There are some AI stems in |ī| that are attested with both treatments (2.24f). The same vowel replacements take place before the preterite suffix |-p(an-)|, but the |-w| is lost after a long vowel (2.24a), and in verbs that have /-əw/ for |ī-w| this becomes |ō|, as if from |əwə| with an inserted |ə| (2.24f).

(2.24) Vowel changes in third person forms
    (a)   é·w and é· (|ā-w|) 'he went' (á·kw 'go (you pl.)'); pret. é·p (|ā-w-p(an-)|) 'he went'
          cf. pá·tama· (|pāhtamā-w|) 'he prayed' (énta-pá·tama·t 'where he prayed')
    (b)   kčinkwehəle· (|kəčīnkwēhlā-w|) 'it is sunrise' (wénči-kčinkwéhəla·k 'east' [B 2x, WS]);
          cf. wsí·ka· (|wəsīhkā-w|) 'the sun sets' (éhəli-wsí·ka·k 'the west')
    (c)   né·e· lə́nəwa (|nēw-ēw| < |-ā-w|) 'he saw a man (obv.)' (B 3x)
    (d)   aə́s·u (|awasī-w|) 'he warmed himself' (pé·-aəs·í·li·t 'as he (obv.) warmed himself')
          cf. má·č·i·w (V) and má·č·i· (|māčī-w|) 'he went home'
    (e)   tahkɔ́·k·u (|takwākī-w|) 'it is fall' (tahkɔ·k·í·k·e 'when it is or was fall');
          cf. aləmá·li· (|aləmālī-w| II) 'the corn is tasseling out'
    (f)   pó·s·u (|pōsī-w|) 'he gets in a boat' (ND; pret. pó·s·o·p B);
          pó·s·i·w (same) (V; pl. po·s·í·ɔk [|pōsī-wak|] B)

The |w| that characterizes the TA w-endings (used for animate objects in the independent modes) does not cause the replacement of a preceding |ā| (2.2d, 5di, 10bd, 19c, etc.).

Before the |y| in first and second person endings of the conjunct order any |ī| is replaced by |ə|; this change affects the stem-final |ī| in any verb and the TA theme sign |ī|, which marks a first person object (**§4.4d**). In |əy| (of this or any origin) the |ə| becomes /i/ and the |y| drops (2.31de).

(2.25) Replacement of |ī| by /ə/ before |y|
    (a)   é·p·ia (|ēpəyā| < |IC+apī-yā(n)|) 'where I am' (é·p·i·t 'where he is')
    (b)   ə́nta-má·č·ia· (|ənta māčəyā| < māčī-yā(n)) 'when I go home' (OA); cf. 24c
    (c)   e·liáne (|ēləyanē| < |IC+əl-ī-yan-ē|) 'when you told me' (é·li·t 'what he told me')

In the sequence |əw| the |ə| remains as /ə/ in a weak syllable (2.26a), but it is replaced by /u/ in a strong syllable (2.26b). The two treatments of |ə| before |w| result in variation in the shape of stems in paradigms of related forms (2.26c). Word-finally |əw| is realized as /-u/ (2.2g, 5a, 8d, 10g, 15h, 24de, 26ab), except that it is retained as /-úw/ or /-əw/ in TA imperatives (2.10g). If a syllable with underlying |əw| is preceded by a weak syllable with a deleted |ə| and followed by a strong syllable, the |əw| seems always to be treated as weak and to have /əw/ (2.26d). This treatment is also found in the word aləwí·i 'more' and others containing the initial |àləw-| 'more', and in a few forms in which the |əw| is in the next to last syllable (2.26e).

(2.26) /ə/ and /u/ for |ə| before |w|
    (a)   lə́nu (|ɸlənəw|) 'man'; pl. lə́nəwak (|ɸlənəw-ak|) (LB)
    (b)   skínnu (|wɸskīlɸnəw|) 'young man'; pl. skinnúwak (|wɸskīlɸnəwak|) (ND)
    (c)   lúwe· (|ɸləwēw|) 'he said'; ntə́ləwe·n (|nɸtələwēn|) 'I said it';
          é·ləwe·t (|ēləwēt| < |IC+ələwē-t|) 'what he said'.
    (d)   ktəma·ksəwá·k·an (|kɸtəmākɸsəwākan|) 'pitiful state' (LB)
    (e)   kkí·skšəwi (|kɸkīskɸšəwī|) 'you (sg.) cut me' (ME 3x); also kki·skšúwi (ME)

§2.10i. Treatment of |ə| before |kw| and |hw|. A |ə| that is not replaced by contraction or otherwise lost becomes /u/ before |kw| or |hw| (2.27abcd, 28d) and before /k·/ or /h/ followed by /ɔ/ or /ɔ·/. Forms related to ones with this treatment typically also have /u/ for |ə| before a /k·/ or

/h/ that is from the underlying |kw| or |hw| and followed by /oˑ/, /u/, or /əw/ (but see 2.27i, 4.27s). These cases of /u/ before /kˑ/ are here analyzed as the result of analogy (2.27efghi), since |ə| is not automatically rounded in these environments (2.27jk). Because these cases of /u/ are from underlying |ə|, they are subject to being lost in related forms exactly like |ə| (2.16cd, 27a).

(2.27) /u/ for |ə| before |kw| and |hw|, and before |k| and |h| in rounding environments

    (a) nšinkáˑlukw (|nə̸-šīnkāl-əkw|) 'he hates me';
        nšinkáˑlkoˑk (|nə̸-šīnkāl-ə̸kōk|) 'they hate me'
    (b) ə́nta-kiˑɔlúkˑwək (|kīwal-əkwək|) 'when she was deceived by him (obv.)' (ME)
    (c) weˑkˑwiˑsˑəmúkˑwək (|wēkwīsəməkwək| < |IC+wəkwīsəm-əkwək|)
        'his (obv.) son (prox.)'
    (d) ahtú (|atəhw|) 'deer', pl. ahtúhoˑk (|atəhōk|) (V, FW, ND, ME)
    (e) ntihəlukˑóˑna (|nə̸t-ihəl-əkōnā|) 'he, she used to tell us (exc.)' (OA, ME)
    (f) nnaˑɔlúkˑoˑk (|nə̸-nāwal-əkōk|) 'they follow me'
    (g) lɔxˑənúkˑu (|wə̸-laxən-əkō(l)|) 'he (obv.) releases him (prox.)'
    (h) kkakˑiˑɔlúkˑəwa (|kə-kakīwal-əkəwā| < |-əkw-əwāw|) 'he deceived you (pl.)' (B)
    (i) nɔkˑalək·əwáˑa (|wə-nakal-əkəwāwa| < |-əkw-əwāw-a|) 'she (obv.) left them' (ME)
    (j) nəməkˑoˑttiéˑpˑi (|nə-məkōtətəyēpī|) 'I ride bareback'
    (k) mpəkˑóˑyəm (|nəpəkōwəm| < |nə-pəkəw-əm|) 'my gum' (OA, ME)

§2.10j. Treatment of |ə| before |nk|. Before |nk| a |ə| becomes /u/ if preceded by |w| (2.28abcde) and becomes |i| otherwise (2.28fg). The |w| that induces the /u/ does not remain before it; it is lost after /aˑ/ (2.28a) or a consonant (2.28d) and replaced by /y/ after /eˑ/ and /iˑ/ (2.28ce). In the locatives of nouns with a second or third person plural possessor (**§4.2d**), Blanchard has the expected /-əwáˑunk/ eight times (2.28b), but /-əwáˑink/ (2.28b, 56c) is much more common (though not found later), an ending apparently influenced by the uncontracted shape of the locative suffix (2.28f). (Compare /-yunk/ and /-ink/ for |-wənk| X/CNJ.NEG [4.94].)

(2.28) /u/ and /i/ from |ə| before |nk|

    (a) saˑkˑiˑmáˑunk (|sākīmāw-ənk|) 'at the king's' (2.36f; |-ənk| LOC);
        cf. saˑkˑiˑmaˑwhéˑtˑe 'if he makes him king' (|sākīmāw| + |-ahē| AI 'make'; |-tē| 'if he')
    (b) kiˑləwáˑunk (|k-īl-əwāwənk|) 'on your (pl.) heads' (|kə–əwāw| 2p, |-ənk| LOC);
        also kiˑləwáˑink (same)
    (c) tənté·yunk (|təntēw-ənk|; |-ənk| LOC) 'in the fire';
        cf. tə́ntay 'fire', but tənté·whe· 'he made fire' (OA) (|təntēw- 'fire' + |-ahē| AI 'make')
    (d) nkɔ́tkunk (|nə̸-kɔtə̸kw-ənk|; |-ənk| LOC) 'on my knee' (V);
        cf. nkə́tˑukw (|nə̸-kətəkw|) 'my knee' (V)
    (e) néˑskɔ-xínkwi-miˑtsahtíˑyunk (|mītəsahətī-wənk|) 'before the big feast' (néˑskɔ PV 'when not yet'; xínkwi PV 'great'; |mītəsahətī-| AI 'eat (coll.)', |-w| NEG, |-ənk| X)
    (f) ahsə́nink (|asən-ənk|) 'on a stone' (|-ənk| LOC); cf. ahsə́n 'stone'
    (g) meˑtˑéˑxˑink (|mētēxənk| < |IC+matēxən-k|; |-k| 0) 'what falls, lands';
        cf. mahtéˑxˑən (|matēxən-w|) 'it falls, lands'

Some instances of /u/ before |nkw| presumably come from underlying |ə| (2.3ce), but this change produces no alternations.

§2.10k. Weakening of |a| between /h/ and /m/ or /n/. An underlying |a| or |wa| is generally replaced by /ə/ if it is in a weak syllable preceded by /h/ and followed by |m| or |n| (or presumably |l|). The effects of this change are seen in the TI(1a) theme sign |-am| (**§3.7e**) and derived stems that incorporate this (2.29ab), the final |-am| TA 'by mouth' (2.29c), the final |-ahanē| II 'flow, be a stream' (2.29d), and the inflection of some nouns (2.29e). There are some exceptions with the quality of the vowel retained (2.29e).

(2.29) /ə/ replacing weak-syllable |a| and |wa| before |m| and |n|
  (a) nkwə́či-kpáhəmən (|kə̸pah-ămən|) 'I tried to close it'; cf. nkəphámən 'I closed it' (AD)
  (b) mpo·tsáhəma· (|nə̸pōtə̸sahămā-w|; |-ahamā| AI 'use, etc.') 'he's wearing boots' (WS);
      cf. təpčehəla·sháma· (|təpə̸čēhlāsə̸hamā-w|) 'he travels by wagon' (LB)
  (c) ntáhəmukw (|nə̸-tahwăm-əkw|) 'he bit me' (OA, ME, LB);
      cf. thɔ́m (|tə̸hwam|) 'bite him!' (V); ntahɔ́ntamən (|nə̸-tahwant-amən|) 'I bit it' (ME)
  (d) si·skəwáhəne· (|sīskəwahănē-w|) 'it is a muddy river' (LB);
      cf. tankháne· (|tankə̸hanē-w|) 'it is a narrow river' (V)
  (e) túhənink (|təhwan-ənk|; |-ənk| LOC) 'on the branch' (OA, LB);
      cf. túhɔn (|təhwan|) 'branch' (V, LB), pl. túhɔna (LB), loc. túhɔnink (LTD ND)

Transcriptions of words that lack this reduction have apparently sometimes been normalized.

§2.11. Loss of intervocalic |w| and |y|. Underlying |w| and |y| are very generally lost between vowels, but with exceptions of various kinds.

§2.11a. Intervocalic |w|. An intervocalic |w| (if it does not undergo contraction to /ɔ/ or /ɔ·/ [**§2.10b**]) is regularly lost (2.12, 13e, 30, 36ab) except in certain environments. It is retained in the underlying sequence |wəy| except where it is lost by analogy (**§2.11e**). And it is retained if it is preceded by /ə/ or /u/ (2.5gh, 12d, 19d, 20ef, 26abc, 27gh, 28b, 29d), or if it is preceded by /o·/ and not followed by /u/ (2.12ad, 19a), or if it is followed by /ə/ (**§2.10e**, end). The retention of /w/ in awé·n 'someone, anyone; person; who?' is unexplained. For né·wa 'four' see (2.15e).

(2.30) Loss of intervocalic |w|
  (a) ne·í·t·e (|nēw-ītē|) 'if he sees me'; cf. kəné·wəl (|kə-nēw-əl|) 'I saw you';
      cf. ne·ó·t·e (|nēw-ātē|) 'when he, she saw him' (B); 2.15b, 2.36e
  (b) wəla·mhitaí·t·e (|wəlāməhtaw-ītē|) 'if he believes me';
      cf. wəla·mhitaó·t·e (|wəlāməhtaw-ātē|) 'if he believes him'
  (c) máta no·wa·ha·í·wəna (|nōwāhāwīwənā|; |-wī| NEG) 'we do not know him';
      cf. máta o·wa·há·wən (|ōwāhāwən|; |-w| NEG) 'he did not know her (then)'
  (d) ne·í·nxke (|nēwīnaxkē|) 'forty'; cf. ne·ó·pxki (|nēwāpaxkī|) 'four hundred' and 2.15e
  (e) nao·kwé·x·i·n (|nawəhkwēxīn|) 'he has (or puts) his head down' (OA, ME)
  (f) i·lá·u (|īlāwəw| < |īlāwī-w|) 'he is a warrior', 1s nti·lá·i (|nət-īlāwī|) (V, OA);
      cf. i·lá·wka·n 'there is a war dance' (ND)
  (g) nkwəs·iá·ukw (|nə-kwəsəyāw-əkw|) 'he sniffed at me' (OA, ME);
      cf. nkwəs·iá·ɔ (|nə-kwəsəyāw-āw|) 'I sniffed at him' (ME)
  (h) kənči·mó·u (|kənčīmōwəw| < |kənčīmōwī-w|; |-ōwī| II) 'it sounds' (B);
      cf. pe·ma·wsó·wi·k (|pēmāwəsōwīk|; |-ōwī| II) 'which is alive, living' (B)
  (i) lo·o·x·we·í·k·e (|lōwōxwēwīkē|) 'when it, they (inan.) had gone by'

Under some conditions and with some variation, when an intervocalic |w| is lost it is replaced by /y/ (**§2.11d**).

§2.11b. Loss of intervocalic |y|. An intervocalic |y| is generally lost (2.31abc), except that after short |a| it is retained before /a/, /ə/, /u/, and /o·/ (2.31ah). When |y| follows |ə| (whether this is original or a replacement of |ī|; 25), the |ə| is replaced by /i/ and (except before /u/ or /o·/) the /y/ drops (2.31def). Word-finally |əy| is realized as /-i/ (2.31f), parallel to the treatment of word-final |-əw| as /-u/ (2.26ab). A |y| is not lost in stem-initial |āy-|, whether this syllable marks reduplication (2.31g) or is part of a stem (e.g. |āyant-| TI(1a) 'desire'). There is some evidence for the optional retention or secondary insertion of /y/ in environments where it is usually lost

(2.31hijk). In the possessed forms of wió·s (|wəyōs|) 'meat, flesh' the |y| was regularly lost, as Blanchard shows consistently, but it was later apparently restored on the basis of the unpossessed noun (2.31.l).

(2.31) Loss and retention of |y|
- (a) e·á·an (|ēyāyan| < |IC+ā-yan|) 'where you (sg.) go';
  cf. čí·p·ayak (|čīpay-ak|) 'ghosts, spirits'; sg. čí·p·ay (|čīpay|)
- (b) é·li·pa·tamá·e·kw (|ēlī pāhtamā-yēkw|) 'how you (pl.) pray'
- (c) me·né·e·kw (|mēnēyēkw| < |IC+mənē-yēkw|) 'what you (pl.) drink'
- (d) é·p·ian (|ēpəyan| < |IC+apī-yan|) 'where you (sg.) are';
  é·p·ie·kw (|ēpəyēkw| < |IC+apī-yēkw|) 'where you (pl.) are'
- (e) e·liáne (|ēləyanē| < |IC+əl-īyanē|) 'when you told me' (with |-ī| 1.OBJ)
- (f) ntə́k·i (|nə-təkəy|) 'my shoulder', pl. ntə́k·ia (|nə-təkəy-a|)
- (g) nta·yahkənó·t·əmən (|nət-āy-akənōt-əmən|) 'I'm talking about it' (OA)
- (h) mo·nši·to·naéhu 'he's shaving' (|mōnšīhtōnayehwī-| AI; cf. wi·tó·naya 'his beard'),
  1s nəmo·nši·to·naéhwi (OA); both forms also heard as if with /ayé/ (OA)
- (i) pe·yé·yu 'it comes'; pe·ye·í·k·e 'when it comes' (B pe·ye·- ⟨prer-⟩ 7x; -yu: §2.11d);
  cf. pe·e·yó·u 'it came' (pe·e·yó·wi·k 'one that comes') (OA, ME); B pe·e·- ⟨prr-⟩ 3x
- (j) akó·=tá [n]ne·yɔ·í·yɔk 'I didn't see them (anim.)' (AP; both [y]'s noted as "clear")
- (k) e·yá·a 'where I went' (ND in LTD)
- (l) no·ó·s·əm (|nōyōsəm| < |nə-wəyōs-əm|; 2.19) 'my flesh' (B 5x),
  o·ó·s·əm 'his flesh' (B 3x);
  cf. no·yó·s·əm 'my meat', ko·yó·s·əm 'your (sg.) meat', o·yó·s·əm 'his meat' (V)

§2.11d. Intervocalic /y/ replacing |w|. Where intervocalic |w| has been lost (§§2.10b, 11a) there is sometimes a /y/ in its place. This secondary /y/ appears before /u/ or /o·/ after /i·/ (2.28e, 32abc) or /e·/ (2.13e, 28c, 31h, 32def). It is probably best taken as directly replacing |w| in these environments, rather than as being inserted to break up a potential vowel sequence. A /y/ that directly replaces |w| is not present after /a/, /a·/, or /o·/ before /u/ or /o·/ (2.30efghi). (The sequence /i·yo·/ is not attested.)

(2.32) Replacement of |w| by /y/ before /u/ or /o·/
- (a) hakí·yu (|ahkīwəw| < |ahkīwī-w|) 'he is of earth'; cf. énta-xínkwi-mpí·i·k (|nəpīwī-k|)
  '(in, on) the ocean' (V, ME [with /ə́nta-/]; lit., 'where the great water is')
- (b) tɔ·kí·yu (|wətahkīwəw| < |wətahkīwī-w|) 'he has land' (cf. 2.34g);
  cf. no·thakí·i (|nōtahkīwī| < |nə-wətahkīwī|) 'I have land' (OA)
- (c) same·lií·yunk (as if |samēləyīw-ənk|) 'in Samaria' (B ⟨Sumrliewf⟩)
- (d) nné·yukw (|nə-nēw-əkw|) 'he saw me' (LB)
- (e) xkwé·yunk (|axkwēw-ənk|) 'woman (loc.)' (2.10e)
- (f) ne·yo·k·wənák·at (|nēwōkwənakat-w|) 'it is four days' (2.15e, 2.30d)

Similarly, an intervocalic |w| is replaced by /y/ after all long vowels before /əm/ (2.33), in all examples the suffix |-əm| POSS.TH that marks the possessed theme of some nouns (**§4.2a**). The possessed themes of stems in a short vowel followed by |w| or |y| are restructured to have a long vowel and treated the same way. Stems in |-ay| replace this with /-e·y/ (as if with |-ēw|; 2.33c), stems in |-əy| replace this with /-i·y/ (as if with |-īw|; 2.33d), and stems in |-əw| are reshaped to /-o·y/ (2.33e). (Possessed themes are not attested for the few stems in |-aw| and |-ōw| that exist.)

(2.33) Replacement of |w| by /y/ before |-əm| POSS.TH
- (a) ksa·k·i·má·yəm (|kə-sākīmāw-əm|) 'your (sg.) king' (B);
  nsa·k·i·ma·yəmə́na (|nə-sākīmāw-əmənā|) 'our (exc.) chief' (AP); cf. 2.28a

(b) o·ski·xkwé·yəma (|wə-wəskīxkwēw-əma|) 'one of his unmarried young women'
(c) wtəskɔnté·yəmink (|wə̆təskwantēwəmənk| < |wət-əskwantay-əmənk|) 'at his door'; cf. skɔ́ntay (|əskwantay|) 'door', loc. skɔ́ntenk (|əskwantay-ənk|) (B, ND)
(d) nəmɔní·yəm (|nəmwanīwəm| < |nə-mwanəy-əm|) 'my money'; cf. mɔ́nia 'coins'
(e) no·skinno·yəməná·na·k (|nōskīlə̊nōwəmənānāk| < |nə-wəskīlənəw-əmənānāk|) 'our (exc.) young men' (ME); cf. 2.26b

§2.11e. Intervocalic /y/ for |w| by analogy. In some grammatical environments a /y/ appears to have replaced |w| by analogy.

Underlying |wəw| with a metrically weak |ə| is, as a general rule, realized as /ww/ (2.2d, 5j, 14d, 19a, 20cd, 22c), but in some cases a realization as /yəw/ between vowels (with unoriginal /y/) has apparently been produced by analogy to forms in the same or parallel paradigms that have /-yu/ (as if |-yəw|) word-finally as the realization of |-wəw| (2.13e, 34abcd). This /y/ appears in the independent indicative third person plural of AI verbs with stems in |-īwī|, |-ēwī|, and |-āwī| (2.34abcde), and for some speakers in the plural forms of II verbs with stems in |-ōwī| (2.34f) and presumably other shapes, if they exist. This /y/ does not appear with AI stems in |-ōwī|, however, in either the verbal inflection or derived nouns (2.14d), and for some speakers it is not present in the II: ankəlúwwa (|ankəlōwəwa| < |ankəlōwī-wa|) 'they (inan.) died' (ME). A /y/ with apparently a similar origin is found before |-əwāw| 2p,3p.poss in stems that have /-i·w/ or /-e·w/ before |-ənān| 1p,12.POSS (2.34gh).

(2.34) Analogical secondary /y/ before /ə/
(a) xkwí·yəwak (|xkwīwəwak| < |xkwīwī-wak|) 'they (anim.) are green, unripe' (OA, ME); sg. xkwí·yu (|xkwīwəw|) '(anim., inan.) is green, unripe'
(b) ɔwəla·p·é·yəwak (|wawəlāpēwəwak| < |wawəlāpēwī-wak|) 'they are good natured'; sg. wəla·p·é·yu (|wəlāpēwī-w|) (V)
(c) wənči·k·ané·yəwak (|wənčīkanēwəwak|) 'they recite their visions in the Big House'; sg. wənči·k·ané·yu (V)
(d) né·yəwak (|nēwəwak| < |nēwī-wak|) 'there are four of them (anim.)' (WP); cf. 2.15e, 2.30d. Also ne·wí·ɔk (CW in Speck 1931:130), a unique form.
(e) i·lá·yəwak (|īlāwəwak| < |īlāwī-wak|) 'they are warriors' (V); cf. 2.30f (sg. without /y/)
(f) wəla·p·ensó·yəwa (|wəlāpēnsōwəwa| < |wəlāpēnsōwī-wa|) 'they (inan.) are blessed' (B)
(g) kta·kí·yəwa (|kət-ahkīw-əwā|) 'your (pl.) land' (OA); cf. nta·kí·wəna (|nət-ahkīw-ənā|) 'our (exc.) land', ntá·kia (|nət-ahkəy-a|) 'my lands'
(h) kkwəshaté·yəwa 'your (pl.) tobacco' (ME); cf. nkwəshaté·wəna 'our (exc.) tobacco' (ME); nkwəshátay 'my tobacco'

The TA stems that replace |w| by /y/ before the inverse ending /-ukw/ (**§2.11d**, 32d) extend this /y/ to the forms with |-əkw| INV in which the |ə| is lost (forms with longer inverse endings and the derived passive stems), giving /-yk-/ by analogy (instead of /wk/) (2.35a, 2.46a, 4.67t). This analogical /y/ also appears in the stems in |-āw|, which do not have /y/ before /-ukw/ (2.35bc), and in the forms that have the passive theme sign |-əkē|, which never has rounding of the |ə| (2.35de). The /y/ in /yk/ is devoiced (i.e. [y̥]) and raises the preceding /e·/ (normally an open [ɛ·]) to [eⁱ]; earlier transcriptions of this voiceless /y/ as /h/ are probably incorrect (B, Voegelin 1946 §2.12), although at least one speaker had this pronunciation, without the vowel raising (ND).

(2.35) Analogical secondary /y/ before /k/
(a) takó· nne·ykó·u (|nə-nēw-əkōwī|; [nneⁱykó·o]) 'he does not see me' (ME) (cf. 2.32d); kəne·ykwə́s·i (|kə-nēwəkwəsī|) 'you (sg.) are seen, visible' (ME); né·ykɔt 'it is seen' (ME); cf. ⟨nrvkot⟩ B 12x (as if [nɛ·hkɔt]), né·hkɔt (ND)

(b) nkukwsiá·yko·k (|nə-kwəkwəsəyāw-əkōk|) 'they kept sniffing me' (ME) (cf. 2.30g)
(c) nəməlá·yko·k (|nə-məlāw-əkōk|) 'they smelled me';
  cf. nəməlá·ɔ (|nə-məlāw-āw|) 'I smelled him (her)'
(d) kəne·ykéhəmɔ (|kə-nēw-əkēhmwā|) 'you (pl.) were seen' (AP) (cf. 2.32d)
(e) nəməlá·yke (|nə-məlāw-əkē|) 'I was smelled'

The cluster /wk/ is otherwise tolerated (2.30f).

In earlier work on Unami a /y/ was generally written between /i·/ or /e·/ and /ɔ/ or /ɔ·/, and was sometimes written after /i/ before a vowel, but since no consistently contrastive intervocalic /y/ is discernible in these environments it has not been written here, and transcriptions are normalized without it. The one environment where this [y] is often heard, at least from some speakers, is between /e·/ and a stressed /ɔ́·/: nne·[y]ɔ́·ɔk 'I saw them (anim.)' (LB); cf. kəne·ɔ́·ɔk 'you (sg.) see them' (ME) and ne·ɔ́·t·e 'if he sees him' (ND), with no [y]. Blanchard sometimes writes ⟨e⟩ in the value of /y/ after /e·/ before /ɔ(·)/ and /a(·)/, but writings without this are more common.

§2.11f. Treatments of |wəy|. In an underlying sequence |wəy| that is not affected by analogy the |w| is retained because of the |ə| (**§2.11a**), but the |əy| is realized as /i/ (**§2.11b**): ká·wia (|kāwəyāw|) 'porcupine'; ɔwiálahsu (|wawəyāhlasəw|) 'whirlwind'.

In the paradigms of TA stems ending in a post-vocalic |w|, the stem would have had variants with and without /w/ before the suffix |-ī| 1.OBJ (marking first person objects; **§4.4d**): the stem would have lost the |w| where this suffix was retained as /i·/ or shortened to /i/, but would have retained the |w| before the /i/ that replaced |ə| before |y| (**§2.11b**), as well as word-finally (2.10f, 36ac). For the most part, TA stems leveled out this opaque distribution by generalizing the shape without the /w/ before /i/ and /i·/ (2.36abcde). The |w| is, however, retained by some speakers (notably OA) in the stems in |ēw| before an /i/ that reflects a |ə| (2.36e), and by all speakers in all stems in |w| before the /i/ in the suffix /-ie·k·-/ (|-əyēk|) of the prohibitive (4.108), which does not contain |-ī| 1.OBJ (2.36bc).

Verbs of being derived by the suffix |-ī| AI 'be' from noun stems ending in underlying vowel plus |w| also drop the |w| from forms that would originally have preserved it (2.36f), except after |ə| (2.36g).

(2.36) Retention and loss of |w| in TA and AI stems
  (a) kəlóstaw (|kələs̸taw|) 'listen to him (you sg.)';
    kələstái·l (|kələs̸taw-īl|) 'listen to me (you sg.)'
  (b) wəla·mhítai·l (|wəlāməhtaw-īl|) 'believe me (you sg.)';
    ć·li- máta wəla·mhitaíhti·t (|wəlāməhtaw-īhətīt|) 'because they do not believe me';
    wəla·mhitaiáne (|wəlāməhtaw-əyanē| < |-ī-yanē|) 'if you (sg.) believe me';
    káči wəla·mhitawié·k·e·kw (|wəlāməhtaw-əyēkēkw|) 'don't believe him, them (you pl.)'
  (c) pənáw 'look at him, them (you sg.)' (V, ME);
    káči pənaí·han (|pənaw-īhan|) 'don't look at me (you sg.)' (OA);
    pənaiáne (|pənaw-əyanē| < |-ī-yanē|) 'if you (sg.) look at me' (OA);
    káči pənawié·k·ač (|pənaw-əyēkač|) 'don't look at him, them (you sg.)' (OA)
  (d) wi·č·e·iáne (|wīčēw-əyanē|) 'if you (sg.) come with me' (ME);
    é·li- .. -wi·č·é·ie·kw (|wīčēw-əyēkw|) 'as you (pl.) have been with me' (B)
  (e) kəne·íhəna (|kə-nēw-īhmənā|) 'you see us' (OA);
    ənta-ne·íhti·t (|ēnta nēw-īhətīt|) 'when they saw me' (OA);
    é·li-né·ian (|ēli nēw-əyan| < |-ī-yan|) 'because you (sg.) see me' (B);
    ənta-né·wian (|ēnta nēw-əyan|) 'when you (sg.) saw me' (OA; archaic retention of |w|);
    ne·wiáne (|nēw-əyanē|) 'if you (sg.) see me' (OA; archaic retention of |w|);

ónta-né·wienk (|ēnta nēw-əyēnk|) 'when you saw us' (OA; archaic retention of |w|)
  (f) sa·k·í·ma (|sākīmāw|) 'chief; prince, king', pl. sa·k·i·má·ɔk (|sākīmāw-ak|); sa·k·i·ma·i·ké·i (|sākīmāw-īhkēwī|) 'among kings' (with |-īhkēwī| loc. pl.); sa·k·i·ma·iáne (|sākīmāwəyanē| < |sākīmāwī-yanē|) 'if you are the chief (or king)'
  (g) we·skinnəwiáne (|wēskīlənəwəyanē| < |IC+wəskīlənəwī-yanē|) 'when you were a young man'

The same variation in shape arose in the stem |kawī-| AI 'sleep', which is found with and without the /w/ in Blanchard. In later sources this variation was leveled out in favor of the form of the stem that has /w/, and in fact this generalization of the variant with /w/ had already begun in Blanchard's day.

(2.37) Variation in |kawī-| AI 'sleep'
  (a) énta-kaí·t 'when he was asleep' (B); né·li-kawí·t 'as he (she) slept' (V)
  (b) kaí·kw 'sleep (you pl.)!' (B); kawí·kw (ME)
  (c) kaí· 'he (she) sleeps' (B 2x); kawí·w (V), kawí· (B 2x, OA, ME)
  (d) né·li-kawía (|nēli kawəyā| < |kawī-yā(n-)|) 'while I slept' (V; archaic retention of |w|)
  (e) kkáwi 'you sleep' (B, V, OA; ME with [k:] 2x)

§2.12. Other miscellaneous phonological changes.
Some variation in surface forms results from changes of limited scope in underlying shapes. Some of the underlying sequences affected have multiple outcomes without clear conditioning.

§2.12a. Treatment of |w| potentially followed by |h|. The sequence /wh/ is tolerated after a vowel other than /u/ or /o·/ if the following vowel is not |a| or |ā|, but there is some variation (2.28c, 2.38abc). If there is no preceding vowel (either word-initially or because an underlying vowel has been lost), the |w| and |h| metathesize to /hw/ before any vowel except |a| or |ā| (2.38def), but /kwh/ was sometimes heard from some speakers (5.12x). If /o·/ precedes the potential postvocalic /wh/, the |w| is dropped (2.43f). If the potential postvocalic /wh/ is followed by |a| or |ā| it is replaced by /hh/ after a short vowel (2.38gh) and by /h/ after a long vowel (2.38ij) or a consonant (2.6c; 38kl), and the following vowel becomes /ɔ/ or /ɔ·/ (**§§2.1e, 10b**). (No example with a preceding short vowel and a following |ā| is citable.)

(2.38) Potential |w| followed by |h|
  (a) wi·s·a·whémpəs 'yellow dress' (ND)
  (b) kɔwhitehó·ɔ |wə-kawəhtehw-āwa| 'he hit him knocking him down' (LB)
  (c) akó· ɔ·whe·í·ɔk 'they (hens) aren't laying' (OA); the /wh/ in this stem was earlier heard as /hw/ (OA, FW) and /h/ (ME).
  (d) hwíkahša (|wəhkaša|) 'his fingernail (or fingernails)' (V, OA, LB); cf. nhíkahšak (|nəhkašak|) 'my fingernails' (OA)
  (e) kát·a-=č -khwítamən (|kwəhtamən|) 'you must (ought to) be afraid of it' (OA); cf. nkwí·tamən (|nəkwəhtamən|) 'I'm afraid of it' (OA)
  (f) pi·mxkhwí·k·an (|pīməxkwəhīkan|) 'stirring paddle'
  (g) nšuhhómən (|nə-šəwəh-amən|) 'I salt it' (ME; confirmed by OA); cf. šəwáha 'salt it (you sg.)' (OA)
  (h) alahhótəwak (|alawahtəwak|; 5.75m) 'they (coll.) go hunting' (OA, ME; stem also V); cf. alái· (|alawī-w|) 'he hunts' (ME, ND)
  (i) we·homá·s·u (|wēwəhamāsəw|) 'he lets people know' (OA; ND 3p and X)
  (j) kpəč·e·hó·s·u (|kəpəčēwəhāsəw|) 'he acts foolish' (V, LB; stem in B)
  (k) nkəp·a·khómən (|nə-kəpāhkwəh-amən|) 'I locked it' (BS)
  (l) na·hóke· (|nāwahkē-w|) 'he (she) followed after' (B, ME); cf. ná·ɔli·l 'follow me' (B)

The verb má·whu (V, OA) 'he attends a dance' (stem apparently |māwahwī-) is variable, perhaps to some extent because of uncertain phonemic interpretation: má·whwi·n (V), má·whi·n (OA, AP), and má·hwi·n (V, FW) 'there's a dance, a stomp dance'; [énta]-má·wink 'when or where there was a dance' (LB).

§2.12b. Treatment of |x| following |w|. If not followed by |a| or |ā|, the sequence /wx/ is kept word-medially after both vowels (2.39a) and consonants (2.39bc), but it is metathesized to /xw/ in an initial syllable, with or without a preceding consonant (2.39de). If a potential /w/-/x/ is followed by |a| or |ā|, this sequence becomes /xɔ/ (2.39f) or /xɔ·/ (2.39gh).

(2.39) Potential |w| followed by |x|

    (a) təma·kwé·wxe·s (|təmāhkwēwaxēs|) 'beaverhide' (V)
    (b) kwənəmxkwxe·s (|kwənəmə̆xkwaxēs|) 'otter hide' (OA)
    (c) ló·kwxi·n (|wə̆lākwaxīn-w|) 'he lives until evening' (OA)
    (d) xwi·s·əmə́s·a (|wə̆-xīsəməs-a|) 'his or her younger sibling or siblings' (B, V, ME);
        cf. naxí·s·əməs 'my younger sibling' (V)
    (e) káči kxwí·han (|kwax-īhan|) 'don't be afraid of me (you sg.)' (ME) (cf. 2.15d)
    (f) é·li-kxɔ́hti·t (|ēlī kwax-āhə̆tīt|) 'because they feared him, them' (B)
    (g) xɔ́·nsa (|wə̆-xans-a|) 'his or her older brother or brothers'
    (h) ntak·ɔ·kxɔ́·na (|nə̆t-akwāhkwaxān-a|, with |-axā-| 'have ear') 'my earwax (pl.)' (ME);
        cf. ahkí·nxe· (|akīn-| 'sharp (pl.)' + |-axā| 'have ear' + |-w| 3) 'he has sharp ears' (ME)

Blanchard writes ostensible /kxw-/ (as in 2.39e) successively as ⟨qxw-⟩ (Mt 10.26), ⟨kwx-⟩ (Mk 6.50), and ⟨qx-⟩ (Lk 12.4), but presumably these are all spellings of /kxw-/. It is unlikely that ⟨kwx-⟩ writes an archaic pronunciation with /kwx-/ ([kʷx]), since Blanchard consistently writes /kw/ with his letter ⟨q⟩ (or if not before a vowel sometimes as ⟨k⟩, especially in the early pages), so this is best seen as simply a printing error for ⟨kxw-⟩. The spelling ⟨qx-⟩ parallels the much more frequent ⟨qv⟩ (as if /kw-h/) that Blanchard came to favor to write /khw/ (pp. 11-214), replacing earlier ⟨kvw⟩ (5x, pp. 6-44): e.g. ⟨trvaqvekamaqvetet⟩ writing /te·ha·khwikama·khwíti·t/ 'when it casts a shadow over them'. Even so, the spellings ⟨qv⟩ and ⟨qx⟩ are best not taken literally, but as similar abstract notations that take advantage of the existence of ⟨q⟩ in the alphabet. The writing ⟨qv⟩ uses the letter for /kw/ and the letter for /h/ to spell the equivalent of English "kwh," but in English "wh" spells /hw/; in effect, Blanchard's spellings show the clusters /khw/ and /kxw/ being decomposed into a labialized [k] (a /kw/) and an /h/ or /x/, which is correct in the abstract but most likely not on the surface. Another piece of evidence for Blanchard's perception of where the labialization was in such clusters and where it should be written is his initial writing of xwi·s·əmə́s·a 'his younger sibling' (2.39d) with ⟨wx-⟩, after which he wrote forms of this word seven times with ⟨xw-⟩. Again, the influence of English "wh" is evident.

§2.12c. Replacement of |y| by |h|. The sequence /yh/ occurs in some words (2.16a), but |əy| and |h| assimilate to /ihh/ (2.40ab). Similarly, |əy| and |s| assimilate to /ihs/ (2.40c).

(2.40) |y| followed by |h| or |s|

    (a) məkihhá·s·u (|məkəyahāsəw|) 'he has sores' (LB);
        cf. məkí (|məkəy|) 'scab, sore', pl. məkía (|məkəya|) (OA); mwə́k·ia 'his sores' (B)
    (b) mpa·ktíhhɔ (|nə̆pākə̆təyahwāw|) 'I spanked him (once)' (OA)
    (c) məkíhsu (|məkəyə̆səw|) 'he is scabby' (OA), 'he has acne' (LB)

§2.12d. Underlying |ōx| and |ōxw|. Given that /x·w/, /x·ɔ/, and /xɔh/ as a weak syllable tend to be preceded by |ō| (2.41ab), and that /x(·)w/ is otherwise extremely rare, it might seem that ostensible underlying |ōxw| could be produced from a more abstract |ōx| by a phonological rule that adds |w| (Goddard 1979: Foreword xvii and 24, rule U-19e [which should be restricted to word-medial position]). Against this, however, are not only the rare cases of /xw/ (in a strong syllable /x·w/) without a preceding |ō| (2.41c), but also a number of cases of /x(·)/ (not /x(·)w/) after /o·/ (2.40de). This distribution indicates that underlying |ōxw| has been lexicalized, that it has become part of the underlying form.

(2.41) Examples of |xw| (with and without |ō|) and |ōx| (without |w|)
  (a) kšó·x·we· (|kəšōxwēw|) 'he walks fast' (OA)
  (b) mpəntó·x·ɔla (|nə-pəntōxwal-āw|), mpəntúxɔhto·n (|nə-pəntōxwat-ōn|) 'I took him, it in' (ME)
  (c) laxwéhəle· (|laxwēhlēw|) '(anim., inan.) scatters' (V)
  (d) kó· wto·x·í·i (|wətōxīwīw|) 'he has no father' (ME; OA with akó·);
    cf. nó·x (|nōx|) 'my father' (V, ME, FW), ó·x·ɔ (|ōxwal|) 'his or her father' (V, ME)
  (e) akó· no·x·i·s·əməs·í·i (|nōxīsəməsīwīw|) 'I have no younger sibling' (OA) (2.39d);
    cf. nó·x·wi·s (|nōxwīs|) 'my grandchild' (ME, ND)
  (f) ki·š·ó·x·ink (kí·š·o·x |kīšōx| 'sun, moon', |-ənk| loc.) 'sun, moon (loc.)'; P '— months':
    ki·š·ó·x·ink 'like the sun' (B); palé·naxk ki·š·ó·x·ink 'for five months' (OA)

§2.12e. Secondary /hi/. Vowel-coloring and the metathesis of underlying |əh| produce /hi/ alternating with /i·/ (2.5 l, 6e) and /hu/ alternating with /o·/ (2.5m) before voiceless consonants, but there are also cases of an ostensibly metathesized /hi/ before a /kw/ (2.21c, 42ab), an environment in which /hu/ would be expected. This anomalous /hi/ can be analyzed as having an underlying |ih|, with |i| being a segment that behaves exactly like |ə| except that before /kw/ it is realized as /i/ or /i·/, depending metrical factors. There are also cases of apparent metathesized /hi/ in forms in which underlying |əh| does not fit the morphological structure (2.42c). These two types of aberrant /hi/ occur where related forms have /i·/, and they have evidently arisen by analogy to the widespread alternation between /i·/ and /hi/ (from |əh|). The /hi/ alternates in related forms with an /i·/ that in the first type was originally an underlying |īh| (2.42ab), and in the second type could be taken as an underlying |əh| on the basis of just the phonology (2.42c).

(2.42) Anomalous, secondary /hi/
  (a) ləkhíkwi (|ələkihkwi|) PV 'to {such} an extent';
    cf. ntəlkí·kwi 'I .. to (such) extent' (|nət-ələkihkwī|; originally |nət-ələkīhkwī|)
  (b) hwík·wi (|wihkwəy|) 'chin' (OA, LB) (2.21c);
    cf. kwəní·kwie· 'he has a long chin' (|kwənihkwəyā-w|; originally |kwənīhkwəyā-|)
  (c) thitpí·kat 'it is a cold night' (OA) (as if |təhtəpəhkat-w|, but cf. |tah-| 'cold');
    cf. wəli·tpí·kat 'it's a nice night' (|wəlītəpəhkat-w|, taken as |wələhtəpəhkat-w|)

§2.12f. Treatment of |-(ə)hmənā| 1p,12. The suffix |-(ə)hmənā| 1p,12 (independent indicative m-ending, first person plural [4.19]) is realized as /-həna/ (as if from |-hnā|, having lost the |mə|; 43abcd), except if it occurs after a consonant and |əh| is metathesized to /hú/ (**§2.5**; 43ef, cf. 5n). This can be considered a regular phonological change, as this underlying sequence does not occur elsewhere.

(2.43) The realizations of |-(ə)hmənā| 1p,12
  (a) nəmi·kəmɔ·s·íhəna (|nəmīhkəmwāsīhmənā|) 'we (exc.) worked'
  (b) ktáhəna (|kətāhmənā|) 'we (inc.) go'
  (c) ko·le·ləntamúhəna (|kōlēləntaməhmənā|) 'we (inc.) are joyful'
  (d) ko·wahəlúhəna (|kōwāhələhmənā|) 'we know you'
  (e) kši·e·ləməlhúmana (|kəšīwēləmələhmənā|) 'we grieved for you'
  (f) takó· kéku mpəthamo·húmana (|nəpətahamōwəhmənā|) 'we (exc.) caught nothing'

In forms like (2.43c) and (2.43d), the presence of the underlying |mə| accounts for why the vowel before the /h/ is /ú/ (as before the second plural suffix in 2.5hn) and not /í/.

§2.12g. Assimilation of |m| before |k| and |t|. An underlying |m| assimilates to /n/ (pronounced [ŋ]) before |k|, and to /n/ before |t|. These sequences arise when a verb stem or theme sign ending in |m| is followed by |-k| 3s (used instead of |-t| 3 after a consonant) (2.44acd); by the prohibitive suffix /-kh/ (the variant of usual |-h| PROH in this environment) (2.44b); by the indefinite object suffix |-kē| AI (2.44e); by the diminutive suffix |-tī| (2.45a); by the reciprocal suffix |-tī| AI (2.45b; **§5.8m**); or by the causative suffix |-təl| TA (2.45c, 5.87).

(2.44) /nk/ from |m-k|
    (a) pəntánke (|pəntankē|) 'when he (she) heard it' (< |-am| TH.1a, |-k| 3, |-ē| SUBJ);
        cf. pə́ntame·kw 'what you (pl.) hear' (with |-am-ēkw| < |-am| TH.1a, |-ēkw| 2p)
    (b) káči kələnínkhe·kw (|kələnənkahēkw|) 'don't carry it (you pl.)' (cf. 3b)
        (with |-ənkahēkw| < |-əm| TH.1b, |-kah| ← |-h| PROH, |-ēkw| 2p)
    (c) nénke (|nēnkē|) 'when he (she) saw it' (< |nēm-| TI(3) 'see', |-k| 3, |-ē| SUBJ);
        cf. nné·mən (|nə-nēm-ən|) 'I saw it' (with |nə–ən| 'I – it')
    (d) kahtunkɔ́nke (|katənkwām-k-ē|) 'if he (she) is sleepy' (OA) (with |-k| 3, |-ē| SUBJ);
        cf. kahtúnkɔ·m 'he (she) is sleepy', kahtunkɔ·má·ne 'if I'm sleepy' (OA)
    (e) kənči·tánke· (|kənčīhtānkē-w|) 'he encourages people' (< |kənčīhtām-| TA + |-kē| AI);
        cf. nkənči·tá·ma (|nə-kənčīhtām-āw|) 'I encourage him' (OA)

(2.45) /nt/ from |m-t|
    (a) kahtunkɔ́ntu (|katənkwām-| AI + |-tī| DIM, |-w| 3) 'he (she) (dim.) is sleepy' (OA)
    (b) naxkúntəwak (|naxkōntəwak| < |naxkōm-| TA + |-tī| AI recip. **[§5.8m]**, |-wak| 3p) 'they answered 'yes' to each other' (OA);
        cf. nnaxkó·ma (|nə-naxkōm-āw|) 'I answered him' (V, OA, LB)
    (c) wənentəlúk·o·n (|wə-nēntəl-əkōn|) 'he (obv.) showed it to him' (*lit.*, 'made him see it'): |nēntəl-| TA < |nēm-| 'see' + |-təl| TA 'cause to' (5.87e; |wə–əkōn| 'obv. – it to him')

§2.12h. Metathesis of |w| and |k| 3,0. Potential |wk| is metathesized to |kw|. The conditions for this change occur when |-k| 3 (the substitute for |-t| 3 used after a consonant) or |-k| 0 follows |-(ō)w| NEG (2.46abc) or |-aw| TH.TI(2), the theme sign of the Class 2 TI (2.46de). In the TI(2) ending the |a| is lengthened to |ā| as part of this process.

(2.46) Metathesis of |w| and |k| to |kw|
    (a) máta ne·ykɔ́t·o·kw (|nēwəkwatōkw|) '(inan.) which is not visible'
        (< (IC) + |nēwəkwat-| II + |-ōw| NEG, |-k| 0)
    (b) máta ki·š·i·k·í·k·we (|kīšīkīkwē|) 'if he is not born'
        (< |kīšīkī-| AI + |-w| NEG, |-k| 3, |-ē| SUBJ)
    (c) máta nəno·stamɔ́k·we (|nə̀nōsətamōkwē|) 'if he does not understand it'
        (|nə̀nōsət-| TI(1a) + |-am| TH.TI(1A), |-ōw| NEG, |-k| 3, |-ē| SUBJ)
    (d) we·lháta·kw (|wəlahtākw|) 'what he has' (< IC + |wəlaht-| TI(2) + |-aw| TH.TI(2), |-k| 3)
    (e) we·ɔ·tá·k·we (|wēwāhtākwē|) 'when he (she) knew it'
        (< IC + |wəwāht-| TI(2) + |-aw| TH.TI(2), |-k| 3, |-ē| SUBJ)

§2.12i. Replacement of |t| by |č|, |h|, and |s|. In certain combinations |t| is replaced by |č| before |ī|, although the sequence |tī| is widely found. This replacement takes place in stem composition (2.49a) and when the suffixes |-t| 3, |-at| 2s–3, or |-ənt| X–3 are followed by |-īk| anim. pl. or |ī(l)| obv., inan. pl. (2.47abc). The same replacement takes place word-finally in prohibitive forms (2.47de), which can be analyzed as having a modal suffix |-∅| PROH whose presence is indicated only by this effect.

(2.47) Replacement of |t| by |č| in inflectional endings
(a) pa·lsí·č·i·k 'sick people' ((IC) + |pāləsī-| AI + |-t| 3, |-īk| anim. pl.);
cf. pá·lsi·t 'one who is sick, a sick person' ((IC) + |pāləsī-| AI + |-t| 3)
(b) e·lanko·máč·i·k 'your (sg.) relatives' (IC+ |əlankōm-| TA + |-at| 2s–3, |-īk| anim. pl.)
cf. e·lankó·mat 'your (sg.) relative' (IC+ |əlankōm-| TA + |-at| 2s–3)
(c) ki·k·e·hənči·k 'the ones that were cured' ((IC) + |kīkēh-| TA + |-ənt| X–3, |-īk| anim. pl.)
cf. ki·k·é·hənt 'the one that was cured' ((IC) + |kīkēh-| TA + |-ənt| X–3)
(d) káči ahkəni·mié·k·ač 'do not pronounce judgment on them'
(|akənīm-| TA + |-əyēk| PROH, |-at| 2s–3, |-∅| PROH)
(e) káči li·x·í·hi·č 'he must not come down' (|līxī-| AI + |-h(ī)| PROH, |-t| 3s, |-∅| PROH)

A |t| becomes |h| before the conjunct suffix |-k| 0 (2.48ab). A word-final |-ahk| resulting from this is reduced to |-ah|, and the |-h| is lost in the regular way (2.48cd; **§2.9c**); see also Goddard (1979:129). Alternatively, a |ə| is inserted between a stem-final |t| and |-k| 0 (2.48a).

(2.48) Replacement of |t| by |h| before |k|, and loss of the |k|
(a) wé·lhik '(what is) good' (wēləhk < IC + |wəlat-| II + |-k| 0); cf. wəlát 'it is good'
also wé·ltək '(what is) good' (wēlə̥tək < IC + |wəlat(ə)-| II + |-k| 0)
(b) naxo·k·wənakháke 'in, after three days' (|naxōkwənakahkē|
< |naxōkwənakat-| II + |-k| 0, |-ē| SUBJ); see 48c
(c) é·li·ke·x·o·k·wənák·a 'in a few days' (|kēxōkwənakah| < |kēxōkwənakat-| II + |-k| 0);
cf. naxo·k·wənák·at 'it is (has been) three days'
(d) me·xkpé·k·a 'wine' (B), 'Red River' (OA) (*lit.* 'red liquid') (|mēxkəpēka|
< |maxkəpēkat-| II + |IC–k| 0/PPL(INsg))

A |t| is replaced by |s| before the final pair |-əhkaw| TA, |-əhk| TI(1a) 'act on by foot or body'. The same replacement takes place before |-əp-| 'water' in one form (5.28a(1)).

(2.49) Replacement of |t| by |s| before certain finals
(a) kpe·x·o·shika·k·o·né·ɔ 'it comes near you (pl.)' (|kəpēxōsəhkākōnēwā|
< |pēxōsəhkaw-| TA + |kə–əkōnēwā| 0–2p; stem |pēxōt-| 'near' + |-əhkaw| TA);
cf. pe·x·o·č·íhəle· 'it comes near' (|pēxōt-| 'near' + |-īhlā| II 'come, go' + |-w| 3,0)
(b) a·phishíko· 'go to meet him (you pl.)' (|āpəht-| + |-əhkaw| TA + |-ō| 2p–3/IMP);
cf. á·phit 'on the way, before getting to the destination' (V. ME)

The implied underlying |āpəhsəhkaw-| TA (2.49b) has an otherwise non-existent underlying |hs|.

§2.12j. Other restricted processes of cluster reduction. In a number consonant sequences that arise in secondary derivation or in inflection the first consonant is replaced by |h|.

A nasal consonant before |l| becomes |h|; this occurs when an AI stem (or its initial element) ending in |m| or |n| adds the abstract final |-l| TA (2.50ab). This can also be seen when the TI Class 1 theme signs (1a |-am|, 1b |-əm|) are followed by the imperative singular suffix |-l| 2s.IMP (2.51ab). (This would also be expected in the imperatives of stems ending in |m|, but none are citable.) These TI endings are always word-final, and in this position the |-hl| is reduced to a potential |-h|, which is regularly lost (**§2.9c**). The existence of the intermediate-stage |-h| is shown, however, by the fact that the TI(1b) ending |-əh| is realized as /-i/, with coloring of the |ə| to /i/ (cf. 2.5il). (No word ends with an underlying |ə| or a phonemic /ə/.)

(2.50) Replacement of nasal consonant by |h| before |l|
(a) tá=háč=k kúhəla·n? 'So, where did you (sg.) get it (anim.) from?' (Blanchard 1834a:12)
(|kōhlān| < |wəhl-| TA 'get from {smwh}', |kə–ān| 2s–3+0s;
|wəhl-| TA < |wəm-| AI 'come from {smwh}' + |-l| TA); cf. tá=háč kúntən 'where do you get it from?' (B; |kōntən| < |wənt-| TI(3), |kə–ən| 2s–0+0s)

(b) nuhəláːčiːk (|nōhlāčīk|) 'ones who breastfeed (an infant)' (|nōhl-| TA < |nōn-| + |-l| TA); cf. nóːneˑ 'it (infant) nurses' (|nōnē-| AI < |nōn-| + |-ē| AI)

(2.51) Word-final |-hl| from |m| + |l| replaced by |-h|
    (a) wəleˑlə́nta (|wəlēləntah|) 'be happy (you sg.)' (|-ah| < |-am| TH.TI(1A) + |-l| 2s.IMP)
    (b) wéˑtˑəni (|wētənəh|) 'pick it up (you sg.)' (|-əh| < |-əm| TH.TI(1B) + |-l| 2s.IMP)

When a TA stem in |l| is followed by the indefinite object suffix |-kē| AI (2.44e), the |l| is replaced by |h|, giving |hk| (2.52ab).

(2.52) Replacement of |l| by |h| before |k|
    (a) mpíˑkeˑ (|nəpīhkē-w|) 'he's doctoring someone with a sweatbath' (OA) (|nəpīhkē-| AI < |nəpīl-| TA + |-kē| AI; also in nenpíˑkeˑs (|nēhnəpīhkēs|) 'sweat doctor'); cf. kənə́pˑiˑla 'you (sg.) sweat him, doctor him with a sweatbath'
    (b) káči khwithikéˑheˑkw 'do not forbid anyone' (|kwəhtəhkē-| AI + |-hēkw| 2p.PROH; |kwəhtəhkē-| AI 'forbid or admonish people' < |kwəhtəl-| TA + |-kē| AI); cf. kkwiˑtəláˑɔ (|wə-kwəhtəl-āwa|) 'he admonished or forbade him, them' (B; ME)

§2.12k. Irregular preterite singular ending. The first and second singular suffix of the m-endings (|-(ə)hm|), which is dropped in word-final position (in the ordinary independent indicative forms), combines with the preterite suffix |-p| (< |-p(an-)|) as |-(ə)həmp|.

(2.53) First and second singular preterite
    (a) ntələwéˑhəmp (|nət-ələwē-həmp|) 'I said' (B, Jn 10.34 ⟨Ntclwrvump⟩; LTD ND) (|ələwē-| AI 'say', |nət–həmp| 1s/IND.PRET)
    (b) nsoˑpsíhəmp (|nə-sōpəsī-həmp|) 'I was naked' (B ⟨-vwmp⟩, as usual)
    (c) nóˑmhəmp (|nōməhəmp|) 'I came from (someplace)' (|wəm-| AI 'come from', |nə–əhəmp 1s/IND.PRET)
    (d) ktahɔˑlíhəmp (|kət-àhwāl-īhəmp|) 'you (sg.) loved me' (|kə–īhəmp| 2s–1s/IND.PRET)
    (e) kəneˑwəlúhump (|kə-nēw-ələhəmp|) 'I saw you (sg.)' (|kə–ələhəmp| 1s–2s/IND.PRET)

§2.13. The realization of the pronominal prefixes (and homophonous syllables). In the inflection of both nouns and verbs there are pronominal prefixes, indicators of first, second, and third person that attach to the beginning of stems. On nouns they indicate the person of the possessor, and on verbs they indicate the subjects of intransitives and one of the two arguments of transitive verbs in the paradigms of the independent order.

The underlying forms of the prefixes are |nə-| 1, |kə-| 2, and |wə-| 3. When one of these is added before a stem there are often changes in the shape of the prefix or the stem, or both, and there is some variation between speakers. (There are similar changes in stems that begin with syllables of the same shape [2.67].) The most archaic pronunciations have word-initial geminate consonants in some cases, but for some speakers some or all of these are not distinguished from single consonants. The most explicit pronunciations from the most conservative speaker, Martha Ellis, are given in (2.54), with some variants; the notation "same" means 'same as in the column to the left'. These have been used in the phonemic transcription of Blanchard's spellings, which never indicate geminates. Notes on speaker variation are given below.

(2.54) Combinations of pronominal prefixes and initial syllables

		Ca(ˑ)-	Ce(ˑ)-	Cə-	(Cəm-)	(Cəp-)	Ci-	Co-	Cɔ(ˑ)-	Cu-
/p/	1	mpa(ˑ)-	mpe(ˑ)-	mpə-	*same*	*same*	mpiˑ-	mpoˑ-	mpɔ(ˑ)-	mpu-
	2	kpa(ˑ)-	kpe(ˑ)-	kpə-	*same*	*same*	kpiˑ-	kpoˑ-	kpɔ(ˑ)-	kpu-
	3	pɔ(ˑ)- ppɔ(ˑ)-	pwe(ˑ)-	pwə-	pwəm-	pup-	pwiˑ-	ppoˑ-	ppɔ(ˑ)-	ppu-

		[Ca(·)-	Ce(·)-	Cə-	(Cəm-)	(Cəp-)	Ci-	Co-	Cɔ(·)-	Cu-]
/k/	1	nka(·)-	nke·-	nkə-	*same*	*same*	nki·-	nko·-	nkɔ(·)-	
	2	kka(·)-	kke·-	kkə-	*same*	*same*	kki·-	kko·-	kkɔ(·)-	
	3	kɔ(·)-	kwe·-	kwə-	kum-	kup-	kwi·-	kko·-	kɔ(·)-	
/kwi·/										
	1						nkwi·-			
	2						kkwi·-			
	3						kkwi·-			
/t/	1	nta(·)-	nte(·)-	ntə-			nti·-	nto·-	ntu-	
	2	kta(·)-	kte(·)-	ktə-			kti·-	kto·-	ktu-	
	3	tɔ(·)-	wte(·)-	wtə-; tən-, təl-			wti·-	wto·-	wtu-	
/s/	1	nsa(·)-	nse·-	nsə-			nsi·-	nso·-		
	2	ksa(·)-	kse·-	ksə-			ksi·-	kso·-		
	3	sɔ(·)-	wse·-	wsə-			wsi·-	wso·-		
/š/	1	nša(·)-	nše·-	nšə-			nši·-	nšo·-		
	2	kša(·)-	kše·-	kšə-			kši·-	kšo·-		
	3	šɔ(·)-	wše·-	wšə-			wši·-	wšo·-		
/l/	1	nla(·)-	nle·-	nlə-			nli·-	nlo·-	(or ll- for nl- in all)	
	2	kəla(·)-	kəle·-	kələ-			kəli·-	kəlo·-		
	3	lɔ(·)-	wəle·-	wələ-			wəli·-	wəlo·-		
/m/	1	nəma(·)-	nəme·-	nəmə-	*same*		nəmi·-	nəmo·-	nəmɔ·-	
	2	kəma(·)-	kəme·-	kəmə-	*same*		kəmi·-	kəmo·-	kəmɔ·-	
	3	mɔ(·)-	mwe·-	mwə-	mum-		mwi·-	mmo·-	mmɔ·-	
/n/	1	nna(·)-	nne·-	nnə-			nni·-	nno·-		
	2	kəna(·)-	kəne·-	kənə-			kəni·-	kəno·-		
	3	nɔ(·)-	wəne·-	wənə-			wəni·-	wəno·-		
/w/	1		nəwe·-	no·- (nu-), nəwə-			nəmi·-			
	2		kəwe·-	ko·- (ku-), kəwə-			kəwi·-			
	3		wwe·-	o·-, wwə-, wə-			wwi·-			
/ɔ(·)/			|wa|		|wā|					
	1		nɔ-, nəwa-		nɔ·-					
	2		kɔ-, kəwa-		kɔ·-					
	3		wɔ-, wwa-		wɔ·-					

Before an underlying word-initial vowel, a |t| is inserted after a prefix; with some exceptions this is treated the same as a stem-initial |t|.

The prefix |wə-| 3 undergoes the most varied treatments. It is reduced to |w|, and this |w| metathesizes with a following consonant, if this would produce a possible cluster (/pw/, /kw/, /mw/) before a permissible following vowel (/i/, /i·/, /e/, /e·/, or most cases of /ə/) (2.55a-l), or if the |w| would combine with a following |a| or |ā| as /ɔ/ or /ɔ·/ (2.55m-r).

(2.55) Metathesis of the |w| of |wə-| 3

    (a) pwihpəntaɔ́·ɔ 'he used to hear him' OA (1s mpihpə́ntaɔ OA)
    (b) pwi·k·ənəmə́na 'he tore them into small pieces' B (mpi·kšə́mən 'I cut it up' OA)
    (c) pwéči-kto·x·ɔlawwá·ɔ 'they brought him out' B (péči PV 'coming (this way)')
    (d) pwé·t·o·n 'he brought it' B, V, LB (1s mpé·t·o·n V, OA, ME)
    (e) pwə́mska·n 'he passed there' (AP; written [pwʊm-]) (see also 2.59e)
    (f) kwíši-mətakhɔwwɔ́·ɔ 'they had covered him up' V (kíši PV 'finish, already')
    (g) kwi·kəná·ɔ 'he touched him' V (1s nkí·kəna V, LB)
    (h) kwe·k·ó·nəm 'his thing' (commonly with obscene sense) ND (ke·k·ó·na 'things' LB)

(i) kwət·ənə́mən 'he pulled it out' V (1s nkət·ənə́mən V)
(j) mwí·laxk 'his hair' B, V, LB (nəmí·laxk 'my hair' V, OA, LB)
(k) mwé·k·ən 'he gave it away' (B, ME) (1s nəmé·k·ən B, ME)
(l) mwə́ne·n 'he drank it' ME (1s nəmə́ne·n B, ME)
(m) ná pə́·n (|wə-pā-n|; |wə–ən| 3s/SBD) 'then he came' ME (short [p]; 1s mpá·n |nə-pā-n|)
(n) tɔhpé·k·əm (|wə-tahəpēkw-əm|) 'his well' OA (thúp·e·kw 'well' (ntahpé·k·əmink 'in my well' OA)
(o) kɔhé·s·a (|wə-kàhēs|) 'his mother' (nkáhe·s 'my mother')
(p) šɔmənəmə́na (|wə-šamən-əmənə|) 'she annointed them (inan.)' (nšámənukw 'she annointed me')
(q) lɔx·əná·ɔ (|wə-laxən-āwa|) 'he released him' (kəlax·ənáwwa=č 'you (pl.) must untie it (anim.)')
(r) nɔxko·má·ɔ (|wə-naxkōm-āwa|) 'he answered them' (kənaxkó·ma=héč 'did you answer him?' V)

Blanchard also attests forms in which |wə-| 3 does not metathesize with |t|, |s|, |š|, or |n| and contract with a following /a/ or /a·/ (2.56). In these cases the prefix has the same treatment as before syllables with the other vowels. Blanchard has at least one example of /w-/ being retained before |t| along with contraction to /ɔ·/ (2.56a), and a form from ER also attests this treatment: wtɔ·tá·p·ia 'his bow'. One speaker (ME) was heard (in one recording session) to have the same dual realization of this prefix with |p| (2.58ghi). The forms without metathesis are generally in the earlier pages of the *Harmony*, but /wəna-/ is overwhelmingly preferred in forms of the word for 'hand' (18x), with /nɔ-/ found only once (2.56c).

(2.56) Retained /wt-/, /ws-/, and /wən-/ before /a/ and /a·/ in Blanchard
  (a) wta·pto·ná·k·an 'his order' (1x, p. 12), wta·pto·ná·k·anink 'in his law' (1x, p. 14) (a·pto·ná·k·an 'word'); wtɔ·pto·ná·k·an ⟨wtoptonakun⟩ (1x, p. 20), tɔ·pto·ná·k·an (31x [all forms], first on p. 6)
  (b) wsa·k·i·ma·ɔ́·k·an 'his kingdom' (6x to p. 76) (sa·k·i·ma·ɔ́·k·an 'kingdom'); sɔ·k·i·ma·ɔ́·k·an (33x [all forms], first on p. 64)
  (c) wənáxk 'his hand' (4x, pp. 68-183), wənáxkink 'in his hand' (5x, pp. 10-217), wənáxka 'his hands; hands' (3x, pp. 196-216), wənaxkí·li·t 'his or her (obv.) hand' (4x, pp. 51-106), wənaxkəwá·ink 'in their hands' (2x, pp. 20-67); nɔ́xkal 'his hands' (1x, p. 143)
  (d) wəna·ɔlawwá·ɔ 'they followed him' (2x, pp. 52, 58), neg. wəna·ɔla·iwwá·ɔ (p. 100) nɔ·ɔlawwá·ɔ (4x, pp. 69-147)

Blanchard also has an example of retained /wš-/ in a derived verb of possession that incorporates the third person prefix (2.67d).

If the conditions for metathesis are not present, |wə-| 3 is generally retained as /w-/ before /t/, /s/, /š/, and /w/ (2.57abcde), and as /wə-/ before /n/ and /l/ (2.57fg).

(2.57) |wə-| 3 retained as /w-/ or /wə-/
  (a) wtó·n (|wə-tōn|) 'his mouth; the mouth' (V)
  (b) wso·khámən (|wə-sōkah-amən|) 'she poured it'
  (c) wšinká·t·amən (|wə-šīnkāt-amən|) 'he hates it'
  (d) wwe·t·ənə́mən (|wə-wētən-əmən|) 'he picked it up' (ME, tape)
  (e) ná=nə wwənčí·ai·n (|wə-wənčīyayī-n|) 'that's where he belongs' (OA, confirmed)
  (f) wəni·č·á·na 'his child' (nní·č·a·n 'my child')
  (g) wəló·s·əmən (|wə-lōs-əmən|) 'he burns it' (OA) (kəló·s·əmən 'you (sg.) burn it' V)

Initial geminate /ww/ was usually clear in the speech of ME and could be heard after a consonant as well as after a vowel, and it was occasionally heard from OA. It thus seems questionable that the /w-/ always "disappear[ed]" before /w/ in the speech of WL (Voegelin 1946:141-142).

In many forms obtained from ME (who recorded several sets of contrasts) |wə-| 3 assimilates completely to /p/, /k/, and /m/, resulting in clear word-initial geminates (2.58), and /mm-/ was also heard from OA (2.58o) and SP (2.58q). In ME's speech geminate /pp-/ and /kk-/ were, if anything, perceived as longer than medial /p·/ and /k·/ although not closing a preceding syllable. (The /kk-/ from /wə-/ 3 + /k-/ [2.58jklm] was identical to the /kk-/ from /kə-/ 2 + /k-/ [2.64].) In three or four forms recorded in one session she pronounced underlying |wəp-| as /wp-/, with a voiceless /w/ before the /p/, although on other occasions /pp-/ was heard (2.58ghi), and two of the cases of /wp-/ had /ɔ/ or /ɔ·/ replacing |a| or |ā| in the following syllable (2.58hi) (cf. Blanchard's /wtɔ·-/ in 2.56a). The potential word-initial geminates were commonly heard as single consonants, however, and single consonants were probably the norm for some speakers. Voegelin (1946:140) stated explicitly that /k-k-/ was reduced to /k-/ in Willie Longbone's speech. The words in (2.58) were heard with the geminates (or /wp-/) audibly pronounced.

(2.58) |w| of |wə-| 3 assimilated to /p/, /k/, and /m/

/pp-/
- (a) ná ppó·s·i·n 'then he got in (a boat or vehicle)' (ME)
- (b) ní ppo·t·a·č·í·k·an 'his whistle' (ME)
- (c) né·k·a ppo·kwənəmən 'he broke it (as, a stick)' (ME)
- (d) ní ppɔ́·m 'his thigh'; cf. ní pɔ́·m 'the ham' (ME) (mpɔ́·m 'my thigh' V, OA)
- (e) ní ppúnkəm 'his gunpowder' (ME) (púnkw 'ashes, dust, gunpowder')
- (f) né·k·a ppuhwə́nəmən 'he pulled it out' (ME) (mpuhwə́nəmən 'I pulled it out' OA)

/wp-/ and /pp-/
- (g) né·k·a wpɔ·wənəmən 'he tries but can't lift or carry it' (ME, tape) (1s mpɔ·wənəmən) (cf. ná ppɔ·wənəmən 'then he tried but couldn't lift or carry it' ME)
- (h) né·k·a wpɔwə́nəmən 'she sifted it' (ME, tape) (1s mpawə́nəmən V, ME) (cf. ná ppɔwə́nəmən 'then she sifted it' ME)
- (i) né·k·a wpɔ·ta·há·a 'he defeated him' (ME, tape) (1s mpa·tá·ha V, OA) (cf. ná ppɔ·tá·ha·n 'then he defeated him' ME)

/kk-/
- (j) né·k·a kkó·na (or kkó·nəma) 'his ice' (ME) (kí· kkó·n(əm) 'your ice'; kó·n 'ice')
- (k) né·k·a kké·k·əma 'his wampum beads' (ME) (ké·k·ək 'wampum beads'; cf. 2.55h)

/kkw-/
- (l) ná kkwí·təla·n 'he told him not to do it' (ME); also 'you' (2.64g)
- (m) á·phit ná kkwə́tki·n 'he went so far and came back' (ME); also 'you' (2.64h)
- (n) kkwí·s·a 'his or her son or sons' (OA, ME)

/mm-/
- (o) né·k·a ní mmɔ́·kələm 'that's his hammer' (ME; also OA) (mɔ́·kəl 'hammer')
- (p) ní mmó·t·ay 'his stomach, belly' (ME)
- (q) takó· mmo·nəna·í·ɔ 'he didn't pluck it (anim.)' (SP)

In some environments /u/ appears instead of /wə/ (/pup-/, /kup-/, /kum-/, /mum-/ in 59abcd; cf. 55eil). Also, expected /pwəm-/ has often been perceived as /pum-/ (2.59e), and Voegelin (1946:141) stated that |wə-| disappeared completely before |pəm-| and |pən-|, giving /pəm-/ (2.59f) and /pən-/ (2.59g). It is not clear if these differences reflect real variation among speakers or simply imprecision in hearing and transcribing.

(2.59) |w| of |wə-| 3 contracted with |ə| to /u/
- (a) pup·a·mihəla·né·ɔ (|wə-pəpāmīhlā-nēwā|) 'they fly there' (ME)
- (b) kuphɔwwá·ɔ (|wə-kəpahw-āwəwāwa|) 'they shut them in' (OA)
- (c) kumó·tke·n (|wə-kəmōtəkē-n|) 'he stole it' (OA) (1s nkəmó·tke·n)
   (Note: some speakers have [k]kamó·tke·n 'you stole it', kɔmó·tke·n 'he stole it' V.)
- (d) nkəmé·e nə́ mumka·la·khómən (nkəmé·e 'always'; nə́ 'that (inan.)';
   |wə-məməkālāhkwah-amən|) 'she constantly scraped it out' (ME)
- (e) ná=yu šúkw púmska·n. ('here'; 'only'; |wə-pəməskā-n|) 'He only walked by here.'
   (OA; written with a rounded [ə]) (see also 55e)
   púmska·n (?) 'he walks by (then or there)' (V; written ⟨pə́mska·n⟩)
- (f) ná púmɔ·n. (?) 'Then he shot him.' (V; written ⟨pə́mo·n⟩ 2x)
   pumɔ́·ɔ (?) 'he shot him' (V; written ⟨pëmo:´o⟩)
   pumó·t·amən (?) 'he shot it' (V, written ⟨pəm-⟩ [Voegelin 1946:141])
- (g) pwənúntəla·n 'he showed it to him' (B; ⟨pwnwntulan⟩ 4x, pp. 10-68,
   ⟨pwunwntulan⟩ 2x, pp. 153-187, ⟨pwunw[n]tulan⟩ p. 216)
   pwənuntəla·né·ɔ (?) 'they showed it to him' (Voegelin 1939, 5:2; [pan-] typo for [pën-])

The prefix |wə-| 3 is usually lost before an intercalated |t| followed by /əl/ or /ən/, but there are cases of /w/ retained in these environments and of |w| lost in other sequences before intercalated |t| and stem-initial |tə-|. In his early notes Voegelin (1939, 5:3) described /tə-/ as the regular treatment of |wə-| 3 and a following |tə-|, with instances of /wtə-/ being due to analogy, but later he described /wtə-/ as normal and the omission of the /w-/ as an unexplained exception (Voegelin 1946:141). Blanchard's occasional writings of ⟨t-⟩ for expected /wt-/ are most likely inaccurate.

(2.60) Loss of |wə-| 3 before /təl-/, /tən-/, and intercalated |t|
- (a) tə́li-mahtá·wsi·n (|wət-əlī matāwəsī-n|) 'that he is a sinner'
   (|-əlī| [= lí PV '{so}' after a prefix], |matāwəsī-| AI 'sin, be a sinner', |wət–n| 3s/SBD);
   tə́li (B 300x) (cf. 2.61a)
- (b) təlá·p·ani·l (|wət-əl-āpanīl|) 'he said to them' (B 3x, pp. 19-75) (cf. 2,61b);
   təlá·p·ani 'he (she) said to him, her, or them' (B 98x, pp. 6-194) (cf. 2,61b)
- (c) ná=nə tə́nta-pá·tama·n. (ná=nə 'that is'; |wət-ənta pāhtamā-n|) 'There he prayed.' (B)
   (|-ənta| [= táli PV '{smwh}' after a prefix], |pāhtamā-| AI 'pray', |wət–n| 3s+0s/IND);
   tə́nta (B 81x)
- (d) tənnə́mən (|wət-ələn-əmən|) 'he did it' (B 4x, OA, ME)
- (e) tənna·há·ɔnink 'on his right (side)' (B 5x, pp. 175-221)
   (|ələn-| 'ordinary' + |-āhē| AI+O 'throw' + |-wan| noun formative; |-ənk| loc.)
- (f) tənna·p·e·ó·k·anink (B; |wət-ələnāpēwākan-ənk|) 'his soul (loc.)' (ləna·p·e·ó·k·an 'soul')
- (g) ti·lá·yəma (|wət-īlāw-əma|) 'his officers' (B p. 201) (í·la |īlāw| 'warrior');
   ti·la·yəməwá·ɔ 'their officers' (B p. 183)
- (h) ná .. tətpí·taɔ·n (|wə-tətəpīhtaw-ān|) 'then he made signs to him' (B p. 178);
   tətpahó·ɔ 'he points at him' (V) (cf. 2.61f)
- (i) tuxkwé·yəma 'his sister or sisters' (V, ND)
   (|wət-əxkwēw-əma|: archaic possessed form of xkwé· 'woman')
- (j) tələmánkan 'his [upper] arm' (V); tələmánkanink 'on his upper arm' (ND)

(2.61) Retention of |wə-| 3 before /təl-/, /tən-/, and intercalated |t|
- (a) wtə́li-=č -núnše·n (B; |wət-əlī nōnšē-n|; =č FUT) 'for her to give birth'
   (|-əlī| [= lí PV '{so}' after a prefix], |nōnšē-| AI 'give birth', |wət–n| 3s/SBD);
   wtə́li (B 3x, pp. 10-12) (cf. 2.60a)

(b) wtəláˑpaniˑl (|wət-əl-āpanīl|) 'he said to them' (B 1x, p. 18);
wtəláˑpani 'he said to him' (B 1x, p. 21) (cf. 2.60b)
(c) wtənnaˑháˑɔnink 'on his right (side)' (B p. 6);
wtənnaˑhaˑɔníˑliˑt 'on his (obv.) right (side)' (B 3x, pp. 194-205) (cf. 2.60e)
(d) wtənnaˑpˑéˑyəmal 'his people' (B 4x, pp. 9-80), wtənnaˑpˑéˑyəma (B 2x, pp. 63, 143; ME 2x) (ntənnaˑpˑéˑyəmak 'my folks' V, with single [n]) (cf. 2.60f)
(e) wtiˑláˑyəma (B p. 159), wtiˑlaˑyəmíˑna (B p. 78) 'his officers' (cf. 2.60g, 4.12b)
(f) wtətpiˑtaˑkˑəwáˑɔ 'they made signs to him' (B forms 4x, pp. 7-38);
wtətpáhəmən 'he's pointing at it' (V) (cf. 2.60h)
(g) wtuxkwéˑyəma, wtuxkwéˑyəmal, wtuxkweˑyəmíˑna 'his sisters' (B 5x) (cf. 2.60i, 4.12c)
(h) wtələmánkan 'his [upper] arm' (V) (cf. 2.60j)

In the prefix |nə-| 1 the |ə| is lost before a voiceless consonant other than /x/, and before |n| and |l| (2.62). Before /x/ the |ə| is replaced by /a/ (2.62g). The |n| assimilates to /m/ before |p| (2.62a), and for some speakers it assimilates to /l/ before /l/ (2.62k). Initial /nn-/ (2.62i) was heard from WL (V), OA, ME, and ER. Initial /nl-/ was retained by ME and LB (2.62j). Initial /ll-/ (2.62k), with assimilation, was heard from WL (V) and OA and appears to be indicated by Blanchard (who writes only ⟨l-⟩).

(2.62) Prefix |nə-| 1 before voiceless consonants, |n|, and |l|
(a) mpákˑama (|nə-pakam-āw|) 'I hit him' (V) (pahkám 'hit him, them (you sg.)' AD)
(b) ntáˑnəs (|nə-tānəs|) 'my daughter' (B)
(c) nčíˑkˑənaˑn (|nə-čīkən-ān|) 'I took it away from him' (V)
(d) nkə́tˑukw (|nə-kətəkw|) 'my knee' (V, FW, ND)
(e) nsaˑkˑiˑxˑiˑnhúməna (|nə-sākīxīn-əhmənā|) 'we (exc.) are sticking out' (V)
(f) nšinkáˑla (|nə-šīnkāl-āw|) 'I hate him' (V, OA)
(g) naxíˑsˑəməs (|nə-xīsəməs|) 'my younger brother or sister' (V, LB; pl. B, ND)
(h) nhákˑay (|nə-hakay|) 'myself' (B, V, OA, AP, ME)
(i) nnáˑwəla (|nə-nāwal-āw|) 'I followed him or her' (V, OA); cf. 2.27f
(j) nlaxahkwə́na (|nə-laxakwən-āw|) 'I loosen it (anim., as a belt)' (ME)
(k) lləmátahpi (|nə-ləmàtapī|) 'I'm sitting down' (OA)

In the prefix |kə-| 2 the |ə| is lost before any voiceless consonant (2.63, 64).

(2.63) Prefix |kə-| 2 before voiceless consonants other than |k|
(a) kpaˑhóke (|kə-pāwahkē|) 'you are friendly' (V) (3s paˑhókeˑ)
(b) któˑn (|kə-tōn|) 'your mouth' (V) (ntóˑn 'my mouth')
(c) ktamə́ntxa (|kət-amətaxā|) 'you don't listen, don't mind' (OA) (3s amə́ntxeˑ)
(d) kčíˑkˑaniˑn (|kə-čīkən-īn|) 'you (sg.) took it away from me' (V); cf. 2.62c
(e) ksoˑkhámaneˑn (|kə-sōkah-amənēn|) 'we (inc.) poured it' (V) (3s wsoˑkhámən)
(f) kšinkáˑləl (|kə-šīnkāl-əl|) 'I hate you (sg.)' (OA) (wšinkaˑláˑɔ 'he hates him' B, V; 62f)
(g) kxíˑsˑəməs 'your (sg.) younger brother or sister' (B, V); cf. 2.62g
(h) khákˑay (|kə-hakay|) 'yourself' (B, ME); cf. 62h

(2.64) Prefix |kə-| 2 before |k|
(a) kíˑkkáwi (|kə-kawī|) 'you're sleeping, you're asleep' (ME, ER)
(b) akóˑkkawíˑi (|kə-kawīwī|) 'you're not asleep' (SP)
(c) ná kkáxptoˑn (|kə-kaxpət-ōn|) 'then you tied it' (ME)
(d) ná kkóxˑɔˑn (|kə-kwax-ān|) 'then you were afraid of him' (ME)
(cf. ná kóxˑɔˑn 'then he was afraid of him' ME 2x; 2.15d)
(e) kíˑkkɔˑxkwsúnkɔˑm (|kə-kwāxkwəsənkwām|) 'you're snoring' (ME)
(kɔˑxkwsúnkɔˑm 'he's snoring')

(f) ná kkə́ntka·n (|kə-kəntəkā-n|) 'then you danced' (ME, OA)
   (cf. ná kə́ntka·n 'then there was a dance' ME, OA)
(g) ná kkwí·təla·n (|kə-kwəhtəl-ān|) 'you told him not to do it' (ME); also 3s (2.58.l)
(h) á·phit ná kkwə́tki·n (|kə-kwətəkī-n|) 'you went so far and came back' (ME); also 3s (2.58m)
(i) wá kkáhe·s 'your (sg.) mother' (AP), ná kkáhe·s (ME, ER)

When followed by a stem-initial |wə-| the prefixes contract |ə-wə| to |ō| (2.19, 31j, 65a-l), with certain exceptions (2.20cdef, 66ab). In Blanchard this contraction does not take place where the expected |ō-| from the contraction of |wə-| 3 would have been shortened to a word-initial /u-/ before |nt| or |nč|. In this environment |wə-| 3 is always retained, originally giving /wwə-/ (2.57e), and this transcription has been used in the edition of Blanchard (2.20cd, 66ab). Recent speakers extended this non-contraction to include the first and second person as well (2.20ef, 66cd), with a small residue of exceptions that retain contraction to /u/ with |nə-| 1 and |kə-| 2 (2.65jkl).

(2.65) Contraction of prefixes with stem-initial |wə-|
(a) no·le·lə́ntam (|nə-wəlēləntam|) 'I am glad' (2s ko·le·lə́ntam, 3s wəle·lə́ntam);
   ná .. o·le·ləntamənéɔ (|wə-wəlēlənt-amənēwā|) 'then they were glad'
(b) no·t·aníhi·n (|nə-wətanihī-n|) 'I pulled it' (ME)
   (wehə́nči-wtaníhink payaxkhí·k·an 'trigger', lit. 'that by which the gun is pulled' ME)
(c) no·wá·to·n (|nə-wəwāht-ōn|) 'I know it' (B et al.; 3s o·wá·to·n |wə-wəwāht-ōn|)
   (kɔ́t·a-wwá·to·n |wə-kata wəwāht-ōn| 'he wanted to know it' B)
(d) no·txúk·o·k (|nə-wətax-əkōk|) 'they come to me' (B)
   (tɔx·í·t·e |wətax-ītē| 'if he comes to me' B)
(e) no·thakí·i (|nə-wətahkīwī|) 'I have land' (OA; tɔ·kí·yu |wətahkīwī-w| 'he has land' OA)
(f) no·yamxkhámən (|nə-wəyàmaxkah-amən|) 'I mixed it, stirred it' (OA)
   (cf. wiámxki |wəyamv̆xkī| P 'mixed' [|v̆| = |a| or |ə|])
(g) tá=háč núnči-wwa·tó·ne·n 'how do we know it?' (B ⟨tu vuh nwnhi watwnrn⟩;
   tá WH; =háč Q; |nə-wənčī wəwāht-ōnēn|)
(h) tá=háč kúnči-wwá·hi·n? 'How do you know me?' (B ⟨Ta vuh kwnhi waven?⟩;
   tá WH; =háč Q; |kōnčī wəwāhīn| < |kə-wənčī wəwāh-īn| <
   |wənčī| PV 'from {smwh}', |wəwāh-| TA 'know', |kə–īn| 2s–1s+0s/IND)
(i) kuntamo·lənéɔ 'I tell you (pl.) it' (B ⟨kwntamwlunro⟩ 2x;
   |kōntamōlənēwā| < |wəntamaw-| TA 'tell', kə–ələnēwā| 1s–2p+0s/IND)
(j) ná=ni núntəne·n 'that's where we got it' (OA; ná PRES, ní 'that (inan.)';
   |nə-wənt-ənen| < |wənt-| TI(3) 'get from {smwh}', |nə–ənēn| 1p–0₍₃₎+0s/IND)
(k) t=éč kuntənéɔ 'where'd you (pl.) get them?' (ER; tá WH; =héč Q;
   |kə-wənt-ənēwā| < |wənt-| TI(3) 'get from {smwh}', |kə–ənēwā| 2p–0₍₃₎+0s/IND)
(l) ná=ni núhəla·n 'that's where I got him' (ME; ná PRES, ní 'that (inan.)';
   |nə-wəhl-ān| < |wəhl-| TA 'get from {smwh}';

(2.66) Non-contraction of prefixes with stem-initial |wə-|
(a) nə́ni wwə́nči-luwe·néɔ, ".." 'because of that they said, ".."' (B ⟨Nuni wunhi lwrnro⟩;
   nə́ni 'that (inan.)'; |wə-wənči ələwē-nēwā| < |wənči| 'from {smthg}', |ələwē-| 'say',
   |wə-nēwā| 3p+0s/IND)
(b) wwəntamáɔ·n 'he told him' (B ⟨wuntamaon⟩; |wə-wəntamaw-ān|, |wə–ān| 3s–3´+0s/IND)
(c) nəwəntamáɔ·n (|nə-wəntamaw-ān|) 'I'm showing him, teaching him' (BF)
(d) kəwəntélahto·n (|kə-wəntēhlat-ōn|) 'you bring it to a boil' (ME)

Stems that begin with underlying |wa-| or |wā-| have phonemic /ɔ-/ and /ɔ·-/ (2.15fghi), but they add the prefixes as if to a stem that begins with a consonant, with some variation. Examples are in (2.15fghi).

Stems that begin with phonemic /h/ when there is no prefix add the prefixes before the underlying stem-initial vowel or |wa-|, with the stem-initial syllable adjusted for its occurrence after a weak-vowel syllable (2.5cd, 8a, 13e, 34g).

In stems that begin with syllables of the same shape as the pronominal prefixes there are similar changes in some cases. Stem-initial |wə-| is treated like the prefix |wə-| 3 and undergoes the same metathesis (2.19c, 32b, 39c, 65de, 67a), except that monosyllabic stems and initials (**§3.1b**) never metathesize the |w| and the second consonant; these exceptions are |wəm-| AI 'come from' (2.67b), |wəl-| 'well, etc.' (2.5e, 30b, 34b, 34f, 36b), and |wət-| 'pull' (2.65b, 2.67c). Blanchard attests a derived verb of possession that incorporates |wə-| 3 into the stem but archaically retains /wša·-/ (2.67d; cf. 2.56). One stem pair begins with /nək-/ for some speakers (2.67d) and with /nak-/ for others (2.67f); in both cases the unprefixed shape is /nk-/. Other stems with |nak-| weaken the |a| to /ah/ in an initial syllable (2.67g). Stems with |nat-| delete the |a| (2.67h), but dependent nouns (**§4.2b**) with /n-/ 1 before stem-initial |at-| have /naht-/ (2.67i). In stems beginning with /nən-/ the vowel is never lost, showing that this syllable has generalized its metrically strong shape and has an underlying |nə̀n-| (2.67j). (No stem begins with /kək-/.)

(2.67) The treatment of stems beginning with |wə-|, |nə-|, and |na-|
- (a) sɔ·me·lə́ntam (|wəsāmēlənt-am|) 'he's taking it seriously' (OA)
  (1s no·s·a·me·lə́ntam |nə-wəsāmēlənt-am|)
- (b) táli- nčí·sas †nčo·tí·yunk -mmán 'that Jesus came from Judaea'
  (|wət-əlī wəm-ən| < |əlī| PV '{so}', |wəm-| AI 'come from', |wət–ən| 3s/SBD; cf. 53c)
- (c) wtá·č·i·l 'drag him (you sg.)' (ME)
  (ko·t·a·č·í·li=č 'you must drag me' ME)
- (d) wša·khuk·wí·ɔno·p 'he had a coat' (B 1x, p. 18; cf. ša·khuk·wí·ɔn 'coat');
  (cf. šɔ·khuk·wi·ɔnəwá·ɔ ⟨jokvwqeunwao⟩ 'their garments' [B 1x, p. 164])
- (e) nkalá·t·e (|nəkal-ātē|) 'if he leaves her' (B)
  (wənək·alá·ɔ |wə-nəkal-āwa| 'he left him' B; nnə́k·ala |nə-nəkal-āw| 'I left him' V, OA)
- (f) nkalá·t·amo·kw (|nakal-ātamōkw|) 'let's leave her behind (you pl.)' (ME)
  (kənak·alək·éhəna 'we were left behind', nɔk·alawwá·a 'they left her' ME)
- (g) nahkíhəle· (|nakīhlā-w|) 'he stopped' (OA, ME; 1s nnak·íhəla)
- (h) nto·nánke (|natōn-ankē|) 'if he seeks it' (B) (nnat·ó·namən 'I looked for it' OA, AD);
  nto·xtá·k·we (|natōxət-ākwē|) 'if he asks for it' (B) (nnat·ó·xto·n 'I call for it' OA);
  nto·t·əmo·lé·k·we (|natōtəmaw-əlēkwē|) 'if I ask you (pl.)' (B)
  (nɔt·o·t·əmaɔ́·ɔ 'he asked him' B)
- (i) nahtuhé·p·i 'my body' (wahtuhé·p·i 'his body; the body'; ahtuhé·p·i 'body' B)
  nahtánkw 'my brother-in-law (male speaking)' (wahtánkɔ 'his brother-in-law' ME)
- (j) nəno·stánke (|nə̀nōsət-ankē|) 'if he understands it'
  é·li-nənaɔ́hti·t (|əlī nə̀naw-|, |IC–āhətīt|) 'how they recognized him'

§2.14. Variation in stem shape with and without prefixes. The addition of a pronominal prefix often affects the metrical structure of a word (**§§2.3, 2.4, 2.4a**). The variations in shape that are produced, even extreme ones, may be retained, but they also may be partially or wholly leveled out by the generalization of either the unprefixed shape or the prefixed shape, or by a combination of the two. The leveling of this variation has clearly continued to spread through the language, being more evident in the twentieth century than in Blanchard's materials.

Prefixes are sometimes followed by a stem-initial syllable that is absent from unprefixed forms (2.6abc, 2.68, 5.34nop). This alternation in shape originated when the stem-initial syllable was lost in word-initial position. Such syllables always have a short vowel (|a| or |ə|) and include any consonant that precedes this; in at least one case the lost syllable includes also the |x| of an |xk| cluster that follows the vowel (2.6a). In most if not all cases, however, the alternation has presumably been restructured and is better described as the irregular addition of a syllable when a prefix is present. This is shown by the fact that there may be variation in the shape of the additional syllable, and in fact some of these stems or stems with the same initials are also found regularized, with no variation in the underlying form (2.6c, 2.68h).

(2.68) Stems with an added syllable after prefixes
- (a) sənémhɔ·n '(large) metal spoon'; ntas·ənémhɔ·n 'my —' (OA)
- (b) múx·o·l 'boat'; ntámxo·l 'my boat' (V)
- (c) skɔ́ntay 'door'; wtəskɔnté·yəmink 'at his door' (B; 2.33c)
- (d) təmá·k·an 'road'; nəmət·əmá·k·an 'my road' (OA, ME)
  (derived from mətəme· 'he takes the road'; 1s nəmə́t·əme;
  cf. təmí·k·e· 'he enters a house': 1s ntəmí·k·e, but note 5.89b)
- (e) tá·x·an 'piece of wood, firewood'; nəmət·á·x·an 'my —' (V, OA, ME)
- (f) skí·xkwe 'young woman'; o·ski·xkwé·yəma 'one of his young women' (B; 2.10a, 2.33b)
- (g) xkɔ́hke· (|kwa̢xkăkā-w|) 'he crossed the water'; 1s nkɔ́xkahka (|nə̢-kwaxka̢kā|) (OA)
- (h) kɔ́t·a-kí·kai·n (|wə-kata (na̢)kəhkayī-n|) 'he wants to borrow it' (OA);
  nnakhíkai·n (|nə-nakəhkayī-n|) 'I borrowed it'; also nkí·kai·n 'I borrowed it' (OA)
- (i) xinkɔhkəní·mi·l 'glorify me!'; nəmax·inkɔhkəní·mukw=č 'he will glorify me' (B)

In stems in which weak and strong short-vowel open syllables alternate, weak and strong would be expected to be reversed after a prefix, but it is common for the expected alternation in the shape of a stem to be wholly or partially leveled out. For example, the predicted pattern of alternation is found in the stem for 'to sit' in Blanchard (2.69a) but has been leveled out in later materials (2.69b), as also in other words even in Blanchard (2.69c). The same leveling is found also in some transitive stems that have the accent of the unprefixed forms generalized to the prefixed forms (2.69de).

(2.69) Retention and leveling of weak and strong syllables
- (a) ləmátahpi 'sit down (you sg.)' (⟨lumutavpi⟩ B);
  wələmahtáp·i·n 'he, she sat (there, then)' (⟨wulumuvtupen⟩ 2x, ⟨wulumutupen⟩ 1x B)
- (b) ləmátahpi 'sit down (you sg.)' (AD, ME);
  nləmátahpi 'I sat down', nləmátahpi·n 'I sat (there, then)' (ME; OA with /ll-/ 2.62k)
- (c) mahtant·ó·wi·t 'one who is a devil' (⟨mavtuntwet⟩ B)
  takó·=tá ní· nəmahtant·o·wí·i '*I* am not a devil' (⟨nmavtuntwei⟩ B)
- (d) mpawə́nəmən 'I sifted it' (V, ME);
  ktə́li-=á·-pawə́nk·o·n (|kət-əlī pawən-əkōn|; =á· POT) 'so that he can sift you' (B)
- (e) mpuhwə́nəmən 'I pulled it out' (OA);
  nkwə́či-phwə́nəmən 'I tried to pull it out' (OA)

A more complex adjustment in stem shape after a prefix is found when the first syllable of the stem has the shape expected after a prefix but the rest of the stem has the shape it has when there is no prefix. This combination of treatments may result in an anomalous intervocalic short consonant (2.70abcde), a strong short-vowel syllable following another strong syllable (2.70fghij), or a consonant cluster that otherwise would not occur (2.70k). In such cases speakers sometimes gave or accepted alternative pronunciations.

(2.70) Partial unprefixed stem shape after a prefix
- (a) nkwətakwté·i 'I'm climbing a hill' (3s kwtakwté·yu) (OA)
- (b) nnəkatší·mukw 'he ran away and left me' (nkatší·mu 'he ran away') (OA)
- (c) skápsu 'he's wet' (1s nsəkápsi) (OA)
- (d) mpəsakpélahto·n 'I stuck it on' (short /s/; OA) (psak·wíhəle· 'he sticks on' V)
- (e) nsəpánkwe (also nsəp·ánkwe) 'I blinked (once)' (3s spánkwe·) (OA)
- (f) llax·ák·wəna 'I loosened it (anim., as a belt)' (laxak·wíhəle· 'it loosened') (OA); also accepted: llaxahkwə́na
- (g) mpənaxahkwéhəla 'I fell off the log when it shifted' (3s pənaxahkwéhəle·) (OA)
- (h) nəmək·ənhamə́ne·n 'we picked them up (rocks)' (OA) (məkənhámo·kw 'gather them up (the pieces) (you pl.)' B)
- (i) no·yamxkhámən (|nōyàma̧xka̧hamən|) 'I mixed it, stirred it' (OA) (wiamxkhí·k·an |wəyama̧xka̧hīkan| 'stirrer' [OA])
- (j) ntalúhi·n 'I choked on it' (3s alúhu 'he choked on food, drink') (OA); also ntálhwi·n (OA)
- (k) ntalxhité·x·əma 'I knocked it (anim., as a bucket) empty' (OA); implying alaxhité·x·əm 'knock it (anim.) empty (you sg.)!' (unattested)

In some cases a syllable with a short vowel followed by a voiced consonant is treated as weak after an underlying weak syllable that loses its vowel, and the following syllable is then strong (2.26de, 2.71).

(2.71) Weak vowel after syncopated short vowel
- (a) málsanakw 'flint arrowhead', pl. malsanák·ɔk (OA)
- (b) phɔlə́lo·k 'they (trees) are sappy and have loose bark', sg. phɔ́ləl (ME)

§2.15. Static words, syllables, and segments. In some words there are short vowels and consonants where long phonemes would otherwise be expected. The short vowels in such cases are metrically strong; they may bear an accent and are not subject to weakening. The words, syllables, and segments with this characteristic can be called STATIC. This is the term used for a similar feature of Menominee, where the vowels in some words are not subject to regular lengthening and shortening, with certain exceptions (Bloomfield 1962:94). The Unami phenomenon is remarkable for being present not merely in whole words, but also in some syllables and single segments. Some words that do not have a segment that could be long but have a recessive accent are also classed as static as a way to explain this feature (2.74kl). Some words that are partly static but contain long vowels seem to conform to recurring templates.

Demonstrative pronouns and some other noun substitutes are static (2.72), as are many free particles (2.73), which often also function as prewords (preverbs and prenouns [2.74], and preparticles [2.75]). The intransitive verb corresponding to one static preverb is static, but with a strong /ə/ instead of /i/ (2.74o). Several particles contain a static diminutive suffix /-íti/ or /-íči/ (2.76). Nouns are ordinarily not static, but nouns containing the formal diminutive suffixes /-səs/ and /-čəč/ are static (2.77), as are some vocative forms (mostly of kinship terms, 2.78), loanwords (2.79), and nicknames and the like (2.80). Words in these lists that are marked with the initials LB and ND have sound clips in the Lenape Talking Dictionary (LTD); other speakers' initials are added in some cases to indicate the speakers that phonetic details were checked with in person or on other recordings, or who used a particular form or variant.

(2.72) Static demonstratives and noun substitutes
    (a)   wáka 'this (abs. anim.)'
    (b)   náka 'that (abs. anim.)'
    (c)   yó·ki 'these (anim.)' (also yó·k)
    (d)   né·ki 'those (anim.)' (also né·k)
    (e)   yúkwe 'now'
    (f)   níke 'then' (earlier néke [B])
    (g)   íka 'there' (not deictic)
    (h)   kéku 'something, anything; what?' (cf. ke·k·ó·ni [B], ke·k·ó·na [LB] 'things')
    (i)   tákɔ·k 'the other, another (anim., inan.)' (anim. pl. takɔ́·ki·k, obv. takɔ́·ki)

(2.73) Static free particles
    (a)   a·šíte 'instead, in contrast' (LB)
    (b)   káči 'don't'
    (c)   ká·xəne 'I wonder if, (to see) whether; really'; ká·xane (OA); ká·xani (ME).
    (d)   kóčəmink 'outside' (LB)
    (e)   lápi 'again' (V, OA, ME); cf. láp·i (ND)
    (f)   líte 'he thinks' (ntíte 'I think', ktíte '(that's what) you think') (OA)
    (g)   máta 'not' (tá in tá=á· 'would not')
    (h)   me·txáki 'soon after, almost immediately' ("quickly")
    (i)   nihəláči 'one's own, on one's own, oneself'
    (j)   ni·núči 'for a long time, since some time back'
    (k)   núči 'since' (OA, ME); also núči PV 'set about'
    (l)   péxu 'soon' (> xú FUT)
    (m)   pe·xúči 'really close' (ME)
    (n)   píši 'it is so' (LB)
    (o)   téxi 'utterly' (B)
    (p)   wəláki 'exactly, just' (OA)
    (q)   xkwíči 'on top' (OA, ME, LB)

(2.74) Static prewords
    (a)   ála PV 'stop, cease' (contrast á·lai, á·la PV 'be unable to')
    (b)   amáči PV 'bad (pl.)'
    (c)   čípi PN, PV 'dreadful; in an awful way, bad, etc.'
    (d)   kahtí and káhti PV 'almost', with prefix nkáti (contrast káhta PV 'want to', nkát·a)
    (e)   kíši PV 'have (done)'
    (f)   ktəmáki PV: nkət·əmáki-lə́s·i 'I'm living a pitiful life' (OA)
    (g)   kwčí PV 'try', with prefix nkwə́či (OA, ME)
    (h)   mə́si P, PV 'all'
    (i)   péči PV 'come to' (ME: píči)
    (j)   səki PN 'black': səki-təmá·kwe 'Black Beaver'
    (k)   táli P, PV '{smwh}'
    (l)   wə́li PV 'good, well'
    (m)   wiáki PV 'have plenty to, enough and to spare'
    (n)   wíči P, PV 'along with (another, others)'; wíči, kíči PN (with prefix) 'his, your fellow'
    (o)   wi·šíki PV 'working hard at'
         (cf. wi·šə́ksu 'he works hard' ME; wi·šə́ksi 'do your best!' B, LB)

(2.75) Static numeral preparticles
- (a) kwə́ti PP 'one' (cf. kwə́t·i P)
- (b) níši PP, PV 'two' (cf. ní·š·a P)
- (c) náxi PP, PV 'three' (cf. naxá P)

(2.76) Particles with a static diminutive suffix
- (a) ke·xíti 'a little bit' (B, ME, LB [with very clear short /x/])
- (b) ki·xkíti 'closer' (B, OA, ME)
- (c) ləkhikwíči 'a little way, not far away' (ME)
- (d) mahtíti 'only a little, not much, barely' (B, V, ME)
- (e) nəkhikwíti 'close by, a short distance' (B, V), nəkhukwíti (ME)
- (f) ɔhələmíči 'not far, a short ways off' (B, ME, LB)
- (g) panke·íti 'a little piece' (B)
- (h) pəphake·íti 'little pieces' (B)
- (i) tankíti P, PV 'a little bit, a little' (B, ME)
- (j) ta·txíti 'few, a little' (B)
- (k) thakíti 'for a little while' (B, OA)
- (l) txíti 'a little' (V, LB)
- (m) xɔləníti (B ⟨xoluneti⟩; Speck 1931:114) and xuləníti (B ⟨xwluneti⟩; OA) 'very soon'; also reduced forms xunníti and xuníti (OA), xɔnníti (V) (all from older ⟨pecho linitti⟩ "directly, in a little while" [Brinton and Anthony 1889:11])

(2.77) Nouns with static formal diminutive suffixes
- (a) aésəs '(wild) animal' (pl. aesə́s·ak)
- (b) hiló·səs 'old man' (OA in LTD), pl. hilo·sə́s·ak (LB; clear contrast of /s/ and /s·/)
- (c) xa·wší·səs 'old woman' (ND), pl. xa·wši·sə́sak (LB) (contrast 2.77b)
- (d) pi·laéčəč 'boy' (WL recording, ME, LTD ND), pl. pi·laečə́č·ak (LB)
- (e) xkwé·čəč 'girl' (xkwe·čə́č·ak 'girls' LB)

(2.78) Static vocatives
- (a) məsa· 'older sister!'
- (b) muxó·msa· 'grandfather!' (ND)
- (c) núxa· 'father!' (V, FW, ME); also núx·a· (ND)
- (d) šísa· '(maternal) uncle!'
- (e) pi·láeči 'boy!' (LB)

(2.79) Static loanwords
- (a) kápi 'coffee'
- (b) kátən 'cotton'
- (c) katúhɔ 'Cherokee' (< Shawnee katoʔhwa)
- (d) képəč 'cabbage' (LB) (pl. kepə́č·ak)
- (e) mpáki 'buggy'
- (f) nčí·sas 'Jesus' (WS)
- (g) pákit 'pocket' (LB) (pɔkít·əmink 'in his pocket' ND)
- (h) pələ́či·s 'pants' (LB) (mpə́lči·s 'my pants'); also 'underwear' (ME) (< English *britches*)
- (i) pó·ši·s 'cat' (ME, ND, LB) (from dialectal Munsee *pó ší·s*, adapted from Dutch); also pó·š·i·s (OA)
- (j) púčəl 'chief's assistant; warparty cook' (< English *butcher*)
- (k) típa·s 'chicken, hen, rooster' (< Swedish *tippa*, used to call chickens)
- (l) wəšá·ši 'Osage' (OA, ME, LB) (< Shawnee *hošá·ši*); also wəšá·š·i (ND)

(2.80) Static nicknames and the like
   (a) mélimwi·s 'crybaby' (OA, ND)
   (b) me·tsísi 'Minnie Fouts'
   (c) ópike·s (woman who lived in a white house northwest of Washita, Okla.)
   (d) pinaé·tət 'Col. Jackson (the last traditional head chief)' (cf. 2.77d)
   (e) tápan 'Charlie Webber' (for wi·t·a·p·anó·x·we)

The characteristic phonetic features that are often found in static words include short vowels that are not subject to weakening or syncope (that is, /a/ and /ə/ that are retained as strong vowels); short high vowels (/i/ and /u/); short consonants between strong vowels, particularly the otherwise rare short voiceless fricatives /s/, /š/, and /x/; and recessive accent. In underlying forms static sequences and segments are indicated by underlining.

The contrast between the lower numbers as preparticles and as free particles is noteworthy (2.75abc); the number for 'four' has a similar contrast but without distinctive static features: né·wi PP 'four' (cf. né·wa P). It is also worth noting that words related to hiló·səs 'old man' (2.77b) that do not have a stem in /-səs/ have a normal long /s·/: nəmihəló·s·əm 'my husband' (AD, LB); hilo·s·iáne 'when you are old' (B; /s·/ from OA, ME).

3. Grammatical Categories

§3.1. The morphological processes of the language (principally the addition of inflectional prefixes and suffixes) indicate the grammatical categories, though the relation between form and meaning may be complex. The units of form (the morphemes) ordinarily indicate more than one category of meaning, and the categories are typically indicated by more than one morpheme in the language and often by more than one morpheme in a word, either in combination or redundantly.

§3.1a. Parts of Speech. There are four parts of speech: nouns, verbs, pronouns, and particles. Nouns and verbs each have distinctive patterns of inflection, and these have several subtypes. Pronouns are of several distinct types and function as various kinds of substitutes and stand-ins for nouns and the pronominal categories of inflection. Particles, which (with one exception) are not inflected, fall into crosscutting syntactic and functional categories.

§3.1b. Stem Components. The stems of nouns, verbs, and particles consist of one or more component parts. The basic component parts are INITIALS, MEDIALS, and FINALS. A PRIMARY stem may consist of (1) an initial; (2) an initial and a final, or (3) an initial, a medial, and a final. A SECONDARY stem is one derived from another stem; it consists of a primary stem (or a theme made on one) and a secondary final, or a secondary stem and a secondary final. A stem component may itself be derived, but the subparts of a stem component are not constituents of the stem, but only of the component.

§3.1c. Grammatical Categories. The core inflection of nouns marks the nominal categories of gender (**§3.2**), number (**§3.3**), obviative (**§3.4**), and absentative (**§3.5**). Gender is an inherent, lexical category; number and absentative status are freely selected; and the obviative is governed by morphological, syntactic, and discourse factors. The seven pronominal categories are those indexed by the emphatic personal pronouns (**§3.6**). In addition, there is an indefinite person marked by inflection or indicated by stem derivation but with no pronoun (3.11). Nouns may also be inflected for the pronominal category of a possessor (**§4.2a**). Verbs are inflected for the nominal and pronominal categories of their arguments (**§3.7a**), as well as for inherently verbal categories (**§4.4**).

§3.2. Gender. The distinction between the ANIMATE and INANIMATE genders is pervasive and fundamental in Unami, as in all Algonquian languages. The labels are conventional and can be misleading. Essentially, the animate gender is the high gender and the inanimate the low gender. Nouns for all humans, animals (members of the animal kingdom), spirits, heavenly bodies, trees, and fruit (including large berries and root vegetables) are animate, as well as ones for many other things (3.2–3.4), including nouns that are personified (e.g., as possessors [Goddard 2019: 98-9]). The inanimate is the gender of the rest of the nouns, including those for abstract concepts (3.5.1).
(3.1) Animate nouns (predictable categories)
    (a)   lə́nu 'man'
    (b)   máxkw 'bear'
    (c)   ó·č·e 'fly'
    (d)   manə́t·u 'spirit, manitou, god, God'
    (e)   alánkw 'star'
    (f)   kí·š·o·x 'sun, moon'

(g) xáx·a·kw 'sycamore'
(h) á·p·ələš 'apple' (from Mun *á pĕləš*, from Dutch *appel*, pl. *appels*)
(i) e·k·ó·k·ɔləs 'raspberry' (V, FW, ND)
(j) o·lé·pən 'onion'
(k) hɔ́pəni·s 'potato'
(l) tanáp·əs 'turnip' (from English *turnips*)

(3.2) Animate nouns (objects)
(a) e·mhɔ́·nəs 'spoon'
(b) é·ška·nš 'needle'
(c) čí·čankw 'mirror' (archaic: 'spirit')
(d) či·x·amɔ́·k·an 'comb'
(e) hápi·s 'tumpline'
(f) hatá·p·i 'bow'
(g) hó·s 'kettle'
(h) húkɔ·n 'pothook'
(i) hupɔ́·k·an 'pipe'
(j) ké·kw 'wampum bead'
(k) mahte·hí·k·anak 'prayersticks' (FW)
(l) ma·nšá·p·i 'bead'
(m) məkó·s 'awl; nail'
(n) məsínkw 'false-face'
(o) ɔ́·wta·s 'doll'
(p) pahkantí·k·an 'drumstick'
(q) pámpi·l 'paper' (from Munsee, from dialectal Dutch *pampier*)
(r) psi·ká·ɔn 'feather worn on head'
(s) selahtí·k·anak 'pick-up-sticks'
(t) təpčéhəla·s 'wagon'

(3.3) Animate nouns (natural phenomena)
(a) kó·n 'ice, snow'
(b) máhələs 'flint'
(c) mó·šukw 'hailstone, icicle'

(3.4) Animate nouns (body parts and the like)
(a) é·həs 'bivalve shell' (pl. éhsak)
(b) hɔ́kahte·s '(animal) stomach'
(c) hɔ́k·e·s 'bark'
(d) lle·la·ɔ́·kwələnč 'my middle finger'
(e) má·x 'vulva' (nəmá·x 'my vulva', mɔ́·x·a 'her vulva' V; "female genitalia, including the vulva, vagina, womb" [ND in Miller 1977:150, with pl. /má·x·ak/])
(f) mí·k·wən 'feather' (pl. mí·k·wənak)
(g) nəma·má·ɔn 'my eyebrow' (OA) (nəma·má·wənak 'my eyebrows' V)
(h) nəmək·əná·kwələnč 'my thumb' (ME)
(i) nhíkxkɔn 'my shin' (pl. nhíkxkɔnak V, ME)
(j) nhík·aš 'my fingernail' (hwíkahšak 'fingernails, hoofs, claws')
(k) nhwíč·u 'my calf (of the leg)' (pl. nhwíčəwak)
(l) nkɔ́t·ukw 'my knee' (pl. nkɔ́tko·k)
(m) nkí·tələnč 'my thumb' (V, OA) (kwi·tələ́nča 'his thumb or thumbs' V)

    (n) nté· 'my heart' (V, OA) (wté·hak 'hearts' V, OA)
    (o) ɔnánu 'cheek' (V) (ɔnánəwak 'cheeks' V, ME) (variants in 4.7g)
    (p) pəmúwe 'boil, pimple' (ND, LB) (pl. pəmuwé·ɔk V)
    (q) pəp·é·kwsu 'kidney' (LB) (mpəp·e·kwsó·yəmak 'my kidneys' OA)
    (r) sanı́·kw 'snot' (V, ND), sáni·kw (FF)
    (s) šə́mu 'horn' (LB) (pl. šə́məwak V, LB)
    (t) wəlúnkɔn 'wing' (pl. kəlúnkɔnak 'your wings')
    (u) wí·skɔn 'elbow' (V) (wí·skɔnak 'elbows' V)
    (v) wi·tó·nayak 'whiskers' (V) (ki·tó·nayak 'your beard' OA, wi·tó·naya 'his beard' LB)
    (w) wi·x·ak 'pubic hairs' (V)
    (x) xé·s 'skin (epidermis); (animal) skin, hide' (xé·s·ak 'pelts, hides' V)

(3.5) Inanimate nouns
    (a) aló·ns 'arrow'
    (b) ka·xkamó·na 'hackberries' (OA, WS)
    (c) kšı́·k·an 'knife'
    (d) kwšá·tay 'tobacco'
    (e) ma·laxkwsı́·t·a 'beans' (V, OA)
    (f) mí·laxk 'hair (of the head)'
    (g) mí·na 'huckleberries' (V, FW)
    (h) mpɔ́·m 'my thigh' (2.58d)
    (i) nhikı́·ɔn 'my nose' (LB)
    (j) nhítaɔk 'my ear'
    (k) ɔ·kháti·m 'mulberry, mulberries' (V, ME)
    (l) pəma·wsəwá·k·an 'life'
    (m) wí·lahkay 'his penis'
    (n) xáskwi·m 'corn' (animate as corn in the field [ME])
    (o) xkwə́n 'liver'

The inanimate is also the gender of the formally pronominal subjects of impersonal verbs: énta-kšəlánte·k 'in the heat of the day' (*lit.*, 'when it (inan.) was hot (weather)').

An animate singular pronoun can be translated 'he' ('him, his') or 'she' ('her'), or more fully 'he or she', or still more completely 'he, she, or animate it'. For concision, especially perhaps where there are complications like multiple references, or simply to keep the language of a source, the translation 'he' is often used here (by convention), but other translations are used to reflect the original context of a form, or when only the female sex is possible, or to make explicit the fact that both sexes are possibilities. The conventional gloss for the inanimate is 'it', but a more accurate translation would be 'it (inanimate)', since many things referred to as 'it' in English are not inanimate in Unami.

§3.3. Number. A contrast between singular and plural is variously marked on nouns, pronouns, and verbs (3.6).

(3.6) Singular and plural distinguished
    (a) lə́nu 'man'; lə́nəwak 'men' (animate)
    (b) wá 'this (anim.)'; yó·k 'these (anim.)'
    (c) ahsə́n 'stone'; ahsə́nal (B), ahsə́na (B, others) 'stones' (inanimate)
    (d) yú 'this (inan.)'; yó·l 'these (inan.)'
    (e) pé·p 'he, she came'; pé·p·ani·k 'they came' (B)
    (f) wə́nči-=č -pəmə́ska·t 'so that he can walk' (B); né·li-pəməskáhti·t 'as they walk' (B)

(g) pé·mska·t 'one who walks'; pep·a·mská·č·i·k 'those that walked' (B)
  (h) no·wá·ha 'I know him, her'; no·wa·há·ɔk 'I know them (anim.)' (B)
  (i) nəmanní·to·n 'I made it'; nəmanni·tó·na 'I made them (inan.)' (ME)
  (j) kti·t·é·ha 'you (sg.) think'; kti·t·e·háhəmɔ 'you (pl.) think' (B)

In many inflectional categories, however, there is no contrast between singular and plural (3.7).

(3.7) Singular and plural not distinguished
  (a) mwí·s·a 'his or her older sister or sisters' (V)
  (b) nhiláte 'if you (sg.) kill him, her, it (anim.), or them'
  (c) nhíl 'kill him, her, it (anim.), or them'
  (d) kəmaxko·lhúməna 'we found you (sg., pl.)' (OA)

The few places in Blanchard where there seems to be number discord probably have specific explanations. The apparent singular verb with a plural subject in (Mt 10.30) is most likely just a misprint (a missing ⟨u⟩). The singular verb with postposed ellí·i 'both' in (Lk 7.42) seems to be just awkward phrasing; 'each' has been added in the translation. The singular subject with a plural verb in Mt 26.36 appears to be idiomatic, implying the meaning 'and the others'; similarly in Jn 3.30 (2x). Representative singulars (with plural meaning) are common, however.

§3.4. Obviative. A contrast between PROXIMATE and OBVIATIVE is marked on animate nouns and demonstratives and on verbs (3.8ab). The proximate is the default category. The obviative is a secondary third person used if there is a proximate noun or pronoun in the same immediate context (usually defined as the same clause); it does not distinguish singular and plural, but there is a rare suffix that marks an obviative plural (**§4.2g**). If an animate noun is possessed it is always obviative, either with an obviative suffix (3.8cd) or with a suffix indicating an obviative possessor (3.8e). Although there is no inanimate obviative inflection on nouns, a verb with a subject that is an inanimate noun possessed by a third person has obviative marking in a few cases in Blanchard's translation (4.21f, 4.64c). Obviative subjects are often not marked on verbs.

(3.8) Obviative marking
  (a) ná ehalo·ká·lənt təlá·ɔ né·l xkwé·ɔ ... (Mt 28.5+)
      'the angel (prox.) said to the women (obv.)'
        (ná ehalo·ká·lənt 'the one sent (prox.)'; təlá·ɔ '(prox.) said to (obv.)';
        né·l xkwé·ɔ 'the woman or women (obv.)')
  (b) mé·či a·č·i·mo·lxúkwke né·l i·lá·ɔ, ... (Mk 15.45+)
      'After the captain (obv.) had reported to him (prox.), ...'
        (mé·či a·č·i·mo·lxúkwke 'after (obv.) had reported to (prox.)';
        né·l i·lá·ɔ 'the warrior (obv.)')
  (c) kkwí·s·al 'his or her son or sons (obv.)' (B)
  (d) kkwí·s·a 'his or her son or sons (obv.)' (B, OA, ME)
  (e) wwe·t·əná·p·ani mi·məntət·al, ɔ́·k kɔhe·s·í·li·t. (Mt 2.14)
      'he (prox.) took the baby (obv.) and his (obv. [i.e., the baby's]) mother.'
        (wwe·t·əná·p·ani '(prox.) took (obv.)'; mi·məntət·al 'baby (obv.)'; ɔ́·k 'and';
        kɔhe·s·í·li·t '(obv.)'s mother [obv.]')

An expected or actual obviative may be, or be treated as, proximate. This often occurs when a new subject or focus of interest would otherwise be obviative, but it can even be so within the clause (e.g., in Mk 8.38, 18.29), as commonly when a noun possessed by a third person is what is the focus of interest and is construed as proximate; these have been called "honorary proximates" (4.21n). There may be an unexpected proximate that is an adjunct giving the topic of a direct quote (3.15h). A participle with an unmarked obviative head may take a proximate verb (Jn

3.34). There are also examples of an indefinite noun being referred to with a proximate plural form in sentences where an obviative (undifferentiated for number) would be expected (4.24c).

§3.5. Absentative. Crosscutting the categories of gender, number, and obviation is the absentative. The absentative is used to refer to someone or something that is dead, departed, absent, missing, or asleep.

(3.9) Uses of the absentative
   (a) náka nkahé·s·a (|nə-kahēs-a|) 'my late mother' (OA)
       (náka 'that (abs. anim.)'; |nə-| 1, |-kahēs| 'mother', |-a| abs. anim. sg.)
   (b) nuhəmínka (|nə-ōhəm-ənka|) 'my late grandmothers' (OA)
       (|nə-| 1, |-ōhəm| 'grandmother', |-ənka| abs. pl./obv.)
   (c) ánkəla (|ankəl-w-a|) 'he is dead' (B)
       (ankəl- AI 'be dead', |-w| 3,0, |-a| abs. anim. sg.)
   (d) ankəlúnka (|ankəl-w-ənka|) 'they are dead' (B)
       (|ankəl-| AI 'be dead', |-w| 3,0, |-ənka| abs. pl.,obv.)
   (e) kawí·ɔ 'he is asleep' (V, OA); kawí·a (ME)
       (|kawī-| AI 'sleep', |-w| 3,0, |-a| abs. anim. sg.)
   (f) linksúwa náka kó·na. 'The snow has melted.' (OA)
       (|lənkəsī-| AI 'melt', |-w| 3,0, |-a| abs. anim. sg.; náka 'that (abs. anim.)';
       |kōn-| AN 'snow', |-a| abs. anim. sg.)
   (g) txihəlé·e níke mpíe. 'The water is all gone.' (OA)
       (|taxīhlā-| AI,II 'be all gone', |-w| 3.0, |-e| abs. inan. sg.; níke 'that (abs. inan.)';
       |nəpəy-| IN 'water', |-e| abs. inan. sg.)
   (h) txihəle·yúnka ta·x·anínka. 'The wood (pl.) is all gone.' (OA)
       (|taxīhlā-| AI,II 'be all gone', |-w| 3,0, |-ənka| abs. pl.,obv.;
       |(mə)tāxan-| IN 'piece of wood', |-ənka| abs. pl.,obv.)

§3.6. Pronominal Persons. The seven basic pronominal categories, or persons, are defined by the emphatic pronouns (3.10). Following the gloss of each form is the full descriptive name and the abbreviated label used in glosses. The first plural exclusive ("1p") excludes the one (or those) addressed, while the inclusive ("12") includes them.

(3.10) Emphatic pronouns and pronominal categories

ní·	'I'	first person singular	(1s)
kí·	'you (sg.)'	second person singular	(2s)
né·k·əma, né·k·a	'he, she'	third person singular	(3s)
ni·ló·na	'we (exc.)'	first person plural, exclusive	(1p)
ki·ló·na	'we (inc.)'	first person plural, inclusive	(12)
ki·ló·wa	'you (pl.)'	second person plural	(2p)
ne·k·əmá·ɔ, ne·k·á·ɔ	'they (anim.)'	third person plural	(3p)

The longer forms of the third person pronouns (with /-əm-/) are older. Blanchard has only /ne·k·əmá·ɔ/ (3p), but both /né·k·əma/ and /né·k·a/ (3s). The longer third plural form has later pronunciations with vowel assimilation (/ne·k·əmá·a/ OA; /ne·k·əmɔ́·ɔ/ WP, BF), but the shorter variant was only heard as /ne·k·á·ɔ/ (OA, ME, AD, ND).

   The seven emphatic pronouns are the only independent personal pronouns, and they refer only to people or personified beings. They always add some degree of emphasis, focus, or contrast to the bare pronominal notion, but two of them may not be used together to emphasize two arguments of the same verb. The nominal categories (of §§3.2-4) intersect the pronominal categories in the animate third persons (3s, 3p) and supply further differentiation to include inanimates (0s, 0p) and obviatives (3´, 0´), which have no corresponding pronouns in the emphatic set.

The indefinite person (X) corresponds to English 'one' or 'people' (or colloquial 'they', 'you', or 'we') when used in an indefinite or general sense rather than to refer to specific individuals. Intransitive and transitive verbs may be inflected for an indefinite subject, and transitive verbs make derived intransitives that indicate an indefinite object. A transitive verb with an indefinite subject is typically the equivalent of an English passive verb with no expressed agent, but the indefinite is not a completely unspecified argument, since the indefinites on different verbs that are in construction with each other refer to the same indefinite person or persons, as in (3.11).

(3.11) Coreferential indefinites
    (a) néwwe· móni lí- íka -laníhi·n. '... he saw people tossing money into it.' (Mk 12.41)
          (néwwe· 'he saw (indef.)' [< |nēw-| TA 'see' + |-əwē| AI (marking indefinite object)], |–w| 3s/IND]; móni 'money'; lí-laníhi·n 'that (indef.) threw it {smwh}' [|əlī| PV '{so}', |əlanihī-| AI+O 'throw O2 {smwh}', |–ən| X/SBD]; íka 'there' [not deictic])
    (b) táli- .. -khwithíke·n mihəma·e·nəmáɔ·n móni †sí·sal (Lk 23.2)
         'for him to forbid people to collect money for Caesar'.
         (|əlī| PV '{so}', |kwəhtəhkē-| AI 'forbid people'
         [< |kwəhtəl-| TA 'forbid' + |-kē| AI (marking indefinite object)], |wət–n| X/IND; |Rih+| HAB, |māwēnəmaw-| TA+O 'collect O2 for', |–ān| X–3/SBD)

§3.7. Verbs: Formal and Syntactic Types. Unami verbs can be classified according to their formal properties and according to their syntactic properties, the syntactic roles of their arguments. These classifications in part coincide and in part do not, giving additional subclasses. Verbs may also have syntactic relationships with obliques and adjuncts, which are not arguments.

§3.7a. Arguments. The arguments for which verbs may be inflected are SUBJECT, PRIMARY OBJECT (first object), and SECONDARY OBJECT (second object). The primary object corresponds to the direct object of an English verb that has no indirect object, or to an English indirect object, and the secondary object corresponds to the direct object of an English verb that also has an indirect object. For example, in the Unami translations of the English sentences (1) *I hit him.* (2) *I gave it to him.* and (3) *I stole it from him.*, a Unami primary object corresponds to *him*, and a Unami secondary object corresponds to *it* (3.12).

(3.12) Primary and secondary objects
    (a) mpák·ama 'I hit him' (V, AD); inflection |nə–ā-w| 'I – him (anim. sg. primary obj.)'
    (b) nəmí·la·n 'I gave it to him' (B, ME); |nə–ā-n| 'I – him (+ inan. sg. secondary obj.)'
    (c) nkamó·t·əma·n 'I stole it from him' (V); |nə–ā-n| 'I – him (+ inan. sg. secondary obj.)'
Certain intransitive stems that are syntactically transitive also mark a secondary object (**§3.7f**).

§3.7b. Obliques. Some verbs, prewords, and particles take an oblique complement, either obligatorily or optionally. Obliques are typically the syntactic complements of certain initials (**§3.1b**) and verb stems. Initials having an oblique valence (the formal property of taking an oblique complement) are RELATIVE ROOTS. A relative root is glossed with a label indicating the type of oblique it takes enclosed in curly braces ({..}); this is intended to indicate that the gloss is a place-holder, a variable rather than a translation. There are also verb stems without a relative root that take an oblique valence, in most case optionally; these can be considered to contain a virtual relative root (3.13(2), (4), (8)). A definite oblique may be inflected for by an n-ending (3.13(6)b, (7)c, (8)b), and an oblique may be the head of a participle, the verb form that makes relative clauses (3.13(2)b, (4)b).

(3.13) Relative roots and obliques
  (1) |əl-| 'to {smwh}' (i.e., 'to somewhere'); '{so}' (i.e., 'in such way'), '{such}' (also |əš-|)
    (a) hák·ink lí-súk·o·p 'he spat on the ground'
        (hák·ink 'ground (loc.)'; |əli| PV 'to {smwh}', |sukw-| AI 'spit', |-wəp| 3s/IND.PRET)
    (b) mux·ó·link lí-pó·s·o·p 'he went aboard a boat'
        (mux·ó·link 'boat (loc.)'; |əli| PV 'to {smwh}', |pōsī-| AI 'embark', |-wəp| 3s/IND.PRET)
    (c) íka lilahtá·ɔk 'they went there by boat'
        (íka 'there' [not deictic]; |əlīhlatā-| AI 'go to {smwh} by boat', |–wak| 3p/IND)
    (d) ná=nə ləs·í·t·e 'if that is what he (she) does'
        (ná PRES; nɔ́ 'that (inan.)'; |ələsī-| AI 'do {so}, be {so}', |–tē| 3s/SBJ)
    (e) nə́ni e·lsí·č·i·k 'ones like that'
        (nə́ni 'that (inan.)'; |ələsī-| AI 'do {so}, be {so}', |IC–čīk| 3/PPL(ANpl))
    (f) íka šíhələ· 'he ran to it' (íka 'there, to it'; |əšīhlā-| AI 'run to {smwh}', |-w| 3s/IND)
  (2) With virtual |əl-| 'to {smwh}'
    (a) íka ntá 'I went there' (íka 'there' [not deictic]; |ā-| AI 'go to {smwh}', |nə(t)–| 1s/IND)
    (b) é·a·t=č 'the way he will go' (|ā-| AI 'go to {smwh}', |IC–t| 3s/PPL(OBL); =č FUT)
  (3) |(-ən)tal-| '{smwh}' ('somewhere'); |talī|, |(-ən)ta| PV
    (a) nɔ́ táli 'there'; nə́ni táli 'there, in that place' (nɔ́, nə́ni 'that (inan.)'; táli P '{smwh}')
    (b) nɔ́ táli o·t·é·nink 'in that town'
        (nɔ́ 'that (inan.)'; táli P '{smwh}'; o·t·é·nink 'town (loc.)')
    (c) pa·tamwe·i·k·á·ɔnink táli-amankí·xsu 'he spoke with a loud voice in the temple'
        (pa·tamwe·i·k·á·ɔnink 'temple (loc.)';
        táli PV '{smwh}', |amankīxəsī-| AI 'speak loudly', |-w| 3s/IND)
    (d) máta=háč ktəle·khi·k·anəwá·ink tale·kha·s·í·i 'isn't it written in your law?'
        (máta NEG; =háč Q; ktəle·khi·k·anəwá·ink 'your (pl.) law (loc.)';
        |(-ən)talēkahāsī-| II 'be written {smwh}', |-wī| 0s/IND.NEG)
  (4) With virtual |tal-| '{smwh}'
    (a) íka ahpú 'he was there'
        (íka 'there' [not deictic]; |apī-| AI 'be {smwh}', |-w| 3s.IND)
        (Cf. pí·li awé·n ahpú 'someone else exists', with |apī-| AI 'be, exist')
    (b) é·p·ia 'where I am' (|apī-| AI 'be {smwh}', |IC–yā(n-)| 1s/PPL(OBL))
    (c) íka ləmátahpo·p ya·p·é·i mənəp·é·k·unk 'he sat on the shore of the sea'
        (íka 'there' [not deictic]; ya·p·é·i 'on the shore'; mənəp·é·k·unk 'lake (loc.)';
        |ləmatapī-| AI 'sit {smwh}', |-wəp| 3s/IND.PRET)
        (Cf. lápi ləmátahpo·p 'he sat down again', with |ləmatapī-| AI 'sit (down)'.)
    (d) le·mahtáp·i·t 'where he's sitting' (ME)
  (5) |(-ən)tax-| '{so many}, {so much}'
    (a) éntxi-ne·ɔ́hti·t 'as many (obv.) as they saw'
        (|(-ən)taxi| PV '{so many}', |nēw-| TA 'see', |IC–āhətīt| 3p–3´/PPL(OBL))
    (b) ní·š·a·š txí·nxke txúwak 'there were seventy of them (anim.)'
        (ní·š·a·š P 'seven'; |taxīnaxkē| P '{so many} tens';
        |(-ən)taxī-| AI 'be {so many}, |–wak| 3p/IND)
  (6) |sahk-| '{so far}', '{so long}'
    (a) yúkwe sháki 'until now', lit. 'as far as now' (yúkwe 'now'; |sahkī| P '{so far}')
    (b) tá=háč ksá·ki-witahpi·mələné·ɔ. 'How long will I be with you (pl.)?' (tá WH; =háč Q;
        |sahkī| PV '{so long}', |wītapīm-| TA 'be with', |kə–ələnēwā| 1s–2p+0s/IND)

(c) se·kháke·t 'while she was gone'
    (|sahkahkē-| AI 'be away {so long}', |IC–t| 3s/PPL(OBL))
(d) se·ksí·t·ank 'a foot (unit of measure)' (*lit.*, 'as long as one's foot is')
    (|sahkəsītā-| AI 'have foot {so long}', |IC–ənk| X/PPL(OBL))

(7) |wənt-| 'from {smwh}' ('from somewhere or something, because of something')
  (a) pəna·kčéhəli yú wə́nči 'jump down from here'
      (|pənākəčēhl-| AI 'jump down', |-əh| 2s/IMP; yú 'here'; wə́nči P 'from {smwh}')
  (b) yú wáin mpínk wénči-manní·tunk 'the wine that had been made from water'
      (yú 'this (inan.)'; wáin 'wine (inan.)'; mpínk 'water (loc.)' (2.21a);
      |wənči| PV 'from {smwh}', |màlənīht-| TI(2) 'make', |–ōnk| X–0/PPL(INsg))
  (c) takó· nə́ni núnči-pá·wən 'I did not come because of that'
      (takó· NEG; nə́ni 'that (inan.)';
      |wənči| PV 'from {smwh}', |pā-| AI 'come', |nə–wən| 1s+0s/IND.NEG)
  (d) ləpwe·innúwak wénči-kčinkwéhəla·k wenči·aí·č·i·k 'wise men who were from the east'
      (ləpwe·innúwak 'wise men'; wénči-kčinkwéhəla·k 'east' [4.67h];
      |wənčīyayī-| AI 'be from {smwh}, belong {smwh}', |IC–čīk| 3/PPL(ANpl))
  (e) xínkwi-ahsə́n uxkwe·k·ánkanink wənta·ptúnke 'if a large stone were tied from his neck'
      (xínkwi PN 'big', ahsə́n 'rock'; uxkwe·k·ánkanink 'his neck (loc.)';
      |wəntāhpət-| TI(2) 'tie from {smwh}', |–ōnkē| X–0/SBJ)

(8) With virtual |wənt-| 'from {smwh}'
  (a) ná=ni hwilát·e 'if you (sg.) get him there' (ME)
      (ná=ni 'that (is)'; |wəhl-| TA 'get from {smwh}', |–àtē| 2s–3/SBJ)
  (b) nə́ni núntəne·n móni 'we got money from that' (V)
      (nə́ni 'that (inan.)'; |wənt-| TI(3) 'get from {smwh}', |nə–ənēn| 1p–0+0/IND)

§3.7c. Instrumental Obliques. Distinct from the constructions involving overt or virtual relative roots are those with INSTRUMENTAL obliques, though they are also linked to semantically appropriate verbs (3.14) or particles. Like the oblique complements of relative roots, instrumental obliques may be indexed by an n-ending, if definite (3.14c), and may be the heads of participles (3.14de).

(3.14) Instrumental obliques
  (a) kaxpí·s·o·p sə̣kahsə́na hwiká·t·ink (Mk 5.4) 'he had been bound <u>with irons</u> on his legs'
      (|kaxpīsī-| AI 'be tied', |–wəp| 3s/IND.PRET; sə̣kahsə́na 'irons';
      hwiká·t·ink 'his leg or legs (loc.)')
  (b) wí·l čí·t·ane·k hémpəs wi·xkwe·ptí·k·e·n (Jn 11.44) 'he had his head tied around <u>with a thick cloth</u>.' (wí·l 'his head'; |čītanē-| II 'be strong', |IC–k| 0/PPL(INsg); hémpəs IN 'cloth'; |wīxkwēpətīkē-| AI+O 'wrap by tying', |–n| X/IND)
  (c) pók·ama·n (Jn 18.10) 'he struck him <u>with it</u>' (|pakam-| TA 'hit', |wə–ān| 3s–3´+0s/IND)
  (d) takó· kéku kkənnəmó·wi <u>anshi·k·é·an</u> (Jn 4.11) 'You don't have anything <u>(for you (sg.)) to scoop up water with</u>' (takó· NEG; kéku 'something, anything';
      |kələn-| TI(1b) 'have', |kə–əmōwī| 2s–(0)/IND.NEG;
      |ansahīkē-| AI 'scoop up (water)', |(IC)–yan| 2s/PPL(<u>IN</u>sg))
  (e) wi·xkwe·pti·k·énkəp wí·l (Jn 20.7) 'what his head (O2) had been bound up with'
      (cf. 3.14b; |–nkəp| X/PPL.PRET(<u>IN</u>sg))

§3.7d. Adjuncts. Distinct from both kinds of obliques are adjuncts, which are not syntactically linked to any word (the way a subject, object, or oblique is) but rather qualify an element of a sentence semantically, usually by narrowing or specifying its reference. Translations of the link include: 'regarding' (3.15a "towards"; also 'for'), 'because of' (3.15b), 'of' (3.15cd: also "among"), 'with (there being)' (3.15e), 'than' (with a standard of comparison; 3.15f), and 'referring to' (explaining what is inside a direct quote; 3.15gh "of, regarding").

(3.15) Adjuncts with no morphological link to a verb
- (a) awé·n=č máta .. nuntae·lənsí·t·e ke·tanət·ó·wi·t sɔ·k·i·ma·ɔ́·k·an ... (Lk 18.17)
    'if someone is not .. humble towards God's kingdom ...'
- (b) .. é·li-kankwi·láhti·t xinkwe·ləmukwsəwá·k·an. (Mk 15.10)
    '.. because they were jealous of him because of the fame.'
    (|əlī| PV '{so}', kankwīl-| TA 'be jealous of', |IC–āhətīt| 3p–3´/CC;
    xinkwe·ləmukwsəwá·k·an 'fame')
- (c) nál=ná ni·k·a·ní·x·ink wé·mi entxíhti·t móni mehəma·e·nínki·k. (Lk 19.2)
    'He was the leader among all the tax-collectors.'
    (nál PRES; ná 'that (anim.)'; |nīkānīxīn-| AI 'be leader', |IC–k| 3s/PPL(ANsg);
    wé·mi 'all'; |taxī-| AI 'be {so} many', |IC–hətīt| 3p/PPL(OBL); móni 'money';
    |Rih+| HAB, |māwēn-| TI(1b) 'collect', |IC–ənkīk| 3–0/PPL(ANpl))
- (d) ntak·e·kinke·ɔ́·k·an, takó· ní· nihəláči, šúkw ná pe·t·alo·ká·li·t. (Jn 7.16)
    'My doctrine is not my own, but of the one that sent me.'
- (e) wə́nči-=č ní·š·a ší=tá naxá awé·ni·k wé·mi a·pto·ná·k·ana -wəla·məwe·i·ná·k·ɔ. (Mt 18.16)
    'so that with two or three people every word shall be seen to be true.'
- (f) .. é·li aləwí·i ktəla·ɔhtíhəmɔ xé·li čo·ləntət·ak. (Mt 10.31)
    '.. as you are worth more than many little birds.'
    (aləwí·i P 'more'; |əlāwatī-| AI 'be worth {so}', |kət–hmwā| 2p/IND)
- (g) káči awé·n luwé·he·kw 'kó·x·əna' (Mt 23.9) 'do not say of anyone 'our (inc.) father''
    (káči 'don't'; awé·n 'someone'; |əlawē-| AI 'say {so}', |–hēkw| 2p/PROH;
    kó·x·əna 'our (inc.) father')
- (h) təlá·ɔ, ehəle·khi·k·é·č·i·k, "kéku=háč ne·t·o·t·əmáe·kw?"
    'He said to them, regarding the scribes (prox.), "What are you asking them about?"'
    (|əl-| TA 'say {so} to', |wət–āwa| 3s–3´/IND;
    |Rih+| HAB, |əlēkahīkē-| AI 'write', |IC–čīk| 3/PPL(ANpl);
    kéku 'what?'; =háč Q; |natōtəmaw-| TA+O 'ask about O2', |IC–ēkw| 2p–3/PPL(INsg))

Even though words do not have an inherent property of taking an adjunct, however, an adjunct may be indexed on a verb by its inflection, either as agreement or pronominally. A definite adjunct may be inflected for by an n-ending (3.16, 4.19), like a definite oblique (3.13(6)b, (7)c, (8)b) or instrumental oblique (3.14c). The n-ending usually has a peripheral suffix showing agreement with the adjunct (3.16a, 4.45), but Blanchard has two occurrences of this construction with the obviative suffix /-a/ leveled out, as if it were replaced by an inanimate singular (3.16b).

(3.16) Adjuncts indexed by n-endings
- (a) e·k·e·kí·mənt takó· tɔləwí·i-ləs·í·wəna e·k·e·ki·mkúk·i. (Jn 13.16)
    'The one instructed is not greater than the one who instructs him.'
    (|akēhkīm-| TA 'teach', |IC–ənt| X–3/PPL(ANsg);
    takó· NEG; |àləwīwī| PV 'more', |ələsī-| AI 'be, do {so}', |wət–wəna| 3s+3´/IND.NEG;
    |akēhkīm-| TA 'teach', |IC–əkwəkī| 3´–3s/PPL(OBV))
- (b) takó· alo·ká·k·an tɔləwí·i-ləs·í·wən nehəla·lkúk·i (Jn 15.20)
    'the servant is not greater than his master'
    (|àləwīwī| PV 'more', |ələsī-| AI 'be, do {so}', |wət–wən| 3s+0[!]/IND.NEG)

Also, an adjunct may be the head of a participle (3.17). Examples include adjunct heads that refer to nominals inside quoted speech (3.17b; Jn 8.54, 9.19) or to the agent of a passive (3.17c).
(3.17) Adjuncts as heads of participles
- (a) ehánkəlink (Mk 16.18) 'what people die from (i.e., poison)'
  (< |Rih+| HAB, |ankəl-| AI 'die', |IC–ənk| X/PPL(INsg))
- (b) nál=tá wáni e·ləwe·á·nəp, "no·t·é·ka·kw ..." (Jn 1.30)
  'This is the one of whom I said, "He comes after me ..."'
  (nál PRES(ANsg); =tá FOC; wáni 'this (anim.)';
  |ələwē-| AI 'say {so}', |IC–yānəp| 1s/PPL.PRET(ANsg))
- (c) šinka·lké·ankw (Lk 1.71, 1.74) 'our (inc.) enemy (*lit.*, the one we are hated by)'
  (< |šīnkāl-| TA 'hate', |(IC)–əkēyankw| X–12/PPL(ANsg))

§3.7e. Intransitive and Transitive Verbs. Verbs typically come in pairs, with intransitive verbs having one stem for animate subjects (the animate intransitive, AI) and another for inanimate subjects (the inanimate intransitive, II), and transitive verbs having one stem for animate primary objects (the transitive animate, TA), and another for inanimate primary objects (the transitive inanimate, TI). In most cases the genders are marked by different intransitive or transitive finals, but a final may be paired with different finals in different stem pairs.
(3.18) Intransitive stem pairs
- (a) šenkí·x·i·n AI 'he, she, or it (animate) lies (reclines)'; šenkí·x·ən II 'it (inanimate) lies'
  (final pair: |-xīn| AI, |-xən| II 'lie'; also generic 'be positioned, undergo, etc.')
- (b) máxksu AI 'he, she, or it (animate) is red'; máxke· II 'it (inanimate) is red'
  (final pair |-əsī| AI, |-ē| II 'be')
- (c) či·má·kwsu AI 'he (etc.) smells bad'; či·má·k·ɔt II 'it smells bad'
  (final pair |-əsī| AI, |-at| II 'be')
- (d) wələ́s·u AI 'he (she) is good, good-looking'; wələ́t II 'it is good'
  (final pair: |-əsī| AI, |-ət| II 'be')
- (e) wínkəl AI 'he (esp. it, animate) tastes good'; wínkan II 'it tastes good'
  (final pair |-əl| AI, |-an| II 'be (of taste, etc.)')
- (f) pəníhəle· (|pənīhlā-| + |-w| 3s,0s) AI,II 'he, it fell off, fell down'
  (final |-īhlā| AI,II 'fall, fly, move rapidly')

Many AI stems are not matched by an II, and the many II stems of impersonal verbs lack AI's. Apparently, however, an II can be derived from an AI with the desired meaning if one does not exist as a primary stem (3.19).
(3.19) II stems derived from AI stems
- (a) kənči·mó·u II 'it (a trumpet) sounds' (|kənčīmōwəw| < |kənčīmōwī-| + |-w| 3s,0s)
  (< |kənčīmwī-| AI: kənči·mu 'it (animal, bird) makes its sound'; 2.30h)
- (b) pe·yé·yu II 'it comes', pe·e·yó·u II 'it came' (2.31i. Note: the glosses are contextual.)
  (< |pā-| AI 'come': pé· 'he came').

Although there are a few transitive stem pairs that are irregular or show a unique pattern, most are formed with one of a large set of final pairs (Voegelin 1946:152-154). These include abstract markers of transitivity, both causative and applicative, and finals with concrete meanings, especially instrumentals, or that fall into small sets with vaguer affinities. The TI stems sort into four formal classes: Class 1a (TI(1a), with endings that contain the theme sign |-am|); Class 1b (TI(1b), with theme sign |-əm|); Class 2 (TI(2), with theme sign |-aw| ~ |-ō| ~ |-ā..w|); and Class 3 (TI(3), with no theme sign).

(3.20) Transitive stem pairs
  (a) nkwət·ama TA 'I taste it (anim.)', nkwət·ántamǝm TI 'I taste it (inan.)'
      (final pair: |-am| TA, |-ant| TI(1a) 'act on by mouth')
  (b) mpák·ama TA 'I hit him'; mpak·ántamǝn 'I hit it'
      (final pair: |-am| TA, |-ant| TI(1a) [applicative])
  (c) nkat·á·la 'I want him'; nkat·á·t·amǝn 'I want it'
      (final pair: |-l| TA, |-t| TI(1a) [applicative])
  (d) nná·la TA 'I went after him, went to get him', nná·t·ǝmǝn TI(1b) 'I went after it'
      (final pair: |-l| TA, |-t| TI(1b) [applicative])
  (e) nkə́phɔ (stem |kəpahw-|) TA 'I shut him in', nkəphámǝn (stem |kəpah-|) TI(1a) 'I shut it'
      (final pair: |-ahw| TA, |-ah| TI(1a) 'act on by tool')
  (f) mpə́ntaɔ (stem |pəntaw-|) TA 'I hear him', mpə́ntamǝn (stem |pǝnt-|) TI(1a) 'I hear it'
      (final pair: |-taw| TA, |-t| TI(1a) 'hear')
  (g) mpí·lǝna TA 'I cleaned him by hand', mpi·lǝnə́mǝn TI(1b) 'I cleaned it by hand'
      (final pair: |-ǝn| TA, |-ǝn| TI(1b) 'act on by hand' [unique pattern])
  (h) mpi·lí·ha TA 'I cleaned him', mpi·lí·to·n TI(2) 'I cleaned it'
      (final pair: |-(ī)h| TA, |-(ī)ht| TI(2) [causative])
  (i) nkaxpí·la TA 'I tied him', nkaxpto·n TI(2) 'I tied it'
      (final pair: |-pīl| TA, |-pǝt| TI(2) 'tie')
  (j) mpé·š·ǝwa (|pēšǝw-|) TA 'I brought him', mpé·t·o·n (|pēt-|) TI(2) 'I brought it' (unique)
  (k) nné·ɔ (|nēw-|) TA 'I saw him', nné·mǝn (|nēm-|) TI(3) 'I saw it' (unique)
  (l) nǝmúhɔ (|mǝhw-|; perhaps also nǝmóhɔ) TA 'I ate him', nǝmí·č·i·n (|mīčī-|) TI(3) 'I ate it' (unique)

Class membership is not predictable from the shape of the TI stem, but there are some patterns. For example, the most common instrumental finals of the shape |-ǝC| are all inflected in Class 1b (|-ǝn| TI(1b) 'act on by hand' [3.20g], |-ǝs| TI(1b) 'act on by fire, heat' (2.57g), and |-ǝš| TI(1b) 'act on by cutting edge' [2.55b]), but in the same class are |nāt-| TI(1b) 'go after' (3.20d) and |-ōt| TI(1b) 'act on by speech' (2.14a, 4.15a), while in a different class are |pǝn-| TI(1a) 'look at' (4.35) and |-ǝsǝt| TI(1a) 'hear' (4.39nv, 4.99g). All Class 2 stems end in |t|, but there are also stems in |t| in Class 1a (3.20a), Class 1b (3.20d), and Class 3 (2.50a, 2.65jk).

§3.7f. Secondary Object. Some AI stems take a secondary object, either optionally or obligatorily. Secondary objects have the same syntax as the objects of TA and TI verbs, but the gender of a secondary object does not select one of a pair of stems or finals; the same stem is used for secondary objects of both genders. There are also TA stems that optionally or obligatorily take a secondary object. Stems that take a secondary object are referred to as AI+O and TA+O stems.

(3.21) Verbs with secondary object
  (a) nɔ́ni·n (|wanī-| AI+O 'forget', |nǝ–ǝn| 1s+0s/IND) 'I forgot it' (OA, LB; 2.15fg)
  (b) nɔní·na (|wanī-| AI+O 'forget', |nǝ–ǝna| 1s+3s.abs/IND) 'I forgot about her (abs.)' (V)
  (c) kǝmí·li·n wá xé·s. 'You gave me this hide.' (ME;
      |mīl-| TA+O 'give O2 to', |kǝ–īn| 2s–1s+3s/IND; wá 'this anim.'; xé·s AN 'hide')
  (d) takó· kǝmi·lí·i mpí 'you did not give me water' (B)
      (takó· NEG; |mīl-| TA+O 'give O2 to', |kǝ–īwī| 2s–1s/IND.NEG; mpí 'water')

Conversely, there is also a class of TI stems that either optionally or obligatorily do not take a syntactic object. These are called objectless TI verbs (abbreviated TI-O; e.g., 4.38gh).

The very few TI(3) verbs are also syntactic transitives without theme signs, but they differ from verbs with secondary objects in being paired with TA stems and used only for inanimate objects (3.20kl).

§3.7g. Inanimate Subject with Non-Sentient Object. For an inanimate subject of a transitive verb, the TA inverse inflection is used only in the case of an inanimate acting on a sentient animate object. If an inanimate is acting on a non-sentient animate or an inanimate, the ordinary TA or TI inflection is used, exactly as if the subject were animate.

(3.22) Animate inflection for inanimate transitive subject
- (a) nə́=á· wáin to·xkhikaɔ́·ɔ po·t·a·lá·s·a 'the wine would tear the skin bag' (Lk 5.37; nə́ 'that (inan.)'; =á· POT; wáin 'wine'; |tōxkəhkaw-| TA 'tear', |wə–āwa| 3s–3´/IND; po·t·a·lá·s·a 'skin bag (obv.)')
- (b) kpúntəm pa·tá·to· télən púntink 'your pound earned ten pounds' (Lk 19.16; kpúntəm 'your pound (of money)'; |pāhtāht-| TI(2) 'earn', |-ōw| 3s–(0)/IND; télən P 'ten'; púntink P 'pound(s)')
- (c) yó·ni té·he·k tɔ́ləmi-pali·tó·nal yó·li skí·kɔl. 'This cold begins to destroy this grass.' (1834:17; yó·ni 'this (inan.)'; té·he·k 'what is cold (inan.)'; aləmi PV 'begin', |palīht-| TI(2) 'destroy', |wə–ōnal| 3s–0p/IND; yó·li 'these (inan.)'; skí·kɔl 'grass (inan. pl.)')

4. Inflection

§4.1. There are distinct inflectional patterns for nouns (§4.2), pronouns (§4.3), and verbs (§4.4).

§4.2. Inflection of Nouns. In the inflection of nouns there is a single word-final suffix that indicates the gender and number of the noun, and if it is obviative or absentative, or both. In the non-absentative paradigm a zero suffix is used in the singular of both genders. In the absentative the genders are distinguished in the singular, but the same suffix is used for both plurals and the obviative. These word-final suffixes, which are also used on verbs (with some variation; §4.6, 4.6a), are the PERIPHERAL (or outer) suffixes. (A zero [-Ø], the absence of an overt suffix, marks a form by contrast within the paradigm.)

(4.1) Peripheral suffixes (on nouns)

Animate	Inanimate
|-Ø| anim. sg.	|-Ø| inan. sg.
|-ak| anim. pl. (also |-āk|)	|-a| inan. pl. (older |-al|)
|-a| (older |-al|) obv. (sg., pl.)	

Absentative

|-a| abs. anim. sg.	|-ē| abs. inan. sg.
|-ənka| or |-ənkakē| abs. anim. or inan. pl., obv.	

For |-ak| anim. pl. the variant |-āk| anim. pl. was used by some speakers (OA, ME) after the suffix |-ənān-| 1p,12 (4.3, 5, 20, 21). The long form of the absentative non-singular suffix (|-ənkakē|) was used by WL, ND, and ME, and the short form (|-ənka|) by Blanchard, WL, OA, and FW.

Adjustments in shape take place when the noun suffixes are added to noun stems. A stem-final |w| contracts with |-a| (obv., inan. pl., or abs. anim. sg,) to /-ɔ/. (The stem of nó·x 'my father' is treated as either |ōxw-| or |ōx-| in inflection [4.2g, 4.52d] and as |ōx-| in derivation [2.41d, 4.64f].) A post-consonantal |w| contracts with |-ak| anim. pl. to /-o·k/ with some stems, and to /-ɔk/ with others; at least one stem has both treatments (4.2l). With the absentative suffix |-ənka(kē)| stems in |-əw| contract to |ō| (giving /-únka(hke)/); other stems ending in |w| (or treated so) have contraction to /-únka(hke)/, with /y/ inserted after a front vowel. With no overt suffix a stem-final |w| is lost except after |k| or archaically after /-e·/ (2.10ae), and stem-final |h| and |hw| are also lost (2.11a, 4.2d).

Before overt suffixes a singular in /-a/ has a stem in |-āw| (4.2f), and a singular in /-e·/ (archaic /-e·w/) or /-e/ has a stem in |-ēw| (2.10a, 4.2c). (Voegelin's practice of inserting /y/ between the resulting /e·/ and /ɔ/ has been followed in the past, but a distinctive [y] appears to be only rarely pronounced in this phonological environment, and /y/ is not written here.) One stem with /-e·/ has |-ēh| (2.11a). A singular in /-i/ has a stem in |-əy| (4.2o) or |-īw| (4.2p); a singular in /-u/ has a stem in |-əw| (4.2abq), |-ōw| (4.2r), or rarely |-əhw| (4.2d); and inanimate nouns with singulars in /-ay/ may have stems in either |-ay| (4.2w) or |-ēw| (4.2x). Singulars ending in a voiceless consonant may have stems with either a short or a long consonant before suffixes, but the only large set of stems with a short voiceless consonant before the suffixes are some with singulars in /-kw/ (4.2ku). The only stem noted that keeps a short /s/ is in (2.77c); otherwise /-s/ alternates with /-s·-/, and this is assumed to be the case with the personal names in Blanchard (4.2mn). A stem-final syllable may be weak before a suffix, affecting the shape of the stem (4.2hilv).

Nouns formed with the noun final |-m| 'seed, berry, fruit' do not take |-a(l)| inan. pl. but may show agreement as either singular or plural (4.2z). The noun kéku 'thing, things' corresponding to the pronoun kéku 'something' (4.18) has the same peculiarity.

(4.2) Noun paradigms

Animate

	(a) 'man'	(b) 'young man'	(c) 'woman'	(d) 'deer'
sg.	lənu (|ələnəw|)	skínnu	xkwé·	ahtú (|atəhw|)
pl.	lənəwak	skinnúwak	xkwé·ɔk	ahtúho·k
obv.	lənəwa	skinnúwa	xkwé·ɔ	ahtúhɔ
	lənəwal (B)		xkwé·ɔl (B)	
abs. sg.	lənəwa	skinnúwa	xkwé·ɔ	ahtúhɔ
abs. pl./obv.	lənúnka (B, OA)		xkwe·yúnka	ahtuhúnka
	lənúnkahke (ME)	skinnúnkahke (V)	(OA)	(V, OA)

	(e) 'old man'	(f) 'chief; king'	(g) 'my father'	'his father'
sg.	hiló·səs (2.77b)	sa·k·í·ma (2.36f)	nó·x	—
pl.	hilo·sə́s·ak	sa·k·i·má·ɔk	—	—
		sa·k·i·má·ak (ME)		
obv.	hilo·sə́s·a	sa·k·i·má·ɔ	nó·x·ɔ (B, OA, ME)	ó·x·ɔ (B, ME)
		sa·k·i·má·a (ME)		
abs. sg.	hilo·sə́s·a	sa·k·i·má·ɔ	nó·x·a (OA, ME)	—
			nó·x·ɔ (OA)	
abs. pl./obv.	hilo·səs·ínka	sa·k·i·ma·únka		o·x·únka (B)
				o·x·ínka (OA)

	(h) 'tree'	(i) 'knee'	(j) 'bear'	(k) 'log'
sg.	hít·ukw (2.16c)	nkə́t·ukw 'my —'	máxkw	məsá·kw
pl.	hítko·k	nkə́tko·k 'my —'	máxkɔk	məsá·kɔk
obv.	hítkɔ	kwə́tkɔ 'his —'	máxkɔ	məsá·kɔ

	(l) 'whiteman'	(m) 'David' (B)	(n) 'Moses' (B)
sg.	šəwánakw	nté·pit	mó·šəš
pl.	šəwánahko·k (V, OA)	—	—
	šəwánahkɔk (B, OA, ME)		
obv.	šəwánahkɔ	nte·pít·al (2x)	mo·šə́š·a (1x)
abs. sg.		nte·pít·a (15x)	mo·šə́š·a (21x)

	(o) 'American elm'	(p) 'Munsee'	(q) 'louse'	(r) 'spirit'
sg.	lɔ·k·anahó·nši	mwə́ns·i	xáyhu	manə́t·u
pl.	lɔ·k·anahó·nšiak	mwəns·í·ɔk (OA)	xayhúwak	manət·ó·wak
		mwəns·í·ak (ME)		

Inanimate

	(s) 'pc. of wood'	(t) '(pc. of) meat'	(u) 'bottle'	(v) 'shoe'
sg.	tá·x·an	wió·s	hákhakw	čí·p·akw
pl.	tá·x·ana	wió·s·a (LB)	hakhákɔ	čípahkɔ
abs. sg.		wió·s·e		
abs. pl.	ta·x·anínka			

	(w) 'town'	(x) 'fire'	(z) 'seed'
sg.	o·té·nay	tə́ntay	xkáni·m (nə́ xkáni·m 'that seed' [B])
pl.	o·té·naya	tənté·ɔ (|təntēw-a|)	xkáni·m (né·l xkáni·m 'those seeds' [ME])

A rare case of a stem with two treatments is škákw 'skunk': pl. šká·kɔk (OA), šká·k·ɔk (ME, ER). The loanword só·p 'soap' shows the same variation: nsó·pəm, nsó·p·əm 'my soap' (OA).

§4.2a. Possessed Nouns. Nouns may be inflected for one of the seven pronominal persons (**§3.6**) or a third person obviative as a possessor. The grammatical relationship of possessor to possessed includes not only ownership, but also kinship, affinity, authority (and its inverse), whole-to-part, and so forth. A possessor is marked by a pronominal prefix (**§2.13**), with or without a pluralizer; the pluralizers are CENTRAL (or inner) suffixes, coming before the peripheral suffix of the core inflection (4.3). (A plural peripheral suffix is sometimes not used after a plural central suffix [e.g., Lk 10.20].) An obviative possessor, singular or plural, is marked by the third person prefix and a central suffix |-īlīt| obv., with no peripheral suffix. Nouns always marked for a possessor (most kinship and body-part terms) are DEPENDENT. The third person prefix may be used on an unpossessed dependent noun, but there is some secondary differentiation of this form, and some variation. Some non-dependent nouns add a possessed-theme marker |-əm| after the stem, but the use of |-əm| POSS.TH is unpredictable and again somewhat variable.

(4.3) Inflection for possessor

	prefix	(noun stem)	poss. theme	pluralizer (and obviative)
1s	|nə-| 1		(|-əm|)	|-∅| sg.
2s	|kə-| 2		(|-əm|)	|-∅| sg.
3s	|wə-| 3		(|-əm|)	|-∅| sg.
1p	|nə-| 1		(|-əm|)	|-ənā(n-)| 1p,12
12	|kə-| 2		(|-əm|)	|-ənā(n-)| 1p,12
2p	|kə-| 2		(|-əm|)	|-əwā(w-)| 2p,3p
3p	|wə-| 3		(|-əm|)	|-əwā(w-)| 2p,3p
3´	|wə-| 3		(|-əm|)	|-īlīt| obv. poss.

The pluralizers |-ənā(n-)| 1p,12 and |-əwā(w-)| 2p,3p have the longer form (with the second |n| or |w|) before an overt suffix; the short forms occur word-finally, with shortening of the |-ā| (**§2.9**). The phonological realization of the prefixes before stems of different shapes is described and exemplified in (**§2.13**). The variation in the shape of stems after prefixes is illustrated in (**§2.14**).

The paradigms in (4.4) and (4.5) are constructed as examples. Initials indicate the authorities for the forms that are attested for these nouns, with asterisked initials for inflections attested on other nouns (usually for only a single source). Supporting data for the constructed forms and variant endings are added, and three forms of other nouns with archaic endings are included. The inanimate noun in (4.4) is usually found with |-əm| POSS.TH, but Blanchard has tɔp·ó·nəwa 'their bread'. The animate noun in (4.5) is a dependent noun and hence has no unpossessed form.

(4.4) Possessed inanimate noun (ahpɔ́·n 'bread; loaf of bread'; ahpá·nši 'pole'; xkán 'bone'; mhúkw 'blood'; múx·o·l 'boat'; lače·s·əwák·an 'possessions, clothing')

	sg. noun	pl. noun
1s	ntap·ó·nəm 'my bread' (LB)	ntap·ó·nəma 'my loaves' (V*); ntap·a·nší·yəma 'my poles' (ME)
2s	ktap·ó·nəm 'your (sg.) bread' (LB)	ktap·ó·nəma 'your (sg.) loaves' (V*)
3s	tɔp·ó·nəm 'his or her bread' (LB)	tɔp·ó·nəma 'his or her loaves' (V*)
1p	ntap·ɔ·nəmə́na 'our (exc.) bread' (ND)	ntap·ɔ·nəmənána 'our (exc.) loaves' (V*) (nsi·t·əná·nal 'our (exc.) feet' B [s.b. /k-/])

12   ktap·ɔ·nəmə́na 'our (inc.) bread' (V*)   ktap·ɔ·nəmənáˑna 'our (inc.) loaves';
                                                 ko·xkanəmənáˑna 'our (inc.) bones' (ME)
2p   ktap·ɔ·nəmúwa 'your (pl.) bread' (V*)   ktap·ɔ·nəməwá·ɔ 'your (pl.) loaves';
                                                 kəškinkəwá·ɔ 'your (pl.) eyes' (B)
                                                 (kše·t·o·nəwɔ́·ɔ 'your (pl.) lips' V)
3p   tɔp·ɔ·nəmúwa 'their bread';   tɔp·ɔ·nəməwá·ɔ 'their loaves';
     mmo·kəmúwa 'their blood' (B)   tɔmxo·ləwá·ɔ 'their boats' (B) (cf. 2.68b)
                                                 (wše·t·o·nəwɔ́·ɔ 'their (pl.) lips' V)
                                                 wtəlahče·s·əwa·k·anəwá·ɔl 'their goods' (B)
3´   tɔp·ɔ·nəmíˑli·t 'his, her, or their (obv.) bread or loaves' (B*; V* 1x)
     (wəškinkwíˑli·t 'his (obv.) eyes, face; their (obv.) eyes, [faces]' B)

(4.5) Possessed animate noun (|-nīčān| 'child', later esp. 'daughter'; mímə·ns 'child'; others)
     sg. noun   pl. noun
1s   nníˑč·a·n 'my child' (B, OA, ME)   nníˑč·á·nak 'my children' (V, OA, ME)
2s   kəníˑč·a·n 'your (sg.) child' (B, ME)   kəni·č·á·nak 'your (sg.) children' (B)
3s   wəni·č·á·na 'his or her child or children (obv.)' (B, V)
     (wəni·č·á·nal B 2x)
1p   nni·č·á·nəna 'our (exc.) child' (OA)   nni·č·a·nəná·nak 'our (exc.) children' (B, V*)
                                                  (ntami·mə·nsəməná·na·k 'our (exc.)
                                                  children' OA, ME)
12   kəni·č·á·nəna 'our (inc.) child' (OA)   kəni·č·a·nəná·nak 'our (inc.) children' (B, V*)
                                                  (ktami·mə·nsəməná·na·k 'our (inc.)
                                                  children' ME)
2p   kəni·č·á·nəwa 'your (pl.) child' (OA)   kəni·č·a·nəwá·ɔk 'your (pl.) children' (B)
                                                  ([k]kahe·s·əwɔ́·ɔk 'your (pl.) mothers' V;
                                                  ktənno·yəməwá·ak 'you women's or girls'
                                                  brothers' ME [see 4.6c])
3p   wəni·č·a·nəwá·ɔ 'their child or children (obv.)' (B)
     (kɔhe·s·əwɔ́·ɔ 'their mother or mothers (obv.)' V, LB;
     wəni·č·a·nəwá·a 'their child or children (obv.)' OA, ME*)
     wtehəwá·ɔl 'their hearts' (B)
3´   wəni·č·a·níˑli·t 'his, her, or their (obv.) child or children [obv.]' (B 'her (obv.) foal' 2x)

The variation in these endings includes archaic |-al| inan. pl. and |-al| obv. for |-a| (B; 4.4:3p, 4.5:3p); /-a·k/ anim. pl. for /-ak/ after /-ənān-/ 1p,12 (OA and ME; 4.5:1p, 12); and /-əwɔ́·-/ for /-əwá·-/ 2p,3p before a peripheral suffix (V and LB; 4.4, 4.5:2p, 3p) OR /-a/ inan. pl., /-a/ obv., and /-ak/ anim. pl. for /-ɔ/ and /-ɔk/ after /-əwá·-/ 2p,3p (OA and ME; 4.4, 4.5:2p, 3p).

Some of the possessed forms of stems ending in an underlying |w| or |y| adopt a shape other than the one that appears before a plural or absentative suffix. Stems ending in a |w| preceded by a long vowel replace the |w| with /y/ before |-əm| POSS.TH and |-əwā(w-)| 2p,3p (2.33ab, 34h, 61de). Before |-əm| POSS.TH, |-ənā(n-)| 1p,12 and |-əwā(w-)| 2p,3p, stems in |-əy| replace this with |-īw| (2.34g, 4.6a); stems in |-ay| replace this with |-ēw| (4.6b); and stems in |-əw| replace this with |-ōw| (4.6c). The underlying |w| in these reshaped stems is treated like an original underlying |w| and replaced by /y/ before /əm/ (§2.11d, 2.33cde, 4.6c) or /əw/ (§2.11e, 2.34g, 4.6a).

(4.6) Possessed forms of nouns with stems in |-y| or |-əw|
     (a) hák·i 'land' (|ahkəy|), ntá·kia (|nət-ahkəy-a|) 'my lands': nta·kí·wəna (|nət-ahkīw-ənā|)
          'our (exc.) land', kta·kí·yəwa (|kət-ahkīw-əwā|) 'your (pl.) land' (2.34g)

(b) nəmóˑtˑay 'my stomach, belly' (**§2.10f**): kəmoˑtˑeˑwənáˑna 'our bellies' (OA)

(c) lə́nu (|ələnəw|) 'man': ntənnóˑyəm (|nət-ələnōw-əm|) 'my (a female's) brother'

§4.2b. Dependent Nouns. Dependent nouns always have a possessive prefix, at least in their underlying forms (4.7). For nouns that are not kinship terms (or 'friend' or 'relative') the third person prefix is used both to mark a third person possessor and as the default prefix when there is no possessor (4.7abc). If the noun is animate the unpossessed form differs from the third person singular form by lacking the obviative suffix and taking a proximate plural (4.7a), but for an inanimate noun there is no difference (4.7bc). Stems that begin with an underlying vowel do not have a |t| inserted before it; the prefixes occur in the shortened forms |n-| 1, |k-| 2, and |w-| 3 (4.7c), with |w-| 3 being dropped before |ō| (4.7d). In some cases variation in the phonological treatment of the third person prefix appears to differentiate the two forms, at least for some speakers, ostensibly making the nouns non-dependent ('thigh' 2.58d). In a number of nouns there is reshaping of prefixes with divergent treatments and leveling of variants. For example, nouns that have an unpossessed form that begins with /ɔ-/ (originally from |wə-| 3 added to a dependent noun stem that begins with |a|) in some cases generalize the /ɔ/ after all prefixes, including a /w-/ that contrastively marks a third person possessor (4.7e). This may also happen in a kinship term, which has no unpossessed form (4.7f). Alternatively there may be a variant paradigm with the original /a/ retained in all possessed forms, including after |wə-| 3 (4.7fg), and there is at least one alternate unpossessed form with initial /a-/ (2.67i). In other cases the prefixes may be added to the original unpossessed form, effectively making the noun non-dependent (2.15i). Nouns with metathesized /hi/ in the first syllable of the first and second person forms (and /hwi-/ with |w(ə)-| 3) may remain as dependent nouns (4.7h), or may add the prefixes to the unpossessed form that incorporates |w(ə)-| 3, giving either /-hwi-/ or /-wiˑ-/ (4.7i).

(4.7) Dependent nouns

(a) ntéˑ 'my heart', ktéˑ 'your (sg.) heart', wtéˑha 'his or her heart (obv.)';
wtéˑ '(a) heart', wtéˑhak 'hearts' (variously V, OA, ND)

(b) ntóˑn 'my mouth', któˑn 'your (sg.) mouth', wtóˑn 'his or her mouth; (a, the) mouth' (V)

(c) níˑl 'my head', kíˑl 'your (sg.) head', wíˑl 'his or her head; (a, the) head', wíˑla 'heads'

(d) nóˑx 'my father', kóˑx 'your (sg.) father', óˑxˑɔ 'his or her father'

(e) ɔlákhakw 'palate', nɔlákhakw 'my palate', wɔlákhakw 'his or her palate' (OA)

(f) nɔhtánkw 'my (male's) brother-in-law'; wɔhtánkɔ 'his brother-in-law' (OA);
cf. nahtánkw 'my (male's) brother-in-law', wahtánkɔ 'his brother-in-law' (ME)

(g) ɔnánu 'cheek', pl. ɔnánəwak (V, ME); wɔnánəwa 'his cheek or cheeks' (OA);
cf. wanánu 'cheek' (ND), pl. wanánəwak (OA); wanánəwa 'his cheek or cheeks' (V);
also wánanu 'cheek' (LB); nánanu 'my cheek' (pl. nananúwak) (V)

(h) nhíkˑaš 'my fingernail', hwíkahša 'his fingernail(s)', hwíkahšak 'fingernails, hoofs' (V)

(i) nhwíčˑu 'my calf', khwíčˑu 'your calf', hwíčəwa 'his calf, calves' (V);
also nəwíˑčəwak 'my calves' (OA)

§4.2c. Absentative Possessed Nouns. A possessed noun may have an absentative suffix. Some examples are given in (4.8).

(4.8) Absentative possessed nouns

(a) nkahéˑsˑa 'my late mother' (V)

(b) kɔheˑsˑínka 'his or her late mother' (V)

(c) nəmuxˑoˑmsənáˑna 'our (exc.) grandfather (abs.)' (B)

(d) nkiˑkayoˑyəmənaˑnínkahke 'our (exc.) ancestors of old' (ME)

(e) kəmuxˑoˑmsənaˑnínka 'our (inc.) grandfather (abs. obv.), or grandfathers (abs. pl.)' (B)

(f) ko·x·əwá·ɔ 'your (fore)father (abs.)' (Jn 8.56);
    [k]kahe·s·əwɔ́·ɔ 'your (pl.) late mother' (V)
(g) ko·x·əwa·únka 'your (pl.) (fore)fathers (abs.)' (B)
(h) o·x·əwa·únka 'their (fore)fathers (abs.)' (B);
    kɔhe·s·əwɔ·únka 'their late mother or mothers' (V)

§4.2d. Locative. Nouns, including possessed nouns, have a locative form marked by the word-final suffix |-ənk| LOC (2.19h, 21, etc.). Locative forms indicate spatial and conceptual relationships that, depending on context, can be glossed 'in', 'on', 'at', 'to', 'from', 'like', etc. The locative suffix is added in the slot of the peripheral suffixes, and the categories that they specify are thus not indicated in locative forms. The number of the noun is thus ambiguous in the locative form: wənáxkink 'his hand or hands (loc.)' (B). (There is also, however, an optional, explicit locative plural suffix [§4.2e].) The suffix is /-ink/ except when the |ə| contracts with a stem-final |w| or |y| (2.28f, 29e, 33c, 41f, 55n, 56ac, 60efj, 61c, 68c, 79g; 4.9).

Stems in |-aw| and |-əw| have contraction to |ō| (2.19h, 22f); stems in |-əy| generally have contraction to |ī| (2.8a, 21ab; an exception is in 2.21c); and stems in |-ay| generally have contraction to |ē| (**§2.10f**; 2.33c), though some simply add /-ink/ (4.9ab). Stems in |-Cw| have contraction to /-Cunk/ (2.28d). Stems ending in a |w| preceded by |ī| or |ē| have /-yunk/ (2.28c, 32e), while stems in |-āw| have /-á·unk/ (2.28a). The central suffix |-əwāw| 2p,3p contracts with the locative to either /-əwá·unk/ (2.28b) or /-əwá·ink/ (2.28b, 2.56c).

The noun stem has the same shape as before the plural suffix, if this differs from the singular (4.9c). Uniquely, the noun o·t·é·nay 'town' drops the |-ay| in the locative (4.9d). Lexicalized participles add the locative suffix like noun stems (4.9e).

(4.9) Additional locative forms with /-ink/
(a) khíkaink 'old lady (loc.)': wténk=á· kəní·p·ai ná khíkaink 'stand behind that old lady' (OA) (wténk 'behind'; =á· POT; kəní·p·ai 'you stand'; ná 'that (anim.)'; sg. khík·ay 'old lady')
(b) ɔhší·x·aink 'in a nest' (LB), wɔší·x·aink 'in her nest' (ME) (sg. ɔhší·x·ay 'nest')
(c) wi·k·əwáhəmink 'in the house, building' (sg. wí·k·əwam, pl. wi·k·əwáhəma)
(d) o·t·é·nink 'in the town' (sg. o·t·é·nay; 4.2w)
(e) ehəntali·p·wínkink 'on the table' (B, ME, ND); sg. ehəntalí·p·wink 'table' (ME) (|èhəntalīpwīnk| 'where one habitually eats' < |IC+Rih+əntalīpwī-(ə)nk| < |Rih+| HAB, |(ən)talīpwī-| AI 'eat {smwh}', |IC–ənk| X/PPL(OBL))

§4.2e. Locative Plural. Nouns and lexicalized participles make explicit locative plurals with the suffix |-īhkēwī| LOC.PL, realized as /-i·ké·i/ (B, V) or /-i·ké·e/ (1960's) (cf. 2.13ab). This tends to imply several or numerous things, but it is attested also for only two (4.10h), and note (4.10j).

(4.10) Locative plural forms
(a) kwə́škwəš·i·ké·i 'to or among the hogs' (kwə́škwəš 'hog')
(b) mahči·k·ami·k·wi·ké·i 'among the graves' (mahčí·k·ami·kw 'grave')
(c) lí ki·t·i·s·i·ké·i 'to your friends' (kí·t·i·s 'your (sg.) friend')
(d) wə́nči wé·mi o·t·e·nai·ké·i 'from all the towns' (o·t·é·nay 'town')
(e) sa·k·i·ma·i·ké·i 'among kings' (sa·k·í·ma 'king')
(f) enkələk·i·ké·i 'among the dead' (enkələ́k·i·k 'the dead (pl. ppl.)')
(g) pehpalo·ka·s·i·t·i·ké·i 'among the criminals' (pehpalo·ká·s·i·t 'one who is a criminal')
(h) nɔ·panəmi·ké·i 'in my lungs' (nɔ·panə́mak 'my lungs') (V)
(i) ahsəni·ké·e 'on or among rocks' (OA, ND, LB) (ahsə́n 'rock')
(j) kəni·č·a·nəwa·i·ké·i P 'on your and their descendants' (Blanchard 1842:8.1)

This suffix is related to |-īhkē| II 'be an abundance of': ahsəní·ke· 'there are many rocks, it is a rocky place' (OA, LB), énta-ahsəní·ke·k 'where it was stony' (B; OA with ə́nta-: "it was nothing but rocks"; cf. 4.10i); also énta ahsəni·ké·i (B). Another synonymous doublet is təme·i·ké·i 'among wolves' and énta-təme·í·ke·k (both B). The suffix |-īhkēwī| LOC.PL is, however, used on many nouns (not to mention participles) that do not make derived verbs of this kind.

§4.2f. Vocative. In a limited number of cases nouns have vocative forms, used in direct address. Ordinary nouns may be used in this function otherwise. A number of kinship terms have vocative singular forms. Most of these have a suffix /-a·/ added to a reduced form of the noun; the first person prefix is omitted and the stem has static features (2.78abcd, 4.11ac). In one case the noun has the usual shape it has before a suffix (4.11b). Two of these vocatives have divergent shapes that cannot be derived from the possessed nouns, one having the unique suffix /-a·s/ (4.11ce). The vocatives of two words for 'friend' are also irregular (4.11fg). There are also vocatives with the vocative diminutive suffix /-t·i/, which either replaces the diminutive /-t·ət/ or is added to the usual vocative; these indicate endearment rather than small size (4.11bcfhij). The word for 'male friend' also has a vocative in which this /-t·i/ has apparently been refashioned into the objurgative suffix /-t·ie/, literally 'butt' (4.11f, 5.50a; also in 4.11m). The vocative of nkwí·s 'my son' is the regular diminutive nkwí·t·ət (OA, ME). Other vocative singulars are rare (4.11k). A few nouns are attested with the vocative plural suffix |-ətōkw| (4.11.lmnopq).

(4.11) Vocative forms
- (a) úmma· 'grandmother!' (LB; cf. nó·həm 'my grandmother'); ME described this as used by some "Dewey" Delawares.
- (b) núhəma· 'grandmother!' (OA, ND, ME), also nuhəmá·t·i (OA, ME)
- (c) ána· 'mother!' (cf. nkáhe·s 'my mother'); also aná·t·i
- (d) xá·nsa· 'older brother!' (cf. naxá·ns 'my older brother')
- (e) xát·a·s 'younger brother or sister!' (cf. naxí·s·əməs 'my younger brother or sister'; 62g); also át·a·č (probably with the same meaning, though glossed as for opposite sex) (OA)
- (f) nčú 'my friend! (male to male)'; also nčó·t·i (B 1834a 3x), nčó·t·ie (B 2x, ME; 4.11m); cf. ní·t·i·s 'my (male) friend (of a male)'
- (g) í·č·u 'my friend! (female to female)'; cf. ní·č·o·s 'my (female) friend (of a female)'
- (h) nuxá·t·i 'father' (endearing; also used in Christian prayers) (cf. 78c)
- (i) nkahé·t·i 'aunt!' (cf. nkahé·t·ət 'my father's or mother's sister')
- (j) no·x·wí·t·i 'grandchild!' (cf. nó·x·wi·s 'my grandchild', dim. no·x·wí·t·ət)
- (k) áška 'attendant!' (FW; cf. áška·s 'ceremonial attendant (in the Big House)')
- (l) mi·mə́nsto·kw 'children!' (B 2x; mí·mə·ns 'child')
- (m) nčo·t·ié·sto·kw 'my friends!' (B, ME; cf. 4.11f)
- (n) ntəlanko·má·wto·kw 'my kinsmen!' (B; KJV "you my friends")
- (o) ni·mahtə́t·o·kw 'my brothers!' (B 1834b:8.12 ⟨Ne Matitwk⟩)
- (p) ni·mahtə́sto·kw 'my brothers!' (Speck 1931:122)
- (q) ntuxkwe·yəmə́t·o·kw 'you women!', *lit.*, 'my sisters (voc.)' (ME)

§4.2g. Obviative Plural. A derivational suffix is added to nouns to mark them as explicitly obviative plural and not singular. This is found as /-í·na/ (B, ME; 4.12abcde) and on one noun as /-í·nay/ (B 2x; 4.12e). (Presumably kkwi·s·í·nal 'his sons' [1834b:18.10] should be kkwi·s·í·na.)

(4.12) Obviative plural
- (a) aesəs·í·na 'animals (obv. pl.)' (ME) (sg. aésəs ·'(wild) animal')
- (b) wti·la·yəmí·na 'his officers (obv. pl.)' (B) (cf. 2.60g, 2.61e)
- (c) wtuxkwe·yəmí·na 'his sisters (obv. pl.)' (B) (cf. 2.61g)

(d) nči·lo·sələm tɔ·ní·na 'daughters (obv. pl.) of Jerusalem' (B; used as a vocative)
(e) wi·mahtí·nay 'his brothers (obv. pl.)' (B 2x); wi·mahtí·na (B 1842 2x)

§4.3. Inflection of Pronouns. The words classed as pronouns have a range of functions as deictics and other noun-substitutes.

The emphatic pronouns (3.10) have first and second person forms with pronominal prefixes and plural-marking suffixes; the third person forms are suppletive, with plural marked by |-wā| (unaccompanied by a prefix). There are no peripheral suffixes. There is, however, a collective plural form for the first plural inclusive that adds /-o·kw/: ki·ló·no·kw 'we (inc., the whole group of us)' (cf. the use of /-o·kw/ in the inclusive imperative, §4.12a).

A second set of emphatic pronouns (4.13) with the added meaning 'also' has first and second person forms made on a stem -é·pe (sg.), -e·p- (pl.); the plurals have variation in accent and shape. The third person equivalents have the emphatic pronoun followed by né·, which is also found with the first singular; the attested combinations are given.

(4.13) Emphatic pronouns ('too' set)

né·pe (né·pe=tá=né· V)	'I too, I also'
ké·pe	'you (sg.) too'
né·k·a né·	'he too, she too'
né·pəna	'we (exc.) too'
ké·pəna	'we (inc.) too'
ké·pəwa (V, ME), ke·pó·wa (LB)	'you (pl.) too'
ne·k·əmá·ɔ né·	'they (anim.) too'

There appears to be some evidence that the first and second plural forms with initial stress also have variants with the stress shifted to the second syllable.

The reflexive pronoun resembles a possessed noun, but with some irregularities. It is used for reflexive primary objects, and the first and second person forms are used for secondary objects, in equational sentences, and as non-volitional subjects. Blanchard has locative forms. It is treated as either animate or inanimate, and the plural forms occur with and without a plural peripheral suffix. The same word is also used as an inanimate noun: nhák·ay 'my body'.

(4.14) Reflexive pronouns (forms)

nhák·ay;	'myself; me'
nhák·enk (B)	'me (loc.)'
khák·ay;	'yourself; you (sg.)'
khák·enk (B)	'you (sg.) (loc.)'
hɔk·ay IN, hɔ́kaya AN;	'himself, herself'
hɔ́k·enk (B)	'him (loc.)'
hɔk·aí·li·t (B)	'him (obv.)' (hɔk·aí·li·t wə́nči 'from him (obv.)' 2x)
nhak·ayə́na (ME),	'ourselves (exc.); us (exc.)'
nhak·ayəná·nak (B);	
nhak·ayəná·nink (B)	'us (exc.) (loc.)'
khak·ayə́na (ME)	'ourselves (inc.); us (inc.)'
khak·ayúwa (B);	'yourselves; you (pl.)'
khak·ayəwá·ink (B)	'you (pl.) (loc.)'
hɔk·ayúwa (B, V, ME),	'themselves'
hɔk·ayəwá·a (OA, ME);	
hɔk·ayəwá·unk (B),	'them (loc.)'
hɔk·ayəwá·ink (B)	

(4.15) Reflexive pronouns (examples)
 (a) nihəláči ntak·ənó·t·əmən nhák·ay 'I tell of my own self' (B)
   (nihəláči P 'own; myself, yourself, himself'; |akənōt-| TI(1b) 'tell about')
 (b) wsíhəwe·n nhák·ay 'he wins me' (V; |sihəwē-| AI+O 'win O2')
 (c) nihəláči mpi·la·wso·há·la nhák·ay 'I make my own self holy' (B)
   (nihəláči P 'own, etc.'; pīlāwəsōhāl-| TA 'make holy, sanctify')
 (d) nɔhɔ·lxého nhák·ay (|wahwālaxehw-| TA 'pierce ears of') 'I pierced my own ears' (OA)
 (e) wə́nči nhák·enk 'from me, concerning me' (B; wə́nči P 'from {smwh}')
 (f) lə́nu nhák·ay 'I'm a man' (V)
 (g) mpe·t·a·k·o·né·ɔ khák·ay 'they brought you to me' (B; |pētaw-| TA+O 'bring O2 to')
 (h) kéku=háč ktəlahkəní·ma khák·ay? 'What do you say about yourself?' (B)
   (kéku 'what?'; =háč Q; |əlakənīm-| TA 'tell about {so}')
 (i) nkát·a·nhilá·ne·n nhak·ayə́na (or) nkát·a·nhitó·ne·n nhak·ayə́na
   'we (exc.) are going to kill ourselves' (ME)
   (|kata| PV 'be going to, want to'; |nəhl-| TA or |nəht-| TI(2) 'kill')
 (j) ke·nahkí·to·kw khak·ayúwa 'watch yourselves' (B) (|kēnakīht-| TI(2) 'watch over')
 (k) mái-pənúntəlo· khak·ayúwa 'go show yourselves to them' (B)
   (|mawī| PV 'go and'; |pənōntəl-| TA+O 'show O2 to')
 (l) hákink təlaníhi·n hɔ́k·ay 'he threw himself down' (B)
   (hákink P 'down'; |əlanihī-| AI+O 'throw O2 to {smwh}')
 (m) wšehəlalá·ɔ hɔ́kaya 'he hanged himself' (B) (|šēhlal-| TA 'hang')

The other words that can be classed as pronouns distinguish the nominal categories. Those that modify or substitute for a noun take their inflectional categories from it.

There are two sets of demonstrative pronouns, which distinguish the same categories as the peripheral suffixes (4.1). Each non-absentative demonstrative has a weakly emphatic or more definite form that adds /-ni/ after a vowel and /-i/ after a consonant; Blanchard has variants with the /k/ or /l/ repeated. At least some of the extended forms in /-ni/ have variants without the /-i/.

(4.16) Demonstrative pronouns
 (a) 'This, these'

Animate	Inanimate
wá, wáni 'this (anim. sg.)'	yú, yó·ni (yó·n V, LB) 'this (inan. sg.)'
yó·k, yó·ki, yó·ki·k (B) 'these (anim. pl.)'	yó·l, yó·li 'these (inan. pl.)'
yó·l, yó·li 'this (obv. sg.), these (obv. pl.)'	

Absentative

wáka 'this (abs. anim. sg.)'	[?] 'this (abs. inan. sg.)'
yukáhke 'this (abs. obv.), these (abs. anim. or inan. pl.)'	

 (b) 'that, those'

Animate	Inanimate
ná, náni (nán) 'that (anim. sg.)'	ní, nə́; nə́ni (nə́n) 'that (inan. sg.)'
né·k, né·ki, né·ki·k (B) 'those (anim. pl.)'	né·l, né·li 'those (inan. pl.)'
né·l, né·li, né·li·l 'that (obv. sg.), those (obv. pl.)'	

Absentative

náka 'that (abs. anim. sg.)'	níke 'that (abs. inan. sg.)'
nikáhke, nəkáhke 'that (abs. obv.), those (abs. anim. or inan. pl.)'	

For the inanimate singular absentative /yúke/ was accepted by OA, but no textual or other example is known. It is likely that yúkwe 'now' is a specialized use of the actual form. /níke/ 'then', which is clearly the same word as níke 'that (abs. inan. sg.)', has an older form /néke/ (B).

The interrogative demonstrative has absentative forms.

(4.17) Interrogative demonstrative

Animate	Inanimate
ta·níka 'where is (anim. sg.)?'	ta·níke 'where is (inan. sg.)?'
ta·nikáhke 'where are they?'	

The indefinite-interrogative pronouns have different stems for the two genders; the inanimate has a single invariant form. The interrogative use requires an interrogative enclitic (usually =háč, =héč; also =ksí, =néh, and =nínk).

(4.18) Indefinite-interrogative pronouns

Animate	Inanimate
awé·n 'someone, anyone; who?'	kéku 'something, anything; what?'
awé·ni·k 'who (anim. pl.)?	
awé·ni 'someone, anyone; who (obv.)?'	

These pronouns are also used as nouns but retain their inflectional peculiarities: awé·n 'person' (pl. awé·ni·k), kéku 'thing, things'. In this usage there are animate absentative forms: awe·níka 'person (abs.)', awe·nikáhke 'person (abs. obv.), 'people (abs. obv., abs. pl.)'. There is an irregular possessed form for the inanimate (2.55h, 2.72h).

The word for 'other' is like a pronoun in its inflection and in taking its gender from the noun it modifies or substitutes for (2.72i).

§4.4. Inflection of Verbs (Basic Categories). Verbs are inflected for the nominal and pronominal categories of their arguments (§3.7a), as needed, as well as for the inherently verbal categories of mode (§4.4a), tense (§4.4b), and negative (§4.4c). Transitive verbs have an object marker, called a theme sign (§4.4d). Some verbs mark a distinction between definite and indefinite arguments (§4.4e).

§4.4a. Orders and Modes. The modes of the verb fall into three orders. The INDEPENDENT order has pronominal prefixes, identical with those of possessed nouns (4.3); most but not all forms have one. It also has suffixes that in part resemble those on nouns. It has two modes, the independent INDICATIVE (IND) and the independent SUBORDINATIVE (SBD). The CONJUNCT order uses only suffixes and a vowel ablaut (replacement), called INITIAL CHANGE (IC), and the pronominal suffixes differ almost entirely from those in the independent order. It has five modes: the conjunct indicative or PLAIN conjunct (CNJ), the CHANGED conjunct (CC), the conjunct SUBJUNCTIVE (SBJ), the CHANGED SUBJUNCTIVE (CS), and the PARTICIPLE (PPL). The imperative order has four formally unrelated modes, the ordinary IMPERATIVE (IMP), the negative imperative or PROHIBITIVE (PROH), the INJUNCTIVE (INJ), and the FUTURE IMPERATIVE (FI). The imperative and future imperative have distinct pronominal suffixes, while the injunctive and prohibitive pronominal suffixes are basically those of the conjunct.

The uses of the modes are summarized before each set of paradigms, below.

§4.4b. Preterite and Present. Independent and conjunct forms may have a suffix for a marked or removed past, or preterite (PRET). The marking of the preterite is common in Blanchard but often seems optional; in later materials it becomes rare, and it was barely ever heard in spontaneous use in the 1960's. Blanchard has two conjunct forms that are marked for a PRESENT perfective.

§4.4c. Negative and Prohibitive. The independent and conjunct orders share a NEGATIVE suffix (NEG). This is consistently used in the independent order, but its use in the conjunct order is variable and becomes less over time. The negative suffix that marks the prohibitive is different. Negative and prohibitive forms also require a negative particle.

§4.4d. Theme Signs. In all transitive verbs except those of the very small Class 3 TI the stem is followed by a theme sign.

The four mutually exclusive TA theme signs are essentially object markers, but their selection also depends on the person of the subject and, for one subset of endings, whether the inflection is of the independent or conjunct order. The choice between the first and second theme signs (called DIRECT and INVERSE) is determined by the relative positions of the subject and object on the following person hierarchy (running from highest to lowest): (1) first or second person; (2) indefinite (subject); (3) proximate third person; (4) obviative third person; (5) further obviative; and (6) inanimate (subject). The direct theme sign (theme 1; |-ā| TH.1) marks an object that is lower (one acted on by a subject that is higher). The inverse theme sign (theme 2; |-əkw| TH.2) marks a higher object (one acted on by a lower subject that is not the indefinite person [X]); the variant |-əkē| TH.2.PS is used if the actor is the indefinite person (in effect making passives for the first and second person). The third theme sign (|-ī| TH.3) is used for a first person object with a second person subject, and in the conjunct order also with a third person or indefinite subject. The fourth theme sign (|-əl| TH.4) marks a second person object with a first person subject.

For a TI verb the theme sign is entirely determined by the stem class (**§3.7e**, 3.20).

§4.4e. Absolute and Objective. Independent indicative verbs with third person objects make a distinction between ABSOLUTE forms (used for an indefinite [that is, non-definite] object) and OBJECTIVE forms (used for a definite object, and hence also for a pronominal object). Objective inflections used pronominally occur with no noun object, and similarly absolute forms may be used for an indefinite object that is not referred to by a noun (4.24e), or only by a particle (4.24d). The same distinction is made between definite and indefinite obviative or inanimate subjects with animate objects, and less consistently (and apparently only in elicitation) for animate subjects with first and second person objects. Objectless TI verbs (TI-O; **§3.7f**) are only inflected with absolute forms in the independent indicative. AI+O and TA+O verbs are inflected for a definite secondary object; with an indefinite secondary object their inflection is exactly the same as for AI and TA verbs. (In the glosses of absolute forms the indefinite argument is parenthesized.)

§4.5. Independent Order Paradigms and Examples. The independent order inflections mark subject and primary object with the same three pronominal prefixes as possessed nouns (4.3) and endings that include maximally a theme sign (**§4.4d**), a central suffix (central ending), and a peripheral suffix (4.1). The central endings (4.19) fall into three sets, named for their distinctive formative elements: the M-ENDINGS have |-əhm| M.FMV in the first and second persons, and the W-ENDINGS and N-ENDINGS have |-w|w W.FMV and |-ən(ē)| N.FMV, respectively, throughout. The singular m-ending |-(əhm)| is overt only when irregularly fused with |-p(an-)| PRET (**§2.12k**). The suffix-initial |ə| in these endings is lost after a vowel.

The pronominal categories marked by the central endings are pluralized by suffixes resembling the pluralizers used for the possessors of nouns (4.3): |-∅| sg.; |-ən(ā(n-))| 1p,12 (i.e., |-ən|, |-ənā|, or |-ənān-|); and |-(ə)wā(w-)| 2p,3p (i.e., |-(ə)wā| or |-əwāw-|). The |ə| in these suffixes is absent after a vowel, and in the m-ending |-əhmwā| 2p after a consonant. The variant |-ən| 1p,12 is used in the n-ending if no suffix follows. The variants |-ənā| 1p,12 and |-(ə)wā| 2p,3p are used before a consonant (i.e., before |-p(an-)| PRET), and word-finally in the m-endings and w-endings. The variants |-ənān-| and |-əwāw-| are used before a vowel (when there is an overt peripheral suffix). The endings with |-ən(ē-)| have |-ən| word-finally or before a vowel, and |-ənē| before a consonant (i.e., before |-p(an-)| PRET).

The third person endings in the m-ending set are suppletive, being formed without |-əhm|; they have a central suffix |-w|m 3,0 and a peripheral suffix (4.1). For an indefinite subject (X) the m-ending uses the suffix of the n-endings. Some endings also include |-əlī| obv.; this marks the obviative subject of an intransitive, and in a few forms an obviative object.

(4.19) Independent order central endings

	m-endings	w-endings	n-endings
1s	|-(əhm)|	|-w|w	|-ən(ē)|
2s	|-(əhm)|	|-w|w	|-ən(ē)|
3s	(see 3,0)	|-w|w	|-ən(ē)|
X	|-ən(ē)|	|-w|w	|-ən(ē)|
1p	|-əhmənā|	|-wənā(n-)|	|-ənēn(ā(n)-)|
12	|-əhmənā|	|-wənā(n-)|	|-ənēn(ā(n)-)|
2p	|-əhmwā|	|-wəwā(w-)|	|-ənēwā(w-)|
3p	(see 3,0)	|-wəwā(w-)|	|-ənēwā(w-)|
3,0	|-w|m		

§4.5a. Independent Indicative. Given here are paradigms of the inflections for independent indicative verbs, with an analysis of their component morphemes and selected examples. (The realization of the pronominal prefixes with stems of different shapes is given in 2.54.) The independent indicative mode is used for the main-clause verb of declarative sentences and simple questions. It may also replace another mode used earlier in a sentence (e.g., Lk 13.28, Lk 16.13).

INTRANSITIVE VERBS mark their subjects with a combination of prefixes and suffixes. In (4.20) the inflections are given in underlying form along with paradigms constructed as examples. The inflected forms are either attested or based on those of other verbs; the sources for the less common ones are specified.

The first and second person prefixes are used as in possessed nouns, but there is no prefix in the third person forms. (Uniquely, |əlītēhā-| AI 'think {so}' elides the stem-initial |əl-| after a prefix [3.6j].) The suffixes are the m-ending set (4.19). The third person forms of both genders have an underlying suffix |-w|m that rarely appears on the surface (4.21cd). This is followed by one of the peripheral suffixes (4.1) and may be preceded by |-əlī| obv.

Before the underlying third person suffix |-w|m some stems in |a| (and |-a| TH.1 4.22) replace the |ā| by |ē| (2.24abc, 4.21co), and some stems in |ī| (and |-əlī| obv.) replace the |ī| by |ə| (2.24de; 4.21kl). The two classes of stems in |ā| are consistently distinguished, but a number of stems in |ī| are attested with both treatments (2.24f).

The first and second singular forms have the same ending, and the first plural exclusive and inclusive forms have the same ending. In the paradigms in (4.20) the inflections are given in full, but in some paradigms below, only the first singular and exclusive inflections are given.

(4.20) Independent indicative: AI and II inflections and constructed paradigms

		inflection	|pā-| AI 'come'	|wəm-| AI 'come from {smwh}'	|ankəl-| AI 'die'
AI	1s	|nə–Ø|	mpá	nó·m	ntánkəl
	2s	|kə–Ø|	kpá	kó·m	ktánkəl
	3s	|–w|	pé· (all sources), pé·w (B, V)	úm (B, V; |wəm|), wúm(?) (B ⟨owm⟩)	ánkəl

3´	|–əlǝwa|	pé·lǝwa (4.21e)		(taɔnkǝlə́lǝwa
	(older |–ǝlǝwal|),	(pé·lǝwal [4.21e]),		'(obv.) is lost' B)
	|–ǝlǝw|	pé·lu (B 2x)		
1p	|nǝ–ǝhmǝnā|	mpáhǝna	no·mhúmǝna	ntankǝlúhǝna
12	|kǝ–ǝhmǝnā|	kpáhǝna	ko·mhúmǝna	ktankǝlúhǝna
2p	|kǝ–ǝhmwā|	kpáhǝmɔ	ko·mhúmɔ	ktankǝlúhǝmɔ
3p	|–wak|	pé·ɔk (B)	mmó·k (cf. 2.67b)	ánkǝlo·k
X	|–ǝn|	(kə́ntka·n		(xé·lǝn, xahé·lǝn
		'there is a dance')		'people are many' B)

			|ahtē-| II 'be {smwh}'	|wǝlǝt-| II 'be good'
II	0s	|–w|	hát·e· (older hát·e·w B)	wǝlə́t
	0p	|–wa|	hat·é·ɔ (ND)	wǝlǝ́t·u (B 1834)
		(older |–wal|)		(ɔwǝ́lto·l [2.17c])
	0´s	|–ǝlǝw|	hat·é·lu (4.21f)	

Not given in (4.20) are third person inflections with absentative peripheral suffixes (3.9cdefgh).

   The examples in (4.21) show various details. Stems in |k| add |w| in the first and second singular (4.21a). Stems with the final |-(ī)xīn| AI 'lie, be' drop the |n| in the first and second singular (4.21b). The archaic word-final |w| of the third person singular forms is attested for both the AI (4.21c) and the II (4.21d). Although the obviative forms are rare, there are examples for both the AI (4.21e) and II (4.21f); an inanimate plural obviative is not attested.

(4.21) Independent indicative AI and II (examples)

    (a) llə́p·akw 'I'm weeping' (OA; |lǝpak-| AI); cf. lǝpákw 'he wept', pe·-lǝpák·ǝk 'he's weeping' (OA)

    (b) nšenkí·x·i 'I'm lying down' (OA, ME; |šenkīxīn-|); cf. šenkí·x·i·n 'he, she is lying down'

    (c) pé·w 'he comes' (B 2x, V; |pā-|); áhi-wǝli·t·é·he·w 'he was very good-hearted' (B; |àhī| PV 'very', |wǝlītēhā-| AI); ɔwǝlá·mǝwe·w 'he always told the truth' (B; |wawǝlāmǝwē-| AI); alǝ́mske·w 'he left' (B; |alǝmǝskā-| AI)

    (d) lé·w 'it happens {so}' (B, V; |ǝlē-| II); kšǝp·éhǝle·w 'it flows' (B; |kǝšǝpēhlā-| II)

    (e) kčí·lǝwa 'they (obv.) came out' (B; |kǝčī-| AI, also 4.21m); pa·lsí·lǝwal kkwí·s·al 'his son (obv.) was sick' (B; |pālǝsī-| AI)

    (f) wǝ́li-=á· -lé·lu 'it (obv.) would be safe' (B; |ǝlē-| II, 4.21d)

    (g) nne·máhǝna 'We (exc.) see.' (B; |nēmā-| AI)

    (h) nkǝkhite·lhúmǝna 'there's a whole lot of us (exc.)' (OA; |Rǝ+| REP, |kǝhtēl-| AI)

    (i) kkǝpčáhǝmɔ. 'You (pl.) are foolish.' (B; |kǝpǝčā-| AI)

    (j) kǝlǝpahkúhǝmɔ=č 'you (pl.) will weep' (B; |lǝpak-| AI; =č FUT)

    (k) wi·š·á·s·ǝwak 'they were afraid' (B; |wīšāsī-| AI)

    (l) salá·mǝwak 'they cried out' (B; |salāmwī-| AI)

    (m) kčí·ɔk 'they went out' (B; |kǝčī-| AI, 4.21e)

    (n) luwé·ɔk 'they said' (B, V, OA; |ǝlǝwē-| AI); kwi·kayó·yǝma luwé·ɔk, ... 'His parents said, ...' (Jn 9.20; honorary proximate [§3.4])

    (o) pé·ɔk 'they came, arrived' (B; |pā-| AI)

    (p) íka lilahtá·ɔk 'they went there by boat' (B; |ǝlīhlatā-| AI; also 3.13(1)c)

    (q) áhi-lǝpák·o·k 'they wept loudly' (B; áhi PV, 4.21c, |lǝpak-| AI, |–wak| 3p/IND; 2.16)

TRANSITIVE VERBS also mark their subjects with a combination of prefixes and suffixes (4.22). The absolute TA and TI paradigms have, in addition to the appropriate theme sign

(**§4.4d**), the same person-marking as the AI (4.20); there are no indefinite-subject forms. The objective TA and TI paradigms use the same three prefixes as in possessed nouns, but there is no prefix in the forms for indefinite subject. In the TA direct objective paradigm the w-endings are used, and in the TI objective the n-endings are used (4.19); the nominal categories of the objects are indicated by the peripheral suffixes (4.1). With the TA inverse theme sign the w-endings make objective forms with an animate subject, and the n-endings make objective forms for an inanimate subject, but the nominal categories of the subjects are indicated by peripheral suffixes. The |w| of the inverse theme sign |-əkw| combines irregularly with the |w| of the w-endings (4.19): it contracts to |ō| in the first plural ending and is elided in the other endings.

The objective inverse forms for an inanimate singular subject are identical to the inverse forms marking a definite secondary object or oblique (see below) and to the inverse forms of the subordinative mode (see the full paradigm in 4.48). The inverse theme sign is used with the m-endings for a non-definite subject, in principle of either gender, but outside of the forms with a third person object the evidence that forms with an absolute inflection could be used for a non-definite animate subject is slight and somewhat ambiguous. The sample paradigms here (4.23, 26) and below are constructed. (The 1s and 1p endings are used with |kə-| 2 for 2s and 12.)

(4.22) Independent indicative, TA direct (inflections)

	TA direct absolute	TA direct objective −3s	−3p	−3´
1s	|nə–ā|	|nə–āw|	|nə–āwak|	
3s	|–ēw|			|wə–āwal|, |wə–āwa|
1p	|nə–āhmənā|	|nə–āwənā|	|nə–āwənānak|, |nə–āwənānāk|	
2p	|kə–āhmwā|	|kə–āwəwā|	|kə–āwəwāwak|	
3p	|–ēwak|			|wə–āwəwāwal|, |wə–āwəwāwa|
X		|–āw|	|–āwak|	|–a·ləwa|

(4.23) Independent indicative, TA direct (constructed paradigm of |nōtəm-| TA 'guard')

	TA direct absolute	TA direct objective −3s	−3p	−3´
1s	nnó·t·əma	nnó·t·əma	nno·t·əmá·ɔk	
3s	nó·t·əme·			wəno·t·əmá·ɔ (wəno·t·əmá·ɔl)
1p	nno·t·əmáhəna	nno·t·əmá·wəna	nno·t·əma·wəná·nak, nno·t·əma·wəná·na·k	
2p	kəno·t·əmáhəmɔ	kəno·t·əmáwwa	kəno·t·əmawwá·ɔk	
3p	no·t·əmé·ɔk			wəno·t·əmawwá·ɔ (wəno·t·əmawwá·ɔl)
X		nó·t·əma·	no·t·əmá·ɔk	no·t·əmá·ləwa

Notes to (4.22) and (4.23): The theme sign |-ā| TH.1 is replaced by /e·/ before |-w|ₘ 3,0 of the m-endings but not before |-w|_w sg. of the w-endings (**§2.10h**, 2.24c). Word-final |-w| is lost with shortening of the preceding vowel in the objective ending |-āw| 1s,2s–3s (2.10b). In contrast, although the |-w| is lost in the endings |–ēw| 3s–(3´) (except in a few forms in Blanchard's early primers) and |–āw| X–3s, its loss leaves the preceding long vowel unaffected, as in the AI (2.10cd). The archaic obviative suffix |-al| (/-ɔl/) is only found in Blanchard. For the TA third person passive (indefinite-subject) singular AP used |-ān| (with an n-ending; 4.24p) instead of |-āw| (4.24m), and the corresponding negative |-āwən| was heard from ME. The peripheral suffix

/-aˑk/ anim. pl. in the first plural forms was used by OA and ME; other sources and speakers have /-ak/ (B, V, ND, LB). Some speakers have /wɔ́ˑ/ for /wáˑ/ before /ɔ/, as in possessed nouns (4.4-5; V, ND, LB, AP), and speakers who did not have this pronunciation usually assimilated the /ɔ/ of the word-final suffixes to /a/. Some speakers (V, AP) had /-áwwɔ/ 2p–3s for /-áwwa/. With stems in |aw|, |ēw|, |pw|, |mw|, and |hw| the |w| of the stem and a following /a/ or /aˑ/ assimilate to /ɔ/ or /ɔˑ/, respectively (2.22abcdef, 2.23ad).

(4.24) Independent indicative, TA direct (examples)
    Absolute
    (a) lə́nəwak nnéˑɔ 'I see men' (B) (|nēw-| TA 'see', |nə–ā| 1s–(3)/IND)
    (b) neˑéˑɔk skinnúwa 'they saw a young man (obv.)' (B) (|nēw-| TA 'see')
    (c) nkíˑskaeˑ télən lə́nəwa 'he met ten men (obv.)' (B) (|nakīskaw-| TA 'meet');
          aesə́sˑak kiˑkiˑšˑíˑkˑəneˑ 'he raised animals' (ME; prox. pl. for obv. [§3.4])
    (d) píˑli=áˑ kəməšˑənáhəna 'we might catch another one' (V; |məšən-| TA 'catch';
          píˑli P 'different, other'; =áˑ POT)
    (e) máta nhileˑíˑɔk 'they did not kill any' (B; |nəhl-| TA 'kill', |–ēwīwak| 3p–(3´)/IND.NEG)
    Objective
    (f) nnéˑɔ=č 'I will see him' (B) (|nēw-| TA 'see', |nə–āw| 1s–3s/IND)
    (g) kwiˑkˑeˑháˑɔ 'he cured them' (B) (|kīkēh-| TA 'cure')
    (h) mɔiˑmáˑɔl wəniˑčˑáˑnal 'she weeps for her children' (B) (|mawīm-| TA 'mourn')
    (i) noˑtxáˑwəna=č 'we will come to him or her' (B) (|wətax-| TA 'come to')
    (j) koˑwaˑháwwa 'you know him' (B) (|wəwāh-| TA 'know')
    (k) kɔtˑoˑnalawwáˑɔ 'they wanted to kill him' (B) (|katōnal-| TA 'want to kill')
    (l) wənatˑoˑnaɔwwáˑɔl 'they looked for him' (B; cf. 2.56c) (|natōnaw-| TA 'look for')
    (m) thwə́naˑ 'she was arrested' (B; |tahwən-| TA 'catch')
    (n) weˑkhwiksáˑɔk "they were all burnt up" (AP, referring to the Gnadenhütten massacre)
    (o) maxkaɔ́ˑləwa tɔləmóˑnsa 'his dog was found' (ME)
    (p) nhílaˑn "somebody killed him" (AP)

(4.25) Independent indicative, TA inverse (inflections)

	TA inverse absolute	TA inverse objective 3s–	3p–	3´–
1s	|nə–əkw|	|nə–əkw|	|nə–əkōk|	
3s	|–əkw|			|wə–əkōl|, |wə–əkō|, |wə–əkwa| (2.18)
3´	|–əkwələw|			
1p	|nə–əkwəhmənā|	|nə–əkōnā|	|nə–əkōnānak|, |nə–əkōnānāk|	
2p	|kə–əkwəhmwā|	|kə–əkəwā|	|kə–əkəwāwak|	
3p	|–əkōk|			|wə–əkəwāwal|, |wə–əkəwāwa|

(4.26) Independent indicative, TA inverse (|nōtəm-| TA 'guard'; |pōl-| TA 'escape from')

	TA inverse absolute	TA inverse objective 3s–	3p–	3´–
1s	nnóˑtˑəmukw	nnóˑtˑəmukw	nnoˑtˑəmúkˑoˑk mpóˑlkoˑk	
3s	nóˑtˑəmukw			wənoˑtˑəmúkˑu, wənoˑtˑəmúkˑɔ (wənoˑtˑəmúkˑoˑl) [→]

	[TA inverse	TA inverse objective	]
	[absolute	3–	3p–	3´–]
3´	no·t·əmúk·wəlu po·lkwə́lu		
1p	nno·t·əmukhúmənə mpo·lkúhəna	nno·t·əmuk·ó·na mpo·lkó·na	nno·t·əmuk·o·ná·na(·)k mpo·lko·ná·na(·)k
2p	kəno·t·əmukhúmɔ kpo·lkúhəmɔ	kəno·t·əmúk·əwa kpo·lkúwa	kəno·t·əmuk·əwá·ɔk kpo·lkəwá·ɔk
3p	no·t·əmúk·o·k		wəno·t·əmuk·əwá·ɔ (wəno·t·əmuk·əwá·ɔl)

Notes to (4.25) and (4.26): The variation in the plural and obviative suffixes can be assumed to be as in the direct suffixes (4.22, 4.23), though not every variant is attested for every form. For the variation in the 3´–3s endings see (2.18). The |ə| of |-əkw| TH.2 contracts with a stem-final |aw| to |ā| (**§2.10e**); it contracts with a stem-final |əw| or post-consonantal |w| to |ō| (**§2.10cg**). The |w| of |-əkw| TH.2 is lost before underlying |ə| in a rounding environment (before phonemic /u/, /hu/, or /əw/) either in the underlying form or at the phonemic level. Phonemic /u/ for retained |ə| was generalized in |-əkw| TH.2 (2.27), but note (2.27i, 4.27s). The |ō| of |-əkōnā(n-)| in the first plural endings is presumably due to a virtual |-əkw-ə-wənā(n-)|, with the |w| of the w-ending.

(4.27) Independent indicative, TA inverse (examples)

Absolute (with animate and inanimate subjects)
- (a) mpəntškinkwého·kw kéku 'something stuck me in the eye' (OA; |pəntəškīnkwehw-| TA)
- (b) wəlankuntəwá·k·an ktap·í·ta·kw 'peace is with you (sg.)' (B; |apīhtaw-| TA)
- (c) máxkɔ nhílukw 'a bear or some bears killed him' (Goddard 1979:159; |nəhl-| TA)
- (d) manət·uwwá·k·an ahpí·ta·kw 'a power is in him' (B; cf. b)
- (e) wəla·te·naməwá·k·an məši·ká·k·wəlu e·lanko·má·č·i
     'gladness comes over his relatives (obv.)' (ME; |məšəhkaw-| TA)
- (f) wəla·te·naməwá·k·an nəməshika·khúməna 'happiness comes over us (exc.)' (ME; cf. e)
- (g) enkələlí·t·əp tóxko·k 'one who had died (obv.) comes to them' (B; cf. 4.24i)
- (h) wi·š·a·s·əwá·k·an tóxko·k 'fear came upon them' (B; cf. 4.24i)

Objective (with animate subjects)
- (i) no·txúk·o·k 'they come to me' (B; cf. g)
- (j) kəwenčí·mukw 'he is calling for you (sg.) to come' (B; |wēnčīm-| TA)
- (k) o·txúk·u 'he (obv.) came to him; they (obv.) came to him' (B; cf. g)
- (l) awé·n nəmaxka·k·ó·na 'someone found us (exc.)' (OA, similarly ME; |maxkaw-| TA)
- (m) nšinka·lko·ná·nak 'they hate us (exc.)' (B; |šinkāl-| TA)
- (n) ktahɔ·lkó·na 'he loves us (inc.)' (B; |àhwāl-| TA)
- (o) kəwi·č·i·k·e·mkúwa awé·n 'someone lives among you (pl.)' (B; |wīčīkēm-| TA)
- (p) ksak·a·kwənúk·əwa=č 'he will lead you (pl.)' (B ⟨ksukaqwnwkwuh⟩; |sakāhkwən-| TA)
- (q) palí·i·č ktəlska·k·əwá·ok 'they will drive you away' (B; |ələskaw-| TA)
- (r) wtətpi·ta·k·əwá·ɔ 'he (obv.) made signs to them' (B; |tə̀təpīhtaw-| TA)
- (s) o·t·ənək·əwó·ɔ 'it (obv.) dragged them' (WL recording; |wətən-| TA)

Objective (with inanimate subjects)
- (t) nča·ɔ·k·ənúk·wən 'it made me cry' (OA; |čāwākən-| 'make cry')
- (u) no·lhálkwən "I am kept by it" (Voegelin 1946:150; |wəlahl-| TA 'keep')
- (v) mɔnt·uwwá·k·an ntap·i·tá·k·o·n 'his spiritual power is in me' (B; cf. b)
- (w) kəna·ka·t·amwe·ɔ́·k·an kkəč·o·há·lko·n 'Your faith has saved you.' (B; |kəčōhāl-| TA 'save')

(x) wé·mi awé·n mwəshiká·k·wən ní kəmant·uwwá·k·an 'your spiritual power benefits everyone' (ME; |məšəhkaw-| TA 'benefit; infect')

(y) wənək·alúk·o·n pɔ·lsəwá·k·an 'the illness left him' (B; |nəkal-| TA 'leave')

(z) nanáli né·l wəni·skha·lkó·na awé·n. 'Those are the things that defile a person.' (B; |nīskahāl-| TA 'defile')

(aa) mo·šə́š·a kkwi·tələt·əwá·k·an ntəlkó·ne·n 'Moses's law tells us' (B; |əl-| TA 'say {so} to')

(bb) čɔ·ɔ·k·ənuk·wəné·ɔ 'it made them cry' (OA; cf. t)

(cc) namé·s·ak tɔhwənuk·o·né·ɔ 'it (a net) caught fish' (B; |tahwən-| TA 'catch')

Passives for the first and second person (indefinite-subject forms with a first or second person object) are made with the theme sign |-əkē| TH.2.PS followed by an m-ending.

(4.28) Independent indicative, TA first and second person passive (inflections and forms)

	inflections	forms (|nakal-| TA 'leave behind')
1s	|nə–əkē|	nnak·alə́k·e 'I was left behind'
2s	|kə–əkē|	kənak·alə́k·e 'you (sg.) were left behind'
1p	|nə–əkēhnā| < |–əkē-hmənā|	nnak·alək·éhəna 'we (exc.) were left behind'
12	|kə–əkēhnā| < |–əkē-hmənā|	kənak·alək·éhəna 'we (inc.) were left behind' (ME)
2p	|kə–əkēhmwā|	kənak·alək·éhəmɔ 'you (pl.) were left behind'

(4.29) Independent indicative, TA first and second person passive (examples)

(a) mpe·t·alo·ká·lke 'I was sent here' (B; |pētalōhkāl-| TA 'send hither')

(b) nəmaxká·k·e 'I was found' (AP; |maxkaw-| TA 'find')

(c) mpe·š·ó·k·e 'I was brought' (ME; |pēšəw-| TA 'bring')

(d) ktələwílke=č 'you (sg.) will be called (so)' (B; |ələwīhl-| TA 'name {so}')

(e) nsiho·k·éhəna 'we (exc.) lost, we were beaten' (ME; |sihw-| TA 'defeat')

(f) palí·i ktəlska·k·éhəmɔ 'you (pl.) are driven away' (B; |ələskaw-| TA 'drive {so}')

In the TA paradigms for action between a first person and a second person, the theme sign indicates the person of the object (**§4.4d**), and the central suffix is an m-ending (4.19) that may pluralize either argument. A first person, whether subject or object, is pluralized by |-hmənā|, and a second person, whether subject or object, is pluralized by |-hmwā|, as long as the first person is not plural. The singular m-ending |-(hm)| is used if both subject and object are singular. The pronominal prefix, which does not convey any additional information, is |kə-| 2 in all forms.

(4.30) Independent indicative, TA theme 3 and theme 4 (inflections)

	TA theme 3		TA theme 4
2s–1s	|kə–ī|	1s–2s	|kə–əl|
2p–1s	|kə–īhmwā|	1s–2p	|kə–ələhmwā|
2–1p	|kə–īhmənā|	1p–2	|kə–ələhmənā|
	(always as if |kə–īhnā|)		

(4.31) Independent indicative, TA theme 3 (paradigm of |wīčəm-| TA 'help')

2s–1s kəwí·č·əmi 'you (sg.) help me'
2p–1s kəwi·č·əmíhəmɔ 'you (pl.) help me'
2–1p   kəwi·č·əmíhəna 'you (sg., pl.) help us'

(4.32) Independent indicative, TA theme 4 (paradigms of |wīčəm-| TA 'help'; |maxkaw-| TA 'find'; |nēw-| TA 'see')

1s–2s kəwí·č·əməl 'I helped you (sg.)'
       kəmáxko·l 'I found you (sg.)'
       kəné·wəl 'I see you (sg.)'

[continued →]

[4.32, continued]
- 1s–2p kəwi·č·əməlhúmɔ 'I helped you (pl.)'
  - kəmaxko·lhúmɔ 'I found you (pl.)'
  - kəne·wəlúhəmɔ 'I see you (pl.)'
- 1p–2 kəwi·č·əməlhúmənα 'we helped you (sg., pl.)'
  - kəmaxko·lhúmənα 'we found you (sg., pl.)'
  - kəne·wəlúhənα 'we saw you (sg., pl.)'

(4.33) Independent indicative, TA theme 3 and theme 4 (examples)
- 2s–1s kəné·i=á· 'you (sg.) should see me' (OA; |nēw-| TA 'see')
- 2p–1s kəne·íhəmɔ 'you (pl.) see me' (B)
  - ktahɔ·líhəmɔ 'you (pl.) love me' (B; |àhwāl-| TA 'love')
- 2–1p kəne·íhənα 'you see us' (OA)
- 1s–2s kəné·wəl 'I saw you (sg.)' (B, OA, ME)
  - ko·lhálal 'I keep you' (V; |wəlahl-| TA 'keep')
  - kəmi·kəmɔ·s·əntamo·l 'I worked for you (sg.)' (B; |mīhkəmwāsəntamaw-| TA)
- 1s–2p ko·lhallúhəmɔ and ko·lhaləlhúmɔ 'I keep you (pl.)' (ME)
  - kpənuntələlhúmɔ 'I showed you (pl.)' (B; |pənōntəl-| TA 'show (to)')
  - kpi·p·i·no·lhúmɔ 'I choose you (pl.)' (B; |pīpīnaw-| TA 'choose')
- 1p–2 kəne·wəlúhənα 'we see you (sg., pl.)' (OA)
  - kši·e·ləmɔlhúmənα 'we grieved for you (pl.)' (B; |šīwēləm-| TA 'grieve for')
  - ktap·i·k·o·lhúmənα 'we played music for you (pl.)' (B; |apīkwaw-| TA 'play for')

Transitive inanimate (TI) verbs fall into four formal classes defined by their theme signs (3.20). Class 1a (TI(1a)) has the theme sign |-am| TH.TI(1A); Class 1b (TI(1b)) has |-əm| TH.TI(1B); Class 2 (TI(2)) has |-aw| TH.TI(2) (varying with |-ō| in the independent order, and in one combination |ā..w|); and Class 3 (TI(3)) has no theme sign and adds endings to stems that resemble AI stems. The absolute forms have m-endings, and the objective forms have n-endings followed by peripheral suffixes, which distinguish the number of the object in some cases. Absolute forms are used with indefinite (non-definite) objects and on objectless TI verbs (TI-O).

(4.34) Independent indicative TI absolute (inflections)

	TI(1a)	TI(1b)	TI(2)	TI(3)
1s	|nə–am|	|nə–əm|	|nə–ō|	|nə–|
2s	|kə–am|	|kə–əm|	|kə–ō|	|kə–|
3s	|–amw|	|–əmw|	|–ūw|	|–w|
1p	|nə–aməhmənā|	|nə–əməhmənā|	|nə–ōhnā| < |–ō-hmənā|	|nə–əhmənā|
12	|kə–aməhmənā|	|kə–əməhmənā|	|kə–ōhnā| < |–ō-hmənā|	|kə–əhmənā|
2p	|kə–aməhmwā|	|kə–əməhmwā|	|kə–ōhmwā|	|kə–əhmwā|
3p	|–amōk|	|–əmōk|	|–ōwak|	|–wak|, |–ōk|

The plural endings vary as in the AI (4.20). The TI(1a) and TI(1b) endings for first and second plural have /-múhənα/ or /-mhúmənα/ 1p,12 and /-múhəmɔ/ or /-mhúmɔ/ 2p. The TI(2) endings are always /-úhənα/ 1p,12 and /-úhəmɔ/ 2p.

(4.35) Independent indicative TI absolute (constructed paradigms of |pən-| TI(1a) 'look at'; |məšən-| TI(1b) 'get'; |pēt-| TI(2) 'bring'; |mīčī-| TI(3) 'eat'; |nēm-| TI(3) 'see')

	TI(1a)	TI(1b)	TI(2)	TI(3)	
1s	mpə́nam	nəmə́š·ənəm	mpé·t·u	nəmí·č·i	nné·m
2s	kpə́nam	kəmə́š·ənəm	kpé·t·u	kəmí·č·i	kəné·m
3s	pənám	məšə́nəm	pé·t·o·	mí·č·u	né·m

	[TI(1a)	TI(1b)	TI(2)	TI(3)	]
1p	mpənamúhəna	nəməš·ənəmhúməna	mpe·t·úhəna	nəmi·č·íhəna	nne·mhúməna
12	kpənamúhəna	kəməš·ənəmhúməna	kpe·t·úhəna	kəmi·č·íhəna	kəne·mhúməna
2p	kpənamúhəmɔ	kəməš·ənəmhúmɔ	kpe·t·úhəmɔ	kəmi·č·íhəmɔ	kəne·mhúmɔ
3p	pənámo·k	məšánəmo·k	pe·t·ó·wak	mí·č·əwak	né·mo·k

(4.36) Independent indicative TI objective with singular object (inflections)

	TI(1a)	TI(1b)	TI(2)	TI(3)
1s	|nə–amən(ē-)|	|nə–əmən(ē-)|	|nə–ōn(ē-)|	|nə–ən(ē-)|
2s	|kə–amən(ē-)|	|kə–əmən(ē-)|	|kə–ōn(ē-)|	|kə–ən(ē-)|
3s	|wə–amən(ē-)|	|wə–əmən(ē-)|	|wə–ōn(ē-)|	|wə–ən(ē-)|
3´	|wə–amətlīn(ē-)|	|wə–əmətlīn(ē-)|	|wə–ōlīn(ē-)|	|wə–əlīn(ē-)|
1p	|nə–amənēn(ā(n)-)|	|nə–əmənēn(ā(n)-)|	|nə–ōnēn(ā(n)-)|	|nə–ənēn(ā(n)-)|
12	|kə–amənēn(ā(n)-)|	|kə–əmənēn(ā(n)-)|	|kə–ōnēn(ā(n)-)|	|kə–ənēn(ā(n)-)|
2p	|kə–amənēwā(w-)|	|kə–əmənēwā(w-)|	|kə–ōnēwā(w-)|	|kə–ənēwā(w-)|
3p	|wə–amənēwā(w-)|	|wə–əmənēwā(w-)|	|wə–ōnēwā(w-)|	|wə–ənēwā(w-)|
X	|–amən(ē-)|	|–əmən(ē-)|	|–ōn(ē-)	|–ən(ē-)|

The corresponding inflections for plural object have |-na| (preterite |-nēpanī|) instead of |-n(ē-)|; |-nānī| instead of |-n(ā(n)-); and |-wāwī| instead of |-wā(w-)|. In the twentieth century only WL (V), ME, and SP could distinguish plural from singular objects with a first plural subject, though this was optional and perhaps not spontaneous (4.39qr). No speaker could specify a plural inanimate object with a second or third plural subject, but this inflection is attested in Blanchard both for a TI(1b) (4.39x) and for plural secondary objects (4.40kl). The variants ending with |-ē-| and |-ā(-)| in (4.36) are used before |-p(an-)| PRET (**§4.7**).

(4.37) Independent indicative TI objective, singular object (constructed paradigms: |pən-| TI(1a) 'look at'; məšən-| TI(1b) 'get'; |pēt-| TI(2) 'bring'; |mīčī-| TI(3) 'eat'; |nēm-| TI(3) 'see')

	TI(1a)	TI(1b)	TI(2)	TI(3)	
1s	mpánamən	nəməš·ənámən	mpé·t·o·n	nəmí·č·i·n	nné·mən
2s	kpánamən	kəməš·ənámən	kpé·t·o·n	kəmí·č·i·n	kəné·mən
3s	pwánamən	mwəš·ənámən	pwé·t·o·n	mwí·č·i·n	wəné·mən
3´	pwanamáli·n	mwəš·ənəmáli·n	pwe·t·ó·li·n	mwi·č·í·li·n	wəné·məli·n
1p	mpənamáne·n	nəməš·ənəmáne·n	mpe·t·óne·n	nəmi·č·í·ne·n	nné·məne·n
12	kpənamáne·n	kəməš·ənəmáne·n	kpe·t·óne·n	kəmi·č·í·ne·n	kəné·məne·n
2p	kpənaməné·ɔ	kəməš·ənəməné·ɔ	kpe·t·o·né·ɔ	kəmi·č·i·né·ɔ	kəne·məné·ɔ
3p	pwənaməné·ɔ	mwəš·ənəməné·ɔ	pwe·t·o·né·ɔ	mwi·č·i·né·ɔ	wəne·məné·ɔ
X	pənámən	məšánəmən	pé·t·o·n	mí·č·i·n	né·mən

(4.38) Independent indicative TI absolute (examples)

(a) tántay nkat·á·t·am. 'I want fire.' (Voegelin 1945:105; |katāt-| TI(1a) 'desire')

(b) ní·=tá, nčú, nná·t·əm tántay '*I'm* going after fire, my friend.' (Voegelin 1945:105; |nāt-| TI(1b) 'go after, go to get')

(c) wəlankuntəwá·k·an=ét mpé·t·u 'I must be bringing peace' (B; |pēt-| TI(2) 'bring')

(d) kéku=tá nné·m 'I saw something' (B 1834b, 1842; |nēm-| TI(3) 'see')

(e) té·hi·m nəmí·č·i 'I ate strawberries' (V; |mīčī-| TI(3) 'eat')

(f) kéku=háč kənat·ó·nam? 'What are you (sg.) looking for?' (B; |natōn-| 'seek')

(g) ko·le·lántam=č 'you (sg.) will be glad' (B; |wəlēlənt-| TI(1a)-O 'be glad')

(h) áhi-=č -lí·nam 'bad things will happen to him' (B; |əlīn-| TI(1a)-O 'experience {so}')

(i) íka pé·t·o· mpí·s·o·n 'he brought medicine there' (B; cf. c)

(j) té·hi·m mí·č·u 'he ate strawberries' (V; cf. e)
(k) nkánši-li·namúhəna. 'We (exc.) had a miraculous experience.' (B; cf. h)
(l) té·hi·m nəmi·č·íhəna 'we (exc.) ate strawberries' (V; cf. e)
(m) nkát·a-ne·mhúməna kéku 'we (exc.) would like to see something' (B; cf. d)
(n) kéku kənat·o·namúhəmɔ? 'What are you (pl.) seeking?' (B; cf. f)
(o) šúkw=č kəməš·ənəmhúmɔ aləwí·i-ləs·əwá·k·an 'but you (pl.) shall receive power' (B; |məšən-| TI(1b) 'get, receive')
(p) mái-mhálamo·k mi·č·əwá·k·an 'they went to buy food' (B; |mahl-| TI(1a) 'buy')
(q) kanše·ləntamo·k 'they were astonished' (B; |kanšēlənt-| TI(1a)-O 'be astonished')
(r) té·hi·m mí·č·əwak 'they ate strawberries' (V; cf. e)
(s) né·mo·k kéku 'they see things' (OA; cf. d)

(4.39) Independent indicative TI objective (examples)
(a) mé·či nəmáxkamən 'I have now found it' (B; |maxk-| TI(1a) 'find')
(b) wé·mi kéku nnihəlá·t·amən 'I am lord over (lit., I own) everything' (B; |nīhlāt-| TI(1a) 'own')
(c) nəwe·t·ənəmə́na 'I picked them (inan.) up' (OA; |wētən-| TI(1b) 'take, pick up')
(d) nəwe·t·ənəmə́na né·l ahsə́na 'I picked up the stones' (OA; cf. c)
(e) ní· né·l hítami nné·məna '*I* saw them first' (ME; cf. 4.38d)
(f) kəmáxkamən=č 'you (sg.) shall find it' (B; cf. a)
(g) mɔ́xkamən=č 'he will find it' (B; cf. a)
(h) ppɔ·khitéhəmən nə́ hákhakw 'she broke the bottle' (B; |pwahkəhteh-| TI(1a) 'break or crack (open) by hitting'; for /ə/ from |a| cf. 2.3f)
(i) pɔ·tá·to·n=č mé·x·e·k təntay 'he will earn the great fire' (B; |pāhtāht-| TI(2) 'earn')
(j) wči·skhámənа 'she wiped them (inan.)' (B; |čīskah-| TI(1a) 'wipe')
(k) kwəš·i·xtó·na nsí·t·a 'she washed my feet' (B; |kəsīxət-| TI(2) 'wash')
(l) mwí·č·i·n 'he ate it' (B, V, ME; cf. 4.38e)
(m) mwí·č·i·n nə́ mpí·s·o·n 'he ate that peyote' (OA; cf. 4.38e)
(n) áhi kwəlsət·amə́li·n tɔ·pto·ná·k·an 'she (obv.) listened intently to his talk' (B; cf. v)
(o) kɔ́t·a-wwa·tó·li·n e·lsíhti·t. 'He (obv.) wanted to know what they (prox.) had done.' (B; |kata| PV 'want to', |wəwāht-| TI(2) 'know'; |ələsī-| AI 'do {so}', |IC–hətīt| 3p(OBL))
(p) wé·mi kéku nnəkahtəmə́ne·n 'we left everything' (B; |nəkat-| TI(1b))
(q) nəmaxkamə́ne·n né·l ahsə́na 'we (exc.) found the stones' (ME; cf. a)
(r) nəmaxkamənе ná ni né·l ahsə́na 'we (exc.) found the stones' (ME; cf. a)
(s) no·wa·tó·ne·n 'we (exc.) know it' (B; cf. o)
(t) kəmaxkaməné·ɔ=č 'you (pl.) shall find it' (B; cf. a)
(u) wé·mi=č yó·l kəməš·ənəməné·ɔ. 'You (pl.) shall obtain all these things.' (B; cf. 4.38o)
(v) nə́ni-á· kwəlsət·aməné·ɔ. 'They should listen to *that*.' (B; |kələsət-| TI(1a) 'listen to')
(w) kwənnəməné·ɔ nə́ mpí·s·o·n 'they carried the medicine' (B; |kələn-| TI(1b) 'hold, carry')
(x) wwe·t·ənəməne·ɔ́·i né·l mɔ́nia 'they took those coins' (B; cf. c)
(y) wiwši·ləntamən 'people marry' (B; |Rih+| HAB, |wəsīlənt-| TI(1a)-O 'get married')
(z) mé·či ki·š·í·to·n. 'Now it is finished.' (B; |kīšīht-| TI(2) 'complete making, finish')

In the independent indicative a definite secondary object is indicated on AI+O and TA+O verbs (**§3.7f**; 4.40-41). The object may be a subordinate clause in the subordinative mode (4.40rs). The subject (or inverse object) is marked by an n-ending (4.19), and a plural or obviative object (or inverse subject) may be marked by a peripheral suffix, though an overt peripheral suffix is rarely used after a plural n-ending. The prefixes are as in the TA and TI objective (4.22, 25, 28, 30, 36). After the singular n-ending the peripheral suffixes are |-ak| (B) or |-āk| (V, OA, ME) anim. pl. (cf. the variation after /-ənān-/ 1p,12 in possessed nouns [**§4.2a**]) and |-a| obv. (sg. and pl.) and inan. pl.; after the plural n-endings the suffixes are |-īk| anim. pl. and |-ī| obv. (sg. and pl.) and inan. pl.

The inflection that indicates a definite inanimate singular secondary object is also used to show agreement with the definite oblique complement of an independent indicative verb that contains, or is construed with, a relative root or virtual relative root (**§3.7b**). The oblique complement is most often the inanimate singular demonstrative pronoun nə́ (ní, nə́ni) 'that (inan.)' or the interrogative pronoun tá WH used for content questions ('what?', 'when?', 'where?', 'why?', 'which?', 'how long?', 'how?', and 'how many?'; 4.42fgjowy, 4.44ce); tá WH is always followed by =háč Q (later also =héč and reduced forms). The demonstrative may be used by itself in this construction (4.42lm), but it usually appears after the empty support particle ná PRES; the demonstrative cliticizes to this (as ná=ni or ná=nə) but may be separated by an enclitic (e.g., =č FUT, =máh PST, =tá FOC) or a semantically weak particle (e.g., ɔ́·k 'and', yúkwe 'now' as an intensifier). Although ná is glossed 'presentational' and ná=nə (ná=ni) is often best translated as the Given term of an equational sentence, ná=nə is sometimes simply a reinforced and hence slightly emphatic demonstrative (as translated in 4.42akpqu), and some cases clearly cannot involve an equational sentence: ɔ́·k ná=nə ləs·í·t·e 'and if that is what he does' (B; *lit.*, 'and if he does *that*'). The oblique may also be a participle having an appropriate relative root as its head (4.42s). The inflection used for the oblique complement of a relative root may also mark a definite verbal adjunct (in the observed cases a standard of comparison; 4.45) or an instrumental oblique (3.14c)

Less commonly, tá WH is the complement of a verb without an n-ending; tá=háč ktá? 'Where are you going?' (B; cf. 4.42g).

There is some systematic variation in the use of the suffixes |-ən(ē)| (singular and indefinite; 4.19) and |-ənēwā(w-)| (second and third plural) outside of these canonical functions that they have in the TI objective paradigm of the independent indicative (4.36-37). In the independent indicative AI+O and TA+O forms having an objective peripheral argument (4.40-41) and those marking a definite oblique (4.42-44), as well as in the subordinative paradigms (**§4.5b**), the plural suffix |-ənēwā(w-)| can be used to indicate the equivalent of a third plural peripheral argument with a first singular or indefinite subject (or inverse object). Conversely, the singular suffix |-ən(ē)| is sometimes used also for a third plural. In Blanchard, inverse forms with n-endings always have contraction of |-əkw-ən(ē-)| to |-əkōn(ē-)|, but speakers in the 1960's had contraction to |-əkōn(ē-)| only in the first plural and (in some cases) before |-a| inan. pl.

With an indefinite subject (X) there is no absolute form, and AI+O and TA+O verbs can be inflected for any plural secondary object, though the plural suffix appears to be optional (4.40n).

(4.40) AI+O with definite secondary object (examples)
    (a) nəwáni·n 'I forgot it' (ME, ND, LB; |wanī-| AI+O 'forget'); cf. nɔ́ni·n 'I forgot it' (OA)
    (b) nəwaní·na·k 'I forgot them (anim.)' (ME)
    (c) nəwaní·na (né·l) 'I forgot them (inan.)' (ME)
    (d) wwaní·na 'he forgot him, them (obv.), them (inan.)' (ME)
    (e) nəwaní·ne·n 'we forgot him, them' (ME)
    (f) kəwani·né·ɔ 'you (pl.) forgot him, it, them' (ME)
    (g) ki·ló·wa=á· wəláha kkəš·í·xta·ɔhti·ne·ɔ́·i. '*You* ought better to wash them (feet, inan.) for each other.' (B; |kəšīxətāwatī-| AI+O 'wash O2 for each other', |kə–nēwāwī| 2p+0p)
    (h) wwani·né·ɔ 'they forgot him, them (obv.), it, them (inan.)' (B, ME)

(i) o·lana·ke·né·ɔ ehahkwihtí·č·i 'they spread their clothing on the ground' (B; |wəlanāhkē-| AI+O 'spread as a mat'; |Rih+| HAB, |akwī-| AI+O 'wear', |IC–hətīčī| 3p/PPL(INpl))

(j) mwe·k·əne·ɔ́·i=č 'they shall hand him (obv.) over' (B; |mēk-| AI+O 'give (away)')

(k) kkwəskuwale·whe·ne·ɔ́·i 'they put heavy loads on their (obv.) backs' (B; |kwəsəkəwalēwahē-| AI+O 'make O2 carry a heavy load on the back')

(l) o·lana·ke·ne·ɔ́·i 'they spread them (small branches, inan.) on the ground' (B; cf. i)

(m) mí·lti·n 'it was given away' (ME; |mīlətī-| AI)

(n) mi·ltí·na (or mí·lti·n) ahkwí·ana 'blankets (inan.) were given away' (ME; cf. m)

(o) tipá·s·ak mi·ltí·na·k 'chickens (anim.) were given away' (ME; cf. m)

(p) wəlana·ké·na·k xé·s·ak. 'Hides (anim.) were spread as mats.' (ME; cf. i)

(q) hákink=č lanihí·nak 'they (anim.) will be thrown down' (B; |əlanihī-| AI+O 'throw {so}, to {smwh}')

(r) nɔxpí·k·i·n kɔk·e·p·ínkɔ·n 'he was born blind' (B; |naxpīkī-| AI+O 'be born with O2', |wə–ən| 3s+0s; for the second verb see 4.49p)

(s) ɔ́·k·á· nəmi·x·anɔ́s·i·n nəwihí·nəwe·n. 'And I would be ashamed of begging.' (B; |mīxanəsī-| AI(+O) 'be ashamed (of O2)', |nə–ən| 1s+0s; for second verb see 4.49c)

(4.41) TA+O with definite secondary object (examples)

(a) nəmí·la·n 'I gave it to him, them' (B, ME; |mīl-| TA+O 'give O2 to')

(b) nəmi·lá·na 'I gave him (obv.), them (inan.) to him' (OA)

(c) nəmi·la·né·ɔ né·l a·pto·ná·k·anal 'I gave them the words' (B)

(d) nəmi·lkó·na 'he gave (obv.) to me' (OA)

(e) mpe·t·a·k·o·né·ɔ khák·ay 'they brought you (sg.) to me' (B; |pētaw-| TA+O 'bring O2 to')

(f) nkəmo·t·əmuk·o·ne·ná·ni 'they stole him (obv.) from us (exc.)' (B; |kəmōtəm-| TA+O 'steal O2 from')

(g) kəmi·lí·na·k=á· 'you ought to give them (anim.) to me' (OA)

(h) kəmi·lí·ne·n=á· 'you ought to give him, it, them (anim., inan.) to us' (OA)

(i) kəmíllən=č 'I will give it to you (sg.)' (B)

(j) kəmilləné·ɔ 'I give it to you (pl.)' (B)

(k) kəmillána·k 'I gave them (anim.) to you (sg.)' (OA)

(l) nəmí·lke·n 'it is given to me' (V ms.) (cf. móni nəmí·lke 'I get paid money' V ms.)

(m) nəmahəlama·k·é·na 'I sell them (inan.)' (V ms.; lit., 'they are bought from me'; |mahlamaw-| TA+O 'buy O2 from')

(n) mhalamáɔ·n 'he sold it' (V; lit., 'it was bought from him'; cf. m)

(o) mi·la·né·ɔ=č pəma·wsəwá·k·an 'life shall be given to them' (B; verb also V)

(4.42) AI and II with definite oblique (examples)

(a) ná=nə ntəli·kí·spwi·n 'I got full on it' (OA; |əlī| PV '{so}', |kīsəpwī-| AI 'be full')

(b) alɔ́·t ná=nə núnči·pá·n. 'Yet that is the very reason why I came.' (B; |wənčī| PV 'from {smwh}', |pā-| AI 'come')

(c) ná=nə ntəlsi·n. 'That's what I am.' (B; |ələsī-| AI 'be {so}, do {so}')

(d) ná=tá=nə ntəle·ləmúkwsi·n ní·, .. 'That's how I was created to be, ..' (ME; |ələləməkwəsī-| AI 'be created so')

(e) mé·či ná=ni ntəntxi- kéku -lúwe·n. 'Now that's all I have to say.' (ME; |(ən)taxī| PV '{so much}', |ələwē-| AI 'say {so}'; kéku 'something')

(f) tá=háč kəwí·k·i·n? 'where do you live?' (B; |wīkī-| AI 'dwell {smwh}')

(g) tá=háč ktá·n? 'Where are you going? Where did you go?' (ME; |ā-| AI 'go to {smwh}')

(h) ná=nə tɔllaehɔ́·s·i·n 'that's the way he acted' (OA; |àyəlaehwāsī-| 'act {so}' < |Ra+| PL, |əlaehwāsī-| 'do {so}' AI)
(i) ná=nə tɔ́·n 'that's where he went' (OA; cf. g)
(j) tá=háč tɔ́·n kí·t·i·s? 'Where is your friend going?' (B 1834a; cf. g)
(k) ná=nə tí·ha·n 'he always goes over there' (OA; |Rīh+| HAB, |ā-| AI 'go to {smwh}')
(l) lɔ́·məwe nə́ tí·a·n 'he went there long ago' (OA; |Rī+| EXT, |ā-| AI 'go to {smwh}')
(m) á·pči=č nə́ tɔ́p·i·n. 'he will stay there always' (B; |apī-| AI 'be {smwh}')
(n) ná·máh=nə tíhahpi·n 'he used to stay there' (OA; |Rih+| HAB, |apī-| AI 'be {smwh}')
(o) tá=háč wtəlsi·n=č ná mi·mə́ntət? 'What will that child do?' (B; cf. c)
(p) ná=nə mɔi·k·e·n. 'and there he spent the night.' (B; |mawīkē-| AI 'spend night {smwh}')
(q) ná=nə tə́nta-pá·tama·n. 'There he prayed.' (B; |talī|, |(-ən)ta| PV '{smwh}', |pāhtamā-| AI 'pray')
(r) ná=nə wwənčí·ai·n 'that's where he belongs' (OA; |wənčīyayī-| AI 'be from {smwh}, belong {smwh}')
(s) má·wsu e·lhukwe·x·i·nəlí·t·əp wələmahtáp·i·n 'one sat where his (obv.) head had lain' (B; |ələhkwēxīn-| AI 'lie with head {so}'; |ləmatapī-| AI 'sit {there}')
(t) ná=tá nə́ní ktəli-=č -naxkuntí·ne·n 'That's the way we'll agree ..' (ME; |əlī| PV '{so}', |naxkōntī- AI 'agree with each other')
(u) ná=nə pwəminni·né·ɔ 'And they stayed there.' (B; |pəmīlənī-| AI 'be staying {smwh}')
(w) tá=héč tɔllí·ksi·n né·k ma·nšá·p·iak? 'What color are those beads?' (OA; |àyələhkəsī-| < |Ra+| PL, |ələhkəsī-| 'be {such} (bright) color' AI)
(x) ná=tá=nə lé·. 'That's just what happened.' (WL; |əlē-| II 'be {so}, happen {so}')
(y) tá=háč txí ahpɔ́·na hát·e·? 'How many loaves of bread are there?' (B; |ahtē-| II 'exist')

(4.43) TA with definite oblique (examples)
(a) ná=nə ntəlí·ha·n 'that's what I did to him' (OA; |əlīh-| TA 'do {so} to')
(b) ná ɔ́·k nə́ né·pe ntəlkí·kwi-=č -pəma·wso·há·la·n awé·n ... 'In that same powerful way also I, too, shall give life to someone ...' (B; |ələkihkwī| PV 'to {such} an extent', |pəmāwəsōhāl-| TA 'cause to live')
(c) ná=nə le·lá·i tɔ́həla·n. 'he set him in the middle there.' (B; |ahl-| TA 'put {smwh}')
(d) ná=nə sɔ́·ki- mahtant·ó·wal -ahkwe·č·íhko·n. 'For that long the devil tempted him.' (B; |sahkī| PV '{so} long', |akwēčīh-| TA 'tempt')
(e) ntəla·né·ɔ 'I tell it to them' (B; |əl-| TA 'say {so} to')
(f) yɔ́·k wəša·ší·ɔk nə́ni ntəlkwəné·ɔ 'these Osages tell me that' (OA; |əl-| TA 'say {so} to')
(g) ná=ni ktə́nta-pənó·lane·n 'that's where we looked at you, watched you' (OA; |talī|, |(-ən)ta| PV '{smwh}', |pənaw-| TA 'look at')

(4.44) TI with definite oblique (examples)
(a) ná=ni nəwə́nči-pé·t·o·n 'that's why I brought it'; 'that's where I brought it from' (OA; |wənčī| PV 'from {smwh}' [3.13(7)], |pēt-| TI(2) 'bring')
(b) ná=yúkwe=ní šé· ntə́ntxi-ahkənó·t·əmən. 'That's all I have to tell about it.' (ME; |(ən)taxī| PV '{so much}', |akənōt-| TI(1b) 'tell about')
(c) tá=háč tənnə́mən 'what did he do?' (B; |ələn-| TI(1b)-O 'do {so}')
(d) ná=č=nə́ lápi tənnə́mən 'He will do the same thing again' (B)
(e) tá=háč=á· ktənnəməné·ɔ 'what would you (pl.) do?' (B)
(f) ná=húnt ná=nə tənnə́mən nikáhke pi·laečəč·ínka. 'Then that's what those boys did.' (OA)

(4.45) Inflection for definite adjunct (examples)
(a) ktaləwa·p·ensí·nak kíči-xkwé·ɔk 'you (sg.) are more blessed than your fellow women' (B; |àləwāpēnsī-| AI 'be more blessed', |kət–nak| 2s+3p/IND)

(b) aləwí·i ktəla·ɔhti·ne·ɔ́·i·k čo·ləntət·ak. 'You (pl.) are worth more than the little birds.'
   (B; aləwí·i P 'more'; |əlāwatī-| AI 'be worth {so}', |kət–nēwāwīk| 2p+3p/IND)

(c) e·k·e·ki·mkwəs·i·t takó· tɔləwí·i-ləs·í·wəna ehahke·kinké·s·a 'the student is not more than the teacher'
   (B; aləwí·i PV 'more', |ələsī-| AI 'be {so}', |wət–wəna| 3s+3´/IND.NEG)

§4.5b. Subordinative. The subordinative mode of the independent order uses the n-endings for the AI (4.46), TA (4.47), and TI, and no peripheral suffixes. (Since the TI subordinative inflections are exactly the same as those for the TI indicative objective with singular object (4.36) they are not repeated here for this second function.) The subordinative inflections are thus identical to those of indicative verbs with definite oblique complements (4.42-44). The AI form with indefinite subject has |–ən(ē-)| X, the same as in the indicative mode, and likewise the II subordinative has |–w|, the same m-ending |-w|ₘ as the indicative and with the same treatments and effects. This can be used with no peripheral suffix for a plural as well as a singular subject (4.49j, 4.50f), but the ostensible indicative form with a plural inflection is also found in contexts where the subordinative would be expected (4.49e, 4.50g).

As in the AI+O and TA+O, the suffix |-ənēwā(w-)| 2p,3p is also used optionally to indicate the equivalent of a third plural peripheral argument with a first singular subject or inverse object, or with an indefinite subject, and the singular |-ən(ē)| is sometimes used with third plural subjects.

The subordinative mode makes subordinate clauses that are complements of higher verbs or other predicates, including some particles; in some constructions subordinative inflection is used with a pleonastic |əlī| PV '{so}'. Uses without this preverb include as a complement of certain verbs (for example, *want*, *let*, *be glad*, and *be difficult*), or of sentence-initial ná 'then' (as if 'and then it was that') and other particles, and as nominalizations functioning as secondary objects. (Blanchard also has six instances of the indicative used after ná 'then', and several cases of a subordinative without ná in clauses describing subsequent action.) Uses of the subordinative with |əlī| PV '{so}' include as a complement of certain other verbs (for example, *say, tell, know, think, see*, and *hear*), in purpose clauses, and after focus-fronted nominals. The verb |wəlīxən-| II 'be right or lawful' takes both kinds of complements, and Blanchard has a few examples of a missing |əlī| PV in constructions that almost always have it. The subordinative is considered a separate mode of the independent order rather that a specialized function of an oblique since, with or without |əlī| PV '{so}', it functions like a verbal mode and is otherwise unlike a verb with an oblique. There is, however, an idiom that has a subordinative verb with |əlī| PV '{so}' after ná PRES with a meaning like 'And with that', 'And so', or 'And proceeded to'. Voegelin (1946:149-150) called the subordinative suffix -n the "directive predicator," referring to the use that "directs attention to a collocated noun or particle as the focus of attention."

In certain idioms the subordinative may appear as a main-clause verb (4.52). By itself it may be the equivalent of 'let (first or third person subordinative subject) do so', or a statement of the speaker's immediate intent. With káč·i 'but' the meaning is 'went right ahead and' (ME).

The AI inflections in (4.46) are also the inflections for the TI(3). The |ə| written at the beginning of the endings drops after a vowel. For the selection of the variants of the endings given with underlying segments in parentheses, see the discussion before example (4.19).

(4.46) Subordinative: AI and II (inflections and forms)

	inflections	forms (|pā-| AI 'come'; |pənīhlā-| II 'fall')
1s	|nə–ən(ē-)|	mpá·n
2s	|kə–ən(ē-)|	kpá·n (B)
3s	|wə–ən(ē-)|	pó·n (B)
3´	|wə–əlīn(ē-)|	pó·li·n

	[inflections	forms]
1p	|nə–ənēn(ā(n)-)|	mpá·ne·n
12	|kə–ənēn(ā(n)-)|	kpá·ne·n
2p	|kə–ənēwā(w-)|	kpa·né·ɔ
3p	|wə–ənēwā(w-)|	pɔ·né·ɔ (B)
X	|–ən(ē-)|	pá·n
0	|–w|	pəníhəle· (OA)

(4.47) Subordinative TA (inflections)

	TA direct		TA inverse		TA theme 3
1s–3	|nə–ān(ē-)|	3–1s	|nə–əkwən(ē-), –əkōn(ē-)|	2ș–1s	|kə–īn(ē-)|
2s–3	|kə–ān(ē-)|	3–2s	|kə–əkwən(ē-), –əkōn(ē-)|	2p–1s	|kə–īnēwā(w-)|
2s–3´	|kə–ālīn(ē-)|			2–1p	|kə–īnēn(ā(n)-)|
3s–3´	|wə–ān(ē-)|	3´–3s	|wə–əkwən(ē-), –əkōn(ē-)|		
X–3	|–ān(ē-)|				
X–3´	|–ālīn(ē-)|				
1p–3	|nə–ānēn(ā(n)-)|	3–1p	|nə–əkōnēn(ā(n)-)|		TA theme 4
12–3	|kə–ānēn(ā(n)-)|	3–12	|kə–əkōnēn(ā(n)-)|	1s–2s	|kə–ələn(ē-)|
2p–3	|kə–ānēwā(w-)|	3–2p	|kə–əkwənēwā(w-)|, |kə–əkōnēwā(w-)|	1s–2p	|kə–ələnēwā(w-)|
3p–3´	|wə–ānēwā(w-)|	3´–3p	|wə–əkwənēwā(w-)|, |wə–əkōnēwā(w-)|	1p–2	|kə–ələnēn(ā(n)-)|

(4.48) Subordinative TA (forms of |nōtəm-| TA 'guard')

	TA direct		TA inverse		TA theme 3
1s–3	nnó·t·əma·n	3–1s	nno·t·əmúk·wən, nno·t·əmúk·o·n	2ș–1s	kənó·t·əmi·n
1s–3p	nno·t·əma·né·ɔ	3p–1s	nno·t·əmuk·wəné·ɔ, nno·t·əmuk·o·né·ɔ	2p–1s	kəno·t·əmi·né·ɔ
2s–3	kənó·t·əma·n	3–2s	kəno·t·əmúk·wən, kəno·t·əmúk·o·n	2–1p	kəno·t·əmí·ne·n
2s–3´	kəno·t·əmá·li·n				
3s–3´	wənó·t·əma·n	3´–3s	wəno·t·əmúk·wən, wəno·t·əmúk·o·n		
X–3	nó·t·əma·n				
X–3p	no·t·əma·né·ɔ				
X–3´	no·t·əmá·li·n				
1p–3	nno·t·əmá·ne·n	3–1p	nno·t·əmuk·ó·ne·n		TA theme 4
12–3	kəno·t·əmá·ne·n	3–12	kəno·t·əmuk·ó·ne·n	1s–2s	kəno·t·əmálən
2p–3	kəno·t·əma·né·ɔ	3–2p	kəno·t·əmuk·wəné·ɔ, kəno·t·əmuk·o·né·ɔ	1s–2p	kəno·t·əmələné·ɔ
3p–3´	wəno·t·əma·né·ɔ	3´–3p	wəno·t·əmuk·wəné·ɔ, wəno·t·əmuk·o·né·ɔ	1p–2	kəno·t·əməlóne·n

(4.49) Subordinative, without |əlī| PV '{so}' (examples)

Complement of a verb

(a) nkat·á·t·amən ko·la·mhitai·né·ɔ 'I want you to believe in me' (B; |katāt-| TI(1a) 'want', |nə–amən| 1s–0s/IND; |wəlāməhtaw-| TA 'believe', |kə–īnēwā| 1s–2p/SBD)

(b) takó· kɔt·a·t·amo·wəné·ɔ wšehəlá·li·n 'they did not want for them (obv.) to be hanging up' (B; |šēhlā-| AI 'hang', |wə–əlīn| 3´/SBD)

(c) nnó·lhant mpáskwi·n 'I'm lazy about standing up.' (Goddard 1979:48; |pasəkwī-| AI 'stand up', |nə–ən| 1s/SBD)

(d) lé·ləm ehankəlák·i·k ppɔ·khakehɔ·né·ɔ enkələ́lí·č·i. 'let the dead bury the dead.' (B;
|əlēləm-| TA 'let', |-∅| 2s–3/IMP; |pwahkahkehw-| TA 'bury', |wə–ānēwā| 3p–3´/SBD)

(e) kóna lí·namo·kw ellí·i aləmí·k·ənu 'let both (inan.) continue growing' (B;
kóna lí·namo·kw 'let (inan.) (you pl.)'; ellí·i 'both'; |aləmīkən-| II 'grow', |–wa| 0p/IND)

(f) máta=háč wəli·x·ənó·wi laxə́na·n 'Is it not right for her to be untied?' (B; máta NEG;
=háč Q; |wəlīxən-| II 'be right', |-ōwī| 0s/IND.NEG; |laxən-| TA 'untie', |–ān| X–3/SBD)

(g) áhɔt nkɔ·nšî́·pha·n 'it is hard for me to hide from him' (ME;
|àhwat-| II 'be difficult', |-w| 0s/IND; |kwānšīpah-| TA 'hide from', |nə–ān| 1s–3/SBD)

Complement of a particle (ná 'then'; kwə́la(h) '(I) wish')

(h) ná nkəs·ínkwe·n 'then I washed my face' (B;
|kəsīnkwē-| AI 'wash one's face', |nə–ən| 1s/SBD)

(i) ná tɔlə́mska·n 'then he departed' (B 3x; |aləməskā-| AI 'depart', |wət–ən| 3s/SBD)

(j) ná=húnt né·l ahsə́na pəníhəle·. 'Then, they say, the stones fell.' (OA; né·l 'those (inan.)';
|asən-| 'stone', |-a| INpl; |pənīhlā-| II 'fall', |–w| 0/SBD)

(k) ná nčí·khɔ·n 'Then I'll scrape them (hides, anim.).' (ME;
|čīkahw-| TA 'scrape', |nə–ān| 1s–3/SBD)

(l) ná nčí·sas wwe·t·ənə́mən ahpó·na 'then Jesus took the loaves' (B;
|wētən-| TI(1b) 'take', |wə–əmən| 3s–0/SBD)

(m) kwə́la nné·məne·n 'we (exc.) wish to see it' (B; |nēm-| TI(3) 'see', |nə–ənēn| 1p–0/SBD)

(n) kwə́lah=á· nəwi·č·əmə́k·e·n 'I wish I would be helped' (OA;
|wīčəm-| TA 'help', |nə–əkēn| X–1s/SBD)

(o) kwə́lah=á·=tá kəmí·li·n hó·s. 'I'd like you to give me a bucket.' (ME;
|mīl-| TA+O 'give O2 to', |kə–īn| 2s–1s+3s/SBD; hó·s 'kettle, bucket (anim.)')

Nominalization as secondary object

(p) nɔxpí·k·i·n kɔk·e·pínkɔ·n 'he was born blind' (B; for the first verb see 4.40r;
|(k)akēpīnkwā-| AI 'be blind', |nə–ən| 1s/SBD)

(q) ó·k=á· nəmi·x·anə́s·i·n nəwihí·nəwe·n. 'And I would be ashamed to beg.' (B; for the first
verb see 4.40s; |Rih+| HAB, |wīnəwē-| AI 'beg', |nə–ən| 1s/SBD)

(4.50) Subordinative, with |əlī| PV '{so}' (examples)

Complement of a verb or particle

(a) tóhi-lá·ɔl, tə́li-=č íka -pá·n 'He implored him to come there' (B;
|àhī| PV 'very much', |əl-| TA 'say {so} to', |wət–āwal| 3s–3´/IND;
|əlī| PV '{so}', |pā-| 'AI 'come', |wət–n| 3s/SBD; =č FUT; íka 'there')

(b) mé·či ktəlləné·ɔ·p ktə́li-ne·i·né·ɔ, 'I have told you that you see me' (B;
mé·či 'now, already'; |əl-| TA 'say {so} to', |kət–ələnēwāp| 1s–2p+0s/IND.PRET;
|əlī| PV '{so}', |nēw-| TA 'see', |kət–īnēwā| 2p–1s/SBD)

(c) no·wá·tɔ·n tə́li-=č -pá·n 'I know that he will come' (B; |wəwāht-| TI(2) 'know',
|nə–ōn| 1s–0s/IND; |əlī| PV '{so}', |pā-| 'AI 'come', |wət–n| 3s/SBD; =č FUT)

(d) káči li·t·e·há·he·kw, ktə́li-=á· -ahkəno·t·əmo·ləné·ɔ 'do not think that I would accuse you'
(B: káči 'don't'; |əlītēhā-| AI 'think {so}', |–hēkw| 2p/PROH; =á· POT;
|əlī| PV '{so}', |akənōtəmaw-| TA 'tell about', |kət–ələnēwā| 1s–2p/SBD)

(e) wəne·ó·ɔl tə́li-šenki·x·í·nəli·n 'he saw him lying there' (B; |nēw-| TA 'see',
|wə–āwal| 3s–3´/IND; |əlī| PV '{so}', |šēnkīxīn-| AI 'lie', |wət–əlīn| 3´/SBD)

(f) mpəntamə́na né·l ahsə́na lí-pəníhəle·. 'I heard the stones fall.' (OA;
|pənt-| TI(1a) 'hear', |nə–aməna| 1s–0p/IND; see 4.49j, here with |əlī| PV '{so}'). Also:

(g) mpəntamə́na né·l ahsə́na lí-pənihəlé·ɔ. 'I heard the stones fall.' (OA; cf. f;
|pənīhlēwa| < |pənīhlā-| II 'fall', |–wa| 0p/IND)

(h) káči čane·ləntánkhan ktə́li-wé·t·əna·n 'do not be reluctant to take her (as a wife)'
  (B: káči 'don't'; |čanēlənt-| TI(1a)-O 'be reluctant', |-ankahan| 2s–0/PROH;
  |əlī| PV '{so}', |wētən-| TA 'take', |kət–ān| 2p–3/SBD)

(i) takó· wəli·x·ənó·u ktə́li-kələ́nəmən ktap·í·nay. 'It's not right for you to carry your bed.'
  (takó· 'not'; |wəlīxən-| II 'be right', |–ōwī| 0s/IND.NEG;
  |əlī| PV '{so}', |kələn-| TI(1b) 'carry', |kət–əmən| 2s–0/SBD; apīnay 'bed', |kət–| 2s)

(j) é·li- máta -tépi-ləs·í·ɔ, ktə́li-=á· -káski-təmí·k·e·n.
  'as I am not worthy enough to have you (lit., for you to be able to) come in.'
  (|əlī| PV '{so}', tépi PV 'enough', |ələsī-| AI 'be {so}', |IC–wā| 1s/CC.NEG; máta 'not';
  |əlī| PV '{so}', |kàskī| PV 'be able to', |təmīkē-| AI 'enter', |kət–n| 2s/SBD; =á· POT)

(k) wanə́š·i ktə́li-pə́ntai·n 'thank you for listening to me' (B; wanə́š·i P 'thank you';
  |əlī| PV, |pəntaw-| TA 'hear', |kət–īn| 2s–1s/SBD)

Purpose clause
(l) ná=nə́ ntə́lsi·n, ktə́li-=č -pí·lsi·n. 'That's what I do for you to be clean.' (B;
  ná PRES, nə́ 'that (inan.)'; |ələsī-| AI 'do {so}', |nət–n| 1s+0s;
  |əlī| PV 'so', |pīləsī-| AI 'be clean', |kət–n| 2s/SBD)

(m) məšá·ke· tə́li-=á· -mí·tsi·n 'he sat down to eat' (B;
  |məšahkē-| AI 'take a seat', |–w| 3s/IND;
  |əlī| PV 'so', |mītəsī-| AI 'eat', |wət–n| 3s/SBD; =á· POT)

(n) kkəkxpto·né·ɔ·č, ktə́li-=č -lo·s·əməné·ɔ. 'You must tie them in bundles to burn them.'
  (B; |Rə+| REP, |kaxpət-| TI(2) 'tie', |kə–ōnēwā| 2p–0/IND; =č FUT (2x);
  |əlī| PV 'so', |lōs-| TI(1b) 'burn', |kət–əmənēwā| 2p–0/SBD)

(o) nə́ni=č ktihələnəməné·ɔ, ktə́li-=č -məša·li·né·ɔ. 'That's what you must always do in
  order to remember me.' (nə́ni 'that (inan.)'; =č FUT (2x);
  |Rih+| HAB, |ələn-| TI(1b)-O 'do {so}', |kət–əmənēwā| 2p–0+0s/IND;
  |əlī| PV 'so', |məšāl-| TA 'remember', |kət–īnēwā| 2p–1s/SBD)

(p) tə́li-=á· -nhíla·n 'in order to kill him'
  (|əlī| PV 'so', |nəhl-| TA 'kill', |wət–ān| 3s–3´/SBD; =á· POT)

With focus-fronted nominal
(q) ní· ntə́li-ló·s·əmən 'I'm the one who burned it' (Voegelin 1946:150;
  ní· 1s/EMPH; |əlī| PV 'so', |lōs-| TI(1b) 'burn', |nət–əmən| 1s–0/SBD)

(r) nčá·n čečhɔ·pwənúwe·t ntə́li-pe·t·alo·ka·lkó·ne·n 'it's John the Baptist who sends us' (B;
  nčá·n 'John'; |Rih+| HAB, |čahwāhpwənəwē-| AI 'baptize people', |IC–t| 3s/PPL(ANsg))
  |əlī| PV 'so', |pētalōhkāl-| TA 'send hither', |nət–əkōnēn| 3–1p/SBD)

(s) awé·n=háč ktə́li-pahkámko·n? 'who is it that hit you?' (B; awé·n 'who?'; =háč Q;
  |əlī| PV 'so', |pakam-| TA 'hit', |kət–əkōn| 3–2s/SBD)

(t) nčí·sas=tá ntə́li-ki·k·éhko·n. 'It was Jesus that cured me.' (B; nčí·sas 'Jesus' [WS];
  =tá FOC; |əlī| PV 'so', |kīkēh-| TA 'cure', |nət–əkōn| 3–1s/SBD)

(u) nál nán ntə́li-wé·t·əna·n 'that's the one (anim.) I picked out' (OA;
  nál PRES; nəni 'that (anim.)'; |əlī| PV 'so', |wētən-| TA 'take', |wət–ān| 3s–3´/SBD)

Blanchard does not use the construction in (4.50u) but rather has the presentational pronoun
nánal (or nál) with an indicative verb or a participle (**§6.5c**).

(4.51) Subordinative with ná PRES and |əlī| PV '{so}' (examples)
  (a) ná tə́li-tpáhɔn e·k·e·ki·má·č·i 'And with that he pointed to his disciples'
    (B; ná PRES; |əlī| PV '{so}', |təpahw-| TA 'point at', |wət–ān| 3s–3´/SBD;
    |akēhkīm-| TA 'teach', |IC–āčī| 3s–3´/PPL(OBV))

(b) ná tə́li- palí·i -a·né·ɔ. 'And with that they went away.'
   (B; ná PRES; |əlī| PV '{so}', |ā-| AI 'go to {smwh}', |wət–newā| 3p/SBD)
(c) ná tə́li-alə́mska·n. '… and so departed.' (B; ná PRES;
   |əlī| PV '{so}', |aləməskā-| AI 'depart', |wət–n| 3s/SBD)
(d) ná tə́li-pá·tama·n, ná kə́nč puphaké·nəmən, ná tə́li-kək·ələ́ntəla·n. 'And he proceeded to pray, before breaking it into pieces and, with that, handing it out to them.' (B; ná PRES; |əlī| PV '{so}', |pāhtamā-| AI 'pray', |wət–n| 3s/SBD; ná 'then' + kə́nč = 'only then'; |Rə̀+| REP, |pahkēn-| TI(1b) 'break in pieces by hand', |wət–əmən| 3s–0/SBD; ná PRES; |əlī| PV '{so}', |Rə̀+| REP, |kələntəl-| TA 'cause to hold O2', |wət–ān| 3s–3´/SBD)

(4.52) Subordinative as main verb (examples)
   Statement of intent
   (a) nəmái-no·t·améns·i·n. 'I'm going fishing.' (B; KJV "I go a fishing.")
       (|mawī| PV 'go to', |nōtamēnsī-| AI 'fish', |nə–n| 1s/SBD)
   (b) kəwi·č·e·wələ́ne·n. 'We're coming with you.' (B; KJV "We also go with thee.")
       (|wīčēw-| TA 'accompany', |kə–ələnēn| 1p–2/SBD)
   (c) ko·t·e·kó·lən. 'I'm going to follow you.' (B; KJV "I will follow thee")
       (|wətēhkaw-| TA 'follow', |kə–ələn| 1s–2s/SBD)
   (d) yúh=tá, mpáskwi·n, nó·x·ink ntá·n. 'Alright, I'm getting up and going to my father's.'
       (B; KJV "I will arise and go to my father")
       (yúh 'alright'; =tá FOC; |pasəkwī-| AI 'get up', |nə–n/SBD;
       |nōx-| 'my father', |-ənk| LOC; |ā-| AI 'go to {smwh}', |nə–n/SBD)
   (e) yúh=tá nəwi·t·a·hé·ma·n 'alright, I'll help her' (B; KJV "I will avenge her")
       (yúh P 'alright'; =tá FOC; |wītāhēm-| TA 'help', |nə–ān| 1s–3/SBD)
   With the meaning 'let (subject) do so'
   (f) ke·k·e·p·inkɔ́·č·i·k tɔləmo·x·ɔla·né·ɔ ke·k·e·p·inkɔ·lí·č·i. 'Let the blind lead the blind.'
       (B; |(k)akēpīnkwā-| AI 'be blind', |IC–čīk| 3/PPL(ANpl) and |IC–līčī| 3´/PPL(OBV);
       |aləmōxwal-| TA 'lead', |wət–ānēwā| 3p–3´/SBD)
   (g) lahápa ní· hítami ntalə́mska·n, nəmái-phɔkhakéhɔ·n nó·x.
       'let me first go and bury my father' (B; lahápa P 'for now, taking the time';
       ní· 1s/EMPH; hítami P 'first'; |aləməskā-| AI 'depart', |nət–n| 1s/SBD;
       |mawī| PV 'go to', |pwahkahkehw-| TA 'bury', |nə–ān| 1s–3/SBD; nó·x 'my father')

§4.6. Conjunct Order Paradigms and Examples.

The five modes of the conjunct order (**§4.4a**) are used for various kinds of subordinate or dependent clauses, with one used also idiomatically as a main verb. The central pronominal suffixes are entirely distinct from those of the independent order. (Prefixes are not used.) The theme signs (**§4.4d**) are basically the same, but with a few differences in distribution. The peripheral suffixes, used only to mark heads of participles (**§4.6a** end), are variants of those used on possessed nouns (4.1) and independent order verbs (4.40-41, 45). Two of the conjunct modes have a word-final suffix |-ē| SBJ.

Three of the conjunct modes have initial change (IC). This is usually the replacement of an underlying short first vowel with |ē|, but in at least one set of stems a phonemic /i/ from an underlying |ī| is replaced (4.64kn). Also, initial change on the reduplicant |Rih+| HAB always has phonemic /e/ (**§5.4d**). The stems |ā-| AI 'go to {smwh}' and |pā-| AI 'come' add |ēy| before |ā| (3.13(2)b, 4.62e). For many verb stems with a short vowel in the first syllable, however, initial change is optional or not used at all. (Initial change that is present in the underlying abstract representation of the morphology but for whatever reason not overt is given as "(IC)."). If there is a preverb (or preverbs) the initial change is on the first (or only) one.

(4.53) Conjunct modes: formation and uses
   Plain conjunct (CNJ): no IC, no modal suffix. For the complement of certain particles; rare.
   Changed conjunct (CC): IC, no modal suffix. Referring to actual events in conditional clauses with certain initials.
   Subjunctive (SBJ): |-ē| SBJ, no IC. For hypothetical conditions, future or past; also idiomatic with certain particles.
   Changed subjunctive (CS): |-ē| SBJ, and IC. For 'when' clauses with past reference.
   Participle (PPL): IC and head-marking peripheral suffixes. Internally headed relative clauses.
Because initial change cannot be shown on many stems and is often omitted on other stems, there is extensive homonymy between forms that would differ only by its presence or absence. There is also always homonymy between a changed conjunct and a participle with a singular head. As a consequence the changed conjunct tends to occur with énta PV 'when' after Blanchard.

There are basic conjunct order central suffixes for all persons, and a set of three that are used only in TA forms with third person objects. The third person plural and obviative endings include the suffix |-t| 3. The variant |-k| 3 is used after AI stems and TI themes that end in a consonant.

(4.54) Conjunct order central suffixes

	basic set	TA with third person object
1s	|-ā(n-)|	|-àk| 1s–3
2s	|-an|, |-àn|	|-àt| 2s–3
3s	|-t| 3, |-k| 3	
X	|-ənk|	|-ənt| X–3
1p	|-ēnk|	
12	|-ankw|	
2p	|-ēkw|	
0	|-k|	
3p	|-hətīt| (< |-hətī| pl. + |-t| 3); also ostensible |-əhtīt|, |-əhətīt|, and |-əhətīt|	
3′	|-əlīt| (< |-əlī| obv. + |-t| 3)	

The suffix |-ā(n-)| 1s is (almost always) /-á·n-/ before a vowel in all periods, and /-a/ word-finally, but one speaker (OA) had /-a·/ word-finally. (Blanchard has two additional rare variants before |-p(an-)| PRET; §4.7.) The suffixes |-àk| 1s–3 and |-àt| 2s–3 are always metrically strong (see §2.3-4), while |-an| 2s is accented against the usual pattern (hence |-àn| 2s) only in one phonological environment (when the metrically strong short vowel in the preceding syllable is followed by a voiced consonant, or no consonant) and apparently in one morphological environment (when followed by |-p(an-) PRET). After a vowel the |ə| in |-ənk| X and |-əlīt| 3′ is elided but the other suffix-initial vowels have a |y| inserted before them. An underlying |ī| is replaced by |ə| before this |y|, the |ə| is colored to /i/, and the |y| is lost. After other vowels (|ā| and |ē|) the |y| is lost without a trace. (In earlier transcriptions /y/ was sometimes written in these forms after /i/ and /e·/, but it is probably never pronounced distinctly.) The variant |-k| 3s is used after a consonant. The suffixes |-k| 3 and |-k| 0 are added directly after |n| and |m|, giving |nk| (pronounced [ŋg], word-finally [-ŋk]) (§2.12g). After other consonants a |ə| is inserted before |-k| 3s. In II stems a stem-final |t| combines variously with |-k| 0: a |ə| may be inserted, giving |tək|, or |-k| 0 may be added directly, giving both |hk| and |h|. Ostensible |-hətīt| 3p is used after a vowel (|hət| realized as /ht/); |-əhtīt| 3p (|əht| realized as /hit/) is used after a consonant preceded by a long vowel (or, rarely, a metrically strong short vowel); |-əhətīt| 3p (|əhət| realized as /iht/) is used in most cases after a short-vowel syllable. The |k| of |-k| 3 and |-k| 0 combines with |-w| NEG as |kw|. The TI Class 2 theme sign |-aw| TH.TI(2) combines with |-k| 3 as |-ākw| (2.46de). A regularized |-āt| was heard from FW (Goddard 1979:134); CW had |-ōt| (Speck 1931:110), presumably from Munsee, where this was a dialectal variant (Goddard 2015:213).

The use of the TA theme signs in the conjunct differs in details from their use in the independent order (**§4.4d**). The direct theme sign (theme 1) |-ā| TH.1 appears overtly before a consonant (giving, for example, |-āt| 3s–3´ and |-āhətīt| 3p–3´) but is dropped before a vowel (giving |-àk| 1s–3, etc.). The underlying presence of |-ā| TH.1 before the vowel-intial suffixes is evident, however, in negative forms in which |-w| NEG intervenes: né·ləma ne·t·o·xtaɔ́·ɔt 'before you (sg.) ask him' (|natōxətaw-| TA 'ask', |IC–āwat| 2s–3/CC.NEG < |-ā| TH.1, |-w| NEG, -àt| 2s–3). Endings for first singular object have |-ī| TH.3 if the subject is a third person animate (|–īt| 3s–1s, etc.), an indefinite (|–īnk| X–1s), or (in Blanchard's day) an inanimate (|–īk| 0–1s). In the twentieth century the inflection for an inanimate subject had |-əkw| TH.2 (|–əkwā(n-) | 0–1s).

In the conjunct, in addition to being a component of the third person obviative ending |-əlīt| 3´ (4.53), the suffix |-əlī| obv. was used to mark obviative objects of first and second persons (three examples in Blanchard; 4.65k) and of the indefinite (the obviative passive; 4.62f, 4.65j).

§4.6a. Plain Conjunct and Subjunctive Paradigms. The sample paradigms (4.55-59) are constructed, but sources or the number of attestations are given for attested forms. The forms given as plain conjunct (4.55, 56, 58) are mostly found after preverbs with initial change; for the true plain conjunct see (4.60). The TA forms for 3–1s and X–1s (with |-ī| TH.3) are put with the inverse forms proper (those with an inverse theme sign, |-əkw| TH.2 or |-əkē| TH.2.PS).

(4.55) Plain conjunct and subjunctive of AI and II (|pā-| AI 'come'; |ləmatapī-| AI 'sit'; |pənīhlā-| II 'fall')

	Plain conjunct	Subjunctive
1s	pá·a (B, V, ME), -a· (OA)	pa·á·ne
	ləmatahpía	ləmatahpiá·ne
2s	pá·an	pá·ane (ME)
	ləmatahpían (ME)	ləmatahpiáne
3s	pá·t (B, V, ME)	pá·t·e (B, V, OA, ME)
	ləmátahpi·t (B 2x)	ləmatahpí·t·e (B)
		šenki·x·ínke 'if he lies down' (|šēnkīxīn-| AI 'lie')
		ankələk·e 'if he dies' (B; |ankəl-| AI 'die')
3´	pa·lí·t	pa·lí·t·e (B)
X	pánk	pánke
1p	pá·enk (V, ME)	pa·énke (OA)
12	pá·ankw	pa·ánkwe (B, ME)
2p	pá·e·kw (B)	pa·é·k·we (B)
3p	páhti·t (21x)	pahtí·t·e
0	pəníhəla·k (B)	pənihəlá·k·e

(4.56) Plain conjunct TA (forms of |nōtəm-| TA 'guard'; |mīl-| TA 'give to')

TA direct		TA inverse		TA theme 3	
1s–3	nó·t·əmak	3–1s	nó·t·əmi·t	2s–1s	no·t·əmían
2s–3	nó·t·əmat	0–1s	nó·t·əmi·k (archaic),	2p–1s	no·t·əmíe·kw
			no·t·əmúk·ɔ, mí·lkɔ	2–1p	no·t·əmíenk
3s–3´	nó·t·əma·t	3,0–2s	no·t·əmúk·ɔn,	TA theme 4	
			mí·lkɔn	1s–2s	no·t·əmálan
3´–3˝	no·t·əmá·li·t	3´,0–3s	no·t·əmúk·uk,	1s–2p	no·t·əmále·kw
X–3	nó·t·əmənt		mí·lkuk	1p–2	no·t·əmálenk

Inflection

	TA direct		TA inverse	
X–3´	no·t·əmá·link			
1p–3	nó·t·əmenk	3,0–1p	no·t·əmúk·wenk, mí·lkwenk	
12–3	nó·t·əmankw	3,0–12	no·t·əmúk·ɔnkw, mí·lkɔnkw	
2p–3	nó·t·əme·kw	3,0–2p	no·t·əmúk·we·kw, mí·lkwe·kw	
3p–3´	no·t·əmáhti·t	3´,0–3p	no·t·əmukhwíti·t, mi·lkwíhti·t	

	TA first and second person passive
X–1s	nó·t·əmink
X–2s	no·t·əmək·é·a, mi·lké·a
X–1p	no·t·əmək·é·enk, mi·lké·enk
X–12	no·t·əmək·é·ankw, mi·lké·ankw
X–2p	no·t·əmək·é·e·kw, mi·lké·e·kw

(The endings /-á·li·t/ 3´–3″, /-a·link/ X– 3´, and /-i·k/ 0–1s are from related forms in Blanchard.)

(4.57) Subjunctive TA (forms of |nōtəm-| TA 'guard'; |mīl-| TA+O 'give O2 to')

	TA direct		TA inverse		TA theme 3
1s–3	no·t·əmák·e	3–1s	no·t·əmí·t·e	2s–1s	no·t·əmiáne
2s–3	no·t·əmát·e	0–1s	no·t·əmuk·ó·ne	2p–1s	no·t·əmié·k·we
				2–1p	no·t·əmiénke
3s–3´	no·t·əmá·t·e	3–2s	no·t·əmúk·ɔne, mi·lkóne		TA theme 4
		3´–3s	no·t·əmúkwke, mi·lkúk·e	1s–2s	no·t·əməláne
				1s–2p	no·t·əməlé·k·we
X–3	no·t·əmə́nte			1p–2	no·t·əməlénke
X–3´	no·t·əma·línke				TA first and second person passive
1p–3	no·t·əménke	3–1p	no·t·əmuk·wénke, mi·lkwénke	X–1s	no·t·əmínke
12–3	no·t·əmánkwe	3–12	no·t·əmuk·ónkwe, mi·lkónkwe	X–2s	no·t·əmək·e·á·ne, mi·lke·á·ne
2p–3	no·t·əmé·kwe	3–2p	no·t·əmuk·wé·kwe, mi·lkwé·k·we	X–1p	no·t·əmək·e·énke, mi·lke·énke
3p–3´	no·t·əmahtí·te	3´–3p	no·t·əmukhwití·t·e, mi·lkwihtí·t·e	X–12	no·t·əmək·e·ánkwe, mi·lke·ánkwe
				X–2p	no·t·əmək·e·é·k·we, mi·lke·é·k·we

(The ending /-a·línke/ X–3´ is attested by a changed subjunctive in Blanchard; 4.62f.)

(4.58) Plain conjunct TI (forms of |pən-| TI(1a) 'look at'; |məšən-| TI(1b) 'get'; |pēt-| TI(2) 'bring'; |mīčī-| TI(3) 'eat'; |nēm-| TI(3) 'see')

	TI(1a)	TI(1b)	TI(2)	TI(3)	
1s	pənáma	məšənəma	pé·t·aɔ	mí·č·ia	né·ma
2s	pənáman	məšənəman	pé·t·aɔn	mí·č·ian	né·man
3s	pənánk	məšənink	pé·t·a·kw	mí·č·i·t	nénk
3´	pənáməli·t	məšənəmáli·t	pe·tó·li·t	mi·č·í·li·t	né·məli·t
1p	pənámenk	məšənəmenk	pé·t·aenk	mí·č·ienk	né·menk
12	pənámankw	məšənəmankw	pé·t·aɔnkw	mí·č·iankw	né·mankw
2p	pənáme·kw	məšənəme·kw	pé·t·ae·kw	mí·č·ie·kw	né·me·kw
3p	pənamíhti·t (B)	məšənəmíhti·t	pe·t·úhti·t	mi·č·íhti·t	ne·mhíti·t
X	pənámink	məšənəmink	pé·t·unk	mí·č·ink	né·mink

(4.59) Subjunctive TI (forms of |pən-| TI(1a) 'look at'; |məšən-| TI(1b) 'get'; |pēt-| TI(2) 'bring'; |mīčī-| TI(3) 'eat'; |nēm-| TI(3) 'see')

	TI(1a)	TI(1b)	TI(2)	TI(3)	
1s	pənamá·ne	məšənəmá·ne	pe·t·aó·ne	mi·č·iá·ne	ne·má·ne
2s	pənamáne	məšənəmáne	pe·t·aóne	mi·č·iáne	né·mane
3s	pənánke	məšənínke	pe·t·á·k·we	mi·č·í·t·e	nénke
3′	pənaməlí·t·e	məšənəməlí·t·e	pe·t·o·lí·t·e	mi·č·i·lí·t·e	ne·məlí·t·e
1p	pənaménke	məšənəménke	pe·t·aénke	mi·č·iénke	ne·ménke
12	pənamánkwe	məšənəmánkwe	pe·t·aónkwe	mi·č·iánkwe	ne·mánkwe
2p	pənamé·k·we	məšənəmé·k·we	pe·t·aé·k·we	mi·č·ié·k·we	ne·mé·k·we
3p	pənamihtí·t·e	məšənəmihtí·t·e	pe·t·uhtí·t·e	mi·č·ihtí·t·e	ne·mhití·t·e
X	pənamínke	məšənəmínke	pe·t·únke	mi·č·ínke	ne·mínke

Participles (4.53) basically have the pronominal inflection of the other conjunct modes and a peripheral suffix indicating the head. The peripheral suffix is |-∅| if the head is singular (anim. sg. or inan. sg., including oblique) or a first (presumably) or second person, and the ending is then the same as in the plain or changed conjunct (4.55, 4.56, 4.58). If the head is a third plural subject (or object in an inverse or passive form), |-īk| anim. pl. is added to the corresponding third singular (|-t| 3s), or to |-ənt| X–3, replacing |-t| with |-čīk|; the variants of |-hətīt| 3p are not used. In all other cases the head is marked by one of the suffixes |-īk| anim. pl., |-ī| inan. pl., or |-ī| obv. added to the shape of the ending that precedes the final /-e/ in the subjunctive and changed subjunctive (4.55, 4.57, 4.59), replacing |-t| with |-čīk| or |-čī|, except that |-ī| obv. is sometimes omitted from obviative participles, both those with |-əlī| obv. (4.65.l, 4.75rs, 4.99.l) and those without this (4.65mn; Jn 3.34). Initial change is present on the stems that mark it.

§4.6b. Conjunct Examples. A selection of forms inflected for the conjunct modes is given in the following tables.

(4.60) Plain conjunct (examples)
  (a) kóč=háč čhɔ·pwənəwé·an 'why do you baptize people' (B)
  (b) kóč=háč ləpák·an? 'why are you weeping?' (B)
      (synonymous with: kéku=háč wénči-ləpák·an? [B])
  (c) kóč=háč nkálian? 'why have you abandoned me?' (B)
  (d) kwáč=háč nhaká·lian? 'Why do you rely on me?' (B)
  (e) kóč=háč máta mhalá·s·i·k 'why wasn't it sold?' (B)

Apparently the plain conjunct is only found in examples from Blanchard like those in (4.60). The word kóč 'why?' (18x; kwáč 2x) is very likely a lexicalized allegro pronunciation of kéku(=háč) wénči- (4.60b) with added =háč Q. (The LTD has /kúč/ 'why?' from LB as a one-word utterance.) In the longer expression for 'why?' the verb is an oblique participle, with optional IC on the preverb (wénči- or wə́nči-). If this explanation is correct, a true plain conjunct may not exist in the language.

The changed conjunct is used with certain initials (incorporated into stems or in preverbs) or adverbial free particles to denote actual contingent or conditional events or circumstances. Apparently initial change, if possible, is always present, but there is evidence that it should be analyzed as lexicalized on the particles used and not part of the modal inflection (and it is so analyzed in 4.61). For example, the ostensible initial ne·l- 'as, while' can be taken as lexicalized in changed conjunct forms, although it seems likely to have been formed from the relative root |əl-| '{so}' (3.13(1)) with initial change and fusion with nə́ 'that (inan.)'. Similarly, in changed conjunct forms the preverb énta- 'when (in the past)' (later ə́nta-) is probably lexicalized as such, since, although this was originally the irregular changed form of táli PV '{smwh}' and can be used to mean 'where', the meaning 'when' is idiosyncratic, being associated only with this construction and the nearly synonymous use of the changed subjunctive. The preverb é·li 'as, because' is ostensibly |əlī| PV '{so}' with initial change, but the fact that there is a free particle é·li 'as, for' commonly used with an independent indicative suggests that the preverb has been lexicalized in this case as well. The free particle né·skɔ 'before; yet' is followed by a changed conjunct verb (with IC if possible).

(4.61) Changed conjunct (examples)
- (a) né·li-kaí·t (B), né·li-kawí·t (V) 'while he was sleeping' (|nēlī| PV 'while', |ka(w)ī-| AI 'sleep', |(IC)–t| 3s/CC)
- (b) ne·lo·x·wéhti·t 'as they walked' (B; |nēl-| 'while', |-ōxwē| AI 'walk', |(IC)–hətīt| 3p/CC)
- (c) wé·t·ami-mái-mhalamɔ·s·íhti·t 'while they were occupied with going to buy' (B; |wətamī| PV 'be busy', /mái/ PV 'go to', mahlamwāsī- AI 'buy', |IC–hətīt| 3p/CC)
- (d) ə́nta-mi·tsían 'when you (sg.) are eating' (Goddard 1979:50; /ə́nta/ PV 'when', |mītəsī-| AI 'eat', |(IC)–yan| 2s/CC)
- (e) énta-ahke·kínke·t 'when he was teaching' (B; /énta/ PV 'when', |akēhkīnkē-| AI 'teach', |(IC)–t| 3s/CC)
- (f) énta-mái-thwə́nie·kw 'when you (pl.) came to arrest me' (B; /énta/ PV 'when', /mái/ PV 'go to', |tahwən-| TA 'arrest', |(IC)–əyēkw| 2p–1s/CC)
- (g) mé·či ə́nta-ká·xkte·k xáskwi·m 'when the corn has dried' (ME; mé·či P 'already'; /ə́nta/ PV 'when', |kāxkətē-| II 'dry by heat', |(IC)–k| 0/CC)
- (h) éntxən-pá·t 'whenever he comes' (Goddard 1979:50; /éntxən/ PV 'every time', |pā-| AI 'come', |(IC)–t| 3s/CC)
- (i) éntxən-təmí·k·e·t 'every time he went inside' (OA; /éntxən/ PV 'every time', |təmīkē-| AI 'enter (structure)', |(IC)–t| 3s/CC)
- (j) é·li-pá·lsi·t 'as she was sick' (B; |ēlī| PV 'as', |pāləsī-| AI 'be sick', |(IC)–t| 3s/CC)
- (k) né·skɔ=á· mi·tsí·ɔn 'before you eat' (OA; /né·skɔ/ P 'before', =á· POT; |mītəsī-| AI 'eat', |(IC)–wan| 2s/CC.NEG)
- (l) né·skɔ ke·š·i·lənčé·li·t 'before they (obv.) washed their hands' (B; /né·skɔ/ P 'before'; |kəšīlənčē-| AI 'wash one's hands', |IC–līt| 3´/CC)
- (m) né·skɔ='ká pe·áhti·t 'before they got there' (OA; /né·skɔ/ P 'before'; íka 'there'; |pā-| AI 'come', |IC–hətīt| 3p/CC)
- (n) ə́nta-páhti·t 'when they came' (OA, ME; /ə́nta/ PV 'when', |pā-| AI 'come', |(IC)–hətīt| 3p/CC)

The changed subjunctive is freely used to indicate an actual past event subordinate to a succeeding past event; it can also be used for a timeless general condition. Like the changed conjunct, it may be used with énta (ə́nta) PV 'when', éntxən PV 'whenever', and né·skɔ P 'before'. In such cases the difference in meaning can be subtle, but some examples suggest that using a changed subjunctive for the contingent event presents it as discrete, implying a temporal sequence, whereas if a changed conjunct is used the two events are seen as simultaneous, perhaps components of a single, multi-part event or activity. In other cases, however, there is no discernible difference between the two modes.

(4.62) Changed subjunctive (examples)
- (a) pe·naí·t·e 'when he looked at me' (B; |pənaw-| TA 'look at', |IC–ītē| 3s–1s/CS)
- (b) mé·či e·ləmskahtí·t·e 'after they left' (B; mé·či 'already'; |aləməskā-| AI 'depart', |IC–hətītē| 3p/CS)

(c) mé·či me·š·ənəmhití·t·e 'after they received it' (B; mé·či 'already';
   |məšən-| TI(1b) 'get, receive', |IC–əməhtītē| 3p–0₍₁ᵦ₎/CS)
(d) mé·či ne·no·stamihtí·t·e 'after they had understood it' (B; mé·či 'already';
   |nənōsət-| 'understand', |IC–aməhətītē| 3p–0₍₁ₐ₎/CS)
(e) íka pe·ahtí·t·e 'when they got there' (B, V; íka 'there';
   |pā-| AI 'come', |IC–hətītē| 3p/CS)
(f) we·li·x·əma·línke 'when he (obv.) was laid to rest' (B;
   |wəlīxəm-| TA 'lay nicely, appropriately', |IC–ālīnkē| X–3´/PPL(OBV))
(g) tenkti·t·iá·ne núči 'from the time I was small' (ME;
   |tankətītī-| AI 'be small', |IC–yānē| 1s/CS; núči P 'since')
(h) énta-ahke·kinké·t·e 'when he taught' (B;
   /énta/ PV 'when', |akēhkīnkē-| AI 'teach', |(IC)–tē| 3s/CS)
(i) énta-a·mwi·kəná·t·e 'when he raised him up' (B;
   /énta/ PV 'when', |āmwīhkən-| TA 'raise', |(IC)–ātē| 3s–3´/CS)
(j) éntxən- o·t·é·nink -pá·t·e 'whenever he came to a town' (B;
   /éntxən/ PV 'every time', |pā-| AI 'come', |(IC)–tē| 3s/CS; o·t·é·nink 'town (loc.)')
(k) né·skɔ e·té·k·e yú hák·i 'before the earth existed' (B; /né·skɔ/ P 'before';
   |ahtē-| II 'exist', |IC–kē| 0/CS; yú 'this (inan.)'; hák·i 'earth')
(l) pwe·khakeho·t·ihtí·t·e 'when they bury each other' (B;
   |pwahkahkehōtī-| AI 'bury each other', |IC–hətītē| 3p/CS)
(m) ké·t·a-áləmi-kəmpahkwihəlá·k·e 'when they are going to start growing leaves' (B;
   |kata| PV 'going to', |aləmī| PV 'begin', |kəmpakwīhlā-| II 'grow leaves', |IC–kē| 0/CS)

The subjunctive marks a hypothetical condition in the future ('if' or 'when'); with an indication of past tense (or even without this if set in the past) it refers to an unfulfilled condition in the past. It is also used as a main verb in an idiom (4.63pqr). Sometimes in the speech of ME |-ē| SBJ was /-i/ instead of /-e/ (4.63f), apparently by assimilation to an /i/ earlier in the word.

(4.63) Subjunctive (examples)

Conditional ('if')
(a) ankhitá·k·we 'if he loses it' (B; |ankəht-| TI(2) 'lose', |–ākwē| 3s–0₍₂₎/SBJ)
(b) kí· li·t·e·há·ane 'if you want to' (ME; kí· 2s/EMPH;
   |əlītēhā-| AI 'think {so}', |–yanē| 2s/SBJ)
(c) ni·š·ihtí·t·e 'if they are two' (B; |nīšī-| AI 'be two', |–hətītē| 3p/SBJ)
(d) lanihínke 'if he is thrown' (B; |əlanihī-| AI+O 'throw {so}', |–nkē| X/SBJ)
(e) xù aləmo·x·ɔlát·e 'if you (sg.) take him (OA; xú FUT;
   |aləmōxwal-| TA 'take away', |–ātē| 2s–3/SBJ)
(f) pa·ta·hiáni 'if you (sg.) defeat me' (ME; |pāhtāh-| TA 'defeat', |–əyanē| 2s–1s/SBJ)
(g) ɔ́·k ná=nə́ ləsí·t·e 'and if that is what he does' (B; ɔ́·k 'and'; ná PRES, nə́ 'that (inan.)';
   |ələsī-| AI 'do {so}', |–tē| 3s/SBJ)

Temporal ('when', etc.)
(h) xú pá·t·e, kənihəlá·wəna. 'When he comes, we shall kill him.' (V; xú FUT;
   |pā-| AI 'come', |–tē| 3s/SBJ)
(i) xú ki·š·i·k·ié·k·we 'when you (pl.) grow up' (OA; xú FUT;
   |kīšīkī-| AI 'grow', |–yēkwē| 2p/SBJ)
(j) kíši- ne·ó·k·wəni -kəntkahtí·t·e 'after they have danced for four days' (V;
   kíši PV PERF, |kə́ntəkā-| AI 'dance', |–hətītē| 3p/SBJ; ne·ó·k·wəni 'for four days')
(k) kə́nč áhi-pa·tama·é·k·we 'unless you pray hard' (B; KJV "but by prayer"; kə́nč 'unless';
   áhi PV 'very much', |pāhtamā-| AI 'pray', |–yēkwē| 2p/SBJ)

Past hypothetical
- (l) šá·e=á·=máh lié·k·we 'if you (pl.) had told me in the first place' (Voegelin 1945, 4.36; šá·e P 'right away'; =á· POT; =máh PST; |əl-| TA 'say {so} to', |–əyēkwē| 2p–1s/SBJ)
- (m) xú kíši-aləmo·x·ɔlát·e 'if you have already taken him' (OA; xú FUT; kíši PV PERF, |aləmōxwal-| TA 'take away', |–àtē| 2s–3/SBJ)
- (n) məšənəmá·ne '(so that in that case) when I got it (I would have ...)' (B; |məšən-| TI(1b) 'get', |–əmānē| 1s–0$_{(1a)}$/SBJ)
- (o) pa·á·ne '(so that in that case) when I came back (I would have ...)' (B; |pā-| AI 'come', |–yānē| 1s/SBJ)

Main verb (idiom)
- (p) kə́nč pa·tama·á·ne. 'I have to pray.' (OA; kə́nč 'unless, until'; |pāhtamā-| AI 'pray', |–yānē| 1s/SBJ)
- (q) yúkwe=tá kə́nč tahkɔp·o·ha·lke·ánkwe=kə́nč. 'Now we must get legally married.' (ME; yúkwe 'now'; =tá FOC; kə́nč 'unless'; |takwapōhāl-| TA 'unite in marriage', |–əkēyankwē| X–12/SBJ)
- (r) mé·či=tá kə́nč aləmska·ánkwe yú wə́nči. 'Now we must go away from here.' (V; mé·či 'already'; =tá FOC; kə́nč 'unless'; |aləməskā-| AI 'depart', |IC-yankwē| 12/SBJ; yú 'this (inan.); here', wə́nči 'from {smwh}')

The formation of participles is summarized at the end of **§4.6a**. The head may be any argument of the verb: subject (4.64abeghikmnpqstuvwx, 4.65abcdfgh, 4.66ab), primary object (4.64jlt, 4.65eh, 4.66c), secondary object (4.40i, 4.64fq,aa, 4.65i, 4.66f), or oblique (3.13(2)b, (3)d, (5)bd, (6)a, (7)cd; 3.15b, 4.9e, 4.67), as well as possessor of subject (4.64cd), instrumental oblique (3.14d), one of the conjoined subjects (4.64p), and adjunct (3.15d), including agent of a passive (4.64o) or topic of quote (3.17b). A third-person participle may qualify a vocative noun (e.g., Lk 13.34 2x, 19.17, Mt 22.18, 25.26). Some participles are used with a mirative function, either alone or in an equational sentence (4.64be). The examples are sorted by the nominal categories (**§3.1c**) of the head. A non-third person head is marked like an inanimate singular.

(4.64) Participle (proximate examples)

Animate singular
- (a) ké·pča·t lə́nu 'foolish man' (B; |kəpəčā-| AI 'be foolish', |IC–t| 3/PPL(ANsg); lə́nu 'man')
- (b) šé· ná pé·a·t 'here he comes' (B, ME; šé· 'here!'; ná 'that (anim.)'; |pā-| AI 'come', |IC–t| 3/PPL(ANsg))
- (c) sunso·kté·li·k wənáxk 'one whose hand was withered' (B; /sunso·kte·-/ II 'be withered', |(IC)–līk| 0´/PPL(ANsg); wənáxk 'his hand')
- (d) ni·š·í·nxke txə́n télən txá·pxki entxí·li·t wsɔ·čələ́ma 'one who had twenty thousand soldiers' (B; ni·š·í·nxke '20', txə́n '{so many} times', télən txá·pxki '1,000'; |(ən)taxī-| AI 'be {so many}', |IC–līt| 3´/PPL(ANsg); wsɔ·čələ́ma 'his soldiers')
- (e) é·ləmi-na·hihəlá·t·a 'There he goes down the river!' (OA; |aləmī| PV 'begin', |nāhīhlā-| AI 'go rapidly downstream', |IC–ta| 3/PPL(ANsg.ABS))
- (f) we·t·ó·x·ink 'the father' (B; |wətōxī-| AI+O 'have as father', |IC–nk| X/PPL(ANsg))
- (g) ke·č·íhəlala·t 'the one who exposed him' (B; |kəčīhlal-| TA 'expose', |IC–āt| 3–3´/PPL(ANsg))
- (h) we·ó·ha·t le·khí·k·ana 'one who knew books' (B; |wəwāh-| TA 'know', |IC–āt| 3–3´/PPL(ANsg); le·khí·k·ana 'book(s) (obv.)')
- (i) we·la·mhítaɔ·t 'one who believes him' (B; |wəlāməhtaw-| TA 'believe', |IC–āt| 3–3´/PPL(ANsg))

(j) ehɔ́·lak 'the one I love' (B; |àhwāl-| TA 'love', |IC–àk| 1s–3/PPL(ANsg))
(k) nehəlá·lkən 'your master' (B; |nīhlāl-| /nihəla·l-/ TA 'own', |IC–əkwan| 3–2s/PPL(ANsg))
(l) we·t·ó·x·əmənt 'the father' (B; |wətōxəm-| TA 'have as father', |IC–ənt| X–3/PPL(ANsg))
(m) ehɔ́·t·ank 'who loves it' (B; |àhwāt-| TI(1a) 'love', |IC–ank| 3–0/PPL(ANsg); cf. 4.65c)
(n) ké·t·a-nihəlá·t·ank 'the one who is going to own it' (B; KJV "the heir"; |kata| PV 'going to', |nīhlāt-| TI(1a) 'own', |IC–ank| 3–0/PPL(ANsg))
(o) šinka·lké·ankw 'our enemy' (B; |šīnkāl-| TA 'hate', |(IC)–əkēyankw| X–12/PPL(ANsg))
(p) mé·li ne·xkuntíhti·t 'Mary, who was engaged to him' (B; |naxkōntī-| 'be engaged to each other', |IC–hətīt| 3p/PPL(ANsg))

Animate plural
(q) milláni·k 'the ones (anim.) I gave you (sg.)' (OA; |mīl-| TA+O 'give O2 to', |IC–əlanīk| 1s–2s/PPL(ANpl))
(r) ké·t·a-wíči-pa·tamá·č·i·k 'ones who desired to join in the prayer' (B; |kata| PV 'going to', /wíči/ PV 'along with (others)', |pāhtamā-| AI 'pray', |IC–čīk| 3/PPL(ANpl))
(s) we·i·mahtəntí·č·i·k 'brothers' (B; |wəwīmatəntī-| AI 'be brothers', |IC–čīk| 3/PPL(ANpl))
(t) wé·mi nehəla·lák·i·k 'all (anim.) that are mine' (B; wé·mi 'all'; cf. k; |IC–àkīk| 1s–3/PPL(ANpl))
(u) kenná·č·i·k 'the ones carrying him' (B; |kələn-| TA 'hold', |IC–āčīk| 3–3´/PPL(ANpl))
(v) metahkəni·má·č·i·k 'ones who accuse him' (B; |matakənīm-| TA 'say bad things about', |IC–āčīk| 3–3´/PPL(ANpl))
(w) we·txa·tpáni·k 'the ones that had come to visit her' (B; |wətax-| TA 'come to', |IC–ātəpanīk| 3–3´/PPL.PRET(ANpl)
(x) we·la·mhitánki·k 'ones who believed in it' (B; |wəlāməht-| TI(1a) 'believe', |IC–ankīk| 3–0₍₁ₐ₎/PPL(ANpl))
(y) me·š·ənínki·k 'ones who have received it' (B; |məšən-| TI(1b) 'get', |IC–ənkīk| 3–0₍₁ᵦ₎/PPL(ANpl))
(z) we·lhatá·k·wi·k 'those who keep it' (B; |wəlaht-| TI(2) 'keep', |IC–ākwīk| 3–0₍₂₎/PPL(ANpl))
(aa) mi·lianpáni·k 'the ones (anim.) that you (sg.) gave me' (B; |mīl-| TA+O 'give O2 to', |IC–əyanəpanīk| 2s–1s/PPL.PRET(ANpl))

(4.65) Participle (obviative examples)
Obviative with |-ī| obv.
(a) ke·t·o·p·wi·lí·č·i 'the hungry (obv.)' (B; |katōpwī-| AI 'be hungry', |IC–līčī| 3´/PPL(OBV))
(b) enkələ lí·č·i 'the dead (obv.)' (B; |ankəl-| AI 'die', |IC–əlīčī| 3´/PPL(OBV))
(c) pe·t·alo·ka·li·lí·č·i 'the one (obv.) that sent me' (B 5x; |pētalōhkāl-| TA 'send hither', |(IC)–īlīčī| 3´–1s/PPL(OBV))
(d) ke·tanət·o·wi·lí·č·i 'God (obv.)' (B; |kəhtanətōwī-| AI 'be great spirit', |IC–līčī| 3´/PPL(OBV))
(e) e·k·e·ki·mahtí·č·i 'their (prox.) disciples (obv.)' (B; |akēhkīm-| TA 'teach', |IC–āhətīčī| 3p–3´/PPL(OBV))
(f) wi·č·e·ykúk·i 'those (obv.) that were with him (prox.)' (B 5x; |wīčēw-| TA 'accompany', |IC–əkwəkī| 3´–3s/PPL(OBV))
(g) ehɔ·lkwihtí·č·i 'those (obv.) that love them (prox.)' (B; |àhwāl-| TA 'love', |IC–əkwəhətīčī| 3´–3p/PPL(OBV))
(h) mehɔ́·č·i 'the one (obv.) he ate' (ME; |məhw-| TA 'eat', |IC–āčī| 3s–3´/PPL(OBV))
(i) mi·lí·č·i 'the ones (obv.) he gave me' (OA; |mīl-| TA+O 'give O2 to', |(IC)–īčī| 3s–1s/PPL(OBV))

(j) ke·t·a·la·línki 'the one (obv.) who was desired' (B;
|katāl-| TA 'desire', |IC–ālīnkī| X–3´/PPL(OBV))

(k) e·lanko·ma·liénki 'our people (obv.) (*lit.*, relatives)' (B;
|əlānkōm-| TA 'have as a relative', |IC–āləyēnkī| 1p–3´/PPL(OBV))

Obviative without |-ī| obv.

(l) pi·lsí·li·t '(who is) holy (obv.)' (B 6x; |pīləsī-| AI 'be clean', |(IC)–līt| 3´/PPL[OBV])

(m) ne·óhti·t 'the one (obv.) they (prox.) saw' (B;
|nēw-| TA 'see', |(IC)–āhətīt| 3p–3´/PPL[OBV]; form not otherwise used as a participle)

(n) pa·tamá·k·uk=č 'the one (obv.) who will pray to him (prox.)' (B;
|pāhtamaw-| TA 'pray to', |(IC)–əkwək| 3´–3s/PPL[OBV]; also 3´–3s/PPL(ANsg))

(4.66) Participle (second person and inanimate examples)

Second person

(a) e·ləwa·p·énsian wé·mi e·xkwé·ian 'you who are the most blessed of all you women
(|àləwāpēnsī-| AI 'be more blessed', |IC–yan| 2s/PPL;
wé·mi P 'all'; |axkwēwī-| AI 'be a woman', |IC–yan| 2s/PPL [representative singular])

(b) we·t·o·x·əmólenk 'you who are our father'
(|wətōxəm-| TA 'have as father', |IC–əlēnk| 1p–2/PPL)

(c) ki·ló·wa le·p·ó·e·kw 'you wise ones'
(ki·ló·wa 2p/EMPH; |ləpwā-| AI 'be wise', |IC–ēkw| 2p/PPL)

(d) ki·ló·wa wi·pó·mie·kw 'you (pl.) who are eating with me' (cf. c;
|wīhpōm-| TA 'eat with', |(IC)–əyēkw| 2p–1s/PPL)

Inanimate singular

(e) mé·x·e·k '(that, inan.) which is big' (B; |maxē-| II 'be big', |IC–k| 0/PPL(INsg));
cf. maxé· 'it is big'.

(f) máxke·k '(that, inan.) which is red' (B, ME; |maxkē-| II 'be red', |(IC)–k| 0/PPL(INsg));
cf. máxke· 'it is red'.

(g) ehó·t·ank 'what he loves' (B; |àhwāt-| TI(1a) 'love', |IC–ank| 3s–0/PPL(INsg); cf. 4.64m)

Inanimate plural

(h) ehɔ·ɔhtí·k·i 'ones (inan.) of great value' (B;
|àhwāwatī-| II 'be very valuable, be expensive', |IC–kī| 0/PPL(INpl))

(i) e·ləwihəlá·k·i 'the ones (inan.) that were left over' (B;
|àləwīhlā-| II 'be left over', |IC–kī| 0/PPL(INpl))

(j) ehahkwiá·ni 'my garments' (B; |Rih+| HAB, |akwī-| AI+O 'wear', |IC–yānī| 1s/PPL(INpl))

(4.67) Participle with oblique head (examples)

(1) |əl-| '{so}', 'to {smwh}'

(a) é·li·kahtá·la·t 'in a way to desire her' (B;
|əlī| PV '{so}', |katāl-| TA 'desire', |IC–āt| 3s–3´/PPL(OBL))

(b) kéku=á· é·li·čani·máhti·t 'some way they could accuse him' (B; kéku 'something';
=á· POT; |əlī| PV '{so}', |čanīm-| TA 'accuse', |IC–āhətīt| 3p–3´/PPL(OBL))

(c) e·li·t·é·ha·t 'his will' (B; |əlītēhā-| AI 'think {so}', |IC–t| 3s/PPL(OBL))

(d) e·lalo·ká·lian 'what you sent me to do' (B;
|əlalōhkāl-| TA 'send {so}, to {smwh}', |IC–əyan| 2s–1s/PPL(OBL))

(e) e·li·x·əmá·link 'how he (obv.) was laid' (B;
|əlīxəm-| TA 'lay {so}', |IC–ālīnk| X–3´/PPL(OBL))

(f) ennəmíhti·t 'what they did' (OA; also with =č FUT [B] and with =á· POT [OA];
|ələn-| TI(1b)-O 'do {so}', |IC–əməhətīt| 3p–0$_{(1b)}$/PPL(OBL))

(2) |wənt-| 'from {smwh}' (hence 'because of {smthg}'); 'in {such} direction'
 (g) wentalo·ká·link 'where I was sent from' (B;
   |wəntalōhkāl-| TA 'send from {smwh}', |IC–īnk| X–1s/PPL(OBL))
 (h) wénči-kčinkwéhəla·k 'the east' (*lit.*, 'in the direction of the sunrise') (B, WS;
   |wənčī| PV 'from {smwh}', |kəčīnkwēhlā-| AI 'rise (of the sun)', |IC–k| 0/PPL(OBL))
 (i) wénči-či·tkwə́s·i·t 'because he remained silent' (B;
   |wənčī| PV 'from {smwh}', |čītəkwəsī-| AI 'be silent', |IC–t| 3/PPL(OBL))
 (j) kéku wénči-kələstáe·kw? 'Why do you listen to him?' (B; kéku 'something; what?';
   |wənčī| PV 'from {smwh}', |kələsətaw-| TA 'listen to', |IC–ēkw| 2p–3/PPL(OBL))
 (k) kéku wə́nči-wi·š·á·s·ie·kw? 'why are you afraid?' (B; kéku 'something; what?';
   |wənčī| PV 'from {smwh}', |wīšāsī-| AI 'be afraid', |IC–yēkw| 2p/PPL(OBL))
 (l) kéku=háč wénči-luwé·an 'why do you say?' (B; kéku 'something; what?';
   |wənčī| PV 'from {smwh}', |ələwē-| AI 'say {so}', |IC–yan| 2s/PPL(OBL))
 (m) kéku=háč wə́nči-lát 'why do you tell them?' (B; kéku 'something; what?'; =háč Q;
   |wənčī| PV 'from {smwh}', |əl-| TA 'tell {so}', |IC–àt| 2s–3/PPL(OBL))
 (n) nə́ni wénči-lə́le·kw 'that's why I say to you' (B; nə́ni 'that (inan.)';
   |wənčī| PV 'from {smwh}', |əl-| TA 'tell {so}', |IC–əlēkw| 1s–2p/PPL(OBL))
 (o) wénči- nə́ -lúwe·t 'why he said that'; (as a clause) 'which is why he said that' (B;
   |wənčī| PV 'from {smwh}', |ələwē-| AI 'say {so}', |IC–t| 3s/PPL(OBL); nə́ 'that (inan.)')
 (p) wénči-=č -po·ní·mi·t 'so that he will stop talking about me' (B; =č FUT;
   |wənčī| PV 'from {smwh}', |pōnīm-| TA 'cease talking about', |IC–īt| 3s–1s/PPL(OBL))
 (q) wénči-=č -məšá·t·ame·kw 'so that you will remember it' (B; =č FUT;
   |wənčī| PV 'fr. {smwh}', |məšāt-| TI(1a) 'remember', |IC–amēkw| 2p–0$_{(1a)}$/PPL(OBL))
(3) |(-ən)tal-| '{smwh}' (énta PV with IC < IC + |(-ən)talī| PV)
 (r) entale·khá·s·i·k 'where it was written' (B;
   |(-ən)talēkahāsī-| II 'be written', |IC–k| 0/PPL(OBL))
 (s) énta- nehənaɔnké·s·ak -xámənt 'where horses were fed' (B; nehənaɔnké·s·ak 'horses';
   |(-ən)talī| PV '{smwh}', |axam-| TA 'feed', |IC–ənt| X–3/PPL(OBL))
 (t) énta-=č -ne·ykwə́s·ian 'where you will be seen' (B; =č FUT; |(-ən)talī| PV '{smwh}',
   |nēwəkwəsī-| AI 'be seen', |IC–yan| 2s/PPL(OBL); for /yk/ see 2.35)
 (u) lehələmátahpink 'seat' (B; |Rih+| HAB, |ləmatapī-| AI 'sit {smwh}', |IC–nk| X/PPL(OBL))
(4) |(-ən)tax-| '{so many}', '{so much}'
 (v) entxe·kháma·t 'what he owed' (B;
   |(-ən)taxēkahamā-| AI 'owe {so much}', |IC–t| 3s/PPL(OBL))
 (w) éntxi-pi·ihəláhti·t 'everyone who is left; all the rest' (V;
   |(-ən)taxī| PV '{so many}', |pīwīhlā-| AI 'be left over', |IC–hətīt| 3p/PPL(OBL))
   Cf. éntxi-ləpó·č·i·k 'all who are wise' (B;
   |(-ən)taxī| PV '{so many}', |ləpwā-| AI 'be wise', |IC–čīk| 3/PPL(ANsg))
 (x) wé·mi éntxi-pəntá·k·uk 'all (obv.) that heard him' (B; wé·mi 'all';
   |(-ən)taxī| PV '{so many}', |pəntaw-| TA 'hear', |IC–əkwək| 3´–3s/PPL(OBL))
   Cf. wé·mi éntxi-pəntaɔ́·č·i·k 'everyone who hears him' (B; wé·mi 'all';
   |(-ən)taxī| PV '{so many}', |pəntaw-| TA 'hear', |IC–āčīk| 3p–3´/PPL(ANpl))
 (y) éntxi-ne·mhíti·t 'as many as see them (inan.)' (B;
   |(-ən)taxī| PV '{so many}, |nēm-| TI(3) 'see', |IC–əhtīt| 3p–0$_{(3)}$/PPL(OBL))
   Cf. éntxi-nénki·k 'everyone that saw it' (B; same with |IC–kīk| 3–0$_{(3)}$/PPL(ANpl))
 (z) entxíhti·t 'all of them' (B 2x; |(-ən)taxī-| AI 'be {so many}', |IC–hətīt| 3p/PPL(OBL))
   Cf. entxí·č·i·k 'all of them' (B 1x; same AI with |IC–čīk| 3/PPL(ANpl))

(5) |sahk-| '{so far}', '{so long}'
 (aa) se·khaké·a 'for as long as I am away' (B;
  (|sahkahkē-| AI 'be away {so long}', |IC–yā| 1s/PPL(OBL))

Oblique-headed participles on stems with |(-ən)tax-| '{so many}', '{so much}' are found in all periods (4.67wxyz), but if an animate plural is the subject this is more commonly the head, marked with |-īk| anim. pl. (see the forms compared in 4.67wxyz). In Blanchard third plural participles with the preverb éntxi usually inflect for an animate plural head (three exceptions are in 4.67wxy), but with the verb |(-ən)taxī-| AI 'be {so many}' (4.67z) there is an early example with an animate plural head (p. 11) and two later examples with the oblique as the head (pp. 31, 146).

§4.7. Independent and Conjunct Preterite. The preterite is a marked or removed past tense indicated by the suffix |-p(an-)| PRET in endings of the independent and conjunct orders (**§4.4b**). It is attested with the independent indicative and subordinative and all conjunct modes except the changed subjunctive. The examples given are from Blanchard unless indicated otherwise.

The suffix |-p(an-)| PRET follows the central suffixes (4.19, 54) and is itself followed only by a peripheral suffix (|-īk| anim. pl., |-ī| inan. pl., obv., |-a| abs. anim. sg., |-ənka| abs. pl., obv.) or by |-ē| SBJ. In at least some forms, however, the peripheral suffix is not used when it would mark a secondary object (4.71eg) or the head of a participle (4.75pqrs, 4.76pq,aa, 4.78cd, 4.78n). When an animate plural head is not marked on a preterite participle it is indicated by the usual conjunct ending |-hətīt| (4.76aa,bb, 4.78n).

The central suffixes exhibit adjustments in shape before |-p(an-)| PRET. The m-suffix |-w|$_m$ 3,0 is lost, but it leaves behind the effects it has on preceding vowels (2.24af, 2.67d, 3.6e, 4.68hm, 4.69ac). The stems in |-ī| that have /-u/ 3s,0s (< |-əw| ← |-ī-w|) have |ō| before |-p(an-)| PRET, as if from underlying |-ə-w-əp(an-)| (2.24f, 2,67d, 3.13(1)ab, 3.13(4)c, 3.14a, 4.68ci), and |-əlī| obv. is treated the same way (4.68e). A consonant-final stem or theme is followed by |ō| before |-p(an-)| PRET, as if from |-w-əp(an-)| (2.15c,4.68dfj, 4.69opqr). In the pluralizers of the three independent order ending sets (4.19) the optional final consonants are lost, leaving |-(ə)nā| 1p,12 and |-(ə)wā| 2p,3p. Similarly, the w-suffix |-w|$_w$ sg., indef. is lost without a trace (2.60b, 2.61b, 3.8e, 4.69defghmn). The n-suffix |-ən(ē)| sg., indef. takes the shape |-ənē|. After a retained consonant a |ə| is inserted before |-p(an-)| PRET, and in the resulting sequence |kw| is optionally dissimilated to |k|. The formative |-əhm| of the m-endings combines irregularly with |-p(an-)| PRET in the first and second singular to give |-(ə)həmp| (2.53, 4.68a, 4.69wxz,aa). In the conjunct the suffix |-ān| 1s takes the shape |-ā| before |-panē| SBJ.PRET in the two examples of this combination attested by Blanchard (4.74a). In one archaic example |-ān| 1s combines with |-p(an-)| PRET as apparent /-á·k·əp/ (4.78c), while in seven other cases this combination is retained as |-ānəp| (4.75a, 4.77b, 4.78ab). The ending with |-āk| 1s before /-əp/ PRET has a parallel in Northern Unami, which has apparent /-á·k·əp/ ⟨-akup⟩ and /-a·kpáne/ ⟨-akpanne⟩ (Zeisberger 1827:56, 87, 121), beside preterite endings with |-ān| 1s (Zeisberger 1827:77).

(4.68) Independent indicative preterite AI and II (examples)
 (a) mpa·lsí·həmp 'I was sick' (|pāləsī-| AI 'be sick', |nə–həmp| 1s/IND.PRET; mpá·lsi 1s)
 (b) pá·tama·p 'he prayed' (|pāhtamā-| AI 'pray'; pá·tama· 3s)
 (c) kpahá·s·o·p 'he had been imprisoned' (|kəpahāsī-| AI, II 'be shut (in)'; kpahá·s·u 3s, 0s)
 (d) ánkəlo·p 'she died' (|ankəl-| AI 'die'; ánkəl 3s)
 (e) ahpí·lo·p 'he or they (obv.) were (there)' (|apī-| AI 'be {smwh}, exist')
 (f) wəlí·x·əno·p=á· 'it would have been the right thing' (wəlīxən-| II 'be good'; =á· POT)
 (g) nəmi·tsíhəna·p 'we (exc.) have eaten' (|mītəsī-| AI 'eat', |nə–h(mə)nāp| 1p/IND.PRET;
  kəmi·tsíhəna 'we (inc.) eat')

(h) aləmské·p·ani·k 'they headed out' (|aləməskā-| AI 'depart', |–panīk| 3p/IND.PRET; aləmske· 3s)
(i) kí·xki ləmatahpó·p·ani·k 'they had sat nearby' (|ləmatapī-| AI 'sit'; ləmátahpu 3s)
(j) šenki·x·i·nó·p·ani·k 'they were lying down (but they left)' (ME; |šēnkīxīn-| AI 'lie')
(k) áhi-kahto·phɔtí·ne·p 'there was great famine' (|àhī| PV 'very', katōpwahtī-| AI 'be hungry (coll.)', |–nēp| X/IND.PRET)
(l) áhi-maxé·p 'it was very large' (|àhī| PV 'very', |maxē-| II 'be big', |–p| 3,0/IND.PRET)
(m) wənčihəlé·p·ani †taipi·liás·ink 'they (inan.) came from Tiberias' (|wənčīhlā-| II 'come from {smwh}', |–panī| 0p/IND.PRET)

(4.69) Independent indicative preterite TA (examples)

TA direct absolute
(a) xé·li awé·ni wenčí·me·p 'he invited many people (obv.)' (xé·li 'many'; awé·ni 'person (obv.)'; |wēnčīm-| TA 'invite', |–ēp| 3s–(3´)/IND.PRET)
(b) nne·óhəna·p lə́nu 'we (exc.) saw a man' (|nēw-| TA 'see', |nə–āh(mə)nāp| 1p–(3)/IND.PRET; lə́nu '(a) man' [here indefinite])
(c) kələné·p·ani·k ɔ·s·əle·ní·k·ana 'they carried lamps (obv.)' (B 2x; |kələn-| TA 'carry', |–ēpanīk| 3p–(3´)/IND.PRET; ɔ·s·əle·ní·k·ana 'lamp(s) (obv.)')

TA direct objective
(d) nčani·laé·ha·p 'I have offended him' (|čanīlawēh-| TA 'offend', |nə–āp| 1s–3s/IND.PRET)
(e) nke·nahki·há·p·ani·k 'I took care of them' (|kēnakīh-| TA 'take care of', |nə–āpanīk| 1s–3p/IND.PRET)
(f) kəmí·la·p aləwí·i-ləs·əwá·k·an 'you have given him power' (|mīl-| TA+O 'give O2 to', |kə–āp| 2s–3s/IND.PRET)
(g) kənihəla·lá·p·ani·k 'they (anim.) were yours' (lit., 'you (sg.) owned them'; |nīhlāl-| TA 'own', |kə–āpanīk| 2s–3p/IND.PRET)
(h) wwi·t·a·he·má·p·ani 'he helped them (obv.)' (|wītāhēm-| TA 'help', |wə–āpanī| 3s–3´/IND.PRET)
(i) mpəntaɔ́·wəna·p 'we (exc.) heard him' (|pəntaw-| TA 'hear', |nə–āwənāp| 1p–3s/IND.PRET)
(j) kənihəláwwa·p 'you (pl.) killed him' (|nəhl-| TA 'kill', |kə–āwəwāp| 2p–3s/IND.PRET)
(k) pwe·š·əwawwá·p·ani 'they brought him (obv.)' (|pēšəw-| TA 'bring', |wə–āwəwāpanī| 3p–3´/IND.PRET)
(l) wəne·ɔwwá·p·ani·l 'they saw him (obv.)' (|nēw-| TA 'see', |wə–āwəwāpanīl| 3p–3´/IND.PRET)
(m) nkála·p 'he was left' (|nəkal-| TA 'leave behind' [2.67ef], |–āp| X–3s/IND.PRET)
(n) wenči·má·p·ani·k 'they were invited' (|wēnčīm-| TA 'invite', |–āpanīk| X–3p/IND.PRET)

TA inverse absolute (inanimate subject)
(o) wi·š·a·s·əwá·k·an tɔ́xko·p 'fear came over him' (|wətax-| TA 'come to', |–əkōp| (0)–3s/IND.PRET)

TA inverse objective (animate subject)
(p) nəmí·lko·p a·pto·ná·k·an 'he gave me words' (|mīl-| 4.57, |nə–əkōp| 3s–1s/IND.PRET)
(q) kwənnuk·ó·p·ani kɔhé·s·al 'he was being held by his mother (obv.)' (|kələn-| TA 'carry', |wə–əkōpanī| 3´–3s/IND.PRET; |wə-| 3, |-kàhēs-| 'mother', |-al| obv.)
(r) mɔ́i-tɔxkó·p·ani·l 'they (obv.) went to visit him' (|mawī| PV 'go to', |wətax-| TA 'come to', |wə–əkōpanīl| 3´–3s/IND.PRET)
(s) čɔhɔ·pwənuk·əwá·p·ani 'they were baptized by him (obv.)' (B ⟨hvop-⟩ for ⟨hovop-⟩; |čahwāhpwən-| TA 'dunk in water', |wə–əkəwāpanī| 3´–3p/IND.PRET)

TA inverse objective (inanimate subject)
- (t) wwi·č·e·ykó·ne·p 'it was with him'
  (|wīčēw-| TA 'accompany', |wə–əkōnēp| 0s–3s/IND.PRET)
- (u) kəwitahpi·mko·né·na·p 'it lived with us (inc.)'
  (|wītapīm-| TA 'live with', |kə–əkōnēnāp| 0s–12/IND.PRET)
- (v) wwe·mihko·né·ɔ·p 'it killed them all'
  (|wēmīh-| TA 'kill all of', |wə–əkōnēwāp| 0s–3p/IND.PRET)

TA theme 3
- (w) ktahɔ·lí·həmp 'you (sg.) loved me' (|àhwāl-| TA 'love', |kət–īhəmp| 2s–1s/IND.PRET)
- (x) kí·=máh kəwinka·lí·həmp 'you (sg.) used to like me' (ME; kí· 2s/EMPH; =máh PST; |wīnkāl-| TA 'like', |kə–īhəmp| 2s–1s/IND.PRET)
- (y) ktax·amíhəmɔ·p 'you (pl.) fed me' (|axam-| TA 'feed', |kət–īhmwāp| 2p–1s/IND.PRET)

TA theme 4
- (z) kəne·wəlúhump 'I saw you (sg.)' (|nēw-| TA 'see', |kə–ələhəmp| 1s–2s/IND.PRET)
- (aa) ní·=máh kəwinkallúhump 'I used to like you (sg.)' (ME; incorrect in Goddard 1979:147)
  (ní· 1s/EMPH; =máh PST; |wīnkāl-| TA 'like', |kə–ələhəmp| 1s–2s/IND.PRET)
- (bb) kpe·t·o·lhúmɔ·p wəla·č·i·məwá·k·an 'I have brought you (pl.) good news'
  (|pētaw-| TA+O 'bring O2 to', |kə–ələhmwāp| 1s–2p/IND.PRET)
- (cc) ktalo·kallúhəmɔ·p 'I sent you (pl.)' (|alōhkāl-| TA, |kə–ələhmwāp| 1s–2p/IND.PRET)
- (dd) kəne·wəlúhəna·p 'we saw you' (|nēw-| TA 'see', |kə–ələhmənāp| 1p–2/IND.PRET)
- (ee) ktəmi·k·aləlhúməna·p 'we brought you inside'
  (|təmīkal-| TA 'bring or take inside', |kə–ələhmənāp| 1p–2/IND.PRET)

(4.70) Independent indicative preterite TI (examples)

TI absolute (and TI-O)
- (a) no·le·ləntamúhump=máh 'I was happy' (ME; incorrect ending in Goddard 1979:147)
  (|wəlēlənt-| TI(1a)-O 'be happy, glad', |nə–aməhəmp| 1s–(0)$_{(1a)}$/IND.PRET)
- (b) kó·li·li·namúhump 'you (sg.) had good fortune' (B; |wəlī| PV 'well', |əlīn-| TI(1a)-O 'experience {so}', |kə–aməhəmp| 1s–(0)$_{(1a)}$/IND.PRET)
- (c) wəle·ĺəntamo·p 'he was glad, happy' (B, ME; cf. a; |–amōp| 3s–(0)$_{(1a)}$/IND.PRET)
- (d) mhalamó·p·ani·k mpí·s·o·n 'they had bought medicine'
  (|mahl-| TI(1a) 'buy', |–amōpanīk| 3p–(0)$_{(1a)}$/IND.PRET; mpí·s·o·n 'medicine')

TI objective
- (e) kkwi·taméne·p 'he was aftraid of it' (B 2x; would also be 'you (sg.) were afraid of it')
  (|kwəht-| TI(1a) 'fear', |wə–amənēp| 3s–0s$_{(1a)}$/IND.PRET; for kkw- see 2.54, 58)
- (f) o·wa·tó·ne·p 'he knew it' (|wəwāht-| TI(2) 'know', |wə–ōnēp| 3s–0s$_{(2)}$/IND.PRET)
- (g) wəné·məne·p 'he saw it' (|nēm-| TI(3) 'see', |wə–ənēp| 3s–0s$_{(3)}$/IND.PRET)
- (h) tóləmi-nhaka·t·aməné·p·ani 'he set about putting them (inan.) to use' (B; |aləmī| PV 'begin', |nahkāt-| TI(1a) 'use', |wət–amənēpanī| 3s–0p$_{(1a)}$/IND.PRET)
- (i) pwəntaməlí·ne·p '(obv.) heard it'
  (|pənt-| TI(1a) 'hear', |wə–aməlīnēp| 3´–0s$_{(1a)}$/IND.PRET)
- (j) mpəntaməné·na·p 'we (exc.) have heard it' (cf. i; |nə–amənēnēp| 1p–0s$_{(1a)}$/IND.PRET)
- (k) kəne·məné·na·p 'we (inc.) saw it' (cf. g; |kə–ənēnāp| 12–0s$_{(3)}$/IND.PRET)
- (l) kkwi·taməné·ɔ·p 'they were afraid of it' (cf. e; |wə–amənēwāp| 3p–0s$_{(1a)}$/IND.PRET)
- (m) wəne·məné·ɔ·p 'they saw it' (cf. g; |wə–ənēwāp| 3p–0s$_{(3)}$/IND.PRET)
- (n) wwe·t·ənəməne·ɔ·p·ani 'they received them (inan.)' (|wētən-| TI(1b) 'take, receive', |wə–əmənēwāpanī| 3p–0p$_{(1b)}$/IND.PRET)

(4.71) Independent indicative preterite AI+O and TA+O (examples)
  AI+O objective
    (a) wte·psi·né·p·ani 'he was full of it (the Holy Spirit, obv.)'
        (|tēpəsī-| AI+O 'be full of O2', |wə–nēpanī| 3s+3´/IND.PRET)
    (b) kki·spwi·ne·ɔ́·p·ani 'you (pl.) were filled by them (loaves, inan.)'
        (|kīsəpwī-| AI+O 'be full eating O2', |kə–nēwāpanī| 2p+0p/IND.PRET)
    (c) mwe·k·əne·ɔ́·p·ani 'they handed him (obv.) over'
        (|mēk-| AI+O 'give, hand over O2', |wə–ənēwāpanī| 3p+3´/IND.PRET)
  TA+O objective
    (d) wwəntamaɔ́·ne·p 'he informed him about it'
        (|wəntamaw-| TA+O 'inform O1 about O2', |wə–ānēp| 3s–3´+0s/IND.PRET)
    (e) tɔk·əno·t·əmaɔ́·ne·p né·l mi·məntət·al 'she spoke about the baby to them'
        (|akənōtəmaw-| TA+O 'tell O1 about O2', |wət–ānēp| 3s–3´+O2/IND.PRET)
    (f) wé·mi təla·č·i·mo·lxuk·ó·ne·p 'they (obv.) told him about all of that' (wé·mi 'all';
        |əlāčīmōlax-| TA+O 'tell O1 about O2', |wət–əkōnēp| 3´–3s+0s/IND.PRET)
    (g) wči·skantama·k·ó·ne·p mwə́k·ia 'they (obv.) licked his sores'
        (|čīskantamaw-| TA+O 'lick O2 of', |wə–əkōnēp| 3´–3s+O2/IND.PRET)
    (h) kəmi·li·né·p·ani·k 'you (sg.) gave them to me'
        (|mīl-| TA+O 'give O2 to', |kə–īnēpanīk| 2s–1s+3p/IND.PRET)
    (i) kwí·n kpənuntələláne·p 'long have I shown it to you (sg.)' (kwí·n 'for a long time';
        |pənōntəl-| TA+O 'show O2 to', |kə–ələnēp| 1s–2s+0s/IND.PRET)
    (j) kpak·i·t·a·t·amó·ləne·p 'I forgave you (sg.) it'
        (|pakītātamaw-| TA+O 'forgive O2 of', |kə–ələnēp| 1s–2s+0s/IND.PRET)
(4.72) Independent subordinative preterite
    (a) ná mɔ·č·í·ne·p 'then he went home'
        (ná 'then'; |māčī-| AI 'go home', |wə–nēp| 3s/SBD.PRET)
    (b) ná tɔləmska·né·ɔ·p 'then they left' (|aləməskā-| AI 'depart', |wət–nēwāp| 3p/SBD.PRET)
    (c) ná təlá·ne·p 'then he said to them' (|əl-| TA 'say {so} to', |wət–ānēp| 3s–3´/SBD.PRET)
    (d) ná təla·né·ɔ·p 'then they said to him' (cf. c; |wət–ānēwāp| 3s–3´/SBD.PRET)
    (e) ná lá·ne·p 'then he was told' (cf. c; |–ānēp| X–3s/SBD.PRET)
    (f) ná pe·š·əwa·né·ɔ·p 'then they were brought' (cf. 4.29c; |–ānēwāp| X–3p/SBD.PRET)
    (g) ná .. o·txuk·ó·ne·p 'then they (obv.) came to him'
        (|wətax-| TA 'come to', |wə–əkōnēp| 3´–3s/SBD.PRET)
    (h) ná tɔ́ləmi-wi·č·e·yko·né·ɔ·p. 'Then he (obv.) started off with them.'
        (|aləmī| PV 'begin', |wīčēw-| TA 'accompany', |wət–əkōnēwāp| 3´–3p/SBD.PRET)
    (i) né·k·a tə́li-ki·š·e·ləntamáne·p 'he himself was the one who had created it'
        (né·k·a 3s/EMPH;
        |əlī| PV '{so}', |kīšēlənt-| TI(1a) '(divinely) create', |wət–amənēp| 3s–0$_{(1a)}$/SBD.PRET)
    (j) tə́li-pəntaməné·ɔ·p 'that they had heard it'
        (|əlī| PV '{so}', |pənt-| TI(1a) 'hear', |wət–amənēwāp| 3p–0$_{(1a)}$/SBD.PRET)
(4.73) Changed conjunct preterite
    (a) ne·lahpí·t·əp 'while she was there' (|nēl-| 'while', |-apī-| AI 'be', |(IC)–təp| 3s/CC.PRET)
    (b) né·li-pa·tamá·t·əp 'while he was praying'
        (|nēlī| PV 'while', |pāhtamā-| AI 'pray', |(IC)–təp| 3s/CC.PRET)
    (c) é·li- nə́ni -li·x·ínkəp 'for that has been the rule' (nə́ni 'that (inan.)';
        |əlī| PV '{so}', |əlīxən| 'be {so}', |IC–kəp| 0/CC.PRET)

(d) é·li-khwitəlá·t·əp 'because he had admonished him'
      (|əlī| PV '{so}', |kwəhtəl-| TA 'admonish', |IC–ātəp| 3s–3´/CC.PRET)
  (e) né·li-mi·kəntamaə́·t·əp 'while he was working for him'
      (|nēlī| PV 'while', |mīhkəntamaw-| TA 'work for', |(IC)–ātəp| 3s–3´/CC.PRET)
  (f) é·li- .. -péči-mái-wwa·təluk·wé·k·əp 'for he came to teach you about it' (B ⟨kup⟩;
      |əlī| PV '{so}', péči PV 'come to', |mawī| PV 'go to',
      |wəwāhtəl-| TA 'teach', |IC–əkw-ēkw-əp| 3–2p/CC.PRET)
  (g) é·li-wi·t·a·wso·məlé·k·əp 'because I was living among you' (B ⟨kup⟩;
      |əlī| PV '{so}', |wītāwəsōm-| TA 'live along with', |IC–əl-ēkw-əp| 1s–2p/CC.PRET)
  (h) é·li- .. -li·namánəp 'for you (sg.) have seen (it)'
      (|əlī| PV '{so}', |əlīn-| TI(1a) 'see, experience', |IC–amanəp| 2s–0$_{(1a)}$/CC.PRET)
  (i) é·li-mi·č·ié·k·əp 'because you (pl.) ate them (inan.)' (B ⟨kup⟩;
      |əlī| PV '{so}', |mīčī-| TI(3) 'eat', |IC–ēkw-əp| 2p–0$_{(3)}$/CC.PRET)
(4.74) Subjunctive preterite
  (a) ní·=á· máta pa·á·p·ane 'if *I* had not come' (Jn 15.22; ní· 1s/EMPH; =á· POT; máta 'not';
      |pā-| AI 'come', |–yāpanē| 1s/SBJ.PRET; non-negative ending)
  (b) ahpianpáne 'if you (sg.) had been there' (|apī-| AI 'be, exist', |–yanəpanē| 2s/SBJ.PRET)
  (c) lanihinkpáne 'if he had been thrown (there)'
      (|əlanihī-| AI+O 'throw {so}', |–nkəpanē| X/SBJ.PRET)
  (d) lehəle·x·e·ankwpáne 'if we (incl.) had been alive' (B ⟨fqp⟩;
      |lēhlēxē-| AI 'live, be alive', |–yankwəpanē| 12/SBJ.PRET)
  (e) nə́ni·á·=máh ləs·ie·kwpáne 'if you (pl.) had done that' (B ⟨qkp⟩;
      nə́ni 'that (inan.)'; =á· POT; =máh PST; |ələsī-| AI 'do {so}', |–yēkwəpanē| 2p/SBJ.PRET)
  (f) wələstae·kpáne 'if you (pl.) had listened to him' (B ⟨kp⟩;
      |wələsətaw-| TA 'heed', |–ēkw-əpanē| 2p–3/SBJ.PRET)
  (g) wəni·č·a·nəmuk·we·kwpáne 'if you had been his children' (B ⟨qp⟩;
      |wənīčānəm-| TA 'have as child(ren)', |–əkwēkwəpanē| 3–2p/SBJ.PRET)
  (h) šá·e=á·=máh lie·kwpáne 'if you (pl.) had told me in the first place' (V ⟨kp⟩ > ⟨kwp⟩
      [in ms.]; šá·e 'immediately' [correcting Goddard 1979:55]; =á· POT; =máh PST;
      |əl-| TA 'say {so} to', |–əyēkwəpanē| 2p–1s/SBJ.PRET [Voegelin 1945:111, 4.20, 44])
  (i) nə́ li·namihti·tpáne 'if they had seen that' (nə́ 'that (inan.)'; cf. 4.73h;
      |–aməhətītəpanē| 3p–0/SBJ.PRET)
(4.75) Preterite participle (AI, II)
  (a) e·ləwe·á·nəp 'the one of whom I said' (Jn 1.30;
      |ələwē-| AI 'say {so}', |IC–yānəp| 1s/PPL.PRET(ANsg))
      e·ləwe·á·nəp 'what I said' (Jn 3.28; |IC–yānəp| 1s/PPL.PRET(OBL))
  (b) e·ləwé·anəp 'as you have said, what you said' (cf. a; |IC–yanəp| 2s/PPL.PRET(OBL))
  (c) e·p·iánəp 'where you (sg.) were' (|apī-| AI 'be {smwh}', |IC–yanəp| 2s/PPL.PRET(OBL))
  (d) wenta·wsiánəp 'what you (sg.) live off'
      (|wəntāwəsī-| AI 'live from {smwh} [3.13(7)]', |IC–yanəp| 2s/PPL.PRET(OBL))
  (e) pa·lsí·t·əp 'who had been sick' (|pāləsī-| AI 'be sick', |(IC)–təp| 3s/PPL.PRET(ANsg))
  (f) e·ləwé·t·əp 'as he said, what he said' (cf. a; |IC–təp| 3s/PPL.PRET(OBL))
  (g) e·p·í·t·əp 'where he was' (cf. c; |IC–təp| 3s/PPL.PRET(OBL))
  (h) énta-mi·tsí·t·əp 'where he had eaten' (|(-ən)talī| PV '{smwh}' [4.67(3)],
      |mītəsī-| AI 'eat', |IC–təp| 3s/PPL.PRET(OBL))
  (i) ke·kai·tpána 'the one who was the eldest then'
      (|kəhkayī-| AI 'be old', |IC–təp| 3/PPL.PRET(ANsg))

(j) nə́ni wénkəp lə́nu 'the man who came from there' (nə́ni 'that (inan.)';
|wəm-| 'come from {smwh}', |IC–kəp| 3/PPL.PRET(ANsg); lə́nu 'man')
(k) šenki·x·ínkəp 'where he lay' (|šēnkīxīn-| AI 'lie {smwh}', |(IC)–kəp| 3s/PPL.PRET(OBL))
(l) enkələ́k·əp 'one who had been dead' (|ankəl-| AI 'die', |IC–əkəp| 3s/PPL.PRET(ANsg))
(m) we·la·wsi·tpáni·k 'those that led good lives'
(|wəlāwəsī-| AI 'live a good life', |IC–təpanīk| 3/PPL.PRET(ANpl))
(n) wé·mi entxi·tpáni·k 'all those who had been present' (wé·mi 'all';
|(-ən)taxī-| AI 'be {so many}', |IC–təpanīk| 3/PPL.PRET(ANpl))
(o) šaxahka·wsi·tpanínka 'ancient righteous ones'
(|šāxakāwəsī-| AI 'live straight', |IC–təpanənka| 3/PPL.PRET(ANpl.abs))
(p) ke·k·e·p·inkɔ·lí·t·əp 'one (obv.) who had been blind' (B 3x;
|(k)akēpīnkwā-| AI 'be blind', |IC–lītəp| 3´/PPL.PRET)
(q) enkələlí·t·əp 'one (obv.) who had died' (|ankəl-| AI 'die', |IC–əlītəp| 3´/PPL.PRET)
(r) e·li·t·e·ha·lí·t·əp 'ones (obv.) who had thought'
(|əlītēhā-| AI 'think {so}', |IC–lītəp| 3´/PPL.PRET)
(s) a·mwi·lí·t·əp 'who (obv.) had risen' (āmwī-| AI 'arise', |(IC)–lītəp| 3´/PPL.PRET)
(t) e·ləwe·lí·t·əp 'what he (obv.) had said'
(|ələwē-| AI 'say {so}', |IC–lītəp| 3´/PPL.PRET(OBL))
(u) pehpalalo·ka·s·i·li·tpáni 'ones (obv.) who had been criminals'
(|Rih+| HAB, |palalōhkāsī-| AI 'do wrong', |IC–lītəpanī| 3´/PPL.PRET(OBV.abs))
(v) nehəni·k·a·ní·i·we·wsi·li·tpanínka 'the prophets (obv.) of old'
(|Rih+| HAB, |nīkānīwī| PV 'ahead',
|wēwəsī-| AI 'find out things', |IC–lītəpanənka| 3´/PPL.PRET(OBV.abs))
(w) énta·ki·š·i·k·o·hénkəp 'where he had been raised' (|(-ən)talī| PV '{smwh}' [4.67(3)],
|kīšīkōhē-| AI+O 'cause O2 to grow up', |IC–nkəp| X/PPL.PRET(OBL))
(x) e·lé·k·əp 'what happened' (|əlē-| II 'happen {so}', |IC–kəp| 0/PPL.PRET(OBL))
(4.76) Preterite participle (TA direct and inverse)
(a) e·k·əni·mák·əp 'who I was talking about'
(|akənīm-| TA 'talk about', |IC–àkəp| 1s–3/PPL.PRET(ANsg))
(b) e·lák·əp 'as I told them' (|əl-| TA 'say {so} to', |IC–àkəp| 1s–3/PPL.PRET(OBL))
(c) wenči·makpáni·k 'the ones I have invited'
(wēnčīm-| TA 'invite', |(IC)–àkəpanīk| 1s–3/PPL.PRET(ANpl)))
(d) me·ya·ɔ·č·i·mo·lxát·əp 'the one you bore witness for'
(|mayāwāčīmōlax-| TA 'testify for', |IC–átəp| 2s–3/PPL.PRET(ANsg))
(e) kənte·ləmát·əp 'which (anim.) you (sg.) condemned'
(|kəntēləm-| TA 'condemn', |(IC)–àtəp| 2s–3/PPL.PRET(ANsg))
(f) wi·k·i·matpáni·k 'your (deceased) husbands'
(|wīkīm-| TA 'be married to', |(IC)–àtəpanīk| 2s–3p/PPL.PRET(ANpl))
(g) pəntaɔ́·t·əp 'one who heard him (obv.)'
(|pəntaw-| TA 'hear', |(IC)–ātəp| 3s–3´/PPL.PRET(ANsg))
(h) mi·lá·t·əp 'what he had given to him (obv.)'
(|mīl-| TA+O 'give O2 to', |(IC)–ātəp| 3s–3´/PPL.PRET(INsg))
(i) e·lá·t·əp 'as he had said to him (obv.)'
(|əl-| TA 'say {so} to', |IC–ātəp| 3s–3´/PPL.PRET(OBL))
(j) ke·t·o·nala·tpáni·k 'those that wanted to kill him (obv.)'
(|katōnal-| TA 'desire to kill', |IC–ātəpanīk| 3–3´/PPL.PRET(ANpl))

(k) we·t·e·ka·ɔ·tpáni·k 'ones who followed him (obv.)'
   (|wətēhkaw-| TA 'follow', |IC–ātəpanīk| 3–3´/PPL.PRET(ANpl))
(l) pe·t·alo·ka·la·tpáni 'the one (obv.) he has sent (here)'
   (|pētalōhkāl-| TA 'send hither', |(IC)–ātəpanī| 3s–3´/PPL.PRET(OBV))
(m) e·lanko·ma·tpáni 'his relative (obv.)' (*lit.*, 'the one (obv.) he is related to')
   (|əlankōm-| TA 'be related to', |IC–ātəpanī| 3s–3´/PPL.PRET(OBV))
(n) nehəlé·k·əp 'who you (pl.) killed' (|nəhl-| TA 'kill', |IC–ēkwəp| 2p–3/PPL.PRET(ANsg))
(o) ne·ɔhtí·t·əp '(obv.) which they had seen' (cf. 4.65k; |(IC)–āhətītəp| 3p–3´/PPL.PRET)
(p) me·t·e·ləma·lí·t·əp 'ones (obv.) who had thought badly of them (obv.)'
   (|matēləm-| TA 'think badly of', |IC–ālītəp| 3´–3´´/PPL.PRET)
(q) né·tami-ne·ɔ·li·tpáni 'those (obv.) who had seen him (obv.) first'
   (|(n)əhtamī| PV 'first', |nēw-| TA 'see', |IC–ālītəpanī| 3´–3´´/PPL.PRET(OBV))
(r) e·lo·ka·ləntpáni·k 'those that were sent'
   (|alōhkāl-| TA 'send', |–əntəpanīk| X–3/PPL.PRET(ANpl))
(s) e·lalo·ka·ləntəp 'where he was sent' (B;
   |əlalōhkāl-| TA 'send {so}, to {smwh}', |IC–əntəp| X–3/PPL.PRET(OBL))
(t) wi·č·e·ykónəp 'the one who was with you (sg.)'
   (|wīčēw-| TA 'accompany', |(IC)–əkwanəp| 3–2s/PPL.PRET(ANsg))
(u) wi·č·əmukwpáni 'the one (obv.) that helped him'
   (|wīčəm-| TA 'help', |(IC)–əkwəpanī| 3´–3s/PPL.PRET(OBV))
(v) e·lkúk·əp 'what he (obv.) had said to him'
   (|əl-| TA 'say {so} to', |IC–əkwəkəp| 3´–3s/PPL.PRET(OBL))
(w) e·p·i·tá·kwkəp mahtant·ó·wa 'the one the devils (obv.) had been in'
   (|apīhtaw-| TA 'be in', |IC–əkwəkəp| 3´–3s/PPL.PRET(ANsg);
   |matanətōw-| 'devil', |-a| obv.)
(x) mi·lkwé·k·əp 'the one who gave it to you (pl.)'
   (|mīl-| TA 'give O2 to', |(IC)–əkwēkwəp| 3–2p/PPL.PRET(ANsg))
(y) e·lkwé·k·əp 'what he said to you (pl.)'
   (|əl-| TA 'say {so} to', |IC–əkwēkwəp| 3–2p/PPL.PRET(OBL))
(x) e·lkwihtí·t·əp 'what they (obv.) said to them'
   (|əl-| TA 'say {so} to', |IC–əkwəhətītəp| 3´–3p/PPL.PRET(OBL))
(aa) we·txukhwití·t·əp 'those to whom it (inan.) came'
   (|wətax-| TA 'come to', |IC–əkwəhtītəp| 0–3p/PPL.PRET)
(bb) ke·lho·khwití·t·əp 'those that it (inan.) fell on'
   (|kəlahw-| TA 'fall on', |IC–əkwəhtītəp| 0–3p/PPL.PRET)
(cc) ki·š·i·xta·k·e·é·k·əp 'that was prepared for you (pl.)'
   (|kīšīxətaw-| TA+O 'prepare O2 for', |(IC)–əkēyēkwəp| X–2p/PPL.PRET(INsg))

(4.77) Preterite participle (TA themes 3 and 4)
(a) pe·t·alo·ka·lí·t·əp 'the one who has sent me here'
   (|pētalōhkāl-| TA 'send hither', |(IC)–ītəp| 3s–1s/PPL.PRET(ANsg))
(b) mi·lí·t·əp 'what he has given me'
   (|mīl-| TA+O 'give O2 to', |(IC)–ītəp| 3s–1s/PPL.PRET(INsg))
   (cf. mi·lkó·nəp 'the one who gave it to me':
   |mīl-| TA+O 'give O2 to', |(IC)–əkwānəp| 3s–1s/PPL.PRET(ANsg))
(c) e·la·pto·na·liánəp 'what you (sg.) told me'
   (|əlāpətōnāl-| TA 'report to {so}', |IC–əyànəp| 2s–1s/PPL.PRET(OBL))

(d) mi·lianpáni 'the ones (inan.) you (sg.) gave me'
      (|mīl-| TA+O 'give O2 to', |(IC)–əyànəpanī| 2s–1s/PPL.PRET(INpl))
   (e) e·p·i·taí·k·əp '(inan.) that was in me'
      (|apīhtaw-| TA 'be in', |IC–īkəp| 0–1s/PPL.PRET(INsg)
   (f) ellé·k·əp 'what I said to you (pl.)'
      (|əl-| TA 'say {so} to', |IC–əlēkwəp| 1s–2p/PPL.PRET(OBL))
   (g) né·tami-ləlé·k·əp 'what I first said to you (pl.)'
      (|(n)əhtamī| PV 'first', |əl-| TA 'say {so} to', |IC–əlēkwəp| 1s–2p/PPL.PRET(OBL))
(4.78) Preterite participle (TI)
   (a) nehəla·t·amá·nəp '(inan.) which I had'
      (|nīhlāt-| TI(1a) 'own', |IC–amānəp| 1s–0$_{(1a)}$/PPL.PRET(INsg); cf. 4.64kr)
   (b) enkhitaó·nəp 'what I had lost'
      (|ankəht-| TI(2) 'lose', |IC–awānəp| 1s–0$_{(2)}$/PPL.PRET(INsg))
   (c) kéku e·li·namá·k·əp 'things I have seen' (B ⟨rlenumakup⟩ Jn 8.38)
      (kéku 'thing(s)'; |əlīn-| TI(1a) 'see, experience', |IC–amākəp| 1s–0$_{(1a)}$/PPL.PRET(INsg))
   (d) no·ná·k·ana kí· no·na·t·amánəp 'the breasts *you* (sg.) nursed from'
      (no·ná·k·ana 'breasts' (inan. pl.); kí· 2s/EMPH;
      |nōnāt-| TI(1a) 'nurse from', |(IC)–amanəp| 2s–0$_{(1a)}$/PPL.PRET [⟨-nrp⟩ Lk 11.27])
   (e) wénči- .. íka -hataónəp 'a reason for you (sg.) to have put it there'
      (|wənčī| PV 'from {smwh}, because of {smthg}',
      |aht-| TI(2) 'put {smwh}', |IC–awanəp| 2s–0$_{(2)}$/PPL.PRET(OBL); íka 'there')
   (f) mi·kəntánkəp 'what he has done'
      (|mīhkənt-| TI(1a) 'work on, do', |(IC)–ankəp| 3s–0$_{(1a)}$/PPL.PRET(INsg))
   (g) ne·ka·t·ánkəp 'what he relied on'
      (|nahkāt-| TI(1a) 'rely on, put to use', |IC–ankəp| 3s–0$_{(1a)}$/PPL.PRET(INsg))
   (h) éntxi-pəntánkəp 'everything she had heard'
      (|(-ən)taxī| PV '{so much}', |pənt-| TI(1a) 'hear', |IC–ankəp| 3s–0$_{(1a)}$/PPL.PRET(OBL))
   (i) me·š·ənínkəp 'the one who got them'
      (|məšən-| TI(1b) 'get', |IC–ənkəp| 3–0$_{(1b)}$/PPL.PRET(ANsg))
   (j) ennínkəp 'what he did' (|ələn-| TI(1b)-O 'do {so}', |IC–ənkəp| 3–0$_{(1b)}$/PPL.PRET(OBL))
   (k) nénkəp 'the one who saw it' (|nēm-| TI(3) 'see', |(IC)–kəp| 3–0$_{(3)}$/PPL.PRET(ANsg))
   (l) ni·k·a·na·pto·na·t·ankpána 'who (sg., abs.) prophesied about it'
      (|nīkānāpətōnāt-| TI(1a) 'report ahead of time, prophesy about',
      |(IC)–ankəpana| 3–0$_{(1a)}$/PPL.PRET(ANsg.abs))
   (m) máta ke·t·a·t·ankpáni·k 'those that don't want it' (máta NEG;
      |katāt-| TI(1a) 'want', |IC–ankəpanīk| 3–0$_{(1a)}$/PPL.PRET(ANpl))
   (n) anshamihtí·t·əp 'the ones that had dipped it up'
      (|ansah-| TI(1a) 'dip up', |(IC)–aməhətītəp| 3p–0$_{(1a)}$/PPL.PRET)
   (o) ke·nahki·tá·k·əp 'who (sg.) took care of it then'
      (|kēnakīht-| TI(2) 'take care of', |(IC)–ākəp| [< |-ākw-əp|] 3s–0$_{(2)}$/PPL.PRET (ANsg))
   (p) e·li·xtá·k·əp 'as he laid down (in law)'
      (|əlīxət-| 'lay down {so}, set in place {so}', |IC–ākəp| 3s–0$_{(2)}$/PPL.PRET (OBL))
   (q) e·li·namihtí·t·əp 'what they had witnessed'
      (|əlīn-| TI(1a) 'see, experience', |IC–aməhətītəp| 3p–0$_{(1a)}$/PPL.PRET)
   (r) ehələnəmihtí·t·əp 'the way they used to do'
      (|Rih+| HAB, |ələn-| TI(1b)-O 'do {so}', |IC–əməhətītəp| 3p–0$_{(1b)}$/PPL.PRET(OBL))

(s) a·pto·ne·tuhtí·t·əp 'which they reported'
(|āpətōnēht-| TI(2) 'report', |(IC)–ōhətītəp| 3p–0_{(2)}/PPL.PRET(INsg))

(t) mi·č·ihtí·t·əp 'what they ate' (|mīčī-| TI(3) 'eat', (IC)–hətītəp| 3p–0_{(3)}/PPL.PRET(INsg))

§4.8. Present. The present, indicating a present perfective aspect, is attested by Blanchard in a subordinative form (Blanchard 1834b:18.3), a subjunctive (4.79a), a changed conjunct (4.79b), and an oblique-headed participle (Blanchard 1834a:18.7). It is marked by the suffix |-əsa(han-)| PRST in the same position as the preterite suffix. When a further suffix follows (only |-ē| SBJ is attested) the suffix has /-sh-/ for underlying |-sah-| even after a syncopated |ə|.

(4.79) Present

(a) kí· aləmo·x·ɔlatsháne yú wə́nči 'if *you* have taken him from here' (Jn 20.15; |aləmōxwal-| TA 'take away', |–àtəsahanē| 2s–3/SBJ.PRST)

(b) é·li·ki·š·e·ləmá·tsa 'because he had created them' (B 1842:8; |əlī| PV '{so}', |kīšēləm-| TA 'create divinely', |IC–ātəsa| 3s–3´/CC.PRST)

§4.9. Negative Suffix and Particles. The negative of verbs in the independent and conjunct orders is indicated by a negative particle and a suffix |-(ō)w(ī)| NEG added before the central ending (4.19). The suffix includes the |ō| after a consonant, and the |ī| appears before a consonant or word-finally; |-aw| TH.TI(2) has the variant |ō| before it, treated like a stem-final vowel.

The negative particle takó· 'not' has later forms akó· and kó·. There is also máta 'not', which before =á· POT ('would, will') is usually tá. These negative particles do not differ in meaning. takó· 'not' (and its later variants) is almost always used in main clauses, where it tends to occur first and may be followed by =tá FOC; it is sometimes preceded by a sentence-initial particle (like ɔ́·k 'and' or šúkw 'but') or by a noun phrase that is fronted as a focus of interest. máta 'not' generally occurs just before the verb and may follow a preverb; it is favored in subordinate clauses. An added háši P or extended reduplication gives the meaning 'never'. Negative verbs are also used after né·ləma P 'not yet', P,PV 'before' and né·skɔ P,PV 'not yet, before'.

§4.10. Independent Negative. In the independent negative when the plural m-endings follow |-(ō)w(ī)| NEG they are treated as having underlying |-əhm|, giving, for example, /-(o·)húməna/ 1p,12 neg. (from |-(ō)w-əhmənā|) and /-(o·)húmɔ/ 2p neg. (from |-(ō)w-əhmwā|), but the preterite singular m-ending (§2.12k) is treated as |-həmp|, giving, for example, apparent /-o·wí·hump/ 1s,2s pret. neg. (B 197 ⟨-wevwmp⟩), though this is perhaps not distinct from /-o·wí·həmp/. The suffixes |-w|_m 3,0 and |-w|_w (the w-ending formative) are lost word-finally in the underlying form after |-(ō)wī| NEG, and the |ī| is shortened; the resulting word-final /-i/ was usually assimilated to a preceding vowel or |ōw| in the speech of the last speakers (2.12). In the TA inverse objective negative ME gave the shortened ending |-əkōwənānāk| (instead of |-əkōwīwənānāk| 4.85.l), and OA accepted this, but OA later gave the long form of the ending for singular subject, agreeing with the B and V endings with singular and plural subjects (4.85kjmn).

(4.80) Independent indicative negative, AI and II inflections and constructed paradigms

	inflection	|pā-| AI 'come'	|ankəl-| AI 'die'
AI 1s	|nə–(ō)wī|	mpá·i (B)	ntankəló·wi
2s	|kə–(ō)wī|	kpá·i	ktankəló·wi
3s	|–(ō)wī|	pé·i (B, V)	ankəló·wi (B)
3´	|–əlīwī|	pe·lí·i	ankələ́lí·i
1p	|nə–(ō)wəhmənā|	mpa·húməna	ntankəlo·húməna
12	|kə–(ō)wəhmənā|	kpa·húməna	ktankəlo·húməna
2p	|kə–(ō)wəhmwā|	kpa·húmɔ	ktankəlo·húmɔ
3p	|–(ō)wīwak|	pe·í·ɔk (B)	ankəlo·wí·ɔk (B)
X	|–(ō)wən|	pá·wən	ankəló·wən

[continued →]

[4.80, continued]

			|wīhkwē-| II 'end'	|wələt-| II 'be good'
II	0s	|–(ō)wī|	wi·kwé·i (B)	wələt·ó·wi (B), wələt·ó·u (OA)
	0p	|–(ō)wīwa|	wi·kwe·í·ɔ	

(4.81) Independent indicative negative, AI and II (examples)

AI: (a) máta nkak·əlo·né·i 'I do not lie' (B; |(k)akəlōnē-| AI)
    (b) né·ləma=tá ntəpskwilahtá·i 'it is not yet time for me' (B; |=tá FOC; |təpəskwīhlatā-| AI)
    (c) kó· nšenki·x·i·nó·u 'I'm not lying down' (OA; |šēnkīxīn-| AI)
    (d) takó· ko·la·məwé·i 'you (sg.) do not tell the truth' (B; |wəlāməwē-| AI)
    (e) máta=háč ne·má·i? 'does he not see?' (B; =háč Q; |nēmā-| AI)
    (f) máta=háč pəntamá·i? 'does he not hear?' (B; |pəntamā-| AI)
    (g) wáin ɔ́·k kéku áhɔnk, máta=č mi·məné·i. 'Wine and anything strong he will never drink.'
       (B; wáin 'wine'; ɔ́·k 'and'; kéku 'anything';
       |àhwan-| II 'be strong-tasting', |(IC)–k| 0/PPL(INsg); =č FUT; |Rī+| EXT, |məné-| AI)
    (h) kó· šenki·x·i·nó·u 'he's not lying down' (OA; cf. c)
    (i) máta pe·í·a 'he (abs.) did not come' (ME; |pā-| AI, |–wīwa| 3s.abs/IND.NEG)
    (j) takó· pí·li no·s·a·k·i·ma·yəmi·húməna 'we (exc.) have no other king'
       (B; |pīlī| P 'different, other'; |wəsākīmāwəmī-| AI 'have a chief, king')
    (k) akó· íka ntap·i·húməna 'we (exc.) weren't there' (OA; íka 'there'; |apī-| AI)
    (l) kó· nkat·unkɔ·mo·húməna 'we (exc.) are not sleepy' (OA; |katənkwām-| AI)
    (m) kó·=tá ki·ló·na kkát·a·kwtək·i·húməna '*we* (inc.) don't want to go back' (V, with [ka-])
    (n) kó·=tá kkát·a·kwtək·i·húmɔ 'you (pl.) don't want to go back' (V, [ka-]; |kwətəkī-| AI)
    (o) takó· wi·wəla·ta·í·ɔk 'they never put up food' (B; also w. máta; |Rī+| EXT, |wəlahtā-| AI)
    (p) máta haki·he·í·ɔk 'they do not plant' (B; |ahki·hē-| AI)
    (q) takó· tɔmi·mənsəmi·í·ɔk 'they had no children' (B; |wətamīmənsəmī-| AI)
    (r) tá=á· ankəlo·wí·ɔk 'they will not die.' (B; |ankəl-| AI)
    (s) máta=háč .. luwensi·lí·i 'is she (obv.) not named {so}?' (B; |ələwēnsī-| AI)
    (t) ɔ́·k=č tá=á· luwé·wən 'and people (indef.) will not say' (B; |ələwē-| AI)

II: (u) takó· káhta·wi·kwé·i 'it is not going to end' (B; |wīhkwē-| II)
    (v) ɔ́·k=č .. máta wi·i·kwé·i 'and it shall never end' (B; ɔ́·k 'and'; =č FUT; |Rī+| EXT, cf. u)
    (w) máta káski·kwčuk·wihəlé·i 'it could not be shaken' (B; |kwəčəkwīhlā-| II)
    (x) tá=á· .. wələt·ó·wi 'it would not be good' (B; =á· POT; |wələt-| II)
    (y) akó· wələt·ó·u 'it is not good' (OA; cf. x)
    (z) máta=háč wəli·x·ənó·wi 'is it not right?' (B; =háč Q; |wəlīxən-| II)
    (aa) akó· pəməč·ehəlé·e 'it (inan.) is not moving' (OA; |pəməčēhlā-| II)
    (bb) akó· pəməč·ehəle·í·ɔ né·l ahsə́na 'the rocks are not moving' (OA; cf. aa)

(4.82) Independent indicative negative, TA direct (inflections)

	TA direct absolute	TA direct −3	−3p	−3´
1s	|nə–āwī|	|nə–āwī|	|nə–āwīwak|	
3s	|–ēwī|			|wə–āwīwal|, |wə–āwīwa|
1p	|nə–āwəhmənā|*	|nə–āwīwənā|	|nə–āwīwənānak|, |nə–āwīwənānāk|	
2p	|kə–āwəhmwā|*	|kə–āwīwəwā|	|kə–āwīwəwāwak|	
3p	|–ēwīwak|			|wə–āwīwəwāwa|
X		|–āwī|	|–āwīwak|	|–a·līwīwa|*

(4.83) Independent indicative negative, TA direct (examples)
  TA direct absolute negative
   (a) máta no·wa·há·i lə́nu 'I know no man' (B; |wəwāh-| TA 'know')
   (b) takó· kahta·lé·i nta·ktə́la 'he has no need of a doctor (obv.)' (B; |katāl-| TA 'want, need')
   (c) takó· awé·ni ne·é·i 'he saw no one'
         (B; awé·ni 'someone, anyone, person (obv.)'; |nēw-| TA 'see')
   (d) takó· awé·ni kéku le·í·ɔk 'they did not speak to anyone'
         (B; cf. c; kéku 'something, anything'; |əl-| TA 'say {so} to')
  TA direct objective negative
   (e) kó· no·wa·há·a 'I don't know him' (OA; cf. a)
   (f) akó· nəmaxkaɔ́·ɔ 'I didn't find him' (OA; |maxkaw-| TA 'find')
   (g) takó· mpa·tamwe·lxa·í·ɔk 'I do not pray for them' (B; |pāhtamwēlax-| TA 'pray for')
   (h) akó· nəmaxkaɔ·í·ɔk 'I didn't find them' (OA; cf. f)
   (i) takó· khičí·i kəwi·k·i·má·i ' you're not really married to him' (B; khičí·i P 'truly';
         |wīkīm-| TA 'be married to')
   (j) máta=č kəwe·t·əná·a 'you mustn't pick him up' (OA; |wētən-| TA 'take'; =č FUT)
   (k) tá=á· kčani·ma·í·ɔk 'you would not criticize them' (B; |čanīm-| TA 'criticize'; =á· POT)
   (l) máta o·wa·ha·í·ɔl 'he didn't know him' (B; cf. e)
   (m) kó· o·wa·ha·í·ɔ 'he doesn't know him' (OA; cf. e)
   (n) akó· mɔxkaɔ·í·ɔ 'he didn't find him, them' (OA; cf. f)
   (o) kó· no·wa·ha·í·wəna 'we (exc.) don't know him' (OA; cf. e)
   (p) kó· no·wa·ha·i·wəná·na·k 'we (exc.) don't know them' (OA; cf. e)
   (q) kó· ko·wa·ha·íwwa 'you (pl.) don't know him' (OA; cf. e)
   (r) máta=č kəwe·t·əna·íwwa 'you (pl.) mustn't pick him up' (OA; cf. j; =č FUT)
   (s) takó· kéku mwi·la·iwwá·ɔ. 'They did not give him anything.' (B; cf. d;
         |mīl-| TA+O 'give O2 to')
   (t) kó· o·wa·ha·iwwá·a 'they don't know him, them' (OA; cf. e)
   (u) akó· mɔxkaɔ·iwwá·a 'they didn't find him' (OA; cf. f)
  TA third person passive
   (v) takó· káski-wəli·há·i 'she could not be made well'
         (B; |kàskī| PV 'be able to', |wəlīh-| TA 'make well, do good for')
   (w) tá=á· khiki·no·ləwá·k·an mi·la·í·ɔk 'they will not be given a sign' (B; cf. s)

(4.84) Independent indicative negative, TA inverse (inflections)

	TA inverse absolute	TA inverse objective 3–	3p–	3´–
1s	|nə–əkōwī|	|nə–əkōwī|	|nə–əkōwīwak|	
3s	|–əkōwī|			|wə–əkōwīwa|
3´	|–əkwəlīwī|*			
1p	|nə–əkōwəhmənā|	|nə–əkōwīwənā|	|nə–əkōwīwənānak|, |nə–əkōwīwənānāk|	
2p	|kə–əkōwəhmwā|	|kə–əkōwīwəwā|	|kə–əkōwīwəwāwak|	
3p	|–əkōwīwak|			|wə–əkōwīwəwāwa|

(4.85) Independent indicative negative, TA inverse (examples)
  TA inverse absolute negative
   (a) tá=á· téxi kéku kpalihko·húmɔ 'nothing at all will destroy you (pl.)'

TA inverse objective negative with animate subject
  (b) takó· ní· nna·ka·lkó·wi 'he does not trust in *me*'
  (c) tá=á· kte·nha·k·ó·wi 'he will not reward you (sg.)'
  (d) kó· kəmaxka·k·ó·u 'he didn't find you (sg.)' (OA)
  (e) takó· kkáski-šinka·lko·wí·ɔk 'they cannot hate you (sg.)'
  (f) máta ko·wahko·wí·ɔk 'they do not know you (sg.)'
  (g) kó· kəmaxka·k·o·wí·ɔk 'they didn't find you (sg.)' (OA)
  (h) máta .. o·la·mhita·k·o·wí·ɔ 'they (obv.) did not believe him'
  (i) máta o·wahko·wí·ɔ 'they (obv.) did not know about him'
  (j) takó· háši awé·n no·t·alo·ka·k·anəmko·wí·wəna.
      'We have never been the servants of anyone.'
  (k) kó· nne·yko·wí·wəna 'he didn't see us (exc.)' (OA)
  (l) takó· ní·š·a lənəwak nəmaxka·k·o·wəná·na·k 'the two men didn't find us' (ME)
  (m) kó· kəne·yko·wí·wəna 'he does not see us (inc.)' (V)
  (n) tá=á· kkáski- kéku -lihko·wí·wəna 'he won't be able to do anything to us (inc.)' (V)
  (o) máta=háč kəwitahpi·mko·wi·wəná·nak? 'are they not sitting with us?'
  (p) máta=ksí ki·ló·wa aləwí·i ktəlihko·wíwwa? 'ought he not then to treat *you* (pl.) better?'
  (q) kó· kəmaxka·k·o·wíwwa 'he didn't find you (pl.)' (OA)
  (r) kó· kəne·yko·wíwwa 'he didn't see you (pl.)' (OA)
  (s) kó· kəmaxka·k·o·wiwwá·ak 'they did not find you' (OA)
  (t) máta kóski- kéku -luk·o·wiwwá·ɔ 'he (obv.) was unable to speak to them'
TA inverse objective negative with inanimate subject
  (u) máta ktap·i·ta·k·o·wəné·ɔ 'it is not in you (pl.)'
  (v) tá=á· wəni·skha·lko·wəné·ɔ 'it will not defile them'

(4.86) Independent indicative negative, TA first and second person passive (inflections, forms)

	inflections	forms (|nakal-| TA 'leave behind')
1s	|nə–əkēwī|	nnak·alək·é·i 'I was left behind'
2s	|kə–əkēwī|	kənak·alək·é·i 'you (sg.) were left behind'
1p	|nə–əkēwəhmənā|	nnak·alək·e·húməna 'we (exc.) were left behind'
12	|kə–əkēwəhmənā|	kənak·alək·e·húməna 'we (inc.) were left behind'
2p	|kə–əkēwəhmwā|	kənak·alək·e·húmɔ 'you (pl.) were left behind'

(4.87) Independent indicative negative, TA first and second person passive (examples)
  (a) takó· pí·li ntəlalo·ka·lké·i 'I was not sent to anywhere else' (B; pí·li P 'other, different'; \|əlalōhkāl-\| TA 'send to {smwh}')
  (b) akó· nəmaxka·k·e·húməna 'we (exc.) were not found' (OA)

(4.88) Independent indicative negative, TA theme 3 and theme 4 (inflections)

TA theme 3		TA theme 4	
2s–1s	|kə–īwī|	1s–2s	|kə–əlōwī|
2p–1s	|kə–īwəhmwā|	1s–2p	|kə–əlōwəhmwā|
2–1p	|kə–īwəhmənā|	1p–2	|kə–əlōwəhmənā|

(4.89) Independent indicative negative, TA theme 3 and theme 4 (examples)
Theme 3
  (a) máta=háč kéku ktəlí·i? 'Aren't you speaking to me?' (B)
  (b) máta kpəntai·húmɔ 'you didn't hear me' (B)
  (c) máta=á· ko·la·mhitai·húmɔ 'you would not believe me' (B)
  (d) tá=á· kəmaxkai·húmɔ 'you shall not find me' (B)

(e) tá=á· čí·č kəne·i·húmɔ 'you (pl.) will not see me again' (B, V)
(f) né·skɔ kkəlsət·ai·húmɔ 'you do not yet believe me' (B)
(g) takó· ktalápi-káhta-na·ɔli·húməna. 'You (sg.) don't hurry to try and follow us.' (ME)

Theme 4
(h) takó· kəwi·nəwaməló·wi 'I do not ask you (sg.)' (B)
(i) máta kkənte·ləməló·wi 'I do not condemn you (sg.)' (B)
(j) máta ktač·inkxe·to·ló·wi 'I did not disobey you (sg.)' (B)
(k) kó· kəne·wəló·wi 'I do not see you (sg.)' (V)
(l) akó· kəwinkalló·u 'I don't like you (sg.)' (OA)
(m) né·skɔ níke kəne·wəló·u 'before I saw you (sg.)' (OA)
(n) takó· ko·wahəlo·húmɔ 'I don't know you (pl.)' (B)
(o) takó· ktəllo·húmɔ 'I'm not telling you (pl.)' (B)
(p) takó·=tá kki·ɔləlo·húmɔ. 'I didn't cheat you (pl.).' (B)
(q) akó· kəwinkallo·húməna 'we don't like you (pl.)' (OA)
(r) kó· kəne·wəlo·húməna 'we didn't see you (pl.)' (B)

(4.90) Independent indicative negative, TI absolute (inflections)

	TI(1a)	TI(1b)	TI(2)	TI(3)
1s	|nə–amōwī|	|nə–əmōwī|	|nə–ōwī|	|nə–(ō)wī|
2s	|kə–amōwī|	|kə–əmōwī|	|kə–ōwī|	|kə–(ō)wī|
3s	|–amōwī|	|–əmōwī|	|–ōwī|	|–(ō)wī|
1p	|nə–amōwəhmənā|	|nə–əmōwəhmənā|	|nə–ōwəhmənā|	|nə–(ō)wəhmənā|
12	|kə–amōwəhmənā|	|kə–əmōwəhmənā|	|kə–ōwəhmənā|	|kə–(ō)wəhmənā|
2p	|kə–amōwəhmwā|	|kə–əmōwəhmwā|	|kə–ōwəhmwā|	|kə–(ō)wəhmwā|
3p	|–amōwīwak|	|–əmōwīwak|	|–ōwīwak|	|–(ō)wīwak|

(4.91) Independent indicative negative, TI absolute (examples)
(a) takó· nəmaxkamó·wi 'I did not find anything' (B)
(b) takó· kéku kkənnəmó·wi 'you (sg.) don't have anything' (B)
(c) máta kéku maxkamó·wi 'he found nothing' (B)
(d) takó· wwa·t·amó·wi 'he was unaware of himself'
    (B; |wəwāt-| TI(1a)-O 'have sense, be rational')
(e) máta káski-we·t·ənəmó·wi kéku 'he cannot receive anything' (B)
(f) kó·=húnt .. kéku mi·mi·č·í·i kí·šte·k. 'he never ate anything cooked' (OA)
(g) máta=č pəma·wsəwá·k·an ne·mó·wi 'he will not see (eternal) life' (B)
(h) takó· kéku mpəthamo·húməna. 'We (exc.) caught nothing.' (B)
(i) máta=háč·á· nəwenčo·t·əmo·húməna tɔ́ntay 'should we (exc.) not summon fire?' (B)
(j) takó· téxi kéku ko·wa·to·húmɔ 'you (pl.) know nothing at all' (B)
(k) máta maxkamo·wí·ɔk 'they did not find any' (B)
(l) wáin máta wəla·to·wí·ɔk. 'They have no wine.' (B)

(4.92) Independent indicative negative, TI objective with singular object (inflections)

	TI(1a)	TI(1b)	TI(2)	TI(3)	
1s	|nə–amōwən|	|nə–əmōwən|	|nə–ōwən|	|nə–(ō)wən|	
2s	|kə–amōwən|	|kə–əmōwən|	|kə–ōwən|	|kə–(ō)wən|	
3s	|wə–amōwən|	|wə–əmōwən|	|wə–ōwən|	|wə–(ō)wən|	
3´	|wə–aməlīwən|	|wə–əməlīwən|	|wə–ōlīwən|	|wə–(ə)līwən|	
1p	|nə–amōwənēn|	|nə–əmōwənēn|	|nə–ōwənēn|	|nə–(ō)wənēn|	
12	|kə–amōwənēn|	|kə–əmōwənēn|	|kə–ōwənēn|	|kə–(ō)wənēn|	[→]

[4.92, continued]

2p	|kə–amōwənēwā|	|kə–əmōwənēwā|	|kə–ōwənēwā|	|kə–(ō)wənēwā|
3p	|wə–amōwənēwā|	|wə–əmōwənēwā|	|wə–ōwənēwā|	|wə–(ō)wənēwā|
X	|–amōwən|	|–əmōwən|	|–ōwən|	|–(ō)wən|

The corresponding inflections for a plural object are not attested but would have the same relationship to the forms with singular object as in the non-negative paradigms (4.36). The endings for singular, obviative, or indefinite subject would add |-a| inan. pl.; the first plural endings would add |-ānī|, and the second and third plural endings would add |-wī|. The TI objective preterite inflections (attested only by Blanchard) add |-p(an-)| PRET as in (4.70e-n), ending in |-nēp| or |-āp| with a singular object, and in |-nēpanī| or |-āpanī| with a plural object, except that the marking of a plural object with a second or third plural subject was apparently optional.

(4.93) Independent indicative negative, TI objective with singular object (examples)
    (a) máta nkat·a·t·amó·wən 'I do not desire it' (B)
    (b) takó· nəwe·t·ənəmó·wən 'I do not receive it' (B)
    (c) máta ktamantamó·wən 'you (sg.) do not feel it' (B)
    (d) máta=háč ko·la·mhitamó·wən 'don't you (sg.) believe it?' (B)
    (e) takó· háši awé·n pwəntamó·wən 'no one ever heard it' (B)
    (f) máta o·wa·tó·wən 'he did not or does not know it' (B)
    (g) tá=á· tɔnkhitó·wən 'he will not lose it' (B)
    (h) tá=á· kɔ́ski-ne·mó·wən 'he would not be able to see it' (B)
    (i) takó· ni·ló·na nnihəla·t·amó·wəne·n 'we (exc.) do not have the say over it' (B)
    (j) takó· no·wa·tó·wəne·n 'we (exc.) do not know it' (B, also with máta; OA with kó·)
    (k) takó· ko·wa·tó·wəne·n 'we (inc.) do not know it' (B)
    (l) máta kəwe·t·ənəmo·wəné·ɔ 'you (pl.) do not accept it' (B)
    (m) takó· ko·wa·to·wəné·ɔ 'you (pl.) do not know it' (B)
    (n) takó· kɔt·a·t·amo·wəné·ɔ 'they did not want it' (B)
    (o) máta o·wa·to·wəné·ɔ 'they did not know it' (B)
    (p) tá=á· káski-kantható·wən 'it cannot be hidden' (B)

§4.10a. Subordinative Negative. The subordinative negative endings add |-(ō)w(ī)| NEG before the underlying |ə| of the n-ending component of the endings in (4.46) and (4.47), giving underlying |-(ō)wən(ē-)| instead of |-ən(ē-)| throughout, exactly as in the TI (4.92): e.g., təli- máta -ahpí·wən 'that he was not there' (B); təli-=č máta -ne·ma·wəné·ɔ 'that they will not see' (B).

§4.11. Conjunct Negative. In the conjunct endings, |-(ō)w(ī)| NEG combines with the third person suffixes |-t| 3 and |-k| 0 to give |-(ō)kw|; this is a fusion of the variant |-(ō)w| NEG with |-k| 0 or the variant |-k| 3 that is used after a stem or theme that ends in a consonant (4.54). Already in Blanchard's day this irregular ending tended to be avoided by using the corresponding non-negative form, with no vestige of |-(ō)w(ī)| NEG (4.78m), and non-negative conjunct endings were sometimes used with negative particles even outside the third person. This trend continued later, and in the twentieth century negative conjunct endings were rare, and some were not accepted by all speakers. A factor in this development must have been the loss of intervocalic |w| and |y| (**§2.11ab**), as a result of which the original negative forms of AI stems in |-ē| and |-ā| that had |-ēnk| 1p or |-ēkw| 2p became identical with the non-negative forms, and the original negative forms of stems and themes in |-ī| would have differed only in having /i·/ instead of /i/ and the shift of a following /a/-quality vowel to an /ɔ/-quality vowel. Even if these contrasts were made they cannot be recovered from Blanchard's transcriptions (except in a few late examples with ⟨o⟩ written for /ɔ/) because he writes prevocalic /i/ and /i·/ both as ⟨e⟩.

(4.94) Conjunct order negative, AI and II (endings)

	(without |-ē| SBJ)	(with |-ē| SBJ)	(with |-panē| PRET. SBJ)
1s	|-(ō)wā|	|-(ō)wānē|	|-(ō)wāpanē|
2s	|-(ō)wan|	|-(ō)wanē|	
3s,0	|-(ō)kw|	|-(ō)kwē|	
1p	|-(ō)wēnk|*	|-(ō)wēnkē|*	
12	|-(ō)wankw|	|-(ō)wankwē|*	
2p	|-(ō)wēkw|*	|-(ō)wēkwē|	
3p	|-hətīkw|* (etc., see 4.54)	|-hətīkwē|* (etc., see 4.54)	
3´	|-əlīkw|	|-əlīkwē|*	
X	|-(ō)wənk| (/-yunk/ and /-ink/)	|-(ō)wənkē|*	

In tables (4.94) and (4.98) the endings followed by an asterisk (*) are not attested but entirely predictable, though distinct negative endings are not attested for the third person plural in any conjunct paradigm.

(4.95) Conjunct order negative, all modes, AI and II (examples)

AI: (a) é·li- máta -ma·wsí·ɔ 'for I am not (just) one' (B ⟨mawseo⟩)
    (b) énta- máta -kwtək·í·ɔ 'when I did not go back' (V 1946:139, §2.12 ⟨-í·yo⟩)
    (c) máta=č ləs·i·ó·ne 'if I don't do (it)' (B)
    (d) né·skɔ-ankəló·wa 'before I die' (B 1842:18)
    (e) máta íkali pənči·nxke·ó·ne 'if I do not stick my hand in there' (B)
    (f) máta ləs·i·ó·p·ane 'if I had not done (it)' (cf. 4.74a; B)
    (g) wénči-=č máta -káski-kčí·ɔn 'so that you will not be able to get out' (B; ⟨kheon⟩)
    (h) né·skɔ=á· mi·tsí·ɔn 'before you (sg.) eat' (OA)
    (i) máta=x=á· kəlaistí·ɔne 'if in fact you are not Christ' (B; ⟨-eonc⟩)
    (j) é·li- né·ləma nčá·n -kpahá·s·i·kw 'for John had not yet been imprisoned' (B)
    (k) máta ki·š·i·k·í·k·we 'if he is not born' (B)
    (l) awé·n máta pahsuwé·k·we nhák·ay 'if anyone does not deny me' (B)
    (m) né·skɔ e·p·í·k·we 'before he was' (B)
    (n) wə́nči-=č máta -kxuwé·ɔnkw 'so that we would not fear' (B ⟨kxoreuf⟩; if not -é·ankw)
    (o) máta mi·tsi·é·k·we 'if you (pl.) do not eat' (B; if not -ié·k·we)
    (p) énta-=č máta -i·ankəlóli·kw 'where they (obv.) will never die' (B)
    (q) né·skɔ xínkwi-mi·tsahtí·yunk 'before the big feast' (B)
    (r) né·ləma i·ae·ké·yunk 'which has never yet been ridden' (B)
    (s) é·li-=á·.. máta -lo·kahəlá·ink 'how one should not give up' (Lk 18.1)
II: (t) éntxi- máta .. -wənčí·ai·kw 'as many as it does not come from'
    (u) wə́nči-=č máta kéku -taɔ́nkəno·kw 'so that nothing will be lost'

(4.96) Conjunct order negative, TA (endings)

	(without |-ē| SBJ)	(with |-ē| SBJ)
TA direct		
1s–3	|-āwàk|	
2s–3	|-āwàt|	|-āwàtē|
12–3	|-āwankw|	
2p–3	|-āwēkw|	
X–3	|-āwənt|	

[continued →]

[4.96, continued]

	(without |-ē| SBJ)	(with |-ē| SBJ)
TA inverse		
3–2s	|–əkōwan|	|–əkōwanē|
3′–3s	|–əkōkw|	|–əkōkwē|
3–1p	|–əkōwēnk|	
3,0–2p	|–əkōwēkw|	
TA theme 3		
X–1s	|–īwənk|	
TA theme 4		
1s–2s	|–əlōwan|	|–əlōwanē|

Negative conjunct TA endings that are predictable but not attested have been omitted from table (4.96), since it seems more likely than in the case of the AI and TI endings that the unattested endings were not in use.

(4.97) Conjunct order negative, all modes, TA (examples from B)

TA direct
    (a)   é·li- .. tá=á· -káski-mi·kəmɔ·s·əntamaɔ́·ɔk 'for I will not be able to work for him'
    (b)   né·ləma ne·t·o·xtaɔ́·ɔt 'before you ask him'
    (c)   máta pahki·t·a·t·amaɔ·ót·e awé·n 'if you (sg.) do not forgive someone for it'
    (d)   wə́nči-=č máta -káski-maxkaɔ́·ankw? 'so that we (inc.) won't be able to find him?'
    (e)   awé·n máta we·ɔ·há·e·kw 'someone you (pl.) do not know'
    (f)   kéku=háč wénči- máta -wəla·mhitaɔ·é·k·əp? 'How come you didn't believe him?'
    (g)   é·li- .. né·skɔ -mi·lá·wənt 'for he had not yet been given it'
    (h)   é·li- máta -wəla·mhitaɔ́·wənt 'because he was not believed'

TA inverse
    (i)   é·li- tá=á· -káski- .. -wenči·mkó·wan 'because they would not be able to invite you (sg.)'
    (j)   máta kələsta·k·ó·wane 'if he doesn't listen to you (sg.)'
    (k)   né·ləma .. wenči·mkó·wane 'before he called you (sg.)'
    (l)   é·li- .. máta háši -luk·ó·wan 'as it never told you (sg.)'
    (m)   wə́nči-(=á·) máta -kčihəlalúk·o·kw 'so that they (obv.) would not expose him'
    (n)   máta .. wi·č·e·ykó·k·we 'if he (obv.) was not with him'
    (o)   é·li- máta -na·ɔluk·ó·wenk 'because he did not follow us (exc.)'
    (p)   é·li-=k máta awé·n -alo·ka·lkó·wenk. 'Well, because no one hired us (exc.).'
    (q)   wénči-=č .. máta -ne·ykó·we·kw 'so that he won't see you (pl.)'
    (r)   wénči-=č .. máta -wi·xko·lkó·we·kw 'lest it take you by surprise'

TA inverse, passive
    (s)   máta li·xta·k·é·ɔne 'if it were not established for you (sg.)'

TA theme 3
    (t)   é·li- .. máta čí·č -ne·í·yunk 'because I will not be seen any more'

TA theme 4
    (u)   kɔ́č=háč máta káski- yúkwe -na·ɔləló·wan? 'why can't I follow you now?'
    (v)   né·skɔ níke ne·wəló·wan 'before I saw you (sg.)'
    (w)   máta ləló·wane 'if I don't tell you (sg.)' (B 1842:22)
    (x)   máta=č kši·xto·ló·wane 'if I don't wash them for you (sg.)'

(4.98) Conjunct order negative, TI (endings)

	(without |-ē| SBJ)	(with |-ē| SBJ)
1s–0	|-amōwā|	|-amōwānē|
2s–0	|-amōwan|	|-amōwanē|
3s–0	|-amōkw|	|-amōkwē|
1p–0	|-amōwēnk|*	|-amōwēnkē|*
12–0	|-amōwankw|	|-amōwankwē|*
2p–0	|-amōwēkw|	|-amōwēkwē|
3´–0	|-amǝlīkw|	|-amǝlīkwē|*

The TI(1a) endings are shown in (4.98); the TI(1b) endings are the same with |-ǝm| instead of |-am|, and those for TI(2) are the same without the |-am| and with |-ōlīkw| for |-amǝlīkw| 3´–0. The TI(3) endings are the same as for an AI (4.94). The endings without an asterisk are attested for at least one TI class.

(4.99) Conjunct order negative, all modes, TI (examples from B)
  TI(1a) and TI(1b)
  (a) é·li- máta -nto·namó·wa 'for I do not seek it'
  (b) máta háši ši·phamó·wa 'what I never spread out'
  (c) máta háši ši·phamó·wan 'what you (sg.) never spread out'
  (d) máta nǝno·stamó·k·we 'if he does not understand it'
  (e) máta wǝla·mhitamo·wé·k·we 'if you (pl.) do not believe it'
  (f) máta kennǝmo·wé·k·we 'when you (pl.) didn't have it'
  (g) awé·ni máta we·lsǝt·amǝlí·k·wi 'the ones (obv.) who did not believe it' (B ⟨-qc⟩)
  TI(2)
  (h) é·li- máta=á· -káski- .. -ɔ·p·i·tó·wan 'as you would not be able to make it white'
  (i) máta háši kéku tǝ́ta e·tó·wan 'things you never put down anywhere'
  (j) é·li- máta -wwa·tó·wan 'because you do not know it'
  (k) é·li- máta šúkw -po·kwílahto·kw 'since he not only broke it'
  (l) awé·ni máta we·lható·li·kw 'someone (obv.) who does not have one'
  (m) é·li- máta -wǝla·tó·wankw ahpɔ́·n 'because we (inc.) have no bread'
  (n) máta we·ɔ·tó·we·kw 'what you (pl.) do not know about'
  (o) máta wǝli·ke·nahki·to·wé·k·we 'if you (pl.) do not take good care of it'

§4.12. Imperative Order Paradigms and Examples. The four modes of the imperative order are the imperative, the prohibitive (negative imperative), the injunctive, and the future imperative. These share an imperative function but are formed in completely distinct ways. The (ordinary) imperative and the future imperative lack third person forms. The injunctive has forms for inanimate subject. The imperative mode has forms for inclusive subject, and these distinguish a single addressee from a plural addressee and thus furnish the only case of a distinct dual number in the grammar. Some speakers apparently did not use the distinct inclusive form for plural addressee, or used it only optionally, but it is attested by Blanchard, though apparently optional, and the distinction was insisted on by ME and accepted by OA.

§4.12a. Imperative Mode. The imperative mode makes positive commands or requests referring to the present time. In the endings for the AI, TI, and TA theme 3, subjects are marked by |-l| (later -∅) 2s, |-kw| 2p, |-tam| 12d (inclusive dual, i.e. addressed to one), and |-tamōkw| 12p (inclusive plural, addressed to two or more). The TA with third person objects has pronominal suffixes unique to this paradigm. A first person (inclusive) object is marked by |-nēn|, the first plural suffix in the n-endings of the independent order (4.19) but here used without a prefix.

In the imperative singular of AI stems ending in a vowel Blanchard usually has the suffix /-l/, but this is sometimes dropped. Later, imperative singulars without the /-l/ predominate, and the use of /-l/ has an emphatic force. When the /-l/ is absent the stem-final vowel is short (2.9a). Stems with the final |-(ī)xīn| AI 'lie, be' make the imperative singular on the shortened stem in |-(ī)xī| that is used in the indicative first and second singular (4.21b). Some speakers also make the plural imperative on this stem (4.103j). The ending /–i/ 2s of consonant-final AI stems is apparently identical to the singular ending on TI(1b) stems.

Before the TA singular suffix |–∅| 2s–3/IMP stems of certain shapes have irregular treatments. The retention of final /w/ in stems ending in |-aw| is regular, but stems in |w| also retain this after |ē| and |ə| and have a stable word-final /-e·w/ and /-əw/ (2.10fg), or stressed /-úw/. The one stem that ends in |-āw| replaces this with /-aw/ (4.104f). Stems in final |hw| add |-aw|, giving /-hɔw/. In Blanchard's time TA stems ending in |h| used the bare stem in some cases, with the regular loss of the |h| (2.11b), but they also made this form by adding /-aw/ after the |h|, and this was the only inflection used for these stems by some later speakers (OA; 2.11c); at least one speaker replaced the |h| with a retained /w/ if the preceding vowel was unstressed (ND; 2.11c). The singular imperative for |əl-| TA 'say {so} to' adds /l-/ (the word-initial shape of the stem) before the expected shape, which would have had a unique word-initial /ə/ (4.104o). The form for first singular object is |–īl| or |–ī| 2s–1s/IMP, with an optional |-l| as in the AI.

In the TI (1a) and TI (1b) the |m| of the theme signs combines with |-l| 2s/IMP as |-ah| (1a) and |-əh| (1b) (2.51), the |ə| becomes /i/ before |h| (cf. 2.5il), and final |-h| is regularly lost (**§2.9c**; 4.106a). The imperatives of class 3 TI stems are the same as an AI, except that |kwəsəyām-| TI(3) 'smell, take a smell of' is treated like a Class 1a TI with a theme sign |-am| (4.106r).

(4.100) Imperative mode, AI and TI(3) (endings)

AI	vowel-final stem	consonant-final stem
2s	|–l| or |–∅|	/–i/
2p	|–kw|	|–ōkw|
12d	|–tam|	|–ōtam|
12p	|–tamōkw|	|–ōtamōkw|

(4.101) Imperative mode, TA (endings)

TA theme 1 (with |-ā| ~ |-∅| TH.1)

2s–3	|–∅| (with some stem changes)
2p–3	|–o·|
12d–3	|–ātam|
12p–3	|–ātamōkw|

TA theme 3 (with |-ī| TH.3)

2s–1s	|–īl| or |–ī|
2p–1s	|–īkw|
2–1p	|–īnēn|

(4.102) Imperative mode, TI(1a), TI(1b), and TI(2) (endings)

	TI(1a)	TI(1b)	TI(2)
2s–0	|–a| (< |-ah|)	|–i| (< |-əh|)	|–ōl| or |–ō|
2p–0	|–amōkw|	|–əmōkw|	|–ōkw|
12d–0	|–amōtam|	|–əmōtam|	|–ōtam|
12p–0	|–amōtamōkw|	|–əmōtamōkw|	|–ōtamōkw|

(4.103) Imperative mode, AI (examples)
- (a) mí·tsi 'eat (you sg.)!' (B, ME)
- (b) káhta-mí·tsi·l! 'You better eat!' (OA)
- (c) aləmska 'go, depart (you sg.)' (B 1x)
- (d) aləmska·l 'go, depart (you sg.)' (B 5x)
- (e) šenkí·x·i 'lie down (you sg.)' (OA, ME)
- (f) xúk·wi or ɔx·úk·wi 'cough (you sg.)' (OA)
- (g) ma·mí·tsi·kw 'have something to eat (you pl.)' (B)
- (h) kaí·kw (B), kawí·kw (ME) 'sleep (you pl.)'
- (i) šenki·x·í·no·kw 'lie down (you pl.)' (OA)
- (j) šenkí·x·i·kw 'lie down (you pl.)' (ME)
- (k) mé·k·o·kw 'give it (you pl.)' (B, OA)
- (l) xúk·o·kw or ɔx·úk·o·kw 'cough (you pl.)' (OA)
- (m) o·t·é·nink á·t·am 'let's go to town (said to one person)' (ME)
- (n) təmi·k·é·t·am 'let's go inside' (WS)
- (o) íka á·t·amo·kw 'let's all go there' (B)
- (p) kwət·i·t·e·há·t·amo·kw '(everyone) think one thought' (V)
- (q) šenki·x·i·nó·t·amo·kw 'let's all lie down' (ME)
- (r) o·t·é·nink á·t·amo·kw 'let's go to town (said to more than one)' (ME)
- (s) o·t·é·nink lo·ltí·t·amo·kw 'let's all go to town (said to a group)' (ME)

(4.104) Imperative mode, TA theme 1 (examples)
- (a) mí·l 'give it, etc. to him, her, them (you sg.)' (V, OA); also mí·law (OA)
- (b) pənáw 'look at him (you sg.)' (ME; |pənaw-| TA)
- (c) pé·š·əw 'bring him (you sg.)' (2.10g; B, ME, LB; |pēšəw-| TA)
- (d) ayúw 'buy him (you sg.)' (OA; |ayəw-| TA)
- (e) wí·č·e·w 'go with him, go marry him (you sg.)' (2.10f; OA, ME, LB; |wīčēw-| TA)
- (f) kwsíaw 'smell him (you sg.)' (ME; |kwəsəyāw-| TA 'smell, take a smell of')
- (g) pé·haw 'wait for him (you sg.)' (OA; |pēh-| TA)
- (h) wəlí·haw 'make him (you sg.)' (OA, only this; |wəlīh-| TA)
- (i) ná·či·w and na·čí·haw 'bother him (you sg.)' (OA; |nāhčīh-| TA)
- (j) ló·s·aw 'burn him (you sg.)' (OA; |lōsw-| TA)
- (k) ki·kí·skšaw 'cut him up (you sg.)' (OA; |kīhkīskəšw-| TA)
- (l) pəmɔ́w 'shoot him (you sg.)' (V; |pəmw-| TA)
- (m) tətpáhɔw 'point at him (you sg.)' (OA; |tətəpahw-| TA)
- (n) kí·skhɔw 'chop him (a tree) down (you sg.)' (OA; |kīskahw-| TA)
- (o) lɔ́l 'tell him, them (you sg.)' (OA; |əl-| TA [uniquely irregular])
- (p) mí·lo· 'give it [etc.] to him, her, them (you pl.)' (V)
- (q) ná·lo· 'go get him (you pl.)' (ME)
- (r) ahɔ́·lo· 'love them (you pl.)' (V)
- (s) lɔ́· 'tell him, them (you pl.)' (B, OA)
- (t) wi·č·é·yo· 'go with him (you pl.)' (OA)
- (u) pəmɔ́· 'shoot him (you pl.)' (V; |pəmw-| TA)
- (v) pənɔ́· 'look at him, her, them (you pl.)' (V, ME; |pənaw-| TA)
- (w) wə́li-ntɔ́·no· 'search carefully for him (you pl.)' (B; |wəlī| PV 'well', |natōnaw-| TA)
- (x) pé·š·o· 'bring him, them (you pl.)' (V, ME; |pēšəw-| TA)
- (y) nhilá·t·am 'let's kill him' (V)

[4.104, continued]
- (z) mái-=tá -pənaó·t·am 'let's go see them (anim.)' (said between two men; V)
- (aa) mái-nto·naó·t·am 'let's go look for him (said to one)' (ME)
- (bb) ši·k·wi·taó·t·am 'let's take it away from him' (Lk 20.14; follows 4.104cc)
- (cc) nhilá·t·amo·kw 'let's kill him' (Lk 20.14)
- (dd) mái-nto·naó·t·amo·kw 'let's go look for him (said to more than one)' (ME)
- (ee) xamá·t·amo·kw 'let's feed him' (ME)

(4.105) Imperative mode, TA theme 3 (examples)
- (a) lí·l 'tell me (you sg.)' (B)
- (b) lí 'tell me (you sg.)' (OA)
- (c) ktəma·k·é·ləmi·l 'take pity on me' (B 4x)
- (d) ktəma·k·é·ləmi 'take pity on me' (B 2x)
- (e) lé·ləmi·l 'let me, allow me (to); think of me (so)' (B 3x)
- (f) wəntamái·l=ksí 'so, explain to me' (B 1834b:8)
- (g) kələstái·l 'listen to me' (B, B 1842:22)
- (h) kələstái 'listen to me' (B 1834b:9; V)
- (i) mí·li·l 'give it to me' (V)
- (j) ktəma·ksət·ai 'hear me with pity' (ME)
- (k) pənái·kw 'look at me (you pl.)' (ME)
- (l) wi·č·é·i·kw 'come with me (you pl.)' (B, ME)
- (m) tóx·i·kw 'come to me (you pl.)' (B)
- (n) mí·li·kw 'give it (etc.) to me (you pl.)' (B 1834a:13)
- (o) mi·lí·ne·n 'give it to us' (V)
- (p) pənaí·ne·n 'look at us' (ME)

(4.106) Imperative mode, TI (examples)

TI(1a) and TI(1b)
- (a) pəná 'look at it (you sg.)' (ME; |pən-| TI(1a))
  (Note the contrast: pəná ní 'look at that'; pənáh ní 'there it is, that's it')
- (b) kwihəló·t·a 'run after it (you sg.)' (V; |kwīhlōt-| TI(1a))
- (c) naxkó·t·i 'answer (the shout; you. sg.)' (OA; |naxkōt-| TI(1b))
- (d) tunkšé·ni 'open it (e.g., a jar; you sg.)' (ME, LB; |tōnkəšēn-| TI(1b))
- (e) nhaká·t·amo·kw 'rely on it (you pl.)' (B)
- (f) kwiháló·t·amo·kw 'run after it (you pl.)' (V)
- (g) tunkšé·nəmo·kw 'open it (e.g., a jar; you pl.)' (ME)
- (h) ma·é·nəmo·kw 'gather them (you pl.)' (B)
- (i) nto·namó·t·am 'let's look for it (said to one)' (ME 3x)
- (j) mái-nto·namó·t·amo·kw 'let's go look for it (said to more than one)' (ME)
- (k) kwihəlo·t·amó·t·amo·kw 'let's all run after it' (V)
- (l) mái-li·namó·t·amo·kw 'let's all go and see it' (B)

TI(2)
- (m) pi·lí·to·l 'clean it (you sg.)' (B)
- (n) wəlí·tu 'fix it (you sg.)' (AD)
- (o) ke·nahkí·to·kw 'take care of it (you pl.)' (B)
- (p) manni·tó·t·amo·kw 'let's all make them' (B)

TI(3)
- (q) kí· mí·č·i·l! '*You* eat it!' (ME; |mīčī-| TI(3))
- (r) kwsía 'smell it (you sg.)' (ME; |kwəsəyām-| TI(3))
- (s) mí·č·i·kw 'eat it (you pl.)' (B)
- (t) kwsiá·mo·kw 'smell it (you pl.)' (ME; |kwəsəyām-| TI(3))

§4.12b. Prohibitive Mode. The prohibitive mode is used for negative commands. It is always found with the negative particle káči 'don't', which by itself means 'no, I won't' or 'no, we won't' (denying a request; Mt 21.29, Mt 25.9). With a second person subject it forbids or advises against doing something and is generally translatable as 'do not' (or 'don't'). With a third person subject it makes a wish or command that someone not do something, generally translatable as 'don't let'.

The prohibitive suffix follows an AI stem or a transitive theme sign (of TA theme 1, 2, or 3, or of TI(1a), TI(1b), or TI(2)), or the plural marker |-hətī| if it is present. It is usually |-h|, but it is |-kəh| after a stem or theme ending in |m| or |n| (yielding |-nkəh|), and there is a suffix |-əyēk| in the TA for third person object. Before this suffix |-əyēk| the direct theme sign (|-ā| TH.1) does not appear overtly, since it always has the shape |-∅| before a vowel (as in the conjunct; **§4.6**). The prohibitive suffix is |-ək| after an AI stem in |t| (4.110e) or |l|, although it is |-əh| after an AI stem in |k| (4.110b). Beside the TA forms with |-əyēk| and the TI(1a) and TI(1b) forms with |-kəh|, however, there are also doublets with /-h/ after the theme signs |-ā| (4.111e-j), |-amō| (4.112f), and |-əmō| (4.112g). Before |-əyēk| (/-ie·k·-/) a stem-final |w| is retained after a vowel (4.110d), in contrast to the general loss before /i/ of the |w| of these stems in conjunct forms (**§2.11f**).

The prohibitive endings have the basic pronominal suffixes of the conjunct (4.54), but word-final |t| (in |-t| 3s and |-at| 2s–3) is replaced by /č/. This can be explained by positing a word-final modal suffix |-∅| proh. that is only manifest by causing this replacement. In the TA singular with |-āh| instead of |-əyēk| both |-at| 2s–3 and |-an| 2s were heard (4.111efgh). Some additional forms on the inverse theme sign that are not listed here were accepted by OA. Voegelin (1946:149, §5.4) reported the ending /-í·enk/ 2–1p/CNJ.NEG used as a prohibitive, but this is likely an error due to a weak articulation of intervocalic /h/, as only the expected /-í·henk/ 2–1p/PROH was confirmed by speakers. The analysis is uncertain for the verb in /káči pa·í·henk/, apparently 'let us not come', used in Blanchard's two translations of "Lead us not" in the Lord's Prayer.

In these paradigms, the trailing asterisk marks endings which can safely be assumed even though no example is at hand.

(4.107) Prohibitive mode, AI and TI(3) (endings)

2s	|–han|
3s	|–hīč|
2p	|–hēkw|
3p	|–hətīhīč|

(4.108) Prohibitive mode, TA (endings)

TA theme 1 (with |-∅| or |-ā| TH.1)

2s–3	|–əyēkač|
	|–āhan|
2p–3	|–əyēkēkw|
	|–āhēkw|

TA theme 2 (with |-əkw| TH.2)

3–2s	|–əkwəhan|
3–2p	|–əkwəhēkw|

[continued →]

[4.108, continued]
TA theme 3 (with |-ī| TH.3)
2s–1s	|-īhan|
2–1p	|-īhēnk|
2p–1s	|-īhēkw|

(4.109) Prohibitive mode, TI(1a), TI(1b), and TI(2) (endings)

	TI(1a)	TI(1b)	TI(2)
2s–0	|-ankəhan|	|-ənkəhan|	|-ōhan|*
	|-amōhan|	|-əmōhan|*	
3s–0	|-ankəhīč|	|-ənkəhīč|	|-ōhīč|
2p–0	|-ankəhēkw|	|-ənkəhēkw|	|-ōhēkw|
	|-amōhēkw|	|-əmōhēkw|	

(4.110) Prohibitive mode, AI (examples)
  (a) káči məli·mwí·han 'don't cry (you sg.)' (OA)
  (b) káči ləpákhan 'don't weep (you sg.)' (OA)
  (c) káči šenki·x·ínkhan 'don't lie down (you sg.)' (ME)
  (d) káči kɔ·xkwsunkónkhan 'don't snore (you sg.)' (ME)
  (e) káči no·lhántkan 'don't be lazy (you sg.)' (OA, ME); káči no·lhántke·kw (pl.; ME)
  (f) káči káhta-ma·č·í·hi·č 'let him not seek to go home' (B)
  (g) káči məli·mwí·he·kw 'don't cry (you pl.)' (OA)
  (h) káči ləpákhe·kw 'don't weep (you pl.)' (OA)
  (i) káči íkali təmi·k·ehtí·hi·č 'let them not enter it' (B; íkali 'to there')

(4.111) Prohibitive mode, TA (examples)
  (a) káči naxko·mié·k·ač 'don't answer him (you sg.)' (OA)
  (b) káči payaxkhwié·k·ač 'don't shoot him (with a firearm; you sg.)' (OA)
  (c) káči kpahwié·k·ač 'don't shut the door on him (you sg.)' (OA)
  (d) káči wəla·mhitawié·k·e·kw 'don't believe him, them (you pl.)' (B)
  (e) káči naxko·má·han 'don't answer him (you sg.)' (OA)
  (f) káči payaxkhó·han 'don't shoot him (with a firearm; you sg.)' (OA)
  (g) káči nhilá·hat 'don't kill him (you sg.)' (OA)
  (h) káči we·t·əna·hat 'don't pick him up (you sg.)' (OA)
  (i) káči we·t·əná·he·kw 'don't pick him up (you pl.)' (OA)
  (j) káči awé·n mahči·há·he·kw 'don't treat anyone badly (you pl.)' (B)
  (k) káči pəntá·khɔn 'don't let him hear you (sg.)' (ME)
  (l) káči ne·ykúhɔn 'don't let him see you (sg.)' (OA, ME)
  (m) káči awé·n ki·ɔlúkhwe·kw 'Do not let anyone deceive you (pl.)' (B)
  (n) káči məšəní·han 'don't touch me (you sg.)' (B)
  (o) káči sak·wi·hí·han 'don't bother me (you sg.)' (B)
  (p) káči payaxkhwí·han 'don't shoot me (with a firearm; you sg.)' (OA)
  (q) káči awé·n pənaí·hi·č 'don't anyone look at me' (OA)
  (r) káči pənaí·henk 'don't look at us' (OA)
  (s) káči nhilí·henk 'don't kill us' (OA, BS, WS)
  (t) káči mai·mí·he·kw 'don't weep for me (you pl.)' (B)
  (u) káči wəla·mhitaí·he·kw 'don't believe me (you pl.)' (B)

(4.112) Prohibitive mode, TI (examples)
    (a)   káči kpahánkhan 'don't shut it (the door; you sg.)' (OA)
    (b)   káči kanše·ləntánkhan 'don't be amazed (you sg.)' (B)
    (c)   káči sak·we·ləntamó·han 'don't worry (you sg.)' (ND)
    (d)   káči we·t·ənínkhan 'don't pick it up (you sg.)' (OA)
    (e)   káči we·t·ənínkhe·kw 'don't pick it up (you pl.)' (OA)
    (f)   káči kanše·ləntamó·he·kw 'do not be astonished (you pl.)' (B)
    (g)   káči ma·e·nəmó·he·kw 'do not gather it (you pl.)' (B)
    (h)   káči awé·n čpənínkhi·č 'let no one break it apart' (B)
    (i)   káči awé·n wwa·tó·hi·č 'don't let anyone know about it' (B)
    (j)   káči manni·tó·he·kw 'don't make it (you pl.)' (B 1842:10)

§4.12c. Injunctive Mode. The injunctive mode expresses a wish or injunction for a third person subject, either animate or inanimate. The inflection is a plain conjunct ending followed by |-eč| INJ. Injunctive forms thus have the shape of a subjunctive (with the modal suffix |-e| SBJ) followed by the future enclitic /=č/, and this is what they were assumed to be in Goddard (1979). Against this analysis, however, is comparative evidence from Munsee, which has |-əč| INJ (Goddard 2013:105-106), and the fact that it would mean that the enclitic /=č/ FUT very often did not occur in its usual position after the first word of a clause. On the other hand, it seems likely that the injunctive suffix has been influenced by the subjunctive suffix, and Blanchard has three examples of a third person subjunctive apparently used with the meaning of an injunctive (Mt 24.16, Mt 26.42, Lk 12.13), one with =á· POT in a future use and one with a separate /=č/ FUT.

(4.113) Injunctive mode (endings)
  AI
    3s |–teč| (after a vowel); |–keč|* (after a consonant)
    3p |–hətīteč| (and presumably variants as in 4.54)

  II
    0s,0p |–keč|

  TA
    3s–3´ |–āteč|*
    3p–3´ |–āhətīteč|*
    X–3 |–ənteč|
    3,0–2s |–əkwaneč| (attested for 3–2s)
    3,0–1p |–əkwēnkeč| (attested for 3–1p)
    3,0–2p |–əkwēkweč| (attested for 0–2p)
    3s–1s |–īteč|
    3p–1s |–īhətīteč|*

  TI (1a)
    3s–0 |–ankeč|
    3p–0 |–aməhətīteč|*

  TI (1b)
    3s–0 |–ənkeč|
    3p–0 |–əməhətīteč|*

(4.114) Injunctive mode (examples from Blanchard)
  AI
  (a) wəntax á·t·eč 'let him come here'
  (b) pahtí·t·eč 'let them come'
  II
  (c) lé·k·eč 'may it be done'
  (d) xinkɔhkəni·mkɔ́tkeč 'may it be praised'
  (e) li·x·ínkeč 'let it be {so}'
  (f) tunkšehəlá·k·eč 'let them (inan.) open'
  TA
  (g) mhalamúnteč 'let him sell it' (*lit.*, 'let it be bought from him', with |–ənteč| X–3)
  (h) na·čihkɔ́neč 'may he concern himself with you (sg.)'
  (i) ktəma·k·e·ləmúk·ɔneč 'may he take pity on you (sg.)' (B 1842:16)
  (j) wəla·p·enso·ha·lkwénkeč 'may he bless us (exc.)'
  (k) wəlankunso·ha·lkwé·k·weč 'let it make you (pl.) be neighborly'
  (l) wi·č·əmí·t·eč 'she should help me; may she help me'
  TI
  (m) pəntánkeč 'let him hear it'
  (n) čhɔ·pwənínkeč 'let him dip it in'

§4.12d. Future Imperative Mode. The future imperative is used for commands and requests that are contingent on a future or recurring action or event. It is well attested by Blanchard but not found in later sources. It is marked by an ending |–mē| in the singular, and this is pluralized by the insertion of a suffix |–wāw| pl., giving |–mwāwē| (/–mɔ́·e/). The TA direct endings do not have the theme sign |-ā| but insert |ō|; before this |ō| a stem-final |aw| is lost, and |w| after |ē| becomes /y/. AI stems ending in a consonant presumably also inserted |ō|, as after the TI(1a) theme sign, but there appear to be no examples. The TI(1b) endings are assumed to parallel those of the TI(1a). The number of the object is not distinguished; in the examples (4.116) the glosses correspond to the attested uses of the cited forms.

(4.115) Future imperative mode (endings)
  AI
  2s |–mē|
  2p |–mwāwē|
  TA
  2s–3 |–ōmē|
  2p–3 |–ōmwāwē|
  2s–1s |–īmē|
  2p–1s |–īmwāwē|
  TI (1a)
  2s–0 |–amōmē|
  2p–0 |–amōmwāwē|
  TI (1b)
  2s–0 |–əmōmē|*
  2p–0 |–əmōmwāwē|*
  TI (2)
  2s–0 |–ōmē|
  2p–0 |–ōmwāwē|

(4.116) Future imperative mode (examples)
    AI (and AI+O)
      (a) íka á·me 'go there (you sg.)'
      (b) wi·nəwe·mó·e 'ask (you pl.)'
      (c) məne·mó·e 'drink it (you pl.)'
    TA
      (d) wenči·mó·me 'invite them (you sg.)'
      (e) wi·č·e·yó·me 'go with him (you sg.)'
      (f) pahki·t·a·t·amó·me 'forgive him (you sg.)' (pakītātamaw-| TA)
      (g) ahɔ·lo·mó·e 'love them (you pl.)'
      (h) pahki·t·a·t·amo·mó·e 'forgive them (you pl.)' (pakītātamaw-| TA)
      (i) məša·lí·me 'remember me (you sg.)'
      (j) péči-wwa·təli·mó·e 'come and let me know (you pl.)'
    TI
      (k) məša·t·amó·me 'remember it (you sg.)' (B 1842:11)
      (l) naxa·t·amo·mó·e 'beware of it (you pl.)'
      (m) wəli·tó·me 'fix it, arrange it (you sg.)'
      (n) pai·te·xto·mó·e 'knock it off (you pl.)'
      (o) mi·č·i·mó·e 'eat it (you pl.)'

5. Derivation

§5.1. Stem Composition. The STEM of a word is the base form of a word without any inflection added. It may be a PRIMARY STEM or a SECONDARY STEM. All stems except for some primary stems are derived from components: a primary stem is one that is not derived from another stem; a secondary stem is one derived from (and based on) another stem, either primary or secondary. The components of primary stems are INITIALS, MEDIALS, and FINALS. A secondary stem consists of a primary or secondary stem and, almost always, an added secondary final. Noun and verb finals are specialized to one part of speech; they determine the status of the stem as a noun or verb, and for verbs also the inflectional category. Some abstract particle finals, however, not only make free particles but also prenouns and preverbs, which are not particles but components of compounds. A compound (compound stem) consists of a head word preceded by one or more prewords (**§5.9**).

Stem components may, in turn, be derived from stems or components. Initials, medials, and finals may be derived from noun stems or components, and initials and finals may also be derived from verb stems.

§5.1a. Primary Stems. The components of a primary stem are: an initial alone (5.1ab), an initial and a final (5.1cdef), or an initial, a medial, and a final (5.1ghijk). (In analyses of stem-derivation, the underlying forms of the different stem components are distinguished by giving initials with a trailing hyphen, finals with a leading hyphen, and medials with both. The glosses of the components, in single quotes, often represent a range of meanings and possible translations. Particles are treated separately, in **§§5.1h, 5.1i**)

(5.1) Primary stems (examples)

Stem = initial
  (a) máxkw 'bear' (stem and initial |maxkw-| AN 'bear')
  (b) ləpákw 'he weeps' (stem and initial |ləpak-| AI 'weep'; |–w| 3s/IND)

Stem = Initial + Final
  (c) skí·xkwe 'young woman, teenage girl' (|wəsk-| 'young' + |-īxkwēw| AN 'woman')
  (d) či·t·anə́s·u 'he is strong' (|čītan-| 'strong' + |-əsī| AI ABSTR; |–w| 3s/IND)
  (e) winkó·x·we·w 'he likes to go' (B; |wīnk-| 'like' + |-ōxwē| AI 'walk, go'; |–w| 3s/IND)
  (f) pí·kšəm 'he cut (it) up' (|pīk-| 'to pieces' + |-əš| TI(1b) 'cut'; |-əmw| 3s–(0)/IND)
  (g) aləwí·i P, PV 'more' (|àləw-| 'more' + |-īwī| PF ABSTR)

Stem = Initial + Medial + Final
  (h) kwəná·ləwe·w 'he has a long tail'
      (|kwən-| 'long' + |-āləw-| 'tail' + |-ā| AI ABSTR; |–w| 3s/IND)
  (i) kwəná·lahkat 'there is a deep hole, the hole is deep'
      (OA; |kwən-| 'long' + |-ālak-| 'hole' + |-at| II ABSTR; |–w| 0s/IND)
  (j) na·ttá·x·ane·w 'he goes after firewood'
      (V; |nāt-| 'go to get' + |-ətāxan-| 'firewood' + |-ē| AI ABSTR; |–w| 3s/IND)
  (k) ki·ski·k·wéhwe· 'he chopped off the head of (him)'
      (|kīsk-| 'cut, sever' + |-īkwē-| 'neck' + |-ahw| TA 'act on by tool'; |-ēw| 3s–(3´)/IND)
  (l) kši·lənčé·ne·w TA 'he washed the hands of (him) by hand'
      (|kəšī-| 'wash' + |-ələnčē-| 'hand' + |-ən| TA 'act on by hand'; |-ēw| 3s–(3´)/IND)

Initials used as stems are specified for part of speech and inflectional category (5.1ab). Otherwise, the final determines the part of speech and inflectional category of a stem. Finals may be abstract (5.1dghij) or concrete (5.1cefkl). In transitive stems like (5.1fjk) the final specifies the means or type of action that produces the resulting state or condition specified by the initial. The more concrete of such transitive finals are referred to as instrumental finals. It is often convenient to gloss the initial in a transitive stem by a verb and the final by a prepositional phrase (e.g. in 5.1k: 'wash' + 'by hand'), but the initial generally labels a process, configuration, or resulting state, with the final expressing the means as a verbal notion (as if: [final] 'manipulate with the hand to cause' + [initial] 'state of being washed').

A stem consisting of an initial alone is found in many nouns (5.1a), but in only a few, intransitive verbs (5.1b; 5.2).

(5.2) AI stems consisting of an initial with no segmentable final
- (a) mé·kw 'he gives (O2, indef.)' (B); nəmé·k·ən 'I gave it away' (B, ME; 2.55k)
  (|mēk-| AI+O 'give O2 away')
- (b) óx·ukw 'he (she) coughs' (V); nɔx·ukhúmǝna 'we cough' (V)
  (|wàwaxǝkw-| AI 'cough' [see 4.103fl], apparently with /x·/ < |wx| < |wax|)
- (c) wého·l '(dog, wolf) howls'
  (|wehōl-| AI 'howl', apparently with a unique reduplication |weh+|)

A small number of intransitive and transitive verbs have stems that could be taken to contain a recurring abstract final (5.10, 5.12), except that this is not preceded by a recurring initial.

(5.3) AI and II stems without a recurring initial
- (a) |ā-| AI 'go to {smwh}' (2.24a)
  é·w and é· 'he went to {smwh}'
- (b) |pā-| AI 'come' (2.10c, 4.20)
  pé·w and pé· 'he came'
- (c) |apī-| AI 'be {smwh}, exist, remain, be born', |ahtē-| II 'be {smwh}'
  ahpú, hát·e· and hát·e·w (B 1x) '(anim., inan.) is, is there, exists, remains'

(5.4) TA and TI stems without a recurring initial
- (a) |ǝl-| TA 'say {so} to' (4.104o)
  ntə́la 'I told s.o.' (V, ME)
- (b) |mīl-| TA+O 'give O2 to' (4.104a)
  nəmí·la·n 'I gave it to s.o.'
- (c) |pōl-| TA 'escape from'
  po·lkúk·i 'the one (obv.) that escaped from him' (B)
- (d) |ahl-| TA, |aht-| TI(2) 'put {smwh}'
  ntáhəla (B, LB), ntá·to·n (B, OA, ME, LB) 'I put (anim., inan.) {smwh}'
- (e) |kwǝhl-| TA, |kwǝnt-| TI(a) 'swallow'
  nkwíhəla (V), nkwə́ntamən (LB, BS) 'I swallowed s.o., it'
- (f) |nǝhl-| TA, |nǝht-| TI(2) 'kill'
  nníhəla, nní·to·n 'I killed s.o., it'
- (g) |wǝhl-| TA, |wǝnt-| TI(3) 'get from {smwh}'
  núhəla·n 'I got (anim.) from there', kúntən 'you got it from there' (2.50a, 2.65jkl)
- (h) |mahlaw-| TA, |mahl-| TI(1a) 'buy'
  nəmáhəlaɔ, nəmáhəlamən 'I bought s.o., it' (V, LB)
- (i) |pǝnaw-| TA, |pǝn-| TI(1a) 'look at'
  mpə́náɔ 'I look at him', mpə́namən 'I look at it' (V, ND)

(j) |pəntaw-| TA, |pənt-| TI(1a) 'hear, understand'
mpə́ntaɔ 'I hear him, understand him', mpə́ntamən 'I hear it' (LB)
(k) |nēw-| TA, |nēm-| TI(3) 'see'
nné·ɔ, nné·mən 'I saw s.o., it' (B, ME)
(l) |kwax-| TA, |kwəht-| TI(1a) 'fear'
nkɔ́x·a (OA, ME), nkwí·tamən (OA, LB) 'I fear s.o., it'

Also rare are concrete intransitive finals that include no segmentable abstract final (5.11a).

§5.2. Formation of Components. Components may be underived in their basic function, but they are also commonly formed from stems or components. The shape of a stem is often modified in a component derived from it, and a given stem may make derived components of more than one shape. Initials, medials, and finals may include extensions, often semantically vague, that derive them from smaller components. The types of extensions are postradicals (poR; i.e., postinitials), premedials (prM), postmedials (poM), and prefinals (prF). (A connective vowel, |ə| or |ī|, added before a derived medial or final, is analyzed as part of that component rather than as an extension.) Components with and without an extension may have the same meaning or may have different specializations or degrees of productivity. Postradicals, premedials, and prefinals are sometimes derived from medials, but their close semantic link to the component they are attached to shows that they are not separate medials in the constituent structure of the stem. This derivation accounts for almost all apparent cases of two medials in the same stem; an exception, obviously highly marked, is in (5.118a).

§5.2a. Underived Initials. Some initials are not derived from other identifiable components. The types of meanings that underived initials have are illustrated by the following selection of initials that are at least moderately productive, given in their underlying forms. (Numbers and relative roots [3.13] could be added to the list.)

|ahw-| 'very much; difficult', |akw-| 'on', |al-| 'rotten', |ālaw-| 'unable to', |aləm-| 'away, off; begin', |àləw-| 'more', |ānəhkw-| (a·nhukw-) 'in succession', |ans-| 'together, bunched', |apām-| 'around, about', |āpat-| 'lean', |āpət-| 'to death', |ask-| 'raw', |ask-| 'tired', |asp-| 'up', |āt-| 'tell', |čan-| 'bad, wrong', čhɔ·p- (-čohɔ·p-) 'into water, dip', |čīp-| 'bad, awful', |čītan-| 'strong', |čōsk-| 'in water', |ēkw-| 'under', |ēš-| 'through', |ələn-| 'ordinary', |kāh-| 'dry', |kanš-| 'amazing(ly)', |kant-| 'hide', |kata(w)-| 'want, want to, be going to', |kaxk-| 'break', |kāxk-| 'dry', |kēx-| 'few', |kəhk-| 'old (person)', |kəht-| 'great', |kəl-| 'hold', |kəlam-| 'calm, still', |kənt-| 'push', |kəp-| 'close, block', |kəš-| 'fast; hot', |kəšəw-| 'itch, scratch', |kəšīx-| 'wash', |kət-| 'out', |kətəmāk-| 'poor, pitiful', |kīhk-| 'touch', |kīm-| 'secretly', |kīn-| 'sharp', |kīsk-| 'cut, sever, remove', |kīš-| 'finish', |kwəčəkw-| 'move', |kwən-| 'long, tall, deep', |kwəs-| 'measure', |kwəsəkw-| 'heavy', |kwətək-| 'back', |lank-| 'light (of weight)', |lāw-| 'in the middle', |lax-| untie, untangle', |laxaw-| 'forked', |laxwē-| 'scattered', |līx-| 'move down', |mat-|, |mač-| 'bad', |max-| 'big', |maxk-| 'red', |məht-| (mhit-, -mi·t-) 'plain, normal', |mən-| 'islandlike', |məs-| 'all', |mətakw-| 'cover', |nak-| (nk-, -nak·-) 'stop', |nank-| 'tremble', |(n)əhtā(w)-| (hita·-, -ni·ta·-) 'know how to', |nīkān-| 'ahead', ninkəm- 'cute', |nīpā-| 'at night', |nīsk-| 'dirty', |pak-| 'hit', |pàk-| 'flat', |pank-| 'drip', |pas-| 'split, half', |pās-| 'swell', |paxàk-| 'peel, scratch', |paxī-| 'skin, peel', |pēnkw-| 'dry (not wet)', |pēt-| 'coming (this way)', |pəkw-| 'hole (through)', |pəm-| 'along, continuing, by', |pən-| 'down', |pənt-| 'enter', |pəsakw-| 'adhere, (up) against', |pəsənt-| 'buried, submerged', |pīk-| 'to pieces', |pīl-| (1) 'clean', |pīl-| (2) 'different', |pōhkw-| 'break (in two)', |pōhw-| 'beat', |pōn-| 'cease, cease holding', |pwak-| (pɔhk-, -pɔk·-) 'immerse', |sak-| 'hold', |sək-| 'black', |səkàp-| 'wet', |sī-| 'squeeze out or exude liquid', |sīnk-| '(outside) corner', |sīs-| 'pinch', |sōk-| 'pour', |šāpw-| 'through', |šaw-| 'weak', |šāxak-| (šaxahk-) 'straight', |šəw-| (šəw-, -šuw-) 'sour', |tah-| 'cold',

|tahkw-| 'short', |tahw-| 'seize', |takw-| 'together', |tank-| 'small', |tə̀kw-| (tuk(·)w-) 'round', |təm-| 'cut off', |tə̀m-| (təm-) 'enter', |təp-| (usually tətp-) 'point', |tə̀p-| 'around, circling', |tōhk-| 'wake up', |tōnk-| 'open', |wāhləm-| (ɔhələm-) 'far away', |wāl-| 'hole, concave', |wāp-| 'white', |wās-| 'light', |wāxē-| 'light, shine', |wāhkā-| 'around', |wēhkw-| 'completely (destroyed, etc.)', |wəl-| 'well, good, nicely', |wəsk-| 'new, young', |wəšāx-| 'slippery', |wət-| 'pull', |wīhkw-| 'end', |wīnk-| 'like; good', |wīpənkw-| (wi·p·unkw-) 'gray', |wīsak-| 'bitter', |wīsāw-| 'yellow', |wīt-| 'with', |wīxkwē-| 'wrap', |xə̀w-| (xuw-) 'old'.

§5.2b. Initials Formed from Stems. Some initials are formed from the stems of nouns and verbs. The full, underlying shape of the stem may be used without modification, or the stem may be shortened or extended. For example, one variant of the initial for 'woman, female' drops the final |w| (5.5h); one variant of the initial for 'man, male' is extended by |-ē| to rhyme with this initial for 'female, woman' (5.5i; cf. 5.5c); and the initial for 'buffalo' omits the reduplication from the verb stem that underlies the noun (5.5g).

(5.5) Initials formed from noun stems

    (a) xe·s·- '(of) skin' ← xé·s AN 'skin' (|axēs-|; pl. xé·s·ak):
        xe·s·ántəp IN 'scalp' (|-āntəp| IN 'head' [here for 'trophy head'])

    (b) mwe·k·ane·w- '(of) dog' ← mwé·k·ane 'dog' (|mwēkanēw-|; pl. mwe·k·ané·ɔk):
        mwe·k·ané·wči IN 'dog turd' (|-əčəy| IN 'excrement')

    (c) |ələnəw-| '(of) man' ← lə́nu 'man' (|ələnəw-|; pl. lə́nəwak):
        lənəwahémpəs IN 'man's shirt' (ND; |-ahempəs| IN 'shirt, dress, cloth' [5.14a])

    (d) nehənaɔnke·s- 'horse' ← nehənaɔ́nke·s AN 'horse' (|nēhnawankēs-|):
        nehənaɔnkésahpu AI 'is riding a horse' (|-apī| AI 'sit'; for /és/ see 2.7abc)

    (e) |ahēmpəs-| '(of) cloth' ← hémpəs IN 'shirt, dress, cloth' (|ahēmpəs-|; pl. hémpsa):
        hempsi·k·á·ɔn IN 'tent' (|ahēmpəs-| 'cloth' + |-īkāwan| IN 'house, structure')

    (f) sən- '(of) stone, (of) metal' ← ahsə́n IN 'stone' (|asən-|; for the reduction, see 2.6):
        səné·mhɔ·n IN '(large) metal spoon' (|-ēməhwān| IN; cf. e·mhɔ́·nəs 'spoon'; 2.68a)
        səna·mɔ́·nši 'sugar maple, rock maple' (|-āmənšəy| AN 'deciduous tree')
        səníhəle 'sparrow hawk' (ND; |-īhlēw| AN 'bird'; referring to its precipitous stoop)

    (g) si·lie·w- '(of) buffalo' ← si·sí·lie AN 'buffalo' (|sī+sīləyēw-|; pl. si·si·lié·ɔk):
        si·lié·wxe·s 'buffalo hide' (|sīləyēw-| 'buffalo' + |-axēs| AN 'skin, hide' [5.14d])

    (h) |axkwē-| 'female' ← xkwé· 'woman' (|axkwēw-|; pl. xkwé·ɔk):
        xkwéhəle 'female bird, hen' (|axkwē-| 'female' + |-īhlēw| 'bird')

    (i) |ələnəwē-| 'male' ← lə́nu 'man' (|ələnəw-|) + |-ē| poR (cf. 5.5c):
        lənəwéhəle 'male bird, rooster' (|ələnəwē-| 'male' + |-īhlēw| 'bird')

    (j) |məsāhkw-| '(of) log' ← məsá·kw 'log' (|məs-| 'all, wholly' + |-āhkw| 'tree' [5.9d])
        məsa·kwi·k·á·ɔn IN 'log house' (|məsāhkw-| '(of) log' + |-īkāwan| 'house')

(5.6) Initials formed from verb stems

    (a) |nəhl-| 'kill' ← |nəhl-| TA 'kill'
        nhílxkwe· 'he kills a bear' (OA; |nəhl-| 'kill' + |-axkw-| 'bear' [5.7b] + |-ē| AI ABSTR)

    (b) |pans-| 'singe' ← |pans-| TI(1b) 'singe':
        pa·nsi·x·e·k·ané·ksu AI 'he singed his hair (as on arm, legs)' (ME;
        |pans-| 'singe' + |-īxēkənē-| 'hair' [5.7h] + |-əhkəsī| AI 'be burned')

    (c) |mōnš-| 'cut (hairlike)' ← mo·nš- TA 'cut the hair of' (|mōnšw-|):
        mo·nši·to·naéhu 'he's shaving' (2.31h)
            (|mōnš-| 'cut (hairlike)' + |-īhtōnayē-| 'beard' [5.8a] + |-ahwī| AI 'act on self by tool')

(d) |nāt-| 'go to get' ← |nāt-| TI(1b) 'go to get' (3.20d):
   na·ttá·x·ane·w 'he goes after firewood')
   (V; |nāt-| 'go to get' + |-ətāxan-| 'firewood' + |-ē| AI ABSTR; 5.1i)
(e) |paxīn-| '(to) skin' ← |paxīn-| TA 'skin (an animal)'
   pxí·nskwe· 'he's husking corn' (|paxīn-| 'skin' + |-askw-| 'plant, corn' + |-ē| AI ABSTR)
(f) |pakam-| 'hit' ← |pakam-| TA 'hit':
   pahkamá·kwe· 'she's pounding an ash log (for bark basket splints)'
   (OA; |pakam-| 'hit' + |-āhkw-| 'wood' [5.6f] + |-ē| AI ABSTR)
(g) |pwahkah-| 'break' ← |pwahkah-| TI(1a) (|pwahk-| 'break open' + |-ah| 'by tool' TI(1a))
   phɔkhá·e· 'she is hatching (her eggs)' (ME) (|-āw-| 'egg' + |-ē| AI ABSTR)

§5.2c. Initials Formed from Initials. Some initials are derived from other initials by the addition of a post-radical extension. These extensions often match medials in form but typically have an attenuated or subtly different meaning. For example, the longer form of the initial meaning 'push' in (5.7a) probably has a more expressive meaning and may better be translated 'shove'. Some initials with extensions, though, are lexicalized with a distinct meaning (5.7e).

(5.7) Initials formed from initials by extensions
(a) kənčč- |kəntəč-| 'push' ← |kənt-| 'push' + |-əč-| poR (cf. |-əčē-| 'body')
   nkənččənə́mən 'I pushed it' (V 3s; |kəntəč-| 'push' + |-ən| TI(1b) 'by hand')
   (cf. nkəntənə́mən 'I pushed it', ME)
(b) |ələkihkw-| 'to {such} an extent' (2.42a) ← |əl-| '{so}' + |-əkihkw-| poR 'size extent'
   e·lki·khɔkamí·k·e·k 'the extent of the earth' (B 3x;
   |ələkihkwahkamīkē-| II 'be earth {so} big', |IC–k| 0/PPL(OBL) ←
   |ələkihkw-| 'to {such} an extent' + |-ahkamīk-| 'earth' + |-ē| II ABSTR
(c) |(ma)xīnkw-| 'big' ← |(ma)x-| 'big' + |-īnkw-| poR 'eye, face' (here abstract)
   xinkɔhkáni·m 'glorify him!' (B; |(ma)xīnkw-| 'big' + |-akənīm| TA 'talk about'; 2.68i)
   xinkwi·k·á·ɔn IN 'Big House' (|(ma)xīnkw-| 'big' + |-īkāwan| 'house')
   (cf. maxák·i·l 'he is big' ← |max-| 'big' + |-əkīl| AI 'be (such size)')
(d) |mačīhkw-| 'bad' ← |mat-|, |mač-| 'bad' + |-īhkw-| poR ABSTR
   mahčí·kwi P, PN 'bad' (|mačīhkw-| 'bad' + |-ī| PF ABSTR)
   (cf. mahtə́t 'it is bad' ← |mat-| 'bad' + |-ət| II ABSTR)
(e) |askaskw-| 'green' ← |ask-| 'raw' + |-askw|, |-askw-| 'grass, etc.'
   askáskwe· 'it is green' (|askaskw-| 'green' + |-ē| II ABSTR)
   (cf. |askam-| TA 'eat (anim.) raw' ← |ask-| 'raw' + |-am| TA 'eat, bite')
(f) |āšəwāhkw-| 'crossed' ← |āšəw-| 'across' + |-āhkw-| 'sticklike' (cf. 5.6f, 5.9d, 5.19e)
   a·š·əwa·kwtié·p·u 'he sits cross-legged' (OA;
   |āšəwāhkw-| 'crossed' + |-ətəyēpī| AI 'sit' [5.18e])

Some initials are derived by initial change from a synonymous or nearly synonymous initial (5.8ab) or stem (5.8c).

(5.8) Initials derived by initial change
(a) |wēw-| 'know' ← |wəw-| 'know' (in |wəwāh-| TA 'know': no·wá·ha 'I know him')
   wé·wsu 'he knows' (|wēwəsī-| AI 'know', |–w| 3s/IND)
(b) |wēt-| 'take (to oneself)' ← |wət-| 'pull' (2.65b, 2.67c)
   wwe·t·ənə́mən 'he took it, picked it up, accepted it, received it'
   (|wētən-| TI(1b) 'take, etc.', |wə–əmən| 3s–0s/IND)
(c) |kwēx-| 'fearful' ← |kwax-| TA 'fear' (nkɔ́x·a 'I fear him'; OA, ME)
   kwé·xsi·kw 'be on guard (you pl.)!' (B 4x; |kwēxəsī-| AI 'be on guard', |-kw| 2p/IMP

§5.2d. Finals and Medials Not Derived from Stems. Some finals and medials appear not to be derived from a stem or another component in the language. (Evidence from other languages shows that some of these were historically derived from stems that are no longer used independently in Unami.) A selection of these is in 5.9-13.

Noun finals in primary stems have concrete, nounlike meanings (5.9).

(5.9) Underived noun finals
- (a) |-ahksən| 'shoe, footwear' (cf. Mun máhksən 'shoe')
  - lənháksən 'moccasin' (|ələn-| 'ordinary')
  - pakháksən 'sole (of moccasin or shoe)' (OA; |pàk-| 'flat')
- (b) |-anšīkan| 'knife'
  - xinkɔnšíˑkˑan 'sword' (B), xinkɔˑnšíˑkˑan 'big knife' (V) (|(ma)xīnkw-| 'big')
  - amankanšíˑkˑana 'swords' (B; |amank-| 'big (pl.)')
- (c) |-axəmw| 'dog, animal'
  - wə́skxəm 'young animal' (LB; |wəsk-| 'young', here as |wə̀sk-|)
  - khikéˑxˑəm 'old dog, old horse, old animal' (V, LB; |kəhk(ē)-| 'old')
- (d) |-āhkw| 'stick, tree' (cf. hítˑukw AN 'tree', IN 'stick')
  - aˑpˑələ́šˑaˑkw 'apple tree' (|āpələš-| 'apple' [< Mun á pŏləš < Dutch] + |-āhkw| 'tree')
  - məsáˑkw 'log' (|məs-| 'all, wholly' + |-āhkw| 'tree')
- (e) |-āntəp| 'head'
  - xeˑsˑántəp 'scalp' (xeˑsˑ- 'skin'; 5.2a)
  - xkanántəp 'skull' (B [loc.], V; xkan- 'bone')
- (f) |-āpēw| 'person' (cf. Cree nāpēw 'man')
  - lənáˑpˑe 'Delaware Indian', (possessed and derived forms) 'person' (|ələn-| 'ordinary')
- (g) |-āpəy| 'string'
  - sənáˑpˑi 'bail' (|asən-| '(of) stone, (of) metal' [5.5f])
- (h) |-ələnč| 'finger' (cf. Shawnee nileča 'my finger')
  - nkíˑtələnč AN 'my thumb' (V, OA; |kəht-| 'great')
- (i) |-ənčəw| 'bowl, dish' (cf. Munsee -íˑnčəw)
  - taˑxˑanə́nču 'wooden bowl' (táˑxˑan '(piece of) wood', 4.2s)
- (j) |-īhlēw| 'bird'
  - ɔˑpsəwíhəle 'domestic goose' (FW, LB; ɔ́ˑpsu '(anim.) is white')
- (k) |-īm| 'berry, nut, grain'
  - túkˑwiˑm 'walnut' (|təkw-| 'round')
  - páˑkˑiˑm 'cranberry' (V)
  - xáskwiˑm 'corn'
- (l) |-īmənšəy|, |-āmənšəy|, |-ōnšəy| 'deciduous tree'
  - tukˑwiˑmə́ˑnši 'walnut tree'
  - sənaˑmə́ˑnši 'sugar maple'
  - lɔˑkˑanahóˑnši 'American elm' (V, ME, FW, WS)

The verb final in a primary stem may be abstract, with little lexical content beyond generic 'be', 'do', 'cause (to be)', or 'act on' (5.10, 5.12abcd), or it may be significant, usually having a specific prefinal combined with one of the abstract finals and a relatively concrete meaning (5.11). A rare case of a significant final that does not include an abstract final is (5.11a). The prefinals in the finals of primary stems may recur in both members of a linked transitive or intransitive final pair, or in linked intransitive and transitive final pairs, but the formal relationship in some final pairs is irregular or suppletive.

(5.10) Abstract AI and II verb finals and final pairs
   (a) |-ā| AI and II (not replaced by |-ē| before |-w|ₘ 3,0/IND) ABSTR
       ní·ma· 'he takes his lunch' (|nīmā-| AI)
       wsí·ka· II 'the sun sets, it is sunset' (V)
   (b) |-ā| AI and II (replaced by |-ē| before |-w|ₘ 3,0/IND) ABSTR
       húpwe· 'he smokes', 1s nó·pɔ (|wəhpwā-| AI)
       (Also AI and II in 5.11n.)
   (c) |-ē| AI and II ABSTR
       məné·w 'he (she) drinks' (B), nəmáne·n 'I drank it' (ME) (|mənē-| AI(+O))
       pí·ske· II 'it is dark, it is nighttime'
       (II also in 5.10.l.)
   (d) |-ī| AI (not replaced by |-ə| before |-w|ₘ 3,0/IND) ABSTR
       pə́nči·w (V), pə́nči· (B, ND) 'he (she) went in (through a small opening)' (|pənčī-| AI)
   (e) |-ī| AI and II (replaced by |-ə| before |-w|ₘ 3,0/IND) ABSTR
       á·ləmu 'he (she) is afraid' (|āləmī-| AI)
       ló·k·u 'it is evening' (|wəlākwī-| II)
       (AI also in 5.10n.)
   (f) |-əl| AI ABSTR
       ánkəl 'he, she, or it (anim.) dies' (derived final with II: 5.17b)
       (See also 5.10gh.)
   (g) |-əl| AI, |-an| II 'be (so) in taste'
       wínkəl AI, wínkan II '(anim., inan.) tastes good'
   (h) |-əl| AI, |-ət| II ABSTR
       aləl, alət '(anim., inan.) rots, is rotten'
   (i) |-əsī| AI ABSTR
       kəláksu 'he (she) laughs' (V, WS)
       (See also 5.10jklm)
   (j) |-əsī| AI, |-an| II ABSTR
       kwsúkwsu AI, kwsúk·ɔn II '(anim., inan.) is heavy'
       lánksu AI, lánkan II '(anim., inan.) is light (of weight)'
       pénkwsu AI, pénkɔn II '(anim., inan.) is dry (not wet)'
   (k) |-əsī| AI, |-at| II ABSTR
       či·má·kwsu AI, či·má·k·ɔt II '(anim., inan.) smells bad'
       pá·xsu AI, pá·x·at II '(anim., inan.) is split in two pieces'
   (l) |-əsī| AI, |-ē| II ABSTR
       máxksu AI, máxke· II '(anim., inan.) is red'
       kí·ns·u AI, kí·ne· II '(anim., inan.) is sharp' (AI: ME, LB; II: V, OA, LB. BS)
       kšúwsu AI, kšúwe· II '(anim., inan.) itches, is itching' (OA)
   (m) |-əsī| AI, |-ət| II ABSTR
       wələs·u AI, wələt II '(anim., inan.) is good, nice, pretty'
       pí·lsu AI, pí·lət II '(anm., inan.) is clean' (V, B)
   (n) |-ī| AI (~ |-ə|), |-ən| II 'be (so many)'
       txúwak AI, txə́nu II 'there are {so many} of them (anim., inan.)'
       ní·š·əwak 'there are two of them (anim.)' (WP)
   (o) |-an| II ABSTR
       ká·han 'it is shallow' (|kāh-| 'dry')

ó·p·an |wāpan| 'it is daylight'
tó·pan |tōhpan| 'there is frost' (LB)
aón |awan| 'there is fog, mist' (LB)
(Also paired with an AI: 5.10gj, 5.11qr.)
- (p) |-at| II ABSTR
káxkat 'it is broken' (V)
kpát 'it is closed, separated off': énta-kpát·ək 'a room' (B)
(Also paired with |-əsī| AI: 5.10k; after medials: 5.13b2, 5.13c1, 5.19i.)
- (q) |-ən| II ABSTR
(Paired with an AI: 5.10n, 5.11ijmop.)
- (r) |-ət| II ABSTR
(Paired with an AI: 5.10hm, 5.11k.)

(5.11) Significant AI and II verb finals and final pairs
- (a) |-īhl| AI (originally probably 'jump')
á·š·əwil 'he (she) swims' (3p a·š·əwíhəlo·k; ME) (|āšəw-| 'across', but here faded)
|-ākīhl| AI 'jump' (5.18b)
- (b) |-īkāpawī| AI 'stand' (cf. |nīpawī-| AI 'stand', but |-īkā-| and |nī-| would be unique)
ni·š·i·k·a·p·ó·wak 'the two of them stood together' (B; |nīšīkāpawī-| AI)
kkəp·i·k·á·p·ai 'you stand blocking the way' (B; |kəpīkāpawī-| AI)
- (c) |-ənkwām| AI 'sleep'
kahtúnkɔ·m 'he (she) is sleepy' (|katənkwām-| AI)
khitúnkɔ·m 'he (she) sleeps soundly' (LB)
- (d) |-ōxwē| AI 'walk'
kšó·x·we· 'he (she) walks fast' (OA, LB)
aspó·x·we· 'he (she) is walking up (a hill)' (OA)
- (e) |-əkā| AI 'dance'
kə́ntke· 'he (she) dances'
mayá·wke· 'he (she) dances the right way (i.e., counterclockwise)' (ME)
- (f) |-əskā| AI 'go, walk'
alə́mske· 'he (she) left'
pəmə́ske· 'he (she) is walking, he (she) walks by'
- (g) |-akōsī| AI 'climb'
kəntahkó·s·u 'he (she) climbed up (a tree)' (B, OA)
lak·ó·s·u 'he (she) climbs {so}' (B)
- (h) |-əlān| II 'rain'
só·k·əla·n 'it is raining' (|sōk-| 'pour, spill')
kší·la·n 'it rained hard' (|kəš-| < Proto-Algonquian *kešy- 'fast, hot, etc.' [cf. 5.19h])
- (i) |-atən| II (1) 'be a hill, mountain'
énta-túkɔhtink 'Round Hill' (B) (|təkw-| 'round')
énta-maxát·ink 'a high mountain' (B 3x) (|max-| 'big')
- (j) |-atən| II (2) 'be cold, frozen' (5.11p)
- (k) |-ēl| AI, |-ēlət| II 'be in (large) numbers or amount'
xé·lo·k 'they (anim.) are many' (énta-xé·link 'a crowd'), xé·lət 'there is much of it' (B)
xáhe·l 'there is alot of (anim.)' (pl. xahé·lo·k)
- (l) |-əkīl| AI, |-əkihkwən| II 'have (such) size, body' (for |-əkihkw-| see also 5.7b)
e·lkí·lək 'his size, his whole body', e·lkí·kwink 'its size'

(m) |-īxīn| AI, |-īxən| II 'lie, be'; also generic 'be positioned, undergo'
    šenkí·x·i·n AI 'he, she, or it (animate) lies (reclines)'; šenkí·x·ən II 'it (inanimate) lies'
    apahčí·x·i·n AI, apahčí·x·ən II '(anim., inan.) leans over' (OA)
    kančí·x·i·n AI, kančí·x·ən II '(anim., inan.) is hidden' (ME, LTD)
(n) |-īhlā| AI, II 'move rapidly, run, fall, fly, change, become, have become'
    pəmíhəle· AI, II '(anim., inan.) flies by' (|pəmīhlā-| + |-w| 3s,0s/IND)
    pəníhəle· AI, II '(anim., inan.) fell off, fell down'
    kšíhəle· AI, II '(anim., inan.) runs fast, falls fast'
    nankíhəle·w 'he (she) trembles' (V)
    psak·wíhəle· 'he (she) sticks on' (V)
    to·kíhəle·w 'he (she) wakes up' (V)
    wi·kwíhəle·w 'he (she) is tired' (V)
(o) |-axōkw| AI, |-axən| II 'be blown by wind; (wind to) blow'
    aləmxo·kw 'he (she) blew away'
    á·mxən 'it blew down'
    kšáx·ən 'the wind blows'
(p) |-ačī| AI, |-atən| II 'be cold, subjected to cold'
    čá·kahču AI, čá·kahtən II 'he (she), it is frozen' (LB)
    tahkóč·u AI, tahkót·ən II 'he (she) is cold; it is frozen together' (tékɔhtink 'lard')
    kpát·ən II 'it is frozen over, frozen shut' (ND)
(q) |-īhpōkw| AI, |-īhtan| II 'float, be floated'
    pəmí·po·kw AI, pəmí·tan II '(anim., inan.) floats along, by'
    ná·tan 'it floats away' (V)
(r) |-ahōkw| AI, |-ahan| II 'be landed on' (etc.)
    kwənáho·kw '(anim., as a tree) is tall' (OA)
    psə́nthan 'it is snowed under' (V)

(5.12) Underived transitive verb finals
(a) |-(ī)h| TA, |-(ī)ht| TI(2) (causative, etc.)
    |wəwāh-| TA, |wəwāht-| TI(2) 'know': no·wá·ha, no·wá·to·n 'I know s.o., it'
    |pēh-| TA, |pēht-| TI(2) 'wait for': mpé·ha, mpé·to·n 'I waited for s.o., it'
    |palīh-| TA, |palīht-| TI(2) 'destroy, ruin': mpalí·ha, mpalí·to·n 'I destroy s.o., it' (B)
    |kēnakīh-| TA, |kēnakīht-| TI(2) 'take care of':
        nke·nahkí·ha, nke·nahkí·to·n 'I take care of s.o., it' (V)
(b) |-l| TA, |-t| TI(1b)
    |nāl-| TA, |nāt-| TI(1b) 'go after, go to get'; nná·la, nná·t·əmən 'I went after s.o., it'
(c) |-l| TA, |-t| TI(2) ABSTR (causative)
    |pakīl-| TA; |pakīt-| TI(2) 'throw away':
        mpak·í·la, mpak·í·t·o·n 'I threw s.o., it away, down; I divorced s.o.'
    |pansīl-| TA, |pansīt-| TI(2) 'singe': mpa·nsí·la, mpa·nsí·t·o·n 'I singed s.o., it' (ME)
(d) |-āl| TA, |-āt| TI(1a) ABSTR (applicative)
    |məšāl-| TA, |məšāt-| TI(1a) 'remember, think about':
        nəməš·á·la, nəməš·á·t·amən 'I remember s.o., it'
    |pōtāl-| TA, |pōtāt-| TI(1a) 'blow at, on': mpo·t·á·la, mpo·t·á·t·amən 'I blow on s.o., it'
(e) |-(ī)nal| TA, |-(ī)nat| TI(2) 'kill, deal with'
    |katōnal-| TA 'seek to kill': kkat·o·nalíhəmɔ 'you (pl.) want to kill me' (B)
    |kīmīnal-| TA 'kill secretly', |kīmīnat-| TI(2) 'work on secretly':
        nki·mí·nala 'I killed him secretly' (V), nki·mí·nahto·n 'I work on it secretly' (LTD)

(f) |-pīl| TA, |-pət| TI(2); |-īpīl| TA, |-īpət| TI(2); |-āpīl| TA, |-āpət| TI(2) 'tie'
    |kaxpīl-| TA, |kaxpət-| TI(2) 'tie (up)': nkaxpí·la, nkáxpto·n 'I tied s.o., it' (B, V)
    |wəntāpət-| TI(2) 'tie from {smwh}': wwənta·pto·né·ɔ 'they tied it from {smwh}' (B)
    |ansīpət-| TI(2) 'tie together': nta·nsí·pto·n 'I tie it together tight' (V)
(g) |-īxəm| TA, |-īxət| TI(2) 'lay, set; (abstract)'
    |kīšīxəm-| TA, |kīšīxət-| TI(2) 'prepare, make ready':
      nki·š·í·xto·n 'I have prepared it' (B)
    |wəlīxəm-| TA. |wəlīxət-| TI(2) 'put away':
      no·lí·x·əma 'I buried s.o.', no·lí·xto·n 'I put it away' (V)
    |kəšīxəm-| TA; |kəšīxət-| TI(2) 'wash':
      nkəš·í·x·əma (OA), nkəš·í·xto·n (V) 'I wash s.o., it'
(h) |-əm| TA, |-ənt| TI(1a) ABSTR
    |wīčəm-| TA, |wīčənt-| TI(1a) 'help':
      nəwi·č·əma, nəwi·č·əntamən 'I helped s.o., it' (V, LTD)
    |nōtəm-| TA, |nōtənt-| TI(1a) 'watch over, guard':
      no·t·əmá·č·i·k 'those watching them (anim.)', no·t·əntánki·k 'those guarding it' (B)
    |kəmōtəm-| and |kamōtəm-| TA+O 'steal O2 from':
      nkamó·t·əma·n 'I stole it from him' (V)
(i) |-ēləm| TA, |-ēlənt| TI(1a) 'think about, act on by thought'
    |kətəmākēləm-| TA, |kətəmākēləm-| TI(1a):
      nkət·əma·k·é·ləma, nkət·əma·k·e·lə́ntamən 'I take pity on s.o., it' (V)
      ki·š·é·ləme·, ki·š·e·lə́ntam 'he divinely created (s.o., it)' (B [TA pret.])
(j) |-am| TA, |-ant| TI(1a) (1) 'act on by mouth, teeth'
    |kwətam-| TA, |kwətant-| TI(1a) 'taste, try the taste of':
      nkwə́t·ama TA, nkwət·ántamən TI 'I taste s.o., it'
(k) |-am| TA, |-ant| TI(1a) (2) 'act on (in miscellaneous ways [applicative])'
    |pakam-| TA, |pakant-| TI(1a) 'hit': mpák·ama TA, mpak·ántamən TI 'I hit s.o., it'
(l) |-āpam| TA, |-āpant| TI(1a) 'see, act on by sight'
    |ēšāpam-| TA 'see through something': nte·š·á·p·ama 'I see s.o. through something' (V)
    |natawāpam-| TA, |natawāpant-| TI(1a) 'look around for'
      ná nɔt·aɔ·p·ama·né·ɔ 'then they looked around for him' (B)
(m) |-īm| TA. |-ōt| TI(1b) 'act on by speech'
    |akənīm-| TA, |akənōt-| TI(1b) 'talk about':
      ntak·əní·ma, ntak·ənó·t·əmən 'I talk about s.o., it'
(n) |-īm| TA, |-ənt| TI(1a) 'act on by speech (?)' (only in this stem pair)
    |akīm-| TA, |akənt-| TI(1a) 'count; read':
      ahkí·m, ahkə́nta 'count them (anim., inan.) (you sg.)'
(o) |-ən| TA, |-ən| TI(1b) '(act on) by hand'
    |kələn-| TA, TI(1b) 'hold, carry in the hand':
      nkə́nna, nkənnə́mən 'I have, hold, carry s.o., it'
    |palən-| TA, TI(1b) 'drop': pɔlə́nəmən 'he dropped it' (LB)
(p) |-w| TA, |-ōt| TI(1a) 'shoot (with an arrow)'
    |pəmw-| TA, |pəmōt-| TI(1a) 'shoot': mpə́mɔ, mpəmó·t·amən 'I shot s.o., it' (V)
(q) |-šəw| TA, |-t| TI(2); only in:
    |pēšəw-| TA, |pēt-| TI(2) 'bring': mpé·š·əwa, mpé·t·o·n 'I bring s.o., it'

(r) |-ahw| TA, |-ah| TI(1a) 'act on by (something used as) a tool'
 |kəpahw-| TA, |kəpah-| TI(1a) 'shut':
  nkə́pho, nkəpháman 'I shut s.o., it up, I closed it' (V)
 |tə̀təpahw-| TA; |tə̀təpah-| TI(1a) 'point at':
  ntətpáho, ntətpáhəmən 'I point at s.o., it' (V ⟨ham⟩ but see 2.29)
 |māwehw-| TA, |māweh-| TI(1a) 'gather' (initial |māwē-|, with |e| generalized):
  nəma·ehó·ɔk 'I gather them (anim.)', mɔ·éhəmən 'he gathers it' (2.29)

(s) |-pw| TA, |-ht| TI(1a) 'eat'
 |katōpw-| TA, |katōht-| TI(1a) 'want to eat, be hungry for':
  nkat·ó·p·ɔ (V, LB), nkat·ó·tam (LB) 'I want to eat (s.o., it)'

(t) |-əsw| TA, |-əs| TI(1b) 'act on by heat, fire'
 |naxkwəsw-| TA, |naxkwəs-| TI(1b) 'light, set fire to':
  nnáxkwsa, nnaxkwsə́mən 'I lit s.o. (pipe, lantern), it' (OA)

(u) |-asw| TA, |-as| TI(1b) 'act on by heat, fire'
 |salasw-| TA, |salas-| TI(1b) 'fry':
  nsálahsa, nsalahsə́mən 'I'm frying s.o., it' (AD)

(v) |-əšw| TA, |-əš| TI(1b) 'act on by cutting'
 |kīskəšw-| TA, |kīskəš-| TI(1b) 'cut':
  nkí·skša, nki·skšə́mən 'I cut s.o., it' (TA: OA; TI: ME, LB; V with [šk]);
  kwi·skšó·k·wən 'it cut him' (OA)

(w) |-əlaw| TA, |-əl| TI(1a) 'shoot, act on by missile'
 |pasəlaw-| TA, |pasəl-| TI(1a) 'split by shot or missile':
  mpas·əlámən, mpas·əláɔ 'I split s.o. (as, an apple), it' (ME)
 |wələlaw-| TA 'hit with a shot':
  no·ləláɔ 'I hit him (with a gunshot or arrow)' (ME)

(x) |-əhkaw| TA, |-əhk| TI(1a) 'act on by foot or body'
 |šākwəhkaw-| TA, |šākwəhk-| TI(1a):
  nša·kwhíkaɔ (ME), nša·kwhíkamən (LB) 'I kicked s.o., it'
 |sakəsītēhkaw-| TA 'step on the foot of':
  nsaksi·t·é·kaɔ 'I stepped on his foot' (V)

(y) |-əskaw| TA, |-əsk| TI(1a) 'act on by foot or body'
 |kwətəkəskaw-| TA, |kwətəkəsk-| TI(1a) 'drive back':
  nkwətkə́skaɔ, nkwətkə́skamən 'I drive s.o., it back' (OA)

(z) |-(ī)naw| TA, |-(ī)n| TI(1a) 'act on by seeing, perceiving'
 |əlīnaw-| TA, |əlīn-| TI(1a) 'see, experience {so}' (with kóna: 'leave alone, let go'):
  ntəlí·naɔ 'she seemed to me {so}' (ME), ntəlí·namən 'it happened to me (V)'
 |wəlīnaw-| TA, |wəlīn-| TI(1a) 'admire':
  no·lí·naɔ (ND), no·lí·namən (B, ME) 'I admire s.o., it'
 |natōnaw-| TA, |natōn-| TI(1a) 'look for, seek':
  nnat·ó·naɔ, nnat·ó·namən I'm looking for s.o., it' (OA)

(aa) |-əhtaw| TA, |-əht| TI(1a) 'act on by hearing'
 |wəlāməhtaw-| TA, |wəlāməht-| TI(1a) 'believe, obey':
  no·la·mhítaɔ, no·la·mhítamən 'I believe s.o., it'

(bb) |-əsətaw| TA, |-əsət| TI(1a) 'act on by hearing'
 |kələsətaw-| TA, |kələsət-| TI(1a) 'listen to':
  nkəlsə́t·aɔ, nkəlsə́t·amən 'I listen to s.o., it'

The medials that appear to be underived lack a corresponding noun stem or noun final in the language. Some medials can be described as suppletive to noun stems or noun finals with the same meanings (5.13acef). Medials that incorporate the common postmedial |-ē-| are considered underived if they are never found without this (5.13g).

(5.13) Underived medials
   (a) |-ax-| 'ear' (cf. nhítaɔk 'my ear')
         ahké·pxe· 'he (she) is deaf' (1s nkak·é·pxa)
         (|(k)akēp-| 'blocked (pl.)' + |-ax-| 'ear' + |-ā| AI ABSTR, |–w| 3s/IND)
   (b) |-ask-| 'plant, grass'
      .1) tamakskhitéhəma· 'he (she) is hoeing his (her) garden' (OA;
           |tamak-| 'bend down' + |-ask-| 'plant, grass' + |-əhtēh| TI(1a) 'strike with tool';
           secondary derivative with |-amā| AI '(act on) things for oneself' (5.59h); |–w| 3s/IND)
      .2) wəláskat 'there was nice grass' (cf. 2.15c;
           |wəl-| 'good, nice' + |-ask-| 'grass' + |-at| II ABSTR, |–w| 0s/IND)
   (c) |-āk-| 'roof of a house' (cf. wí·k·əwam 'house')
      .1) kwəná·k·at 'it is a high house'
           (ME; |kwən-| 'long, tall' + |-āk-| 'roof' + |-at| II ABSTR, |–w| 0s/IND)
      .2) ktaspa·k·ənəmən 'you raise it up' (of a destroyed structure)
           (B; |àsp-| 'up' + |-āk-| 'roof' + |-ən| TI(1b) 'by hand'; |kət–əmən| 2s–0s/IND)
   (d) |-əč-| 'body, belly; as a ball; (abstract)'
         kpə́č·e· 'he (she) is foolish, crazy'
         (|kəp-| 'blocked' + |-əč-| (abstract) + |-ā| AI ABSTR, |–w| 3s/IND)
   (e) |-īnkw-| 'eye, face' (cf. nə́škinkw 'my eye, face'; also |-əškīnkw(-ē)-| 'eye' [4.27e, 5.8d])
      .1) ahke·p·ínkwe· 'he (she) is blind'
           (|(k)akēp-| 'blocked (pl.)' + |-īnkw-| 'eye' + |-ā| AI ABSTR; |–w| 3s/IND)
      .2) nsɔ·pínkwe 'I closed my eyes'
           (ME; |swahp-| 'close' + |-īnkw-| 'eye' + |-ē| AI ABSTR; |nə–| 1s/IND)
   (f) |-əhkw-| 'head, hair' (cf. ní·l 'my head', mí·laxk 'hair on human head')
         nkəš·i·xhúkɔ 'I washed my head, my hair' (OA; |kəšīxəhkwā-| AI ←
         |kəšīx-| 'wash' + |-əhkw-| 'head, hair' + |-ā| AI ABSTR; |nə–∅| 1s/IND)
   (g) |-əšē-| 'opening' (perhaps basically 'edge, rim')
         tunkšé·ni 'open it (you sg.)' (ME, LB [4.106d];
         |tōnk-| '(spread) open' + |-əšē-| 'opening' + |-ən| TI(1b) 'by hand'; |-i| 2s–0/IMP)
   (h) |-īkam-| 'water' (cf. 5.7fg)
         wəli·k·amíhəle· 'the water became clear'
         (V; |wəl-| 'good' + |-īkam-| 'water' + |-īhlā| II 'move rapidly, become'; |–w| 0s/IND)

§5.2e. Finals and Medials Formed from Stems and Components. Many noun finals are formed from noun stems, and many verb finals are formed from verb stems. Medials, which have only noun-like meanings (either concrete or somewhat abstract and general), are sometimes identical in shape and meaning to noun finals, and in such cases, if there is also a corresponding noun stem, both could ostensibly be derived from it independently (5.14af,). It would seem more reasonable, however, to derive the noun final directly from the noun stem (retaining the part-of-speech categorization; 5.14abcfj) and to derive the medial from the noun final (5.19abcdg). This derivation of the medial is overt when a postmedial extension is added (5.19b(2)fhi). Conversely, however, a noun final may be formed from a medial that ends in |k| by adding |w| (5.16). If a medial matches a noun stem but there is no corresponding noun final, the medial can be described as derived directly from the noun (as in 5.20, 5.21), though the absence of an attested noun final may be an accident, particularly if the noun is non-dependent. (Dependent nouns seem less likely to have corresponding derived finals.) With some sets of related components, the direction of the derivation may be ambiguous (5.14m, 5.16a).

A derived final (or medial) may have an underlying shape identical to that of the stem (nouns: 5.14abcdefg; verbs: 5.17abcde), or it may differ slightly in shape, most commonly by the addition, deletion, or replacement of an initial segment. A component derived from a non-dependent noun often drops an initial consonant (5.14mno) or adds an initial |ə| (5.14hij); it adds an initial |a| if one is present after possessive prefixes (5.14c). There are also verb finals derived from stems that delete an initial consonant (5.17g) or add |a| (5.17f). Rarely there are other changes (5.17h). All finals and medials incorporate a connective |ə| or |ī| when preceded by an underlying consonant if they would otherwise begin with a consonant (5.7e, 5.14hij); these connective vowels are written in the underlying form, but they are not present (or dropped) after a vowel. From the word for 'woman' there is one final that is unaltered (5.14f) and another in which the underlying stem-initial |a| is replaced by |ī| (5.14k). In the noun final for 'man' the stem-initial |ə| is replaced by |ī| (5.14,l), but the noun final for 'person' retains the stem-initial |ə| (5.14g). A component derived from a dependent noun may drop the |h| of an initial cluster (5.21ef; cf. 5.21g).

(5.14) Noun finals from non-dependent noun stems

    (a) |-ahēmpəs| IN (← hémpəs |ahēmpəs-| 'shirt, dress, cloth'; ntahémpəs 'my shirt, dress' ← Mun hé·mpət < Dutch hemd 'shirt, shift'; cf. hémptət 'piece of cloth', with |-tət| DIM)
        lənəwahémpəs IN 'man's shirt' (ND; 5.2c; medial: 5.19a)

    (b) |-ahkəy| 'earth' ← hák·i 'earth'(|ahkəy-|; 2.8a)
        maxkhák·i |maxkahkəy-| 'red dirt, red clay' (BS; |maxk-| 'red' + |-ahkəy| 'earth')

    (c) |-amīməns| 'child', dim. |-amīməntət| ← mí·mə·ns 'child', dim. mi·mə́ntət; ntami·mə́·nsəm 'my child' (OA, ME; cf. 4.5)
        tankami·məntə́t·ak 'little children' (B; |tank-| 'small' + |-amīməntət| 'small child')

    (d) |-axēs| AN 'skin, hide' (← xé·s |axēs-| AN 'skin'; ntáx·e·s 'my skin, my hide')
        təma·kwé·wxe·s 'beaver skin' AN (|təmāhkwēwaxēs|, with |təmāhkwēw-| 'beaver')
          (cf. təmá·kwe |təmāhkwēw| 'beaver')

    (e) |-axkōk| 'snake' (← xkó·k |axkōk-| 'snake'; ntaxkó·k·əm 'my snake' [V])
        maxáxko·k 'Great Serpent' (in story; V, OA, ME; |max-| 'big' + |-axkōk| 'snake')
        xinkwxko·k 'big snake' (ND; |(ma)xīnkw-| 'big' + |-axkōk| 'snake')

    (f) |-axkwēw| AN (← xkwé· |axkwēw-| 'woman')
        khítxkwe 'smart woman' (OA; |kəht-| 'great' + |-axkwēw| AN 'woman')
        kí·kxkwe 'virgin' (B; |kīk-| ('unmarried') + |-axkwēw| AN 'woman')

    (g) |-ələnāpēw| 'person' (← ləná·p·e |ələnāpēw-| 'person; Delaware' [2.61d])
        wəskələná·p·e 'young person' (OA; |wəsk-| 'young' + |-ələnāpēw| 'person')
        khikələná·p·e 'older person' (B; |kəhk-| 'old' + |-ələnāpēw| 'person')

    (h) |-ətəmēw| 'wolf' (← tə́me |təmēw-| 'wolf'; Unalachtigo dialect mətóme·w [§1.3])
        xinkwtə́me '(big) wolf, timber wolf' (FW, ND; |(ma)xīnkw-| 'big' + |-ətəmēw| 'wolf')

    (i) |-əsīpəw| 'river' (← sí·p·u |sīpəw-| 'river')
        xinkwsí·p·u 'big river' (OA; |(ma)xīnkw-| 'big' + |-əsīpəw| 'river')

    (j) |-ətipās| 'chicken' ← típa·s 'chicken' (a loanword; 2.79k)
        səs·aptípa·s 'guinea fowl' (ND; səs·ap- 'spotted' + |-ətipās| 'chicken')
        amanktipá·s·ak 'big chickens' (LB; |amank-| 'big (pl.)' + |-ətipās| 'chicken', |-ak| ANpl)

(k) |-īxkwēw| 'woman' (← xkwé· |axkwēw-| 'woman'; cf. 5.13f)
    skí·xkwe 'teenage girl' (|wəsk-| 'young' + |-īxkwēw| 'woman' [5.1c])
(l) |-īlənəw| 'man' (← lə́nu |ələnəw-| 'man')
    skínnu 'young man' (|wəskīlənəw| ← |wəsk-| 'young' + |-īlənəw| 'man')
(m) |-ālakw| IN 'cave' (← ɔ́·lakw |wālakw-| 'cave' [OA, ME, V]; alternatively: 5.16a)
    səná·lakw 'rock cave' (V; sən-| '(of) stone' [5.2f] + |-ālakw| 'cave')
(n) |-əpəy| 'water' (← mpí |nəpəy-| 'water')
    so·k·əlá·npi IN 'rain water' (LB; |sōkəlān-| 'rain' + |-əpəy| 'water')
(o) |-ākahəkwīwan| 'coat' (← ša·khuk·wí·ɔn |šākahəkwīwan-| 'coat'; underlying form?)
    xinkɔ·khuk·wí·ɔn 'large coat' (B)

(5.15) Noun final from prefinal + final:
(a) |-āhkwələnč| 'finger' (← |-āhkw-| prF 'sticklike' [poR in 5.7f]) + |-ələnč| 'hand, finger')
    nəmək·əná·kwələnč AN 'my little finger' (V)
    (← məkən-| 'last' + |-āhkwələnč| 'finger')
(b) |-əhkwēsīt| 'toe' (← |-əhkwē-| prF 'head' + |-əsīt| 'foot):
    nki·thukwé·s·i·t AN 'my big toe' (V)
    (← |kəht-| 'great' + |-əhkwēsīt| 'toe'; |nə–| 1s)

(5.16) Noun final from medial (with added |w|)
(a) |-ālakw| IN 'cave' ← |-ālak-| 'hole' (5.1i) + |-w| NF (alternatively: 5.14m)
    səná·lakw 'rock cave' (V; sən-| '(of) stone' [5.2f] + |-ālakw| 'cave')
(b) |-əpēkw| 'body of water' ← |-əpēk-| 'water' + |-w| NF (5.7g)
    mənə́p·e·kw 'pond, lake, inland sea' (|mən-| 'islandlike' + |-əpēkw| 'body of water')

(5.17) Verb finals from verb stems
(a) |-alōhkāl| TA 'send' ← |alōhkāl-| TA 'send' (ntalo·ká·la 'I sent him' [B])
    |pētalōhkāl-| TA 'send hither' (← |pēt-| 'coming, hither' + |-alōhkāl| TA 'send'):
    mpe·t·alo·ká·lukw 'he sent me (here)' (B)
(b) |-ankəl| AI 'die, be diseased, disappear', |-ankən| II 'disappear'
    ← |ankəl-| AI (ánkəlo·k 'they died, are dead'), *|ankən|- II (not found)
    |tawankəl-| AI, |tawankən-| II 'be lost' (← |taw-| 'gap' + |-ankəl| AI, |-ankən| II):
    taɔ́nkəl, taɔ́nkən 'he, it is lost'
    |əlankəl-| AI 'die {so}, be diseased {so}':
    e·lánkələk 'the disease he has' (OA); e·lankələ́li·t=č 'how he (obv.) will die' (B)
(c) |-āčīmwī| AI 'tell' ← |āčīmwī-| AI 'tell'
    |pētāčīmwī-| AI 'come and tell' (← |pēt-| 'coming, hither' + |-āčīmwī-| AI 'tell'):
    pe·t·a·č·í·mu 'he reports, comes and tells' (B)
    |kəhtāčīmwī-| AI 'testify, confirm the truth' (← |kəht-| 'greatly' + |-āčīmwī-| AI 'tell'):
    nki·ta·č·í·mwi 'I testify' (B)
(d) |-āpətōnē| AI 'speak' ← |āpətōnē-| AI 'speak' (nta·ptó·ne 'I speak, I talk' [B, OA]
    |kəhtāpətōnē-| AI 'insist' (← |kəht-| 'greatly' + |-āpətōnē| AI 'speak'):
    khita·ptó·ne· 'he insisted' (B)
    |wəlāpətōnē-| AI 'speak well' (← |wəl-| 'well' + |-āpətōnē-| AI 'speak'):
    ko·la·ptó·ne 'you speak correctly' (B; |kə–∅| 2s/IND)
(e) |-āšəwīhl| AI 'swim' ← |āšəwīhl-| AI 'swim'
    |pētāšəwīhl-| AI 'swim hither' (← |pēt-| 'coming, hither' + |-āšəwīhl| AI 'swim'):
    pe·t·a·š·əwíhələk 'one who comes swimming' (ME; |(IC)–ək| 3s/PPL(ANsg))
    |əlāšəwīhl| AI 'swim'{so}, to {smwh}' (← |əl-| '{so}, etc.' + |-āšəwīhl| AI 'swim'):
    ká·mink lá·š·əwil 'he swam across' (OA; ká·mink 'across the river or lake')

(f) |-amīhkəmwāsī| AI ← |mīhkəmwāsī-| AI 'work':
    |əlamīhkəmwāsī-| 'work {so}' (← |əl-| '{so}' + |-amīhkəmwāsī| AI 'work'):
    eˑlamiˑkəmɔˑsˑíˑliˑt=č 'the tasks they (obv.) were to perform' (B; |IC–līt| 3´/PPL(OBL); =č FUT)

(g) |-āpan| II 'be dawn' ← |wāpan-| II (óˑpˑan 'it is daylight, morning, dawn')
    |pētāpan-| II 'dawn to come' (← |pēt-| 'coming, hither' + |-āpan| II 'be dawn'):
    peˑtˑáˑpˑan 'dawn comes'

(h) |-īxənē| AI(+O) 'cook' ← |wīxənī-| AI(+O) 'cook' (3s wíˑxˑənu)
    |wəlīxənē-| AI+O 'cook O2 well': noˑlíˑxˑəneˑn 'I cook it well' (V; |nə–ən| 1s–0s/IND)

Some verb finals are derived by adding a prefinal (which may itself be derived) to an existing final. A prefinal may be derived from a medial with postmedial |-ē-| (5.18e) or without it (5.18j). Prefinals may be abstract (with no obvious added meaning; 5.18b) or may modify the meaning of the basic final (5.18ch). Derived prefinals may be concrete, with their literal meaning (5.18efi), or may have an attenuated or metaphorical use (5.18ag). A final with a meaningful prefinal may itself have an attenuated meaning (5.18d).

(5.18) Verb finals from verb finals

(a) |-ahtakīhlā| AI 'run' (← |-ahtak-| prF "string" + |-īhlā| AI 'move rapidly' [5.11n])
    aləmhatahkihəleˑ 'he's starting to run' (|aləm-| 'away; begin')
    niˑkˑaˑnhatahkíhəleˑ 'he's running at the head' (OA; |nīkān-| 'ahead, (in the) lead')
    pəmaˑtahkíhəleˑ 'he runs along' (V; |pəm-| 'along, continuing, by')

(b) |-ākīhl| AI 'jump' (← |-āk-| prF '?' + |-īhl| AI 'jump(?)' [5.11a])
    |àspākīhl-| AI 'jump up' (← |àsp-| 'up' + |-ākīhl| AI 'jump'):
    aspáˑkˑil AI 'he jumped up' (V; 3p aspaˑkˑíhəloˑk)

(c) |-əhtēxīn| AI, |-əhtēxən| II 'fall or collide with force'
    (← |-əhteˑ-| prF 'by striking' + |-(ī)xīn| AI, |-(ī)xən| II 'lie, fall')
    kšiˑtéˑxˑiˑn AI (ME), kšiˑtéˑxˑən II (B) 's.o., it gets hurt by falling or colliding'
    (|kəš-| 'fast, hot, intense' + |-əhtēxīn| AI 'fall or collide violently')
    kɔxkwhitéˑxˑiˑn 's.o. (heart, vein) has a pulse' (OA;
    |kwaxkw-| 'bounce' + |-əhtēxīn| AI 'fall or collide violently')
    aləmčeˑtéˑxˑən 'it rolled down' (OA;
    |aləm-| 'away' + |-əčē-| 'body; as a ball' + |-əhtēxīn| AI 'fall or collide violently')

(d) |-īnkwēxīn| AI 'look' (← |-īnkw-ē-| 'eye, face' + |-(ī)xīn| AI 'lie, fall')
    aspinkwéˑxˑiˑn 'he looks up' (← |àsp-| 'up' + |-īnkwēxīn| AI 'look')
    kwtəkˑinkwéˑxˑiˑn 'he looks back' (OA; ← |kwətəkw-| 'back')

(e) |-ətəyēpī| AI 'sit, ride (a horse)' (← |-ətəyē-| prF 'rear end' + |-apī| AI 'sit')
    aˑšˑəwaˑkwtiéˑpˑu 'he sits cross-legged' (OA; 5.7f)
    (|āšəwāhkw-| 'crossed' + |-ətəyēpī| AI 'sit (in a position)')
    məkoˑttiéˑpˑu 'he rides bareback' (OA, LB; |məkōt-| implying 'without a saddle';
    cf. məkúčì "pure" (V), məkóˑčì 'exclusively' (LB))

(f) |-akōsīhlā| AI 'climb moving rapidly, climb around' (← |-akōs(ī)-| 'climb'
    [< |-akōsī| AI 'climb' (5.11g)] + |-īhlā| AI 'move rapidly' [5.11n])
    aləmakˑoˑsˑíhəleˑ 'he's climbing around in a tree' (OA; |aləm-| 'away')

(g) |-āhkwahw| TA, |-āhkwah| TI(1a) 'act on by tool against resistance' (see also 2.59d)
    (← |-āhkw-| prF 'wood, solid' + |-ahw| TA, |-ah| TI(1a) 'act on by tool' [5.12r])
    nkəpˑaˑkhómən 'I locked it'
    (OA, BS; |kəp-| 'block' + |-āhkwah-| TI(1a) 'act on by tool against resistance')

nši·p·a·khə́mən 'I smoothed it (using my hands as a tool)'
  (AD; |šīp-| 'smooth' + |-āhkwah-| TI(1a) 'act on by tool against resistance')
(h) |-əhtehw| TA, |-əhteh| TI(1a) 'act on by hitting'
  (← |-əhte·-| 'by striking' [/e/ generalized] + |-ahw| TA, |-ah| TI(1a) [as in (g)])
  |pəhtəhtehw-| TA 'hit accidentally' (|pəht-| 'accidentally' + |-əhtehw| TA 'hit')
    mpi·thitéhɔ 'I hit him by accident' (OA)
  |pwahkəhteh-| TI(1a) 'break by hitting' (|pwahk-| 'break' + |-əhteh| TI(1a) 'hit')
    mpɔ·khitéhəmən 'I hit it so as to break it' (ND; |nə–amən| 1s–0s$_{(1a)}$/IND)
  |pawəhteh-| TI(1a) 'shake, shake the dust off of' (|paw-| 'shake' + |-əhteh| TI(1a) 'hit')
    mpawhitéhəmən 'I shook it (once)' (OA), mpahwitéhəmən 'I dust it off' (ME)
    (|nə–amən| 1s–0s$_{(1a)}$/IND)
    pai·téha 'dust it off!' (ME; |-a| 2s–0$_{(1a)}$/IMP)
(i) |-əšehw| TA, |-əšeh-| TI(1a) 'act on the opening of'
  (← |-əšē-| 'opening' [/e/ as in (h); 5.13g] + |-ahw| TA, |-ah| TI(1a) [as in (g)])
    kupšehɔ́·ɔ (OA), kupšéhəmən (V) 'he covered, closed, put a lid on s.o. (as a pot), it'
    (|kəp-| 'close, block' + |-əšehw| TA, |-əšeh-| TI(1a) 'act on the opening of';
    |wə–āwa| 3s—3´/IND, |wə–amən| 3s—0s/IND)
(j) |-ələnčahw| TA, |-ələnčah| TI(1a) 'act on with the fingers'
  (← |-ələnč-| 'finger' [5.1k, 5.9h] + |-ahw| TA, |-ah| TI(1a) 'act on by tool' [5.12r])
    nni·skələ́nčhɔ, nni·skələnčhámən 'I dirtied s.o., it with my fingers'
    (V; |nīsk-| 'dirty'; |nə–āw| 1s—3s/IND, |nə–amən| 1s—0s/IND)

Medials are often formed from noun finals, which in many cases are themselves derived from a noun stem (**§5.2e**). In cases where there is a related noun, noun final, and medial, two different patterns of derivation may be present; these alternative possible derivations are noted in (5.13m) and (5.16a). Medials derived from noun finals are sometimes identical in shape and meaning (5.19abcdgj), The derived status of a medial is, however, overt when a postmedial extension is present (5.19b(2)fhi). For example, a derived medial used before a final that is not merely abstract generally adds a postmedial |-ē-| (5.19b(2)h, 5.20c, 5.21bcfg). A medial from a noun final ending in |-əy| may delete this (5.19b(2)hi). In some cases a derived medial adds |-ak| (5.19f) or (if an |-əy| is deleted) |-ēk| (5.19i). If no postmedial is used, a close link between the medial and the concrete final may be implied, as if in effect forming a derived final (5.18j), but this is not always the case (5.22g(2)).

(5.19) Medials from noun finals
(a) |-ahēmpəs-| 'shirt, dress, clothing' ← |-ahēmpəs| (5.13a):
    kši·xhémpse· 'she's washing cothing'; nkəš·i·xhémsa 'I'm washing clothes' (OA)
    (|kəšīx-| 'wash' + |-ahēmpəs-| 'clothing' + |-ā| AI ABSTR)
    maxkhémpse· 'she has on a red dress'
    (ND, ME; |maxk-| 'red' + |-ahēmpəs-| 'clothing' + |-ā| AI ABSTR)
(b) .1) |-ahkəy-| ← |-ahkəy| (5.14b)
    talaxhákie· 'he plows' (|talax-| '?' + |ahkəy-| 'earth' + |-ē| AI ABSTR; 1s ntalxá·kie)
    .2) |-ahkē-| 'earth' ← hák·i 'earth, land' (|-ahkē-| ← |-ahk-| [← |ahkəy-|] + |-ē-| poM):
    kwčukhɔkéhəle· 'there's an earthquake' (OA)
    (|kwəčəkw-| 'shake' + |-ahkē-| 'earth' + |-īhlā| II 'move rapidly')
    phɔkhakéhɔ· 'he was buried in the ground' (OA, LB)
    (|pwahk-| 'break' + |-ahkē-| 'earth' + |-ahw| TA 'act on by tool'; |-āw| X–3s/IND)

(c) |-amīməns-| 'child' ← |-amīməns| 'child' (5.13c)
no·t·ami·mə́·nsu 'he (she) is babysitting' (ND)
(|nōt-| 'watch over, guard' + |-amīməns-| 'child' + |-ī| AI ABSTR)
(d) |-axkwēw-| 'woman' ← |-axkwēw| (5.13f)
winkxkwé·e· 'he likes women' (ND)
(|wīnk-| 'like, good, etc.' + |-axkwēw-| 'woman' + |-ē| AI ABSTR)
(e) |-āhkw-| 'sticklike, treelike, woodlike' (5.6f, 5.7f, 5.9d, 5.15a, 5.18g)
kwəná·kwsu 'he, she, or it (anim.) is tall' (|kwən-| 'long' + |-āhkw-| 'treelike' + |-əsī| AI ABSTR, |–w| 3s/IND; or deriving initial |kwənāhkw-| 'tall' with |-āhkw-| poR 'treelike')
(f) |-īlənəw-ak-| ← |-īlənəw| 'man' (5.14,l):
|əlīlənəwakəsī| AI 'be {such} an official, have {such} an official function'
(|əl-| '{so}' + |-īlənəwak-| 'man' +|-əsī| AI ABSTR)
linnuwahkə́s·i·t 'one with official function and authority; an official, an officer' (B)
kéku e·linnuwahkəs·í·č·i·k 'those with some official authority' (B)
(g) |-ətipās-| ← |-ətipās| 'chicken' (5.14j)
nenhiltipá·s·e·t 'chickenhawk' (FW)
(IC + |Rih+| HAB + |nəhl-| 'kill' [5.3a] + |-ətipās-| 'chicken' + |-ē| AI ABSTR; |-t| PPL)
(h) |-əpē-| 'water' ← |-əp-| (← |-əpəy| 'water' [5.13n]) + |-ē-| poM:
kšəp·éhəle· 'water flows fast'
(|kəš-| 'hot; rapid'[cf. 5.11h] + |-əpē-| 'water' + |-īhlā| II 'move rapidly')
(i) |-əpēk-| 'water' ← |-əp-| (← -əpəy| 'water' [5.13n]) + |-ēk-| poM:
kšəp·é·k·at 'it is hot water' (|kəš-| 'hot; rapid' + |-əpēk-| 'water' + |-at| II ABSTR)
kwčukwpe·k·íhəle· 'the water trembles'
(|kwəčəkw-| 'shake' + |-əpēk-| 'water' + |-īhlā| II 'move rapidly')
(j) |-ənčəw-| 'dish' ← |-ənčəw| 'bowl, dish' (5.9i)
kši·x·ə́nčəwe· 'he (she) washes the dishes'
(LB; |kəšīx-| 'wash' + |-ənčəw-| 'dish' + |-ē| AI ABSTR, |–w| 3s/IND)
(5.20) Medials from non-dependent nouns
(a) |-axkw-| 'bear' ← máxkw 'bear' (|maxkw-|; 5.1a)
nhílxkwe· 'he kills a bear' (OA; |nəhl-| 'kill' [5.3a] + |-axkw-| 'bear' + |-ē| AI ABSTR)
(b) |-ətāxan-| 'firewood' ← tá·x·an 'piece of wood, firewood' (|(-mə)tāxan-|; 2.68e)
na·ttá·x·ane·w 'he goes after firewood'
(V; |nāt-| 'go to get' + |-ətāxan-| 'firewood' + |-ē| AI ABSTR; 5.1i, 5.3d)
(c) |-īxēkənē-| 'hair' ← mi·x·é·k·ən 'a hair (of animal, of human body)'
pa·nsi·x·e·k·əné·ksu AI 'he singed his hair (as on arm, legs)' (ME)
(|pans-| 'singe' + |-īxēkənē-| 'hair' + |-əhkəsī| AI 'be burned')
(5.21) Medials from dependent nouns
(a) |-īhtōnay-| and |-īhtōnayē-| 'beard' ← |-īhtōnay| AN 'beard' (wi·tó·naya 'his beard')
kwəni·tó·naye· 'he has a long beard' (B, LB; kwe·ni·tó·naya·t 'one with a long beard')
(|kwən-| 'long' + |-īhtōnay-| 'beard' + |-ā| AI ABSTR, |–w| 3s/IND)
mo·nši·to·naéhu 'he's shaving' (2.31h)
(|mōnš-| 'cut (hairlike)' + |-īhtōnayē-| 'beard' + |-ahwī| AI 'act on self by tool', |–w| 3s/IND)
(b) |-īnaxk-| and |-īnaxkē-| 'hand' ← |-naxk| IN 'hand, (lower) arm' (nnáxk 'my hand')
aspí·nxke· AI 'he (she) raises his (her) hand' (OA, LB; 1s ntaspí·nxke)
(|asp-| 'raise' + |-īnaxk-| 'hand' + |-ē| AI ABSTR)

alli·nxkéhəle· 'he (she) waves (his [her] hand)' (LB)
(|Rā+| CONT + |əl-| '{so}' + |-īnaxkē-| 'hand' + |-īhlā| AI 'move rapidly', |–w| 3s/IND)
  (c) |-əsīt-| and |-əsītē-| 'foot' ← |-sīt| IN 'foot' (nsí·t 'my foot')
    me·me·xksí·t·e· 'he (she) is barefoot' (ME; 1s nəme·me·xksí·t·a)
    (|mēmēxk-| 'bare' [only here] + |-əsīt-| 'foot' + |-ā| AI ABSTR, |–w| 3s/IND)
    e·lsi·t·é·x·ink 'at his feet' (B)
    (|əl-| '{so, to smwh}' + |-əsītē-| 'foot' + |-īxīn| AI 'lie, be'; |IC–k| 3s/PPL(OBL))
  (d) |-əškīnkw-| 'eye' ← |-škīnkw| IN 'eye, face' (nə́škinkw 'my eye, my face')
    ahpi·mškínkwe· 'he (she) is cross-eyed'
    (|Ra-| PL + |pīm-| 'crooked' + |-əškīnkw-| 'eye' + |-ā| AI ABSTR, |–w| 3s/IND)
  (e) |-əkāt-| 'leg' ← |-hkāt| IN 'leg' (nhíka·t 'my leg')
    amankká·t·e· 'he (she) has big legs' (V, ND)
    (|amank-| 'big (pl.)' + |-əkāt-| 'leg' + |-ā| AI ABSTR, |–w| 3s/IND)
  (f) |-əkaxkwanē-| 'shin' ← |-hkaxkwan-| 'shin' (nhíkxkən 'my shin')
    mpo·po·kwkaxkənéhə 'I broke his legs' (B, other forms)
    (|Rv+| REP + |pōhkw-| 'break' + |-əkaxkwanē-| 'shin' + |-ahw| TA 'act on by tool')
  (g) |-īhkaš-| and |-īhkašē-| 'fingernail' ← |-hkaš| AN (nhík·aš 'my fingernail', pl. nhíkahšak)
    ahkɔ·ní·kahše· 'he (she) has long fingernails' (ME; 1s nkak·ɔ·ní·kahša)
    (|(k)akwān-| 'long (pl.)' + |-īhkaš-| 'fingernail' + |-ā| AI ABSTR, |–w| 3s/IND)
    kči·kahše·x·i·n 'his (her) nail has come off (*lit.*, out)' (OA; 1s nkəč·i·kahšé·x·i)
    (|kət-| 'out' + |-īhkašē-| 'fingernail' + |-īxīn| AI 'lie, be (as a result)')

A medial may be formed from a medial by the addition of a premedial, which may be abstract (5.22efg) or may itself be derived from a medial (5.22hi). The premedial may itself have only a vague meaning but may nevertheless narrow the meaning of the medial (5.22eg). More than one premedial may be found with the same base medial, and a difference of meaning is not always apparent (5.22f and 5.22i). As with the medials derived from stems (**§5.1g**), many medials that are not otherwise derived incorporate the postmedial extension |-ē-| (5.22bg(3)h); some medials have this before some abstract finals (5.22a). In rare cases the postmedial |-ē-| is replaced by |-a-| (5.22cd); this substitution apparently takes place only before certain finals.

(5.22) Medials from medials
  (a) |-əčē-| 'body' (← |-əč-| [4.6d] + |-ē-| poM)
    tukwčé·s·u 'he is round-bodied' (V; |təkw-| 'round' + |-əčē-| 'body'+ |-əsī| AI ABSTR)
  (b) |-īnkwē-| (← |-īnkw-| 'eye, face' [5.13e] + |-ē-| poM)
    .1) nsɔ·pinkwé·i 'my eyes are closed' (ME;
    |swahp-| 'close(d)' + |-īnkwē-| 'eye' + |-wī| AI 'be', |nə–∅| 1s/IND)
    .2) shɔpinkwe·x·í·no·k 'they have their eyes closed' (B;
    |swahp-| 'close(d)' + |-īnkwē-| 'eye' + |-īxīn| AI 'lie, be', |–ōk| 3p/IND)
  (c) |-əča-| (← |-əč-| [4.6d] + |-a-| poM)
    ná·č kwi·skčaš·ó·k·o·n 'then he (obv.) shall cut him to pieces' (B 2x; ná 'then'; =č FUT;
    |kīsk-| 'sever' + |-əča-| 'body' +|-əšw| TA 'cut', |wə–əkōn| 3´–3s/SBD)
  (d) |-āntəpa-| (← |-āntəp-| + |-a-| poM)
    mpa·nsantpás·i 'I singed my head' (ME;
    |pans-| 'singe' + |-āntəpa-| 'head' + |-əsī| AI 'be heated, burned', |nə–∅ 1s/IND)
  (e) |-āləhkw-| 'hair' (← |-āl-| prM + |-əhkw-| 'head, hair' [5.13f])
    kwəna·lhúkwe· 'he (she) has long hair' (AD, LB;
    |kwən-| 'long' + |-āləhkw-| 'hair' + |-ā| AI ABSTR; |–w| 3s/IND; 1s nkwəna·lhúkɔ)

(f) |-ēlīnkw-| 'eye' (← |-ēl-| prM + |-īnkw-| 'eye, face' [5.6f])
šae·línkwe· 'his eyes are weak' (ME; |šaw-| 'weak')

(g) |-ətəlīnkw-| and |-ətəlīnkwē-| 'face' (← |-ətəl-| prM + |-īnkw-| 'eye, face' [5.6f])
 .1) kwənət·əlínkwe· 'he has a long face'
    (FW; |kwən-| 'long' + |-ətəlīnkw-| 'face' + |-ā| AI ABSTR; 1s nkwənət·əlínkɔ)
 .2) mpa·ktəlínkhɔ 'I slapped his cheek, face'
    (|pāk-| 'slap' + |-ətəlīnkw-| 'face' + |-ahw| TA 'act on by tool'; |nə—āw| 1s–3s/IND)
 .3) pɔxaktəlinkwe·ná·ɔ 'he scratched up his (obv.) face' (V;
    |paxàk-| 'peel' + |-ətəlīnkwē-| 'face' + |-ən| TA 'by hand', |wə–āwa| 3s–3´/IND)

(h) |-əšēnkwē-| 'eye(lid) edge' (← |-əšē-| prM 'hole, rim' + |-īnkwē-| 'eye, face' [cf. 5.6f])
tuhwənəš·enkwéhəle· 'he has a sty' (1s ntuhwənəš·enkwéhəla)
(ME; tuhwən- [cf. túhɔn 'branch' (2.29e)] + |-əšēnkw-| + |-īhlā| AI 'move rapidly')

(i) |-ālakīnkw-| 'eye' (← |-ālak-| prM 'hole' [cf. 5.1i] + |-īnkw-| 'eye, face' [5.6f])
kəkta·lahkínkwe· 'he has bulging eyes' (OA; "his eyes pop out")
(|Rə̀+| PL + |kət-| 'out' + |-ālakīnkw-| 'eye' + [presumably] |-ā| AI ABSTR)

§5.3. Particles. Many particles consist of a single unanalyzable element (**§5.3a**), but others are formed from components and have an identifiable final or ending (**§5.3b**).

§5.3a. Underived Particles. The unanalyzable particles are mostly free particles (5.23), but there are also a number of enclitics (5.24). Enclitics always follow a phonological host, which is typically the first word in a clause or salient phrase or another enclitic. They are written with a preceding /=/, a word boundary that cannot be realized as a pause. There are as well three preverbs that are unanalyzable, but one has an older form with |-ī| PF (5.23c, 5.27a).

(5.23) Unanalyzable free particles and preverbs
 (a) ála PV 'cease, stop' (2.74a)
 (b) amí·ka P 'later, late, after a long time'
 (c) á·la PV 'be unable to' (V, OA, ME, LB); earlier á·lai (5.27a)
 (d) čí·č P 'again, more' (with negative)
 (e) káhta PV 'want to, be going to' (with prefix: nkát·a)
 (f) kwə́la (kwə́lah=) P 'I wish, I hope'
 (g) lahápa P 'for a while; take the time to; in turn, on the other hand'
 (h) ló·məwe P 'long ago'
 (i) máta (tá=) P 'not'
 (j) péxu P 'soon'
 (k) takó· (akó·, kó·) P 'not'
 (l) tpó·kəwe P 'last night'
 (m) xú P FUT (< péxu 'soon')

(5.24) Enclitics (complete set)
 (a) =á· (=á·m=) POT, (with negative) FUT
    máta=á·. 'It shouldn't be so.' (B)
    tá=á· ɔ·x·e·é·i. 'There will be no light.' (B ⟨taa oxrri⟩)
    awé·n=néh=á·m=ét ... 'Who would possibly ..? (B)
 (b) =č FUT (may have scope over more than one clause)
    kkəptó·na=č 'you (sg.) will be mute' (B)
    kpé·t·o·n=č wí·l. 'You (sg.) must bring his head.' (B)
 (c) =ét 'maybe, must, must have', (in questions) 'possibly'
    kpəč·e·ónkəl=ét. 'He must be out of his mind.' (B)

kí·wsu=ét 'He must be drunk.' (BS; said about someone who appeared to be drunk.)
awé·n=ét=tá wá lə́nu? 'Who can this man be?' (B)

(d) =ə́nt 'nevertheless, despite that' (cf. Mun =ə́nt 'on the contrary')
sa·k·í·ma=ə́nt khák·ay? 'Are you nevertheless a king?' (B; KJV "then")

(e) =háč, =héč Q
kí·=háč nčo·wí·i-sa·k·í·ma? 'Are you king of the Jews?' (B)
ké·x·i=héč kahtənámu 'How old is he?' (OA)

(f) =hánkw (=ánkw) 'always, usually, would' (general truth)
kkɔk·ɔ́·ni-=hánkw -pa·tamáhəmɔ 'you (pl.) always say long prayers' (B)
tɔskántamən=húnt=ánkw nə́ wió·s. 'He always ate the meat raw (they say).' (OA)

(g) =húnt HRSY (not in B)
kwət·ən=húnt tóp·i·n pi·laéčəč. 'One time, the story goes, a boy was born.' (V)
hít·ukw=húnt kí·skham. 'He cut a stick (so the story goes).' (ME)

(h) =ínk (=nínk) Q (in rhetorical or exclamatory questions, implying unusual uncertainty)
tá=háč=ínk=láh e·li·ná·kwsi·t 'what is (he) like?' (B)
tá=háč=ínk=láh ləkhíkwi-áhɔt 'how hard is it?' (B)
kéku=nínk=č=háč ntə́ləwe li·ná·k·ɔt? 'What shall I say it is like?' (B)

(i) =k (=ké=) 'Well'
píši=k ktá 'Yes, indeed, in fact ...' (B)
yú=ké=č ntə́lsi·n. 'Well, this is what I'll do.' (B)
(also 5.24p)

(j) =ksí 'then, So, well (if you're saying THAT)' (question or imperative)
ktaləwí·i-=ksí -lə́s·i·n 'Are you (sg.) then greater than ...?' (B)
kələstái·kw=ksí lahápa 'So, listen to me for a while ...' (B)
(also 5.24l)

(k) =ktá 'instead, rather, indeed' (also ktá [5.24i])
nó·x=ktá nəmax·inkwé·ləmukw. 'It is rather my father that thinks highly of me.' (B)
šé·=ktá ko·lanko·mko·ná·nak. 'Look how well they treat us.' (V)

(l) =láh (in rhetorical questions and mirative statements)
awé·n=ksí=láh? i·láyas=háč khák·ay? 'Who, then? Are you Elias?' (B)
kéku=láh=wáni pahsí·i namé·s. 'Why, here it was half fish!' (V)
(also 5.24h)

(m) =máh PST
ná=máh nčí·sas tə́ləwe·n 'then Jesus said' (B)

(n) =néh 'possibly?' (in skeptical questions)
né·k·a=háč, ší=néh kwi·kayó·yəma? 'Was it him, or possibly his parents?' (B)
(also 5.24a)

(o) =tá FOC (marker of weak focus)
ní·=tá. 'It's me; I am.' (B)
mahtánt·u=tá wáni. 'He is a devil.' (B)
mé·či=tá ánkəla. 'He has died.' (B)
íka=tá á·kw. 'Go there (you pl.).' (B)
tá=á·=tá ankəló·wi. 'He will not die.' (B)
(also 5.24c)

(p) =x 'in fact'
nə́=ké=x 'well, in fact it was (because ...)' (B)

(q) =xán 'however, although' (also xánne·)
   nčó·=xán khák·ay 'Even though you are a Jew ...' (B)

§5.3b. Particle Finals. The abstract particle finals are -i (|-ī|), -í·i (|-īwī|), and -e (|-ē|); there is also a final -i· that is apparently a variant of -í·i (5.27a). Of these, -i PF and -í·i PF commonly make prenouns and preverbs as well as particles, and -e PF combines with medials, which may be primary or derived from noun stems (cf. **§5.2e**). The relative roots (3.13) all make particles and prewords with -i PF. As a secondary final -í·i makes prenouns from nouns and lexicalized participles (5.122, 123). Some particles include the suffix |-ənk| (/-ink/, /-unk/) LOC that makes the locative of nouns (**§4.2d**). Particles and prewords are often static words (**§2.15**).

(5.25) Particles with |-ī| PF (not also used as preverbs)
   (a) ahčínki P 'have a hard time; it is difficult'
   (b) éntxi P 'every'
   (c) ksí·ni P 'unconcernedly'
   (d) kxántki, xántki P 'finally'
   (e) lápi P 'again'
   (f) le·lá·i P 'in the middle'
   (g) mé·či P 'already'
   (h) tá·ɔni P 'although'
   (i) tpəskwi P 'like, likewise' (cf. 5.29f)
   (j) wé·mi P 'all'
   (k) wəláki P 'just'
   (l) xé·li, xahé·li P 'many'

(5.26) Particles incorporating |-ənk| LOC
   (a) čuwé·yunk 'in, on the hills' (cf. ɔhčú 'hill, mountain', loc. ɔhčúnk)
   (b) hukwé·yunk 'above, up above, on high, in or to the sky or heaven' (also hókunk B)
   (c) ká·mink 'across the river, creek, lake'
   (d) kɔ́čəmink 'outside, outdoors'
   (e) lo·wané·yunk 'in, to the north'
   (f) ša·ɔné·yunk 'in, to the south'

(5.27) Preverbs with |-ī| PF
   (a) á·lai PV 'be unable to' (B; cf. 5.23c)
   (b) a·yáhi PV 'previously, formerly, earlier' (B)
   (c) kahtí, káhti PV 'almost' (2.74d; with prefix nkáti)
   (d) káski PV 'be able to'
   (e) má·wəni PV 'collectively, all together'
   (f) níši PV 'two together'
   (g) ɔ·wtámi PV 'is slow in, to'
   (h) wiáki PV 'plenty' (cf. 2.74m, 5.129pp)
   (i) wi·šíki PV 'working hard at'

(5.28) Particles with |-ī| PF used also as preverbs
   (a) áhi P, PV 'very, very much'
   (b) aləwí·i P, PV 'more'
   (c) hápi P, PV 'with, along with, also, in addition'
   (d) hítami P, PV 'first'
   (e) ktəmáki P, PV 'poor; woefully, miserably, in torment'
   (f) ləkhíkwi P, PV 'at {such} time; {so} much'

(g) núči P, PV 'since, starting from'
(h) sháki P 'as far as, until', PV 'until; {so long} (a time)'

(5.29) Particles and prewords with |-īwī| PF
    (a) amǝníˑi P 'nevertheless, despite that, regardless'
    (b) khičíˑi P, PV 'greatly, strongly, etc.'
    (c) laˑwǝnteˑíˑi P 'in the middle of the lodge; in the middle (halfway)' (ME; cf. 5.31,l)
    (d) nalahíˑi P 'upstream, up the river'
    (e) naˑhíˑi P 'downstream, down the river'
    (f) palíˑi P 'away, elsewhere, in or to another place'
    (g) tahkwíˑi P 'together'
    (h) tpǝskwíˑi P 'directly' (cf. 5.25i)

(5.30) Particle with variation in the particle final
    (a) yaˑpˑéˑi P 'on the shore' (B, OA), yaˑpˑéˑiˑ (OA, LB), yaˑpˑeˑíˑi (ME)

A number of concrete particle finals consist of a medial or noun final and |-ē| PF (5.31), including some with a noun final derived from a noun and |-ē| PF (5. 32). In some cases the medial matches an II verb final, presumably being based on an unattested or virtual noun final derived from it (5.31o). A few particles are made similarly but lack an abstract final (5.33).

(5.31) Particle finals derived from medials
    (a) |-ahkamīkwē| PF 'earth' (|-ahkamīk-| 'earth' 5.7b)
        xkwiˑthakamíˑkˑwe 'on earth' (B, ME)
    (b) |-atē| PF 'belly' (cf. |-atay-| 'belly': maxkaskahtáyaˑt 'snake with red underside')
        láˑmahte 'in the womb' (B; |lām-| 'inside, under')
    (c) |-atǝnē| PF 'hill, mountain' (|-atǝnw| NF 'hill': khítahtǝn 'mountain')
      .1) ɔˑsahtǝ́ne 'over the hill' (OA; ɔˑsˑ- 'across, on the other side' [non-shortening /ɔˑ/])
      .2) xkwitahtǝ́ne 'on top of a hill, mountain' (B, FE; |xkwīt-| 'on top of')
    (d) |-axakwē| PF 'log, wood' (|-axakw| NF 'wood': puhéˑxɔkw 'a box' [LB; puhēw-| 'hollow' + |-axakw| NF 'wood'])
        ɔˑsxákˑwe 'on the other side of a log (lying down)' (OA)
    (e) |-ākē| PF 'roof' (|-āk-| 5.13c)
        xkwiˑtˑáˑkˑe 'on the roof, on top of the house' (B; |xkwīt-| 'on top of')
    (f) |-āhkwē| PF 'tree' (|-āhkw-| NF: aláˑkw 'rotten log' V, čelíˑsˑaˑkw 'cherry tree' LB)
        ɔˑsˑáˑkwe 'behind the tree' (OA; ɔˑsˑ- 'across, on the other side')
    (g) |-ālakwē| PF 'hole' (< |-ālakw| NF; 5.14a, 5.16a)
        laˑmáˑlahkwe 'in the hole' (ME; |lām-| 'under, inside')
    (h) |-āpǝxkī| PF '(number times) 100'
        kwǝtˑáˑpxki '100' (|kwǝt-| 'one')
    (i) |-āwankwē| PF 'hill, hillside' (cf. |-āwank-|: pemaˑɔ́nkeˑk 'side of a hill, ridge' [FW])
      .1) aˑphitaˑɔ́nkwe 'below the top of the hill' (B [KJV "the brow"]; áˑphit P 'on the way')
      .2) ɔˑsˑaˑɔ́nkwe 'over the hill' (OA; ɔˑsˑ- 'across, on the other side')
    (j) |-ēlǝnawakī| PF 'set(s), pair(s), kind(s)' (|-ēlǝnawak-| 'sets' [KJV "parts," as shares])
      .1) kwǝtˑennáɔhki 'a single thing, kind, place' (B; |kwǝt-| 'one')
      .2) niˑšennáɔhki 'two sets, two pairs, two kinds' (OA; |nīš-| 'two')
      .3) xeˑlennáɔhki, xaheˑlennáɔhki 'many different kinds or places' (B; x(ah)eˑl- 'many')
    (k) |-ǝnkwē| PF (only in this word)
        laˑmúnkwe 'inside' (B, ND; |lām-| 'under, inside')

(l) |-əntē| PF 'room, inside space of house' (|-ənt-ē| II 'be (such) room': aˑnhukwə́nteˑ 'it is an added-on room, a porch', with |ánəhkw-| 'added-on')
    laˑwə́nte 'in the middle of the floor, room' (B; |lāw-| 'in the middle'; cf. 5.29c)
(m) |-əpē| PF 'water' (|-əp-| 'water' 5.19h)
  .1) xkwíˑspe 'on the water' (B; |xkwīt-| 'on top of'; for /s/, see 2.49)
  .2) šɔ́ype 'at the edge of the water, on the shore' (B 1834b:43.9), šɔ́hpe (V, OA; |wəšayəpē| with |wəšay-| '(at the) edge of'; cf. Mun wšáy(ə̃)pe)
(n) |-əpwāmē| PF 'thigh' (|-əpwām-| 'thigh': xinkwpɔ́ˑmeˑ 'he has a big thigh' V)
    laˑwpɔ́ˑme 'in the middle of the thigh' (OA; |lāw-| 'in the middle')
(o) |-īhtanē| PF 'stream; body of water' (cf. |-īhtan| II 'flow, float, drift')
    laˑíˑtane 'in mid-stream' (V, ME; |lāw-| 'in the middle'); 'in the middle of the lake' (B)
(p) |-īnaxkē| PF '-ty, (number times) ten' (cf. 5.21b)
    neˑíˑnxke 'forty' (|nēw-| 'four')
(q) |-īskwətē|, |-īskwətayē| PF 'fire'
    šawíˑskwte, šawiˑskwtáye 'next to the fire' (ME; /šaw-/ for /šɔ-/ [see next])
(r) |-īxkanawē| PF 'road'
    šɔiˑxkanáe 'on the side of the road' (B; /šɔ-/ 'on the side of' [5.31m.2])
(s) |-ōkwənī| PF 'days' (|-ōkwən-| 'day (as a period pf time)')
    niˑšˑóˑkˑwəni 'for two days' (|nīš-| 'two')

(5.32) Particle finals derived from nouns
(a) |-ahkəyē| PF 'earth' < |-ahkəy| NF (< hákˑi |ahkəy-| 'earth'; 5.14b, 5.19b)
    laˑmhákie 'inside the earth' (B; |lām-| 'inside')
(b) |-ahkīhākanē| PF 'field' < |-ahkīhākan| NF (< hakiˑháˑkˑan |ahkīhākan-| 'field')
    ɔˑshakiˑháˑkˑane 'across the field' (OA; /ɔˑs-/ 'across, on the other side')
(c) |-amēnaxkē| PF 'fence' < |-amēnaxk| NF (< méˑnaxk |(-a)mēnaxk-| 'fence')
    laˑmaméˑnxke 'inside the fence, in the garden' (B ⟨-kc⟩ 2x; |lām-| 'inside')
    |-amēnaxkī| PF 'fence'
    ɔˑsˑaméˑnxki 'on the other side of the fence' (OA; /ɔˑsˑ-/ 'across, on the other side')
(d) |-ənəpēkwē| PF 'lake' < |-ənəpēkw| NF (< mənə́pˑeˑkw 'lake')
    laˑwənəpˑéˑkˑwe 'in the middle of the sea' (B; |lāw-| 'in the middle')
(e) |-īkəwahmē| PF 'house' < |-īkəwahm| NF (< wíˑkˑəwam |wīkəwahm-| 'house')
    laˑmiˑkˑəwáhəme 'inside the house' (B; |lām-| 'inside')
(f) |-ōtēnayē| PF 'town' < |-ōtēnay| NF (< oˑtˑéˑnay 'town')
    laˑwoˑtˑéˑnaye ' in the middle of town' (B ⟨-nyc⟩ 2x; |lāw-| 'in the middle')

(5.33) Particle finals without an abstract final
(a) |-ahkamīkw| PF 'earth' (cf 5.31a)
    wiˑwənthákamiˑkw 'since the world began' (B)
(b) |-atay| PF 'belly' (cf. 5.31b)
    láˑmahtay 'inside (the body)' (ME)

§5.4. Reduplication. There are five basic patterns of reduplication, which derive words from other words by adding a reduplicant, an initial syllable that, generally speaking, includes a repetition of the stem-initial consonant and, in some cases, other changes (Goddard 2011:149-155). The characteristic repetition of a consonant is, however, necessarily absent in stems that begin with a vowel (which insert /h/ or /y/), and in one type (plural reduplication) it appears only in forms that have a prefix or initial change. Reduplication is found on verbs, preverbs, and particles, and on certain categories of nouns derived from verb stems. When reduplication is added to a stem that is already reduplicated the inner reduplication is apparently treated as lexicalized.

The five basic types of reduplication are plural (reduplicant |Ra+| PL), repetitive (repetitive-intensive; |Rə̀+| REP, |Rvh+| REP), continuative (continuative-attenuative; |Rā+| CONT), habitual (|Rih+| HAB), and extended (|Rī+| EXT). In the abstract representation of the reduplicants, the diacritic |R| is a morphophoneme that marks a morpheme as a reduplicant; it indicates a copy of the stem-initial consonant (or in some cases /kw/), if there is one. The plus sign (|+|) indicates a word-internal boundary with certain features peculiar to the respective reduplicants. The labels of the five basic types of reduplication are used for convenience and do not apply literally to all uses, which have greater or lesser ranges of semantic values, including vague and overlapping ones. In particular, the plural and repetitive reduplications intergrade, and the same reduplicant may be used in both functions. There is also a residue of additional types of ostensible reduplication that are not derived from known simpler shapes by an active grammatical rule (**§5.4f**).

The continuative, habitual, and extended reduplications mark grammatical categories with more consistent aspectual meanings than the other two types. Their reduplicants are basically the same for all stems, and stems with these reduplicants are not found lexicalized as independent words without unreduplicated counterparts.

§5.4a. Plural Reduplication. Plural reduplication is used for plural actors (of intransitive verbs), plural body parts (indicated by medials), and multiple actions. It is sometimes optional, and some stems with it are not found unreduplicated.

The plural reduplicant |Ra+| PL is most commonly /a-/ (before a voiced consonant) or /ah-/ (before a voiceless consonant). The reduplicated consonant is only overt if there is a pronominal prefix (giving /-Ca-/ [5.34a] or /-Cə-/ [5.34bce], followed by a long consonant if voiceless) or if there is initial change (yielding /Ce-/ [5.34qrs] or /Ce·-/ [5.34nps]).

A stem-initial |w| is reduplicated as |wa+|, giving /ɔ-/; when this precedes a stem that begins with |wə| followed by a voiceless consonant, it is treated as a strong syllable |wà-| even when there is no prefix, just as if it were the realization of the repetitive reduplicant |Rà+| (5.34fg). Before a stem that begins with |wəl-|, a reduplicant /ɔ-/ may be treated as a weak syllable (5.34h), or a strong syllable (5.34i). The reduplicant |wa+| also has the peculiarity that, where it would be expected to be realized as /ɔ-/ before a stem-initial |wī-|, it appears as /aw-/, with a retained intervocalic /w/ (5.34klm). One form was also recorded with /a-/ instead of /ɔ-/ before /wəl-/ (5.34n).

Stem-initial |kw| usually reduplicates as |k|, but |kw| is also attested (5.34r).

Some stems have plural reduplication with a prefix or initial change but not word-initially (where it was presumably lost phonologically [cf. 2.68]); these seem not to have contrasting forms without reduplication and do not have a salient plural meaning, and in fact some speakers used unreduplicated stems after prefixes (5.34opq).

Two, less common, variants of plural reduplication have the reduplicant |Ra+| PL and, in addition, a vowel change in the stem-initial syllable, replacing a short vowel by either |ā| (5.34qr) or |ē| (5.34stuvwx). The prefixed forms of /ahkɔ·n-/ 'long (pl.)' (the reduplication of |kwən-|) are found with both /-kak·ɔ·n-/ and /-kək·ɔ·n-/, and with IC /kwek·ɔ·n-/ (5.34r).

Some reduplicated initials are based on underlying forms that differ from the corresponding singulars, reflecting an earlier shape (5.34x).

The suppletive initial |amank-| 'big (pl.)' has several attested shapes after prefixes (5.35abcde).

For stems that begin with a vowel there appears to be no plural reduplication distinct from repetitive reduplication (note 5.37c).

(5.34) Plural reduplication

With the vowel of the initial unchanged
- (a) ahki·naní·k·e· 'he's got sharp teeth', 1s nkak·i·naní·k·e, nkak·i·naní·k·a (OA);
   cf. |kīn-| 'sharp'
- (b) amax·ahe·lɔ́ntam 'he suffers torments', 1s nəməmxahe·lɔ́ntam; cf. max- 'big'.
- (c) amayahkí·to·n 'it is wasted' (B), mwəmayak·i·tó·na 'he wastes them' (B);
   only reduplicated (but cf. Mun mayakíhto·w 'he wastes (it)')
- (d) ahpi·mškínkwe· 'he's cross-eyed' (OA; 5.21d); cf. |pīm-| 'twist, twisted, crooked, devious': pi·məwále· 'he's carrying his bundle to one side'
- (e) ahtankala·mwí·t·u 'he hollers a little'; 1s ntət·ankala·mwí·t·i (V); cf. |tank-| 'small'
- (f) ɔwčəli·thwə́na·s 'blackjack oak (one with tangled limbs)' (FW);
   also wewčəli·thwə́na·s (LB)
- (g) kɔwcíhəla 'you have cramps' (|wawəčīhlā-| AI; ME); cf. |wət-| 'pull';
   cf. nɔhči·čəwéhəla 'I have spasms in my calves' (with /ɔhč/ for /ɔwč/) (OA)
- (h) ɔwəlsúwak 'they are good-looking' (|wawələsī-| AI) (V, ME; also wəlɔ́s·əwak [V]);
   cf. 3s wəlɔ́s·u (|wələsī-| AI);
   ɔwə́ltu 'they (inan.) are good' (OA; also wəlɔ́t·u [B, OA]); cf. wələ́t 'it is good';
   ɔ́wəli-kí·šku 'it's good weather (these days)' (OA); cf. wə́li-kí·šku 'it's a good day'
- (i) ɔɔ·x·e·línkwe· 'he has grey eyes' (OA)
- (j) awi·p·unkwškínkwe· 'he has grey eyes' (OA)
- (k) awi·p·unkwsí·č·i·k 'ones who are grey' (V)
- (l) awi·s·a·ɔ́·tae·s 'yellow-flower (a medicine plant)' (FW)
- (m) awəlto·nhé·ɔk "they talk good" (V ⟨awëltu:uhe:´yok⟩)
- (n) kəló·ne· 'he lies, tells a lie', 1s nkak·əló·ne (B, ME), ke·k·əló·ne·t 'a liar' (B);
   cf. 1s nkəló·ne (LB)
- (o) ki·ɔnáskwe· 'he is dizzy', 1s nkak·i·ɔnáskwe (OA); cf. nki·ɔnáskwe (LB)
- (p) kí·wsu 'he is drunk', 1s nkak·í·wsi (ME), ke·k·í·wsi·t 'a drunkard, a drunk' (ND)

With the |ə| in the initial replaced by |ā|:
- (q) ahpá·mske· 'he's walking around', 1s mpəp·á·mska (OA), pep·á·mska·t 'who was walking around' (ME); cf. pəmə́ske· 'he walks (by)'. May be treated as lexicalized and take a second layer of reduplication (5.40n).
- (r) ahkɔ·ní·kahše· 'he's got long nails', 1s nkak·ɔ·ní·kahša (ME); cf. |kwən-| 'long';
   nkək·ɔ·nhakéhəna "we were [always] gone a long time" (Voegelin 1945:114-5, no. 39);
   kwek·ɔ́·nxa·s 'donkey' (FF), kwek·ɔ·nxá·s·ak 'donkeys' (OA), kɔk·ɔ·nxá·s·ak 'mules' (ME) (lit., 'one with long ears')

With the |ə| or |a| in the initial replaced by |ē|:
- (s) ahke·p·ínkwe· 'he is blind', 1s nkak·e·p·ínkɔ (OA, ND); ke·k·e·p·inkɔ́·č·i·k (B ⟨krkrp-⟩ 9x), kek·e·p·inkɔ́·č·i·k (B ⟨kckrp-⟩ 1x) 'blind people'; cf. |kəp-| 'shut, block, seal'
- (t) ahkwe·lpíhəle· '(anim.) rolls or turns over and over' (ND), 1s nkak·we·lpíhəla (ND);
   cf. kwələp·íhəle· 'he turns over' (ND), 'he turns around quickly' (OA)
- (u) ahkwe·t·á·he· 'he's practicing shooting' (kwtá·he· 'he took a practice shot' [ME])
- (v) ame·xkanánəwe· 'he (she) has rosy cheeks' (OA); cf. |maxk-| 'red'
- (w) ame·xkhempsé·ak 'they are wearing red dresses' (ME)
- (x) ane·skə́s·əwak 'they are dark, black' (|(-n)anēsək-| 'black (pl.)') (OA), 3s sə́ksu (V, OA, ND, LB), 2s ksə́ksi (ND); cf. Mun 3s nsə́ksəw, 3p ane·s'kə́sə̄wak; see also (5.36s)

(5.35) |amank-| 'big (pl.)' with prefixes and initial change
  (a) nəməmmankaní·k·a 'I have big teeth' (OA), 3s amankaní·k·e· (OA);
      also regularized: ntamankaní·k·a 'I have big teeth' (OA)
  (b) nəməmmankki·lhúmǝna 'we are big' (ME)
  (c) kəməmmánkxa 'you have big ears' (ME)
  (d) kamankškínkɔ 'you have big eyes' (ME)
  (e) nəmmankka·t·áhǝna 'we have big legs' (V), 3s amankká·t·e· (V)
  (f) memmánkǝwe·k 'that (inan.) which makes loud sounds' (B ⟨mcmufwrk⟩)

§5.4b. Repetitive Reduplication. Repetitive reduplication, which could be labeled more fully repetitive-intensive, typically marks an action or state as having multiple, discrete components, but it is often expressive or intensive. It is sometimes used ostensibly to reinforce a plural, perhaps adding the notion 'all' (5.36abijrs, 5.37c, 5.38h)

The reduplicant for repetitive reduplication takes three basic shapes: |Rə̀+|, |ày+|, and |Rvh+|. It is |Rə̀+| REP on stems beginning with |Ca-| or |Cə-|, or invariant |Cà-| or |Cə̀-|, and on a few others (5.36). A following voiceless consonant may be either short or long (/C/ or /C·/), with no clear conditioning, except that before /ah/ (< weak |a|) or /C/ (other than /w/) only a short consonant is permitted. The repetitive reduplication of |kālōm-| TA 'berate' is found as apparent |kà-| as well as |kə̀-| (5.36t).

(5.36) Repetitive reduplication (consonant-initial stems with a short vowel in the initial syllable)
  Followed by a short /C/ where a long /C·/ is possible:
  (a) yó·k só·čǝlak tə́li-pəpayaxkhɔ·né·ɔ 'these soldiers are the ones that shot them' (OA)
  (b) səsalá·mǝwak 'they scream' (ND)
  (c) nšəša·khwíkamǝn 'I kicked it a few times' (OA)
  (d) šəšəwánahku 'he's speaking English' (OA); cf. šəwánakw 'whiteman'
  Followed by a short /C/ where a long /C·/ is not possible:
  (e) pəpahsíhǝle· 'it's cracking' (ME); cf. pahsíhǝle· 'it split open'
  (f) kwə́kahti-mi·č·í·na 'he would almost eat them (inan.)' (B ⟨qwk-⟩); cf. káhti, kahtí PV
  (g) kəkhité·lo·k 'there's a lot of them (anim.)' (OA); also khité·lo·k
  (h) kukwtá·he· 'he's practicing shooting' (ME); kwtá·he· 'he took a practice shot' (ME)
  (i) ləlpwé·ɔk 'they are (all) smart' (V); 3s ləpwé·
  (j) kəkhité·li=č awé·ni·k nənhilá·ɔk 'a lot of people will get killed' (OA); cf. |nəhl-| TA
  (k) ɔhpəla·nšəmá·nu 'he's speaking French' (V; /ɔh-/ < |wà+wə-|);
      cf. pəlá·nšəma·n 'Frenchman' (< Mun pəlá·nšəma·n < Dutch *fransman*)
  (l) ɔwša·wənó·u 'he's talking Shawnee' (OA); cf. šá·ɔnu (ND), šá·wǝnu (OA) 'Shawnee'
  (m) ná=č ɔwisahkí·ha·n 'then he shall be mocked' (B)
  Followed by a long /C·/:
  (n) kək·ǝlə́ksu 'he's laughing' (OA); cf. kǝlə́ksu 'he laughs' (V, WS)
  (o) kək·ǝlámu 'it (anim. [snow]) is piled up' (OA); cf. kǝlámu (same) (ME)
  (p) kək·ənčí·mu 'he's crowing' (OA); cf. kǝnčí·mu 'it (anim.) crows, neighs, hoots' (LB)
  (q) pup·alhɔ́·ɔ 'he kept missing him' (ME; /pu-/ < |wǝ-pə̀+|); cf. mpálhɔ 'I missed him'
  (r) səs·áp·e· 'it is spotted, speckled' (LB; |sàp-| 'having a spot')
  (s) səs·ǝksúwak 'they are (all) black' (OA'; |sə̀k-| 'black'; cf. 5.34x);
      səs·ǝ́ki-sápsu 'he has black spots' (LB)
  (t) kwək·a·lo·mawwá·ɔ 'they berated them' (B ⟨kwvk-⟩ for ⟨kwk-⟩; also ⟨qwk-⟩ 2x);
      also: kɔk·a·lo·má·a 'he berates him', 1s nkak·a·ló·ma (OA; with |Ra+| PL)

The repetitive reduplicant is |ày+| on stems that begin with |ə-| (5.37cdef) and on some with |a-| (5.37abghi). It appears overtly as /ay-/ before |àhw-| 'very (much), extreme(ly)' (5.37ab). The |y|

assimilates to the following /l/ in stems beginning with |əl-| (5.37cdef) and assimilates to a following /h/ in stems that have /ha-/ metathetized from underlying |ah-| (5.37ghi; for the metathesis, see §2.5). Other stems beginning with |a-| take the reduplicant |Rvh+| (5.38rstu).

(5.37) Repetitive reduplication (stems beginning with |ə-| and some with |a-|)
- (a) ayahúnkɔ·m 'he slept soundly', 1s ntayahúnkɔ·m (OA)
- (b) ntayáhɔhči 'I get cold easily' (OA, ME)
- (c) alləní·i-awé·ni·k 'Indian people' (ME) (|ày+| REP, |ələnīwi| PN 'ordinary' [5.121a])
- (d) alləní·xsu 'he (she) speaks Delaware' (|ày+| REP, |ələnīxəsī-| 'speak normally')
- (e) alla·p·éhəle· 'he (she) is swinging' (ME; |ày+| REP, |əlāpēhlā-| AI 'swing {so}')
- (f) ná=nə tɔllaehó·s·i·n 'that's how he acted' (OA; |ày+| REP, |əlawēhwāsī-| AI 'act {so}')
- (g) é·ləmi-ahhaté·k·e 'when it began to exist' (B; |ày+| REP, |ahtē-| II)
- (h) énta-=č -ahhaphiká·s·i·k 'where it will be trampled on' (B; |ày+| REP, |ahpəhkāsī-| II)
- (i) ahhaphika·ɔhtúwak 'they were stepping on each other' (B; |ày+| REP, |ahpəhkāwatī-| AI)

On stems with an underlying long vowel in the first syllable and on some with |a-| the repetitive reduplicant is |Rvh+| REP (a reduplicated consonant followed by a copy vowel and an underlying |h|). A resulting |hC| cluster has its normal treatments. If the consonant is voiceless, the |hC| is realized as a short consonant, even in the case of |hs| and |hš|, which otherwise appear as /s/ and /š/ between strong vowels only in static words and syllables (§2.15). If the consonant is |l|, |m|, or |n|, a /ə/ is inserted after the /h/ except if the consonant is followed by a voiceless consonant in a secondary cluster (one arising from the loss of a weak |ə|); in this case the |h| is lost (§§2.4, 2.5). If the consonant is |w|, it is lost if it would otherwise result in a cluster /hw/, but the underlying |w| is retained if it contracts with a following |ā| (§2.19b). When the |h| in the reduplicant is retained as /h/, the preceding vowel is always short, even if a strong vowel follows, but in a reduplicant /ah-/ or /ɔh-/ the vowel is not affected by initial change (§4.6; 5.38uvx).

(5.38) Repetitive reduplication (stems with a long vowel in the first syllable, and some with |a-|)
- (a) pa·pa·k·alúhu 'he whoops (several times)'; cf. pa·k·alúhu 'he gives a single war-whoop'
- (b) pi·pí·li 'all different, different from each other'; cf. pí·li 'different'
- (c) to·tunktó·ne· 'he's gaping' (|tōnk-| 'open (a hole)')
- (d) ɔ́nta-ki·ki·š·i·k·íhti·t 'when they grow up' (|kīš-| 'finish')
- (e) nsa·sa·k·ənə́mən 'I kept sticking it out (of somewhere)' (OA; cf. 5.40g)
- (f) sa·sa·p·í·s·ak 'fireflies' (LB; /-s-/ contrasts audibly with /-s·-/);
   cf. sa·p·əléhəle· 'there is lightning'
- (g) si·si·lie 'buffalo'; cf. si·lié·wxe·s 'buffalo hide' (apparently |sīləyē-| AI < |sī-| 'squeeze out or exude liquid' + medial corresponding to E. Ab. wìli 'scent gland, musk gland')
- (h) so·so·psúwak 'they are both or all naked' (OA); só·psu 'he is naked' (B, V, ME)
- (i) ši·ší·p·e· 'it's rubbery, stretchy' (|šīp-| 'stretch, smooth')
- (j) lahəla·ptó·nhe· 'he repeats (in speaking)' (|lāp-| 'again')
- (k) lehəlé·x·e· 'he lives' (lé·x·e· 'he breathes'); cf. Mun lehlé·xe·w 'he's breathing'
- (l) mehəme·te·lə́ntam 'he's grieving hard' (|mēht-| 'to the end')
- (m) kənihəni·š·antpáhəmɔ 'you have two heads each' (V; |nīš-| 'two')
- (n) nəwehe·t·əna·wəná·na·k 'we picked them (anim.) up (in multiple acts)' (OA);
   cf. nəwé·t·əna 'I picked him, her, it (anim.) up' (ME, AD)
- (o) wihi·shitehá·s·u 'it (board) has multiple dents (as from blows by an axe)' (OA);
   cf. wi·shitehá·s·u 'it has a dent', wí·s·e· 'it has a scar'
- (p) ɔhɔ́·lxe· 'he (she) has pierced ears', 1s nɔhɔ́·lxa (OA; also 4.15d);
   cf. ɔ́·le· 'it's a hole' (OA)

(q) ntahas·e·níhi·n 'I keep scattering it' (OA); cf. ntas·é·nəmən 'I scattered it' (ME)
(r) ahaš·áhəle· 'he moved backwards or slid back repeatedly' (LB); cf. ahšáhəle· (for once)
(s) ahaləwí·i P 'more and more'; cf. aləwí·i 'more'
(t) ahaləmxó·k·o·k 'they are blown away by the wind' (OA), 3s aləmxo·kw
(u) ahalhikéhti·t 'their tracks, footprints', e·lhíke·t 'his tracks' (ME; |aləhkē-| AI 'step')
(v) aha·pto·ná·lkən 'the one speaking to you (sg.)' (B; |(IC)–əkwan| 3s–2s/PPL(ANsg));
    cf. nta·pto·ná·la 'I talked to him' (OA)
(w) aha·ptəp·é·ək 'they drown' (OA); a·ptəp·e· 'he drowned' (B, OA)
(x) ahá·mxink 'tumbleweed' (ME); cf. á·mxən 'it blew down, blew over' (LB)

Some stems have shapes that show that they originally included plural or repetitive reduplication but are not treated as such and have no unreduplicated counterpart (5.39).

(5.39) Stems with fossilized plural or repetitive reduplication
(a) |asēn-| TI(1b) 'scatter': ntas·é·nəmən 'I scattered it'; cf. |sē-| in nse·níhi·n 'I sow it' (B)
(b) |alēpwā·m-| TA 'give advice to': ktale·p·ɔ·mkúwa 'he (will) give you (pl.) advice' (B);
    cf. |ləpwā-| AI 'be wise, be smart' (3.38i), |-m| TA 'act on or cause by speech'
(c) |wehēməwāl-| TA 'mock': nəwehe·məwá·la 'I made fun of him'; cf. we·mi P,PV 'all'

§5.4c. Continuative Reduplication. A more inclusive name for the continuative reduplication would be continuative-attenuative. It indicates a continuous action or state, treated as non-segmented, or a protracted or attenuated action; it is often idiomatic.

The continuative reduplicant is |Rā+| CONT, realized as /Ca·+/ before a consonant and as /a·y+/ before a vowel. The only following vowel in known occurrences is |a-|, and before this the /y/ is retained. A following voiceless consonant is long.

(5.40) Continuative reduplication
(a) mpa·p·ənaé·ləma 'I'm thinking about him' (V)
(b) mpa·p·o·kwənəmən 'I gradually broke it' (OA)
(c) nta·t·əmə́š·əmən 'I "take (my) time to cut it off"' (OA)
(d) nta·t·unkšé·nəmən 'I gradually open the door' (OA)
(e) ka·k·əli·x·í·k·e· 'she's taking her time sewing' (OA)
(f) ka·ktəma·k·i·ká·x·i·n 'he lies there pitifully' (ME)
(g) nsa·s·a·k·ənəmən 'I slowly or gradually stuck it out (as a stick out a window)' (cf. 5.38e)
(h) nsa·s·í·k·wəna 'I'm (gradually) rubbing him' (OA)
(i) sa·s·ó·k·əla·n 'there's a slow rain' (FW, LB)
(j) ša·š·enkí·x·i·n 'he's lying down (resting, or for a long time)' (OA),
    nša·š·enkí·x·i=máh 'I was lying down' (OA; =máh PST)
(k) nəmá·məne·n 'I take my time drinking it' (OA)
(l) nəma·mí·tsi 'I am eating' (V); ma·mí·tsi·kw 'have something to eat (you pl.)!' (B)
(m) nna·né·ɔ 'I see him, keep him company; I notice him; I always see him' (OA);
    kó· nna·ne·yko·wí·ɔk "they don't notice me" (OA;
    kó· NEG; |nēw-| TA 'see', |nə–əkōwīwak| 3p–1s/IND.NEG)
(n) a·yahpá·mske· "he kinda walked around a little bit" (OA),
    nta·yahpá·mska 'I'm walking a bit' (OA)
(o) nta·yahkənó·t·əmən 'I'm talking about it' (OA);
    cf. ntak·ənó·t·əmən 'I'm talking about it, I talk or tell about it' (OA)'

§5.4d. Habitual Reduplication. The habitual reduplication indicates habitual or characteristic activity, occupation, or the like. Less commonly it has a perfective semelfactive use, indicating at least one past occurrence (5.41hijk). It is found on some particles (5.41dm).

The habitual reduplicant is |Rih+| HAB, realized as /Cih-/ before a consonant and as /ih-/ before a vowel. The |h| is retained as /h/ except before a consonant cluster other than /Cw/ (5.41hilm) or a voiceless consonant and a syllable with /ah/, notably when the reduplicant is followed by a voiced consonant and /ah/ (5.42f; contrast 2.7g). After the /h/, a /ə/ is inserted before a voiced consonant other than |w| (5.41fgjk), and |w| is lost (5.41no). Uniquely, the stem |ā-| AI 'go {smwh}' has the variant /i·h+/ HAB (5.41t). Also unique is the variant kihahki·hɔke·- of ihahki·hɔke·- AI 'be a deceiver, a hypocrite', *lit.* 'habitually deceive people' (5.41u).

With initial change the reduplicant is |(C)eh-|, always with short /e/; participles with this shape are often lexicalized (5.19g, 5.42fghnop), and there are also nouns formed like participles with habitual reduplication but with |-s| instead of third person |-t| (5.42acdek) and nouns of instrument in |-kan| with habitual reduplication (5.42i).

(5.41) Habitual reduplication (without initial change)
- (a) mpihpə́ntaɔ 'I used to hear him' (OA); cf. mpə́ntaɔ 'I hear him, heard him'
- (b) ntihtəməš·əmə́na 'I always cut them (inan.) off' (OA; |təməš-| TI(1b) 'cut')
- (c) kihkəmó·tke·p 'he had been a thief' (B; |kəmōtəkē-| AI 'steal')
- (d) kwíhkwi·n 'customarily for a long time' (V; kwí·n P 'for a long time')
- (e) nšihša·khwíkamən 'I always did kick it' (OA; |šākwəhk-| TI(1a) 'kick')
- (f) lihəli·khakéhəle· 'the ground is cracking' (OA; |līk-| 'come apart(?)')
- (g) mihəmi·kəmɔ́·s·u 'he works, is a worker' (ME: |mīhkəmwāsī-| AI 'work')
- (h) kəmímhɔ=hə́č si·sí·lie? 'Have you ever eaten buffalo?' (LB)
- (i) nəmímhɔ. 'I have eaten it (anim.)' (ND)
- (j) kənihəné·mən 'you have seen it before' (ND; |nēm-| TI(3) 'see')
- (k) ɔ́·k=hə́č kənihəné·ɔ ᵗe·pəlihámaɔ? 'and have you seen Abraham?' (B; |nēw-| TA 'see')
- (l) nkəmé·e nnink·ála 'I always leave him' (OA; < /nink·-/ < |nihnək-|; |nəkal-| TA 'leave')
- (m) nink·əmé·i (B), nink·əmé·e (V, OA) 'always'; cf. nkəmé·e 'always'
- (n) ní·=tá xú yúkwe áləmi kəwihi·č·əməlhúmɔ. 'I'm going to help you (pl.) from now on.' (V; /wihī·-/ < |wihwī-|; ní· 'I'; =tá FOC; xú FUT; yúkwe 'now'; áləmi P 'beginning'; cf. kəwi·č·əməlhúmɔ 'I help(ed) you (pl.)'
- (o) wihínki-či·p·a·š·í·mu 'he always has nightmares' (OA; idiomatic use of |wīnkī| PV 'like to')
- (p) ná=máh=nə tíhahpi·n 'he used to stay there' (OA; |apī-| AI 'be {smwh})
- (q) ná=nə ntihələ́nəmən. 'That's what I do, the way I do.' (OA; |ələn-| TI(1b) 'do {so}')
- (r) ná=húnt=nə ihəlí·ha·n 'that's how they used to be treated' (OA; |əlıh-| TA 'treat {so}')
- (s) tá=hə́č ktihə́nta- nə́ -lə́s·i·n? 'Where do you do that?' (B; |-ənta| PV '{smwh}' [3.13(3)])
- (t) ná=nə tí·ha·n 'he always goes over there, he used to go there' (OA; |ā-| AI 'go {smwh}')
- (u) ehahki·hɔ́ke·t (1x; pl. 3x), kehahki·hɔ́ke·t (2x; pl. 1x) 'hypocrite'; kkihahki·hɔ́ke 'you are a hypocrite' (1x; pl. 9x); e·lkí·kwi-ihahki·hɔké·li·t 'how hypocritical (obv.) is' (B)

(5.42) Habitual reduplication with initial change
- (a) pehpəmət·ó·nhe·s 'preacher' (V, OA, ND); cf. pəmət·ó·nhe· 'he's talking, telling, preaching'
- (b) tehtəməš·ínki·k 'the reapers' (B; cf. 5.41b)
- (c) kehkəmó·tke·t (B, OA), kehkəmó·tke·s (OA, LB) 'thief' (cf. 5.41c)
- (d) sehsi·skəwahó·she·s 'potter' (*lit.*, 'clay-pot-maker'); cf. si·skəwáho·s 'clay pot' (ND)
- (e) šehši·k·wí·ta·s 'robber' (B); cf. ši·k·wi·tá·ɔk 'they are robbing' (V)
- (f) léhəlahpi-ki·s·í·č·i·k si·p·əwá·s·ak 'sand plums', *lit.*, 'quick-ripening plums' (|lap-| 'fast')
- (g) mehəmí·č·ink 'food, groceries' (*lit.*, 'what people eat') (B, V, ME); nəmí·č·i·n 'I eat it'

(h) memhálamunt 'merchant' (*lit.*, 'one people buy from') (B, V, OA; |mehmahlamōnt|);
cf. nəmahəlamáɔ·n 'I bought it from him' (|mahlamaw-| TA+O 'buy O2 from')
(i) mehəmo·nši·to·naehí·k·an 'razor' (OA, LB; |mōnš-| 'cut hair', |-īhtōnay-ē-| 'whiskers')
(j) nenhíləwe·t 'murderer' (B, OA; |nehnəhləwēt| < |nəhləwē-| AI 'kill people' [5.101c])
(k) nenpí·ke·s 'sweat doctor' (OA, ME; |nehnəpīhkēs| < |nəpīhkē-| AI 'doctor (people)')
(l) wehi·k·iénkəp 'where we (exc.) used to live' (V; |wehwīkəyēnkəp| < |Rih+| HAB, |wīkī-| AI 'dwell {smwh}', |IC–yēnkəp| 1p/PPL.PRET(OBL); cf. nəwí·k·i·n 'I live there')
(m) ehalaí·č·i·k 'hunters'; cf. alái· 'he hunts'
(n) eskí·tamink 'watermelon' (|ehaskīhtamənk|
< |Rih+|, |askīht-| TI(1a) 'eat raw', |IC–amənk| X–0/PPL(INsg))
(o) ehəntalí·p·wink 'table' (*lit.*, 'where people eat'; 4.9e)
(p) ehe·š·ánte·k 'window' (*lit.*, 'what the sun shines through')
(q) wəntáhkwi ehe·yó·wi·k khak·ayə́na 'over where our bodies go (after death)' (ME)
(|ēyōwī-| II 'go {smwh}', derived from |ā-| AI 'go {smwh}' [3s é·(w)])

§5.4e. Extended Reduplication. What is called, somewhat arbitrarily, the extended reduplication has two discrete functions. In sentences that are not negative it indicates a past time relatively far removed from the present, but in negative expressions it gives the meaning 'never' and may refer to past, present, or future. It is also found on some particles (5.43fhj).

The extended reduplicant is |Rī+| EXT (/Ci·+/ before a consonant, /i·y+/ before a vowel). A following voiceless consonant is long, and the /i·/ is kept long if the following syllable has /ah/ (from a weak |a|). When the stem begins with |əl-|, the sequence |īy+əl-| is reduced to /ill-/ (5.43ijk, 5.44rs). Otherwise, the |y| drops before a vowel (5.43gh, 5.44lmnop), and presumably |īy+ahk-| becomes /i·hak-/ (5.44q). A stem-initial |w| drops before a long vowel (5.44k).

(5.43) Extended reduplication (for removed past)
(a) čínke=ét=tá kpi·p·á·həmp? 'When (some time ago) did you come here?' (B)
(b) nti·t·unkšé·nəmən 'I have already opened it' (OA; cf. 5.40d)
(c) nti·t·əmə́š·əmən=máh=nə́n 'I have already cut it off' (OA; cf. 5.41b)
(d) máta kí·kski- kéku -luwé·i 'he was never able to say anything' (B; **§2.4a**, end)
(e) nši·š·a·khwíkamən 'I have already kicked it' OA)
(f) ni·núči P 'for a long time, since some time back' (2.73j);
cf. núči, nóči P, PV 'beginning, since'
(g) ló·məwe ná tí·a·n 'he went there long ago' (OA; |ā-| AI 'go {smwh}', |wət–ən| 3s/SBD)
(h) i·á·pči P 'still' (cf. |āpət-| 'to death')
(i) illəkhíkwi-ahɔ·lá·t·əp 'as much as he had loved them' (B)
(j) ílli P 'even'; cf. lí (|əlī|) '{so}' (idiomatic)
(k) ná=yó·k ní·š·a illo·xwéhti·t tɔ·né·ɔ 'then those two went the way they had been walking' (V; |əlōxwē-| AI 'walk {so}')

(5.44) Extended reduplication (with a negative)
(a) tá=á· čí·č pí·p·e· 'he'll never come back any more' (OA); pé· 'he comes'
(b) takó· awé·n ki·kahto·p·wí·i 'no one ever used to be hungry' (ME);
cf. kahtó·p·u 'he's hungry'
(c) máta si·s·ihɔ́·i 'nobody could ever beat him' (ME)
(d) kó· si·s·o·psí·i 'he never went without clothes' (OA)
(e) máta si·s·o·k·əla·nó·wi·p 'it never rained' (B)
(f) kó· nši·š·a·khwikamó·wən 'I never did kick it' (OA)
(g) tá=á· awé·n mwi·məné·wən 'no one would ever drink it' (B 1842:23)

(h) kó·nni·nk·alá·a 'I never left him' (OA)
(i) é·li- takó· -wi·wəni·č·a·ní·t·əp 'as she had never had a child' (B)
(j) takó· wi·wəla·ta·í·ɔk 'they never put up food for themselves' (B)
(k) ɔ́·k=č wsa·k·i·ma·ɔ́·k·an máta wi·i·kwé·i 'and his kingdom shall never end' (B)
(l) énta- máta -i·ála-pəmá·wsink 'where one never stops living' (B)
(m) kó· nti·ahkwi·má·a 'I never accused him' (OA)
(n) kó· i·ahpa·mské·e 'he never did walk around' (OA)
(o) máta i·ahki·hóke·t 'who never cheats' (B)
(p) nə́ tə́ntay máta=á· i·a·té·i 'the fire would never go out' (B)
(q) takó· i·haki·he·í·ɔk 'they never plant' (B; ⟨evak-⟩)
(r) akó· nə́ ntilləs·i·wən. 'I've never been that way.'
(OA; akó· NEG; nə́ 'that (inan.)'; |īy+| EXT, |ələsī-| AI 'be {so}', |nət–wən| 1s(OBL))
(s) máta ílle·k 'which has never been' (B)

§5.4f. Rare Patterns of Reduplication. A few words exhibit additional types of ostensible reduplication that are not derived from known simpler shapes by an active grammatical rule.
(5.45) Rare reduplication types
(a) tətá ehe·ləmo·k·wənák·a 'forever and ever' (ME; /ehe·ləm-/ as if |IC+Rih+IC+áləm-|)
(b) kéku=húnt ná píči-kčkčí·t 'there she was, going in and out (of the house)' (ME)
(c) a·məwé·ak píči-kəkčkčihəlá·č·i·k 'bees flying in and out' (ME)
(d) či·č·i·k·o·líhəle· 'it slides around' (OA); cf. či·k·o·líhəle· 'it slides (off)'
(e) či·č·i·k·o·lháma· 'he keeps sliding (on sled)' (OA); cf. či·k·o·lháma· 'he slides downhill'
(f) lahəlápi 'again and again' (B); cf. lápi 'again'
(g) pwe·pahsənəmáɔ·n 'he divided it up for them' (B); cf. mpas·ə́nəmən 'I tore it in two'.

The form in (5.45a) appears to have /eh-/ (|Rih+| HAB with IC) added to a stem that already has |IC| on |aləm-| 'begin, continue'. It is actually, however, a reshaping of the earlier form ehaləmo·k·wənák·a 'forever' used three times by Blanchard. The functionally repetitive reduplication of stems with /kč-/ (from |kət-| 'go out') as /kčkč-/ and /kəkčkč-/ was used only by ME (5.45bc); other speakers had, for example, péči-kə́kči·t (for 5.45b). The reduplication of |čīkōl-| 'slide' as /či·č·i·k·o·l-/ has a repetitive function but a medial long /č·/ (5.45de).

§5.5. Secondary Derivation. Secondary derivation is the derivation of a stem from another stem. A secondary stem is one derived from another stem by means of a secondary final. A secondary stem may be derived from a primary stem or from another secondary stem. In a complex secondary stem, one with multiple formal layers of derivation, not all the ostensible intermediate stems may be attested or even likely as independent words, and in such cases complex secondary finals may function as unitary components of the resulting derived stem.

The part-of-speech classifications of the stem that is the base of the derivation and of the resulting, derived stem determine the type of secondary derivation (**§5.5a-d**, **§5.6**, **§5.7**, **§5.8**).

§5.5a. Nouns Formed from Nouns. Some noun stems are derived from nouns with the same basic meaning by the addition of suffixes that mark the noun as diminutive (**§5.5b**), pejorative (**§5.5c**), or objurgative (**§5.5d**).

§5.5b. Diminutives. The characteristic consonant making diminutives for all parts of speech is |t|, which is always a long |t·| in environments where this is permitted, except in static words (2.76, 2.80d).

Diminutive nouns are freely formed with the suffix |-ətət| DIM. Before this, stems in underlying |-Vw| and |-Vy| have contraction (5.46fghi), except for xkwé· 'woman', which also differs from the other nouns in |-Vw| in having a stressed long /é·/ and archaically a retained final

/w/ (2.10e, 5.46j). Stems in |-s| replace this with |-tət| (5.46klmn). The words for 'boy' and 'girl' replace final /č/ with /š/ before |-ətət| (5.46op).

In most cases a noun with |-ətət| has a literal diminutive meaning, but with some kinship terms this suffix indicates a more distant relative (5.46ek).

(5.46) Diminutive nouns with |-ətət|
- (a) hitkwə́t·ət 'stick', pl. hitkwət·ə́t·a; cf. hít·ukw 'tree', pl. hítko·k
- (b) mənəp·é·kwtət 'pool' (B); cf. mənə́p·e·kw 'lake'
- (c) mínkwtət 'little seed'; cf. mínkw 'seed'
- (d) ahpó·nt·ət 'piece of bread, little bread, biscuit' (B, OA); cf. ahpó·n 'bread'
- (e) nó·xtət 'my father's brother'; cf. nó·x 'my father'
- (f) mwe·k·ané·t·ət 'little dog'; cf. mwé·k·ane 'dog' (|mwēkanēw-|)
- (g) o·t·e·né·t·ət 'little town'; cf. o·t·é·nay 'town' (|ōtēnay-|)
- (h) ma·nša·pí·t·ət 'little bead' (OA); cf. ma·nšá·pí 'bead', pl. ma·nšá·pí·ak
- (i) mpí·t·ət 'small amount of water' (V); mpí 'water' (|nəpəy-|)
- (j) xkwé·wtət 'little woman' (ND); cf. xkwé· (archaic xkwé·w) 'woman'
- (k) nkahé·t·ət 'my aunt (father's or mother's sister)'; cf. nkáhe·s 'my mother'
- (l) e·mhɔ́·nt·ət 'little spoon' (OA); cf. e·mhɔ́·nəs AN 'spoon'
- (m) namé·t·ət 'little fish'; cf. namé·s 'fish'
- (n) mi·mə́ntət 'small child, baby' (cf. 5.14c); cf. mí·mə·ns (dial. mí·məns) 'child'
- (o) pi·laečə́štət 'little boy'; cf. pi·laéčəč 'boy' (2.77d)
- (p) xkwe·čə́štət 'little girl'; cf. xkwé·čəč 'girl' (2.77e)
- (q) wté·htət 'little heart' (OA), wte·htə́t·a 'his little heart' (V 1946:156)

When a non-dependent diminutive noun is possessed, the possessed-theme marker |-əm| (**§42a**) precedes the diminutive suffix |-ətət| DIM if what precedes the diminutive suffix in the unpossessed noun is the full non-diminutive noun stem (5.47a) or the full stem with contraction (5.47b). If the diminutive suffix is fused with the noun stem by replacing a stem-final |s| (as in 5.46klmn), either it is followed by the |-əm| (the diminutive being, in effect, treated as an independent word; 5.47cd), or it follows the possessed non-diminutive theme (5.47e)

(5.47) Possessed diminutive nouns
- (a) ntap·ɔ·nəmə́t·ət 'my little piece of bread' (OA; cf. 5.46d)
- (b) nəma·nša·p·i·yəmət·ə́tak 'my little beads' (OA); nəma·nša·pí·yəmak 'my —' (cf. 5.46h)
- (c) ntahemptə́t·əm 'my rag' (OA); cf. hémptət 'piece of cloth' (5.14a)
- (d) nte·mhɔ·ntə́t·əm 'my little spoon' (OA; cf. 5.46.l, 5.47e)
- (e) nte·mhɔ·ns·əmə́t·ət 'my little spoon' (OA; cf. 5.47d)

The vocatives of some kinterms incorporate a diminutive suffix /-t·i/ (4.11hij)

Many nouns with a diminutive flavor incorporate a purely formal diminutive suffix, especially /-əs/ (5.48) or |-sə̀s| (2.77abc). The words for 'boy' and 'girl' uniquely have |-čə̀č| (2.77de, 5.46op). Words with |-sə̀s| and |-čə̀č| have static features.

(5.48) Nouns with a formal diminutive suffix |-(ə)s|
- (a) méki·s 'sheep, goat'
- (b) memmák·a·s (ME), memmék·a·s (LB) 'butterfly'
- (c) mí·li·s 'phoebe'
- (d) ɔ́·k·wəs 'fox'
- (e) pəpxɔ́k·wəs 'eastern red cedar'
- (f) púnkwəs 'mosquito'
- (g) xaní·k·wəs 'chipmunk' (V); cf. xáni·kw 'squirrel'

The ostensible agent nouns with |-əs| (5.62) can be taken as having the formal diminutive suffix |-(ə)s|, but nouns with the agentive suffix |-s| (5.66) lack any diminutive flavor.

§5.5c. Pejoratives. A handful of nouns have been recorded with a suffix |-šəš| (either added or replacing |-səs|) that gives a pejorative meaning. Presumably this could be used on other nouns as well.

(5.49) Nouns with a pejorative suffix
- (a) lənó·š·əš 'no-good man, old so-and-so' (ND)
- (b) hiló·š·əš 'nasty old man' (V; /š·/ conjectured from 5.49a); cf. hiló·səs 'old man'
- (c) xkó·kšəš 'hateful snake' (V); cf. xkó·k 'snake'

With a similar flavor is mi·mə·nšak 'children!' (cf. mí·mə·ns 'child'), said to have been used jokingly by an old man along with the objurgative verbs in (5.118cd).

§5.5d. Objurgatives. Other nouns with a pejorative meaning have objurgative noun finals. Objurgative forms are made from nouns and verbs by the addition of elements referring to intimate bodyparts. Their use adds the rough equivalent of a swear word or expletive. They range in strength (from mildest to strongest) from 'rear end, butt', to 'anus, rectum', to 'penis', to 'female parts'. For examples in verb stems see (5.118).

(5.50) Objurgative nouns
- (a) nčó·t·ie 'my friend (voc.) (male to male)' (4.11f); cf. |-təy-| 'rear end' (very mild).
- (b) pi·lae·č·a·lahkí·t·i "bad boy" (V); cf. pi·laéčəč 'boy', |-ālakītəy-| 'rectum'
- (c) xko·k·a·lahkí·t·i "disgusting snake" (V); cf. xkó·k 'snake', |-ālakītəy-| 'rectum'
- (d) xko·kšé·t·i "darned old snake" (V); cf. xkó·k 'snake', |-əšētəy| 'anus'
- (e) hilo·š·é·t·i '(darned) old man' (ME)
- (f) hilo·š·alák·ay '(damned) old man' (ME; worse than 5.50e)
- (g) mpas·alák·ay 'damn bus' (FW from Jim Shaw, used when he had just missed the bus); cf. mpás 'bus', |-alakay| 'penis' (cf. unpossessed noun: alák·ay 'penis' [V, ER])
- (h) mwiálahkay (a strong insult to a man) (ER; |mwəy-| 'excrement', |-alakay| 'penis'; cf. 5.118f)
- (i) we·lxo·s·alak·ayak "bunch of studs" (ER; cf. wé·lxo·s 'stallion')
- (j) səkahkóle·s 'black person' (|sək-| 'black', /ahkóle·s/ 'a Swede' [attested as ⟨Akoores⟩, Campanius 1696:140]; |akw-| 'wear clothing', |-al-| 'penis', |-ē| AI [5.118f], |-s| [5.66])
- (k) səkahkɔle·wšé·t·iak '(damned) black people' (OA; cf. 5.50de)

The noun finals in these words are not the heads of the ostensible compounds (modified by the initials), but it is rather they that modify the ostensible initial, the way a diminutive suffix would.

§5.6. Secondary Derivation: Nouns Formed from Verbs. The types of nouns that are formed from verb stems include nouns of instrument and the like, abstract nouns, and agent nouns. In addition, participles (which are inflected verb forms; §4.6a, 4.64) function as nouns, and some participles that are lexicalized have taken on features of noun morphology, both in inflection and in further derivation.

Nouns that refer to the instrument or means used, or broadly to the product (what is made, made to happen, or caused to be produced), and nouns that provide a label for the action or process denoted are made with abstract secondary noun finals that end in |-ən| (in most cases /-n/) or, rarely, |-ənay|.

§5.6a. Nouns with |-ən| NF. A few nouns have |-ən| NF added directly to an AI stem. Before |-ən| NF, |ē| is replaced by |a| (5.51abcd) and presumably also |ā| (5.51g).

(5.51) Nouns with |-ən| NF added to an AI stem
- (a) ahpí·k·ɔn (|apīkwan|) "flute" (i.e., end-blown Woodland flageolet)
    < ahpí·k·we· (|apīkwē-| AI) 'he's playing a "flute" (1s ntap·í·k·we)

(b) kwəláꞏkan (|kwəlahkan|) 'tabooed food item'
   < kwəláꞏkeꞏ (|kwəlahkē-| AI) 'is forbidden, restricted by taboo' (1s nkwəlháke)
(c) leꞏkhíꞏkꞏan (|əlēkahīkan|) 'book, writing' < leꞏkhíꞏkꞏeꞏ (|əlēkahīkē-| AI) 'writes'
(d) ahkəntíꞏkꞏan (|akəntīkan|) 'number(s)' (V, BS) < ahkəntíꞏkꞏeꞏ AI 'counts' (OA, LB)
(e) kɔhɔ́ꞏkꞏan (|(ta)kwahākan|) 'mortar' (2.6c) < kɔhɔ́ꞏkꞏeꞏ AI 'grinds corn in a mortar'
(f) iꞏláꞏwkaꞏn (|īlāwəkān|) 'war dance' (used as the name of the dance)
   < iꞏláꞏwkeꞏ (|īlāwəkā-| AI) 'he does the war dance' (iꞏlaꞏwkáꞏčꞏiꞏk 'war-dancers')
   (Cf. the homophonous verb form: iꞏláꞏwkaꞏn 'there is a war-dance'; |-ən| X [4.19, 20].)
(g) ahpɔ́ꞏn (|apwān|) 'bread' < |apwē-| AI 'roast' (only in ahpweꞏmíꞏna 'roasting ears' [ME])

§5.6b. Nouns with |-ənay| NF. Three nouns have |-ənay| NF. One adds |-ənay| NF to an AI stem in |-ī| (5.52a); one adds this after an archaic, consonant-final TI(3) final that survives only in derived nouns (5.52b); and one is based on an unused verb and has the short form /-n/ before the locative ending (5.52c).

(5.52) Nouns with |-ənay| NF added to an AI or TI(3) stem
   (a) ahpíꞏnay 'bed' (|apīnay|; attested as ahpíꞏnenk 'on a bed', tɔpꞏíꞏnay 'his bed' [B])
   (b) kwiꞏpꞏələ́nay (|(a)kwīpələnay|) 'hoe' (*'thing tied against'; |-pəl| TI(3) 'tie')
   (c) oꞏtéꞏnay 'town' (loc. oꞏtéꞏnink; 4.9d); AI stem not in use.

§5.6c. Nouns with |-wən| NF. Some AI verbs in |-ī| add |-wən| NF, with contraction: |-ī-wən| > |-ə-wən| > |-ōn| (5.53). Other nouns in |-ōn| likely have the same derivation but lack a known corresponding verb (5.53defghi).

(5.53) Nouns with |-wən| NF
   (a) anáꞏnsoꞏn 'mattress' (cf. ə́nta-anáꞏnsiꞏt 'where he lay (on bedding)')
   (b) ktaꞏptiꞏksoꞏn 'sweat' < ktaꞏptíꞏksu 'sweats'
   (c) sahkaxꞏéhoꞏn 'earring' < sahkaxꞏéhu 'wears earrings' (ND)
   (d) kəlamaꞏpíꞏsꞏoꞏn 'belt' (with |-āhpīsī| AI 'be tied, tie self'; cf. |kaxpīsī-| AI 'be tied')
   (e) kpáhoꞏn 'door' (< *|kəpahī-| AI 'shut oneself in' with |-ahī| AI < |-ahw| TA 'by tool')
   (f) məloꞏkwéhoꞏn 'pillow' (with |-ahī| AI; cf. 5.53c)
   (g) mpíꞏsꞏoꞏn 'medicine' (< *|nəpīsī-| AI 'be doctored' < |nəpīl-| TA 'doctor' [5.104.l])
   (h) šaꞏpꞏwələnčéhoꞏn 'ring' (with |-ahī| AI; cf. 5.53c)
   (i) xáꞏnsoꞏn 'bed' (cf. 5.53a)

§5.6d. Nouns with |-wan| NF. There are also nouns formed with |-wan| NF; before this |ī| is retained (5.54a) and |ē| is replaced by |ā| (5.54c). The final |-īkāwan| 'house, building' that can be derived as part of a verb stem in (5.54c) most commonly appears in nouns formed by primary derivation where there is no corresponding verb (5.54def). Some other nouns ostensibly with |-wan| NF are also not from a verb (5.54g).

(5.54) Nouns with |-wan| NF
   (a) škíꞏɔn 'urine' (WT)
   (b) psiꞏkáꞏɔn AN 'feather worn on head' (< psíꞏkaꞏ AI 'wears a feather on his head')
   (c) hempsiꞏkꞏáꞏɔn 'tent' (< hempsíꞏkꞏeꞏ 'camps in a tent'; with |-īkē| AI 'dwell, etc.')
   (d) məsaꞏkwiꞏkꞏáꞏɔn 'log house' (< məsákw 'log')
   (e) paꞏtamweꞏiꞏkꞏáꞏɔn 'temple' (B) (< |pāhtamwē-| < |pāhtamā-| AI 'pray' [**§5.6h**])
   (f) maiꞏkꞏeꞏiꞏkꞏáꞏɔn 'inn' (B) (< maíꞏkꞏeꞏ AI 'stays the night, camps')
   (g) wiꞏsꞏaniꞏkꞏáꞏɔn 'gum (in mouth)' (with |-anīkē| AI or |-anīkā| AI 'have (such) teeth')

§5.6e. Nouns with |-kan| NF. In addition to the |-kan| derived from |-kē| in AI stems (5.51cde), there is an underived |-kan| NF that is added to AI stems (or virtual stems) to make nouns (5.55). Before |-kan| NF a stem-final |ē| becomes |ā| (5.55bcdefg); a stem-final |ā| that is not replaced by |ē| in third person independent order forms is replaced by an intermediate-stage |wē| (as in all derivatives of such verbs; cf. 5.54e), and the potential |ē| in this is in turn also replaced by |ā| (5.55h).

(5.55) Nouns made with |-kan| NF
- (a) hupó·k·an 'pipe' (< húpwe· 'smokes', 1s nó·pɔ; |wəhpwā-| AI)
- (b) a·pto·ná·k·an 'word' (< a·ptó·ne· 'speaks')
- (c) a·thilo·há·k·an 'winter story' (< a·thiló·he· 'tells a winter story')
- (d) haki·há·k·an 'field, garden' (< hakí·he· 'plants, farms')
- (e) talaxhakiá·k·an 'plow' (< talaxhákie· 'he plows')
- (f) təmá·k·an 'road', nəmət·əmá·k·an 'my road' (< mətə́me· 'takes the road'; 2.68d)
- (g) pəntahsəná·k·an 'tobacco pouch' (< *|pəntasənē-| AI 'put stones (i.e., shot) in')
- (h) či·xhamó·k·an (|čīxahamwākan|) 'comb' (OA, LB) (< či·xháma· 'combs own hair'; OA)

§5.6f. Nouns with |-īkan| NF. There is also a common secondary final |-īkan| NF that is added to TI stems to make nouns of instrument and the like. Although for some nouns with this final there is an intermediate stage with the detransitivizing final |-īkē| AI (5.51cd), in most cases this stage is not attested, and the noun is effectively derived directly from the TI stem (5.56). A stem-final |t| is usually retained before this final (5.56cd), but in at least one case it is replaced by |č| (5.56f).

(5.56) Nouns made with |-īkan| NF
- (a) kəlahí·k·an 'trap' (< |kəlah-| TI(1a) 'trap')
- (b) kpəš·ehí·k·an 'lid' < kpəš·éham 'closes the opening of (it) with a lid'
- (c) maxke·elahtí·k·an (|maxkēwēhlatīkan|) '(U.S.) flag'
  (< |maxk-| 'red' + |-ēwēhlā| II 'echo, flap noisily' + |-t| TI(2) 'cause to' [5.78])
- (d) pahkantí·k·an AN 'drumstick' (< |pakant-| TI(1a) 'hit')
- (e) payaxhí·k·an 'gun' (< |payaxkah-| TI(1a) 'shoot by firearm';
  pɔyxkhámən 'he shoots it (with a gun)' [LB], *'strikes it with a lightning bolt')
- (f) po·t·a·č·í·k·an 'whistle' (< |pōtāt-| TI(1a) 'blow on')

§5.6g. Nouns with |-ākan| NF. A few nouns have instead |-ākan| NF added to a TI stem; the intermediate stage |-ākē| AI (5.51e) is not attested for those in (5.57).

(5.57) Nouns made with |-ākan| NF
- (a) nkwəntá·k·an 'my throat' (< |kwənt-| TI(1a) 'swallow'; nkwə́ntamən 1s–0s/IND [LB])
- (b) khikhá·k·an 'boundary marker; state' (V, OA; CW) (< |kəhkah-| TI(1a) 'mark the boundary of' [B])

§5.6h. Nouns with |-wākan| NF from primary stems. Very productively abstract nouns are made from AI verbs by adding |-wākan| NF. (The examples in 5.58 are from primary stems, ones not formed by secondary derivation.) Nouns of this shape are also made from objectless TI verbs (in all cases with |-am| TH.1a), which are syntactically intransitive (5.58mn), and from |mīčī-| TI(3) 'eat', which has the vowel-final stem shape otherwise found only in AI verbs (5.58t). The final vowel of an AI stem is replaced as before |-w| 3 (**§2.10h**; 5.58abcdefghij), except that a stem-final |ā| that does not change to |ē| in third person independent indicative forms (cf. 2.24a) is replaced by |wē| (5.58k), as in all derivatives of these stems (cf. 5.54e, 5.55h, 5.75p, 5.79d, 5.82, 5.83c, 5.98a). Consonant-final AI stems and TI themes insert |ə| (5.58lmn). Stems in |-ōwī| make nouns ending in /-wwá·k·an/, with a geminate /ww/ that is the regular contraction of |-wəw-| (with |-ōwə-w-| < |-ōwī-w-|; 2.14, 5.58op). Stems in |-āwī| and |-ēwī| (in all cases verbs of being [**§5.7a**]) have haplology of the expected |-wəw-| to |-w-| (5.58rst), as if |-ākan| were added directly to the noun stem. (There is a verb |sākīmā-| AI 'be king', but this was perhaps back-formed from the noun for 'kingdom' (5.58t).)

(5.58) Abstract nouns made with |-wākan| NF from primary stems
  (a) ləhəle·x·e·ɔ́·k·an 'life' (< |lēhlēxē-| AI 'live'; 3s ləhəlé·x·e·)
  (b) mahta·ke·ɔ́·k·an 'fighting, war' (< |matahkē-| AI 'fight'; 3s mahtá·ke·)
  (c) wəla·məwe·ɔ́·k·an 'truth' (wəlá·məwe· AI 3s; |-ē|)
  (d) maxkpehəle·ɔ́·k·an 'measles' (maxkpéhəle· AI 3s; |-ā|)
  (e) ke·na·məwá·k·an 'prayer of thanks' (< |kēnāmwī-| AI 'give thanks'; 3s ke·ná·mu)
  (f) wəla·te·naməwá·k·an 'happiness' (< |wəlahtēnamī-| AI 'be happy'; 3s wəla·té·namu)
  (g) luwe·nsəwá·k·an 'name' (< |ələwēnsī-| AI 'be named {so}'; 3s luwé·nsu)
  (h) sala·məwá·k·an '(loud) weeping' (< |salāmwī-| AI 'cry loudly'; 3s salá·mu)
  (i) ahpo·s·əwá·k·an 'roasted meat' (ME) (< |apōsī-| AI+O 'roast, bake'; 3s ahpó·s·u)
  (j) wi·s·əwá·k·an 'fat' (ME) (< |wīsī-| AI 'be fat'; 3s wí·s·u)
  (k) pa·tamwe·ɔ́·k·an 'prayer' (< |pāhtamwē-| < |pāhtamā-| AI 'pray', 3s pá·tama·)
  (l) ankələwá·k·an 'death' (< ánkəl 'dies')
  (m) ši·e·ləntaməwá·k·an 'sorrow' (< ši·e·ləntam 'is sorry, sorrowful, upset')
  (n) pəna·eləntaməwá·k·an 'thought(s), plan(s)' (< pəna·eləntam 'thinks')
  (o) a·s·uwwá·k·an 'song' (LB) (< |āsōwī-| AI 'sing'; 3s a·s·ó·u [2.14d])
  (p) manət·uwwá·k·an 'spiritual power' (B), kəmant·uwwá·k·an 'your power' (ME)
    (< |manətōwī-| AI 'be a spirit, have spiritual power')
  (q) ahɔ·p·e·ɔ́·k·an 'wealth' (< |ahwāpēwī-| 'be rich'; ehɔ·p·é·i·t '(one) who is rich')
  (r) ləna·p·e·ɔ́·k·an 'soul' (B, V) (as if < |ələnāpēwī-| AI 'be a person' < ləná·p·e 'person')
  (s) sa·k·i·ma·ɔ́·k·an 'kingdom' (< sa·k·í·ma 'chief; king, prince')
  (t) mi·č·əwá·k·an 'food' (< |mīčī-| TI(3) 'eat')

§5.6i. Nouns with |-wākan| NF from derived AI verbs. Abstract nouns cannot be made directly from transitive verbs (except for the special cases of those treated as intransitives, as noted in **§5.6h**). Abstract nouns are, however, freely made from AI verb stems that are formed on transitive verbs in any of several ways by secondary derivation (5.59, 5.60). On the secondary final |-(ə)tī| AI RECIP, which makes reciprocals but also passives with indefinite subject (**§5.8m**), abstract nouns are made that may have a reciprocal (5.60jk), active (5.60jk), or passive (5.60a-i) meaning; more examples are in (5.114-116).

(5.59) Abstract nouns made with |-wākan| NF from secondary AI stems in |-ē| and invariant |-ā|
Nouns from stems with |-kē| AI (detransitivizer; 5.102) added to TA in |m|
  (a) ahke·kinke·ɔ́·k·an 'teaching' (|akēhkīnkē-| AI 'teach people' < |akēhkīm-| TA 'teach')
  (b) wi·k·inke·ɔ́·k·an 'marriage' (|wīkīnkē-| AI < |wīkīm-| 'be married to' [5.102e])
  (c) wi·penke·ɔ́·k·an 'adultery' (|wīhpēnkē-| AI < |wīhpēm-| TA 'sleep with'; B 1x); also
    ki·mí·i-wi·penke·ɔ́·k·an 'unfaithfulness, adultery' (B 2x; ki·mí·i P 'secretly' [5.127])
Nouns from stems with |-kē| AI (detransitivizer; 5.102) added to a TA in |l| (with |l-k| > |hk|)
  (d) ki·hɔke·ɔ́·k·an 'deception' (|kīwahkē-| AI < |kīwal-| TA 'deceive')
Nouns from stems with |-əwē| AI (detransitivizer; 5.101) added to a TA
  (e) luwe·ɔ́·k·an 'saying, word(s), a voice' (|ələwē-| AI 'say {so}', 3s lúwe·w, lúwe·;
    < |əl-| TA 'say {so} to')
  (f) ki·k·ehawe·ɔ́·k·an 'curing power' (KJV "virtue") (|kīkēhəwē-| AI < |kīkēh-| TA 'cure')
  (g) pa·tahəwe·ɔ́·k·an 'victory' (|pāhtāhəwē-| AI < |pāhtāh-| TA 'defeat')
Nouns from stems with middle-reflexive |-amā| AI (see **§5.6h**, 5.104) added to a TI(1a) stem
  (h) nhaka·t·amwe·ɔ́·k·an 'faith' (← |nahkātamā-| AI < |nahkāt-| TI(1a) 'put to use, rely on'

(i) ktəle·khamwe·ó·k·an 'your debt' (|kət-| 2s; ← |əlēkahamā-| AI 'have a debt'
< |əlēkahamaw-| TA 'owe O2 to', *lit.* 'write down O2 for')
(j) nihəla·t·amwe·ó·k·an 'freedom' (← nihəlá·t·ama· AI 'he is of age, is free to act, has
authority' < |nīhlāt-| TI(1a) 'own, be master of, be lord of, have the say over')
(k) o·wa·t·amwe·ó·k·an 'his wisdom' (|wə-| 3s; ← |wəwātamā-| virtual AI
< wwá·t·am 'is smart, has sense, is aware of himself')

(5.60) Abstract nouns made with |-wākan| NF from stems with |-(ə)tī| AI RECIP
(a) ahke·kəntəwá·k·an 'teaching' (|akēhkīntī-| AI < |akēhkīm-| TA 'teach')
(b) ahɔ·ltəwá·k·an 'love' (|àhwālətī-| AI < |àhwāl-| TA 'love');
tɔhɔ·ltəwá·k·an 'his love'
(c) ktəma·k·e·ləntəwá·k·an 'mercy (received)' (< |kətəmākēləm-| TA 'pity');
kwət·əma·k·e·ləntəwá·k·an 'his mercy (shown)'
(d) mawəntəwá·k·an 'mourning' (|mawīntī-| AI < |mawīm-| TA 'cry for, mourn')
(e) naxkuntəwá·k·an 'agreement, bargain, covenant' (< |naxkōm-| TA 'answer, say yes to')
(f) wəlankuntəwá·k·an 'peace' (< |wəlankōm-| TA 'be on good terms with, at peace with')

§5.6j. Nouns with |-w| NF from AI and TA verbs. A noun final |-w| NF forms agent nouns from some AI stems and TA themes; this resembles the inflection |–w| 3s/IND (4.20), except that when it is lost word-finally a preceding long vowel is shortened (**§2.9b**). For the examples identified the underlying verbs are transparent but not attested.

(5.61) Agent nouns with |-w| NF
(a) mhúwe 'cannibal monster' (< *|mwahəwē-| AI 'eat people')
(b) təmá·kwe 'beaver' (< *|təmāhkwē-| AI 'cut trees')

Some nouns can be described as agent nouns like those in (5.61) with the stem-final |-ēw| deleted and replaced by the formal diminutive suffix |-əs| (5.48).

(5.62) Agent nouns with |-əs| NF
(a) təmáskwəs 'muskrat' (< *|təmaskwē-| AI 'cut grass, plants')
(b) wi·nínkwəs 'mink' (< *|wīnīnkwē-| AI 'have a dirty face')

A secondary final |-āw|, formed by adding |-w| NF to the TA direct theme sign |-ā|, makes nouns denoting the undergoer from TA stems (5.63). At least one such verb is possessed, denoting what would be the object of the verb (5.63b). This derivational |-āw| NF is homophonous with inflectional |–āw| X–3/IND, but (as with |-w| NF) when the |w| is lost word-finally the |ā| is shortened to /-a/ (**§2.9b**). Most examples of nouns formed this way are women's names (5.63defg); the meanings of these are esoteric and often obscure (Goddard 1991).

(5.63) Nouns of undergoer with |-āw| NF
(a) aha·nhukɔ·č·í·ma 'interpreter' (V ⟨ha·nhɔk·ɔ·č·í·ma⟩, /ah-/ in the AI participle;
aha·nhukw- 'in succession' + |-ācīm| TA 'tell')
(b) ntəlanko·má·wto·kw 'my kinsmen (voc.)'
(B; KJV "my friends"; |nət–ətōkw| 1s+VOC.PL; < |əlankōm-| TA 'be related to ({so})')
(c) šinki·p·í·la 'stretched hide' (|šənk-| '(lying) flat' + |-īpīl| TA 'tie'; in
šinki·p·í·la təma·kwé·wxe·s alánkɔk 'stretched beaverhide stars (a constellation)' [V])
(d) ahpa·mé·ləma (Old Lady Drum; |apām-| 'along' + |-ēləm| TA 'think of, use thought on')
(e) pe·t·aé·kaɔ (Old Lady Paticow; |pēt-| 'coming' + |-awē-| '?' + |-əhkaw| TA 'move, etc.')
(f) sa·k·anaxkí·naɔ (Mary Bascomb; |sāk-| 'emerge' + |-anaxk-| 'treetop' + |-īnaw| TA 'see')
(g) xe·lsát·aɔ (Stella Parton's grandmother; |(ma)xēl-| 'many' + |-əsətaw| TA 'hear')

There is one dependent noun, not productively formed, that can be seen to be made from a TA stem by adding a secondary final |-əkw| that is formed from the TA inverse theme sign |-əkw| by

adding a virtual |-w| NF (which makes the stem a noun but is lost, like an inflectional |w|, in this environment [**§4.5a**, 4.25]). Other languages have this noun meaning 'parents' and show that the verb it is based on meant 'cause to be born' (cf. Ojibwe niigi- AI 'be born', niigi'- TA 'bear').
(5.64) Noun of undergoer with |-əkw| NF
    (a) nni·k·íhko·k 'my kin (pl.)' (OA)

§5.6k. Lexicalized participles. Participles are freely used as nominals, either modifying nouns (or equivalently in apposition with them) or independently (4.64, 4.65). In addition to regularly formed participles, there are participles that are lexicalized as, in effect, separate words, a status indicated overtly by the use of some inflections and derivational suffixes copying or influenced by those used on nouns.

(5.65) Lexicalized participles
    (a) ehəntalí·p·wink 'table' (indef. ppl.); loc. ehəntali·p·wínkink 'on the table' (4.9e);
           possessed form ntehəntali·p·wínkəm 'my table' (V; accepted by OA, FW)
    (b) enkələk·i·k 'the dead' (pl. ppl.): pl. loc. enkələk·i·ké·i 'among the dead' (4.10f)
    (c) pehpalalo·ká·s·i·t 'one who is a criminal' (sg. ppl.):
           pl. loc. pehpalalo·ka·s·i·t·i·ké·i 'among the criminals' (4.10g)
    (d) memhálamunt 'merchant, seller (*lit.*, one bought from)': memhalamúnči 'sellers (obv.)'
           has the participial suffix |-ī| obv. (4.65) but not the participial ending |-ālīnkī| (4.65j);
           verb of being (**§5.7a**) memhalamunti·- AI 'be a merchant': énta-memhalamúntink 'in
           the market (*lit.*, where people are merchants)', and other forms.
    (e) we·t·ó·x·əmənt 'the father (*lit.*, one had as father)': we·t·o·x·əmə́nči 'the father (obv.)';
           we·t·o·x·əmə́ntink '(to, from) the father (loc.)'
    (f) ki·š·e·ləmúk·ɔnkw 'God; *lit.*, our (inc.) creator' (|(IC)–əkwankw| 3–12/PPL(ANsg)):
           > |kīšēləməkwankwī-| II 'be God': ki·š·e·ləmuk·ónko·p 'it was God' (|-w-əp| 0s/PRET)

§5.6.l. Agent nouns in |-s|. Resembling participles and in some cases the doublets of participles are agent nouns derived from AI verbs with a suffix |-s| AGTV instead of the inflectional third person |-t|. These have initial change where possible and have habitual reduplication where appropriate (5.42acdek, 5.66fghij). This agentive suffix |-s| is distinct from the formal diminutive suffix |-əs| (5.48, 5.62).

(5.66) Agent nouns in |-s|
    (a) kwe·ni·škwə́naya·s 'mountain lion' (V, LB; |kwənīšəkwənayā-| AI 'have a long tail')
    (b) me·x·e·lká·t·a·s 'centipede' (V; |(ma)xēləkātā-| AI 'have many legs')
    (c) təpčéhəla·s AN 'wagon, car' (|təpəčēhlā-| AI, II 'roll')
    (d) kehkəmó·tke·s 'thief' (|kəmōtəkē-| AI 'steal'); beside kehkəmó·tke·t (5.42c)
    (e) kukwčuk·wipahkíhəla·s 'cottonwood' (OA; V ⟨kɔkwčək·w-⟩;
           |Rə+| REP + |kwəčəkwīpakīhlā-| AI 'have leaves move')
    (f) nehənaónke·s 'horse' (|Rih+| HAB + *|nawankē-| AI 'carry people on the back';
           the verb is obsolete, but cf. Mun nehnayó·nkəs 'horse' < |nayōm-| TA 'carry on back')
    (g) nehəni·sktó·nhe·s 'clown' (V, LB; |Rih+| HAB + |nīskətōnahē-| AI 'talk dirty')
    (h) pehpəmət·ó·nhe·s 'preacher' (|Rih+| HAB + |pəmətōnahē-| AI 'talk, tell, preach'; 5.42a)
    (i) wehí·nəwe·s 'beggar' (V; |Rih+| HAB + |wīnəwē-| AI 'beg')
    (j) wewtə́nəwe·s 'water spirit' (LB; |Rih+| HAB + |wətənəwē-| AI 'pull people (under)')

§5.7. Secondary Derivation: Verbs Formed from Nouns. Several categories of verbs are formed from noun stems, including verbs of being or becoming (5.67), verbs of having as an attribute (5.68), verbs of speaking a language (5.69), verbs of making or acquiring (5.70), and verbs of possession (5.71, 5.72).

§5.7a. Verbs of Being or Becoming. Verbs that mean 'to be' or 'to become' are made by adding to the stem of a noun an abstract final |-ī| AI, II or |-īwī| AI, II. The final is |-ī| after a stem in |-ēw|, |-āw|, |-ōw|, or |-əw| (5.67abcde), and it is apparently either |-ī| (5.67fg) or |-īwī| (5.67h) after other consonants, without enough examples to determine what conditions the choice. In the case of at least some nouns referring to substances the verb of being has the shape of a verb of having an attribute (5.68mnop).

Verbs of being are also made on lexicalized participles (5.65d).

(5.67) Verbs of being or becoming
- (a) |àhwāpēwī-| AI 'be rich' (ahɔ·p·é·yu 'is rich, well off')
  < |àhwāpēw-| (ahɔ́·p·e) 'rich person' (B)
- (b) |ələnāpēwī-| AI 'be a Delaware' (é·li-ləna·p·é·ian 'because you are a Delaware')
  < |ələnāpēw-| (ləná·p·e) 'person; Delaware'
- (c) |sākīmāwī-| AI 'be chief, king' (nčo·wí·i-sa·k·i·ma·iáne 'if you are the king of the Jews')
  < |sākīmāw-| (sá·k·í·ma) 'chief; king'. (There is also |sākīmā-| AI [in sa·k·i·má·t·e 'when he was king'], perhaps backformed from sa·k·i·ma·ɔ́·k·an 'kingdom'.)
- (d) |matanətōwī-| AI 'be a devil' (mahtant·ó·wi·t 'one who is a devil') < mahtánt·u 'devil'
- (e) |(wə)skīlənəwī-| AI 'be a young man' (we·skinnəwiáne 'when you were a young man')
  < |(wə)skīlənəw-| (skínnu) 'young man'
- (f) |(m)əhlōsī-| AI 'be an old man' (hilǿ·s·u 'he is old', hilo·s·iáne 'when you are old')
  < |(m)əhlōs-| (cf. hilǿ·səs 'old man'; see **§2.15**, end)
- (g) |kəlaistī-| AI 'be Christ' (kəlaistiáne 'if you are Christ') < kəláist 'Christ'
- (h) |šəwanakwīwī-| AI 'be a white person' (|aləwí·i káhta-šəwanahkwi·í·ɔk. 'They would rather be white people.') < |šəwanakw-| (šəwánakw) 'white person'

§5.7b. Verbs of Having as an Attribute. Verbs that mean 'to have as a condition or attribute' are made by adding |-ōwī| AI, II to the stem of a noun (5.68abcdefg), except that the final is |-əwī| after stems in |-əw| and |-əy| (with contraction to |-ōwī| [5.68hijk] and |-īwī| [5.68op]), and in at least one case it is |-ī| (5.68.l; cf. **§5.7a**). Some stems with these shapes have the meaning 'be, become' (5.68mnop) or are found with both meanings (5.68q).

(5.68) Verbs of having as an attribute
- (a) ahpi·k·ó·u 'he's got fleas' (FW) < |apīkw-| (ahpí·kw) 'flea'
- (b) hikənē·s·ó·u 'he's got nits' (ME) < |əhkənēs-| (híkəne·s) 'nit'
- (c) ko·nó·u 'it has snow on it' (LB) < kó·n 'snow, ice'
- (d) mi·x·e·k·ənó·u 'he is hairy, it is hairy' (ME) < mi·x·é·k·ən 'a hair'
- (e) xkanó·u 'it is bony' < xkán 'bone'
- (f) o·kwe·yó·u 'it has maggots in it' (FW) < |ōhkwēw-| (ó·kwe) 'maggot'
- (g) si·khe·yó·u 'it is salty' < |sīkahēw-| (sí·khay) 'salt' (cf. 2.28c, 4.2x)
- (h) si·skó·u 'he's all muddy; it's muddy' < |sīskəw-| (sí·sku) 'mud'
- (i) šumó·u 'has horns' (OA) < |šə́məw-| (šə́mu, pl. šə́məwak) 'horn'
- (j) wi·lsó·u 'it has fat, is fatty' (ME) < |wīləsəw-| (wí·lsu) 'fat', "plain animal fat"
- (k) xayhó·u 'he has lice' < |axayəhw-| (xáyhu) 'louse'
- (l) mhúk·u 'he's bleeding' (OA) < |məhkw-| (mhúkw) 'blood'
- (m) ahsənó·u 'she turned to stone' (ME) < |asən-| (ahsə́n) 'stone'
- (n) kwəla·kanó·u 'it is forbidden (as food)' < kwəlá·kan 'tabooed food item' (5.51b)
- (o) hakí·yu (|ahkīwī-w|; 2.32a) 'he is of earth' (B; KJV "is earthly") < |ahkəy-| 'earth'
- (p) mpi·i·- 'be water' (|nəpīwī-| II) < |nəpəy-| (mpí) 'water':
  énta-xínkwi-mpí·i·k 'in the ocean', *lit.* 'where the big water is'

(q) wio·s·ó·u 'it is meaty, has meat on it' (LB); takó· wio·s·o·wí·i 'it does not have flesh' (B); wio·s·ó·o·p 'it became flesh' (B ⟨Wewswp⟩)

§5.7c. Verbs of Speaking a Language. Verbs that mean 'to speak a (particular) language' are made by adding |-ī| AI to nouns that name a tribe or nationality, with repetitive reduplication. In some of these the reduplication is made on an underlying |wə-| prefixed to the noun (5.69bc).

(5.69) Verbs of speaking a language
    (a) šəšəwánahku 'he's speaking English' (5.36d)
    (b) ɔhpəla·nšəmá·nu 'he's speaking French' (5.36k)
    (c) ɔwša·wənó·u 'he's talking Shawnee' (5.36.l)

§5.7d. Verbs of Making. Verbs of making or acquiring (in the normal way for normal use) are made by adding |-ahē| AI to the underlying shape of the noun (5.70). This contracts with a stem-final |əy| or |əw| as if it were underlying |-əhē| (5.70cg).

(5.70) Verbs of making or acquiring
    (a) ahpó·nhe·w 'he (she) makes bread' (V) < ahpó·n 'bread'
    (b) čó·lə·nshe·w 'he hunts birds' (V) < čó·lə·ns 'bird'
    (c) hakí·he· 'he gardens, farms, plants' < |ahkəy-| (hák·i 'dirt, earth')
    (d) o·t·e·nayahe·- AI 'form a town' < |ōtēnay-| (o·t·é·nay) 'town': wi·t·o·t·e·nayahe·má·č·i·k 'his fellow townsmen' (5.99j)
    (e) ó·lhe·w 'he digs a hole' (V) < *ɔ·l- 'hole' (as an initial in: ɔ·lpé·k·at 'waterhole')
    (f) pxaš·i·k·anáhe· 'he slices meat thin and dries it' (OA) < pxaš·i·k·an 'dried meat'
    (g) si·skó·he· 'he makes clay (moistened dirt)' (B) < |sīskəw-| (sí·sku) 'mud'
    (h) tənté·whe· 'he (she) makes fire' < |təntēw-| (tə́ntay 'fire'; 2.28c)

§5.7e. Verbs of Possession (AI). Verbs of possession are made by adding |-ī| AI to the third-person-possessed themes of nouns: the possessed form with the third person prefix and the possessed-theme marker |-əm|, if any, but no inflectional suffix. A dependent noun with third-person-possessed forms that begin with |wī-| or |ō-| adds, respectively, |wə-| (5.71fghi) or |wət-| (5.71j) as a derivational prefix (cf. inflectional |wə-| 3 [4.3]), giving word-initial /wwi·-/ (5.71i) or /wto·-/ (5.71j). These verbs of possession are used as intransitives and with a secondary object as AI+O's (**§3.7f**).

(5.71) Verbs of possession (AI)
From dependent nouns
    (a) |wənīčānī-| AI 'have a child', AI+O 'have O2 as a child'
        (< wəni·č·á·na 'his, her child', nní·č·a·n 'my child' [2.57f]):
        wəni·č·á·nu 'he (she) has a child; she gives birth' (AI, |–w| 3s/IND);
        we·ni·č·á·ni·t 'his mother' (B; AI+O, |IC–t| 3s/PPL(ANsg));
        we·ni·č·á·nink '(one who is) the child' (B; AI+O, |IC–nk| X/PPL(ANsg))
    (b) |wəkàhēsī-| AI 'have a mother' (< nkáhe·s 'my mother', kɔhé·s·a 'his, her mother'):
        ko·k·ahé·s·i 'you have a mother' (V; AI, |kə–| 2s/IND)
    (c) |wəkwīsī-| AI 'have a son', AI+O 'have O2 as a son'
        (< nkwí·s 'my son', kkwí·s·a [|wəkwīsa|] 'his or her son'): we·k·wí·s·ian 'a son of yours' (B; |IC–yan| 2s/PPL(ANsg)); we·k·wí·s·ink 'the son' (B; AI+O, |IC–nk| X/PPL(ANsg))
    (d) |wətaləmōnsī-| AI+O 'have O2 as an animal'
        (< ntáləmo·ns [~ -muns] 'my dog, horse, or other animal', tɔləmó·nsa 'his, her animal'):
        we·t·aləmúnsi·t 'owner of them (sheep), it (donkey)' (B; AI+O, |IC–t| 3s/PPL(ANsg))
    (e) |wətānī-| AI 'have a daughter', AI+O 'have O2 as a daughter'
        (tó·na [|wətāna|] 'his (her) daughter'; cf. ntá·nəs 'my daughter', with |-əs| [5.48]):
        we·t·á·nink 'the daughter' (B; AI+O, |IC–nk| X/PPL(ANsg))

(f) |wəwītīsī-| AI '(male to) have a male friend', AI+O '(male to) have O2 as a male friend' (< wi·tí·s·a 'his male friend', ní·t·i·s 'my male friend (male speaking)'):
no·wi·tí·s·i 'I have a friend' (V; AI, |nə–| 1s/IND);
tá=á· ko·wi·t·i·s·í·wən 'you will not be his friend' (B; AI+O, |kə–wən| 2s+3s/IND.NEG)

(g) |wəwīmatī-| AI+O '(male to) have O2 as a brother' (< wí·mahta 'his brother(s)'):
we·i·mahtí·č·i·k 'his (obv.) brothers (prox.)' (B 1842; AI+O, |IC–čīk| 3p/PPL(ANpl))

(h) |wəwīləmwī-| AI 'have a sibling-in-law of the opposite sex' (wí·ləmə 'his sister-in-law, her brother-in-law', ní·ləm 'my sibling-in-law of the opposite sex'):
no·wí·ləmwi 'I (a woman) have a brother-in-law' (OA; AI, |nə–| 1s/IND)

(i) |wəwīpītī-| AI 'have teeth' (< wí·p·i·t 'his, her tooth', ní·p·i·t 'my tooth'):
máta wwi·p·i·tí·i 'he has no teeth' (ME; AI, |–wī| 3s/IND.NEG)

(j) |wətōxī-| AI 'have a father', AI+O 'have O2 as a father' (< ó·x·ɔ 'his or her father'):
wtó·x·u AI 'has a father' (V; AI, |–w| 3s/IND);
we·t·ó·x·ink 'the father' (B; AI+O, |IC–nk| X/PPL(ANsg))

From non-dependent nouns

(k) |wətalōhkākanī-| AI 'have a servant', AI+O 'have O2 as a servant' (< tɔlo·ká·k·ana 'his servant' < alo·ká·k·an 'servant'):
tɔlo·ka·k·aní·t·e 'if he has a servant' (B; AI, |–tē| 3s/SBJ);
ko·t·alo·ka·k·ani·né·yɔ 'he is your (pl.) servant' (AI+O, |kə–ənēwā| 2p+3/IND)

(l) |wətahkīhākanī-| AI 'have a field' (tɔ·ki·há·k·an 'his field' < haki·há·k·an 'field'):
we·thaki·há·k·ani·t 'the field owner' (B; AI, |IC–t| 3s/PPL(ANsg))

(m) |wətōtēnayī-| AI 'have a town' (< wto·t·é·nay 'his town, city' < o·t·é·nay 'town, city'):
we·t·o·te·naí·č·i·k 'townspeople' (B; AI, |IC–čīk| 3p/PPL(ANpl))

(n) |wəwašīxayī-| AI 'have a nest' (< wɔš·í·x·ay 'its nest' [ME] < ɔhší·x·ay 'nest'):
wɔš·i·x·ayúwak 'they have nests' (B; AI, |–wak| 3p/IND).

(o) |wəwālakwī-| AI 'have a hole' (< ó·lakw 'hole'):
wɔ·lahkúwak 'they have holes' (B; AI, |–wak| 3p/IND)

(p) |wətamīmənsəmī-| AI 'have a child, children' (< tɔmi·mə́·nsəma 'his or her child' [and esp. 'children'] < mí·mə·ns 'child'):
tɔmi·mə́·nsəmu 'he has children' (OA; AI, |–w| 3s/IND); also neg. pl. (B; 4.81q);
no·t·ami·mə́·nsəmi 'I have children' (OA; AI, |nə–| 1s/IND)

(q) |wəsākīmāwəmī-| AI 'have a chief, a king' (< sɔ·k·i·má·yəma 'his chief' [V] < sa·k·í·ma [|sākīmāw-| (see 2.33a)] 'chief, king'; cf. ksa·k·i·má·yəm 'your king'):
takó· pí·li no·s·a·k·i·ma·yəmi·húmənа 'we (exc.) have no other king' (B; AI, |nə–wəhmənā| 1p/IND.NEG; takó· 'not'; pí·li 'other, different')

From an unattested (historically dependent) noun

(r) |wəwīkī-| AI 'have a house' (*wí·k 'house' also in wí·khe· 'builds a house' [see §5.7d]):
né·k·a wwí·k·u 'he has a house' (ME, with [ww-]; AI, |–w| 3s/IND);
we·i·k·í·č·i·k 'the house-owners' (B; AI, |IC–čīk| 3p/PPL(ANpl))

§5.7f. Verbs of Possession (TA). There are also verbs of possession that are TA's, which are formed like their AI counterparts but with the secondary final |-əm| TA instead of |-ī| AI. If the possessed noun takes the possessed-theme marker |-əm|, only one |-əm| is used (5.72ef). As with other TA's, AI reciprocal verbs may be derived from these verbs (5.72gh).

It is likely that TI verbs of possession could also be made, but the only example found is an objectless TI (with |-ənt| TI-1a instead of |-əm| TA) used as an intransitive: wši·lə́ntam TI-O 'he (she) gets married' (ME; cf. |wəsīləm-| TA 'have as father-in-law, nši·líhəlo·s 'my father-in-law'

[with |-īhlōs| 'old man' (cf. 4.2e, 5.67f)]). This TI-O has been lexicalized, as shown by the irregular derivation, the shifted meaning, and the existence of a derived final with this meaning (no·skši·ləntam 'I'm newly married' [|wəsk-| 'new' + |-əšīlənt| TI(1a)-O 'get married']).
(5.72) Verbs of possession (TA)
　From dependent nouns
　　(a) |wənīčānəm-| TA 'have as child' (cf. |wənīčānī-| AI 'have a child'; 5.71a):
　　　we·ni·č·a·nəmúk·we·kw 'you (pl.) who are their offspring' (|IC–əkwēkw| 3–2p/PPL);
　　　wəni·č·a·nəmuk·we·kwpáne 'if you (pl.) had been his children'
　　　　(|–əkwēkwəpanē| 3–2p/SBJ.PRET)
　　(b) |wəkwīsəm-| TA 'have as son' (cf. |wəkwīsī-| AI 'have a son'; 5.71c):
　　　we·k·wí·s·əmənt 'the son' (|IC–ənt| X–3/PPL(ANsg))
　　(c) |wətōxəm-| TA 'have as father' (cf. |wətōxī-| AI 'have a father'; 5.71j):
　　　we·t·ó·x·əmənt 'the father' (|IC–ənt| X–3/PPL(ANsg));
　　　we·t·o·x·əmə́lenk 'you who are our father' (|IC–əlēnk| 1p–2/PPL);
　　　we·t·o·x·əmə́lan 'O father of mine' (|IC–əlan| 1s–2s/PPL)
　From non-dependent nouns
　　(d) |wətalōhkākanəm-| TA 'have as a servant' (cf. |wətalōhkākanī-| AI 'have a servant'
　　　 < tɔlo·ká·k·ana 'his servant' < alo·ká·k·an 'servant' [5.71k]):
　　　we·t·alo·ka·k·anə́mkuk 'one he (obv.) has as a servant' (|IC–əkwək| 3´–3s/PPL(ANsg));
　　　we·t·alo·ka·k·anəmkúk·i 'one (obv.) he is a servant of' (|IC–əkwək| 3´–3s/PPL(OBV));
　　　o·t·alo·ka·k·anə́mko·n 'he is the servant of it' (|wə–əkōn| 0s–3s/IND)
　　(e) |wətamīmənsəm-| TA 'have as a child' (cf. |wətamīmənsəmī-| AI 'have a child' [5.71p]):
　　　ktə́li-=á· -tɔmi·mənsəmúk·o·n 'so that you (sg.) may be his child' (|kə–əkōn| 2s–3/SBD)
　　(f) |wəsākīmāwəm-| TA 'have as a chief or king'
　　　(cf. |wəsākīmāwəmī-| AI 'have a chief, a king' [5.71q]):
　　　o·s·a·k·i·ma·yəmúk·o·l '(obv.) will have him as king' (|wə–əkōl| 3´–3s/IND)
　Reciprocal verbs (§5.8m) derived from TA verbs of possession
　　(g) |wəwīmatəm-| TA '(male to) have as a brother' (< wí·mahta 'his brother or brothers';
　　　cf. wəwīmatī-| AI+O '(male to) have O2 as a brother' [5.71g]):
　　　> |wəwīmatəntī-| AI 'be brothers': ní·š·a we·i·mahtəntí·č·i·k 'two brothers' (B; 4.64s)
　　(h) |wəwītəkəxkwəm-| TA '(female to) have as a sister' (< wi·tkúxkɔ 'her sister or sisters'):
　　　wwi·tkuxkwə́ntəwak AI 'they are sisters' (|–wak| 3p/IND; /ww-/ assumed)

§5.8. Secondary Derivation: Verbs Formed from Verbs. The derivation of a secondary verb stem from a verb may simply add information about the action or the subject, but in most cases it changes the valence structure of the verb, variously adding and subtracting subjects and objects, or altering their roles. The derived verbs that do not have a changed valence structure are diminutive, pejorative, and collective verbs, and inanimate intransitive verbs for which there is no primary stem. Those that do have changed valences are causative, applicative, double-object, benefactive, and joint-action verbs (which add an object); detransitive, middle-reflexive, passive, and reciprocal verbs (which remove an object or convert it to a subject); and verbs of environmental effect (which derive an AI from an II).

§5.8a. Diminutive Verbs. Diminutive verbs are made by adding the secondary final |-tī| DIM after an intransitive stem or transitive theme. This is added directly after a nasal (with |m| assimilating to /n/) and is preceded by |ə| after other consonants. It is transparent to the replacement of |ā| by |ē| before the suffix |-w| 3,0 (2.24). (The diminutive suffix is not used with the theme sign |-əl| TH.4.) Whem |-tī| DIM is added to a stem that ends with the abstract final |-əsī| AI, the |s| in this final is replaced by |t| (5.73cn).

In the TA the diminutive suffix is followed by the regular TA pronominal suffixes (in their underlying shape; 4.22) in the independent indicative (those seen in direct forms), but by AI pronominal suffixes in the conjunct.

With TI verbs the diminutive suffix refers to the subject, but with TA verbs it refers to the object of direct forms and (in the usage of OA) to the subject of inverse forms. Voegelin (1946:155), however, glosses diminutives on theme 2 and theme 3 as referring to first person objects, and ME rejected these forms for any use (5.73wx). It should also be noted that, although diminutive verbs appear to be freely formed, most examples were obtained by elicitation (the unmarked ones being from OA).

The diminutive generally implies small size or very young age, but it may also be used because of the inherent meaning of the initial (e.g., |tank-| 'small' or |tahkw-| 'short'; 5.73hior) or of the stem (5.73tu).

(5.73) Diminutive verbs

AI verbs

  (a) kawí·t·u 'the little one sleeps' (|kawī-| AI);
      kawí·t·əwak 'the little ones sleep'

  (b) nɔhtawwe·í·t·i 'little I am talking Ottawa' (V, with ⟨w⟩ for /ww/ [ND])

  (c) thakɔ·kwtí·t·u 'he (she) is short' (|tahkwāhkwəsī-| AI)

  (d) kahtunkóntu 'the little one is sleepy' (|katənkwām-| AI; 2.45a)

  (e) ləpáktu 'the little one is crying' (|ləpak-| AI; 3s ləpákw)

  (f) a·š·əwíltu 'the little one is sleeping' (|āšəwīhl-| AI)

  (g) pé·t·u 'the little one comes' (|pā-| AI)

  (h) tanktɔ·né·t·u 'he (she) has a small mouth' (|tankətōnā-| AI);
      ntanktɔ·ná·t·i 'I have a small mouth'

  (i) thakwi·xkɔyaé·t·u 'he has a short neck' (ME)

  (j) énta-kəntká·t·ie·kw 'when you little fellows were dancing' (V)

  (k) kpa·tama·t·íhəmɔ=héč 'are you little fellows praying?' (V)

  (l) kkat·o·p·wí·t·i 'you're hungry (little one)' (ME)

  (m) no·wí·t·i 'come here (little one)!'

  (n) mi·ttí·t·i 'eat (little one)!' (ME; |mītəsī-| AI)

II verbs

  (o) tanké·t·i·k 'the small one' (B)

  (p) énta-sap·é·t·i·k 'the little spot' (B)

  (q) mahta·p·əwé·t·u 'it is thin (soup)' (|matāpəwē-| II)

  (r) thakɔkahtə́t·u 'it (a house) is low' (ME; |tahkwākat-| II)

  (s) náni li·nakɔhtə́t·u 'the little thing looks like that' (|əlīnākwat-| II)

  (t) lankántu 'it is light of weight' (|lankan-| II)

  (u) ká·hantu 'it is shallow' (|kāhan-| II)

TA verbs

  (v) nəwe·t·əná·t·u 'I picked up the little one' (|wētən-| TA);
      nəwe·t·əná·t·əwak 'I picked up the little ones';
      wwe·t·əná·t·əwa 'he picked up the little one(s)';
      kəwe·t·əna·t·í·wəna 'we (inc.) picked up the little one';
      wwe·t·əna·t·i·wwá·ɔ 'they picked up the little one(s)';

énta-we·t·əná·t·ia 'when I picked up the little one'
énta-we·t·əná·t·ian 'when you (sg.) picked up the little one'
énta-we·t·əná·t·i·t 'when he (she) picked up the little one'
- (w) mpak·amúkwtu 'the little one hit me' (|pakam-| TA; rejected by ME);
mpəpahkamkwət·u 'the little one hit me repeatedly';
mpəpahkamkwət·í·wəna 'the little one hit us (exc.) repeatedly'
- (x) énta-wəlahəlá·t·ian 'when you (sg.) kept the little one' (V)
no·lhalkwə́t·u 'he kept little me' (V);
ko·lhalí·t·i 'you kept little me' (V; rejected by ME)

TI verbs
- (y) pwəpahkantánti·n 'the little one hit it repeatedly'
- (z) pwəpahkantantí·na 'the little one hit them (inan.) repeatedly'

§5.8b. Pejorative Verbs. Pejorative verbs are made by adding a secondary final |-šī| PEJ after an intransitive stem or a transitive theme sign. When |-šī| PEJ is added to a stem that ends with the abstract final |-əsī| AI, the |s| in this final is replaced by |š| (5.74ef). The formation of pejoratives parallels that of diminutives, but there are many fewer attested forms. For some speakers, the TI(1a) theme sign |-am| is replaced by |-ā| before this (5.74k).

The pejorative implies that someone or something is disapproved of, undesirable, or ugly.

(5.74) Pejorative verbs
- (a) čəməš·í·š·u 'the "old thing" is flirting' (ND; < čəmə́s·u 'he flirts')
- (b) pé·š·u 'the undesirable one came'
- (c) énta-pá·š·i·t 'when the undesirable one came'
- (d) kəməmanki-pak·ani·k·á·š·i 'your teeth are too wide' (said to Beaver; Michelson 1912)
- (e) nəmax·ahi·na·kwší·š·i 'I am ugly' (said by Beaver; Michelson 1912)
- (f) ni·ski·na·kwší·š·əwak 'they are dirty looking' (|nīskīnākwəsī-| AI)
- (g) xínkwi-pak·é·š·u 'the ugly thing is too wide' (Beaver's tail; Michelson 1912)
- (h) (nánə) li·nakɔhtə́š·u 'the ugly thing looks like that' (|əlīnākwat-| II; same)
- (i) nnihəlá·š·əwa 'I killed the undesirable one' (|nə–ā-wa| 1s–3s.abs + |-šī| PEJ)
- (j) wwe·kwi·tá·nši·n 'the undesirable one ate it all up' (ME)
- (k) wwe·kwi·tá·š·i·n 'the undesirable one ate it all up' (OA)

§5.8c. Collective Verbs. Collective verbs are made on AI stems to indicate the action or condition of a large group; they take a plural or indefinite subject and can often be translated with 'all', 'everyone', or '(all) together'. There is also a collective made on |mīčī-| TI(3) 'eat', which has the shape and inflection of an AI. These verbs almost always refer to human actors, but reference to animals is also possible (5.75g).

The collective stem is formed by a suffix |-ōlətī| AI (replacing stem-final |ī|), or (metrically conditioned) |-ahətī| AI or |-ahtī| AI (added after a consonant or replacing a vowel). The collectives of 'go' and 'come' are uniquely irregular (5.75ab): The variant |-ahətī| is used after a metrically weak syllable and is always realized with /aht/ (or /ɔht/); the variant |-ahtī| is used after a metrically strong syllable and is always realized with /hat/ (or /hɔt/), with a short /t/. Stems ending in an |ā| that is not changed to |ē| in third person independent indicative forms replace this with |wē| (elided to |w|; 5.75p). These suffixes have shapes that suggest the reciprocal (|-ətī| AI; **§5.8m**) of a causative (|-l| TA [5.77] or |h| TA [5.78]), as if literally 'have each other (do so)', but collective stems do not match how such derived stems would be made productively. They also resemble, but are distinct from, the conjunct third person pluralizer |-hətī| (and variants; 4.54).

(5.75) Collective verbs
　Irregular
　　(a)　loˑltúwak 'they all go {smwh}' (|əlōlətī-| AI; coll. of |ā-| AI 'go {smwh}')
　　(b)　peˑltúwak 'they all came back' (|pēlətī-| AI; coll. of |pā-| AI 'come')
　Stems with |-ī| replaced by |-ōlətī|
　　(c)　aˑmoˑltínke 'when people all rise up' (B; coll. of |āmwī-| AI)
　　(d)　kčoˑltúwak 'they all come out' (V, ME; coll. of |kəčī-| AI)
　　(e)　maˑčˑoˑltúwak 'they (all) went home together' (ND; coll. of |māčī-| AI; cf. 5.75i)
　Stems in a consonant, adding |-ahtī| after a metrically strong syllable
　　(f)　ləpakhátəwak 'they are all weeping' (OA) (also w. X);
　　　　peˑ-ləpakhátink 'they are all weeping' (OA)
　　(g)　wehoˑlhátəwak 'they are howling' (OA; |wehōl-| AI);
　　　　wehoˑlhátiˑn 'the dogs are all howling' (OA)
　Stems with |-ā| after a metrically strong syllable, replaced by |-ahtī|
　　(h)　aˑpčílhátəwak 'they all have whooping cough' (AD; |āpəčīhlā-| AI);
　　　　aˑpčilhátiˑn 'everyone has whooping cough' (AD: "like an epidemic")
　Stems with |-ī| after a metrically strong syllable, replaced by |-ahtī|
　　(i)　maˑčhátəwak 'they are all going home' (ME; |māčī-| AI; cf. 5.75e)
　　(j)　áhi-=č -wiˑšˑaˑshátiˑn 'there will be great terror' (B; |wīšāsī-| AI 'be afraid')
　　(k)　mpíˑsˑoˑn miˑčhátiˑn 'there is a peyote ceremony' (OA; |mīčī-| TI(3) 'eat'; mpíˑsˑoˑn 'medicine; peyote')
　　(l)　paˑphátəwak 'they're playing with each other' (ME)
　　(m)　alahhɔ́təwak 'they all hunt' (OA, ME; |alawī-| AI 'hunt'; /hhɔ/ < |wha| [2.38h])
　　(n)　məliˑmhɔ́təwak 'they're all crying' (OA; |məlīmwī-| AI 'cry')
　　(o)　kahtoˑphɔ́tiˑn 'there is a famine' (B; |katōpwī-| AI 'be hungry')
　Stem with |-ā| (that is not replaced by |ē|) > |wē| > |wā| (after a metrically weak syllable):
　　(p)　kpaˑtaməhtíhəna 'we (inc.) are praying together' (V; |pāhtamā-| AI)
　Stem with |-ē| after a metrically weak syllable, replaced by |-ahətī|
　　(q)　mənahtúwak 'they are all drinking' (OA; |mənē-| AI)
　Stems with |-ī| after a metrically weak syllable, replaced by |-ahətī|
　　(r)　xínkwi-miˑtsahtúwak 'they had a great feast' (B; |mītəsī-| AI 'eat')
　　(s)　áhi-ktəmaˑksáhtiˑn 'there is great misery' (B; |kətəmākəsī-| 'be miserable' AI)

§5.8d. II Verbs Derived from AI Stems. Intransitive verbs typically come in pairs, with different stems for the AI and the II, or the same stem may be used for both genders. For verbs that typically have only an animate subject and lack an II counterpart for the AI, an II may be derived from the AI by the addition of a secondary final.

AI stems ending in |-ī| (3s -uˑ) replace this with |-ōwī| II (0s -óˑu, 0p -óˑyəwa).

AI stems in |-ē| add |-yōwī| (0s -yóˑu) or (less commonly) |-wī| (0s /-yu/), with some doublets and ambiguous transcriptions. In the singular independent forms Blanchard's ⟨-rb⟩ is transcribed as /-éˑyu/, and ⟨-rw⟩ as /-eˑyóˑu/, the same as ⟨-rbw⟩. The interpretation of ⟨-rw⟩ as the equivalent of ⟨-rbw⟩ rests on the contrast with ⟨-rb⟩ (though this should probably not be assumed to be completely consistent), doublets of one word with ⟨-rbw⟩ (2x) and ⟨-rw⟩ (5.76i), and also the fact that an early reader of the Bartlesville Public Library copy marked the occurrence of this spelling in (5.76.l) with a caret to indicate that a letter was missing.

AI stems in |-ā| with 3s -aˑ replace this with |wē| and add |-yōwī| (5.76.l).

The stem |ā-| AI 'go {smwh}' has |ēyōwī-| II (5.42q).

The stem |pā-| AI 'come' has the doublets pe·yé·yu 'it comes' (B) and pe·é·yu (ME), and also pe·ye·í·- (B) and pe·e·í·- (B), with evidence also for pe·e·yó·wi·- (OA, ME) (2.31i).

(5.76) II verbs derived from AI stems

AI stems in |ī|: |-ōwī| II
  (a) kənči·mó·u '(trumpet) sounds' (< kənčí·mu 'it (anim.) makes its sound', |kənčīmwī-| AI)
  (b) kənthó·u 'it flies' (< kə́nthu '(bird) flies', |kəntahwī-| AI)
  (c) wi·s·ó·u 'it's fatty, too fat' (ND, ME; < wí·s·u 'he's fat', |wīsī-| AI)
  (d) to·panamó·u 'it's got frost on it' (ME; < |tōhpanamī-| AI 'have frost' 5.117c)
  (e) wəla·p·ensó·yəwa 'they (inan.) are blessed' (for the /y/, see 2.34f;
        < wəla·p·é·nsu 'he (she) is blessed', |wəlāpēnsī-| AI)

AI stems in |ē|: |-ēyōwī| II
  (f) aspo·x·we·yó·u (B ⟨uspwxwrbw⟩) 'it (cloud) rises up' (< |-ōxwē| AI 'walk, go')
  (g) luwe·yó·u (B ⟨lwrw⟩) 'it said {so}' (< lúwe· 'says {so}'; |əlǝwē-| AI 'say {so}')
  (h) pəma·wso·ha·ləwe·yó·u (B ⟨pumawswvalwrbw⟩) 'it gives life'
        (< |pəmāwəsōhāləwē-| AI 'cause people to live')
  (i) wəla·məwe·yó·u (B ⟨wlamwrbw⟩ (2x), ⟨wlamwrw⟩ 1x) 'it (saying, word) is true'
        (< |wəlāməwē-| AI 'tell the truth')

AI stems in |ē|: |-ēwī| II
  (j) |əlōxwēwī-| 'go {smwh}': lí-=á· palí·i -lo·x·wé·yu 'that it might pass away' (B ⟨lwxwrb⟩)
  (k) pe·t·o·x·wé·i·- II 'come': pe·t·o·x·wé·i·k '(inan.) that comes' (B)

AI stem in |-ā| (3s /-a·/): |-wē-yōwī| II
  (l) nihəla·t·amwe·yó·u (⟨nevlatamwrw⟩) 'it is free, autonomous'
        (< nihəlá·t·ama· AI 'he is free, is is own man, has authority' [B])

§5.8e. Causatives. Causatives are transitive verbs that are derived from intransitive or transitive stems and indicate that the subject in some way causes, brings about, or provides the occasion for the action of the base verb. In some cases the combination of an AI final with a causative secondary final has become established as a transitive final that can be used freely with a narrower meaning and regardless of whether a corresponding intransitive verb is in use.

In a few cases a causative is made with the secondary final |-h| TA (|-ht| TI(2)), but more common is |-l| TA (|-t| TI(2)). Before |-h| TA, |ē| is unchanged (5.77a) or replaced by |ə| (5.77b); in one stem, which is presumably no longer synchronically derived, |ā| is replaced by |ē| (5.77c). Before |-l| TA there are various vowel changes, some isolated: |ē| is replaced by |ā| (5.78a) or |a| (5.78bcdef); |ī| (perhaps only if in |Cwī|) is replaced by |ō| (5.78gh), and one stem in |ē| is treated as if it had |-ehwī| (5.78i); in single stems |ī| and |awī| are replaced by |a| (5.78jk).

Causatives are made productively from AI stems by means of secondary finals that incorporate |-ahē| AI 'make' (**§5.7d**). In the simplest case, the stem adds |-ahē| AI (as |-əhē|) after an intercalated |-w| (which can be identified on some level with the noun final |-w| that makes agent nouns; **§5.6j**), and the ostensible secondary final |-wəhē| makes a causative AI+O stem from the AI (5.79). Before |-wəhē| AI+O stem-final |ī| is replaced by |ə|, with contraction of |əwə| to |ō| (5.79a). (Uniquely, the verb |kawī-| AI 'sleep' makes a causative with the loss of the stem-final vowel and |-ənahē| AI+O (5.80).) Much more commonly, however, this secondary final is made explicitly transitive by adding |-l| TA (|-t| TI(1a)), giving |-wəhāl| TA (|-wəhāt| TI(1a)); both stages of this derivation are found for the stem in (5.79a, 5.81i). The stems in |-ī| that do not use |-l| use |-wəhāl|, with contraction of |-ə-wəhāl| to |-ōhāl| (5.81); one stem has been found with both secondary finals (5.78g, 5.81b). After stems in other vowels the |w| in this final either metathesizes (giving /-hɔ·l/; 5.82) or, more commonly, disappears completely (giving /-ha·l/;

5.82, 5.83). Before these finals stems in which |ā| is replaced by |ē| in the independent indicative third person replace it with |ē| (5.79b), and those in which |ā| is kept in the third person replace it with |wē| (5.79d, 5.82, 5.83c).

A stem ending in a consonant adds the secondary final |-əmahāl| TA (5.84a; the only example), and |-mahāl| TA is found after |ē| in at least one case (5.84b).

Several AI causatives are found with a suffix |-ōhkē| that replaces a stem-final |ī| (5.85); this seems usually to be an AI+O, but it is an AI on a reciprocal (5.85e). This suffix has the shape of a detransitive with |-kē| AI (5.102) of a causative |-l| TA (cf. 5.78g), but the intermediate TA stage is not attested. In one case (5.85b) there is a synonym with |-wəhāl| TA (5.81g). The examples from Blanchard (5.85cd) are assumed to have a short /k/ on the basis of the examples from OA (5.85ab) and V (5.85e).

One TI causative is found that is made on a TA with a passive meaning, the equivalent of a causative based on an explicit derivational passive (5.86; cf. 5.81h).

(5.77) Causatives derived from AI stems with |-h| TA, |-ht|, TI(2)
   (a) |kīkēh-| TA 'cure': kwi·k·e·há·ɔ 'he cured him, her, them'
        (B; < |kīkē-| AI 'be cured, be healed, heal up', 3s kí·k·e·)
   (b) |mənəh-| TA 'give a drink to': mənihkóne 'if he gives you (sg.) a drink'
        (B; |-əkwanē| 3–2s/SBJ; < |mənē-| AI 'drink', 3s məné·)
   (c) |pēh-| TA, |pēht-| TI(2) 'wait for, expect to come':
        mpé·ha, mpé·to·n 'I waited for him, it' (OA; < |pā-| AI 'come', 3s pé·)

(5.78) Causatives derived from AI stems with |-l TA|, |-t| TI(2)
   (a) |kīkāl-| TA 'visit (to bring comfort), go to see about':
        kki·k·a·líhəmɔ·p 'you (pl.) came to see about me' (B: < ki·k·e·- AI 'be healed')
   (b) |aləmōxwal-| TA 'take away, lead away': aləmo·x·ɔlá·t·e 'if he leads him'
        (B; < aləmó·x·we· AI 'starts walking, walks away' [with narrowed meaning];
        or < |aləm-| 'begin, along' + |-ōxwal| TA 'take along, lead')
   (c) |əlōxwal-| TA, |əlōxwat-| TI(2) 'take to {smwh}': təlo·x·ɔlá·ɔ 'he brought him (there)';
        təluxɔhto·né·ɔ 'they took it there' (B; < |əlōxwē-| AI 'go {so, to smwh}';
        or < |əl-| '{so, to smwh}' + |-ōxwal-| TA, |-ōxwat-| TI(2) 'take along, lead')
   (d) |kətōxwal-| TA 'bring, take, lead out': kwət·o·x·ɔlá·ɔ 'he leads them out'
        (B; < |kət-| 'out' + |-ōxwal-| TA 'take along, lead')
   (e) |təmīkal-| TA, |təmīkat-| TI(2) 'bring, take in': təmi·k·alá·ɔ 'she took him inside' (B),
        mpéči-təmíkahto·n 'I brought it in' (OA; < |təmīkē-| AI 'enter')
   (f) |səkàpəpal-| TA, |səkàpəpat-| TI(2) 'wet': tánta-skappalá·ɔ 'he wet it (anim.) {smwh}'
        (< *|səkàpəpē-| AI, but skáp·e· II 'it is wet' reshaped as /skap·-/ 'wet' + /-e·/ II 'be')
   (g) |ki·səpo·l-| TA 'fill (by feeding)': kwi·spól·a·n 'he filled them with it'
        (B; < |ki·səpwi·-| AI 'be full, eat one's fill': 1s nkí·spwi, 3s kí·spu, 3p ki·spúwak)
   (h) |šāpwələnčehōl-| TA 'put ring on': ša·p·wələnčehó·lo· 'put a ring on his finger (you pl.)'
        (< *|šāpwələnčehwī-| AI 'wear a ring'; cf. ša·p·wələnčého·n 'ring (for the finger)' LB)
   (i) |čīpakwehōl-| TA 'put shoes on': čipahkwehó·lo· 'put shoes on his feet (you pl.)'
        (< čípahkwe· 'he (she) wears or puts on shoes', AI |-ē| treated as if |-ehwī| (3s /-éhu/)
   (j) |māčal-| TA, māčat-| TI(2) 'take home': nəmá·č·ala 'I took him home' (V),
        nəmáčahto·n 'I took it back home' (OA; < |māčī-| AI: má·č·i· 'he, she went home')
   (k) |nīpal-| TA, |nīpat-| TI(2) 'make stand; set out (trees)':
        nní·p·ala 'I stood him up', nnípahto·n 'I stood it up' (OA; < |nīpawī-| AI 'stand')

(5.79) Causatives derived from AI stems with |-wəhē| AI+O
    (a) |kīšīkōhē-| AI+O 'raise O2': énta-ki·š·i·k·o·hénkəp 'where he had been raised'
        (B; |(-ən)talī| PV '{smwh}', |IC–nkəp| X/PPL.PRET(OBL); < |kīšīkī-| AI 'grow, mature')
    (b) |ačīnkaxēwəhē-| AI+O 'make disobedient': tə́li-ahčinkxé·whe·n 'make disobedient'
        (B; < |ačīnkaxā-| AI 'be disobedient')
    (c) |kwəsəkəwalēwəhē-| AI+O 'make carry a heavy load on the back':
        kkwəsəkəwale·whe·ne·ɔ́·i 'they put heavy loads on their (obv.) backs'
        (B; |wə–nēwāwī| 3p+3´/IND; < |kwəsəkəwalē-| AI 'carry a heavy load on the back')
    (d) |nīhlātamwēwəhē-| AI+O 'make free': ké·t·a-nihəla·t·amwé·whe·t 'the one who is going
        to set them free' (B; |IC–t| 3s/PPL(ANsg); < |nīhlātamā-| AI 'be free')

(5.80) Causative derived from an AI stem with |-ənahē| AI+O
    (a) |kawənahē-| AI+O 'put to sleep': ɔ́nta- awé·n káhta -kawə́nhe·t. 'When someone wants
        to put him or her to sleep. (ND; < |kawī-| AI, 3s kawí·)

(5.81) Causatives derived from AI stems with |-wəhāl| TA, |-wəhāt| TI(1a)
    (a) |kəčōhāl-| TA 'save, ransom' (< |kəčī-| 'go out'):
        kčo·há·la·=č 'he shall be saved' (B; |–āw| X–3s/IND; =č FUT);
        derivative: kčo·ha·ltəwá·k·an 'salvation' (with |-ətī| AI RECIP [**§5.8m**])
    (b) |kīsəpōhāl-| TA 'fill (by feeding)' (< |ki·səpwi·-| AI 'be full, eat one's fill' [cf. 5.78g]):
        kwi·spo·há·lkwən 'it filled him up' (ME; |wə–əkwən| 0s–3s/IND)
    (c) |wəlahtēnamōhāl-| TA 'make happy' (< |wəlahtēnamī-| AI 'be happy'):
        wehwəla·te·namo·há·ləwe·s 'comforter' (B; |-əwē| AI [5.101]; **§5.6.l**)
    (d) |wəlankōnsōhāl-| TA 'make friendly' (< |wəlankōnsī-| AI 'be friendly, be neighborly'):
        wəlankunso·ha·lkwé·k·weč 'let it make you (pl.) be neighborly'
        (B; |–əkwēkweč| 3,0–2p/INJ)
    (e) |wəlāpēnsōhāl-| TA 'bless' (< |wəlāpēnsī-| AI 'be blessed', 3s wəla·p·énsu):
        no·la·p·enso·há·lukw 'he blesses me' (B; |nə–əkw| 3s–1s/IND)
    (f) |takwapōhāl-| TA 'marry (two people)' (< *|takwapī-| AI 'sit together'):
        nta-tahkɔp·o·ha·lké·enk 'when we (exc.) were married (by the official)'
        (ME; |IC–əkēyēnk| X–1p/CC); reciprocal stem (with passive meaning): 5.113d
    (g) |alāxīmōhāl-| TA 'take over the task of O1 to give them a rest'
        (< |alāxīmwī-| AI 'rest', 3s ala·x·í·mu; cf. 5.85b):
        nəpé·h=tá ala·x·i·mo·há·li 'Come take my place!' (OA; |–ī| 2s–1s/IMP)
    (h) |(ma)xīnkwakənīməkwəsōhāl-| TA 'glorify, *lit.*, cause to be talked about as great':
        nəmax·inkɔhkəni·mkwəs·o·há·lko·k 'they cause me to be glorified'
        (B; < |(ma)xīnkwakənīməkwəsī-| AI 'be talked about as great, be honored'; cf. 5.86)
    (i) |kīšīkōhāt-| TI(1a) 'raise' (< |kīšīkōhē-| AI+O 'raise O2' < |kīšīkī-| AI 'grow up'):
        > kwi·š·i·k·o·ha·t·amaɔ́·ɔ 'he raises (some) for him' (B; |kīšīkōhātamaw-| TA+O; 5.94)

(5.82) Causatives derived from AI stems with |-wəhāl| TA (/-hɔ·l/) and |-hāl| TA (/-ha·l/)
    (a) |nīhlātamwēwəhāl-| and |nīhlātamwēhāl-| TA 'make free'
        (< |nīhlātamā-| AI 'be free, be one who makes their own decisions'):
        (1) nihəla·t·amwe·hɔ·lkɔ́ne 'if he makes you (sg.) free' (B; |–əkwanē| 2–2s/SBJ);
        (2) kənihəla·t·amwe·ha·lko·né·ɔ 'it makes you (pl) free' (B 2x; |kə–əkōnēwā| 0–2p/IND)
    (b) |wəšīləntamwēwəhāl-| and |wəšīləntamwēhāl-| TA 'give in marriage'
        (< *|wəšīləntamā-| AI < |wəšīlənt-| TI(1a)-O 'get married' [**§5.7f**]), with |Ra+| PL):
        (1) ɔwši·ləntamwe·hɔ·ltɔ́p·ani·k 'they gave each other in marriage' (B);
        (2) ɔwši·ləntamwe·ha·ltɔ́p·ani·k 'they gave each other in marriage' (B)

(5.83) Causatives derived from AI stems with |-hāl| TA
    (a) |kəntəwēhāl-| TA 'convert': ktəli-=á· .. -kəntəwe·ha·la·né·ɔ 'in order for you (pl.) to convert him (to the practices of a Jewish sect)' (B; |kət–ānēwā| 2p–3/SBD; < |kəntəwē-| AI 'be a Christian', *lit.* apparently 'shout out, sing out')
    (b) |(k)akwēpīnkwēhāl-| TA 'make blind (literally or figuratively)': kɔk·e·p·inkwe·ha·lkəwá·ɔ 'he (obv.) blinded them' (B; |wə–əkəwāwa| 3´–3p/IND; < |(k)akwēpīnkwā-| TA 'be blind')
    (c) |nēmwēhāl-| TA 'cause to see, give sight': é·li-ne·mwe·há·lkɔn 'how he made you see' (B; |IC–əkwan| 3–2s/PPL(OBL); < |nēmā-| AI 'see', 3s né·ma·)
(5.84) Causatives derived from AI stems with |-(ə)mahāl| TA
    (a) |tawankələmahāl-| TA 'cause to get lost': tehtaɔnkələmhá·ləwe·s 'will-o-the-wisp', *lit.* 'one that gets people lost'; < |tawankəl-| AI 'be lost' (ND; |-əwē| AI [5.101]; §5.6.1)
    (b) |lēhlēxēmahāl-| 'save, bring back to life': lehəle·x·é·mha·l khák·ay 'save yourself'; (B; < |lēhlēxē-| AI 'live', 3s lehəlé·x·e·; 5.38k)
(5.85) Causatives derived from AI stems in |ī| with |-(ō)hkē-| AI(+O)
  AI+O
    (a) |wīsōhkē-| AI+O 'fatten (animal)': nəwi·s·ó·ke·n 'I fattened it' (OA; |nə–n| 1s+3s/IND; wi·s·o·kénki·k 'fattened ones' (B, KJV "fatlings"; |(IC)–nkīk| X/PPL(ANpl); < |wīsī-| AI 'be fat', 3s wí·s·u)
    (b) |alāxīmōhkē-| AI+O 'take over the task of O2 to give them a rest': ntala·x·i·mó·ke·n 'I took his place (he being tired)' (OA; |nə–n| 1s+3s/IND; < |alāxīmwī-| AI 'rest', 3s ala·x·í·mu)
    (c) |mawōsəmōhkē-| AI+O 'take (animal) to water' (*lit.*, 'make or have go and drink'): máta=háč=hánkw .. mɔwo·s·əmo·ké·wəna 'does he not take them (obv.) to water?' (B; máta 'not'; =háč Q; =hánkw 'usually, etc.'; |wə–wəna| 3s+3´/IND.NEG; < *|mawōsəmwī-| AI 'go to drink' [cf. nkat·ó·s·əmwi 'I'm thirsty'])
    (d) |mīhkəmwāsōhkē-| AI+O 'trouble, cause to have to do something': káči mi·kəmɔ·s·o·ké·han khák·ay 'don't trouble yourself' (B; |–han| 2s/PROH; < |mīhkəmwāsī-| AI 'work', 3s mi·kəmó·s·u)
  AI (on a reciprocal stem)
    (e) |kwətəskāwatōhkē-| AI 'race horses': kwtəska·ɔhtó·ke· 'he races horses' (V; < |kwətəskāwatī-| AI 'race (each other)', X kwtəská·ɔhti·n 'there's a race')
(5.86) TI causative derived from a TA taken as a passive
    (a) |(ma)xīnkwakənīmahāt-| TI(1a) 'glorify, *lit.*, cause to be talked about as great' (5.81h): xinkɔhkəni·mhá·t·a 'glorify it!' (B; |–a| 2s–0/IMP); nəmax·inkɔhkəni·mha·t·améne·p 'I glorified it' (B; |nə–amənēp| 1s–0s/IND.PRET)

Causatives are also derived from transitive stems; they may be based formally on either the TA or TI with no difference in function. In the examples encountered, a TI(1a) stem in |t| adds |-əl| TA (5.87a); a TI(2) stem either adds |-əl| TA (5.87b) or (in at least one case) |-ā-hl| TA (incorporating the theme sign as |ā|; 5.87c); a TI(1b) stem in |n| and a TI(3) stem in |m| add |-təl| (giving |-ntəl|; 5.87de); and a TA stem in |-aw| adds |-əntəl| TA, with contraction to |-ōntəl| (5.87f). There is one example of a causative from a TI(1a) theme with the theme sign |-am| retained and ostensible contraction of |-am-ī-wəhāt| TI(1a) (cf. 5.81) to |-amōhāt| (5.87g).
(5.87) Causatives derived from transitive stems
    (a) |kwəhtəl-| TA(+O) 'admonish, forbid': khwítəl! 'admonish them!' (B; |–∅| 2s–3/IMP; < |kwəht-| TI(1a) 'fear'); derivatives: |kwəhtəhkē-| AI 'forbid' (5.102b), khwitələt·əwá·k·an 'law' (5.114d)

(b) |wəwāhtəl-| TA+O 'let know O2': o·wá·tələ·n 'he let him know it'
    (B; |wə–ān| 3s–3´+0s/IND; < |wəwāht-| TI(2) 'know')
(c) |ahtāhl-| TA+O 'turn O2 over to, let have O2': tɔ·tahəlá·ne·p 'he turned it over to them'
    (B; |wət–ānēp| 3s–3´+0s/IND.PRET; < |aht-| TI(2) 'put {smwh}')
(d) |kələntəl-| TA+O 'hand O2 out to': ná kwələ́ntələ·n 'then he handed them out to them'
    (B; |wə–ān| 3s–3´/SBD; < |kələn-| TA,TI 'hold')
(e) |nēntəl-| TA+O 'cause to see O2, show O2 to':
    wənéntələ·n hók·ay 'he appeared to him' (B; hók·ay 'himself' [4.14];
    |wə–ān| 3s–3´+0s/IND; < |nēm-| TI(3) 'see');
    derivative: |nēntəsī-| AI 'show oneself' (5.104m)
(f) |pənōntəl-| TA+O 'cause to look at O2':
    mpənúntələ·n 'I showed it to him' (V; |nə–ān| 1s–3s+0s/IND; < |pənaw-| TA 'look at');
    derivative: |pənōntəhkē-| AI 'reveal O2 to' (5.102e)
(g) |wəlāpēntamōhāt-| TI(1a) 'bless': o·la·p·entamo·há·t·amən 'he blessed it'
    (B; |wə–amən| 3s–0s/IND; < |wəlāpēnt-| TI(1a) 'enjoy' [Zeisberger], implying a
    corresponding causative TA 'cause to enjoy or benefit')

§5.8f. Applicatives. Applicatives are transitive verbs derived from AI stems that variously add notions like 'to', 'on', 'for', 'about', 'by means of', or 'in relation to' the object. Before the applicative final |-l| TA, |-t| TI(1a) stem-final |ē| is replaced by |ā| (5.88abcde). Stem-final |ī| is retained in some stems (5.88fg) and becomes |ā| (5.88hi) in others. The replacement of |t| by |č| in (5.88g) is apparently unique. Before |-m| TA, |ē| is replaced by |a| (5.89). Before |-aw| TA |ē| is lost (5.90). Before |-htaw| TA, |-ht| TI(1a), and |-htam| TA there are no changes in the stem (5.91, 5.92). Some applicative finals are irregular and apparently isolated (5.93).

(5.88) Applicatives derived from an AI stem with |-l| TA, |-t| TI(1a)
(a) |wəlāpətōnāl-| TA 'say something good, nice, or favorable to or about':
    no·la·pto·na·lá·wəna 'we say nice words to persuade him' (B; |nə–āwənā| 1p–3s/IND);
    ko·la·pto·ná·la 'you make polite excuses to him' (B; |kə–ā| 2s–3s/IND);
    no·la·pto·ná·la 'I said good words about him' (V; |nə–ā| 1s–3s/IND)
    (B; < |wəlāpətōnē-| AI 'put in a good word' [V], 'speak correctly')
(b) |matāpətōnāl-| TA, |matāpətōnāt-| TI(1a) 'speak evilly about, say bad things about'
    mɔt·a·pto·na·lá·ɔ 'he said bad things about him' (B; |wə–āwa| 3s–3´/IND);
    mahta·pto·na·t·ánke 'if he says bad things about it' (B, mistranslating "swear by";
    |–anke̅| 3s–0/SBJ; < |matāpətōnē-| AI 'talk evilly,' "curse and .. swear")
(c) |lēxāl-| TA 'breathe on': wəle·x·a·lá·ɔ 'he breathed on them' (B; |wə–āwa| 3s–3´/IND;
    < |lēxē-| AI 'breathe')
(d) |pəmətōnahāt-| TI(1a) 'preach about' (|pəm-| 'along' + |Ra+| PL > |(p)apām-| [5.34q]):
    pup·a·mto·nha·t·améne·p 'he preached about it' (B; |wə–amənēp| 3s–0s/IND.PRET;
    < |pəmətōnahē-| AI 'preach', 3s pəmət·ó·nhe·)
(e) |wīnəwāt-| TI(1a) 'ask for': nəwi·nəwá·t·amən 'I beg for it' (V; |nə–amən| 1s–0s/IND;
    < |wīnəwē-| AI 'ask (for something), pray, beg')
(f) |šəkīt-| TI(1a) 'urinate on': wšək·í·t·amən 'he peed on it'
    (ME, FE; |wə–amən| 3s–0s/IND; < |šəkī-| AI 'urinate', 3s škí· [ME: animal only])
(g) |maskəčīt-| TI(1a) 'defecate on': mɔskčí·t·amən 'he dirtied it, defecated on it'
    (ME; |wə–amən| 3s–0s/IND; < |maskətī-| AI 'defecate', 3s másktu)
(h) |āsōwāl-| TA 'sing to': nta·s·o·wá·la 'I sang to him' (V; |nət–āw| 1s–3s/IND;
    < |āsōwī-| AI 'sing')

(i) |šahwēləmwāt-| TI(1a) 'have doubts about':
káči šhwe·ləmɔ·t·ánkhe·kw 'Don't be doubtful about it.' (B; |–ankahēkw| 2p–0/PROH;
< |šahwe·ləmwī-| AI 'have doubts, lose one's will')

(5.89) Applicatives derived from an AI stem with |-m| TA
(a) |kīwīkam-| TA 'visit' (OA, ME, ND, LB):
ki·i·k·amá·č·i 'the one (obv.) she was visiting' (ME; |(IC)–āčī| 3s–3´/PPL(OBV);
< |kīwīkē-| AI 'go visiting')
(b) |(mə)təmīkam-| TA 'go into the house of': wtəmi·k·amá·p·ani 'she went to his house',
mwət·əmi·k·amá·p·ani 'he came in to where she was' (B; |wə–āpanī| 3s–3´/IND.PRET;
< |təmīkē-| AI 'enter (a dwelling)'; not attested as |mətəmīkē-| AI [cf. 2.68d])
(c) |wīnəwam-| TA 'beg': wwi·nəwamá·ɔ 'he begged him' (B; |wə–āwa| 3s–3´/IND;
< |wīnəwē-| AI 'ask (for something), pray, beg')

(5.90) Applicatives derived from an AI stem with |-aw| TA
(a) |apīkwaw-| TA 'play music for': ktap·i·k·o·lhúməna 'we played music for you'
(B; |kət–ələhmənā| 1p–2/IND; < |apīkwē-| AI 'play a "flute," music', 3s ahpí·k·we·)
(b) |ēnahaw-| TA+O 'pay O2 to': wé·mi=č kte·nhó·lən 'I will pay you all of it' (B; =č FUT;
wé·mi 'all'; |kət–ələn| 1s–2s(+INsg)/IND; < |ēnahē-| AI 'pay', nté·nhe 'I paid' [OA])
(c) |wəlawīkaw-| TA 'arrange a place for O1 to spend the night':
kɔ́t·a-wəlai·k·aɔwwá·ɔ 'they intended to arrange a place for him to stay'
(B; |kata| PV 'going to'; |wə–āwəwāwa| 3p–3´/IND; < *|wəlawīkē-| AI 'arrange a place
to stay' [< |wəl-| 'well, arranged' + |mawīkē-| AI 'spend the night, camp'])
(d) |wīkahaw-| TA 'build a house for': ktə́li-wi·khá·k·e·n 'for it to be built for you'
(ME; |kət–əkēn| X–2s/IND; < |wīkahē-| AI 'build a house', 3s wí·khe·)

(5.91) Applicatives derived from an AI stem with |-htaw| TA, |-ht| TI(1a)
(a) |apīhtaw-| TA, |apīht-| TI(1a) 'be in': e·lkí·kwi- .. -ahpí·tama 'as much as I am in it' (B;
|ələkihkwī| PV 'to {such} extent', |IC–amā| 1s–0/PPL(OBL)|; < |apī-| AI 'be {smwh}');
tɔp·i·ta·k·ó·p·ani 'it (obv.) was with him, in him' (B; |wət–əkōpanī| 3´–3s/IND.PRET)
(b) |nīkānīhtaw-| TA 'go before': kəni·k·a·ni·tá·k·əwa 'he is going ahead of you (pl.)'
(B; |kə–əkəwā| 3s–2p/IND; < |nīkānī-| AI 'go ahead, go in the lead, be the leader')
(c) |tə́təpīhtaw-| TA 'make signs to': wtətpi·tá·k·u 'he (obv.) signed to them (lit., him)'
(B; |wə–əkō| 3´–3s/IND; < tə́tpi· 'he's using sign language' [LB])
(d) |kīšənāhkwəsōhkēhtaw-| TA 'make O2 ready for':
wénči-=č -ki·š·əna·kwso·ké·tunt 'so that they (obv., O2) will be made ready for him'
(B; =č FUT; |wənčī| PV 'from {smwh}', |IC–ənt| X–3/PPL(OBL);
< *|kīšənāhkwəsōhkē-| TA 'make O2 ready' < |kīšənāhkwəsī-| AI 'be ready'; cf. 5.85)

(5.92) Applicatives derived from an AI stem with |-htam| TA
(a) |nīkānīhtam-| TA 'go before' (cf. 5.90b):
nni·k·a·ni·tama 'I passed him, went in ahead of him' (OA; |nə–āw| 1s–3s/IND);
wəni·k·a·ni·tamá·ɔl=č 'he will go before him' (B; |wə–āwal| 3s–3´/IND); cf. 5.91b.
(b) |təkawəsīhtam-| TA 'regard favorably': ktəkawsí·tamukw 'he regards you favorably'
(B, KJV "thou hast found favour with [him]"; |kə–əkw| 3s–2s/IND;
< tkáwsu [Zeisberger:] 'he is gentle, good-natured, mild, well-minded')

(5.93) Applicative derived from an AI+O stem with |-māl| TA (irregular)
(a) |əlanēhəmāl-| TA 'throw {smwh}':
hákink=č ktəlanehəmá·lke 'you shall be thrown down' (B; hákink 'down below';
=č FUT; |kət–əkē| X–2s/IND; < |əlanihī-| AI+O 'throw {smwh}')

§5.8g. Double-Object Verbs. Double-object verbs are derived from transitive stems; the original object becomes a secondary object, and the added object is the primary object. Double-object verbs are formally derived from TI stems, but they function as if derived from the final pair jointly, and the secondary object may be of either gender. They generally indicate that the action is performed on the secondary object for, to, or of the primary object.

Double-object verbs are productively formed from TI(1a) and TI(1b) stems by adding a suffix |-aw| TA after the TI theme (giving |-amaw| TA and |-əmaw| TA). They are made from TI(2) stems by adding |-aw| TA without the TI(2) theme sign |-aw|, that is with a single |-aw| instead of the potential |-aw-aw|. Uniquely, the stem |nəht-| TI(2) is treated like a TI(1a) (5.95h). The suffix |-aw| TA is also added directly to a TI(3) stem ending in a consonant (5.96).

Some verbs have the shape of a double-object verb but are apparently not based on a simple transitive stem (5.97).

(5.94) Double-object verbs derived from TI(1a) and TI(1b) themes
  (a) |pahwàtəhtehamaw-| TA+O 'strike O2 off of O1 with a blow, chop O2 off of O1':
      pəhɔthitehəmáɔ·n hwitaɔk·í·li·t 'he chopped off his ear' (B; |wə–ān| 3s–3´+0s/IND;
      < |pahwàtəhteh-| TI(1a) 'strike off with a blow'; hwitaɔk·í·li·t 'his (obv.) ear')
  (b) |čīskahamaw-| TA+O 'wipe O2 of, for O1': wčI·skhamáɔ·n 'she wiped them (of him)'
      (B; |wə–ān| 3s–3´+0/IND; < |čīskah-| TI(1a) 'wipe'. The inflection for secondary
      object does not mark it as plural (cf. 4.40n); 'of him' is implied by the context.)
  (c) |sōkahamaw-| TA+O 'pour O2 on O1': ná wé·mi íka wso·khamáɔ·n wi·lí·li·t 'then she
      poured all of it on his head' (B; |wə–ān| 3s–3´/SBD; < |sōkah-| TI(1a) 'pour';
      ná 'then'; wé·mi 'all'; íka 'there (pleonastic)'; wi·lí·li·t 'his (obv.) head [loc.]')
  (d) |pəmətōnahātamaw-| TA+O 'preach O2 to O1':
      ntáli-=č -pəmət·o·nha·t·amáɔ·n 'for me to preach it to them' (B; =č FUT; |əlī| PV '{so}',
      |nət–ān| 1s–3+0s/SBD; < |pəmətōnahāt-| TI(1a) 'preach about' (5.88d)
  (e) |katātamaw-| TA+O 'desire O2 of O1': kahta·t·amáɔ·n 'it was desired of him'
      (B; |–ān| X–3s+0s/IND; < |katāt-| TI(1a) 'want, desire')
  (f) |akənōtəmaw-| TA+O 'tell or talk to O1 about O2': tɔk·əno·t·əmáɔ·n 'he talked to them
      about it' (B; |wət–ān| 3s–3´+0s/IND; < |akənōt-| TI(1b) 'talk about');
      ktak·əno·t·əmo·ləné·ɔ 'I tell you (pl.) about him' (B; |kət–ələnēwā| 1s–2p+3s/IND)
  (g) |nəkatəmaw-| TA+O 'leave O2 behind for O1': kənəkahtəmo·lhúmɔ 'I leave (some)
      behind for you' (B; |kət–ələhmwā| 1s–2p/IND; < |nəkat-| TI(1b) 'leave behind')
  (h) |tōnkəšēnəmaw-| TA+O 'open O2 for O1': tunkše·nəmáɔ·n=č. 'it shall be opened for
      him' (B; =č FUT; |–ān| X–3s+0s/IND; < |tōnkəšēn-| TI(1b) 'open')

(5.95) Double-object verbs derived from TI(2) stems
  (a) |kəšīxətaw-| TA+O 'wash O2 for O1': tólɔmi-kši·xtáɔ·n wsí·t·a 'she began to wash his
      feet (wsí·t·a)' (B; |àləmī| PV 'begin', |wə–ān| 3s–3´+0/IND; < |kəšīxət-| TI(2) 'wash')
  (b) |kīšīkīhtaw-| TA+O 'give birth to O2 for O1': kki·š·i·k·í·ta·kw=č we·k·wí·s·ian 'she will
      bear you a son' (B; =č FUT; |kə–əkw| 3s–2s/IND; < |kīšīkīh-| TA, |kīšīkīht-| TI(2) 'cause
      to be born' < |kīšīkī-| AI 'be born'; we·k·wí·s·ian 'one you have as a son' [5.71c])
  (c) |lāpahtaw-| TA+O 'restore O2 to': é·li-la·phata·k·é·an 'because you are paid back'
      (B; |əlī| PV '{so}', |IC–əkēyan| X–2s/CC; < |lāpaht-| TI(2) 'put back'/)
  (d) |əlīxətaw-| TA+O 'set O2 for O1 ({so})': máta li·xta·k·é·one 'if it were not established
      for you' (B; máta 'not'; |–əkēwanē| X–2s/SBJ.NEG; < |əlīxət-| TI(2) 'set, place ({so})')
  (e) |səkàpəpataw-| TA+O 'wet O2 for O1': ktáli-skappat·aí·ne·n 'that you wet it for us'
      (ME; |əlī| PV '{so}', |kət–īnēn| 2–1p/SBD; < |səkàpəpat-| TI(2) 'wet')

(f) |tahəpataw-| TA+O 'cool O2 for O1': thəpahtaí·t·eč 'let him cool it for me'
(B; |–īteč| 3s–1s/INJ; < *|tahəpat-| TI(2) 'cool (with water)')

(g) |pētaw-| TA+O 'bring O2 to O1': pé·t·aɔ· '(a blind man) was brought to him' (B; |–āw| X–3s/IND), pe·t·aɔ́·na 'they (obv.) were brought to him' (B; |–āna| X–3s+3´/IND; < |pēšəw-| TA, |pēt-| TI(2) 'bring')

(h) |nəhtamaw-| TA+O 'kill O2 for O1': kəni·tamáɔ 'you killed (a fat calf) for him'
(B; |kə–āw| 2s–3s/IND; < |nəhl-| TA, |nəht-| TI(2) 'kill')

(5.96) Double-object verb derived from a TI(3) stem
(a) |nēmaw-| 'see O2 of O1': nné·maɔ. 'I saw his thing.' (ME; |nə–āw| 1s–3s/IND)

(5.97) Ostensible double-object verbs not derivable from TI stems
(a) |mīhkəmwāsəntamaw-| TA 'work for': nəmi·kəmɔ·s·əntamáɔ 'I'm working for him, serving him' (B; |nə–āw| 1s–3s/IND; cf. |mīhkəmwāsī-| AI 'work', 3s mi·kəmɔ́·s·u)

(b) |mīhkəntamaw-| TA 'do things for': mwi·kəntamaɔ́·p·ani 'she did things for them'
(B; |wə–āpanī| 3s–3´/IND.PRET; KJV "serve," "minister unto")

(c) |wəntamaw-| TA 'tell': wəntamaí·ne·n 'tell us' (B; |–īnēn| 2–1p/IMP)

§5.8h. Benefactives. True benefactives indicate that an action is done on behalf of someone. They are formed from AI stems by the final |-lax| TA, with adjustments in shape found in other derivatives. The meaning diverges or is idiomatic in the case of |ačīmōlax-| TA 'tell' (5.98c), although this sometimes has the contextual meaning 'be a witness for'.

(5.98) Benefactives
(a) |pāhtamwēlax-| TA 'pray on behalf of': pɔ·tamwe·lxá·ɔ 'he prayed on their behalf'
(B; |wə–āwa| 3s–3´/IND; < |pāhtamā-| AI, 3s pá·tama· [see §5.6h, 5.58k])

(b) |wīnəwēlax-| TA 'ask on behalf of': kəwi·nəwe·lxələné·ɔ 'I ask for it for you (pl.)'
(B; |kə–ələnēwā| 1s–2p/IND)

(c) |ačīmōlax-| TA 'tell': a·č·i·mo·lxié·k·we 'if you tell me' (B; |–əyēkwē| 2p–1s/SBJ;
< |ačīmwī-| AI 'tell'); tɔ·č·i·mo·lxawwá·ɔ 'they recounted to them (what they had seen)' (|wət–āwəwāwa| 3p–3´/IND)

§5.8i. Joint-Action Verbs. Verbs for doing something together with someone else can have a derived stem with the initial |wīt-| or a stem compounded with the corresponding preverb wíči PV 'with' (cf. wíči P 'with'). The transitive verbs have the secondary final |-m| TA, before which there are various adjustments in shape of the intransitive stem or (in the case of objectless TI's) the included theme sign. Two transitive stems incorporate |wīt-| irregularly (5.99no). Although the intransitives are not inflected for an object, they often imply the meaning 'along with the other person or people (in the context)'.

(5.99) Verbs of joint action or inclusion
AI and preverb wíči
(a) |wíči awasī-| AI: wíči-aɔ́s·u 'he warmed himself with the others' (B; |-w| 3s/IND)

(b) |wíči mītəsī-| AI: wíči-mi·tsó·p·ani·k 'they ate along with the others'
(B; |–wəpanīk| 3p/IND.PRET)

(c) |wíči wəlēlənt-| TI(1a)-O: wé·mi wíči-wəle·ləntamó·p·ani·k 'they were all happy along with her' (B; wé·mi 'all'; |-amōpanīk| 3p–(0)₍₁ₐ₎/IND.PRET)

AI and initial |wīt-|
(d) |wītalāmwī-| AI: wi·t·alá·mu 'he joins the crying or hollering'
(OA; |-w| 3s/IND; with |-alāmwī| AI 'cry, yell')

(e) |wītakīməkwəsī-| AI: witahki·mkwə́s·u 'he was counted in'
(B; |-w| 3s/IND; cf. |akwīməkwəsī-| AI 'be counted')

(f) *|wītalōhkē-| AI 'work with another or others': > causative (cf. 5.78) |wītalōhkāl-| TA: nəwi·t·alo·ká·la 'I hired him to work with someone' (OA; |nə–āw| 1s–3s/IND)

TA and preverb wíči
- (g) |wiči āmwīm-| TA: kəwíči-=č -a·mwi·mkúwa 'she will rise up along with you (pl.)'
    (B; =č FUT; |kə–əkəwā| 3s–2p/IND; < |āmwī-| AI 'rise up, arise')
- (h) |wiči wəlēləntaməwīm-| TA: wíči-wəle·ləntaməwí·mi·kw 'rejoice with me'
    (B; |–īkw| 2p/IMP; < wəle·ləntam TI(1a)-O 'is happy, glad')

TA and initial |wīt-|
- (i) |wītāwəsōm-| TA: nəwi·t·a·wsó·ma 'I live with him'
    (OA; |nə–āw| 1p–3s/IND; < |-āwəsī| AI 'live');
    sé·ki-wi·t·a·wsó·mat 'while you (sg.) are with him'
    (B; |sahkī| PV '{so long}'; |IC–at| 2s–3/PPL(OBL))
- (j) |wītōtēnayahēm-| TA: wi·t·o·t·e·nayahe·má·č·i·k 'his fellow townsmen'
    (B; |(IC)–āčīk| 3p–3´/PPL(OBV); < *|ōtēnayahē-| AI 'make a town' [5.70d]);
    wwi·t·o·t·e·nayahe·má·ɔ 'they treated him as a fellow townsman'
    (B; |wə–āwa| 3s–3´/IND; subject is a representative singular)
- (k) |wītəhkwēpīm-| TA: wwi·thukwe·p·i·mawwá·ɔ=č 'they shall sit with them'
    (B; =č FUT; |wə–āwəwāwa| 3p–3´/IND; < |-əhkwēpī| AI 'sit, be in a sitting position')
- (l) |wītōsəmwīm-| TA: wi·t·o·s·əmwi·má·t·e 'if he drinks with them'
    (B; |–ātē| 3s–3´/SBJ; < |-ōsəmwī-| AI 'drink' [cf. 5.85c])
- (m) |sahkī wītapīm-| TA: sé·ki-witahpi·mák·əp 'while I was with them'
    (B; |sahkī| PV '{so long}'; |IC–àkəp| 1s–3/PPL.PRET(OBL); < |-apī| AI 'be, stay')
- (n) |wīhpēm-| TA 'sleep with': nəwi·pé·ma 'I sleep with him' (V; |nə–āw| 1s–3s/IND)
- (o) |wīhpōm-| TA 'eat with': wi·po·má·t·e 'if he eats with them' (B; |–ātē| 3s–3´/SBJ)

§5.8j. Detransitives. Detransitives are AI verbs that suppress the object of a transitive verb and refer to the activity in general or as directed towards indefinite animate or inanimate objects. Many detransitive stems are found in participles or in derived agent nouns in |-s| (5.42, 5.66dfghij). General detransitives add |-īkē| AI to a TI stem (5.100); they usually refer to performing the action on indefinite objects or, less commonly, people, and they may be used with a secondary object, with only a subtle if any difference in meaning from the underlying TI. Indefinite intransitives refer to action on an unspecified person or people (5.101-103). A large class of these are made by adding |-əwē| AI to a TA stem (5.101). Another set adds |-kē| to a (real or virtual) TA stem in |-l|, with |l| + |k| becoming |hk| (2.52, 5.102abc), or to a stem in |-m|, giving |-nkē| (2.44, 5.102defg). Still another set replaces the |-aw| of a TA stem with |-āsī| AI (5.103).

(5.100) General detransitives in |-īkē| AI
- (a) |akəntīkē-| AI 'count': ahkəntí·k·e· 'he's counting' (OA; < |akənt-| TI(1a) 'count; read': tɔk·əntaməné·ɔ 'they read it' [B; |wət–amənēwā| 3p–0/IND])
- (b) |wīxkwēpətīkē-| AI+O 'wrap and tie O2': wi·xkwe·ptí·k·e·n 'it was bound up'
    (B; |–n| X+0s/IND; < |wīxkwēpət-| TI(2) 'wrap and tie': nəwi·xkwe·ptó·ne·p 'I wrapped it up' [B; |nə–ōnēp| 1s–0s/IND.PRET])
- (c) |čahwāhpwənīkē-| AI 'baptize': čhɔ·pwəní·k·e·kw 'baptize, perform baptisms (you pl.)!'
    (B; |–kw| 2p/IMP, < |čahwāhpwən-| TA 'baptize, *lit.* dunk in water': kčɔhɔ́·pwəni 'you baptize me' [B; |kə–ī| 2s–1s/IND]; cf. 5.101g)
- (d) |natōnīkē-| AI 'search': nto·ní·k·e· 'he's looking for somebody' (OA;
    < |natōn-| TI(1a) 'seek': nɔt·ó·namən 'he seeks it' [B; |wə–amən| 3s–0s/IND])

(e) |əlēkahīkē-| AI 'write' : le·khí·k·e· 'he (she) writes, is writing' (ME;
< |əlēkah-| TI(1a) 'write': təle·khámən 'he wrote it' [B; |wət–amən| 3s–0s/IND]);
ehəle·khí·k·e·s 'scribe' (B; |ehəlēkahīkēs| < |IC+|, |Rih+| HAB, [stem], |-s| AGTV [5.66j])

(f) |kəlīxahīkē-| AI 'sew': nkəli·xhí·k·e 'I'm sewing' (OA; |nə–| 1s/IND,
< |kəlīxah-| TI(1a) 'sew': nkəli·xhámən 'I sewed it' [ND; |nə–amən| 1s–0s/IND])

(g) |čīkahīkē-| AI 'sweep': či·khí·k·e· 'he's sweeping' (AD;
< |čīkah-| TI(1a): ó·li·či·khámən 'she swept it up nicely' [ME; |wə–amən| 3s–0s/IND])

(h) |təmaskahīkē-| AI 'cut grass, mow': təmaskhí·k·e· 'he's cutting the grass' (OA;
< |təmaskah-| TI(1a): ntəmáskham TI(1a)-O 'I'm hoeing' [ME; |nə–am| 1s–(0)/IND])

(i) |təpahīkē-| AI 'point': tpahí·k·e· 'he's pointing' (ME; < |təpah-| TI(1a) 'point at':
ntətpáhəmən 'I point at it' [V ⟨ham⟩ but see 2.29; with repetitive reduplication])

(j) |sīlənehīkē-| AI 'do the milking': sinnehí·k·e· 'she milks the cow(s)' (ME;
< virtual TI matching |sīlənehw-| TA 'milk')

(5.101) Indefinite intransitives in |-əwē| AI
Verb forms

(a) |ələwē-| AI 'say {so}': lúwe· 'he says {so}' (< |əl-| TA 'say {so} to')

(b) |kwānšīpahəwē-| AI 'hide': kɔ·nši·phúwe· 'he hides' (V; < |kwānšīpah-| TA 'hide from':
ə́nta-kɔ·nši·pháhti·t 'when they hide from them (obv.)' [ME; |IC–āhətīt| 3p–3´/CC])

(c) |nəhləwē-| AI 'kill a person, people': nhíləwe· 'he kills someone' (< |nəhl-| TA 'kill');
káči nhiləwé·han 'do not murder anyone' (B; káči 'don't'; |–han| 2s/PROH);
nenhíləwe·t 'a murderer' (B, OA; |Rih+| HAB [5.42j], |IC–t| 3s/PPL(ANsg))

(d) |pēhəwē-| AI 'wait for someone': péhəwe· 'he waits' (V;
< |pēh-| TA 'wait for': mpé·ha 'I waited for him' [OA; |nə–āw| 1s–3s/IND])

(e) |sihəwē-| AI 'win, beat someone': síhəwe· 'he won' (ME, LB;
< |sihw-| TA 'beat, defeat': nsíhɔ 'I beat him' [ME; |nə–āw| 1s–3s/IND])

(f) |wəlankōnsōhāləwē-| AI 'make people be friends':
wehwəlankunso·ha·ləwé·č·i·k 'peacemakers, lit., those that make people be friends' (B;
< |Rih+| HAB, |wəlankōnsōhāl-| TA 'make friendly, neighborly', |IC–čīk| 3p/PPL(ANpl);
< |wəlankōnsī-| AI 'be friendly' [5.81d])

(g) |čahwāhpwənəwē-| AI 'baptize people': ə́nta-čhɔ·pwənúwe·t 'where he was baptizing
people' (B; |(-ən)talī| PV '{smwh}' [4.67(3)], |IC–t| 3s/PPL(OBL);
< |čahwāhpwən-| TA 'baptize, lit. dunk in water' [cf. 5.100c])

Derived nouns

(h) wewtənəwe·s 'water spirit' (LB; |wehwətənəwēs| <
|IC+|, |Rih+| HAB, |wətənəwē-| AI 'pull people (under)', |-s| AGTV [5.66j];
< |wətən-| TA 'pull, drag': o·t·ənək·əwɔ́·ɔ 'it (obv.) dragged them' (WL; 4.27s)

(i) pehpo·kčí·ləwe·s 'stink bug' (ME; |pehpōkəčīləwēs| <
|IC+|, |Rih+| HAB, |pōkəčīləwē-| AI 'fart on people', |-s| AGTV [5.66];
< |pōkəčīl-| TA 'fart on' < |pōkətī-| AI 'fart', 3s pó·ktu [cf. |čī-l| < |tī| in 5.88g])

(j) šəško·lo·há·ləwe·s 'teacher' (ME; |šəšəkōlōhāləwēs| <
|(IC)+|, |Rə+| REP, |šəkōlōhāləwē-| TA 'teach people in school', |-s| AGTV [5.66];
< |šəkōlōhāl-| TA 'teach O1 in school': nšək·o·lo·há·la 'I schooled him' (ME);
< |šəkōlī-| AI 'go to school', 3s škó·lu [LB])
(LB has the variant: šəško·lhá·ləwe·s 'teacher')

(5.102) Indefinite intransitives in |-kē| AI

    TA in |-l| > |-hkē| AI

    (a) |kəlōhkē-| AI 'swear': kəló·ke·w 'he swears' (V;
        < |kəlōl-| TA 'swear at': nkəló·la 'I cussed him' [OA; |nə–āw| 1s–3s/IND])

    (b) |kwəhtəhkē-| AI 'forbid': káči khwithiké·he·kw 'do not forbid anyone' (B);
        < |kwəhtəl-| TA(+O) 'admonish, forbid' (5.87a)

    (c) |nāwahkē-| AI 'follow': na·hóke· 'he followed' (B, ME); < |nāwal-| TA 'follow':
        nɔ·ɔlawwá·ɔ 'they followed him' [B; |wə–āwəwāwa| 3p–3´/IND]; cf. 2.56d)

    (d) |nəpīhkē-| AI 'doctor (people), doctor someone with a sweatbath': 3s mpí·ke· (OA);
        |nehnəpīhkēs|: nenpí·ke·s 'sweat doctor' (OA, ME; |IC+|, |Rih+| HAB, -s| AGTV [5.42k]);
        < |nəpīl-| TA 'doctor by sweating': kənáp·i·la 'you (sg.) sweat him, doctor him with a
        sweatbath' (OA, FW; |kə–āw| 2s–3s/IND]); mpí·l 'doctor him!' (OA; |–∅| 2s–3/IMP])

    (e) |pənōntəhkē-| AI 'reveal O2 to': kpənunthike·né·ɔ 'you (pl.) reveal it to people' (B);
        < |pənōntəl-| TA+O 'cause to look at O2' (5.87f)

    TA in |-m| > |-nkē| AI

    (f) |kwīlōnkē-| AI 'be lonesome': kwi·lúnke· AI 'he (she) is lonesome' (V);
        < |kwīlōm-| TA 'be lonesome for': nkwi·ló·ma 'I am lonesome for him' [V; cf. 5.102a])

    (g) |wīčənkē-| AI 'help, help people': nəwi·č·ínke 'I'm helping people' (ND; |nə–∅| 1s/IND);
        < |wīčəm-| TA 'help': nəwí·č·əma 'I helped him' (V; cf. 5.102a)

    (h) |wīkīnkē-| AI 'be married': wi·k·ínke·p 'she had been married'
        (B; |–p| 3s/IND.PRET; also with |-wākan| NF [5.59b]); < |wīkīm-| TA 'be married to':
        wi·k·í·mat 'your wife, your husband' (B; |(IC)–at| 2s–3/PPL(ANsg))

    (i) |wīhpēnkē-| AI 'sleep with someone': énta-ki·mí·i-wi·pénke·t 'when she was committing
        adultery' (B; énta PV+IC 'when', ki·mí·i PV 'secretly', |IC–t| 3s/CC)
        < |wīhpēm-| TA 'sleep with': nəwi·pé·ma 'I sleep with him' (V; cf. 5.102a)

    (j) |kələntəhkē-| AI+O 'give O2 to people to have': kwələnthiké·ne·p 'he gave it to people
        to have' (B; |wə–nēp| 3s+0s/IND.PRET); < |kələntəl-| TA+O 'hand O2 out to' (5.87d)

(5.103) Indefinite intransitives in |-āsī| AI (replacing |-aw| TA)

    (a) |pənāsī-| AI 'look on': pəná·s·u 'he looked on' (B;
        < |pənaw-| TA 'look at': pənáw 'look at him, them (you sg.)' [V, ME])

    (b) |pəntāsī-| AI 'listen': pənta·s·í·č·i·k 'who were listening' (B; |(IC)–čīk| 3p/PPL(ANpl)
        < |pəntaw-| TA 'listen to': kpəntaó·ɔk 'you hear them' (B; |kə–āwak| 2s–3p/IND);
        cf. pəntá·s·u II 'it is heard' (5.195g)

    (c) |pakītātamāsī-| AI+O 'forgive O2': pahki·t·a·t·amá·s·u 'he forgives O2 (sin)' (B);
        < |pakītātamaw-| TA(+O) 'forgive (O2)':
        pahki·t·a·t·amaót·e 'if you forgive him (for O2)' (B; |–atē| 2s–3/SBJ)

    (d) |wəntamāsī-| AI+O 'tell about O2':
        ɔ́·k=č kuntama·s·i·né·ɔ nhák·ay 'and you (pl.) shall bear witness to me'
        (B; |kə–nēwā| 2p+0s/IND; ɔ́·k 'and'; =č FUT; nhák·ay 'me' [4.14];
        < |wəntamaw-| TA 'tell' [5.97c])

§5.8k. Middle-Reflexives. A middle-reflexive denotes an action or state performed on or brought about for the subject, or an action or state brought about by an internal process. The subject may be an actor, an undergoer, or an experiencer, typically with a specialized or idiomatic link to the meaning of the verb. A middle-reflexive is most often an AI derived from a TA, but for some verbs there is also an II.

The middle-reflexives do not have a shape uniquely distinct from other intransitives (cf. Goddard 1979:63-66), but on formal and semantic grounds several types and stem shapes can be recognized as falling into this category.

(5.104) Middle-reflexives (types and examples)
Stems with invariant |-ā| in AI (cf. **§2.10h**) beside |-aw| in TA
  (a) |pāhtamā-| AI 'pray': 3s pá·tama·;
      < |pāhtamaw-| TA 'pray to': mpa·tamáɔ 'I pray to him' (V)
  (b) |wəlahtā-| AI 'put up food for oneself': takó· wi·wəla·ta·í·ɔk 'they never put up food'
      (B; < *|wəlahtaw-| TA 'put up for' < |wəlaht-| TI(2) 'put away, put up (food); keep')
  (c) |nīpatā-| AI 'have an erection': 3s nípahta· < *|nīpataw-| TA 'stand O2 up for';
      < |nīpat-| TI(2) 'stand up': nnípahto·n 'I stand it up')
  (d) |pōhwənəmā-| AI 'beat a drum': 3s púhənəma· (OA, LB), puhənə́ma· (OA);
      < *|pōhwənəmaw-| TA 'beat for' < *|pōhwən-| TI(1b) 'beat'; cf. puhəní·k·an 'drum'
Stems with |-mwī| AI (beside |-m| TA)
  (e) |-īmwī| AI 'speak, vocalize': |ačīmwī-| AI 'tell a story', 3s a·č·í·mu (V);
      < |-īm| TA 'act on by speech' (5.12m): ntak·əní·ma 'I talk about s.o.'
Stems with |-nsī| AI (beside |-m| TA)
  (f) |-ēlənsī| AI 'think of oneself': |tankēlənsī-| AI (*lit.*, 'think oneself small'):
      tanke·ló̜nsu (B), tanke·lə́·nsu (V) 'he is humble'; < |tankēlənt-| TI(1a) 'think small':
      tanke·ləntánke hɔ́k·ay 'if he thinks little of himself' (B; |(IC)–ankē| 3s–0/SBJ; 4.14)
  (g) |wəlankōnsī-| AI 'be friendly', 3s wəlankó·nsu AI (V; < |wəlankōm-| TA 'be on good
      terms with, be at peace with, be good to, treat well, apologize to, acknowledge'
Stem with |-pwī| AI 'eat' (beside |-pw| TA 'eat')
  (h) |katōpwī-| AI 'be hungry', 3s kahtó·p·u (V, ME, AD);
      < |katōpw-| TA 'want to eat, be hungry for': nkat·ó·p·ɔ 'I want to eat (anim.)' (V, LB)
Stems with |-sī| AI (beside |-l| TA)
  (i) |kīmīnasī-| AI 'kill secretly', 3s ki·mí·nahsu (V); < |kīmīnal-| TA 'kill secretly':
      nki·mí·nala 'I killed him secretly' (V; |nə–āw| 1s–3s/IND)
  (j) |naxāsī-| AI 'be watching, be on guard', 3s naxá·s·u, 1s nnax·á·s·i (OA);
      < |naxāl-| TA 'watch out for': naxá·lo· 'watch out for them' (B; |–ō| 2p–3/IMP)
  (k) |-pīsī| AI 'be tied': |kaxpīsī-| AI 'be tied up', 3s kaxpí·s·u (OA)
      < |-pīl| TA 'tie': |kaxpīl-| TA 'tie up', nkaxpí·la 'I tied him up' (V)
  (l) *|nəpīsī-| AI 'do one's doctoring' (in mpi·s·o·n 'medicine' [5.53g]);
      < |nəpīl-| TA 'doctor' (see 5.102d)
  (m) *|nēntəsī-| AI 'show oneself' (in |nēntəsīhtaw-| [with applicative |-htaw| TA 5.91]:
      wənentsi·taɔ́·ɔ 'he appeared to him, her, them')
      < |nēntəl-| TA+O 'cause to see O2, show O2 to' (5.87e)
Stems with |-sī| AI, |-tē| II 'be heated, burned' (beside |-sw| TA 'act on by heat, fire')
  (n) |lōsī-| AI, |lōtē-| II 'burn': 3s ló·s·u, 0s ló·t·e· (V); < |lōsw-| TA, |lōs-| TI(1b) 'burn':
      wəlo·s·a·né·ɔ 'they burned him up' (V; |wə-lōsw-ānēwā| 3p–3´/SBD),
      wəlo·s·o·k·u 'he (obv.) burned him' (ME; |wə-lōsw-əkō(l)| 3´–3s/IND);
      wəló·s·əmən 'he burns it' (OA; |wə-lōs-əmən| 3s–0s/IND)

§5.8l. Derived Passives. When AI and II passives are derived from transitive stems, the passives for both genders are based on either the TA or the TI. TI(1a), TI(1b), and TI(2) stems add |-āsī| AI, II, and TA stems add |-əkwəsī| AI and |-əkwat| II. Most passive stems in |-āsī|, however, are II's. Stems ending in |-īnākwəsī| AI, |-īnākwat| II 'seem, appear' (as if passive stems from |-īnaw| TA 'perceive') and |-əhtākwəsī| AI 'use the voice, shout' (as if a passive stem from |-əhtaw| TA 'hear') are best taken as having lexicalized finals with these shapes (5.108, 109).

(5.105) AI and II passive stems derived from TI(1) stems

TI(1a) stems in |-ah| (cf. 3.20e, 5.12r)
  (a) kpahá·s·u AI 'he was imprisoned', II 'it was closed'
  (b) phɔkhakehá·s·u AI 'he is buried'
  (c) psakhwitehá·s·u AI 'he was crucified'
  (d) le·khá·s·u II 'it is written' (cf. le·khá·s·u AI 'takes a picture' V)
  (e) či·khá·s·u II 'it is swept out'
  (f) ma·ehá·s·u II: e·lkí·kwi-ma·ehá·s·i·k 'the time when they (inan.) are gathered' (B)

TI(1a) stems in |-C| with TA in |-Caw| (cf. 3.20f, 5.12x)
  (g) pəntá·s·u II 'it is heard' (cf. 5.103b)
  (h) maxká·s·u II 'it is found'
  (i) haphiká·s·u II 'it is trampled on': énta-=č -ahhaphiká·s·i·k 'where it will be trampled on'
  (j) tahči·ká·s·u II 'it has been oppressed'
  (k) mhalá·s·u II 'it was sold'

TI(1a) stems in |-nt| with TA in |-m| (cf. 3.20ab)
  (l) pi·ɔntá·s·u II 'it is left uneaten'
  (m) pahki·t·e·ləntá·s·u II 'it is forgiven'
  (n) wəle·ləntá·s·u II 'it is acceptable'
  (o) ahkəntá·s·u II 'it is counted'

TI(1b) stems in |-C| with TA in |-Cw| (3.20, 5.12tv)
  (p) lo·s·á·s·u: e·lkí·kwi-lo·s·á·s·i·k 'the time when they are burned'
  (q) énta-winki·ma·khwiksá·s·i·k 'altar (where incense was burned)'
  (r) təmšá·s·u and təməš·á·s·u 'it is cut' (harvested)

TI(1b) stems in |-ən| TA, TI 'by hand' (3.20g, 5.12o)
  (s) énta-čhɔ·pwəná·s·i·k paíntal 'when cups are washed'
  (t) phwəná·s·u 'it is pulled up'
  (u) šaxahkəná·s·u 'it is made straight'
  (v) tahkwəná·s·əwa 'they are mixed together'
  (w) wəntəná·s·u 'it was taken from' (B)
  (x) ehə́nta-a·š·unte·ná·s·i·k 'where it is traded'
  (y) mehəma·e·ná·s·i·k 'what is collected'

TI(1b) stem in |-ōt| TI with TA in |-m| (5.12m)
  (z) ahkəno·t·á·s·u 'it is told about': e·k·əno·t·á·s·i·k 'what is spoken of'

(5.106) II passive stems derived from TI(2) stems
  (a) kanthatá·s·u 'it is hidden'
  (b) manni·tá·s·o·p 'it was made, it was built'
  (c) wəli·tá·s·u 'it is made nice'

(5.107) AI and II passive stems derived from TA stems with |-əkwəsī| AI, |-əkwat| II
  (a) ahki·mkwə́s·u AI 'is counted': takó· ahki·mkwəs·i·í·ɔk 'they (anim.) were not counted'
  (b) |akēhkīməkwəsī-| AI 'be taught': e·k·e·ki·mkwəs·í·č·i·k 'disciples (*lit.*, ones taught)'
  (c) mi·lkwə́s·u AI+O 'is given (O2) (by a higher power)':
      ktá·pi·=č yó·l wé·mi -mi·lkwəs·i·né·ɔ. 'You (pl.) will be given all these things in the bargain.' (B; |ahpī| PV 'along with (it), in addition', |mīləkwəsī-| AI+O 'be given O2', |kət–nēwā| 2p+0/IND; =č FUT; yó·l 'these (inan.)'; wé·mi P 'all')

(d) ne·ykwə́s·u AI, né·ykɔt II 'is seen, appears' (ME)
(e) nihəla·lkwə́s·u 'he is not free to act (*lit.*, is owned)' (B)
(f) pəntá·kwsu, pəntá·k·ɔt 'he, it is heard': pənta·khɔ́ke 'when it was heard about' (B)
(g) wwahkwə́s·u AI, wwáhkɔt II 'he, it is known' (B, ME)
(h) |(ma)xīnkwēləməkwəsī-| AI 'be thought great': xinkwe·ləmukwsí·č·i·k 'noblemen'
(i) |(ma)xīnkwakənīməkwəsī-| AI 'be praised, be glorified': xinkɔhkəni·mkwəs·í·t·e 'when he was glorified'; maxinkɔhkəni·mkwəs·í·t·eč 'let him be praised';

(5.108) Stems with |-īnākwəsī| AI, |-īnākwat| II 'seem, appear'
(a) li·ná·kwsu, li·ná·k·ɔt 'he, it looks {so}, like (someone, something)': e·li·ná·kwsi·t 'what he is like, looks like'
(b) ni·ski·ná·kwsi·t 'the foul one', ni·ski·ná·k·ɔt 'it looks filthy'
(c) kanši·na·kwsúwak 'they (anim.) are marvelous to behold' (B)
(d) ktəma·k·i·ná·k·ɔt 'it looks pitiful'
(e) xahi·ná·kwsu 'he, she is ugly' (V, OA, LB)

(5.109) Stems with |-əhtākwəsī| AI, |-əhtākwat-| II 'have a sound, use the voice, be a voice'
(a) či·phitá·k·ɔt 'it sounds strange' (LB)
(b) |ələwēhtākwəsī-| AI, |ələwēhtākwat-| II 'be heard speaking {so}': e·ləwe·tá·kwsi·t 'his voice' (B); luwe·tá·k·ɔt 'it (a voice) is heard to say {so}' (B)
(c) manunkhita·kwsúwak 'they shout angrily' (B)
(d) xa·whita·kwsu 'he shouts': tɔ́ləmi·xa·whita·kwsi·né·ɔ 'they began shouting (sbd.)' (B)

§5.8m. Reciprocals. AI reciprocals are made from TA verbs and typically are used to indicate an action that plural subjects do to each other, though they are also sometimes inflected for a singular subject. The action is not always literally reciprocal, and may rather be performed by some of a group on others. With an indefinite subject and in derived abstract nouns reciprocal stems often have a passive meaning.

Reciprocal stems are formed on TA stems ending in |-l|, |-h|, |-ēw|, or |-Cw| with a suffix |-ətī| AI (5.110abcdef); the stems ending in |-Cw| have contraction to |-Cōtī| (5.110ghi). TA stems in |-Caw| have contraction to |-Cāwatī| (5.110jklm). TA stems in |-m| add |-tī| AI, and the |m| is assimilated to |n| (2.45b; 5.110nopqrstu). TA stems in |-ən| add |-əntī|, giving |-ənəntī| (5.114c).

(5.110) Reciprocals on different stem shapes
  With uncontracted |-ətī| AI
(a) šinka·ltúwak 'they hate each other' (B; |šīnkāl-| TA)
(b) nhiltúwak 'they killed each other' (OA; |nəhıl-| TA)
(c) kahto·nalə́t·əwak 'they attack each other' (B; |katōnal-| TA)
(d) ktəlihti·né·ɔ 'you do it for each other' (B; |əlīh-| TA 'treat{so}, do {so} for')
(e) məšihtúwak 'they infect each other, are contagious' (V; *|məšīh-| TA)
(f) ne·wtúwak 'they saw each other' (OA; |nēw-| TA)
  With |-ətī| AI and contraction to |-ōtī|
(g) čani·nehó·t·əwak 'they disputed among themselves' (B; |čanīnehw-| TA)
(h) payaxkhó·t·əwak 'they shot each other' (AD; |payaxkahw-| TA 'shoot with firearm')
(i) pəmi·nehó·t·əwak 'they argued, quarreled' (B, OA; |pəmīnehw-| TA)
  With |-ətī| AI and contraction to |-āwatī|
(j) ahkahəmá·ɔhti·kw 'share it among yourselves' (B; |akahamāwatī-| AI+O 'distribute O2 to each other', |–kw| 2p/IMP; < |akahamaw-| TA+O 'distribute O2 to')
(k) kkəš·i·xta·ɔhti·ne·ɔ́·i 'you wash them for each other' (B; |kəšīxətāwatī-| AI+O 'wash O2 for each other', |kə–nēwāwī| 2p+0p/IND; < |kəšīxətaw-| TA+O 'wash O2 for')

(l) nnak·i·ska·ɔhtíhəna 'we met each other' (OA;
|nakīskāwatī-| AI 'meet each other', |nə–hmənā| 1p/IND; < |nakīskaw-| TA 'meet')

(m) pəna·ɔhtúwak 'they looked at each other' (OA; |pənāwatī-| AI < |pənaw-| TA 'look at')

With |-tī| and |-m-tī| > |-ntī|

(n) naxkúntəwak 'they answered each other' (OA; < |naxkōm-| TA)

(o) pahkántəwak 'they're hitting each other' (OA; < |pakam-| TA)

(p) wəlankúntəwak 'they are good to each other' (V; < |wəlankōm-| TA)

(q) wi·č·ə́ntəwak 'they're helping each other' (OA; < |wīčəm-| TA)

(r) wi·péntəwak 'they are sleeping together' (V; < |wīhpēm-| TA)

(s) no·wi·č·o·s·əntíhəna 'we (women) are friends' (OA; < |wəwīčōsəm-| TA; cf.4.11g)

(t) no·wi·t·i·s·əntíhəna 'we (men) are friends' (OA; < |wəwītīsəm-| TA; cf. 4.11f)

(u) wwi·tkuxkwə́ntəwak 'they are sisters' (OA; < |wəwītəkəxkwəm-| TA; see 5.72h)

(5.111) Reciprocal with singular inflection

(a) xé·li=č awé·n .. amə́ntahkənə́ntu 'many people will betray each other' (B; < |amə́ntakənīm-| TA; =č FUT; xé·li 'many'; awé·n 'person (sg. for pl.)')

(5.112) Reciprocal form not literally reciprocal

(a) ahhaphika·ɔhtúwak 'they were stepping on each other' (B; < |ày+ahpəhkaw-| TA; 5.37i)

(b) e·nha·ɔhtúwak 'they're paying each other' (OA; < |ēnahaw-| TA)

(c) lə́t·əwak 'they said {so} to each other' (< |əl-| TA)

(d) wte·ka·ɔhtúwak 'they go single file' (OA; < |wətēhkaw-| TA 'follow behind')

(5.113) Reciprocal stems with indefinite subject

Reciprocal meaning

(a) énta-wi·púntink 'at a feast' (B; |(-ən)talī| PV '{smwh}' [4.67(3)], |wīhpōm-| TA 'eat with', |-tī| AI RECIP, |IC–nk| X/PPL(OBL);
lit., 'where (on one occasion) people eat with each other')

(b) ehə́nta-mhalamá·ɔhtink 'in the market' (B; |Rih+| HAB, |(-ən)talī| PV '{smwh}' [5.113a], |mahlamaw-| TA 'buy (O2) from', |-ətī| AI RECIP, |IC–nk| X/PPL(OBL);
lit., 'where people (customarily) buy from each other')

Passive meaning

(c) mí·ltink 'which is given' (B; < |mīl-| TA+O 'give O2 to', |-ətī| AI RECIP, |(IC)–nk| X/PPL(INsg))

(d) énta-tahkɔp·o·há·ltink 'at the wedding' (B; < |takwapōhāl-| TA 'marry' [5.81f])

(e) ehə́nta-nhíltink 'the place of (customary) execution' (B; |nəhl-| TA 'kill' [5.110b])

Abstract nouns derived from reciprocal stems are commonly nominalizations with the basic meaning of the underlying verb (5.60). They may refer to the verbal notion being performed (5.114) or being experienced (5.115), and the possessor may be the agent (5.116abcdef) or the undergoer (5.116gh).

(5.114) Nouns derived from reciprocal stems (ostensibly active)

(a) ahke·kəntəwá·k·an 'teaching' (< |akēhkīm-| TA 'teach'; see 5.60a)

(b) čani·laentəwá·k·an 'offences' (< |čanīlawēm-| TA 'offend, torment verbally')

(c) čhɔ·pwənəntəwá·k·an 'baptism (being performed)' (see 5.116e; cf. 5.115b)

(d) khwitələt·əwá·k·an 'law' (< |kwəhtəl-| TA(+O) 'admonish, forbid'; 5.87a)

(e) lankuntəwá·k·an 'kinship' (V; < |əlankōm-| TA 'be related to ({so})':
ntəlankó·ma 'I'm related to him' [V, WS])

(f) lehəle·x·e·mha·ltəwá·k·an 'salvation' (< |lēhlēxēmahāl-| TA 'save the life of')

(g) nhiltəwá·k·an 'murder; killing' (Mt 15.19, Lk 9.31; < |nəhl-| TA 'kill')

(h) mawəntəwá·k·an 'mourning' (< |mawīm-| TA 'mourn, weep for')
  (i) pahki·t·a·t·ama·ɔhtəwá·k·an 'forgiveness' (< |pakītātamaw-| TA+O 'forgive for O2')
  (j) sak·wi·laehtəwá·k·an(a) 'persecutions' (< |sàkwīlawēh-| TA 'persecute, torment')
  (k) tahpantəwá·k·an 'commandment' (< |tapām-| TA 'instruct in what is right' [ME])
  (l) we·mihtəwá·k·an 'massacres' (< |wēmīh-| TA 'kill all of' [B])
  (m) wəlankuntəwá·k·an 'peace' (< |wəlankōm-| TA 'be on good terms with, at peace with')
  (n) wə́ski-naxkuntəwá·k·an 'new covenant' (wə́ski PN 'new'; cf. 5.60e)
(5.115) Nouns derived from reciprocal stems (with passive meaning)
  (a) ahkwe·č·ihtəwá·k·an 'temptation, being tempted'
        (< |akwēčīh-| TA 'tempt': káči ahkwe·č·i·hié·k·ač 'do not (you sg.) tempt him')
  (b) čhɔ·pwənəntəwá·k·an 'baptism (being undergone)' (Lk 3.3, Lk 12.50; 5.100c, 5.116e)
  (c) kčo·ha·ltəwá·k·an 'salvation', *lit.* 'being rescued' (< |kəčōhāl-| TA 'rescue'; 5.81a)
  (d) ktəma·k·e·ləntəwá·k·an 'mercy (received)' (Mt 9.13; 5.60c)
  (e) nto·t·əma·ɔhtəwá·k·an 'judgment, being judged' (i.e., 'examination, being asked')
        (< |natōtəmaw-| TA 'ask')
(5.116) Nouns derived from reciprocal stems (possessed forms)
  Possessor = agent
  (a) kəmi·ltəwá·k·an 'your gift (given)' (< |mīl-| TA+O 'give O2 to'; cf. 4.40m)
  (b) kwət·əma·k·e·ləntəwá·k·an 'his mercy (shown)' (cf. 5.60c, 5.115d)
  (c) wšinka·ltəwá·k·an 'his hatred' (< |šīnkāl-| TA 'hate'; 2.63f)
  (d) tɔhɔ·ltəwá·k·an 'his love' (|àhwālətī-| AI < |àhwāl-| TA 'love'; cf. 5.60b)
  (e) nčá·n wčɔhɔ·pwənəntəwá·k·an 'John's baptism' (nčá·n 'John'; cf. 5.100c)
  (f) ntap·antəwá·k·an 'my commandment' (cf. 5.114k)
  Possessor = undergoer
  (g) kwəč·o·ha·ltəwá·k·an 'his salvation, his being saved' (cf. 5.115c)
  (h) kte·nha·ɔhtəwá·k·an 'your reward (received)'

§5.8n. Verbs of Environmental Effect. Some II verb stems make AI derivatives that indicate that the subject experiences in the normal way (or one of the normal ways) what the II verb would describe. These verbs are made with a final |-namī| AI added after a vowel, or |-amī| AI added after |-n|. If the II verb is not impersonal, the derived AI may take its notional subject as a secondary object (5.117f). An II verb may be derived from the AI (5.117c). This final is also found added to the lexicalized participle of an II (5.117d).

(5.117) Verbs of environmental effect and the like with |-(n)amī| AI
  (a) |katənamī-| AI 'be (so many) years old' (< kahtə́n II 'be (so many) years', P 'year(s)'):
      níši-kahtənámu 'he is two years old' (níši PV 'two')
  (b) |sōkəlānamī-| AI 'get rain, get caught in the rain' (< |sōkəlān-| II 'rain': só·k·əla·n 'it
      rains'): so·k·əlá·namu 'he got caught in the rain' (V), 'he got rain' (ME)
  (c) |tōhpanamī-| AI 'have frost' (< |tōhpan-| II 'be frost': tó·pan 'there is frost'):
      > to·panamó·u 'it's got frost on it' (ME; 5.76d)
  (d) |wāxēyēkamī-| AI 'have light' (< ɔ·x·é·e·k 'light', a lexicalized II participle):
      wénči-=č -ɔ·x·e·e·k·amíe·kw 'so that you (pl.) shall have light' (B)
  (e) |wīnēnamī-| AI 'have snow' (< wí·ne· II 'it's snowing'):
      wi·né·namu AI 'he has snow'
  (f) |wəlīkənamī-| AI+O 'have O2 grow well as a crop' (< |wəlīkən| II 'grow well'):
      eski·tamínka no·li·k·ənámi 'I grew some good watermelons' (ME)

§5.8o. Objurgative Verbs. Verbs with an affective pejorative meaning like that of objurgative nouns (**§5.5d**) are formed with medials that refer literally to intimate bodyparts (or are otherwise not found). These range in force from mild disapproval to more serious insults.
(5.118) Objurgative verbs
   (a) |(ma)xalētəyā-| AI 'be a glutton' (< |(ma)x-| 'big', |-alē-| 'penis', |-təy-| 'rear end', |-ā| AI):
      xalé·t·ie· 'he is a glutton' (WT; LTD "greedy"); maxale·t·ié·ɔk 'they are gluttons' (V); me·x·alé·t·ia·t 'glutton' (B). The literal meaning is as if '(be a) damn big-butt'.
   (b) |kəlōnəšētəyā-| AI 'be a liar' (< |kəlōn-| 'lie', |-əšētəy-| 'butt-hole', |-ā| AI):
      kəlo·nš·é·t·ie· 'he's a damn liar' (ER); normal: kəló·ne· 'he tells a lie'
   (c) |kəšətaxkēhlā-| AI 'go fast' (< |kəš-| 'intense, fast', |-ətaxkē-| '?', |-(ī)hlā| AI 'go fast'):
      kšətxkéhəla·kw "step a little faster" (ER); normal: kšíhəle· 'goes fast, runs'
   (d) |matalālakītəyēhw-| TA 'overtake, catch up to' (< |matal-| [TA] 'overtake' + |-ālakītəyē-| 'butt-hole' + |-ahw-| TA 'act on by tool'): hu ləníti kəmat·ala·lahki·t·ieho·k·éhəna 'pretty soon we're going to be overtaken' (ER); normal: xú xántki kəmat·alək·éhəna
   (e) káči pa·kše·t·ie·x·ínkhan 'don't fall down on your butt!' (ME; káči 'don't'; |pāk-| 'slap', |-əšētəyē-| 'butt-hole', |-(ī)xīn| AI 'fall', |-kəhan| for |-han| 2s/PROH)
   (f) |mwəyalē-| AI (|mwəy-| 'excrement', |-al-| 'penis', |-ē-| AI): mwiále· 'he's lazy, good-for-nothing' (ME), kəmwíale 'you're afraid to fight, cowardly' (ME; cf. 5.50h)
   (g) |čītəkwāxē-| AI 'shut up' (|čītəkw-| 'shut up', |-āx-| 'vagina', |-ē| AI):
      či·tkó·x·e 'shut the hell up!' (used between women) (JR); normal: či·tkwə́s·i 'shut up!'

Most objurgative verbs are conventional, but the ones in (5.118cd) were known as what was said jokingly by an old man to urge some children riding on a forced march during the Civil War.

Some objurgatives are attested with the substitution of meaningless |-əlē-| for |-alē-| 'penis'. The variant in (5.119a) was used by two women, while the one in (5.119b) was used by two men, one of whom (FW) explained that it was "not a cussword."
(5.119) Objurgative verbs euphemistically altered
   (a) |(ma)xəlētəyā-| AI 'be a glutton' (cf. 5.118a):
      kəmax·əlé·t·ia 'you're greedy (eating)' (ME), xəlé·t·ie· "he is greedy" (LB).
   (b) |šākwəlētəyā-| AI 'be stingy with food' (|šākw-| 'stingy', |-əlē-| '?', |-təy-| 'butt', |-ā| AI):
      ša·k·wəlé·t·ie· 'he's stingy with food' (FW; V pl.): normal: šá·kwsu 'he is stingy'

§5.9. Compounds. Some words are compounds, which are concatenations of more than one phonological word; there are compound nouns, compound verbs, and particle compounds. Although compound words comprise more than one phonological word and therefore contain one or more word boundaries, they behave like single words for purposes of inflection and within the functional structure of the larger sentence.

Each compound has a single head word (a head noun, head verb, or head particle) preceded by one or more prewords (prenouns, preverbs, or preparticles). Except for some preverbs (5.23ace), prewords have an abstract final -i PF or -í·i PF, but despite being made formally with these finals that also make particles, and sometimes being homonymous with particles, they are functionally not particles (**§5.3**) but components of compounds.

The components of a compound may be adjacent to each other, or they may be discontinuous, with intervening words (or clauses: e.g., Mk 2.19) that are not part of the compound. Adjacent components are written with a hyphen separating them instead of a space. When the components are discontinuous, they are flagged by hyphens, which are written with a following space (or /=/; **§5.3a**) after a preword, and with a preceding space before a preword or the head word.

§5.9a. Compound Nouns. Prenouns are derived from initials, which may themselves be derived from the stems of nouns or verbs. Most prenouns that are based on underived initials have -i PF (5.120), but some have -í·i PF (5.121). A prenoun with -í·i PF that modifies a noun that is derived from a verb can be taken as a particle used as a prenoun in the same way that it would be used with the underlying verb (5.127). Prenouns can apparently be freely made from noun stems (5.122) and lexicalized participles (5.123) by the addition of -í·i PF, and some prenouns are made this way from a locative noun or particle (5.124). Much less common are prenouns made from verb stems, which are based on an intermediate stage that is formally an agent noun made with |-w| NF (5.61; presumably with |-əw| after a consonant). Prenouns are made in this way directly from intransitive verb stems (5.125ab) and presumably, like preverbs, TI themes; they are made from TA verbs by using the derived reciprocal stem (cf. 5.113cde, 5.114-115; 5.125cd). A prenoun may precede a possessed noun (B 1842:11.4, 16.1).

Particles with -í·i PF that are derived from nouns can be considered a specialized use of the homonymous prenoun; particles of this type may be postposed to a noun (5.126ab) or used predicatively (5.126cde).

The head noun of a compound noun may be a lexicalized participle (5.122ah). In these cases the initial change that marks the participle (if overt) is on the head noun (formally a participle) rather than on the prenoun (e.g., on 'priests' in 5.120e). In contrast to this, when a participle is made from a compound verb the initial change (if overt) is on the preverb (5.129mvwaannppss).

(5.120) Prenouns with underived initials and -i PF
- (a) čípi PN 'terrible, horrible, dreadful, dangerous' (2.74c):
    - čípi-aésəs 'dangerous animal' (B 1842)
    - čípi-kéku 'terrible thing' (i.e., whiskey; B 1834a)
    - čípi-awé·n 'dreadful person' (V)
- (b) máhči PN 'bad':
    - máhči-kéku 'bad thing' (i.e., liquor; OA)
    - máhči-ləs·əwá·k·an 'wrong-doing' (B 1834a:13);
        here presumably from máhči PV (in a noun from máhči-ləs·u 'does wrong, etc.')
- (c) mahčí·kwi PN 'bad':
    - mahčí·kwi-kéku 'bad thing or things' (B, OA, ME)
    - mahčí·kwi-hítkunk 'bad tree (loc.)' (B; hít·ukw 'tree', |-ənk| loc.)
- (d) máxki PN 'red':
    - máxki-sí·p·u 'Red River' (V; sí·p·u 'river')
- (e) mayá·i PN 'true' (B 5x; cf. 5.121b):
    - mayá·i-ɔ·s·ahkame·í·i-ahpɔ́·n 'the true bread of heaven' (B)
    - mayá·i-wehi·hunké·č·i·k 'the chief priests'
- (f) səki PN 'black' (2.74j):
    - səki-təmá·kwe 'Black Beaver' (OA)
- (g) ší·ki PN 'good':
    - ší·ki-lə́nu 'good man' (B 1834a, V)
    - ší·ki-təpčéhəla·s 'a fine wagon' (ME; loc. 'in a chariot' [B 1842])
    - ší·ki-hítkunk 'good tree (loc.)' (B)
- (h) wəski PN 'new':
    - wəski-naxkuntəwá·k·an 'new covenant' (B; KJV "the new testament")
    - wəski-po·t·a·lá·s·ink 'in a new skin bag' (B)

(i) wíči PN 'fellow' (with pronominal prefix, making a dependent noun):
   wiči-alo·ká·k·ana 'his fellow servant or servants' (B)
   kíči-xkwé·ɔk 'your fellow women' (B)
(j) xínkwi PN 'big' (pl. amánki); also as PV (cf. 5.129rr):
   xínkwi-ɔ́·lakw 'big cave' (OA)
   xínkwi-sa·k·í·ma 'great king' (B)
   xínkwi-o·t·é·nink 'to a big town' (B)
   amánki-awé·ni·k 'big people' (OA)
   amánki-ahpo·t·í·k·ana 'large roasting sticks' (V)
(k) xúwi PN 'old':
   xúwi-a·pto·ná·k·ana 'old words, sayings; the ancient law' (B)
   xúwi-kə́mpahkɔ 'old leaves' (OA)

(5.121) Prenouns with underived initials and -í·i PF
(a) ləní·i PN 'ordinary':
   ləní·i-lə́nu 'an ordinary man' (KJV "a man")
   ləní·i-ahɔ·p·e·ɔ́·k·an 'ordinary wealth'
   ləní·i-awé·ni·k 'Delaware Indians at Anadarko' (V; *lit.*, 'ordinary people'; cf. 5.37c)
(b) maya·í·i PN 'true':
   maya·í·i-ahɔ·p·e·ɔ́·k·an 'true wealth' (B ⟨myaei⟩ 1x; cf. 5.120e)

(5.122) Prenouns from noun stems and -í·i PF
(a) ahpɔ·ní·i PN 'of bread' (< ahpɔ́·n 'bread'):
   ahpɔ·ní·i-pá·ste·k 'yeast for bread'
(b) a·məwe·í·i PN 'of bees' (< á·məwe 'bee'):
   a·məwe·í·i-šó·k·əl 'honey (*lit.*, bee sugar)'
(c) ləpwe·ɔ·k·aní·i PN 'of knowledge' (< ləpwe·ɔ́·k·an 'knowledge'):
   ləpwe·ɔ·k·aní·i-tunkše·kɔ́·k·an 'the key of knowledge'
(d) mahtant·o·wí·i PN 'of the devil or devils' (< mahtántu 'devil'):
   mahtant·o·wí·i-sa·k·í·ma 'Chief of the Devils' (cf. 5.122h)
(e) mhukwí·i PN 'of blood' (< mhúkw 'blood'):
   mhukwí·i-hák·i 'the land of blood'
(f) mɔnií·i PN 'of money; of silver' (< mɔ́ni 'money'):
   mɔnií·i-nó·t·e·s 'money bag'
(g) ɔpahsəní·i PN 'of white stone' (< *ɔpahsən 'white stone', translating 'alabaster'):
   ɔpahsəní·i-hákhakw 'white-stone bottle'
   ɔpahsəní·i-si·k·á·xkwtət 'white-stone box'
(h) sa·k·i·ma·í·i PN 'of chief, king' (< sa·k·í·ma 'chief, king'):
   sa·k·i·ma·í·i-lehələmatahpínkink 'on thrones' (i.e., royal chairs)
   sa·k·i·ma·í·i-mahtant·ó·wa 'the king of devils (obv.)' (cf. 5.122d)
(i) si·skəwí·i PN 'of clay' (< sí·sku 'mud, clay'):
   si·skəwí·i-hó·s·ak 'clay pots' (also si·skəwahó·s·ak [B; sg. 5.42d])
(j) wəla·məwe·ɔ·k·aní·i PN 'of truth' (< wəla·məwe·ɔ́·k·an 'truth'):
   wəla·məwe·ɔ·k·aní·i-manə́t·u 'the truth spirit'

(5.123) Prenouns from lexicalized participles and -í·i PF
(a) ehaləmo·k·wənak·aí·i PN 'of eternity' (< e·ləmo·k·wənák·a 'eternal; for eternity' [II]):
   ehaləmo·k·wənak·aí·i-pəma·wsəwá·k·anink táli 'in eternal life'

(b) ehalo·ka·ləntí·i PN 'of the messenger' (< ehalo·ká·lənt 'messenger', *lit.*, 'one sent'):
ehalo·ka·ləntí·i-mənəp·e·kwtə́t·ink 'the pool of the messenger (loc.)'
(c) enkələk·í·i PN 'of the dead' (< énkələk 'one who is dead', pl. enkəlák·i·k):
enkələk·í·i-xkána ó·k 'the bones of the dead'
(d) ke·kayəmhe·t·í·i PN 'of the ruler(s)' (< ke·kayə́mhe·t 'ruler', used variously):
ke·kayəmhe·t·í·i-a·pto·ná·k·an 'the laws of the rulers'
(e) ke·tanət·o·wi·t·í·i PN 'of God' (< ke·tanət·ó·wi·t 'God', *lit.*, 'one who is the great spirit'):
ke·tanət·o·wi·t·í·i-awé·n 'a person of God'
ke·tanət·o·wi·t·í·i-pa·tamwe·i·k·á·ɔnink 'the temple of God (loc.)'
(f) lo·winkí·i PN 'of the Passover' (< ló·wink 'Passover'
< |lōwī-| AI 'pass through', |(IC)–nk| X/CC):
lo·winkí·i-mekí·t·ət 'the Passover lamb'
(g) nehəla·lkɔnkwí·i PN 'of our lord, of the Lord' (< nehəla·lkɔnkw 'our Lord'
< |nīhlāl-| TA 'own, be master of', |IC–əkwankw| 3–12/PPL(ANsg)):
nehəla·lkɔnkwí·i-wi·k·əwáhəmink 'the Lord's house'
nehəla·lkɔnkwí·i-ehalo·ká·lənt 'an angel (*lit.*, messenger) of the Lord'

(5.124) Prenoun from locative noun or particle
(a) mpinkí·i PN (< mpínk 'in the water' < mpí 'water' + |-ənk| loc.):
mpinkí·i-xkó·k 'water snake' (OA)
(b) ɔ·s·ahkame·í·i PN 'of heaven' (< ɔ·s·áhkame P '(in) heaven'):
ɔ·s·ahkame·í·i-sa·k·i·ma·ɔ́·k·an 'the kingdom of heaven' (cf 5.126b)

(5.125) Prenouns from verb stems with |-w| NF
(a) ala·x·i·məwí·i PN 'of resting' (< |alāxīmwī-| AI 'rest', 3s ala·x·í·mu):
ala·x·i·məwí·i-kí·škwi·k 'day of rest' (B; also ala·x·i·məwe·í·i PN, rhyme of 5.124b)
(b) manunksəwí·i PN 'of being angry' (< |manōnkəsī-| AI 'be angry', 3s manúnksu):
manunksəwí·i-ki·škúwal 'days of anger' (B; kí·šku 'day', pl. kí·škúwa(l))
(c) no·t·amensəwí·i PN 'of fishing' (< |nōtamēnsī-| AI 'fish (with a spear)'):
wəno·t·amensəwí·i-hémpəs 'his fisherman's shirt' (B; hémpəs 'shirt'; |wə–∅| 'his')
(d) tahkɔp·o·ha·ltəwí·i PN 'of being married, of wedding' (< |takwapōhālətī-|; AI 5.113c):
tahkɔp·o·ha·ltəwí·i-lač·e·s·əwá·k·an 'wedding garb' (B; lač·e·s·əwá·k·an 'clothing')

(5.126) Derived particles matching prenouns with -í·i PF
(a) payaxkhi·k·aní·i P 'of gun' (< payaxkhí·k·an 'gun'):
mpúnkum payaxkhi·k·aní·i 'my gunpowder' (OA; púnkw 'powder', |nə–əm| 'my')
(b) ɔ·s·ahkame·í·i P 'of heaven' (cf 5.124b):
sa·k·i·ma·ɔ́·k·an ɔ·s·ahkame·í·i 'the kingdom of heaven' (B; cf. 5.124b)
(c) ke·tanət·o·wi·t·í·i P 'of God' (cf. 5.123e):
ná lə́nu takó· ke·tanət·o·wi·t·í·i 'That man is not of God.' (B; ná 'that (anim.)';
lə́nu 'man'; takó· NEG)
(d) ahtuhwí·i P 'of deer' (< ahtú |atəhw| 'deer'):
ahtuhwí·i ná xé·s 'the hide (I use) is a deerhide' (*lit.*, 'of deer')' (OA; ná 'that (anim.)',
xé·s 'hide')
(e) ala·x·i·məwí·i P 'of rest' (cf. 5.125a):
ala·x·i·məwí·i=tá yúkwe kí·šku 'today is the day of rest' (B; =tá FOC; yúkwe 'now,
today'; kí·šku 'day' [5.125b])

(5.127) Prenoun in -í·i PF with a derived noun (equivalent to a particle with the underlying verb)
  (a) ki·mí·i PN 'secret' < ki·mí·i P 'secretly':
    ki·mí·i-wi·penke·ó·k·an 'unfaithfulness, adultery' (B 2x); also without this:
      wi·penke·ó·k·an 'adultery' (B 1x; < |wīhpēnkē-| AI 'sleep with someone' [5.59c])

§5.9b. Compound Verbs. Preverbs are derived from initials, which may themselves be derived. A large number of preverbs based on underived initials have -i PF, but a few end in -a or -í·i PF. Some preverbs are derived from nouns or verbs with -í·i PF in the same way that prenouns are derived.

One group of preverbs has grammatical functions, being used in certain constructions or as the equivalent of a higher verb taking the head verb as a complement (5.128).

A preverb may be separated from the head verb or another preverb by an enclitic or other word that is not a preverb. This is especially true of the more abstract preverbs that mark subordinate clauses (5.128enpx).

(5.128) Preverbs with grammatical functions
  (a) ála PV 'cease' (2.74a):
    ála-kšáx·ən 'the wind quit blowing' (B, ME)
    ála- kéku -lúwe· 'he stopped talking' (ME)
    ála-=hunt -aós·u 'he got warmed up enough' (ME)
  (b) áləmi PV 'begin, start; continuing, away' (ntáləmi 1, tóləmi 3; with IC é·ləmi):
    áləmi-mahta·ptó·ne· 'he began to swear' (B)
    áləmi-kčí·l. 'Go on out!' (V)
    áləmi-pó·o·p 'she became pregnant' (B)
    ná tóləmi-kči·né·ɔ 'then they went out' (B)
    ná tóləmi-čə́p·wi·n 'then he disappeared off into the crowd' (B)
    ná tóləmi-lá·n 'then he continued, saying to them ...' (B)
    é·ləmi-ló·wank 'this winter' (OA)
  (c) ápi PV 'come from, have done, have been':
    ápi-mi·kəmɔ·s·i·lí·t·e 'when he (obv.) comes from his work' (B)
    ápi-hakí·he· 'he got through making a garden' (OA)
    e·lkí·kwi- .. -ápi-ne·ykwə́s·i·t 'at the time when he has appeared' (B)
  (d) á·lai PV (younger á·la) 'be unable to':
    mé·či á·lai- íka -lo·x·ɔlahtí·t·e 'after they had been unable to bring him to him' (B)
    tá=á· tó·lai-lǝs·í·wən 'he would not be unable to do it' (B)
    tó·la-ne·ɔwwá·ɔ 'they saw him no more' (*lit.*, 'could not see him') (B)
    á·la-né·ma 'he can't see' (LB)
    á·la-wí·x·ənu 'she is having her period' (*lit.*, 'she can't cook') (LB)
  (e) énta PV (with IC; younger ə́nta) 'when' (in a changed conjunct or changed subjunctive verb; see **§4.6b**):
    énta-ahke·kínke·t 'when he was teaching' (B)
    énta-ahke·kinke·á·ne 'when I was teaching' (B)
    énta- íka -pá·t 'when he arrived there' (V)
    ə́nta-pí·ske·k 'after dark' (OA)
    ə́nta-ne·wə́nte 'when he was seen' (ME)
  (f) éntxən PV (with IC) 'every time' (in a changed conjunct):
    éntxən-ó·p·ank 'every morning, every day' (B, ME)

  éntxən-náxi-kahtínk 'every three years' (OA)
  éntxən-kahtá-məné·t mpí 'every time he wanted to drink some water' (V)
  éntxən-wé·t·ənink 'every time he picked it up' (ME)
(g) éši PV 'every (time that), whenever' (in a changed conjunct):
  éši-kí·škwi·k 'every day' (B)
  éši-tpəskwíhəla·k 'whenever it is the right time' (B)
  éši-ɔ́·p·ank 'every morning' (ND)
(h) káhta PV 'want to, be keen to, be about to' (nkát·a 1, kɔ́t·a 3, with IC ké·t·a):
  káhta-áləmi-ála-hat·é·k·e hák·i 'when the world is about to cease to exist' (B)
  káhta-ki·š·əná·kwsi·kw 'be keen to be ready (you pl.)' (B)
  nkát·a-na·pənála 'I'm going to go over and get after him' (OA)
  tɔ́ləmi-káhta-čani·lae·ma·né·ɔ 'they began to seek to provoke him' (B)
  ké·t·a-lɔ́s·ian 'what you intend to do' (B)
(i) káski PV 'be able to' (with |Rī+| EXT [§5.4e]: ki·kski):
  ná=nə šúkw nkáski-ləs·í·ne·n. 'That's just what we were able to do.' (B)
  káski-lé·k·e 'if it were possible' (B; |əlē-| II 'be {so}')
  akɔ́· káski-ála-mi·tsí·i. 'He couldn't stop eating.' (OA)
  máta kí·kski-pəmɔ́ska·t 'one never able to walk' (B)
(j) khwíta PV 'be afraid to' (kkwí·ta 3):
  kkwí·ta-nto·xtaɔ·né·ɔ 'they were afraid to ask him about it' (B)
  é·li-khwíta-khwíle·kw mo·x·wé·t·ət 'because you're afraid to swallow a little bug' (B)
(k) kíši PV 'have (done)' (nkíši 1, kwíši 3, with IC kíši):
  kwət·ennáɔhki nkíši-ləs·i 'I have done one thing' (B)
  mé·či kkíši-lələné·ɔ 'I have already told you' (B)
  mé·či kwíši-li·ha·né·ɔ 'they have already done it to him' (B)
  kíši- nɔ́ -luwé·t·e 'after he (she) said that' (B)
(l) kwčí PV 'try to, try and' (nkwə́či 1, kkwə́či 2,3):
  awé·n kwčí-wwa·tá·k·we 'if anyone tries to know it' (B 1842)
  kkwə́či- íka -lo·x·ɔlawwá·ɔ 'they tried to bring him to him' (B)
  nkwə́či-ma·e·ná·ak 'I tried to gather them up' (ME)
  nkát·a-kwčí-ntɔ́·ma 'I'm trying to call him' (OA)
(m) ləkhíkwi PV '{so} much; at {such} time' (ntəlkí·kwi 1, təlkí·kwi 3, with IC e·lkí·kwi):
  nɔ́ ləkhíkwi-ki·š·əná·kwsi·kw 'be ready to that extent (you pl.)' (B)
  ktəlkí·kwi-ahɔlləné·ɔ 'I love you (that) much' (B)
  e·lkí·kwi-a·p·əwát·ək 'how easy it is' (B)
  e·lkí·kwi-mahta·wsíhti·t 'how sinful they were' (B)
  e·lkí·kwi-ahɔ́·lat khák·ay 'as much as you love yourself' (B)
  e·lkí·kwi-təmšá·s·i·k 'the time when they are reaped' (B)
  ehələkhíkwi-ma·éhɔ·t 'at the times when she gathers them' (B)
(n) lí PV '{so}', 'to {smwh}' (ntə́li 1, tə́li 3, with IC é·li):
  mux·ó·link lí-pó·s·o·p 'he went aboard a boat' (B; 3.13(1)b)
  hák·ink lí-məšá·ke·kw. 'Sit down on the ground (you pl.)!' (B)
  íka ntə́li-ktə́k·i wé·ma. 'I'm going back where I came from.' (B)
  ɔ·ká·i=č ntə́li-mó·nhɔ 'I'll dig around it' (B)

In a changed conjunct:
  é·li-kí·ɔla·t ləna·p·é·ɔ 'for he deceives the people' (B)
  é·li-lə́le·kw wəla·məwe·ɔ́·k·an 'because I tell you the truth' (B)
  é·li-wəlá·ta·kw xinkɔnší·k·an 'since he had a sword' (B)
  ko·x·əwa·únka é·li-nhilahtí·t·əp 'it was your forefathers that killed them' (B)
With a subordinative complement:
  lí-nhíla·n '(he sent orders) for them to be killed'
  ná=č ɔ́·k nə́ .. lí-áspəna·n 'that is how he shall be lifted up'
  nčí·sas=tá ntəli-ki·k·éhko·n. 'It was Jesus that cured me.'
  məšá·ke· təli-=á· -mí·tsi·n 'he sat down to eat'

(o) mái PV 'go to, go and' (nəmái 1, mɔ́i 3, with IC mé·i):
  mái-mhálamo·k mi·č·əwá·k·an 'they went to buy food' (B)
  nəmái-tó·kəna 'I go to wake him up' (B)
  nə́ pɔ·né·ɔ, mái-čhɔ·pwəná·ɔk 'they came there, coming to be baptized' (B)
  lí-=á· -mái-ki·k·e·há·li·n 'so that he (obv.) would be cured (by the one going there)' (B)
  é·li- .. -péči-mái-lehəle·x·e·mhá·la·t 'for he came to save them' (B)
  énta-mái-thwə́nie·kw 'when you (pl.) came to arrest me' (B; 4.61f)
  kéku=háč mé·i-pənáme·kw? 'What did you (pl.) go to see?' (B)

(p) né·li PV 'as, while' (with changed conjunct) (B):
  né·li-kaí·t 'while he slept' (B)
  né·li-pa·tamá·t·əp 'while he was praying' (B)
  né·li-se·níhi·t 'as he sowed' (B)
  né·li-ala·x·i·məwí·i-kí·škwi·k 'during the day of rest' (B)
  né·li-máhči-lə́s·ian 'when you are evil; given that you are evil' (B)
  né·li- máta -pé·ha·t 'while he is not waiting for him' (B)

(q) péči PV 'come to, come and':
  péči-təmi·k·e·lí·t·e 'when she (obv.) came in' (B)
  péči-pənas·ihtí·t·e 'when they came down from the height' (B)
  péči-kčí·l! 'come out!' (B)
  kpéči-lúkw 'he sends you this message (as follows)' (B)
  pwéči-né·ma·n 'and he came back seeing' (B)

(r) pɔ́·i PV 'be unable to':
  tá=á· kéku kpɔ́·i-ləs·i·húmɔ. 'Nothing would be impossible for you to do.' (B)
  é·li- .. máta -pɔ́·i- kéku -lə́s·i·t. 'Since nothing is impossible for him to do.' (B)

(s) sháki PV '{so long} (a time)' (ksá·ki 2, sɔ́·ki 3, with IC sé·ki; |sahkī| [3.13(6), 5.28h]):
  kwə́t·i á·wəlink šúkw sháki-mi·kəmɔ́·s·əwak 'they only worked for one hour' (B)
  tá=háč ksá·ki-witahpi·mələné·ɔ. 'How long will I be with you?' (B)
  ná=nə sɔ́·ki- .. -ahkwe·č·íhko·n 'for that long he (obv.) tempted him' (B)

(t) šínki PV 'not want to, refuse to':
  šínki-kələ́ksu 'he didn't want to laugh' (V)
  kšínki-lé·ləmi 'you refused to let me' (B)
  šínki-kələsta·k·wé·k·we ma·e·x·we·é·k·we 'if he refuses to listen to you (pl.)' (B)

(u) táli PV '{smwh}' (ntə́nta 1, tə́nta 3, with IC énta [more recent ɔ́nta]) :
  kɔ́čəmink táli-pa·tamá·p·ani·k 'they were praying outside' (B)
  ehə́nta-ma·éhəlank ntə́nta-pəmət·ó·nhe 'I preached in synagogues' (B)
  ná=č=nə́ ntə́nta-ne·yko·né·ɔ. 'That's where they will see me.' (B)

énta-ma·ehəláhti·t 'where they gathered' (B)

íka énta-ma·ehəlá·či·k 'the people (who were) gathered there' (B)

énta-luwentá·s·i·k xkanántpink 'a place called "Skull Place"' (B; *lit.*, 'where it is named "At the Skull"'; |ələwēntāsī-| II 'be named {so}')

(v) tépi PV 'be able to, be capable of, be fit to, be enough (to)':

ntépi-=tá -ləs·í·ne·n. 'We can.' (B)

tépi-=á· šúkw -pahkí·to·n. 'It would only be fit to be thrown away.' (B)

tépi-ləs·i·t 'one who is capable' (B)

tépi-=á· ahsən -pe·t·á·henk ləkhíkwi 'the distance that a stone could be thrown' (B)

é·li- máta -tépi-ləs·í·ɔ 'as I am not worthy enough' (B)

(w) txí PV '{so many}, {so much}' (ntəntxi 1, ktəntxi 2, təntxi 3, with IC éntxi; |(-ən)taxī|):

ihikalíči lápi txí-məné·w. 'He drinks a little more each time.' (B 1834b:8; ihikalíči 'a little more repeatedly'; lápi 'again')

kwət·a·š txí-kahtənámu 'he's six years old' (OA; kwət·a·š 'six')

tá=č=háč ktəntxi-mi·li·né·ɔ 'how much will you (pl.) give me?' (B)

aləwí·i·=č ntəntxi-məšənəmúhəna. 'We will get more.' (B)

ná=ní təntxi-maya·ɔ·č·í·mwi·n 'that is how much he testifies to' (B)

éntxi-=č awé·n -wé·t·ənink xinkənší·k·an 'as many people as shall take up the sword' (B)

éntxi-ne·óhti·t 'as many (obv.) as they saw' (|IC–āhətīt| 3p–3´/PPL(OBL)) (B)

éntxi-mi·liáni·k 'as many (anim.) as you gave me' (|IC–əyanīk| 2s–1s/PPL(ANpl)) (B)

wé·mi éntxi-lóle·kw 'everything I told you to do' (|IC–əlēkw| 1s–2p/PPL(OBL)) (B)

(x) wənči PV 'from {smwh}' (núnči 1 [later nəwənči], wwənči 3, with IC wénči, wənči):

íka wənči-kčí·ɔk 'they went out from there' (B)

ankələwá·k·anink=č wənči-á·mwi· 'he will rise up from death' (B)

tépi wənči-nhíla·n. 'It's enough reason for him to be killed.' (B)

nəni wwənči-luwe·né·ɔ 'because of that they said ...' (B)

kəwínki-=háč=á· -wənči-ánkələn ní·? 'Would you be willing to die for me?' (B)

tá=háč=á· wənči-lé·w? 'how would it happen?' (B)

wénči-pí·lhik 'because of which it is holy' (B)

wənči-=č .. -wəla·mhítame·kw 'so that .. you (pl.) will believe it' (B)

ná=nə núnči-pá·n 'that is the very reason why I came' (B)

palé·naxk íka núnči-pa·tá·tu 'I have earned five from them' (B)

tá=háč kúnči-wwá·hi·n? 'How come you (sg.) know me?' (B)

nánə nəwənči-li·t·é·ha·n 'that's why I think ...' (OA)

(y) wínki PV 'like to, want to, be willing to':

nəwínki-ánkəl 'I am willing to die' (B)

wwínki-ne·ɔwwá·p·ani 'they were glad to see him' (B)

takó· wwínki-məné·wən 'he did not want to drink it' (B)

é·li- .. -wínki-=á· -laxəna·t 'as he would be willing to release him' (B)

Preverbs that do not have grammatical functions have a wide range of meanings, often matching initials and free particles. In cases where homonymous preverbs and particles are known, or when there are no occurrences with a prefix or initial change, the part of speech of a particular word may be uncertain. Some preverbs appear to be restricted to use with very few verbs (e.g., 5.129t) or with an empty verb that essentially makes a verb from a particle (|ələsī-|

AI, |əlē-| II 'be {so}'; e.g. 5.129hu). Some preverbs are essentially prenouns that have become preverbs secondarily in compound verbs derived from compound nouns (5.130).

(5.129) Other underived preverbs (asterisked forms are not attested without a prefix)
    (a) áhi PV 'very' (5.28a; examples: 4.21cq, 4.38h, 4.39n, 4.63k, 4.68kl, 5.75js):
        áhi-wi·š·á·s·əwak 'they were very frightened' (B)
    (b) ahpá·mi* PV 'around, about' (pup·á·mi 3; cf. ahpá·mi P):
        pup·á·mi-ahke·kínke·n 'he goes around teaching (there)'
    (c) aláx·i* PV 'empty' (tólxi 3; cf. aláx·at II 'it is empty'):
        tólxi- palí·i -ləskaó·ɔl 'he sent the rich away empty'
    (d) aləwí·i PV 'more, to a greater degree, further':
        aləwí·i-lás·u 'he is greater', aləwí·i-lé· 'it is more, it is greater'
        aləwí·i-wəlát 'it is better'
    (e) ánči PV 'more, over again':
        ánči-é· 'he went on further'
        káski-ánči-məšá·kwsu 'he can attain a greater height'
        ánči-mi·lí·ne·n nhaka·t·amwe·ó·k·an 'give us more faith'
        ntánči- mpí íka -laníhi·n 'I add some more water in it' (OA)
        lápi ánči-skás·əma· 'he relit his pipe' (ME; lápi 'again')
    (f) a·p·a·č·i* PV 'in return' (kta·p·a·č·i 2):
        tá=á· kta·p·a·č·i- kéku -li·húmɔ 'you won't speak to me in return'
    (g) á·p·əwi PV 'easily':
        á·p·əwi-sá·k·ən 'it easily sprouted'
    (h) čáni PV 'wrong'
        nčáni-lás·i 'I have done wrong'
    (i) čípi PV (pl. ahčípi) 'bad, dangerous' (cf. 5.120a)
        čípi-lé· 'it is dangerous, it is a bad situation, it is powerful' (B, ME)
        ə́nta-ahčípi-lə·k, -ahčípi-ləs·íhti·t awé·ni·k 'when evil things happened and people were evil' (OA: "bad things")
    (j) čí·t·ani PV 'strong'
        é·li- tɔ·pto·ná·k·an -čí·t·ani-lé·k 'as his words had power'
        čí·t·ani-kəle·lə́ntamo·kw 'hold it firmly in your minds' (B)
    (k) čə́čpi PV 'different from each other' (čpi P 'different')
        čə́čpi-luwé·ɔk 'they gave differing accounts'
        lí-čə́čpi-lé· wé·mi yú táli 'that different things are happening all over here'
    (l) hápi PV 'in addition, along with (it)' (ktá·pi 2; cf. hápi P 'in addition')
        ktá·pi=č yó·l wé·mi -mi·lkwəs·i·né·ɔ. 'You (pl.) will be given all these things in addition.'
        é·li=á· tá·mse .. -hápi-phwə́nəme·kw nə́ hwí·t 'for you (pl.) could sometimes pull up the wheat with them'
    (m) hítami PV 'first' (wəní·tami 3, with IC né·tami; cf. hítami P)
        wəní·tami-kánši- kéku -laehɔ·s·í·ne·p 'he performed his first miracle'
        né·tami-mi·kəmɔ·s·í·č·i·k 'the first workers'
    (n) káhti PV 'almost' (also kahtí; nkáti 1 [2.74d])
        káhti-we·kwi·há·ɔk 'they almost killed them all' (OA)
        nkáti-nhíla 'I pretty near killed him' (OA)

(o) kánši PV 'marvelous, wonderful'
    kkánši-li·namúhəna 'we have seen something wonderful'
    kánši-ləs·í·t·əp 'who did marvelous things'

(p) kší PV 'quickly, hard' (nkə́ši 1, kwə́ši 3)
    nkə́ši-pahkántamən 'I hit it hard' (OA)
    ná kwə́ši-lí·x·i·n 'then he quickly came down' (B)

(q) ktəmáki PV 'pitifully, woefully, miserably, in torment' (nkət·əmáki 1)
    ktəmáki-lí·nam 'a miserable fate befalls him' (B)
    nkət·əmáki-lə́s·i 'I'm living a pitiful life' (OA)

(r) kwə́ni PV 'long' (with |Ra+| PL: ahkó·ni [kkək·ó·ni 2])"
    kwə́ni-pí·ske· 'it's been dark for some time' (ME)
    ə́nta-kwə́ni-tpó·kwi·k 'when the nights are long' (OA)
    ahkó·ni-lehəle·x·é·p·ani·k 'they lived long' (B 1842:20)
    kkək·ó·ni-=hánkw -pa·tamáhəmɔ 'you (pl.) always say long prayers' (B)

(s) kwí·la PV 'at a loss; in a quandary'
    kwí·la-le·lə́ntam 'he didn't know what to do' (B)
    kwí·la-lə́s·əwak 'they were at a loss' (B)
    nkwí·la- kéku -xáma 'I have nothing to feed him' (B)

(t) lá·i PV 'in the middle':
    lá·i-tpó·ku 'it is midnight'

(u) ló·wi PV 'past'
    ló·wi-lé· II 'it is past, it is over' (B)

(v) máhči PV 'bad' (kəmáči 2, with IC méči; pl. amáči [/č/ LB])
    máhči-lí·namo·p 'he had bad fortune' (B)
    máhči-ləs·í·t·e 'if he is evil' (B; máhči [V, OA])
    kəmáči-lə́s·i 'you are evil' (B)
    né·l méči-wi·č·əmúkwki 'the one who behaved badly in helping him' (B)
    amáči-luk·wé·k·we 'if they say bad things to you' (B)

(w) mayá·i PV 'right, as should be, exactly'
    kəmayá·i-lə́s·i 'you did just what you were supposed to'
    ntə́li-mayá·i-lə́s·i·n 'that I do it exactly'
    kəmayá·i-lúwe 'you speak plainly'
    me·á·i-ləs·i·tpáni·k 'ones who were properly behaved (i.e., virgins)'

(x) mə́si PV 'all' (mwə́si 3)
    mə́si-é·p 'he went all over' (B)
    nəmə́si-lí·ha 'I tease him' (*lit.*, 'I do everything to him') (OA)
    mwə́si- kéku -lənəməné·ɔ 'they are doing everything' (OA)

(y) nalái* PV 'peacefully' (cf. Mun naláwi· P 'peacefully')
    nnálai-ánkələn 'that I die peacefully' (B)

(z) náxi PV 'three'
    náxi-kahtənámu 'he's three years old' (OA)

(aa) náxpi PV 'with O2'
    kənáxpi-=hánkw -ke·na·mwi·né·ɔ 'you (pl.) give thanks with them' (B)
    nóxpi-nhaké·wsi·n 'she sought help with (i.e., by spending) it' (B)
    né·xpi-pə́ntame·kw 'what you hear it with' (B)

(bb) né·wi PV 'four'
  né·wi-puhé·e· 'it has four rooms' (OA)
  éntxən-né·wi-kahtínk 'every four years' (OA; |katən-| II 'be year(s)')
(cc) níši PV 'two; two together'
  níši-kahtənámu 'he is two years old' (OA)
  níši-ki·škwí·k·e 'after two days' (B)
  níši-kɔhɔ·k·é·ɔk 'the two of them pound corn in a mortar together' (B)
(dd) nó·čkwe PV 'freely'
  kənó·čkwe-milləné·ɔ 'I gave it to you freely' (B; ⟨knwhi⟩, confused with the next)
(ee) nú·či PV 'since, starting from' (ni·núči PV 'for a long time')
  náxi-kahtən nnúči-máhəmai-pənáɔ 'I have been coming to look at it (anim.) for three years' (B)
  nə́ wənúči-ke·nahkí·ha·n 'from then on he took care of her' (B)
  wəni·núči-káhta-ne·ó·p·ani 'he had wanted to see him for a long time' (B)
(ff) ɔ·wtámi PV 'slow'
  é·li-ɔ·wtámi-pəna·eləntamíhti·t 'as they were slow in thought' (B)
(gg) pahkánči PV 'exactly, completely, perfectly'
  pahkánči-lé· 'it happens exactly, is fulfilled, comes true'
(hh) só·mi PV 'too much'
  só·mi-áhi-sak·we·ləntam 'it (anim.) is extremely troubled' (B)
  só·mi-kanše·ləntamo·k 'they were so astonished (that ...)' (B)
(ii) tankíti PV 'little'
  ktankíti-nhake·wsíhəmɔ 'you (pl.) have little faith' (B)
(jj) tpə́skwi PV 'like'
  tpə́skwi-lé· 'it was like' (B; with subordinative or participial complement)
(kk) txí PV '{so many}' (used as an empty placeholder for the numbers above 'four')
  áləmi- ahpá·mi xí·nxke -txí-kahtənamo·p 'he began to be about thirty years old' (B)
(ll) wé·mi PV 'all'
  kəwé·mi-məši·ka·k·ó·ne·n 'it came over all of us' (B)
(mm) wé·t·ami PV (with IC) 'be busy with'
  wé·t·ami-mái-mhalamɔ·s·íhti·t 'while they were occupied with going to buy' (B; 4.61c)
(nn) wə́li PV 'well, carefully, good' (nó·li 1, ó·li 3, with IC wé·li)
  nə́ni wə́li-wwa·taé·k·we 'if you know that well' (B)
  wə́li- kéku -káski-né·m 'he could see things well' (B)
  nó·li-ke·nahkí·to·n 'I took good care of it' (B)
  ó·li-nto·t·əmaɔ́·p·ani·l 'he carefully asked them' (B)
  wé·li-ləs·i·t awé·n 'a good person' (B)
(oo) wə́ski PV 'newly, anew' (with IC wé·ski and wə́ski)
  máta lápi wə́ski-ki·š·i·k·í·t·e 'if he is not born again anew'
  wé·ski-ki·š·í·k·i·t 'the new-born one' (B)
  né·l wə́ski-ne·ma·lí·č·i 'the newly seeing one (obv.)' (B)
(pp) wiáki PV 'abundantly' (with intensifier |-ask-|: weyákski [with IC]; B ⟨wceukski⟩)
  wiáki-mí·č·əwak ahpɔ́·n 'they have plenty of bread to eat'
  weyákski-wi·k·inké·č·i·k 'ones who are promiscuous' (KJV "adulterers")
(qq) wíči PV 'along with the other or others' (5.99abcgh)
  né·pe=č nəwíči- íka -ahpí. 'I shall also be present, too.' [→]

wé·mi wíči-wəle·ləntamó·p·ani·k. 'they were all happy along with her.' (5.99c)
kəwíči-=č -a·mwi·mkúwa 'she will rise up along with you'
- (rr) wi·šíki PV 'working hard at'
wi·šíki-wə́li-no·tí·k·e·t 'the one working hard at watching the house' (B)
kéhəla ke·xennáɔhki kəwi·šíki-lami·kəmɔ́·s·i 'you work hard at quite a few things' (B)
- (ss) xínkwi PV 'big', also maxínkwi (pl. amánki); cf. 5.120j
xínkwi-mi·tsahtúwak 'they had a great feast' (B)
énta-xínkwi-mpí·i·k 'in the ocean', *lit.* 'where the big water is' (V, ME)
máta=á· maxínkwi-ahčinkxá·t·e 'if he were not disobedient in a major way' (B)
kəmax·ínkwi-čanəstamúhəmɔ 'you (pl.) greatly misunderstand' (B)
me·x·ínkwi-ləs·i·t 'the mighty one' (B)
amánki-=hánkw -má·whwi·n. 'There were big dances.' (V;
 cf. má·whi·n 'there is a (stomp) dance' [OA, AP])
énta-amánki-mpí·i·k 'in the oceans' (V)

(5.130) Preverb from prenoun
- (a) ní·ski-manət·ó·wi·t 'an unclean spirit' (*lit.*, 'the one who is an unclean spirit') (B);
< ní·ski-manə́t·u 'an unclean spirit'

(5.131) Preverb from free particle
- (a) kémələk kəməmsəč·é·i-khwilawwá·ɔk 'you swallow camels whole' (B);
< məsəč·é·i P 'whole, all'

(5.132) Preverbs from verb stems
- (a) ši·e·ləntaməwí·i PV 'sorrowfully'
nni·núči-ši·e·ləntaməwí·i-nto·no·lhúməna 'we've been sorrowfully looking for you forever' (B) < ši·e·lə́ntam 'he is sorrowful, sad, upset'
- (b) ahke·kho·t·əwí·i PV
e·lkí·kwi-ahke·kho·t·əwí·i-kí·škwi·k 'at the time of the day of judgment' (B);
< |akēhkahw-| TA 'separate out, select' (ntak·é·khɔ 'I picked him out';
énta-ahke·khó·t·ink 'in court, *lit.*, where people are judged')

§5.9c. Particle Compounds. In a particle compound the preparticle modifies the head particle. The two components are semantically linked, but each has the shape of a free particle. They thus differ structurally from compound nouns and verbs, in which the two components are different parts of speech. It is also the case, however, that a preparticle may modify a prenoun: áhi-ní·ski-kéku 'a very foul thing' (with ní·ski PN; B). Here áhi-ní·ski 'very foul' behaves like a prenoun, though derived from a particle compound.

The prewords in (5.133) are static words (**§2.15**). The number words (2.75) contrast with non-static particles that are used attributively: kwə́t·i kí·škwe 'one day (ago)' (OA, LB); ní·š·a kí·škwe 'two days (ago)' (OA).

(5.133) Particle compounds
- (a) áhi PP 'very (much):
áhi-alap·a·í·i 'very early in the morning' (B)
áhi-hwə́ska 'extremely' (B; hwə́ska 'very, extremely')
áhi-kwə́la 'I greatly wish' (with subordinative complement) (B)
áhi-nihəláči 'completely on his own' (B)
áhi-wə́li 'in a very good way' (B)
áhi-xé·li 'a great many' (B)

(b) kéxi PP 'a few, several' (matching ké·x·a P 'a few, several; how many?'):
   kéxi-kahtəné·e 'for a few years' (OA), 'for several years' (ME)
   mé·či kéxi-kí·škwe 'over the last few days' (B; mé·či 'now, already')
(c) kwə́ni PP 'for the length of'
   kwə́ni-kí·škwe 'all day' (OA)
   kwə́ni-kí·š·ukw 'during the day' (B)
   kwə́ni-tpó·kw 'during the night, all night long' (B)
(d) kwə́ti PP 'the whole (period of time)'; archaic nkwə́ti (matching kwə́t·i P 'one')
   kwə́ti-kí·škwe 'all day' (B, V, OA, ME, LB)
   nkwə́ti-kí·škwe 'all day long' (B 1x)
   kwə́ti-tpó·kwe 'all night' (B 1x)
(e) náxi PP 'three' (matching naxá P)
   náxi-kí·škwe 'in three days' (B 6x)
   náxi-kí·škwe 'for three days' (B)
   náxi-tpó·kəwe 'for three nights' (B)
(f) níši PP 'two' (matching ní·š·a P)
   níši-phake·í·i 'two pieces (of something)' (ME)
(g) txí PP '{so many}' (used as a placeholder for the numbers above 'four'; cf. 5.129kk)
   kwə́t·a·š txí-kí·škwe 'for six days' (B 1842)
   ní·š·a·š txi-kí·škwe 'in seven days' (B).
   ní·š·a·š txí-kahtəné·i 'for seven years' (B)
   palé·naxk txí-ki·š·ó·x·unk 'for five months' (B)

6. Sentence Structure

§6. In this section various topics relating to the structure of sentences are described and exemplified.

§6.1. Kinds of Sentences. Sentences express predications, in a broad sense, which may be positive, negative, interrogative, or imperative. They may be verbal sentences, with a verbal predicate, but there are also substantive and equational sentences, which are verbless predications.

Sentences may combine as the clauses of a complex sentence. In complex sentences, the central predication is the main clause, and its verb (if it has one) is the main verb. The clause of a verb that is nominalized (as a participle) is treated syntactically as a noun phrase, which may be attributive to another noun. The clauses other than the main clause that are not nominalized are subordinate clauses, which may be conditional clauses (including temporal clauses and purpose clauses) or complements of various kinds.

The order of elements in a sentence is not entirely free, but it is variable. Outside of some cases where there are fixed or very strong preferences, the order of words may have a discourse function, determined by, for example, emphasis, givenness, or topicality (focus). Also, it is characteristic of components, including compounds, that they may be discontinuous (**§6.6**), in which case they are interspersed with words that are not part of them. Such discontinuous constituents effectively scramble the word order of components.

§6.2. Sentence Components. The words in a sentence are nouns, verbs, and particles (which may be compounds), and a word of any type may be the head of a phrase: a noun phrase, a verbal phrase, or a particle phrase. A noun phrase has a noun, overt pronoun, or other nominal and its associated words. A verbal phrase consists of a verb and its modifiers, but it does not include the noun phrase for any argument, or any verbal complement. Particle phrases consist of particles and (in the case of some formed from relative roots) their complements. The verb and its object do not form a constituent, unlike the verb phrase of some formal grammatical theories.

§6.2a. Noun Phrases. A noun phrase may consist of a noun, or a pronoun, particle, or participle with a nominal function, along with any associated determiners (such as a demonstrative pronoun or quantifier) or other modifiers, or it may be a determiner or modifier without a noun. It may also consist of two or more noun phrases that are conjoined, or with one naming a possessor or a loosely linked adjunct.

(6.1) Noun phrase without a noun or participle

One word
   (a) yó·k 'these (people)': yó·k=á· mi·č·íhti·t 'what these people could eat'
   (b) né·l 'those (obv.)': nčí·sas təlá·ɔl né·l 'Jesus said to them'
   (c) ní·š·a 'two': ní·š·a=č mhičí·i ahpúwak. 'Two will be out in the open.'
   (d) wé·mi 'all (of them)': kwi·k·e·há·ɔ wé·mi 'he healed them all'
   (e) a·lə́nte 'some (of them)': a·lə́nte=č nhilá·ɔk 'some will be killed'

Two words or more
   (f) ní·š·a ki·ló·wa 'two of you'
   (g) a·lə́nte ki·ló·wa 'some of you'
   (h) né·k ní·š·a 'those two'

- (i) nə́ txí 'that many'
- (j) ahpá·mi=ét né·wən télən txá·pxki 'maybe about four thousand'
- (k) kwət·á·pxki ɔ́·k palé·naxk txí·nxke ɔ́·k naxá 'a hundred and fifty-three (of them)'

(6.2) Noun phrase with a noun or participle

One word
- (a) mahtánt·u 'a devil; the devil':
    - mahtánt·u=tá wáni. 'He is a devil.'
    - mahtánt·u íkali pə́nči·p 'the devil entered him'
- (b) mɔ́ni 'money': mɔ́ni=č kəmillúhəna. 'We'll give you money,'
- (c) we·í·k·i·t 'the house-owner' (participle)

Determiner or quantifier (word or phrase) and noun (or noun phrase)
- (d) ná lə́nu 'that man'
- (e) ní·š·a mɔni·t·ə́t·a 'two small coins'
- (f) xé·li kwəškwə́š·ak 'many hogs'
- (g) ní·š·a ší=tá naxá awé·ni·k 'two or three people'
- (h) yó·l ní·š·a tahpantəwá·k·ana 'these two commandments'
- (i) ke·k·e·p·inkɔ́·č·i·k ní·š·a lə́nəwak 'two blind men'

Noun and relative clause (with participle) or other qualifier
- (j) kó·x ɔ·s·áhkame é·p·i·t 'your father who is in heaven' (kó·x 'your (sg.) father'; ɔ·s·áhkame '(in) heaven'; |apī-| AI 'be {smwh}', |IC–t| 3s/PPL(ANsg
- (k) kó·x·əwa ná ɔ·s·áhkame 'your (pl.) father in heaven' (kó·x·əwa 'your (pl.) father'; ná 'that (anim.)'; ɔ·s·áhkame '(in) heaven')
- (l) ná kó·x ɔ·s·áhkame 'your father in heaven'
- (m) kó·x ɔ·s·áhkame 'your father in heaven'
- (n) pí·li nəmekí·s·əmak 'other sheep of mine' (pí·li P 'different, other')

(6.3) Quantifier and adjunct
- (a) ní·š·a e·k·e·ki·má·č·i 'two of his disciples'
- (b) a·lə́nte yó·k ni·p·aí·č·i·k 'some standing here' (*lit.*, 'some of these who are standing')
- (c) má·wsu yó·k tanke·lənsí·č·i·k 'one of these meek ones'

(6.4) Possessor and possessed
- (a) yó·k wtehəwá·ɔ 'the hearts of these people'
- (b) mi·mə́nsak tɔp·ɔ́·nəwa 'the children's bread'
- (c) nčí·sas kɔhé·s·a 'Jesus's mother'
- (d) sɔ·k·i·ma·ɔ́·k·anink ke·tanət·ó·wi·t "in the kingdom of God" (KJV)
- (e) ó·x·ɔ ɔ́·k né·l kɔhé·s·a ná xkwé·čəč 'the girl's father and mother'
- (f) xínkwi-sa·k·í·ma wto·t·é·nay 'the great king's city' (KJV: "the city of the great King")
- (g) we·t·alo·ka·k·anə́mkuk nehəla·ləwe·lí·č·i 'the Lord's servant' (two participles, *lit.*, 'one that the master (obv.) has as a servant')

§6.2b. Verbal Phrases. A verbal phrase consists of a verb and its modifiers, if any. Modifiers may be adverbial (with a range of meanings modifying the verbal notion) or grammatical (associated with certain verbal categories, such as the negative or prohibitive).

(6.5) Verb with adverbial particle
- (a) šá·e pəntákɔhto·p 'it was immediately heard about'
- (b) ki·mí·i=č mpo·ní·ha. 'I shall leave her alone in secret.'
- (c) lápi=č nəməš·ənə́mən 'I'll get it back again'
- (d) pé·p pi·ske·wəní·i 'he came at night'

(6.6) Verb with negative or prohibitive particle
- (a) takó· tɔmi·mənsəmi·í·ɔk 'they had no children' (B; |wətamīmənsəmī-| AI 'have child')
- (b) takó·=tá kki·ɔləlo·húmɔ. 'I didn't cheat you (pl.).' (Mt 20.13)
- (c) akó· pa·pi·í·yɔk 'they didn't play, they were not playing' (OA)
- (d) kó· káski- ílli -mai·k·e·í·yɔk 'they couldn't even camp' (OA)
- (e) kó·=tá nkáski- nə́ -lənəmó·wən. 'I can't do that.' (OA)
- (f) máta nnənaɔ́·i·p. 'I did not know who he was.' (B)
- (g) é·li máta no·wa·há·i lə́nu. 'For I know no man.' (B)
- (h) máta=á· ko·la·mhitai·húmɔ 'you won't believe me' (B)
- (i) tá=á· kɔ́ski-ne·mó·wən 'he would not be able to see it' (B)
- (j) tá=á·=tá ankəló·wi 'he will not die' (B)
- (k) káči kəlo·né·han 'do not lie' (B)

(6.7) Verb with complement of relative root
- (a) mux·ó·link lí-po·s·í·ɔk 'they got into a boat' (|əlī| PV; 3.13(1))
- (b) hák·ink lí-a·lo·lahtehəlé·ɔk 'they threw themselves face-down on the ground'
- (c) hɔ́k·enk núnči-wəle·lə́ntam 'I am pleased because of him' (|wənčī| PV; 3.13(7))
- (d) ahke·kho·t·əwá·k·an núnči-pá·n 'I come for judgment'
- (e) íka táli-pəmət·ó·nhe·p 'he preached there' (|talī| PV; 3.13(3))
- (f) kɔ́čəmink táli-pa·tamá·p·ani·k 'they were praying outside'
- (g) aləwí·i=č ntə́ntxi-məšənəmúhəna. 'We will get more.' (|taxī| PV; 3.13(5))
- (h) kwə́t·i á·wəlink šúkw sháki-mi·kəmɔ́·s·əwak 'they only worked for one hour' (|sahkī| PV; 3.13(6))

Verbs may be conjoined, with or without a conjunction. Most commonly the conjunction used is ɔ́·k 'and, or', but ší 'or' (always followed by an enclitic, usually as ší=tá) is also found.

(6.8) Conjoined verbs

With no conjunction:
- (a) nso·psí·həmp, ktak·ɔníhəmɔ·p. 'I was naked, and you clothed me.'
- (b) wənək·alá·ɔ, lápi palí·i é·, mái-pá·tama·. 'And he left them and went away again, going to pray.'

With a conjunction:
- (c) ko·wa·háwwa, ɔ́·k kəne·ɔ́wwa 'you know him, and you see him'
- (d) né·li-pa·lsían, ɔ́·k né·li-kpahá·s·ian 'while you were sick or in prison'

§6.2c. Particle Phrases. In a particle phrase a particle modifies another particle, or a particle that contains a relative root is preceded or followed by its complement. There may be additional modifiers or conjoined elements. The particle lí 'to {smwh}' is found with a locative particle or with a locative noun, which functions as a particle (6.9fghi). In some cases the head particle in such a construction takes an uninflected noun, presumably as an adjunct (6.9mno).

Particle phrases with a numeral as the first word (6.9ab) differ from particle compounds, in which the numeral is expressed by a preparticle (5.133def). In expressions with numerals above four, the particle phrase includes a particle compound with the numeral placeholder *txí* PV,PP '{so many}' (5.133g).

(6.9) Particle phrases
- (a) naxá náhənəm '75 cents' (OA; náhənəm P '25 cents' [as a noun: 'raccoon'])
- (b) naxá ki·š·ó·x·ink ahpá·mi 'for about three months' (B; ki·š·ó·x·ink P 'months') (cf. náxi-kí·škwe 'in three days, for three days')
- (c) áhi xé·li 'a great many' (B); better taken as a compound (5.133a)

(d) nə́ txí 'that amount, that many' (B)
(e) aləwí·i txí 'more, a greater amount' (B)
(f) lí e·k·wəlúnkɔne '(to) under her wings' (B)
(g) lí nčo·wi·ké·i 'to the Jews' (B; nčo·wi·ké·i P 'among the Jews')
(h) lí ɔ́·lahkunk 'into a pit' (B)
(i) wé·mi lí wəla·məwe·ɔ́·k·anink 'to all truth' (B)
(j) wə́nči o·t·é·nink 'out of the city' (B)
(k) nə́ wə́nči mux·ó·link 'from the boat' (B)
(l) mpínk wə́nči ɔ́·k či·čánkunk 'from water and the spirit' (B)
(m) wə́nči nhák·enk; wə́nči nhák·ay 'about me; concerning me' (B)
(n) wə́nči šaxahka·wsəwá·k·an 'because of righteousness' (B)
(o) wə́nči čí·čankw ɔ́·k wəla·məwe·ɔ́·k·an 'by spirit and truth' (B)
(p) wə́nči ya·p·é·i 'from the shore' (B)

§6.3. Verbless Sentences. Substantive and equational sentences are predications but lack a main verb. These differ from verbless sentences in which a verb may be said to be missing, either because it is an omitted repetition that can be supplied from a parallel sentence (6.32), or because it is a sentence fragment (such as an answer to a question or an exclamatory reference).

Sentences with the presentational particle šé· are given here together (6.10j-r), but while some of these are clearly substantive sentences, others could be analyzed as equational sentences with the following demonstrative as the Given term (**§6.3b**).

§6.3a. Substantive Sentences. Substantive sentences state (or deny or question) the existence or attributes of someone or something without the use of a verbal predicate.
(6.10) Substantive sentences.
Particles only
(a) kɔhán, mé·či yúkwe 'indeed, it is already now' (Jn 16.32)
Noun phrase
(b) ni·k·a·ní·i-=tá -wé·wsi·t, ... 'He's a prophet, ...' (Mk 6.15)
(c) né·tami-nhiləwé·t·əp 'he was the first to commit murder' (Jn 8.44)
(d) lə́nəwa=máh tɔ·ki·há·k·anink hítkɔ .. 'In a certain man's field was a tree ..' (Lk 13.6)
With particle as attribute
(e) la·múnkwe enkələk·í·i-xkána 'inside are the bones of the dead' (Mt 23.27)
(f) xé·li we·t·e·kaɔ·tpáni·k 'there were many who followed him' (Mt 4.25)
(g) e·k·e·ki·má·č·i xé·li 'many were his disciples' (Lk 6.17)
(h) ta·txíti me·xkánki·k 'there are few that find it' (Mt 7.14)
Negative
(i) tá=á· ní· xó·ha 'I would not be alone' (Jn 16.32)
Presentational (with šé· 'See!, Look!; here is; there is')
(j) šé· yúh: 'it is this (as follows): ...' (Mk 12.31); šé· yó·ni.' This is it.' (Lk 17.23)
(k) šé· nə́ wəlé. 'That's it over there.' (Lk 17.23)
(l) šé· wá lə́nu! 'Here is the man.' (Jn 19.5; KJV "Behold the man!")
(m) šé· ná kəláist. 'Here is Christ.' (Mt 24.23)
(n) šé· ná nkáhe·s ɔ́·k naxi·s·əmə́s·ak. 'There is my mother and my brothers.' (Mt 12.49)
(o) šé· yú ntap·antəwá·k·an: ... 'This is my commandment: ...' (Jn 15.12)
(p) šé· yú e·lá·t·əp. 'This is what he said.' (Jn 1.20)
(q) šé· yó·l ní·š·a amankanší·k·ana. 'Here are two swords.' (Lk 22.38)
(r) šé· nə́ni ke·tanət·ó·wi·t mwi·kəmɔ·s·əwá·k·an, ... 'This is the work of God. ...' (Jn 6.29)

Interrogative
- (s) ní·=háč ..? 'Is it me?' (Mk 14.19)
- (t) nihəláči=háč wəni·č·a·nəwá·ɔ, ší=háč pí·li awé·ni? 'Is it their own children, or is it someone else?' (Mt 17.25)

§6.3b. Equational Sentences. Equational sentences state (or deny or question) the equivalence of the referents of two noun phrases, one stating the known entity (the Given) and the other the predicated new information about it (the New). If the New term of the equation is definite, it follows the Given term (6.11), and if the Given term is a personal pronoun, it is an emphatic pronoun (6.11abcdg). If the New term is indefinite, it precedes the Given term (6.12), and if this is a personal pronoun, it is a reflexive pronoun (6.12c-h). If the pronoun that is the Given term is emphasized, pronouns of both kinds may be used together (6.13a), or an emphatic pronoun may be used alone (6.13b). There are some other patterns (e.g., Jn 10.16).

(6.11) Equational sentences (Given + New)
- (a) ní· kəláist. 'I am Christ.' (Lk 23.2)
- (b) ní· ke·tanət·ó·wi·t kwí·s·a. 'I am the son of God.' (Mt 27.43)
- (c) ní· wisahki·múnši 'I am the vine' (Jn 15.5)
- (d) ki·ló·wa tuhənət·ét·a 'you (pl.) are the branches' (Jn 15.5)
- (e) we·t·ó·x·əmənt xó·ha nehəlá·t·ank 'the father alone is the one in control of it' (Acts 1.7)
- (f) máta=háč náni kəláist? 'Is he not Christ? (Jn 4.29)
- (g) kí·=háč nčo·wí·i-sa·k·í·ma? 'Are you king of the Jews?' (Jn 18.33)

(6.12) Equational sentences (New + Given)
- (a) mahtánt·u=tá wáni. 'He is a devil.' (Lk 7.33)
- (b) †same·líí·i-lənu náni. 'He was a Samaritan man.' (Lk 17.16)
- (c) sa·k·í·ma nhák·ay. 'I am a king.' (Lk 23.2)
- (d) mé·či khík·ay nhák·ay. 'Now I'm an old lady.' (OA; cf. 6.13b)
- (e) ó·k=č e·k·e·ki·mák·i·k khak·ayúwa. 'and you will be my disciples.' (Jn 15.8)
- (f) takó· .. alo·ká·k·anak nhak·ayəná·nak 'we are not servants (who ..)' (Lk 17.10)
- (g) nčó·=háč nhák·ay? 'Am I a Jew?' (Jn 18.35)
- (h) awé·n=háč khák·ay? 'Who are you?' (Jn 1.19)

(6.13) Equational sentences with New term emphasized
- (a) ki·ló·wa=č ni·t·í·s·ak khak·ayúwa '*You* will be my friends' (Jn 15.14)
- (b) ... é·li khík·ay mé·či ní·. '... because *I'm* old *lady* now.' (OA; ní· also emphasized)

§6.4. Subordinate Clauses. A subordinate clause is one that is dependent on a higher verb or clause. Of the two basic types, conditional clauses (including temporal clauses) give the circumstances of the event or action of the main clause, while complement clauses (including purpose clauses) add information that is presented as integral to the action specified by the main clause and completing the thought. There are also clauses centered on participles, but these are more or less complex noun phrases, rather than being dependent on a higher verb or sentence.

§6.4a. Conditional Clauses. Conditional clauses convey a notion of 'if', 'unless', or the like. Temporal clauses specify 'when', 'while', 'after', 'before', or the like. A subjunctive verb is used to refer to a future condition or time (4.63), and a changed conjunct (4.61) or changed subjunctive (4.62) is used for past time or a general condition. The unique example of a subjunctive present is in (4.79a). 'For' or 'because' may be indicated by é·li PV (with IC) in a changed conjunct verb (4.73cdfghi) or by é·li P with an indicative (3.15f, 6.6g). 'Because' is also rendered with wénči PV (with IC [3.13(7)], 4.67i), and wénči PV (with IC) is also used with =č FUT or =á· POT for 'so that' (4.67pq; also as wənči [4.95nu, 4.97m, 5.128x]).

§6.4b. Complement Clauses. Verbs and certain particles take verbal complements in the subordinative mode, with or without the preverb |əlī| '{so}'. Complements without |əlī| PV '{so}' are found if the main-clause verb is, for example, 'want', 'let, allow', and 'be hard, difficult' (4.49a-g), and also after ná P 'then (it was that)' (4.49h-l) and kwə́la(h) P '(I) wish' (4.49m-o). Complements with |əlī| PV '{so}' are found after, for example, 'know', 'say', 'tell, implore', 'think', 'see', 'hear', 'be reluctant', and 'be not worthy' (4.50a-j), and also after wanə́š·i P 'thank you' (4.50k). Complements both with and without |əlī| PV '{so}' are found after 'be right or lawful' (4.49f).

Subordinative verbs without |əlī| PV '{so}' are also found as nominalized verbs used as secondary objects (4.49pq).

Purpose clauses have a subordinative verb with the preverb |əlī| '{so}' (4.50.l-p).

Complements of verbs of saying, thinking, and the like are ordinarily in direct discourse (as if quoted words; 6.14). In some cases, however, a verb of saying takes a complement in indirect discourse, in the independent indicative with no mark of subordnation (6.15).

(6.14) Direct discourse complement
    (a) təle·ləmawwá·ɔl, "awé·n[i]=ét wəne·ɔ́·ɔl." (Lk 1.22) 'They thought he must have seen some being.' (*Lit.*, 'They thought about him, "He must have seen some being."')
    (b) təle·ləmawwá·p·ani, "nál=ét wá kəláist?" (Lk 3.15) 'They wondered if he could be Christ.' (*Lit.*, 'They thought about him, "Could he possibly be Christ?"')

(6.15) Indirect discourse complement
    (a) lə́l, ntáspi lí nó·x·ink, ké·pəwa ko·x·əwá·ink (Jn 20.17)
        '.. (and) tell them I am going up to my father, and your father also, ..'

§6.5. Sentence-Initial Focus and Emphasis. New or otherwise important information may be highlighted by occurring first (of the major components) in the sentence, before the verb. This FOCUS position is used is several ways. For example, if a noun object provides new information it ordinarily precedes its verb, and since the noun will be previously unmentioned it is prototypically indefinite, and the verb accordingly has absolute inflection if it is in the independent indicative (4.24a, 4.38ac, 4.69a, 4.91bcg). When an indefinite object instead follows its verb, it seems typically to be the case that the sentence-initial position is occupied by another highly salient sentence component, such as a subordinate clause (4.24bc, 4.69b), a contextually contrastive subject (4.69c), or an emphatic pronoun (4.38b).

§6.5a. Focus-Fronting. Emphasized words or phrases may occur sentence-initially with an enclitic after the first word of the rest of the sentence that, in effect, separates the two parts (6.16), as enclitics are typically found after the first word of a sentence or clause (**§5.3a**). An enclitic may also occur with the fronted component (6.16fg).

(6.16) Focus-fronted subject or object (underlined) followed by enclitic host
    (a) <u>we·t·o·x·ínki</u> pwe·t·alo·ká·lku=č ntəlsəwá·k·anink. (Jn 14.26)
        'He will be sent by the father to act for me (*lit.*, 'in my power').'
    (b) <u>pí·lhik či·čankəwá·k·an</u> kɔ́·txukw=č, ... (Lk 1.35) 'A holy spirit (inan.) shall visit you, ...'
    (c) .. <u>ɔ́·k e·ləwe·ləmúkwsi·t tɔləwí·i·ləs·əwá·k·an</u> kəwi·wəni·ká·k·o·n=č. (Lk 1.35 cont.)
        '.. and the power of the one who is most highly regarded shall envelop you.'
    (d) .., <u>kó·x·əwa ɔ·s·áhkame é·p·i·t</u> tá=á· kpak·i·t·a·t·ama·k·o·wəné·ɔ kčana·wsəwa·k·anúwa. (Mk 11.26) '.., your father who is in heaven will not forgive you your sins.'
    (e) .. šúkw <u>či·čánkɔ</u> tá=á· kɔ́ski-nhila·iwwá·ɔ. (Mt 10.28) '.. but the soul they cannot kill.'
    (f) <u>wé·mi</u>=č <u>entxa·ké·i·t</u>, tələwéntamən=č wí·k·ia pa·tamwe·i·k·á·ɔn (Mt 21.13, Mk 11.17)
        'All nations shall call my house a house of prayer.'
                                                                            [→]

(g) .., ó·k=č ko·le·ləntaməwa·k·anúwa, tá=á· awé·n kči·k·ənuk·o·wəné·ɔ. (Jn 16.22)
  '.., and your joy no one will take from you.'

§6.5b. Focus Peg. Another way of indicating emphasis is with the empty support particle (or focus peg) ná P PRES followed by a demonstrative pronoun, a collocation that is often fronted in a focus construction (4.42-44, 4.50q-t) but sometimes refers to a fronted nominal (6.17a), follows another fronted nominal (6.17bc), or is merely emphatic (6.17d).

(6.17) ná P PRES not in sentence-initial focus position
   (a) mpínk, mpí é·te·k, ná=nə təlaníhi·n. (V) 'In the water, in a body of water (*lit.*, a place where there is water), is where she threw it.'
   (b) .., né·k·a=č né· ná=nə tóp·i·n (Jn 12.26) '.., he, too, shall be in the same place.'
   (c) ké·pəwa=č ná=nə ktəli·naməné·ɔ .. (Lk 13.3)
       'You (pl.) shall also have the same thing happen to you ..'
   (d) .., kwi·k·e·há·ɔ ná=nə táli. (Mt 21.14) '.. and he healed them in that very place.'

§6.5c. Presentational Pronoun. The presentational deictic pronoun nánal 'he, she, it is the one who', sometimes shortened to nál, has the forms in (6.18). This is found only in Blanchard, and the position of the accent is conjectured. The verb with it is either an independent indicative (6.19cjknl) or a participle (6.19blmp). It is most commonly sentence-initial and followed by a demonstrative pronoun, but it may be preceded by a conjunction or a negative particle, and it can also be found in subordinate clauses (6.19pq) and in a verbless complement clause (6.19o).

(6.18) Forms of nánal (nál) 'he, she, it is the one that'

animate sg.	nál	nánal ⟨nunul⟩, ⟨nu nul⟩
animate pl.	náli·k	nanáli·k ⟨nunulek⟩, ⟨nu nulek⟩
obviative	náli	nanáli ⟨nunuli⟩, ⟨nunul li⟩, ⟨Nunule⟩
inanimate sg.	nál	nánal
inanimate pl.	[not found]	nanáli ⟨nunuli⟩, ⟨nunul li⟩, ⟨nunul le⟩

(6.19) Examples of nánal (nál) 'he, she, it is the one that'
   (a) nəni haki·há·k·an, nál nəni pe·mhakamí·k·e·k; .. (Mt 13.37)
       'the field, *that* is the world; ..'
   (b) nál=tá wáni e·k·əni·mák·əp, .. 'This is who I was talking about ..'
   (c) náli·k né·k o·txawwá·ɔ .. (Jn 12.21) 'It was they who came to (Philip, who ..)'
   (d) .., náli né·l kwəlsót·aɔ. (Jn 9.31) '.., he is one he listens to.'
   (e) .., nánal ná mahtánt·u; .. (Mt 13.39) '.., that is the devil; ..'
   (f) nánal yó·ni nahtuhé·p·i (Lk 22.19) 'This is my body, ..'
   (g) é·li nánal=tá wáni e·ləwé·t·əp 'For this is the one he said it of, ..'
   (h) .., nanáli·k né·k ni·mahtəs·ak '.., (Mt 12.50) they are my brothers, ..'
   (i) ..; ó·k nə mahčí·kwi·xkáni·m, nanáli·k né·k me·t·a·wsí·č·i·k. (Mt 13.38)
       '..; and the bad seed, those are the sinners.'
   (j) nanáli né·l †ke·yápas wənənaó·ɔ, .. (Jn 18.15) 'He was one that Caiaphas knew, ..'
   (k) nanáli=á· né·l awé·n tohɔ·lá·ɔ .. (Mk 12.33) 'He is who a person should love ..'
   (l) nanáli né·l ehɔ·lá·č·i nčí·sas, .. (Jn 21.20)
       'He (obv.) was the one that Jesus loved, (who ..)'
   (m) nanáli ehɔ·la·tpáni. (Jn 13.23) 'He (obv.) was the one he (prox.) loved.'
   (n) nanáli né·l wəni·skha·lkó·na awé·n. (Mt 15.20)
       'Those are the things that defile a person.'
   (o) o·wa·hawwá·ɔ lí nánal nehəlá·ləwe·t. (Jn 21.12) 'They knew that he was the Lord.'

(p) .., é·li- we·t·ó·x·əmənt nanáli né·l -ntó·naɔ·t pa·tamá·k·uk=č. (Jn 4.23; see 4.65n)
'.., for the father seeks the one who will pray to him.'
(q) .., é·li- wé·mi awé·n éntxi·t nanáli né·l -ntó·nank. (Lk 12.30)
'.., for those things are what everyone that exists seeks after.'

§6.5d. Presentational Particle as Emphatic. The presentational particle šé· P PRES has been exemplified in (6.10j-r). In Blanchard this is essentially and almost exclusively sentence-initial, being otherwise found only after a conjunction and after a fronted nominal. In the twentieth century šé· was also frequently used as a relatively weak emphatic reinforcement after demonstrative pronouns (6.20).

(6.20) šé· P EMPH
(a) ná=yúkwe=ní šé· ntə́ntxi-ahkənó·t·əmən. 'That's all I have to tell about it.' (ME)
    (ná P PRES; yúkwe EMPH (*lit.*, 'now'); ní 'that (inan.)'; šé· EMPH;
    |(ən)taxī| PV '{so much}', |akənōt-| TI(1b) 'tell about', |nət–əmən| 1s–0+0s/IND)
(b) 'nə́pe·h=tá íka alənəmó·t·am yú šé· ə́nta-tayá·xkhwi·t yó·l šé· məsá·kɔ, ...
    'Let's hold on to this here when he crosses over on these logs, ...' (ME)
    (nə́pe·h=tá 'alright, let's'; íka 'there'; |alən-| TI(1b) 'hold on to', |–əmōtam| 12–0/IMP;
    yú 'this (inan.)'; šé· P EMPH;
    /ə́nta/ PV 'when', |tayāxkwahī-| AI+O 'cross (as a bridge)', |(IC)–t| 3s/CC);
    yó·l 'these (inan.)'; šé· P EMPH; məsá·kɔ 'logs')

§6.6. Discontinuous Constituents. It is common for the components of a compound, a noun phrase, or a subordinate clause to be DISCONTINUOUS, separated by words that are not components of the constituent. Although the words may appear to be in scrambled order, however, the discontinuities may be thought of as having the effect of binding together the overall sentence by, to some degree, counteracting the normal looseness of the rather free word order.

A discontinuous noun phrase with a locative meaning often consists of íka 'there' or íkali '(to) there' before a verb as essentially a place-holder, with a full noun phrase after the verb (6.28).

(6.21) Discontinuous particle compound
(a) náxi-=č -kí·škwe 'in three days (in the future)'

(6.22) Discontinuous compound verb
With enclitic after preverb
(a) ni·k·a·ní·i-=tá -wé·wsi·t. (Mk 6.15) 'He's a prophet.'
(b) nehəni·k·a·ní·i-=ét -wé·wsi·t. (Mt 14.5; Mt 21.46+) 'He must be a prophet.'
(c) nehəni·k·a·ní·i-=á· -we·wsí·t·e,... (Lk 7.39) 'If he is a prophet, (he would) ..'
(d) ktaləwí·i-=ksí -lə́s·i·n nəmux·o·msəná·na (Jn 8.53)
    'Are you greater than our (exc.) grandfather of old ..?'
(e) áhi-=máh -pó·i·p. (Lk 2.5) '..; she was far along in her pregnancy.'
With noun phrase after preverb
(f) sé·ki- wi·k·əwáhəmink -táli-winki·ma·khwiksə́mank. (Lk 1.10)
    'while the incense was burned in the building.'
(g) wtépi-=á· yó·l ahsə́nal -wə́nči-ki·š·i·há·ɔl mi·mə́nsa, ... (Mt 3.9)
    'he would be able to make children from these stones'
With two, three, four, or many words after preverb
(h) é·li- né·ləma nčá·n -kpahá·s·i·kw. (Jn 3.24) 'For John had not yet been imprisoned.'
(i) é·li- máta la·í·tane -ahpíhti·t, ... (Jn 21.8) 'as they were not out in the middle, ...'

(j) kúnči- máta hítami nə́ni -ləlo·wəné·ɔ·p, ... (Jn 16.4)
'I didn't tell you that in the beginning because (of it) ...'
(k) ɔ́·k é·li- ná=nə lí kí·xki -hát·e·k. (Jn 19.42) 'and as it was near that place.'
(l) ɔ́·k=č
wénči- tákta kéku wi·nəwamé·k·we we·t·ó·x·əmənt wə́nči ntəlsəwá·k·an -mí·lkwe·kw.
(Jn 15.16) 'and so that whatever you ask the father for by my power he will give you.'

With words after each of two preverbs
(m) wə́nči-=č máta -káski- kéku -luwé·ɔn, .. (Lk 1.20; possibly -luwé·an)
'.. so that you will not be able to speak, ..'
(n) é·li- ki·š·e·ləmúwe·t máta -pɔ́·i- kéku -lə́s·i·t. (Lk 1.37)
'.., since nothing is impossible for God do to.'
(o) tə́li- šúkw -wə́nči- ahaləwí·i -xa·whita·kwsí·li·n, ... (Mt 27.24)
'that they only shouted all the more because of it, ...'

(6.23) Discontinuous noun phrase (demonstrative and participle)
Across particle, noun, or verb
(a) ɔ́·k <u>ná</u> máta <u>we·t·ó·x·əmənt</u> (Jn 5.23) 'they also do not (honor) <u>the father</u>'
(b) né·k má·wsu <u>télən</u> ɔ́·k <u>ní·š·a entxí·č·i·k</u>. (Jn 6.71) '.. one <u>of those twelve</u>.'
(c) <u>ná nə́</u> təli·naməné·ɔ <u>e·lə́ntəp</u>. (Mk 14.16)
'Then they saw what they had been told (they would).'
(d) ná <u>ná</u> kwə́č·i·n <u>e·k·e·ki·mkwə́s·i·t</u> we·ɔ́hkuk †ke·apás·a, ... (Jn 18.16)
'Then <u>the disciple</u> that Caiaphas knew went out, ...'
Across two conjoined verbs
(e) šé· yú núnči- yú -táli-ki·š·í·k·i·n ɔ́·k núnči-pá·n <u>entalá·wsink</u>:... (Jn 18.37)
'This is why I was born in <u>the world</u> and why I came here: ...'

(6.24) Discontinuous noun phrase (noun or pronoun and participle)
(a) <u>lə́nu</u> o·txá·p·ani <u>ni·skankələ́k·əp</u> (Mt 8.2) '<u>a man who had the nasty disease</u> came to him'
(b) tə́li- <u>nčí·sas</u> -aləwí·i-txí·li·n <u>e·k·e·ki·má·č·i·l čhɔ·pwəná·č·i·l</u>, náni nčá·n, ... (Jn 4.1).
'that there were more of <u>Jesus's disciples that he baptized</u> than of John's, ...'
(c) ɔ́·k <u>nčí·sas</u> máta wwi·č·e·yko·wí·p·ani <u>e·k·e·ki·ma·tpáni</u>, ... (Jn 6.22)
'and <u>Jesus's disciples</u> were not with him, ...'
(d) <u>ké·pəwa</u>=č ahpúwak <u>me·č·ihkwé·k·wi·k</u>. (Jn 15.20)
'there will be <u>those that treat you badly, too</u>.'

(6.25) Discontinuous noun phrase (particle and noun or participle)
(a) <u>wé·mi</u> pwənúntəla·n <u>nihəlá́či e·lalo·ká·s·i·t</u>. (Jn 5.20)
'he shows him <u>everything he himself has done</u>'
(b) <u>wé·mi</u> kwi·k·e·há·p·ani <u>pa·lsi·lí·č·i</u> 'he cured <u>all the sick</u>' (Mk 4.23)
(c) <u>ké·x·a</u> wəlahəlé·p·ani·k <u>name·t·ə́t·al</u> (Mk 8.7) 'they had <u>a few small fish</u>'
(d) ɔ́·k=č <u>aləwí·i</u> pwənúntəla·n <u>me·x·inkwi·ná·k·ɔ laehɔ·s·əwá·k·an</u>, .. (Jn 5.20)
'And he will show him <u>deeds of an even greater kind</u>, ..'

(6.26) Discontinuous noun phrase (possessor and possessed noun)
(a) <u>ná kó·x·əwa</u> mahčí·kwi <u>pwəna·eləntaməwá·k·an</u> (Jn 8.44)
'<u>The thoughts of that father of yours</u> are evil, ..'
(b) tákta kéku <u>awé·n</u> čuhoté·li·k <u>wté·hink</u> (Mt 12.34) 'whatever fills <u>someone's heart</u>'
(c) <u>ná lə́nu</u> aləwí·i máhči·lé·w <u>hɔ́k·enk</u> (Mt 12.45) 'it is worse <u>in that man's body</u>'
(d) <u>ké·pəwa</u>=č ahpúwak we·la·mhitánki·k <u>kta·pto·na·k·anúwa</u>. (Jn 15.20)
'there will be those that believe <u>your words, too</u>.'

(6.27) Discontinuous noun phrase (locative)
Across a verb
   (a) íka ntəli-ktək·i wé·ma. (Mt 12.44) 'I'm going back where I came from.'
   (b) ná íka təli-kčí·n kɔhé·s·ink, Mk 6.24 'Then she went out to her mother ...'
   (c) ná íka təli-po·s·i·né·ɔ mux·ó·link ki·mí·i. (Mk 6.32)
      'Then they secretly got on board a boat.'
   (d) íka təli-šuhəmáɔ·n wsi·t·í·li·t nči·sás·a, ... (Jn 12.3) 'She rubbed it on Jesus's feet, ...'
   (e) lkali a·lo·lahtéhəle· wsi·t·í·li·t nči·sás·a, ... (Lk 17.16)
      'He threw himself face-down at Jesus's feet'
Across verb and particle
   (f) wé·mi awé·n íka ma·éhəle·p alap·a·í·i pa·tamwe·i·k·á·ɔnink (Lk 21.38)
      'Everyone gathered in the temple early in the morning, ..'
   (g) né·ləma málahši nihəláči čəphiko·wí·i táli wté·hink, ... (Mt 13.21)
      'It has not yet, as it were, taken root in his own heart, ...'
Across verb and object
   (h) íka lalo·ká·le·p nčo·wí·i-ke·kayəmhe·lí·č·i nči·sás·ink (Lk 7.3)
      'he sent some Jewish leaders to Jesus'
(6.28) Discontinuous noun phrase (oblique complement of the included relative root)
   (a) məsəč·é·i wənči kči·t·anəs·əwá·k·anink. (Mk 12.30) 'with all your strength'
   (b) nə́ táli xinkwi·k·á·ɔnink (Lk 1.8) 'in the house of worship'
   (c) wé·mi lí wəla·məwe·ó·k·anink (Jn 16.13) 'to all truth'
   (d) yú táli xkwi·thakamí·k·we (Mk 2.10, Mt 13.22) 'here on earth'
      (xkwi·thakamí·k·we P 'on (the surface of) the earth')
   (e) mənəp·é·k·unk táli ká·mink (Jn 6.25) 'on the other side of the sea'
      (mənəp·é·k·unk 'sea (loc.)'; ká·mink P 'on the other side of the water')
   (f) wé·mi táli éntxink o·t·é·naya (Mt 11.1) 'in all the towns there were'
      (wé·mi P 'all'; éntxink 'how many there are' [II oblique ppl.]; o·t·é·naya 'towns')
   (g) yú táli entalá·wsink (Mt 12.32), yó·ni táli entalá·wsink (Mt 16.19) 'in this world',
      yú táli hák·ink (Mt 18.18) 'here on earth'; also (6.23e)
   (h) yú táli énta-wínkəle·k (Lk 16.24) 'in this blazing fire'
(6.29) Discontinuous subordinate clause
   (a) ílli mɔč·ípahkɔ nnuntae·lənsi·n llax·ənəmáɔ·n. (Lk 3.16)
      'I feel unworthy even to untie his *shoes*.'
(6.30) Two discontinuous clauses intertwined
   (a) wénči-=č ké·pəwa .. íka -lo·x·ɔlək·é·e·kw tə́ta=á· či·mí·i é·p·ie·kw. (Lk 16.9)
      'so that you (pl.) also .. will be brought to wherever you will be forever.'
      (Omitted: tá·mse kwí·la-ləs·ié·k·we 'when at some point you are no more')

§6.7. Gapping. When verbs are conjoined they may share modifiers or other associated or component words. The shared words are found only once, it seems always with the first verb, and are GAPPED (omitted) with the second verb, but they are construed with both verbs. A gapped word is understood as being the same with the second verb as with the first, except that the pronominal prefix on a gapped preverb may be different (6.31g). Also, in at least one case é·li- PV 'as' is gapped after a verb with é·li P 'as' (Mk 1.22). There is no gapping of verbal arguments, as there is simply ordinary pronominal reference when a lexical argument is not repeated, but an oblique may be gapped when it would repeat a lexical object (6.31a).

Also, the head verb of a compound verb may be gapped stranding the preverb, which may retain a pronominal prefix, and omitting the inflectional ending, even if it would have been different (6.32).

(6.31) Conjoined verbs with gapping

    With gapped oblique complement
- (a) nə́ni wə́li-wwa·taé·k·we ɔ́·k ləs·ié·k·we (Jn 13.17) 'if you know that well and do it'

    With gapped negative or prohibitive particle
- (b) máta=háč=á· .. kwət·əma·k·e·ləma·í·ɔ .. ɔ́·k mwi·la·í·ɔ kéku wé·lhik? (Mt 7.11)
  'Would he not take pity on them and not give them good things?'
- (c) máta=háč=á· ɔ·s·əle·ní·k·ana naxkwsé·i, ɔ́·k ɔ́·li-či·khamó·wən wí·k·əwam, tə́hi-nto·namó·wən ..? (Lk 15.8)
  'would she not light a candle, and sweep the house well, and look for it carefully?'
- (d) káči wəla·mhitawié·k·e·kw ɔ́·k na·ɔlié·k·e·kw (Lk 17.23)
  'don't believe them or follow them'

    With gapped preverb
- (e) né·li-ləmatahpíhti·t ɔ́·k -mi·tsíhti·t 'as they sat and ate' (Mk 14.18)
- (f) énta=á· kehkəmo·tké·č·i·k -tunkše·nəmíhti·t, -kəmo·tkéhti·t (Mt 6.19)
  'where thieves would open and steal them'

    With gapped preverb having a different prefix
- (g) tá=á· nkáski-a·mwí·i ɔ́·k -milló·wi. (Lk 11.7; = kkáski-milló·wi)
  'I would not be able to get up and (be able to) give you any.'

    With gapped preverb along with its oblique complement
- (h) ihikalíči ləkhíkwi-ləpwé·p nčí·sas, ɔ́·k -lək·i·l (Lk 2.52)
  'Jesus gradually became wiser and taller'
- (i) čínke=háč ktə́li-kahto·p·wí·ne·p .. ɔ́·k -kahto·s·əmwí·ne·p ..? (Mt 25.37)
  'when were you hungry .. or thirsty ..?'

    With two gapped preverbs
- (j) wə́nči-=č -káski-wwa·taíe·kw, ɔ́·k -wəla·mhitaíe·kw (Jn 10.38)
  'so that you will be able to know and believe (that ...)'

    With gapped preverb on two verbs
- (k) áləmi-ši·e·lə́ntam, ɔ́·k -nankíhəle·, ɔ́·k -kwsuk·ɔmálsu (Mt 26.37)
  'he began to be sorrowful, and to tremble, and to feel heavy'

    With gapped preverb or preverbs along with negative particle
- (l) énta-=á· máta mo·x·wé·s·ak -pali·túhti·t, ší=tá -maxkalə́t·ək (Mt 6.20)
  'where insects would not destroy them, or they would not rust'
  (|palīht-| TI(2) 'destroy'; |maxkalə́t-| II 'rust')
- (m) é·li- máta=á· -káski- náxpəne kwə́t·i mí·laxk -ɔ·p·i·tó·wan, ší=tá -sək·i·tó·wan (Mt 5.36)
  'as you would not be able to make even one hair white or black'
  (|wāpīht-| TI(2) 'make white'; |səkīht-| TI(2) 'make black')

(6.32) Conjoined verbs: second head verb gapped after preverb with prefix
- (a) nə́ wwə́nči-káhta-thwəna·né·ɔ, šúkw tə́·lai. (Jn 10.39)
  (tə́·lai = |ālawī| PV 'be unable to', |wət-| 3)
  'Because of that they desired to arrest him, but they failed.'
- (b) kə́t·a-nhilá·a, šúkw akó· kə́ski. (OA; kə́ski = |kàskī| PV 'be able to', |wə-| 3)
  'She tried to kill him, but she couldn't.'
- (c) nkát·a-psí-khita·kwčéhəlala·n, šúkw kó· nkáski. (ME; nkáski with |nə-| 1)
  'I tried to grab him around the waist from behind, but I couldn't.'

Bibliography

Beckwith, Miles, and Ives Goddard. 2021. A Glossary to the Delaware Publications of Ira D. Blanchard. Petoskey, Michigan: Mundart Press.

Blanchard, Ira D. 1834a. *Linapi'e Lrkvekun.* Shawnee Mission: J. Meeker.

Blanchard, Ira D. 1834b. *Linapie Lrkvekun, Ave Apwatuk.* Shawannoe Mission: J. Meeker.

Blanchard, Ira D. [and James Conner]. 1837 [completed 1839]. *The History of our Lord and Saviour Jesus Christ.* Shawanoe Baptist Mission: J. Meeker [and John G, Pratt].

Blanchard, Ira D. [and Charles Journeycake]. 1842. *The Delaware First Book.* Second Edition. Shawanoe Baptist Mission Press: J. G. Pratt.

Blanchard, Ira D., and James Conner, translators. 2021. *A Harmony of the Four Gospels in Delaware (1837-1839).* Edited and translated by Ives Goddard. Petoskey, Michigan: Mundart Press.

Bloomfield, Leonard. 1962. *The Menomini Language.* New Haven: Yale University Press.

Brinton, Daniel G., and Albert S. Anthony, eds. 1889. *A Lenâpé-English Dictionary.* Philadelphia: The Historical Society of Pennsylvania. [Second title page has "1888."]

Campanius, Johan. 1696. *Lutheri Catechismus Öfwersatt på American-Virginiske Språket.* Stockholm. [Facsimile reprint: *Martin Luther's Little Catechism translated into Algonquian Indian by Johannes Campanius.* With some notes by Isak Collijn. Stockholm–Uppsala, 1937.]

Goddard, Ives. 1979. *Delaware Verbal Morphology: A Descriptive and Comparative Study.* New York and London: Garland Publishing, Inc.

Goddard, Ives. 1991 Oklahoma Delaware Personal Names. *Man in the Northeast* 41:1-7.

Goddard, Ives. 2013 [2014]. The Munsee of Charles Halfmoon's Translations. *Papers of the 41st Algonquian Conference*, ed. by Karl S. Hele and J. Randolph Valentine, pp. 81-119. Albany: SUNY Press.

Goddard, Ives. 2014. Reduplication in the Delaware Languages. *Papers of the 42nd Algonquian Conference*, ed. by J. Randolph Valentine and Monica Macaulay, pp. 134-158. Albany: SUNY Press.

Goddard, Ives. 2015. Three Nineteenth-Century Munsee Texts: Archaisms, Dialect Variation, and Problems of Textual Criticism. *New Voices for Old Words*, ed. by David J. Costa, pp. 198-314. Lincoln: University of Nebraska Press.

Goddard, Ives. 2019. The Kansas Unami Writings of Ira D. Blanchard, Pioneering Algonquian Linguist. *Papers of the 48th Algonquian Conference*, ed. by Monica Macaulay and Margaret Noodin, pp. 87-106.

Halfmoon, Charles. 1874. *A Collection of Hymns in Muncey and English.* [Second, revised edition.] Toronto.

Hunter, William A. 1974. A Note on the Unalachtigo. *A Delaware Indian Symposium*, ed. by Herbert C. Kraft, pp. 147-152. Pennsylvania Historical and Museum Commission, Anthropological Series 4.

Jameson, J. Franklin. 1909. *Narratives of New Netherland, 1609-1664.* New York: Charles Scribner's Sons. (Reprinted: Barnes and Noble, New York, 1959.)

Lieberkühn, Samuel. 1823. *A Harmony of the Four Gospels, or the History of Our Lord and Saviour Jesus Christ.* Second edition revised. London: W. M'Dowall.

McCoy, Isaac. 1835. *Annual Register of Indian Affairs within the Indian (or Western) Territory.* [No. 1.] Shawanoe Mission.

McMurtrie, Douglas C., and Albert H. Allen. 1930. *Jotham Meeker, Pioneer Printer of Kansas.* Chicago: Eyncourt Press.

Michelson, Truman. 1912. Ethnological and linguistic field notes from the Munsee in Kansas and the Delaware in Oklahoma. NAA MS 2776, National Anthropological Archives, Smithsonian Institution.

Miller, Jay. 1977. Delaware Anatomy: With Linguistic, Social, and Medical Aspects. *Anthropological Linguistics* 19:144-166.

Pilling, James C. 1891. *Bibliography of the Algonquian Languages.* Bureau of [American] Ethnology Bulletin 13. Washington: G.P.O.

Speck, Frank G. 1931. *A Study of the Delaware Big House Ceremony.* Publications of the Pennsylvania Historical Commission 2. Harrisburg.

Voegelin, Carl F. 1939. Linguistic Institute course in Living Language. [In seven parts; title after the second part is "Group for Delaware (an Algonquian language) at the Linguistic Institute"; mimeographed.] Copy in the American Philosophical Society, Philadelphia.

Voegelin, Carl F. 1939a. Delaware songs and texts. Mss. in the American Philosophical Society, Philadelphia.

Voegelin, Carl F. 1945. Delaware Texts. *International Journal of American Linguistics* 11.2:105–119.

Voegelin, Carl F. 1946. Delaware, an Eastern Algonquian Language. *Linguistic Structures of Native America*, by Harry Hoijer et al., pp. 130–157. Viking Fund Publications in Anthropology 6. New York.

Walker, Willard B. 1996. Native Writing Systems. *Handbook of North American Indians*, vol. 17, *Languages.* Washington: Smithsonian Institution.

[Wampum, John B., and H.C. Hogg.] 1847. *Morning and Evening Prayers.* London: SPCK.

Zeisberger, David. 1827. *A Grammar of the Language of the Lenni Lenape or Delaware Indians.* Translated by Stephen Peter Du Ponceau. [Separately issued.] Philadelphia: James Kay, Jun. (Also in *Transactions of the American Philosophical Society*, vol. 3, pt.1, n.s. no. 2, pp. 65-250 + errata.)

Zeisberger, David. 1887. *Zeisberger's Indian Dictionary*, ed. by Eben Norton Horsford. Cambridge: John Wilson and Son, University Press.